MW00581027

Mythologies Without End

Mythologies Without End

The US, Israel, and the Arab-Israeli Conflict, 1917–2020

JEROME SLATER

OXFORD
UNIVERSITY PRESS

Oxford University Press is a department of the University of Oxford. It furthers the University's objective of excellence in research, scholarship, and education by publishing worldwide. Oxford is a registered trade mark of Oxford University Press in the UK and certain other countries.

Published in the United States of America by Oxford University Press
198 Madison Avenue, New York, NY 10016, United States of America.

Library of Congress Cataloging-in-Publication Data
Names: Slater, Jerome, author.
Title: Mythologies without end : the US, Israel, and the Arab-Israeli conflict, 1917–2020 / Jerome Slater.
Description: New York, NY : Oxford University Press, 2021. | Includes bibliographical references.
Identifiers: LCCN 2020017142 (print) | LCCN 2020017143 (ebook) | ISBN 9780190459086 (hardback) |
ISBN 9780190459109 (epub) | ISBN 9780190074609
Subjects: LCSH: Arab-Israeli conflict—History. | Jewish-Arab relations—History. |
Israel—Foreign relations—United States. | United States—Foreign relations—Israel. |
Palestine—Foreign relations—United States. | United States—Foreign relations—Palestine. |
Zionism—Political aspects.
Classification: LCC DS119.76 .S785437 2021 (print) | LCC DS119.76 (ebook) |
DDC 956.04—dc23
LC record available at https://lccn.loc.gov/2020017142
LC ebook record available at https://lccn.loc.gov/2020017143

1 3 5 7 9 8 6 4 2

Printed by Sheridan Books, Inc., United States of America

CONTENTS

PART THREE WAR AND PEACE IN THE ISRAELI-PALESTINIAN CONFLICT

ACKNOWLEDGMENTS

This work grows out of studying, teaching, and writing about US policy, Israel, and the Arab-Israeli conflict for the past fifty years; as well, I was a Fulbright lecturer at Haifa University in 1989 and have visited and lectured in Israel on several other occasions. As a result of my articles in professional journals and general-interest magazines, as well as my blog on the United States and Israel, over the years a number of scholars, journalists, and diplomats have commented on my work; these include Benjamin Beit-Hallahmi, David Bromwich, Helena Cobban, Noam Chomsky, Larry Derfner, Michael Desch, Chas Freeman, Jeremiah Haber, John Judis, Menachem Klein, Jim Lobe, Scott McConnell, John Mearsheimer, Terry Nardin, the late Peter Novick, William Quandt, Cheryl Rubenberg, Stephen Shalom, Henry Siegman, Jordan Michael Smith, Stephen Van Evera, Stephen Walt, Phil Weiss, Alan Wolfe, and David Zweifel.

I am especially indebted to John Mearsheimer, Stephen Walt, and David Hendrickson, who have supported my work for many years; in particular, Mearsheimer urged David McBride, the Social Sciences Editor at Oxford University Press, to invite me to write this book.

A large debt of gratitude is owed to the two outside reviewers of the manuscript, Ilan Pappé and Paul Pillar, whose comments and recommendations were invaluable. As well, three others read and extensively commented on the entire manuscript, to my great benefit: David Hendrickson, Jane Nardin, and my wife, Judith Slater, the latter two themselves scholars and writers (English literature), who made hundreds of invaluable suggestions.

I am also indebted to the following friends who read and commented on one or more of the chapters: Carl Dennis, William Hauser, the late George Hochfield, Ed Katkin, Anne Shapiro, Jim Smith, and David Tarbet.

Finally, this book could not have been written—literally—but for the ongoing rescue work of my brilliant computer specialist, Rob Dege, who tutored me and solved all the (seemingly endless) computer and word processing problems that arose in the course of the five years I have been working on this book.

PROLOGUE

Like almost all Jews of my generation, coming of age in America in the 1940s, immediately after the Holocaust and with anti-Semitism still alive in this country, I thought of myself as a passionate Zionist and rejoiced over the establishment of the state of Israel and its 1948 and 1967 victories over its Arab enemies.

From 1957 to 1960 I served as the anti-submarine warfare officer on a US destroyer. Some years later, after Egypt acquired four submarines from the Soviet Union, I wrote to the Israeli embassy in the United States and offered to serve as an ASW officer on an Israeli destroyer if a new war with Egypt were to break out before the Israelis could train their own people.

My offer was politely declined, and in any case I changed my mind when it became apparent that soon after the 1967 war, Gamal Abdel Nasser, and then his successor Anwar Sadat, were seeking to end the Arab-Israeli conflict, but were being stonewalled by the Israeli government of Golda Meir. I considered writing to Meir to say that if Israel blundered into an unnecessary war with Egypt—which, of course, in 1973 it did—she should consider my offer as canceled.

For the past fifty years I have been studying, teaching, and writing about Israel and the Arab-Israeli conflict, and have many close connections in that country. I've been there many times, served as a Fulbright lecturer at Haifa University in 1989, and given lectures at other Israeli universities. I continue to have many dear Israeli friends. During this time I've become convinced that Israel—with essentially blind US Jewish and government support—is well along the road to both a moral and security disaster. The first step Israel must take to prevent matters from getting even worse is to come to terms with the historical truth. Doing so may even be the sine qua non to providing justice to the Palestinians, to save itself as an enlightened democracy, and perhaps even literally save itself from an attack by fanatical Arab terrorists who have somehow acquired nuclear or other weapons of mass destruction.

The prospects today for a just peace, it must be said, have never been so dim. What then is the purpose of this book? Or even for completely secular Jews, like me, what is the point of thinking of ourselves as part of the Jewish people if we fail to align ourselves with the best values of Western civilization, to which Judaism has made a fundamental contribution? There was a time when it was widely accepted—and not just by Jews—that the Jewish culture and tradition were particularly committed to reason, truth, and justice. Consequently, when Israel was founded, and vowed to be "a light unto the nations," the belief was widespread that it might actually fulfill this promise, or at least try to. Today that seems quaint, if not downright preposterous—but it wasn't always so.

I write now in the hope that an effort at honesty and accuracy might perform some service. I feel something of a personal responsibility: these are, in some sense, my people. Their mythologies have blinded them to the true history of the Israeli-Palestinian conflict, and in their oppression of the Palestinian people they have abandoned enlightened Jewish traditions, which in my (secular) view constitute the best reasons for Judaism to have survived for twenty-five centuries. One can only hope that correcting the historical record can make a contribution to justice as well as truth.

Mythologies Without End

Introduction

Every nation has a narrative or stories about its history that are instilled into its citizens, generation after generation. The narratives explain much about a nation's motivations, policies, and actions. In order to understand why nations behave as they do, then, it is essential to know what they believe about their history. However, no matter how sincerely and deeply held, national narratives often—perhaps typically—are misleading or simply untrue, embodying as they do mythologies that cannot stand up to serious examination and which, therefore, may be disastrous both for the peoples who believe in them and to others who are affected by them.

In what has become a cliché but nonetheless invaluable, Daniel Moynihan famously observed: "Everyone is entitled to their own opinions, but not their own facts." Perhaps in no other major international conflict has the gap between opinions—or "myths," as in this context I shall call them—and demonstrable historical facts been as great as they are in the Arab-Israeli and the Israeli-Palestinian conflicts since the early twentieth century. As a result, perhaps in no other international conflict have these myths, which still dominate Israeli and US political discourse, had such devastating consequences for both peace and justice.

In 1973, Abba Eban, the eloquent Israeli diplomat, said: "The Arabs never miss an opportunity to miss an opportunity," an argument—better said, a myth—that was widely accepted and continues to have a huge impact on how the Arab-Israeli conflict has been understood in Israel, the United States, and most Western states. But that assessment was wrong then, and wrong since—if anything, the converse is close to being the case. One of the central purposes of this book, then, is to correct this myth, both in the interests of historical accuracy and in an effort to pave the way for policy changes in Israel and the United States.

Since the creation of Israel in 1948 there have been some fourteen wars or at least major armed clashes (as well as many smaller ones) between Israel and Arab states, the Palestine Liberation Organization (PLO), and the Islamic militant movements of Hezbollah in Lebanon and Hamas in Gaza. These include the 1948, 1956, 1967, and 1973 wars, principally with Egypt and Syria; the 1978, 1982, 1993, 1996, and 2006 attacks against Hezbollah and the PLO in Lebanon; and five major

Israeli attacks against Arafat and the PLO in the West Bank and Hamas in Gaza (2000–2001, 2002, 2008–9, 2012, and 2014). In addition, for more than fifteen years, the Israeli blockade or "siege of Gaza," as it is widely called, has amounted to economic warfare.

None of these wars and lesser conflicts, probably even the 1948 "Israeli War for Independence," were unavoidable. Israel's independence and security could have been protected had it accepted reasonable compromises on the four crucial issues of the Arab-Israeli and Israeli-Palestinian conflicts: a partition of the historical land of Palestine; Palestinian independence and sovereignty in the land allotted to them in the 1947 UN partition plan, including Arab East Jerusalem; the return of most of the territory captured from the Arab states in the various wars; and a small-scale symbolic "return" to Israel of some 10,000 to 20,000 Palestinian refugees (or their descendants) from the 1948 war.

The historical record, examined in detail in this book, demonstrates that it has been Israel, far more than the Palestinians and the leading Arab states, that has blocked fair compromise peace settlements. As a result, the conflict has continued for some one hundred years, making it one of the world's most important and, at times, most dangerous unresolved international conflicts.

The overall Arab-Israeli conflict can be seen, paradoxically, as one of the world's most difficult, yet simplest international conflict to resolve. By definition difficult, since after a century it still hasn't been settled. On the other hand, the solution is obvious and has been widely understood from the onset of the conflict, even by many and sometimes most of the participants. Two peoples, each having historical, religious, and political claims to the same land are locked into endless conflict: What can be done? For at least seventy-five years, study after study, international commission after international commission, negotiations after negotiations, have come to the same, nearly self-evident conclusion: the land must be divided between the two peoples on an equitable basis: the "Two-State Solution."

There is another paradox: precisely because it has gone on so long and is so potentially dangerous, the Arab-Israeli or Israeli-Palestinian conflict is one of the most studied international conflicts—by historians, political scientists, psychologists, journalists, and in the extensive memoirs and analyses of former political and military leaders. Yet it continues to be misunderstood, especially by the Israelis and their supporters, largely because their dominant historical narrative is the product of mythologies that are misleading or flatly wrong.

According to the conventional Israeli narrative, the story Israelis tell themselves and others, the Arab-Israeli conflict is the consequence of over a century of Arab hatred of the Jews and of their unwillingness to agree to numerous Zionist, Israeli, and international efforts to reach a fair compromise over the historic land of Palestine, starting with the Palestinian and Arab state rejection of the 1937 British Peel Commission compromise plan and, especially, the 1947 United Nations (UN) partition plan.

The UN plan provided for the division of Palestine between the Jews and the Arabs and the creation of the state of Israel. In a spirit of compromise, the Israeli narrative holds, the Zionist leadership accepted the UN plan, but the Palestinians and the neighboring Arab states rejected it and in 1948 launched an unprovoked invasion designed to destroy the new Israeli state.

In the course of the ensuing war, the narrative continues, hundreds of thousands of Palestinians living within Israel's boundaries fled to the neighboring Arab states, ordered or urged to do so by the invading Arab armies, even though the Zionists opposed the Palestinian exodus, hoping to demonstrate that Arabs and Jews could live side by side in the Jewish state. Thus, it is charged, it was the Arab states and the Palestinians who are responsible for creating the still-unresolved Palestinian refugee problem that, along with other issues, continues to block a two-state settlement.

After the 1948 war, the story continues, Israel remained willing to settle the conflict on the basis of generous compromise, but it could find no Palestinian or other Arab leaders with whom to negotiate. Consequently, the narrative holds, the conflict escalated into the Arab-Israeli wars of 1956, 1967, 1973, and 1982, all begun or provoked by continuing Arab rejectionism, terrorism, and unwillingness to live with the Jewish state of Israel.

As well, the refugee issue remained unresolved, largely because it suited the cynical purposes of the Arab states to keep it festering, so as to undermine the security and viability of the Jewish state. As a result, with the aid of neighboring Arab states, especially Egypt and Syria, the Palestinians turned to guerrilla warfare and outright terrorism.

The wall of monolithic Arab hostility was not breached, the Israeli narrative continues, until Anwar Sadat of Egypt decided to make peace with Israel in the late 1970s, followed fifteen years later by King Hussein of Jordan. But even today, it is contended, the Israeli-Palestinian conflict is no closer to being settled because the Palestinians still hope to destroy Israel rather than accept a fair compromise settlement.

So goes the Israeli narrative. However, while there are some elements of truth in it, most of it does not stand up to historical examination. Though other Israeli mythologies will be examined, especially those concerning Zionist ideologies, the primary focus of this book will be on the many lost opportunities for peace in the hundred-year conflict, and it will argue that it is Israel, not the Arabs, which has "never missed an opportunity to miss an opportunity." Unwilling to make territorial, symbolic, or other compromises, Israel has not merely missed but sometimes even deliberately sabotaged repeated opportunities for peace with the Arab states and the Palestinians.

Another focus of the book is on US policy toward Israel, which has provided crucial political, diplomatic, economic, and military support for Israeli policies throughout the history of the conflict. With some exceptions, that support has been close to unconditional—and never more so than today—despite serious arguments that it jeopardizes not only US national interests but Israel's true interests as well. What best explains this remarkable state of affairs is complicated and has been the subject of considerable dispute, as will be discussed in succeeding chapters.

Why Another Book on the Arab-Israeli Conflict?

Despite the vast literature that deals with one aspect or another of the Arab-Israeli conflict, there is no up-to-date book that covers the entire history of the conflict and critically analyzes the major historical issues and controversies from its origins after World War I until the present, especially the lost opportunities for peace and what must change lest future openings also be squandered.

The intended audience for this book includes the educated general reading public; college and graduate students studying the conflict; academicians and journalists with a general interest in international politics and US foreign policy; specialists on the Arab-Israeli conflict who will welcome an overview that incorporates the most important literature on the major historical disputes; and—not least—political leaders, policymakers, and government officials in Israel and the United States.

To these ends, the book will synthesize the vast existing literature on the Arab-Israeli and Israeli-Palestinian conflicts and provide a demythologizing account of their history. Two premises underlie this work: that historical truth is valuable for its own sake, and that a demythologizing history of the Arab-Israeli conflict is an essential prerequisite for changes in Israeli and US policies that could pave the way for a final settlement.

To be sure, at the time of this writing—Netanyahu still in power in Israel, Trump in the United States—the prospects for such changes range from very little to non-existent; even so, it is important to provide the intellectual and psychological bases for reassessments that may take place in the future. As the Israeli historian Shlomo Sand has said in his own demythologizing work, historians cannot know whether changes in long-held attitudes and historical narratives are possible: "All they can do is hope that their books may somehow help to bring about the beginning of change."[1]

In each of the chapters and case studies in this book, the first question addressed will be, What are the facts? Then, what are their implications, especially in terms of the many lost opportunities for peace?

Before beginning, it is necessary to acknowledge that this work is based on the existing literature rather than on original research in the primary documentary sources. This is unavoidable, in the first instance because no one person could write a history of a hundred-year conflict based on original research in the documentary sources.

In any case, most of the relevant Israeli and US documents over the past twenty-five to as long as seventy years are still unavailable. Israel currently does not release its "security-related" government documents for seventy years; consequently, the public records for such cases—which Israel defines very broadly—are available only through 1950.[2] Even so, some Israeli historians have gained access to classified documents—all the more reason a work of this kind must be based on secondary materials. The US government classifies its documentary records for twenty-five to fifty years, depending on their level of "sensitivity"; consequently, the most important ones after 1980 are not available.[3]

As a result, then, this book is primarily a work of synthesis and interpretation of the existing literature. It will cover the entire history of the Arab-Israeli and Israeli-Palestinian conflicts and the US role in them, bringing together the best and most important existing works, with special emphasis given to those of leading Israeli journalists, historians, political scientists, philosophers, and, especially, to the autobiographies, memoirs, and other commentaries by former Israeli government officials, diplomats, military leaders, and intelligence officials.

A word on source citations. Since the work is based on the vast secondary literature—including many hundreds of books, scholarly studies in political science and history journals, and Israeli and American newspaper stories—a strict listing of all the sources would result in many thousands of citations. Therefore, I have cited only those works that fit into one of the following categories: those that are widely regarded as the most authoritative works on the topic; those which I have directly quoted or closely paraphrased; and those in which the quality of the writing and analysis are particularly impressive.

It is also important to acknowledge that I don't read Hebrew. However, almost all the important materials by Israeli writers and in Israeli journals and newspapers, such as *Haaretz*, Israel's most important newspaper, are either written in or translated into English. I am not aware of any claim that an untranslated Hebrew book, article, or document is crucial to understanding the history of the conflict: if it were truly essential, it would soon be available in English.

Plan of Work

The book is both an analytic history of the Arab-Israeli conflict—"a new hundred years war," it might be termed—and a series of arguments that challenges the conventional historical accounts. In each chapter, I will be asking two central questions. First, throughout the history of the conflict what are the facts at issue and the best available evidence? Second, how should we think about those facts? What are their implications, both for accurate history—truth—and public policy?

The Structure of the Book

The first chapter is an overview of US policies in the Arab-Israeli and Israeli-Palestinian conflicts. It examines the various factors that have accounted for the nearly unconditional support that the American government has provided Israel since its founding in 1948; particular attention is paid to the controversial argument that the power of "the Israel lobby" is the most important explanation for US policy. The subsequent historical chapters go into much greater detail on the role of US policies.

The second chapter, "Zionism Reconsidered," reviews the history of Zionism from the end of the nineteenth century to today and examines the validity and persuasiveness of the various arguments that comprise the Zionist ideology. The central argument is that it is crucial to separate what is persuasive and legitimate about Zionism from what is not merely unpersuasive but is devastating both to Israel and the Palestinians.

The book then moves to its man body, the history of the Arab-Israeli and Israeli-Palestinian conflicts. It is divided into three sections. Part I covers the origins and early years of the conflict between Israel and the leading Arab states, as distinct from the Israeli-Palestinian conflict. Chapter 3 examines the onset of the Arab-Israeli conflict, from 1917 through 1947. Chapter 4 discusses the creation of the state of Israel in 1948. These chapters also focus on US policies in this period, from Woodrow Wilson to Harry Truman's decision to recognize and support the creation of a Jewish state in Israel.

Part II is entitled "War and Peace in the Arab-Israeli State Conflict, 1948–2020." Separate chapters focus on the 1948 war; on the lost opportunities for peace in the 1949–56 period; on the 1956 war between Israel and Egypt; on the 1967 war; on the Cold War and the Arab-Israeli conflict in the 1970s; on the Israeli-Egyptian peace settlement in the late 1970s; on the Israel-Jordanian peace settlement in the 1980s; on the Lebanese wars from the late 1970s through the mid-1990s; and on the Israeli-Syrian conflict between 1948 and the present.

Part III is entitled "War and Peace in the Israeli-Palestinian Conflict." It examines the Israeli-Palestinian Conflict, 1917–88; the rise and fall of the "peace process" in the 1975–99 period; the Camp David and Taba negotiations in 2000; the Israeli occupation of the West Bank and Gaza and the rise of Palestinian resistance in the 2000–8 period; the Israeli siege of Gaza and the rise and evolution of Hamas; the attempts to renew the peace process from 2001 through 2016; and the US and the Israeli-Palestinian conflict in the Netanyahu-Trump era, from early 2017 through the present.

The book closes with a summary of its main arguments and their implications for US and Israeli policies. This chapter is quite long. It is divided into two parts, the first third of which is a summary of the argument I have developed in the main body, and the evidence on which it is based. Readers who have read the previous chapters may just wish to skim this section, and then go on to the overall conclusions and policy recommendations. On the other hand, readers who have largely skimmed the main body should find a long summary to be useful. The rest of the Conclusions goes well beyond just presenting the facts and letting readers draw their own conclusions as it explicitly argues the implications of the facts, especially in terms of how the conflict might finally be resolved.

PART ONE

THE ARAB-ISRAELI CONFLICT

1

The United States and the Arab-Israeli Conflict

With rare and short-lived exceptions, since the UN partition of Palestine in 1947, the United States has strongly supported Israel and its policies toward the Arab world, particularly the Palestinians—even when many officials in the US foreign policy establishment have believed that such support is harmful to American national interests.

The US support of Israel has been one of the most remarkable and unprecedented phenomena in the history of American foreign policy. There is considerable debate over what constitutes the best explanation for this story, especially over the role of the "Israel lobby." This chapter provides an introduction to and overview of US policies, which are then discussed in greater detail in the context of the historical review of the Arab-Israeli and Israeli-Palestinian conflicts that constitutes the main body of this work.

In many ways the US backing of a Jewish state is heartening, attesting to the great decline in anti-Semitism in the last seventy-five years and its replacement by what might even be called philo-Semitism and the respected position of the Jewish people throughout American society. There have been recent isolated attacks on Jewish synagogues or other targets, but these have been carried out by lone misfits and have been almost universally condemned in public opinion and by government officials at all levels.

Yet it is also the case that the near-unconditional US support of Israel has enabled that country to spurn repeated opportunities for peaceful settlements of its conflict with the Arab world, secure in the knowledge that even when American governments have disagreed with hard-line Israeli policies, only rarely have they been willing to press for changes in them.

What accounts for this situation? Four major arguments, or sets of arguments, have been offered to explain it: the requirements of morality and shared religious and other values; public and elite opinion, especially that of all American presidents from Woodrow Wilson through Donald Trump; the strategic and national interests of the United States; and the power of the Israel lobby.[1]

In the following pages, I provide an overview of the major factors that are widely held to explain and justify US policies toward Israel, followed by brief evaluations of their validity and persuasiveness. This should be understood as an introduction to later chapters, in which the arguments and issues are examined in the context of specific cases.

For a number of reasons, after its creation in 1948 Israel quickly captured the imagination and sympathy of general as well as elite American opinion, of both political parties, of Congress, and of a succession of presidents. Among those reasons are these:

Holocaust Guilt. There is little doubt that in the early years following the Holocaust, the most important motivation underlying US policy was the widespread and deeply felt belief that the United States had a fundamental moral obligation to support the creation and survival of a Jewish state. At the time, this sense of obligation clearly, and often explicitly, stemmed from a sense of guilt or shame among many policymakers and opinion leaders because the United States had done little or nothing to prevent the Holocaust, or even to mitigate its effects—as it could have, for example, by accepting large numbers of Jewish refugees from Nazism in the 1930s and 1940s.

Shared Values. Supplementing the post-Holocaust moral argument in explaining US policy was the belief that Israel was an outpost of Western civilization in the Middle East, in light of the origins of most of its inhabitants at the time it was created, the perceived cultural and religious affinities (the Judeo-Christian tradition), and the declared values and principles of the new state, particularly regarding the kind of society and political system it proclaimed as its goals.

The Democracy Argument. Israel has benefited from the belief—in the abstract, at least—that the United States should support fellow democracies: from its creation down to today, Israel has been regarded as "the only democracy in the Middle East," an area dominated by military juntas, despotic autocracies, or feudal kingdoms. To be sure, there is an obvious conflict between the belief that supporting democracy should be an important goal in US foreign policies and the fact that during the Cold War the United States repeatedly sought to overthrow, destabilize, or prevent the accession to power of democratically elected but left-wing governments in, for example, Iran, Guatemala, Chile, Nicaragua, and elsewhere. As well, both during the Cold War and perhaps even more so today, especially in the Middle East, the United States has actively supported right-wing dictatorships whose Cold War or present-day policies were aligned with US objectives: Iran under the shah, the numerous murderous but "anti-communist" dictatorships in Latin America, and the military juntas or autocracies in the Middle East—such as Egypt and Saudi Arabia—that support many current US policies.

Be that as it may and whatever the obvious inconsistencies, it is clear that "support of democracies" has played an important role in US attitudes toward Israel.

The Underdog Argument. Israel has benefited from traditional US sympathy for victims or underdogs: in the widely accepted imagery, it was the Israeli David versus the Arab Goliath.

The Religious Arguments. For several reasons, from the onset of the Arab-Israeli conflict, evangelical Christians have strongly supported Israel. At the heart of Christian Zionism, as it has often been termed, is belief in the New Testament teaching that the "return" of the Jews to Palestine—especially Jerusalem—and the reestablishment of "the Nation of Israel" are preconditions for the return of Jesus and the victory of Christianity in the final battle of Armageddon.[2]

In October 2013, a public opinion survey reported that while only 40 percent of American Jews believed that God gave the land of Israel to the Jews in perpetuity, 82 percent of evangelical Christians in the United States—in some estimates numbering 50 million—held that view.[3] Thus, for Christian Zionists, the defense of Israel is a matter of deeply held beliefs and principles.[4] Indeed, it is at least arguable that for Republican officeholders—including Donald Trump—the views of the Christian right are at least as important as those of the American Jewish community.

Public and Elite Opinions. The US government supports Israel, it is often argued, because both opinion elites and the general public believe it should, as repeated surveys have shown. Of particular importance have been the views of American presidents. From the 1917 Balfour Declaration to the creation of the state of Israel, every American president—Wilson, Coolidge, Hoover, Roosevelt, Truman—declared his support for the Declaration and the aspirations of the Zionist movement. Since the creation of Israel in 1948, every American president, Democrat or Republican, from Truman to Trump, has supported not only the basic security of Israel but also most of the policies of the Jewish state.

The Arab Intransigence Argument. A crucial belief of both US governments and public opinion is that only Arab intransigence has blocked an overall peace settlement between Israel and the Arab world, including the Palestinians. Therefore, it is argued, the United States must support Israel, which has no choice but to depend on its military power to avoid being destroyed.

The National Interests Argument. During the 1947–48 period many of the highest officials in the US government, especially in the State and Defense Departments, opposed US recognition of the new state of Israel because they thought it would undermine the critical national interests of the United States in the Middle East. That policy began to change after Israel's overwhelming victory in the 1948 war impressed US military leaders; for example, after the war a member of the Joint Chiefs of Staff wrote a memorandum:

> Existing policy on this subject appears now to have been overtaken by events. The power balance in the Near and Middle East has been radically

> altered. At the time the state of Israel was forming, numerous indications pointed to its extremely short life in the face of Arab League opposition. However, Israel has now . . . demonstrated by force of arms its right to be considered the military power next after Turkey in the Near and Middle East. . . . Palestine remains of strategic importance. . . . The possibility exists that, as the result of its support to Israel, the United States might now gain strategic advantages from the new political situation.[5]

That quickly became the dominant view, and since then US governments have believed that a strong Israel was a "strategic asset" that served the US national interest, defined during the Cold War as containing Soviet expansionism and maintaining access to Middle Eastern oil at reasonable prices, and since the end of the Cold War primarily as fighting "the war on terrorism." Because Israel shared those interests, the two countries have had a de facto alliance.

The Israel Lobby Argument. In contrast with the argument that the national interest explains US policies toward Israel, many have argued that the policies are best explained in terms of domestic politics, in particular by the political power of what has come to be known as "the Israel lobby." Over the years a number of scholarly works have discussed the power of the lobby in government and public opinion, the most important and influential of which is *The Israel Lobby and U.S. Foreign Policy,* the massive work by John Mearsheimer and Stephen Walt; these writings argue that because American policy in the Middle East is antithetical to true US national interests, it is best explained as the consequence of the exceptional power of the "Israel lobby" in the US political system.[6]

Evaluating the Arguments

Aside from their explanatory persuasiveness, it is important not only to examine the arguments about *why* the United States has provided nearly unconditional support for Israeli policies but to analyze whether it *should* have done so, in the past and the present.

The Moral Argument. In light of the circumstances at the time, the moral arguments for supporting the creation of the Jewish state of Israel were strong; indeed, in my view, overwhelming. Moreover, the moral arguments for continuing to support the *existence* of Israel—as opposed to many of its policies—are self-evident. However, the dominant "pro-Israel" view largely ignores the moral issues posed by Israeli policies and behavior toward the Palestinian people and their legitimate rights. In particular, I argue that Israel's refusal to agree to attainable and just compromise settlements with the Palestinians is morally indefensible—not to mention inconsistent with the enlightened national interest of Israel itself. Still, in some respects the moral issues are complex and require an extended evaluation, as are discussed throughout the book.

The Democracy Argument. It is now clear that Israel is a true democracy in its broadest sense only for its Jewish citizens. The Arab-Israeli (or, as some prefer, the Palestinian-Israeli) peoples, roughly 20 percent of the total population of Israel within its pre-1967 boundaries, are citizens and have voting rights, but they face political, economic, and social discrimination. And, of course, Israeli democracy is inapplicable to the nearly 4 million Palestinian Arabs in the West Bank and Gaza, conquered by Israel in June 1967, who are occupied, repressed, and in many ways, directly and indirectly, effectively ruled by Israel.

The Underdog Argument. Israeli and other scholars and military analysts have demonstrated that even at the onset of the Arab-Israeli conflict in 1948, the David and Goliath metaphor was a great oversimplification of the realities on the ground. More important, since then—especially since 1967—Israel has become vastly more powerful than any potential Arab adversary or any plausible combination of Arab states that might be bent on destroying Israel. To state the most obvious point, David now has nuclear weapons, Goliath none. Beyond that, Israeli economic and conventional military power outstrips that of the entire Arab world put together.

The Arab Intransigence Argument. As will be demonstrated, it is pure myth that the major Arab states have refused to accept the existence of Israel: throughout the seventy-year history of the conflict they have repeatedly offered peace settlements on reasonable and legitimate terms, only to be rejected, often out of hand. The central argument of this book, which is developed throughout, is that Israel is primarily responsible for missing or deliberately refusing to explore highly promising opportunities for peaceful settlements.

The National Interests Argument. During the Cold War it was an axiom of US policies that a strongly anti-communist, pro-American, and increasingly powerful Israel served US national interests in countering the threat of Soviet or communist expansionism in the Middle East and even elsewhere.[7] However, I argue (in Chapter 9) that the validity of these perceptions was by no means unchallengeable—in particular, that Israeli policies, far from "containing Soviet expansionism" in the Middle East, opened the door to Soviet military and political alliances with the Arab states. Similarly, I argue (in Chapter 20) that US and Israeli policies in the Middle East have exacerbated the threat of Islamic terrorism to American national interests and security.

As for the relationship between US support of Israel and the United States' national interest in Middle East oil, the matter is complicated. For many years, it was widely believed that these US goals were inconsistent: the fear was that the Arab oil-producing states, particularly Saudi Arabia, the largest and most important one, would refuse to sell oil to the United States because of anger at its support for Israeli policies.

Until the 1970s, though, the dilemma (as policymakers saw it) remained theoretical. As late as 1965 only about 3 percent of US oil consumption came from the Mideast. Moreover, oil was cheap and easily obtainable, since the world's supply of oil exceeded the demand for it. Consequently, had there been an interruption of imported Middle East oil, replacing it would have been relatively easy, by substituting oil from somewhere else, including from US oilfields.

Moreover, most Middle East oil was owned and controlled less by the states in the region than by the world's largest oil corporations, most of them dominated by Americans and supported by the US government. However, the situation began to change after the formation of OPEC (Organization of Petroleum Exporting Countries) in 1960. From the formation of the cartel to the early 1970s, the OPEC states, led by Saudi Arabia, had nationalized most of the oil companies and largely succeeded in taking over the production, pricing, and marketing of Middle East oil.

In the aftermath of the 1973 Arab-Israeli war, in which the United States supported Israel, the power of OPEC grew—and for six months its Arab members sought to cut off oil shipments to the United States and other Western states that had supported Israel. Second, OPEC also used its cartel power to cut oil production and take other steps that dramatically raised the price of oil. These actions, together with the interruption of Iranian oil exports following the 1979 Iranian revolution, resulted in an oil price increase from $3 a barrel in the 1960s to $34 a barrel in 1980. Because of the central role of oil in their economies, the United States and other Western states suffered from considerable inflation, soon followed by a recession.

However, for a number of reasons the problem was short-lived. First, the Arab embargo turned out to be loose and leaky, and a lot of Gulf oil continued to find its way into the United States. Second, it is clear that the Arab OPEC members took note of the growing discussions in the American media that if the economy continued to suffer, the United States might find it necessary to use force—for example, by seizing Persian Gulf oil fields. Third, as radical movements spread in the Middle East, especially after the Iranian revolution in 1979, the Saudis and other conservative monarchies realized that they might need US military support at least as much as the United States needed Persian Gulf oil. Fourth, a number of important new oilfields were discovered and began to be exploited—in Alaska, in Mexico, in Venezuela, in the North Sea, and elsewhere; as a result, by 1984 OPEC's share of world oil production had dropped from 50 percent in the mid-1970s to 33 percent. Fifth, the US government vastly increased its oil stockpiling program, making the country much less vulnerable to oil import stoppages. Finally, the cumulative effect of various alternative energy sources and technologies—the doubling of vehicle fuel efficiency, increased domestic oil production, and the use of natural gas, coal, electrical, and nuclear power—made the United States less dependent on Persian Gulf oil.

As a result of all these developments, the huge oil price increases of the 1970s were largely rolled back as the economy gradually recovered from the 1972–75 recession. Since then the 1973 scenario has not been repeated, nor is it likely to be in the foreseeable future. Regardless of their ideologies, oil-producing states have powerful economic reasons to sell oil to whoever will buy it. Moreover, the oil-producing states have powerful prudential reasons not to challenge the US interest in maintaining Western access to Gulf oil. Today less than 7 percent of US oil has to be imported from the Gulf, and most future projections are for a steadily declining US need for Persian Gulf oil, and indeed for imported oil from anywhere.

As for the terrorism issue, while the once-feared conflict between US support for Israel and access to Arab oil is more remote than ever, that is not the case in the conflict between support of Israel and the war on terrorism.

Since the end of the Cold War and the rapidly declining importance of the oil issue, the United States has defined its primary national interest in the Middle East as fighting Islamic radicalism, especially to prevent terrorist attacks against America's allies and even, since September 11, 2001, against the US homeland itself. The dominant assumption among US policymakers has been that Israel is a major asset and ally in this "war against Islamic terrorism." The contrary view, of course, is that US support for Israel in its conflict with the Palestinians was the major reason for the 9/11 attacks and would likely be for any future Islamic terrorist attacks against this country. Two leading scholars put it this way: "The United States has a terrorism problem in good part because it has long been so supportive of Israel."[8] I examine this issue in Chapter 20.

The Israel Lobby Argument

The term "Israel lobby" is generally understood as referring to organized interest groups—by far the most important of which is AIPAC (American Israeli Public Affairs Committee)—that regularly lobby Congress and the executive branch.[9] The heart of the issue of the explanatory power of the Israel lobby argument is not whether there is an organized, well-financed, and politically powerful pro-Israel lobby (mostly organized Jewish groups, but increasingly also including evangelical Christians), since that is beyond serious dispute. Rather, the question is the *extent* of the Israel lobby's power: Is it the master variable explaining US policies, or is it just one—an important one, to be sure—of a number of factors that explain those policies?

The Israel Lobby: Sources of Its Power

Whatever its extent, the undoubted importance of the Israel lobby is explained by a number of factors. First, an often underestimated factor is the marked decline in US anti-Semitism since the 1940s, one result of which is the general public's sympathy with Jewish support of Israel.[10]

Second, politicians almost always court voters in the American Jewish community, particularly on Israeli-related issues. While Jews are estimated to be only 3 percent of the electorate they cast nearly 5 percent of the vote, with turnout close to 90 percent in most elections.[11] Consequently, the Jewish vote can be important in close elections, particularly in states with substantial Jewish populations, such as New York, New Jersey, Massachusetts, Ohio, Pennsylvania, California, and Florida.

The remarks of political leaders often reveal the weight that they give to the Jewish vote. In 1954, Secretary of State John Foster Dulles told European diplomats that he had just twelve months left to do something about Palestine before another election would make action impossible.[12] And according to two Israeli journalists, in a private conversation, David Ben-Gurion said that John F. Kennedy told him, "You know I was elected by the Jews. I have to do something for them."[13]

Even so, there are sharp limits on the importance of the Jewish vote, which is almost always overwhelmingly Democratic: yet, during their presidencies, Richard Nixon, Ronald Reagan, and George W. Bush, all of whom got less than a third of Jewish votes, were regarded, in turn, as the most "pro-Israeli" presidents ever.[14] And recently Donald Trump—who got just 25 percent of the Jewish vote in the 2016 presidential election—in the eyes of his supporters has surpassed all of his predecessors. Whether, of course, his policies are really good for either Israel or the United States are another matter, as is discussed throughout this book.

Third, Jews are known to be exceptionally heavy political donors—meaning, of course, that their political views count for a great deal. It has been widely estimated that Jews contribute anywhere from 25 to 50 percent of money donated to the campaign funds of the Democratic Party, and as much as 30 percent of those donated to the Republican Party.[15]

Fourth, for reasons described above, in recent years the "pro-Israeli" Christian right has become increasingly powerful in the Republican Party—and can even be legitimately described as part of the Israel lobby, especially on issues relating to the war against Islamic terrorism. In fact, as Israel has moved to the right it has lost support among Democrats but gained support among Republicans. According to one major poll, as of 2014, 73 percent of Republicans support Israel compared with 44 percent of Democrats.[16] Under the circumstances, it is not surprising that during George W. Bush's administrations, Israel "had a direct line into the White House" (mainly through the office of Vice-President Dick Cheney), as Condoleezza Rice, Bush's national security advisor and later secretary of state, wrote in her memoirs.[17]

Fifth, the Israel lobby—AIPAC, in particular—faces no countervailing organized group power. Despite its recent growth, the Arab population of the United States is considerably smaller than the Jewish population, and, equally important, it has no lobby comparable to the Israel lobby. As well, American oil companies with substantial interests in the Middle East, interests at least potentially jeopardized by US support of Israel, have conspicuously refrained from taking on the Israel lobby.[18]

Sixth, American public opinion has strongly supported Israel, from its creation in 1948 through today.[19] Although there have been periods in which support has declined, it soon returns to the long-term averages, roughly 65 percent. Indeed, even when US support of Israel arguably has had detrimental consequences not only for American policies in the Middle East but in the United States itself, support for Israel soon reverted to its long-term norms. Two examples have been widely cited: the Arab oil embargo of 1973 and the 9/11 attacks on the United States. Though it was relatively short-lived, the embargo did cause significant economic damage to the United States for a while. Nonetheless, majorities continued to view Israel favorably and there was little support for a reduction in US government support of Israel. And the pattern was repeated after 9/11.[20]

For all of these reasons, American political leaders have had little incentive to alter US policies in the Arab-Israeli conflict, even when their personal views have differed or were at least more complex. In light of all these factors, it is hardly surprising that the Israel lobby has won a number of significant battles. Among the examples cited by Mearsheimer and Walt and other writers are the following:

- In 1970, strong opposition by AIPAC to the Rogers Plan, a peace settlement effort by Secretary of State William Rogers that incurred strong Israeli displeasure, led Richard Nixon to effectively abandon it. To be sure, there was also strong opposition in Congress, but undoubtedly some of that opposition—though not all—was a result of the lobbying of AIPAC and other Jewish organizations.
- Because of what President Gerald Ford and Secretary of State Henry Kissinger believed to be Israeli intransigence in peace negotiations with Egypt, in March 1975 the administration threatened to "reassess" US policy toward Israel. As part of that reassessment, in the next six months the administration delayed scheduled weapons deliveries and suspended talks on further financial and military assistance to Israel.
- However, in the words of Itamar Rabinovich, a former Israeli ambassador to the United States, "[Israeli prime minister] Rabin fought back by mobilizing the Jewish community and Israel's friends in Israel,"[21] and AIPAC organized an intensive lobbying campaign. In May, seventy-six senators signed a resolution affirming their continued support of Israel and opposing any reassessment of US policy; some senators admitted that they signed the letter only for political reasons. In any case, that ended the Ford/Kissinger efforts to pressure Israel and the administration agreed to most of the aid requested by Israel.[22]
- There have been several cases of successful AIPAC campaigns against congressmen and governors who were regarded as insufficiently pro-Israel.

In the best-known and most important case, in 1984 AIPAC organized a successful campaign to prevent the reelection of Senator Charles Percy, chairman of the Senate Foreign Relations Committee, as he had defied Israel and the lobby by backing a deal to sell sophisticated military aircraft to Saudi Arabia.[23] As J. J. Goldberg observed, the defeat of such politicians "has only happened a handful of times. . . . But that was all that was needed to make the point."[24]

- Presidents have often—but not always—decided not to adopt certain policies or make several high-level appointments that they knew would invite a fight with the lobby. For example, as discussed later, Barack Obama clearly retreated from his initial inclination to adopt what is usually called "more balanced" policies toward Israel and ended by returning to the traditional US policies of near-unconditional support.
- Mearsheimer and Walt point out that since the Israeli capture of the West Bank and Gaza in 1967, all American presidents from Lyndon Johnson through George W. Bush wanted Israel to—at a minimum—stop the expansion of its settlements in the occupied territories. Yet they all failed: "There is much evidence that the lobby is the root of the problem," they argue. "If it is not the lobby," they ask rhetorically, "what does account for the failure of the past eight [now: ten] presidents to put an end to settlement building, or even to make a serious effort in that direction?"[25]

There is no question that their argument is powerful. Yet their concluding rhetorical question is not unanswerable.

The Israel Lobby: Limits of Its Power

Important as it is, the Israel lobby has not been all-powerful. On a number of occasions it has either been defeated outright or, equally important, has itself placed sharp limits on its pressure campaigns and backed away from direct confrontations with determined presidents.

To begin, at least until the Trump administration, the lobby has been far more powerful in Congress than in the executive branch—and it is presidents and their appointees, not Congress, who decide most foreign policy issues. When US presidents have defied the Israel lobby, they usually have prevailed—the fate of the Ford administration's initial effort to "reassess" US policies toward Israel and several other cases notwithstanding.

There are a number of examples of presidential defiance or defeat of the Israel lobby:

- Despite the anger of American Jewish groups, during the 1973 Israeli-Egyptian war, the Nixon administration placed heavy pressures on Israel, including delays in replacing Israeli weapons losses, in a successful effort to stop Israel from completely defeating Egypt and instead to accept a ceasefire that left Egyptian forces in control of parts of the Sinai peninsula.
- Despite being forced to compromise on some issues, the Carter administration repeatedly defied the Jewish lobby on others: on the creation of a homeland for the Palestinians, on the need for Israeli withdrawals from the Egyptian and Syrian territory it had conquered in the 1973 war, on diplomatic overtures to the PLO and Syria, and on its sale of weapons to Saudi Arabia.
- In the early 1980s, the lobby—and the Israeli government—mounted a fierce campaign to oppose the Reagan administration's sale of advanced military aircraft to Saudi Arabia. The administration went ahead anyway.
- During the 1982 Israeli invasion of Lebanon, Ronald Reagan successfully pressured Israel not to invade Beirut or destroy the PLO in Lebanon, by threatening to reassess overall US policy toward Israel.
- In 1991, the lobby was unable to stop George H. W. Bush from withholding $10 billion in US loan guarantees to Israel because of its continued expansion of Jewish settlements in the occupied territories.
- Throughout the administration of George W. Bush, the Israel lobby unsuccessfully pressed for more severe US economic sanctions against Syria and for the military destruction of Iranian nuclear facilities.
- With the enthusiastic support of AIPAC, in September 2013 Barack Obama announced he would seek a congressional resolution authorizing military action against Syria. Consequently, AIPAC "threw an army of lobbyists behind an effort to win a congressional mandate for Mr. Obama's threatened military strike on Syria."[26] Nonetheless, congressional resistance forced Obama to drop the proposed resolution.
- Throughout 2013 the lobby pressed Congress to impose new sanctions against Iran, but when the Obama administration opposed the sanctions, the effort failed: "AIPAC . . . finds itself in a very public standoff with the White House. . . . Its top priority, a Senate bill to impose new sanctions on Iran, has stalled . . . and in what amounts to a tacit retreat, AIPAC has stopped pressuring Senate Democrats to vote for the bill."[27]
- Even more tellingly, in September 2015 AIPAC "threw itself into a $30 million advertising and lobbying effort" to convince Congress to kill the Obama administration's proposed nuclear accord with Iran. However, it "suffered a stinging political defeat" when Congress refused to block the accord.[28]

Comparing Two Explanations: The Israel Lobby or Domestic Politics?

Explanations of the long history of strong US support for Israel often treat the terms "domestic politics" and "the Israel lobby" as if they were synonymous. This is misleading, for *the Israel lobby is just one component, and often not the most important one, in the domestic politics of the US policymaking process toward Israel.*

One way to approach this issue is through a thought experiment: What if there were no Israel lobby at all, no organized, powerful interest groups actively lobbying on behalf of Israel? Would the policy process then be significantly different from what it is today?

No doubt it would be *somewhat* different, but arguably the disappearance of the lobby—or more plausibly, a significant decline in its power—would not lead to much of a change in the fundamentals of US policy toward Israel. That is, the underlying domestic political realities would continue, for the electoral and financial facts of life would still create very strong incentives for politicians to swear allegiance to whatever policies Israel follows. Thus, even without an organized lobby, there would still be the potentially decisive Jewish or wider "pro-Israel" vote in close elections; there would still be large Jewish financial contributions to the most uncritical politicians; there would still be generally favorable attitudes toward Israel among the public (though this may have diminished in the last few years); there would still be strong support of Israel in the media; and there would still be strong support of Israel in Congress.

Moreover, the absence of the Israel lobby would still leave intact the personal beliefs and attitudes of policymakers, including the many genuinely pro-Israel politicians in Congress who don't need to be lobbied, let alone pressured, to support Israel.[29]

In short, the power of the Israel lobby is only a partial and not necessarily the most important explanation of US policies in the Mideast.[30] What, then, constitutes a fuller explanation? As I have previously argued, the full range of US support for Israel, from 1948 through today, is the result of the remarkable convergence of many factors, including felt moral obligations; political and cultural affinities; religious beliefs and identifications (often described as "the Judeo-Christian heritage"); the strong emotional, moral, or ideological views of most American presidents, who didn't need to be lobbied to support Israel; perceived common or parallel national interests, especially the belief that the anti-communist and militarily powerful Israel was a strategic asset for the United States during the Cold War and is now an indispensable ally in the struggle against Islamic radicalism and terrorism; and finally, the influence or power of the Israel lobby as well as other aspects of American domestic politics.

There is no way to measure how much explanatory weight should be assigned to each of these factors—especially since they all work in the same direction and are not balanced by countervailing factors. Moreover, to add to the complexity, the explanatory factors vary in their importance over time, on different issues, and on whether Congress or the executive branch is the primary policymaking institution. Given this complexity, all we can really say is that the explanation for US policy is multicausal.

Of course, the extent to which these American perceptions reflect reality is altogether a different matter—and one that is assessed throughout this book. As the late political essayist Peter Viereck put it, "Reality is that which, when you don't believe in it, doesn't go away."

2

Zionism Reconsidered

Zionism has clashed with the Arab world for over one hundred years. While the dissension with the leading Arab states has largely ended, the core conflict between Israel and the Palestinians is unresolved and there is no solution in sight. Given the insistence of the Zionists to establish a Jewish state in the land of Palestine, *some* conflict was probably inevitable, but it was not at all inevitable that it would result in a century of continuing blood-soaked conflict.

Zionism, which can be regarded as the secular Israeli ideology, in some crucial ways was, and perhaps still is, legitimate and persuasive. In other ways, however—most of them unnecessary for the central Zionist argument and cause, and difficult if not impossible to defend rationally—Zionism has precipitated unnecessary wars with the Arab states and undermined the possibilities for a just settlement of the Israeli-Palestinian conflict.

Typically a small and vulnerable minority in the many countries in which they have lived, for over two thousand years the Jewish people have been repeatedly afflicted by anti-Semitism. As a result, history has taught the Jews that they are never permanently safe anywhere: no matter how long they have apparently been secure and accepted, they remain outsiders, sooner or later to be singled out for mob or government violence or expulsion.

The severity of anti-Semitism has varied widely. Often hardly noticeable except by the Jews themselves, sometimes it goes into long remission, leading to the optimistic belief that it has been eradicated, only to break out again, and often murderously so. Consider the implications of the most murderous anti-Semitism in the modern world; it took place in Germany, which until the rise of Hitler was one of the most advanced of the Western countries and in which Jews seemed to be thoroughly assimilated, prosperous, and prominent. And yet, in the span of only a few years, latent German anti-Semitism broke out again in its most virulent form ever, ending with the Holocaust, an evil so monstrous that even today it remains nearly incomprehensible.

While the Holocaust was unprecedented in its scope and insane ferocity, severe and often murderous anti-Semitism was hardly a new phenomenon. During the eleventh through the sixteenth centuries Jews were repeatedly massacred by the Crusaders. As well, most of the Jewish populations were killed or expelled from Germany in 1182, from England in 1290, from France in 1306 and 1394, from Austria in 1421, from Spain during the Inquisition in 1492, and from Portugal in 1497.

The Spanish case is especially important for understanding the deep historical background of Zionism. For *fifteen* centuries, first under Roman and later under tolerant Islamic rule, Spain had been a haven for the Jews, who were well integrated into its society. Yet, from 1480 to 1492, they were massacred in large numbers and then given the choice of conversion or expulsion, the consequence of which was essentially the end of the Spanish Jewish community.

This history is essential to understanding the rise of the Zionist movement in Europe in the early twentieth century. After waning somewhat in the 1800s, European anti-Semitism intensified, especially in Russia and Eastern Europe, where most of the Jews in the world then lived, and where anti-Semitism was historically common. From the 1880s into the early twentieth century, it became particularly murderous, as pogroms and mob violence were tolerated or even encouraged by the Russian and other regional governments.

Though less murderous, anti-Semitism was also growing in Western Europe. Of particular importance in precipitating the Zionist movement was the "Dreyfus affair" in France, where in 1894 a Jewish army officer was falsely convicted of treason as mobs in the street chanted "Death to the Jews." The intensifying violent anti-Semitism in Europe during this period had two important consequences. First, it led to the emigration of millions of Jews—mostly to the United States, but also to Germany, England, South America, and South Africa. However, from 1882 through 1914, only about 65,000 went to Palestine.

The second consequence was the rise of Zionism and Jewish nationalism, led by Theodore Herzl, an Austrian Jewish lawyer, journalist, and writer who had been thoroughly assimilated into Western society, values, and culture.[1] Influenced in part by the Dreyfus affair, Herzl argued in his 1896 book, *The Jewish State*, and then amplified in his 1902 novel, *Altneuland*, that the assimilation of Jews into their current homelands had repeatedly failed. For example, he wrote, "The whole of history has taught us that never have Jews been in a happier condition than they were in Spain before . . . the Inquisition and Expulsion of the fifteenth century." Thus, Herzl came to believe that violent anti-Semitism was an immutable fact of life: only in a Jewish state with a Jewish army, he concluded, could the Jews cease to be outsiders and have real security.

It is important to emphasize, particularly in light of the current controversy over whether Israel should remain a Jewish state—and exactly what that should entail—that Herzl decidedly did not envision that the Jewish state he called for would be a *religious* one, as opposed to a nationalist and politically Jewish one. Herzl himself was non-observant, at least an agnostic if not an outright atheist.[2]

As well, other early Zionist leaders were nonreligious, if not anti-religious. As one of Israel's leading scholars on Zionism wrote, "Zionism as a national movement that rebelled against historical Judaism was mainly atheistic. The rabbis knew that, and were terrified—and, therefore, almost all of them became avowed anti-Zionists."[3]

In this context, it is vital to emphasize that while Herzl considered a Jewish state to be essential if the Jewish people were to survive recurrent bouts of anti-Semitism, he also insisted that a Jewish state should be an exemplar of civilized values and therefore a benefit to mankind generally. Because that promise was so central to the founder of Zionism, it is worth elaborating with a few examples of his writing:

> Zionism entails not only a yearning to purchase a foothold in the promised land for our tormented people . . . [but] it also represents an aspiration to achieve moral, spiritual goals.[4]

> The world will be liberated by our freedom, enriched by our wealth, magnified by our greatness. And whatever we attempt there to accomplish for our own welfare will react powerfully and beneficially for the good of humanity.[5]

> It [the coming Jewish state] is founded on the ideas which are a common product of all civilized nations. . . . [W]e stand on the shoulders of other civilized peoples. . . . Our motto must therefore be, now and ever: "Man, you are my brother."[6]

Avi Shlaim, a leading Israeli-British historian, summed up the promise of Zionism: "Zionism embodied the urge to create not merely a new Jewish state in Palestine but also a new society, based on the universal values of freedom, democracy, and social justice."[7] Put differently, in the famous words of the Hebrew Bible, repeatedly cited by Israeli leaders, including by David Ben-Gurion and Benjamin Netanyahu: the Jewish state would become "a light unto the nations."

Where to Put a Jewish State

From the early twentieth century onward, the Zionists refused to consider as separable questions the need for a Jewish state and whether such a state had to be in Palestine—and nowhere else. Put differently, the paradox of Zionism is that while the argument for the right and need of the Jews to have a state of their own was strong (though, as will later be discussed, not uncontested, even by a number of non-Zionist Jews), most of the arguments for the right to create that state *in Palestine* were very weak, based as they were on "principles" that cannot withstand close logical or moral analysis. This is not to say that there was no basis at all for the Jewish claim to sovereignty over Palestine: the argument, rather, is that the claim could not be reconciled with the political and religious rights and claims of the indigenous Palestinian people, which were far more persuasive.

Herzl himself initially appeared to consider the question of where the Jewish state should be located as an open one, a practical rather than an ideological or religious issue: "I can tell you everything about the 'promised Land' except its location. This will be left to a conference of outstanding Jewish geographers, who will decide where to set up the Jewish state, after examining all the geological, climatic . . . [and] natural circumstances."[8]

To be sure, Herzl did agree with most other Zionists that in the long run Palestine must become the homeland, nation, and state of the Jewish people: "It is evident," he told the 1903 Zionist Congress, "[that] the Jewish people can have no ultimate goal other than Palestine."[9] At that moment, however, Palestine was not an option, in light of the implacable opposition of its existing rulers, the Ottoman Empire. Thus, Herzl and other practical and nonreligious Zionists concluded that priority must be given to rescuing the endangered Jews of Europe and providing them with safe havens—perhaps in Argentina, he suggested, or someplace else in South America: "I am thinking of giving the movement a closer territorial goal, preserving Zion as the final goal."[10]

Some thought was given to the possible alternatives to Palestine, though almost all of them held little promise. The most serious one was the British government's April 1903 offer to give some 5,000 square miles of what was then British East Africa (today, Kenya and Uganda) as a refuge for the Jewish people. Herzl took the offer seriously and presented it to the Zionist Congress of 1903, recommending that it be seriously investigated as an interim place of immediate and temporary refuge, pending a "return" of the Jews to Palestine. Most of the delegates, however, especially the religious Zionists, opposed any alternative to Palestine—even as a temporary refuge. Consequently, two years later the Zionist Congress decisively rejected any effort to create the Jewish state in any place but biblical Palestine.

Benjamin Netanyahu's grandfather, a rabbi, told his son Benzion why the Zionist movement could never accept the Uganda plan, even if it was feasible:

> For so many centuries the Jewish people had made so many sacrifices for this land, had shed their blood for it, had prayed for a thousand years to return to it, had tied their most intimate hopes to its revival—we considered it inconceivable that we would now betray the generations of Jews who had fought and died for this end.[11]

If the Zionists had accepted the British offer, undoubtedly they would have eventually sought to transform the refuge into a Jewish state, just as later occurred in Palestine; in part for that reason, the offer was bitterly opposed by the British settlers in East Africa. Further, even if their opposition had been overcome, it is likely that a Western-imposed East African Israel would have come into conflict with the post–World War II nationalist uprisings in what became Uganda and Kenya, resulting in an African-Israeli rather than an Arab-Israeli conflict.

It could be argued that despite strong arguments for the creation of a Jewish state, especially in the aftermath of the Holocaust, in practical fact there was no place to put it that did not inflict a grave injustice on another people. But perhaps that was not necessarily the case. In 1941, Lord Moyne, one of Britain's leading colonial officials for the Middle East, suggested to David Ben-Gurion that Jewish refugees could be resettled in East Prussia after Germany was defeated and the area's German inhabitants were expelled. However, Ben-Gurion is said to have responded, "The only way to get Jews to go [to East Prussia] would be with machine guns."[12]

Then, in early 1945, Franklin Roosevelt met with King Ibn Saud of Saudi Arabia to discuss the Palestine issue. According to several accounts, Roosevelt was considering the establishment of "an exclusively Jewish Palestine (with the Arabs bribed to leave)." However, Saud was vehemently opposed and "recommended instead that the Jewish refugees of Nazi oppression be granted the choicest homes and land of the defeated Germans."[13] Quite reasonably Saud asked: "What injury have the Arabs done to the Jews of Europe? . . . Make the enemy and the oppressor pay."[14]

It might have worked: ex-Nazi Germany was probably the only country in which the right of a people not to be expelled to make way for a Jewish homeland could have been morally overridden and where, in practice, a Jewish state might have been successfully imposed: in light of the unconditional surrender of Germany, the subsequent growing awareness of the German people of its collective guilt in the Holocaust and its acceptance of its obligations to the Jewish people, and—hardly least—the long postwar occupation of Germany by the Allied powers.

Nothing came of such proposals, of course, in part because Roosevelt and other Allied leaders quickly came to believe that a full German recovery was essential in order for the war-devastated economies of Western Europe to be rebuilt, but also because a possible "German solution" continued to be completely unacceptable to Ben-Gurion and other Zionist leaders, implacably committed as they were to Palestine.[15]

In any case, it is a reasonable argument that the early search for a better solution than Palestine as the site for a Jewish state was abandoned by the Zionist leaders prematurely and, more important, for the wrong reasons. That is, even if alternatives to Palestine ultimately had proven to be unfeasible, the very willingness to search for them would have required a dissociation of Zionism from biblical theology, and that would have made the need for a just compromise with the Palestinians evident from the start.

Narratives

Every nation constructs a "narrative"—that is, tells a story—about its history, or rather its imagined history. The "collective memories" that constitute such narratives play an important role in creating a commonly shared past and socializing a people into the beliefs—or myths—of their nation-state and society. Explicating such narratives is crucial to understanding why nations caught in "intractable conflicts" think and behave as they do. As the Israeli psychologist and historian Daniel Bar-Tal puts it in his seminal book on national narratives and their dangers:

> The major reasons for the construction of narratives is that human beings in general need a reasoned, coherent, and meaningful story that provides illumination, justification, and explanation of the reality in which they live. This need is especially essential in situations of violent and lasting conflicts.[16]

The problem with national narratives, however, is that no matter how sincere and deeply felt they may be, they invariably include mythologies that can't stand up to serious and dispassionate scrutiny, and which in times of interstate conflicts can have disastrous consequences. In the classical words of the nineteenth-century French philosopher and historian Ernst Renan: "A nation is a group of people united by a mistaken view about the past and a hatred of their neighbors."[17] Or, as Bar-Tal puts it:

> Collective memory is selective, biased, and distortive [and] in time of intractable conflict these features are greatly magnified. . . . [It] omits certain facts, adds doubtful ones, changes the accounts of events, makes biased inferences . . . [and] directs the focus on the past without providing an ability to evaluate properly the present and plan for the future.[18]

In short (as previously observed), in order to understand *why* states behave as they do, especially in national conflicts, one must know their historical narratives. But in order to understand the *realities and consequences* of such conflicts—that is, the historical truths rather than the myths—it is not the narratives that count but the facts.

Nowhere is this more important than in the Arab-Israeli and Israeli-Palestinian conflicts. The matter is so important that the general observation in the Introduction to this book bears repeating: among both Israelis and Americans there has been no other conflict that has been so badly understood, so impervious to the ever-growing and overwhelming historical evidence, and in which the mythology has had such devastating consequences. Demonstrating the validity of this argument—and the obvious policy implications that follow from it—is the single most important purpose of this book.

The Zionist/Israeli Narrative

According to the standard Zionist and then the Israeli narrative, for a number of reasons the land of Palestine rightfully belongs to the Jewish people—and no others, including today's Palestinians. A number of arguments are made to support and justify this claim, some based on religious and ancient territorial claims, others on late nineteenth- and twentieth-century history.

First, it is argued that according to the book of Genesis, God promised Abraham, the patriarch of the ancient Jews, that he and his descendants would have the land of Canaan—largely, ancient Palestine—"for an everlasting possession" (Genesis 17:8). The promise that Palestine would be Jewish for eternity, it is said, was then reaffirmed in the covenant between God and the leaders of the Jewish tribes, Moses and his successor Joshua, who led their followers out of Egypt into the Promised Land, conquered the Canaanites, and established a great Jewish kingdom under King David and his son Solomon in the entire land of Palestine.

The Jews continued to inhabit and rule Palestine for many centuries, the story continues, until the Romans conquered the land in 63 BCE and then in 70 CE destroyed the Jewish temple and largely expelled the Jews from the country. However, it is argued, throughout the next twenty centuries many Jews continued to live and practice their religion there, supplemented on occasion by new waves of Jewish immigration.

Consequently, the Zionist argument holds, there has been an unbroken and legitimate Jewish claim to the land of Palestine—despite the Muslim conquest of the land in the seventh century, the Crusader conquests and rule in the eleventh and twelfth centuries, and the Ottoman conquest in the sixteenth century. The Ottoman Empire then ruled Palestine until the end of World War I, after which the British ruled until they withdrew in 1948. Even so, it is implicit in the Zionist narrative that the Romans, the Arabs, the Christians, the Turks (and others) were the true foreigners in Palestine, no matter how long they had lived and ruled there, and no matter how small—and for long periods, tiny—the Jewish population.

Beginning in the late nineteenth century, the Zionist narrative continues, a sovereign Jewish homeland in Palestine was "reborn." An official Israeli government publication puts it this way: "The land seemed eminently suitable for [this] purpose: a marginal province of the weak Ottoman Empire, sparsely inhabited by a population consisting of various religious groups and seemingly lacking any national consciousness or ambitions of its own; a motherland waiting to be redeemed from centuries of neglect and decay by its legitimate sons."[19]

To be sure, during the first half of the twentieth century there was growing (and often violent) indigenous Arab resistance to the Zionist settlers and claims to sovereignty in Palestine. However, as the Israeli historian Shlomo Sand puts it, "The leaders of the Zionist community portrayed it not as an authentic protonationalist uprising against foreign invasion, but rather as the product of anti-Semitic incitement on the part of hostile Arab leaders."[20]

This narrative then became dominant in Israel—and in many ways still is. As Bar-Tal writes:

> From the moment of the state's establishment in 1948 until the early 1970s, the conflict-supporting narratives were hegemonic and pervasive in all the institutions and channels of communication, whether formal or informal, expressed in leaders' speeches, literature, textbooks, news and commentary in the press and on the radio, and in films and plays.[21]

Thus, according to the dominant Israeli narrative, the Israeli-Palestinian conflict is the consequence of over a century of mindless Arab hatred of the Jews, and an unwillingness to match the Jewish effort to reach a fair compromise over the ancient land of Palestine.[22] The Zionist-Palestinian conflict then escalated into a wider Arab-Israeli conflict, according to the narrative, when the Arabs rejected the 1947 United Nations partition plan, which provided for the division of Palestine between the Jews and the Arabs and the creation of the state of Israel.

In a continuing spirit of compromise, the narrative continues, the Zionist leadership accepted the UN plan, but the Palestinians and the neighboring Arab states rejected it and launched an unprovoked invasion designed to destroy the new Israeli state. In the course of the ensuing war, hundreds of thousands of Palestinians living within Israel's boundaries fled to the neighboring Arab states, supposedly ordered or urged to do so by the invading Arab armies—although the Israeli leadership had urged the Palestinians *not* to leave, seeking to demonstrate that the Palestinians and Israelis could live side by side within a Jewish state.

After the 1948 war, the story continues, Israel remained willing to settle the conflict on the basis of generous compromise, but they could find no Palestinian or other Arab leaders with whom to negotiate. As Abba Eban famously put it, "The Arabs never missed an opportunity to miss an opportunity." The refugee issue remained unresolved, largely because it suited the cynical purposes of the Arab states to keep it festering; the result was the creation of Palestinian guerrilla terrorism, aided by the neighboring Arab states, especially Egypt and Syria. This local and international terrorism led, in turn, to new Arab-Israeli wars in 1956, 1967, and 1973, all of them forced on Israel by Arab aggression.

The wall of monolithic Arab hostility was not breached, the narrative continues, until Anwar Sadat of Egypt decided to make peace with Israel in the late 1970s, followed twenty years later by King Hussein of Jordan. But even today, it is said, the overall Arab-Israeli conflict continues, because neither the Palestinians nor the rest of the Arab states are willing to accept fair compromises.

So goes the Israeli narrative. Its accuracy is quite another issue, which I address throughout this book.

The Palestinian Narrative

The Palestinian narrative is quite simple: except for small minorities of Jews and non-Palestinian Christians, for over 2,000 years the Palestinians had been the indigenous population of the land of Palestine, whether or not ruled by foreign empires: the Romans, the Crusaders, the Ottoman Turks, the British, culminating (in the words of a publication of the Arab Information Center) with "the uprooting and dispossession of an entire nation to make room for . . . Jews from all parts of the world . . . in order to fulfill the political aspirations of Zionism."[23]

Given the two diametrically opposed national narratives, one common argument among observers of goodwill is that since the conflict between the narratives is irresolvable, the only way out of "the tragedy" is for each side to "recognize" each other's narrative. This is the view, for one example, of Uri Avnery—who for over sixty years was one of Israel's leading dissidents—who wrote, "There is not one narrative, but two. Each side is convinced of the absolute justice of its cause . . . [and] neither side can be entirely blamed."[24]

The sentiment is admirable, but it begs the question of the relative historical accuracy of the conflicting narratives. For example, if the Palestinian narrative is largely true and the Israeli narrative is largely false—and that is what this book argues—the burden of revising the narratives would fall far more heavily on Israel, for in that case it would be the Israelis who are not only historically but also morally in the wrong. Given the history of the Jews, it may be understandable that the Israelis see themselves as victims—of the Palestinians, of the Arabs as a whole, and sometimes of the world in general. But however understandable that perspective, it is not only unconvincing but it is devastating to the chances of an Israeli-Palestinian peace agreement: in *this* conflict it is largely the Israelis who are the aggressors and the Palestinians who are the victims.

Aside from the fact that the symmetry of responsibility implied in either the "tragic" or the "conflicting narratives" arguments is unconvincing, it is far from clear that mutual recognition of each other's narrative would do much to resolve the conflict. To be sure, there is a strong argument—accepted even by such severe critics of Zionism as the Israeli "new historian" Ilan Pappé and the late Palestinian-American writer Edward Said—that a Palestinian acknowledgment of the Holocaust and its consequences for the Jews might have a powerfully positive effect on Israeli attitudes and behaviors toward the Palestinians.[25]

Even granting that argument, if the Zionist narrative is mostly historically inaccurate—as is argued here—it would be the Israelis who would need to fundamentally reconsider their narrative of victimization by the Palestinians. However, even if they were to acknowledge the essential truthfulness of the Palestinian narrative, that might not be sufficient to lead to significant changes in Israeli policies, for, as later discussed, many of the most important Zionist leaders—in particular, Vladimir Jabotinsky, David Ben-Gurion, and Moshe Dayan—were surprisingly forthright in acknowledging that the Palestinian "narrative" of Zionist/Israeli dispossession of their rights was accurate; it's just that they believed that the Zionists had no choice but to override those rights.

What's Right and What's Wrong with the Zionist Argument?

The first step in answering that question is to sort out Zionism's good arguments from its bad ones, beginning with the ones drawn from ancient history—or, rather, ancient history as it is understood, or imagined, by adherents of the biblically based Zionist narrative.

The Religious Argument

In theory, the purely religious biblical argument is separable from the essentially historical one (though those who base Zionism's legitimacy on biblical arguments rarely make this distinction). As already noted, the religious argument is simple and straightforward: God promised Palestine to the Jews, forever. That kind of argument, however, will be convincing only to religious literalists and fundamentalists; indeed, it is hardly clear that most of the Jewish people themselves—the great majority of them non-Orthodox or largely secular—are persuaded by the religious argument.

More important, Christians and Muslims also have strong historical connections, claims, and ties to Palestine based on religion and sentiment. That being the case, it is not surprising that the religious Zionist argument has failed to convince the Muslim and most of the Christian world—other than the Christian Zionist fundamentalists— that their own religious claims to the land must be subordinated to those of the Jews.

In short, there is no persuasive general principle that privileges the Zionist claim of ancient religious rights, let alone eternal ones, over the similar claims of Christians and Muslims.

The Historical Argument

The second Zionist argument based on the Bible is a historical rather than a religious one—or, more accurately, as I have summarized earlier, it is based on ancient history as described in the Hebrew Bible.

To begin with, no part of the Zionist/Israeli narrative that is based on the Hebrew Old Testament stands up to serious scrutiny, and in the last few decades the accuracy of nearly every part of that narrative has been decisively rejected by leading historians and archaeologists—*especially* Israeli ones—who have concluded that the biblical account must be regarded as theology and myth rather than genuine history.[26] There is little or no archaeological evidence that the biblical figures who are central to the Zionist/Israeli narrative—Abraham, Moses, David, and

Solomon—existed. And even if they were actual rather than mythical figures, the scholarship has demonstrated that there is little historical or archaeological evidence in support of the "Exodus" myth and other biblical stories: that Palestine was the major homeland of the Jews until they were expelled by the Romans, that Moses and other Patriarchs led the Jews out of Egypt and conquered Canaan (Palestine), and that King David and King Solomon, ruling from Jerusalem, established an extensive Jewish kingdom over most of the land.

In short, as the Israeli archaeologist Israel Finkelstein stated in 2000, it had been "common knowledge among serious scholars for years" that Zionism was based on biblical myths or folktales that were adopted to bolster the political claim that the Jewish people were rightfully and eternally sovereign over the land of Palestine.[27] In 2017, an Israeli journalist reviewed the scholarship and concluded: "It is hard to find a mainstream archaeologist prepared to defend the Biblical description[s]."[28]

The Myth of Original Homeland, Exile, and Expulsion

It is important to examine the biblically based myths in greater detail. To begin, archaeologists and historians have established that there has never been one Jewish "homeland," whether in Palestine or anywhere else. Long before the Roman conquest of Palestine and the subsequent Jewish revolt, there were large Jewish communities in Egypt, Mesopotamia, Asia Minor, and throughout the Mediterranean basin. Moreover, contrary to the myth, there is no evidence that the Jews established political sovereignty or control over ancient Palestine, which was inhabited by a number of peoples, no one of which was dominant.[29]

In 66–70 CE a Jewish rebellion against Roman rule in Palestine was suppressed. Zionist mythology holds that "the Romans may have laid the entire nation waste between AD 70 and 135, slaughtering as many as 600,000 Jews, and carrying off half that number in bondage."[30] This myth is no longer taken seriously by informed historians. In his review of the scholarship, Charles H. Manekin (writing under his pen name Jeremiah Haber), a Hebrew University philosopher and historian, writes that "there is no contemporary evidence—i.e., first and second centuries CE—that anything like an exile took place." Rather, some of the rebels were killed, others died of hunger, and some prisoners became Roman slaves.[31] And over the centuries, most of the Jews who remained in Palestine became Christians, and later Muslims, leaving only a small group that preserved its Jewish identity.

Although the Zionists are correct that there was a continuing Jewish presence, between the first and mid-nineteenth centuries it consisted only of some 5,000 or 6,000 nonpolitical religious fundamentalists in Jerusalem and two or three other towns or villages. Jewish immigration increased somewhat after that, but by the end of the nineteenth century there were still only about 50,000 Jews in Palestine.[32]

More important, even if the Jewish population of Palestine had been far larger, I argue that it would not have established a "right" of permanent sovereignty over the land.

The Myth of the "Diaspora"

However small the Jewish community in Palestine was from the first through most of the nineteenth century, the mythology holds that the Jewish people as a whole were unwillingly confined to exiled communities—the "Diaspora"—in other lands, but maintained their attachment to the land of Palestine and yearned to eventually "return" to it.

One Zionist writer put it this way: "Despite the loss of political independence and the dispersion of the Jewish people, the true home of the Jews remained Jerusalem and the Land of Israel; the idea of eventual return from the four corners of the earth was never abandoned."[33] Or, as the Hebrew Bible (Psalm 137) puts it: "If I forget thee, O Jerusalem, let my right hand forget her cunning."

It is undoubtedly true that *some* kind of a Jewish identification, especially among religious Jews, has resonated throughout diaspora history—"Next year in Jerusalem," and the like—but even during the late nineteenth and early twentieth centuries an overwhelming majority of the East European Jews threatened by anti-Semitism sought to move to the West, particularly the United States, rather than go to Palestine. And today it is clear that the overwhelming majority of the Jewish people do not think of themselves in any meaningful way as a diaspora yearning to "return" to Palestine—else they would have done so, as they now have had the right and (in most cases) the ability to move to Israel for some seventy years.

Suppose the Biblical Mythology Were True?

For the sake of analysis, for the moment let us leave aside the historical and archaeological evidence and assume that the Zionist narrative and the argument on which it is based is accurate: that Palestine was the homeland of the Jewish people who ruled it for many centuries until they were driven out by the Romans, that nonetheless some Jewish communities remained in Palestine for the next 2,000 years, and that the remainder of the scattered Jewish people never stopped yearning and striving for the reestablishment of their homeland and a Jewish state in Palestine—so for all those reasons, the historical land of Palestine eternally belongs to the Jewish people.

That argument, however, is more a matter of special pleading for the Jews than one based on a persuasive and universally applicable principle. For what would the principle be? That lands conquered by force would eternally belong to the "original" inhabitants (whatever that might mean), no matter how many centuries other peoples had been a majority in that land, so long as the previous inhabitants were still a distinguishable people, some small minority of which continued to yearn to "return" to their "homeland"?

The problem for that Zionist argument, of course, is that there is no such universal principle. That is, even if the mythology were true, that would not establish a persuasive modern Jewish claim to the land of Palestine. The argument that an ancient claim to a land has precedence over very long periods of a different reality—in Palestine, eight centuries of Christianity followed by thirteen centuries of an overwhelming Islamic majority—is accepted nowhere else in the world, whether in law, moral reasoning, or plain common sense.

Put differently, there is scarcely any place on earth that at one time or another has not been conquered, subjugated, and populated by other peoples. Yet there is no other place in which it is taken to be a serious argument that even if more than twenty centuries have passed since the expulsion of a people from their homelands, they still retain their right to permanent political sovereignty there, if necessary overriding the political and other rights of the peoples who have inhabited the land since then, including most of its present-day inhabitants. If there was no way to establish some kind of limit to land claims by right of previous inhabitance, there would be no principle that would prohibit endless wars of restitution and protect international stability from the law of the jungle.

To be sure, ascertaining the point at which the passage of time has nullified the legal or moral validity of previous land claims cannot be precise, and certainly there are hard cases—the Zionist claim, however, is not one of them. Today a kind of tacit or commonsense consensus has evolved to establish a rough metaphorical statute of limitations on land claims by right of previous inhabitance. A morally plausible range might look something like this:

- The passage of a few years is not enough to wipe out past rights. Thus, during the 1990s it was widely accepted that the Bosnians had a moral right to reverse the Serbian ethnic cleansing of Yugoslavia—even though such a reversal required the dispossession of Serbs who had relatively recently taken over abandoned homes and villages.
- The passage of, say, sixty or seventy years creates a complex problem, both in principle and in practice. On the one hand, for example, few argue—not even many of the dislocated people themselves—that the ethnic Germans expelled from Czechoslovakia and elsewhere in the aftermath of World War II have a right to return to their pre-war homelands. On the other hand, of course, one of the central issues in the Arab-Israeli conflict, even today, is precisely whether or not the Palestinian people have a legitimate "right of return" to the lands from which they were expelled during the 1947–48 period.[34]
- The longer the passage of time, the less the complexity. Certainly, for example, the passage of 150 years is too long. Thus, while there is no doubt

that while Americans in the nineteenth century illegitimately and forcibly conquered much of what became the United States from Mexico and the Native Americans, it does not follow that Mexico could legitimately reclaim Texas or that today's Native Americans have even the theoretical moral right to reconquer the West.

If this way of looking at the issue is persuasive, then what is left of the Zionist argument that is based on ancient history? For over thirty centuries Palestine (or Canaan) has been repeatedly conquered: by the Assyrians, by the Babylonians, by Alexander the Great, by the Roman Empire, by the Crusaders, by the Arabs, and by the Ottoman Empire. After each of these conquests, the previous inhabitants of the land were subjugated by the new rulers who then held sway, sometimes for centuries.

In light of these facts, some versions of the Zionist argument hold that violent conquests do not invalidate the moral and political rights of the previous inhabitants. Among other problems with that argument, though, is the fact the Jewish Bible itself claims that *the Jews themselves were conquerors*, defeating the previous indigenous peoples of the land of Palestine, the Canaanites.

Given all these issues, who should be regarded as the "rightful" claimants to Palestine? Absent a religious basis ("the Promised Land") accepted by everyone, including those of different nationalities and religions, stopping the clock as it marches backward in time to twenty centuries ago, *neither earlier nor later*, must be completely arbitrary and self-serving.[35]

Put differently, by what objective criteria are the claims of one set of victims—the Jews supposedly driven out of Palestine by the Romans 2,000 years ago—privileged over all other such claims? If the most ancient of the "original" victimization is the criterion, then it must follow that the descendants of the Canaanites—in some accounts, the *Syrians,* whose descendants live in Lebanon today![36]—must have priority over the descendants of the Jews. On the other hand, if more recent victimization is the criterion, then the victims of various conquests of Palestine since the end of the Roman Empire must have priority over the Jews.

Indeed, the great irony of the Zionist narrative is that unlike the alleged Roman expulsion, the Israeli expulsion of the Palestinians is both demonstrable and far more recent—seventy years ago, not 2,000. While it is perhaps arguable whether this history creates a present-day Palestinian "right of return," there can be no doubt that the Palestinian argument is far more historically accurate, intellectually respectable, and arguably far better grounded in moral principle than is its Zionist counterpart.

In sum, the Zionist arguments based on religious claims, biblical mythology, or ancient territorial rights cannot stand up to serious analysis. If Zionism ever had a persuasive claim for a Jewish state, it would have to rest on the modern period, meaning from the late nineteenth century through today.

The Modern Arguments for Zionism

Prior to the United Nations Partition Plan that gave *conditional* international support for the creation of Israel (discussed in Chapter 4), the main modern Zionist arguments for a Jewish state in Palestine are based on the British Balfour Declaration of 1917, the League of Nations Mandate to Britain in 1923, and above all, the Holocaust.

The Balfour Declaration and the League of Nations Mandate

British sympathy for Jewish aspirations in Palestine go back at least to the nineteenth century: in 1875 Lord Shaftesbury, a prominent British politician and religious leader, wrote: "We have here a land teeming with fertility and rich history, but almost without an inhabitant—a country without a people and look! Scattered over the world, a people without a country."[37]

On November 2, 1917, British foreign secretary Arthur Balfour issued the following official statement: "His Majesty's Government view with favor the establishment in Palestine of a national home for the Jewish people, and will use their best endeavors to facilitate the achievement of this object, it being clearly understood that nothing shall be done which may prejudice the civil and religious rights of existing non-Jewish communities in Palestine, or the rights and political status enjoyed by Jews in any other country."

The Balfour Declaration, as it has come to be known, was motivated by a number of factors. First, the British government hoped that it would lead to increased Russian and especially US support for Britain in World War I—both Balfour and Prime Minister Lloyd George believed that the Jews had great power in those countries. Second, they believed that establishing a presumptively friendly and pro-British Jewish homeland in the Middle East would serve Britain's colonial and strategic interests, particularly its interest in retaining control over the Suez Canal, its "gateway to India."

Third, as Ilan Pappé writes, it was possible that "pious Christians, such as British Prime Minister David Lloyd George, were motivated by a wish to facilitate the return of the Jews to precipitate the second coming of the Messiah."[38]

Finally, there is no reason to doubt that Balfour, Lloyd George, and especially Winston Churchill (then a powerful member of the cabinet) were genuinely sympathetic to the plight of European Jewry. As the prominent Israeli historian Benny Morris writes: "Brought up on the Bible and on a belief in the Jews' contribution to Judeo-Christian civilization . . . these [leading British officials] . . . believed that Christendom owed the Jews a debt and that it must atone for two thousand years of persecution by restoring them to their land."[39] As well, most British leaders at that time were not much interested in Arab rights; in 1919 Balfour wrote: "Zionism . . . is rooted in age-long traditions, in present needs, in future hopes of far profounder import than the desires and prejudices of the 700,000 Arabs who now inhabit that ancient land."[40]

In particular, Churchill is said to have been "a lifelong Zionist," who wrote, "It was manifestly right that the scattered Jews should have a national center and a national home in Palestine . . . [which] would be good for the world, good for the Jews, good for the British Empire, but also good for the Arabs who dwell in Palestine. . . . They shall share in the benefits and progress of Zionism."[41]

In any case, the British government was not alone among Western states in believing that there was a strong moral case for the Balfour Declaration. For example, in 1917, Jules Cambon, a leading French government official, stated, "It would be a just and compensatory act to support, with the help of the powers, the revival of the Jewish nation in the land from which it was expelled centuries ago." And in 1920 President Woodrow Wilson stated, "I have become convinced that the allies, with the full assent of our government and people, agree that the foundations for a Jewish community be laid in Palestine."[42]

In light of the powerful support for the Balfour Declaration, the League of Nations incorporated it into the preamble of the 1923 "Mandate" that established British rule over Palestine, stating that "recognition has thereby been given to the historical connection of the Jewish people with Palestine and to the grounds for reconstituting their national home in that country." As a result, since 1917 the Zionist movement has argued that the Balfour Declaration and the League of Nations Mandate provided the modern legal and moral basis for the creation of a Jewish state of Israel.

Though not devoid of merit, in the final analysis that argument is not convincing, for in the first instance the commitment was inconsistent with previous British promises to Arab leaders, who in 1915 were promised they would be granted political independence under an Arab kingdom that would rule Palestine, Transjordan, and other areas if they mounted a revolt against the Ottoman Empire, allied with Germany in World War I.

Second, the Balfour Doctrine was deliberately vague and ambiguous: as has been widely noted, it did not call for a Jewish *state* in Palestine, but only a "national home," however that was to be defined; nor did it define the term "Palestine," whose territory and borders were left undetermined.

Third, the Balfour Doctrine and the League Mandate were conditional, stipulating that the "non-Jewish" communities of Palestine—some 90 percent of the indigenous peoples!—must retain their "civil and religious rights." What constituted "civil rights"? Did they include political rights? If not, why not? The Declaration and the Mandate were silent on these key issues.

Finally, and perhaps most fundamentally, whatever their motives for doing so, neither the British nor the League of Nations—basically a club of colonial powers—had the right to give political control over Palestine to the 50,000 Jews who then lived there, rather than to the 700,000 Arabs.

In short, the Balfour Declaration and the League Mandate were simply unilateral ukases of the leading colonial powers of the time, actions essentially of force, undertaken not only without regard to the rights and feelings of the local inhabitants but indeed in contradiction to the promises made to them earlier. As such, the promises to the Jews—even to the extent that the authors of the mandate were motivated by genuine moral commitment rather than simply colonial national interests—finally had no more legal or moral standing than any other colonialist actions.

Is Zionism Colonialism?

In addition to the clear fact that the support of Western colonialism was crucial to Zionism's success in creating a Jewish state in the Middle East, it is often argued that Zionism *itself* is a form of colonialism—"settler colonialism," as it is commonly put. This is widely charged not only by the Arab world but by many other critics of Israel, among them some Israeli historians.

The connections between Zionism and Western colonialism in the early decades of the twentieth century are undeniable. The early Zionist leaders, Herzl, Chaim Weizmann, and others, products of the colonial age, shared the belief that European colonialism would bring the blessings of Western civilization to a lesser, backward people. Herzl put it this way: a Jewish state would serve as "a rampart of Europe against Asia, an outpost of civilization as opposed to barbarism."[43]

The Jewish immigrants from Europe typically treated the indigenous inhabitants of the land in the same spirit of blindness, indifference, or outright hostility as did colonialist settlers throughout the non-Western world during this period, often resorting to coercion and violence when they faced resistance.

That said, there were also important differences between Zionism and typical Western colonialism, which unlike Zionism had no objective claim of necessity but rather was driven by economic gain or simple greed, the ideological/racist belief in "the white man's burden," or even by the goal of power for its own sake. Still, it is often argued that Zionism's "settler colonialism"—as also occurred in North America and Australia—was no less unjust than other Western forms of colonialism. Whether or not that is persuasive, the more important point is that even before the Holocaust, the case for the creation of an independent Jewish state that had the means to defend itself was well grounded in historical realities—realities that had nothing to do with colonialism.

In an unfortunately rare Arab acknowledgment of the distinctions between Western colonialism and the Jewish predicament, Khaled Diab, an Egyptian journalist, addressed the issue:

> Though Zionists certainly had colonial designs on Palestine, the exclusive focus on Zionist imperialism overlooked the reality that these bedraggled Jews who arrived in Palestine were not just colonists but also refugees,

> oppressed natives fleeing persecution and murder in their homelands.... The inability to understand this element hurt the Palestinian cause because it led Arabs to believe that Zionism was a classical form of European colonialism, and so if they resisted it long enough and hard enough, the newcomers would eventually go home. But Zionism differed.... Jews who came to Palestine felt they had no "home" to return to, and that Palestine was the only home left to them.[44]

Still, it is important to distinguish between the earlier Zionist settling of Palestine and its expansion into the West Bank, Arab East Jerusalem, and Gaza after its conquest of them in 1967, which can certainly be described as illegitimate "settler colonialism," pure and simple.[45]

Zionism and Racism

Closely related to the issue of whether Zionism is colonialism is the issue of whether "Zionism is a form of racism," as stated in a famous—or infamous—1975 UN General Assembly resolution. A storm of protest followed—not only in Israel, but throughout the West—and continued until 1991, when the General Assembly voted to revoke the resolution. Since it is obvious that the votes both for the original resolution and its revocation were the consequence of international political calculations as well as domestic politics, rather than of a careful philosophical inquiry into the nature of racism, it is worth examining the question: *Is* Zionism a form of racism?

With only minor differences, all leading dictionaries, as well as common usage, define "racism" as the belief that one's own race or ethnicity is inherently superior to others. (It is true that the word is sometimes used in other senses, but that just muddies its meaning and usual connotations.) Except for a small minority of religious zealots, Zionist ideology is not based on the belief that the Jews are *superior* to others; on the contrary, it means that they are just more *vulnerable,* or potentially so.

Given that historical reality, it must follow that Zionism is not *inherently* or unavoidably racist. The belief to the contrary seems to be primarily based on three factors. The first is that Israel's "Law of Return" automatically grants citizenship to Jews, and to no others. However, even a number of Western democracies that are generally not regarded as being "racist"—including Finland, Italy, Greece, Ireland, and even Germany—to one degree or another privilege ethnic origin in establishing national citizenship. To be sure, ethnic origin is not a *precondition* for citizenship in those countries—but neither is it in Israel, where about 21 percent of the citizens of that country are Arab.

Second, the insistence by most Israelis that their country must remain a "Jewish state" can be understood to be motivated by anti-Arab racism—and in fact that animus clearly does play a significant role. Nonetheless, at its most fundamental level, the Jewish state concept is based on the belief—an only too plausible belief, and one that has nothing whatever to do with racism—that history demonstrated the need for a state in which the Jewish people control their own destiny.

That said, even if it is persuasive that Zionist ideology is not inherently or necessarily racist (at least in the sense of connoting Jewish racial superiority), the third factor explaining that still widely held belief among critics of Israel is the undeniable evidence that Israeli society in recent decades *has* become increasingly racist. Henry Siegman, a former leader of global Zionism as well as national director of the American Jewish Congress who has become a severe critic of Israel, has put it best: "Netanyahu and his government have proven that although Zionism is not racism, Zionists can indeed be racists."[46]

In light of the trends in Israeli society, it must be acknowledged that the distinction between Zionism and racism may not remain persuasive for much longer.

The Holocaust

I have been arguing that one of the many tragedies of the Israeli-Palestinian conflict is that Zionism's historically inaccurate, irrelevant, or otherwise unpersuasive arguments for privileging the Jewish claims to sovereignty in Palestine over those of its indigenous inhabitants are unnecessary. By the early 1940s, there was one very strong—and, in my view, sufficient—argument: the Holocaust, which rightly convinced most Western governments and their peoples that there was now an overwhelming and urgent moral case for the creation of a Jewish state and a haven for the victims of anti-Semitism.[47]

But why in Palestine? That is a different and morally far more complex matter: the indigenous inhabitants who would lose their political rights were in no way responsible for the Holocaust, let alone for the long history of murderous European anti-Semitism that produced Zionism. As the Palestinians always ask, and—up to a point—persuasively so: Why should we be made to pay for evils we did not commit?[48] The problem, of course, is that *anywhere* a Jewish state was created, essentially by force majeure, would have necessarily and unavoidably overridden the political rights of the majority of the local inhabitants.

It is often argued that another alternative to the creation of Israel might have been the settlement in the United States of most of the Holocaust survivors and other Jewish refugees in Europe; indeed, it was evident that that would have been the first choice of most of the refugees. But there are two problems with that argument. First, there was still much anti-Semitism in the United States, as well as more general anti-immigration sentiment; as a consequence, the country refused to accept large numbers of Jewish refugees.

Second—and relatedly—resettling the refugees in any place other than Palestine would not necessarily have solved the historical problem of Jewish vulnerability when they are a small minority in countries other than their own; this is why at the end of World War II the Zionist leadership was implacably opposed to refugee resettlement in any place other than Palestine.

By 1947, then, the die was cast: if a Jewish state was to be created there was essentially no practical alternative but a partitioned Palestine, especially as hundreds of thousands of surviving Jewish refugees from Europe began arriving in the country and the British were preparing to end their control and their Mandate over it.

Conclusion

Could the Israeli-Palestinian conflict have been averted, or at least settled long ago? The entire history of the Israeli-Palestinian conflict might have been different had the Israelis abandoned most of the Zionist narrative; other than the argument from historical anti-Semitism and the Holocaust, it is largely mythological, and it is both legally and morally irrelevant even it were true. Put differently, all the Zionist arguments for the creation of a Jewish state in Palestine, and only in Palestine, were unconvincing—save the argument of existential necessity, which was both necessary and sufficient to make the case a strong one.

To be sure, even if the Zionists had rested their case on that single argument and the absence of any other practical solution, a grave injustice to the Palestinians was unavoidable. Had the Zionists acknowledged that injustice, however, there were—and perhaps still are—a number of ways it could have been rectified, apologized for, mitigated, compensated, and significantly diminished—all without compromising the existence of a secure and legitimate Jewish state.[49] The failure to have done so is the great moral failure of Zionism, and the standard Zionist narrative continues to be an enormous psychological obstacle, for both the Israelis and the Palestinians, to a peace settlement between them.

3

The Onset of the Israeli-Palestinian Conflict, 1917–47

Prior to the onset of Zionism in the late nineteenth century, there were about 15,000 Jews in Palestine, perhaps 3 percent of the total population. In the next several decades, the Jewish population grew only slightly; when the Balfour Declaration was proclaimed in 1917, the generally accepted estimate was that the total population of Palestine—as that land was defined by the British and a few years later by the League Mandate—was about 750,000, of whom 50,000–60,000 or less than 9 percent were Jewish.[1]

The task of the Zionist leaders, as they saw it, was to create a state in Palestine that would be at least 80 percent Jewish.[2] That would not be an easy task: in the demands of the early Zionist leaders—including Chaim Weizmann (president of the Zionist Organization and the first president of Israel) and later David Ben-Gurion—the Jewish state should include Jerusalem, the West Bank of the Jordan River and stretching beyond that to Amman (all allocated to Transjordan—later, Jordan—in the League Mandate), southern Lebanon, the Golan Heights, and other parts of southern Syria and the Gaza Strip.

In 1918, Zionist leaders joined with British mandate officials to propose that a Jewish Palestine should include southern Lebanon up to the Litani River so that the Zionist state could "control all water resources up to their sources."[3] In 1919, the World Zionist organization made public its map of the intended Jewish homeland (Map 3.1).

In 1920, Weizmann wrote to Winston Churchill, then the British colonial secretary, on the future of Palestine. In the words of William Manchester, Churchill's biographer, he "demand[ed] that the Jewish state's eastern boundary be extended east of the Jordan River to include all of Transjordan (now Jordan)." Transjordan, Weizmann continued, "has from the earliest time been an integral and vital part of Palestine." Manchester adds that Weizmann also wanted Palestine's southern frontier "pushed southward."[4]

As well, Ben-Gurion's expansionist agenda clearly affected Arab perceptions of a Zionist danger, for he continued to adhere to these territorial goals, at least in principle—in fact to even somewhat wider ones, including much of the Egyptian

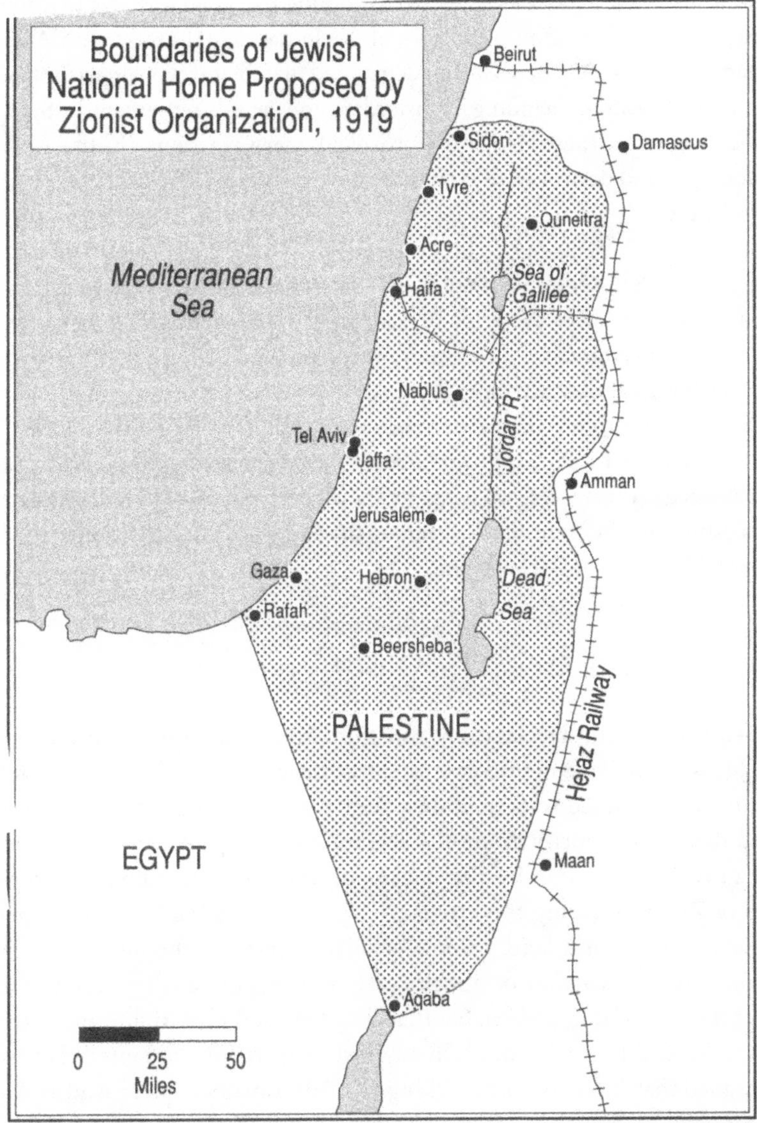

Map 3.1 Boundaries of Jewish National Home Proposed by Zionist Organization, 1919, from Mark Tessler, *A History of the Israeli-Palestinian Conflict*, 2nd ed., 163. Permission granted by Indiana University Press.

Sinai peninsula. Simha Flapan, a peace activist and a political leader in the Israeli Mapam Party as well as a journalist and historian, wrote:

> Ben-Gurion's territorial aims were large. He never tired of reminding his Arab listeners of the historical boundaries of Erez Israel. He had advocated

> these historic boundaries since 1918, quoting the Bible to prove that the Hebrews had settled on both sides of the Jordan. . . . [In talks with Arab leaders in 1934–36] Ben-Gurion demanded that they accept a Jewish state in all of Palestine including Transjordan, and Jewish settlement in Syria and Iraq. . . . [These demands] provoked angry reactions [in the Arab world] . . . and destroyed the last vestiges of trust in the sincerity of Zionist declarations.[5]

As late as 1956, Ben-Gurion reiterated his expansionist goals in a conversation with French officials, prior to the joint British/French/Israeli attack on Egypt in that year. In later years, though, his ambitions were tempered by a pragmatic recognition of the constraints against attaining them.

Whatever their future intentions, the immediate issue facing the Zionists was how their projected state could attain Ben-Gurion's goal of at least an 80 percent Jewish majority. There were two ways: by some combination of Jewish immigration into Palestine and the "transfer"—meaning the emigration or expulsion—of a large number of the Arabs out of Palestine.

"Transfer"

Between the Balfour Declaration and the United Nations partition plan of 1947, Jewish immigration into Palestine steadily grew to about 600,000, but the Palestinians continued to constitute a large majority in the land. The Zionists viewed the Arab majority as an obstacle to Jewish domination and statehood that had to be overcome by one means or another. According to a reputed slogan of Zionism during this period, Palestine was "a land without a people for a people without a land."[6] Some scholars question whether anyone actually said that; but whether or not the early Zionists literally ignored the existence of the Arabs, it is undeniable that they believed their rights and interests were superseded by Jewish ones. In any case, it is well documented that Golda Meir argued that "there is no such thing as a Palestinian people."[7] And as Flapan has observed, such views were not aberrations but "the cornerstone of Zionist policy, initiated by Weizmann and faithfully carried out by Ben-Gurion and his successors."[8]

However they viewed the Palestinians, the Zionists soon realized that it might be impossible to build a Jewish state with a dominant majority solely by increased Jewish immigration: indeed, because of the higher Arab birth rate, the Jews might never achieve even a small majority. Therefore, they began discussing various ways in which the Palestinians could be "transferred"—the preferred Zionist euphemism—out of the country, preferably voluntarily, but by force if necessary.

The scholarship on transfer, especially by Israeli historians, leaves no doubt about its importance in the thinking of every major Zionist leader before and after Israel became a state. One leading Israeli scholar writes:

> The idea of transfer is as old as modern Zionism[;] . . . driving it was an iron logic. There could be no viable Jewish state in all or part of Palestine unless there was a mass displacement of Arab inhabitants, who opposed its emergence and would constitute an active or potential fifth column in its midst. This logic was understood and enunciated, before and during 1948, by Zionist, Arab, and British leaders and officials.[9]

In particular, Theodore Herzl, Chaim Weizmann, and David Ben-Gurion, the three most important leaders in the pre-state era, were all advocates of transfer, including, if necessary, forced transfer.

Herzl. Tom Segev writes: "The hope of emptying Palestine of its Arab inhabitants had been a part of Zionist discourse from its first days. Its earliest incarnation appears in Herzl's diary. 'We shall try to spirit the penniless populations across the border by procuring employment for them in the transit countries, while denying them employment in our own country,' Herzl wrote in June 1895. . . . The evacuation of the Arabs from the territory of the projected Jewish state came up for discussion again and again, in a variety of contexts."[10]

Weizmann. In 1930, Weizmann, the first president of Israel and in Benny Morris's words "the movement's liberal, moderate elder statesman," wrote that an "exchange of populations could be fostered and encouraged" so that the Arabs would "flee into neighboring countries."[11] Similarly, in January 1941 he told other Zionist leaders of his hopes that some 500,000 Palestinians could be transferred into Iraq or Jordan.[12]

Ben-Gurion. If Herzl and Weizmann hoped that the Palestinians could be induced to go elsewhere more or less voluntarily, with economic compensation in one form or another, Ben-Gurion was much more ruthless, or at least unapologetic and blunt. He believed that the Jewish claim to sovereignty over all of Palestine essentially was absolute, for it "stems from the unbreakable bond between the Hebrew people and its historic homeland; from the right of the Jewish nation to independence and national renewal in equal measure to that of the world's other nations; from the status of the Jews in the diaspora as a wandering minority at the mercy of strangers; from the need to find a home for millions of Jewish immigrants; [and] from the underpopulated condition of the land of Israel."[13]

The written record shows that Ben-Gurion repeatedly advocated transfer. Segev writes:

> The Zionists began executing a mini-transfer from the time they began purchasing land and evacuating the Arab tenants. "Up until now we have accomplished our settlement in Palestine by population transfer," Ben-Gurion said in one discussion of the issue. . . . With few exceptions, none of the Zionists disputed the desirability of forced transfer—or its morality. . . . "I do not see anything immoral in it," Ben-Gurion asserted.[14]

Some Zionist historians have questioned whether Ben-Gurion supported the use of force to bring about transfer as opposed to such non-coercive measures as land purchases, but the evidence from Ben-Gurion's diary and other private and public statements shows that while he may have preferred to achieve a Jewish state peacefully and by agreement with the Palestinians, he increasingly understood that was impossible unless he was prepared for major compromises on the Zionist aspirations—which he wasn't. Consequently, there is no doubt that he was perfectly willing to resort to force if necessary. Here are just a few examples:

- A key document, widely cited in the Israeli literature, is Ben-Gurion's 1937 letter to his son in which he defends his willingness to *temporarily* accept the British government's Peel Commission partition plan on the grounds that later the compromise can be discarded by the Zionists, by force if necessary: "We must expel Arabs and take their places, if necessary with the force at our disposal." Even Shabtai Teveth, Ben-Gurion's official biographer, characterizes the letter as making clear that "Ben-Gurion forthrightly embraced territorial expansionism."[15] Another sympathetic biographer, Michael Bar-Zohar, who was granted access to Ben-Gurion's private papers and diaries, quoted from the letter: "A partial Jewish state is not the end, but only the beginning. . . . We shall organize a modern defense force . . . and then I am certain that we will not be prevented from settling in other parts of the country, either by mutual agreement with our Arab neighbors or by some other means."[16]
- In preparing for the 1937 meeting of the Zionist Congress, Ben-Gurion listed the stages of expansion of the pending Jewish state: "immigration . . . systematic, state-controlled settlement . . . a Jewish army . . . [and] *the gradual conquest* of all of Palestine."[17]
- In 1930 Ben-Gurion wrote: "I support compulsory transfer. I don't see anything immoral in it."[18]
- In August 1939 Ben-Gurion told the 20th Zionist Congress that there would now have to be "transfer of a completely different scope. . . . Transfer is what will make possible a comprehensive settlement program. . . . [T]he Arab people have vast empty areas [in Transjordan and Iraq]. . . . Jewish power, which grows steadily, will also increase our possibilities to carry out the transfer on a large scale."[19]

- And in 1941 Ben-Gurion wrote, "Complete transfer without compulsion—and ruthless compulsion at that—is hardly imaginable."[20]

In short, despite his occasional obfuscations on the issue and his belief that it "needed to be done quietly,"[21] Ben-Gurion's diaries, writings, and speeches to Zionist groups demonstrate that he was fully prepared to use force if necessary to expel the Arabs from whatever parts of Palestine the Zionists could include in the projected Jewish state. And, decisively, during the 1947–48 period, that is exactly what happened.

Moshe Sharett, a major Zionist leader in the pre-state period and the second prime minister of Israel, was considerably more liberal than Ben-Gurion and repeatedly clashed with him. Still, he also supported transfer, though not by coercion. Following the flight and expulsion of some 700,000 Palestinians before and during the 1948 war, Sharett wrote to Chaim Weizmann that Israel was determined not only to block any return of the refugees, but in the future "We are equally determined . . . to explore all possibilities of getting rid, once and for all, of the huge Arab minority which originally threatened us."[22]

Was Transfer Morally Acceptable?

Though there were some exceptions, most Zionist leaders believed that the "transfer" of Arabs from Palestine in order to ensure a stable and secure Jewish state was morally acceptable. And not only Zionist leaders: there is no doubt that many respectable non-Zionist and non-Jewish political leaders and well-intentioned intellectuals and writers believed that buying out or bribing the Palestinians to leave was justifiable. Indeed, some even believed that *some* degree of involuntary transfer might be acceptable (see below for my discussion of the Peel Commission report), though it seems highly doubtful—to put it mildly—that anyone would have thought the Zionists were justified in employing the kind of extensive violence that actually occurred.

There were three arguments for the moral acceptability of some form of transfer. The main one—certainly for the Zionists but not only for them—was the alleged necessity of establishing a secure and stable Jewish state in as much of Palestine as was feasible, which was understood to require a large Jewish majority.

The second argument was that no great harm would be done to the Palestinian Arab population that would have to be transferred if that goal were to be reached, because they would be moved—or voluntarily move themselves—only relatively short distances into neighboring Arab states of the same or highly similar culture, economies, customs, religion, language, and even geography.[23]

For example, Chaim Weizmann argued that "the Jewish right has precedence over Arab rights because a Jewish homeland in Palestine is a question of life and death for the Jewish people, while the loss of less than 1 percent of their territory is not decisive for the future of Arabs."[24]

Similarly, Ben-Gurion often argued that for the Jews, Palestine had a different value than it had for the Arabs. As one of his biographers summarized his thinking: "The Arabs had numerous countries; the Jews had only one. One side in this conflict consisted of a fragment of the Arab nation, while the other side included the entire Jewish people, dispersed over the world."[25] In particular, Ben-Gurion believed that the Arabs had little attachment to Jerusalem; in 1929 he wrote that "Jerusalem is not the same thing to the Arabs as it is to the Jews. The Arab people inhabits many great lands."[26]

Israel's third prime minister, Levi Eshkol, who succeeded Ben-Gurion in 1963, was widely considered to be more moderate than Ben-Gurion and other hard-line early Zionist leaders. Yet, in 1967, Eshkol told the Israeli cabinet: "There have always been population exchanges. When coexistence is difficult and countries can't live together, population exchange is the answer. We took in 100,000 Jews from Iraq, let them take in 100,000 Arabs. . . . It's the same language, the same standard [of living], there's water and land. . . . [It] cried out in its justice."[27]

The obvious counterargument to this position was made by Simha Flapan; responding to Weizmann's argument that "the loss of less than 1 percent of their territory is not decisive for the Arabs," Flapan wrote that Weizmann "ignored the fact that for those who lived in Palestine it *was* decisive."[28] Or, consider a contemporary parallel: We don't say that it's not so bad that the Syrians are being driven from their homes today, because they can go to other Arab countries.

Yet, that said, I shall argue that the genuine similarities between Palestine and the neighboring Arab states might not have been morally irrelevant had the actual Israeli "transfer" of the Palestinians in the 1947–48 period not been so violent. Even in that hypothetical circumstance, the forced emigration of hundreds of thousands of Palestinians of course would have constituted an injustice, but at least that injustice would have been mitigated. I develop that argument in Chapter 5.

The third argument made by proponents of transfer was that there have been a number of other precedents for forced exchanges of national populations: typically cited are the 1923 exchanges of Greek and Turkish peoples and the post–World War II transfer of ethnic German minorities in Poland and Czechoslovakia to Germany, and similar population movements between Bulgaria and Turkey as well as between Hungary and Slovakia.[29]

Of course, the citation of these "precedents" hardly constitutes a moral argument, for the fact that similar actions have occurred in the past does not make any of them right, especially since the "transfers" were either the consequences of war or were otherwise accompanied by massive violence.

Other Supporters of Transfer

During the 1917–47 period, support for some kind of transfer was not limited to the Zionists. In 1936, the British government appointed a high-level commission to examine and report on what it could do about the increasingly violent conflict between the Jews and Arabs in Palestine. In July 1937, the Peel Commission (as it became known) issued its report: "An irrepressible conflict has arisen between two national communities within the narrow bounds of one small country. There is no common ground between them. Their national aspirations are incompatible. . . . Neither permits of combination in a single state."

Consequently, the commission recommended that Palestine be partitioned. However, it continued, partition would be feasible only if there was a substantial exchange of populations to ensure that there would be a large majority of Jews in the 20 percent of the country earmarked for a Jewish state and a similar majority of Arabs in the Palestinian state. The commission put it this way: "If Partition is to be effective in promoting a final settlement it must mean more than drawing a frontier and establishing two States. Sooner or later there should be a transfer of land and, as far as possible, an exchange of population . . . *voluntary or otherwise*. . . . [I]n the last resort the exchange should be compulsory" (emphasis added).[30]

Ben-Gurion wrote that he was overcome by "burning enthusiasm" by the Peel recommendation: "I see the realization of this program as an almost decisive stage at the beginning of our full redemption," he wrote in his diary, "and the strongest possible impetus for the step-by-step conquest of Palestine as a whole." . . . He reacted with two words: "compulsory transfer," underlining the words in his diary.[31]

Facing the opposition of the Palestinian Arabs and only lukewarm support from the Zionist leaders, the British government declined to implement the Peel report, but for the first time the idea of some form of transfer—including compulsory transfer—was "accorded an international moral imprimatur" and became "a real possibility and a respectable option."[32]

Perhaps for that reason, in November 1945, former US president Herbert Hoover issued a statement recommending the transfer of Arabs out of some parts of Palestine,[33] a recommendation that was supported by Reinhold Niebuhr, the celebrated liberal American theologian and moral philosopher, who argued that "while Palestine was the logical place for [a] homeland for the Jews, the Arabs have a vast hinterland in the Middle East."[34]

Roosevelt and Transfer

From the outset of his administration in 1933, Franklin Roosevelt strongly supported the establishment of a Jewish state in Palestine. In 1939, Roosevelt proposed to the British government and American Zionist leaders that the Palestinian Arabs should be transferred to a nearby Arab country, such as Iraq. He had in mind, however, a compensated transfer—"a little baksheesh," is how he put it—costing about $300 million, which could be raised by Britain, the United States, and wealthy Western Jews.[35] Eleanor Roosevelt, often more liberal than her husband, on this occasion agreed, writing, "The Arabs will probably be better off if the funds already in hand are used to resettle them in some of the Arab countries."[36]

The British government rejected this plan, however, telling Roosevelt that "no amount of financial inducement would move the Palestinian Arabs."[37] Nonetheless, Roosevelt persisted, saying that in his coming 1945 meeting with King Ibn Saud of Saudi Arabia he intended to argue that "he could not see why a portion of Palestine could not be given to the Jews" in light of the fact that it would be "an infinitesimal part of the whole area."[38]

An American historian of these events concludes: "Roosevelt continued to think of Palestine as a strictly Jewish land. . . . Time and again, his instincts led him to consider ways to move the Palestinian Arabs off the land, to make way for the Jews wishing to return to their rightful home."[39] Indeed, the historian observes, in seemingly believing that no Arabs at all should be allowed to remain in a Jewish state, Roosevelt went even further than most of the Zionist leadership.[40]

Arab Leaders and Transfer

According to British diplomatic records, Benny Morris wrote that by the mid-1940s a number of Arab leaders, including King Abdullah of Jordan and Nuri Said of Iraq, had accepted the logical solution of the Palestine problem as partition, "followed by an exchange of populations. . . . As all involved understood, 'exchange of populations' was a euphemism for transferring the Arabs out of the area of the Jewish state-to-be."[41]

Despite this growing consensus, however, it is highly unlikely that the international supporters of partition and transfer—even including *some* kind of forced transfer, if that had proved necessary—would have supported the kind of Zionist "transfer" that actually occurred in 1947–48.

Palestinian Resistance

From the nineteenth century until the Balfour Declaration, while there were some clashes between the small Jewish population in Palestine and the native Arab population, they were rare and relatively minor.[42] During the 1920s, when the Palestinians began to realize that the Balfour Declaration, the beginning of the British Mandate, and the increasing Jewish immigration would have consequences for their own nationalist aspirations, violent clashes and riots became more frequent. One of the causes of the increasing Palestinian resistance was the Zionist movement's plan to purchase Arab lands and resettle them with the Jewish immigrants. Many of the owners who were willing to sell did not live on their property, or even in Palestine, and the consequence of the sale was often the eviction of the Arabs who actually lived on and cultivated the land. In any case, the Palestinian resistance understood the political implications of the land purchases, the aim of which, as Tom Segev wrote, "was to create a contiguous area of Jewish settlement" in the most fertile sections of Palestine, a key component of the Zionist program to "reclaim" the country: "The Zionist movement had always planned to buy Palestine with money," wrote Segev, so that "as time went by the question of legal right was increasingly beside the point. What people saw was Jews dispossessing Arabs."[43]

During the 1930s, the violence escalated as the Zionist goal of a Jewish state in Palestine was given new urgency and several hundred thousand Jewish refugees from Europe arrived in the country, intensifying the Arab fears—prescient ones, as it turned out—that they were in danger of losing not only their land but also their political rights. Beginning in the 1936 "Arab revolt," as it is customarily termed, the Arabs escalated their attacks on both the Jews and the British occupation forces; the Zionists responded with their own terrorist attacks against both the British and the Arabs. By the time the British finally suppressed the revolt in 1939, more than 1,200 Jews and 5,000 Palestinians had been killed.

Writing about this period, Abba Eban acknowledged that the "thousands of years of Jewish connection [to Palestine]" could not be seen as "totally eliminating thirteen centuries of later Arab-Muslim history. . . . If they had submitted to Zionism with docility they would have been the first people in history to have voluntarily renounced their majority status."[44]

Anti-Semitism and the Palestinian Resistance

It is not difficult to understand that as the Palestinians grew more desperate, many of them—but hardly all, as will shortly be discussed—turned to extremist leaders who advocated violence. One of the most important Palestinian leaders, Hajj Amin al-Husseini, the Grand Mufti of Jerusalem, even sought Hitler's help in defeating the Jews.[45] As a result of this "fatal decision to stake the future of the Palestinian people on the collapse of Britain's rule in the Middle East and on Nazi military victory in the approaching World War II,"[46] it was not surprising that the Jews in Palestine (and elsewhere) believed that the Arab resistance was a function simply of anti-Semitism rather than, as one scholar has put it, the consequence "not of unreasoned hatreds but competing nationalism."[47] Similarly, Benjamin Beit-Hallahmi, one of Israel's most astute psychologists and historians, wrote: "At some point, the natives came to be described as invaders and aggressors. . . . Because of Jewish history, it was easy to see the natives as anti-Semitic Gentiles, engaging in genocide."[48]

The failure of the 1936–39 Arab uprising, the defeat of Nazi Germany, and the determination of the British and later the United Nations to reach a compromise in Palestine resulted in greater realism and moderation among the Palestinians. Some remained violently committed to preventing the establishment of a Jewish state in any part of Palestine, but by the mid-1940s many others had come to the realization that the partition of Palestine was unavoidable.

In one of the most important books on the history of this period, widely considered to be the first major work in the Israeli "New History" movement (to be described in a later chapter), Simha Flapan provides detailed evidence of numerous Palestinian proposals for a peaceful settlement with the Zionists during the 1947–48 period.[49] The matter is so important, challenging as it does a central component of the Zionist narrative, that it is worth quoting from Flapan's work in some detail. Denying that there was monolithic Palestinian extremism, he writes:

> [It] is a myth that the Palestinian leaders were uniformly uncompromising. . . . [T]he evidence is so overwhelming that the question arises how the myth of a Palestinian jihad against the Jews could survive so long. . . . It seems reasonable to assume that had the Jewish leadership so desired, alternative policies towards the Palestinian Arabs . . . could have been adopted. . . . Objective conditions for an alternative policy existed all along [but it was] rejected by the official Jewish leadership.[50]

Flapan concludes: "The Palestinians neither wanted nor believed in war . . . [and] attempted to protect themselves against warfare by the only means at their disposal: local agreements with their Jewish neighbors against mutual attacks, provocations, and hostile acts." As a result hundreds of nonaggression and neutrality pacts were arranged between Arab and Jewish villages, workers, and businesses throughout the country.[51]

In his 1991 review of the evidence, the American scholar Steven Heydemann concluded that Flapan, Morris, and Shlaim "provide graphic evidence of the way in which efforts at accommodation, both with Abdullah and with local Palestinians, were consistently rebuffed by Ben-Gurion, Moshe Dayan and many others in the military establishment who regarded compromise as unnecessary in light of Israel's evident military superiority."[52]

Together with the evidence that calls into question the myth of a coordinated Arab state invasion designed to drive the Jews into the sea, the evidence of pragmatism, realism, and a willingness to compromise among many Palestinians suggests the possibility that the 1948 war might have been avoided—contrary to the Israeli mythology—if the Zionist leadership had been genuinely committed to compromise: that is, to sharing Palestine with the Palestinians.

The Zionist Response: The Iron Wall

Many of the most important Zionist leaders—especially Vladimir (Zeev) Jabotinsky, David Ben-Gurion, and Moshe Sharett during the pre-state period and Moshe Dayan later on—were surprisingly forthright in acknowledging that the Palestinian narrative of victimhood at the hands of the Zionists was well-grounded.

Jabotinsky

Jabotinsky was a Ukrainian Jewish nationalist who became the leader of the right-wing Zionists and the terrorist Irgun group in Palestine during the pre-state era. It was his "Iron Wall" strategy that was adopted by the Zionist movement—and may be said to have remained, in effect if not officially, the dominant philosophy of Israel ever since.[53]

In his main Iron Wall essay, Jabotinsky presciently wrote: "Any indigenous people will fight the settlers as long as there is a spark of hope to be rid of the foreign settlement. That is what the Arabs of the land of Israel are doing and will continue to do, as long as a spark of hope lingers in their heart that they can prevent 'Palestine' becoming the Land of Israel."[54] Therefore, the Arab decision to resist Zionism "was only natural. . . . There was no misunderstanding between Jews and Arabs, but a natural conflict. No agreement was possible with the Palestinian Arabs; they would accept Zionism only when they found themselves up against 'an iron wall,' when armed force gave them no alternative but to accept Jewish settlement."[55]

Importantly, however, Jabotinsky did not advocate permanent suppression of the Palestinians: "Once the Arabs were faced with this 'iron wall' and renounced further opposition," Flapan writes, "Jabotinsky would be ready to give them a fair deal to include full equality of rights," including cultural autonomy and participation in the government as well as the management of the economy: "everything the Jews demanded for themselves in the Diaspora," Flapan adds. In particular, there would be no involuntary "transfer," for the Arabs would not be required to emigrate, "although [Jabotinsky] would not feel overly distressed if they did."[56] Many Israeli critics of the Iron Wall strategy argue that throughout Israeli history its many (acknowledged or de facto) adherents have ignored the conciliatory components in Jabotinsky's arguments.

Ben-Gurion

Although Ben-Gurion and Jabotinsky were often bitterly at odds, their views, at least on the *first* part of the Iron Wall strategy, were quite similar. Like Jabotinsky, Ben-Gurion could put himself in the shoes of the Palestinians and understand their bitter rejection of the Zionist claims to Palestine, but he was equally likely to be blunt and uncompromising in rejecting them and advocating their defeat by whatever force was needed. Especially when speaking privately or before meetings of Zionist leaders, like Jabotinsky, Ben-Gurion often diagnosed the Zionist-Palestinian conflict with startling, even brutal clarity and realism. There are many examples of Ben-Gurion's adherence to Jabotinsky's views, especially in his recognition of the legitimacy of Palestinian claims but the need of the Jews to override them by means of the Iron Wall.

As described by Teveth, in the early 1930s the Arab Executive Committee issued orders that violence should be directed against the British, but not the Jews. These orders were obeyed, which impressed Ben-Gurion and led him to conclude that the Arab uprising was a genuine political movement which had to be respected.[57]

During the 1935–36 Arab revolt, the Palestinians initially mainly targeted the British occupation forces. Writing of this period, Segev comments: "The fact that most Arab attacks in the 1930s were directed against the British bolstered [Ben-Gurion's] view that the Arab Revolt was the product of an organized and disciplined national public acting with political maturity, dedication, idealism, and death-defying bravery." The conclusion he drew, Segev continues, is that the Palestinian fighters deserved to be considered "national liberation fighters facing off against a foreign government. . . . Were he a politically and nationally aware Arab, he would also enlist in the fight."[58]

As for the attacks on the Jews, Ben-Gurion even conceded that the Jews "had to see things with Arab eyes": growing Jewish immigration, economic dominance, "the best lands passing into our hands," and more.[59] On another occasion, he told Zionist leaders: "We and they . . . both want Palestine," so the Arabs' only alternative was to fight: "The cause of the Arabs' war today is primarily their fear of Jewish growth in Palestine, in numbers and in strength that can bring about Jewish rule. And then they will face destruction."[60]

The same analysis led some moderate Jewish leaders to suggest considering some restrictions on Jewish immigration in order to reach a compromise peace with the Palestinians. Ben-Gurion would not hear of it, writing: "It is not in order to establish peace in the country that we need an agreement. . . . [P]eace for us is a means. The end is the complete establishment of Zionism; only after total despair on the part of the Arabs . . . as a consequence of our growth in the country may the Arabs finally acquiesce in a Jewish Erez Israel."[61]

On another occasion, elaborating on this analysis Ben-Gurion said, "Why should the Arabs make peace? If I were an Arab leader, I would never make terms with Israel. That is natural: we have taken their country. Sure, God promised it to us, but what does that matter to them? There has been anti-Semitism, the Nazis, Hitler, Auschwitz, but was that their fault? They only see one thing: we came here and stole their country. Why should they accept that?"[62]

Similarly, Simha Flapan quotes from a 1938 speech to his political party, in which Ben-Gurion said that Arab violence was not mindless terrorism but "a national war":

> Terror is one of the means of war . . . an active resistance by the Palestinians to what they regard as a usurpation of their homeland by the Jews. . . . Let us not ignore the truth among ourselves. . . . [A] people which fights against the usurpation of its land will not tire easily. . . . When we say that the Arabs are the aggressors and we defend ourselves—this is only half the truth. . . . [P]olitically we are the aggressors and they defend themselves. . . . The country is theirs, because they inhabit it, whereas we want to come here and settle down, and in their view we want to take away from them their country.[63]

Flapan then comments: "Ben-Gurion's accurate assessment of the deep-rooted character of the Arab Revolt did not lead him to serious negotiations with the Palestinian Arabs." On the contrary, following the Iron Wall strategy, "it led him to an even more militant line on the need to build up Jewish military strength in order to coerce the Arabs."[64]

However, as had Jabotinsky, Ben-Gurion also addressed the question of what could lead to a settlement with the Arabs. First, the Jews needed to establish facts on the ground: "Only after we manage to establish a great Jewish fact in this country . . . a Jewish force clearly immovable, only then will the precondition for discussion with the Arabs be met."[65]

In short, the two most important Zionist leaders in the pre-state period, Vladimir Jabotinsky and David Ben-Gurion, recognized Palestinian resistance to Jewish dominance in Palestine as fully understandable and based on their correct understanding that Zionism and Palestinian national aspirations were incompatible—but they also believed that the Zionist goals were both more legitimate and necessary, and therefore must be given priority and realized by whatever means were necessary, that is, the Iron Wall.

Sharett

As described by Flapan (and others), Moshe Sharett was the most moderate Zionist leader in the pre-state period, having "a deep understanding of the Arab problem" and conceding that "there is no Arab in Palestine who is not harmed by Jewish immigration and who does not feel himself part of the Great Arab Nation. . . . His reaction cannot be but resistance."[66]

However, Flapan writes, Sharett "confided his doubts and uneasiness of conscience to his diary, only rarely sharing them with his comrades in the leadership of the Labour Party . . . [and agreeing with] the necessity of realizing Zionist aspirations regardless of Arab attitudes and by force if necessary. While understanding that there was a Palestinian people, he felt it was their fate to suffer at the expense of Zionist goals." Flapan then quotes Sharett: "They have other countries."[67]

In later years, reacting to criticism of his hard-line views on Arab rights in Palestine, Menachem Begin, heir to Jabotinsky as the leader of the Irgun, protested: "If this is Palestine and not the land of Israel, then you are conquerors and not tillers of the land. You are invaders. If this land is Palestine, then it belongs to a people who lived here before you came."[68] Of course, Begin meant to discredit that view.

Finally, in a famous 1956 speech eulogizing an ambushed Israeli soldier, Moshe Dayan perfectly captured the spirit of the Iron Wall: "Let us not today cast blame on the murderers. What can we say against their terrible hatred of us? For eight years now, they have sat in the refugee camps of Gaza, and have watched how, before their very eyes, we have turned their lands and villages, where they and their forefathers previously dwelled, into our home." The conclusion he drew, however, was not that Zionist policies should change, but on the contrary that the Israelis must recognize that they had no choice but to redouble their efforts at repressing the Palestinian resistance:

> We are a generation of settlement, and without the steel helmet and the gun's muzzle we will not be able to plant a tree or build a house. . . . That is the fate of our generation. This is our choice—to be ready and armed, tough and harsh—or to let the sword fall from our hands and our lives be cut short.[69]

In short, the Iron Wall concept—together with the premises, values, and historical myths that underlie it—has been and still is the dominant political and military strategy of Zionism. Summarizing its consequences, Flapan wrote that Jabotinsky "left an indelible mark on the Zionist attitudes towards the Arab question":

> He implanted in Jewish psychology the image of the Arab as the mortal enemy, the idea of the inevitability of the conflict and of the impossibility of a solution except by sheer force. . . . Attitudes of this kind could not be maintained without an appeal to the most primitive instincts of fear and self-defense, without unleashing emotions of hate and vengeance, without painting the Arab as a primitive, evil and cruel creature . . . and without inflating feelings of self-righteousness to the point where the whole, absolute truth and justice were on one side only. Once such a psychological structure was erected it served as a partition concealing reality and as a blind obscuring the vision.[70]

The Dissenters

To be sure, there has always been dissent from the prevailing orthodoxy and advocates of non violence and conciliatory policies toward the Palestinians. One such strand of dissent has been "cultural Zionism," or "community Zionism," as it is sometimes known. Herzl and all the dominant Zionist leaders who followed them were "political Zionists," meaning that they were nationalists seeking to establish a Jewish state in Palestine. The cultural or community Zionists rejected nationalism in general and Jewish nationalism in particular, and while they favored the establishment of Jewish religious or cultural communities in Palestine, they opposed the creation of a Jewish *state* there—and they especially opposed the use of force against the indigenous Arabs that they accurately foresaw would accompany it.

The founder of cultural Zionism was Ahad Ha'am, a Russian Jewish philosopher. Ha'am visited Palestine in 1891 and reported that the settlers "behave towards the Arabs with hostility and cruelty [and] trespass unjustly upon their boundaries."[71] Appalled by this behavior, Ha'am prophetically wrote:

> If the time comes when the life of our people in Eretz Israel develops to the point of encroaching upon the native population, they will not easily yield their place. . . . [H]ow careful we must be not to arouse the anger of other people against ourselves by reprehensible conduct. And what do our brethren in Eretz Israel do? Quite the opposite! They were slaves in their land of exile, and they suddenly find themselves with unlimited freedom. . . . This sudden change has engendered in them an impulse to despotism. . . . They deal with the Arabs with hostility and cruelty. . . . We must surely learn, from both our past and present history, how careful we must be not to provoke the anger of the native people by doing them wrong . . . even if [the Arabs] are silent and endlessly reserved, they keep their anger in their hearts. And these people will be revengeful like no other. . . . [T]his society . . . will have to face the prospects of both internal and external war.[72]

Among the leading adherents to Ha'am's vision of cultural Zionism, some of whom were religious and others secular supporters of a binational Jewish-Arab state in Palestine, were the philosopher Martin Buber; the religious leader and founding president of the Hebrew University of Jerusalem Judah Magnes; and the prominent scientist and public intellectual Yishayahu Leibowitz. As well, whether or not they could be considered cultural Zionists, Albert Einstein, the famous philosopher Hannah Arendt, and other "diaspora" leaders became increasingly disenchanted with political Zionism as the direction it was taking became clear. In particular, as early as 1930 Einstein had written: "Only direct cooperation with the Arabs can create a safe and dignified life. . . . What saddens me is less the fact that the Jews are not smart enough to understand this, but rather, that they are not just enough to want it."[73]

In retrospect, were the cultural Zionists, only a small minority during the pre-state period and even less influential after the creation of the state of Israel in 1948, correct in their diagnoses? It is not an easy question. In principle, cultural Zionism's rejection of nationalism and its calls for conciliation and nonviolence could—perhaps should—be seen as appealing and prescient, especially in light of the results of political Zionism in Israel today.

Even with the benefit of hindsight, however, the issue is very difficult, for cultural Zionism offered no solution to the existential Jewish problem: the historical persecution of Jews, a small and essentially defenseless minority in countries other than their own, dependent for their well-being and even survival on the all-too-often disappearing goodwill of the Gentiles.

In 1935, Ben-Gurion met with Judah Magnes, who was willing to consider limits on Jewish immigration for the sake of a peace settlement with the Palestinians—even if it resulted in a state in which the Arabs would retain a 60 percent majority. Needless to say, Ben-Gurion was adamantly opposed to such a settlement, especially in light of what was happening in Europe.[74] In light of the Holocaust it is hard to say that he was wrong, for it is unlikely that a non-state cultural Zionist homeland in Palestine, sharing the country on an equitable basis with the Palestinians, could have met the desperate needs of the European Jewish refugees.

Even if a genuinely binational democratic state could have been established in Palestine—highly unlikely, after so many years of intercommunal violence and outright terrorism—almost certainly the Palestinians would not have agreed to unlimited Jewish immigration. Surely they would have feared that the consequence would be the de facto end of a truly binational state with equal power and rights for all and its replacement with a markedly unequal state under Jewish military, political, economic, cultural, and religious domination: that is, a state like Israel today.

Moreover, going beyond the post-Holocaust problem, even if Magnes's proposal had been acceptable to the Arabs and a binational state with a Jewish minority had been established, it would not have met the felt Jewish need for an independent state that in the future could serve as a refuge for threatened Jewish communities. A "cultural" Zionist homeland—no state and no army—would have been unable to defend itself, let alone serve as a refuge for Jews throughout the world, if and when murderous anti-Semitism again broke out.

In recent years Israeli dissidents are again challenging political Zionism. In a sense, cultural or community Zionism has reappeared—though not by that name—in the form of binationalism or a "one-state solution": the replacement of the Jewish state of Israel with a binational democracy with equal rights for all, sometimes called "Isratine."

It would seem undeniable that the case for political Zionism and the maintenance of an overwhelmingly Jewish state today is considerably less compelling than it was during the first half of the twentieth century. Even so, whether binationalism could be a practical solution either to the historical problem of murderous anti-Semitism or to the Israeli-Palestinian conflict today is another matter, which is discussed in the concluding chapter, Chapter 20.

Whether one should regard the period from the Balfour Declaration through the establishment of a Jewish state in Palestine as a lost opportunity to have averted the Zionist-Palestinian conflict is not certain, for it is not clear that the Palestinians would have agreed even to a "cultural" Jewish homeland, let alone one that opened its doors to the refugees from Nazism.

The word "tragedy" is typically overused in descriptions of the Israeli-Palestinian conflict, for it wrongly implies a symmetry between the Zionist and Palestinian narratives, particularly over the question of why the conflict has persisted since the 1948 creation of the state of Israel. It seems much more persuasive, however, to describe the *origins* of the conflict as a genuine tragedy: two national movements, two peoples, both having legitimate but irreconcilable claims for political sovereignty, majority rule, and cultural and religious predominance in one very small country, the Land of Palestine.

4

The Creation of the State of Israel, 1947–48

The UN Partition Plan

By February 1947, the British government concluded that it had enough of the intractable Zionist-Palestinian conflict and decided to end the Mandate, withdraw from Palestine, and turn over the problem to the United Nations.[1] A United Nations Commission was appointed to investigate the situation and recommend a solution to the General Assembly. The commission found that in light of the irreconcilable nationalist claims to Palestine, there would have to be a compromise, namely, partition: "It is a fact that both of these peoples have their historic roots in Palestine. . . . The basic conflict in Palestine is a clash of two intense nationalisms. . . . Only by means of partition can these conflicting national aspirations [be resolved]."

In essence, the UN Commission concluded—like the Peel Commission earlier and just about every other study or international report since then—that the only feasible way to end the conflict was by what has come to be known as "the two-state solution." Hence, it recommended that Palestine be divided into a Jewish state and an Arab state, with Jerusalem—populated by a roughly equal number of Jews and Palestinians and considered a holy city by Jews, Muslims, and Christians—to become an international city administered by a special commission.

One problem with this solution was that the Jews were only one-third of the population of mandatory Palestine, so that to create a viable state with a Jewish majority, the UN engaged in a kind of gerrymandering, creating the proposed state on some 57 percent of the land, almost twice as large as that proposed by the Peel Commission. And to ensure its economic viability, the Jewish state was allocated most of the best fertile land and most of the coastal areas and ports in Palestine (see Map 4.1).

Even so, the Jews would have only a 55–56 percent majority in their new state, which would consist of about 500,000 Jews and 400,000 Arabs. And, unlike the Peel Commission, the UN body did not recommend that "transfer," even by nonviolent

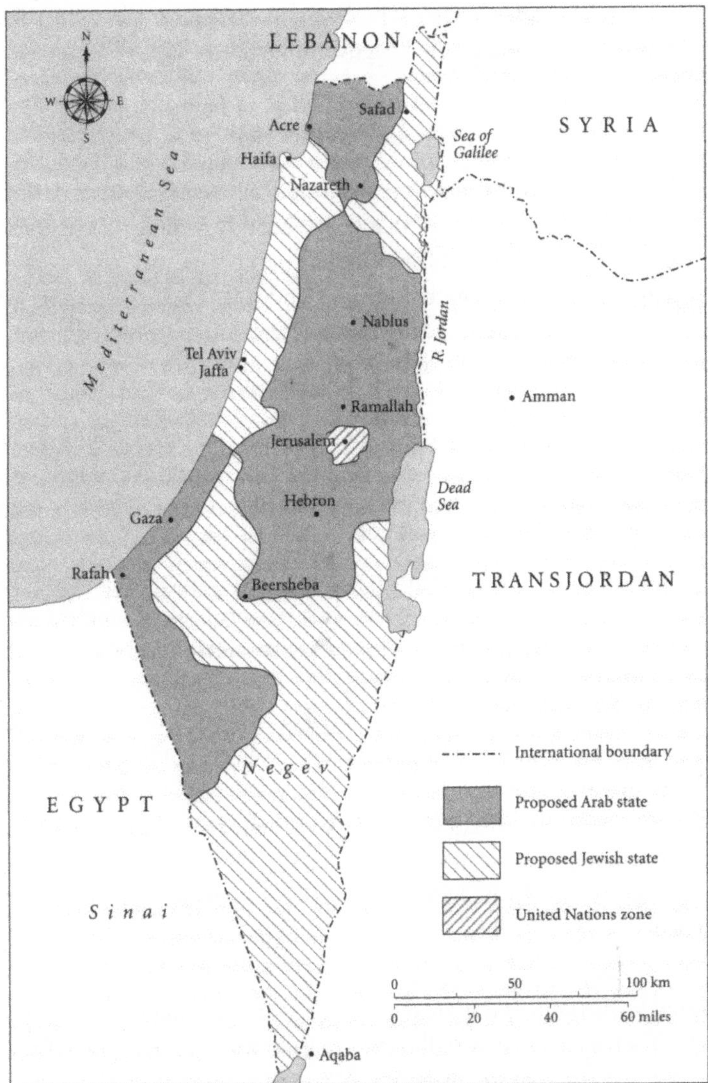

The United Nations partition plan, 1947

Map 4.1 UN Partition Plan, from Shlomo Ben-Ami, *Scars of War*, 33. Permission granted from Ben-Ami.

means, be employed. On November 29, 1947, the UN General Assembly passed a partition resolution supported by a two-thirds majority, which included the United States and the Soviet Union. Indeed, the Truman administration did considerably more than merely support the resolution; most studies of that period conclude that the resolution passed not only because of the genuine acceptance by many states of the moral necessity of a Jewish state but also because of the extensive heavy lobbying by the Zionists and by the US government.[2]

The Zionist Response

The Zionist response to the partition plan, led by Ben-Gurion and the Jewish Agency, by no means demonstrated that they were now willing to accept the forthcoming Jewish state as being established in only part of Palestine. The evidence is irrefutable that Ben-Gurion "accepted" the plan and sold it to his reluctant co-leaders solely as a temporary tactic to allow the Zionists to gain a foothold, from which they would build a state and powerful military forces that could later expand and take over *all* of historical Palestine.

As noted earlier, in the aspirations of Ben-Gurion and other Zionist leaders, the Jewish state would include all of Jerusalem, the West Bank of the Jordan River, a substantial part of the East Bank and western Jordan at least to Amman, the Gaza Strip, southern Lebanon, and the Golan Heights and other parts of southern Syria. Nor were these just "dreams," as some have sought to explain them away, for Ben-Gurion's private papers contained (in the words of his leading biographer) "abundant proof that during the first years following the establishment of the State of Israel, he continued to secretly plan the next stage, in which he would achieve his territorial ambitions."[3] And, of course, in subsequent years the Israelis took advantage of the numerous wars with the Arab states to seize all of those areas, excepting only western Jordan.

In a famous and oft-cited 1937 letter to his son, Ben-Gurion made clear the thinking that would guide his goals and policies in the years to come. In the letter, Ben-Gurion explained why he had decided to acquiesce to the Peel Commission's partition plan:

> A partial Jewish state is not the end, but only the beginning. The establishment of such a Jewish state will serve as a means in our historical efforts to redeem the country in its entirety. . . . We shall organize a modern defense force . . . and then I am certain that we will not be prevented from settling in other parts of the country, either by mutual agreement with our Arab neighbors or by some other means. . . . We will expel the Arabs and take their places . . . with the force at our disposal.[4]

A year later, he told a Zionist meeting that he favored partition because after the establishment of the state, the new state would become strong enough to abolish partition and spread throughout all of Palestine: "I doubt whether there is a single border on the globe that has not changed," he wrote to his party. "Our movement is maximalist. Even all of Palestine is not our final goal."[5]

Ben-Gurion did not change his mind in the next ten years. Shlomo Ben-Ami, a major leader in the Labor Party and a past foreign minister of Israel, makes that unmistakably clear, writing that "the endorsement of partition . . . by Ben-Gurion was essentially a tactical move." He then quotes a 1947 statement of Ben-Gurion to a Zionist leadership meeting: "Does anybody really think that the original meaning of the Balfour Declaration and the Mandate, and indeed, that of the millenarian yearning of the Jewish people, was not that of establishing a Jewish state in the whole of Eretz-Israel?" Ben-Ami continues: "Ben-Gurion's acceptance of the principle of partition, he explained a week later, was an attempt to gain time until the Jews were strong enough to fight the Arab majority."[6]

Moreover, Ben-Gurion and the Zionist leadership simply ignored the part of the partition plan that they opposed, notably the internationalization of Jerusalem and the establishment of a Palestinian Arab state on the West Bank. To avoid the creation of such a state, they secretly agreed to the ensuing takeover of Jerusalem and the West Bank by King Abdullah of Transjordan, in the hope or expectation that this could be reversed in the future.[7] Temporary Hashemite control of the West Bank and the Old City of Jerusalem was regarded by Ben-Gurion as preferable to either the internationalization of Jerusalem or the creation of a Palestinian state; later, when Israel became stronger, an opportunity might present itself for an Israeli takeover of "Judea and Samaria." And, of course, it did just that in the 1967 Arab-Israeli war.

The Palestinian Response

For several reasons, most of the Palestinian leaders, particularly the most powerful one, Amin al-Husseini, the mufti of Jerusalem, rejected the UN partition plan. First, even those who otherwise might have been prepared in principle to accept a compromise partition settlement argued that the UN plan was unfair in its allocation of most of the land of Palestine to the Jews, including 84 percent of its best agricultural arable areas, and 80 percent of the coastline. As the Palestinian-American scholar Walid Khalidi wrote: "For the Zionists, partition was three-quarters of a loaf; for the Palestinians, partition was half a baby."[8]

Second, the Palestinians were well aware of the Zionist plans for expansionism and the centrality of "transfer" in Zionist thinking. Consequently, they did not believe—and were *right* not to believe—that Ben-Gurion and the other leading Zionists would be satisfied with, or abide by, a genuine compromise. They feared, in other words, that the Zionist "acceptance" of the UN plan was disingenuous, that the Zionist leaders were adamantly bent on expanding a Jewish state to include all of biblical Palestine, and that they would simply use a partition compromise as the base from which to expand later—as, of course, they did.

Nor were the Palestinians alone in considering the Zionist position to be cynical. In 1947, Count Folke Bernadotte, a Swedish diplomat who during World War

II had negotiated the release of thousands of prisoners from Nazi concentration camps, including 450 Danish Jews, was appointed by the UN to serve as its mediator in the Arab-Israeli conflict. In August 1949, Bernadotte reported to the General Assembly that the Arabs feared that "a Jewish state in Palestine will not stay within its defined boundaries, and through population pressure resulting from immigration, encouragement and support from world Jewry, and burgeoning nationalism, a threat will be posed not only to Palestine but the entire Arab Near East." It is clear from Bernadotte's other comments and reports that he thought the Arab fears were justified, since military success had led to greater Israeli self-confidence and unreceptiveness to UN mediation efforts.[9]

In any case, many Palestinians were prepared to negotiate a compromise settlement with the Zionists. As several of the Israeli "New Historians" have demonstrated, the failure of the Palestinian revolt of the 1930s and the determination of the British and later the United Nations to enforce a compromise in Palestine resulted in greater moderation and realism among many Palestinians who by the mid-1940s had come to the realization that partition and the creation of a Jewish state in part of Palestine was unavoidable. As a result, a number of Palestinian proposals were made for a compromise settlement; they were ignored by Ben-Gurion and other Zionist leaders because of the Zionist determination, as Simha Flapan put it, "to achieve full sovereignty [in a Palestine] at whatever cost."[10]

Moreover, even if it were the case that the Zionists were ready for compromise but the Palestinians weren't, the issue would be morally complicated: whatever the larger justification for the creation of a Jewish state in Palestine, it is hardly irrelevant that it was the Palestinians who lost their political rights and much of the land they had lived in for centuries.

Did the Palestinians Err in Rejecting the UN Partition?

In considering this question, one must separate the issue of the moral persuasiveness of the Palestinian position from its practical consequences.

The Moral Issues

The Palestinians and their supporters make the case that it was morally unjust for the international community to force them to pay the price for the Nazi Holocaust by creating a Jewish state in what for centuries had been their homeland. On the other hand, the implicit underlying premise of the UN partition plan was that by 1945 the Palestinian plea that they were not responsible for the Holocaust had lost its force. That is, the answer to "why should we have to pay the price" was that a Jewish state, even at the expense of *some* Palestinian political sovereignty, had become a tragic moral necessity, and there no longer was any practical alternative to Palestine.

Put differently, the argument goes, by 1947 a new human reality in Palestine had emerged, however problematic its origins. Further, because the UN partition plan was a response to the historical plight of the Jews in general and the Holocaust in particular, as well as because it was overwhelmingly supported by the world community, it had a far greater moral legitimacy than did the Balfour Plan and the subsequent League of Nations Mandate to Britain, which today are widely seen as simply colonialist impositions.

Of course, these arguments, significant as they were, would have had much greater moral persuasiveness if the Zionists had been content with the compromise UN plan and abided by it. However, because the Palestinians were fully aware that Ben-Gurion and other leading Zionists had no intention of truly accepting the UN compromise and planned to overturn it once they came into power, it is perfectly plausible that it was Israeli expansionism that accounted, at least in part, for the Palestinian resistance to the partition plan.

In that light, it is quite unpersuasive to argue (as do many Israeli right-wingers and their US supporters) that because the Palestinians rejected the UN compromise in 1947, they permanently forfeited their right to a new state of their own. Moreover, even if it had been true that in 1947 the Palestinians, and only the Palestinians, refused all compromise, it is hard to see why that would be a compelling argument for subsequent Israeli intransigence.[11]

For all or at least most of the period since the late 1990s, a majority of the Palestinians and their leaders have generally accepted partition or a two-state solution, which however remote it is today, still retains the same compelling moral and practical logic that has led nearly every outsider of goodwill to recommend it for over seventy-five years.

The Practical Consequences

To be sure, whatever the abstract moral justice of their cause, there is a strong argument that the general Palestinian unwillingness to accept the UN-required compromise turned out to be a terrible mistake in terms of their own interests. As one writer has noted, "From the British government's 1937 Peel Commission partition plan and the UN partition plan of 1947 to UN Security Council Resolution 242 and the Oslo Accords, every formative initiative endorsed by the great powers has given more to the Jewish community in Palestine than the previous one."[12]

In recognition of this history, in 2011 Mahmoud Abbas, Arafat's successor as the most important Palestinian leader and then president of the Palestinian Authority, effectively conceded that the Palestinian rejection of the UN partition was a mistake, because it was the "best offer" the Palestinians had ever received.[13]

Actually, Abbas was inaccurate, for the Peel Commission partition plan had given the Palestinians much more land than did the UN plan. Even so, while in hindsight the Palestinian rejection was a tactical error, they had no way of knowing that neither the UN nor the international community—in particular, the United States—would act to prevent Israel from expanding well beyond the partition boundaries.

The United States and the Creation of Israel

In principle, all American presidents and the US Congress have supported the creation of a Jewish state in Palestine since the Balfour Declaration. In March, 1019, President Woodrow Wilson said: "I am persuaded that the Allied nations, with the fullest concurrence of our own government and people, are agreed that in Palestine shall be laid the foundation of a Jewish Commonwealth."[14] While not officially endorsing the Balfour Declaration, Wilson told leading Zionist officials, in both private and public, that he supported their goals. As one writer has put it: "Although an ardent believer in the liberation of colonized peoples and the right of self-determination, as a devout Christian and the son of a Presbyterian minister Wilson was also deeply attracted to the idea of the "rebirth of the Jewish people . . . as a blessing for all mankind."[15]

In the 1920s, Presidents Calvin Coolidge and Herbert Hoover also declared their support for the Balfour Declaration and the aspirations of the Zionist movement, as did Franklin Delano Roosevelt (FDR). However, Roosevelt's record in supporting the creation of a Jewish state in Palestine was mixed. On the one hand, as argued in Chapter 3, in principle FDR was sympathetic to Zionism and the creation of a Jewish state in Palestine;[16] for a while he even favored a compensated transfer of the Palestinians. On the other hand, he was not willing to put at risk what he considered to be the national interests of the United States.[17]

During the 1940s the most important Arab leader was Ibn Saud, the king of Saudi Arabia. In 1943, Roosevelt wrote to him: "I assure Your Majesty that it is the view of the Government of the United States that no decision altering the basic situation of Palestine should be reached without full consultation with both Arabs and Jews."[18]

In February 1945, Roosevelt met with Ibn Saud and raised the issue of coupling the creation of a Jewish state with major development programs for the Arabs. However, when the king vehemently rejected this idea, Roosevelt quickly backed down, reiterating that he "wished to assure His Majesty that he would do nothing to assist the Jews against the Arabs and would make no move hostile to the Arab people."[19] A few weeks later in his final speech to Congress, Roosevelt said, "On the problem of Arabia, I learned more about that problem—the Muslim problem, the Jewish problem—by talking with Ibn Saud for five minutes than I could have learned in the exchange of two or three dozen letters."

Cordell Hull, Roosevelt's secretary of state, later wrote that FDR "at times talked both ways to Zionists and Arabs, besieged as he was by each camp."[20] In the final analysis, however, the argument of most of his advisors, that the national interests of the United States had to take precedence over the Zionist cause, largely prevailed.

Consequently, in 1949, David Niles, an important aide to Roosevelt, said that there were "serious doubts in my mind that Israel would have come into being if Roosevelt had lived."[21]

Truman

The perceived conflict between the moral issues and the national interest continued during the presidency of Harry Truman. Despite the administration's support for the UN partition resolution, the US government was sharply divided. Most of President Truman's political advisors strongly supported US recognition of and support for the fledgling state of Israel, but almost the entire foreign policy establishment opposed Truman's policies—including Secretary of Defense James Forrestal, Secretary of State George Marshall, Under Secretary Robert Lovett, Chief of Policy Planning George Kennan, and other high State Department officials, including Dean Acheson and Dean Rusk, under secretaries who would later become secretaries of state.

For example, in early 1948, a State Department analysis principally written by George Kennan, head of policy planning, warned that US support for the creation of the state of Israel would harm US national security by undermining US influence in the Arab world, might result in extensive anti-American mob violence in the region, would open the door for the expansion of Soviet influence, would endanger US access to Persian Gulf oil, and would threaten the ability of the United States to retain and expand its military bases in the region.[22]

General Marshall, perhaps the most respected official in the administration, was bitterly opposed to the recognition of Israel. Rejecting Truman's advisor Clark Clifford's argument that not only had the Holocaust created a moral commitment for the United States to support a Jewish state, but "Jewish-Americans were an important voting bloc and would favor the decision," Marshall angrily said:

> I thought this meeting was called to consider an important, complicated problem in foreign policy. . . . I do not think that politics should play any role in our decision. . . . I stated bluntly that if the president were to follow Mr. Clifford's advice, and if I were to vote in the next election, I would vote against the president.[23]

Truman refused to back down. As a US senator and vice-president he had publicly supported Zionist aspirations in Palestine, and all the major studies and insider accounts of Truman's decision to recognize Israel agree that he was moved by the plight of the Jews and was horrified by the Holocaust.[24] Moreover, he deeply believed in the argument that the Bible supported the Zionist claim on Palestine.

Of course, it did not hurt that Truman's moral beliefs coincided with his domestic political interests, especially his hope for Jewish political support. The extent to which this consideration explains Truman's decision to recognize Israel has been the subject of historical dispute, but there can be little doubt that it played a major role in supplementing Truman's moral and religious beliefs. Truman was the underdog going into the 1948 presidential elections, so the Jewish vote and perhaps financial contributions, especially in key states with substantial Jewish populations, like New York and California, might be crucial.[25] Moreover, polls showed there would be little backlash against US recognition of Israel; less than 15 percent of the American public was opposed to the creation of a Jewish state.[26]

Consequently, Truman's political advisors wanted him to recognize Israel, and it is clear that Truman was sensitive to the political considerations and didn't need much persuasion to override the objections of the foreign policy establishment. At one point, Truman met with American diplomats who were opposed to recognition of Israel and told them this: "I'm sorry, gentlemen, but I have to answer to hundreds of thousands who are anxious for the success of Zionism; I do not have hundreds of thousands of Arabs among my constituents."[27]

Actually, Truman initially believed that the fairest solution to the Israeli-Palestinian conflict would be the creation of some kind of binational Jewish Palestinian state or federation; consequently in March 1948 the US government formally proposed the establishment of a UN Trusteeship over Palestine until such a settlement could be reached.[28] However, a storm of protest by the Zionists and their supporters in the United States led Truman to abandon that idea.

Consequently, the arguments of Marshall, Kennan, and the foreign policy establishment that US national interests in the Middle East precluded US recognition of Israel were not so much refuted on their merits as they were simply overridden by the administration. According to Clifford, Marshall, Acheson, Forrestal, and Rusk remained convinced for the rest of their lives that in terms of the national interests, Truman had made the wrong decision.

Were they right? At the time, Kennan's analysis of the issue was very strong; whether—or to what extent—his predictions of the consequences for US interests proved to be correct is still debatable. Even today the relationship between US support of Israel and US national interests is subject to widely varying, even bitterly opposed, evaluations. Examining this issue is one of the main tasks of this book, beginning with Chapter 5.

PART TWO

WAR AND PEACE IN THE ARAB-ISRAELI STATE CONFLICT, 1948–2020

5

The 1948 War

The dominant Israeli narrative, the story the Israelis tell themselves and their unquestioning supporters, is that the Arabs in general and the Palestinians in particular have been nearly wholly responsible for the history of the Arab-Israeli conflict that has led to repeated wars, the first of which broke out immediately after the creation of the state of Israel in May 1948.

In the conventional Israeli narrative (as summarized by Avi Shlaim), despite their disappointment in not being given a state in all Palestine, the Zionists accepted the two-state UN partition plan, but the Palestinians and the neighboring Arab states rejected it and sent seven Arab armies into Palestine, intending to "strangle the Jewish state at birth." When they failed to do so, hundreds of thousands of Palestinians fled to the neighboring Arab states, "mainly in response to orders from their leaders and despite Jewish pleas to stay and demonstrate that peaceful coexistence was possible."[1]

Today, few if any serious scholars and historians—least of all, Israeli ones—subscribe to this story. Beginning in the late 1980s, the Israeli "New History," as it came to be known, demonstrated that there had to be a sweeping reassessment of the entire course of the Arab-Israeli conflict.[2] As a result, the conventional narrative is now recognized as oversimplified and misleading at the least; at worst, it is largely mythology. As Benny Morris, one of the most important and prolific of the New Historians throughout the 1990s, wrote: "No historian today, no matter how conservative, would write like the historians of the previous generation. People would say such a person wasn't serious. Our actions have forced historians as a group to adopt a more critical stance."[3]

The New History emerged in the late 1980s as a result of two developments: the declassification of Israeli, American, British, and UN archives concerning the 1948 war and the early years afterward, and the soul-searching by a younger generation of Israeli scholars and journalists, particularly because of their shock at Israel's behavior in the 1982 Lebanon war.[4] To be sure, even earlier there had been a number of works by Israeli and British writers that had directly challenged the dominant Israeli mythologies, but they had been largely ignored.[5]

In the past, argued the younger generation of historians, the "old historians" either consciously or unconsciously crafted their works so that they mainly supported the dominant Israeli mythology. Thus, they ignored, downplayed, or even failed to recognize the darker side of the Israeli experience, creating a "history," in the judgment of the New Historians, that was merely the propaganda of the victors in the Arab-Israeli conflict.

The New History examined and decisively refuted the main myths in the conventional Zionist-Israeli mythology, the most important of which are these:

- The Zionist leaders accepted the UN partition as a necessary compromise with the Arabs, but the Palestinians and their supporters in the Arab world rejected partition, thus launching the overall Arab-Israeli conflict.
- The Arab states that invaded Israel in May 1948 were united in their main intention, which was to destroy the state of Israel. In something of "a miracle" they failed to do so, because the vastly outnumbered Jews—"David"—somehow defeated the Arab "Goliath."
- The some 700,000 to 750,000 Palestinians who "fled" Israel during the 1948 war did so voluntarily, in the expectation they would soon return after the invading Arab armies conquered Israel.
- Immediately after the 1948 war Israel sought a compromise peace with the Arabs but were met with unyielding Arab rejection, which then left Israel no choice but to defend itself against Arab state aggression in the subsequent 1956, 1967, 1973, and 1982 Arab-Israeli wars, as well as in a number of military conflicts with the Palestinians in the West Bank and Gaza.

The UN Partition Mythology

It is true that most of the Palestinians rejected partition and, following the passage of the UN plan on November 30, 1947, engaged in a number of attacks on the Jews. On the other hand, a number of Palestinians and their local leaders recognized that they could not defy the Zionists and the international community and that partition was unavoidable; consequently, they were prepared to compromise. As Simha Flapan observed: "The evidence is so overwhelming [of local Palestinian attempts to avoid a violent conflict with the Zionists] that the question arises how the myth of a Palestinian jihad against the Jews could survive so long."[6] Flapan notes the many Palestinian villages that sought non-intervention agreements with their Jewish neighbors, with hundreds of non-aggression pacts signed all over the country.[7]

Ben-Gurion was fully aware of these efforts by many Palestinians as well as their Jewish neighbors, admitting that "it is now clear, without the slightest doubt, that were we to face the Palestinians alone, everything would be all right. They, the decisive majority of them, do not want to fight us, and all of them together are unable to stand up to us."[8]

Benny Morris and Avi Shlaim reached similar conclusions. Summing up the evidence, the American scholar Steven Heydemann wrote, "Both Morris and Shlaim provide graphic evidence of the way in which efforts at accommodation, both with Abdullah [the king of Jordan] and with the Palestinians were consistently refused by Ben-Gurion, Moshe Dayan, and many others in the military establishment who regarded compromise as unnecessary in light of Israel's evident military superiority."[9]

In short, as I have previously argued, the evidence is overwhelming that the Zionist leaders had no intention of accepting partition as a necessary and just compromise with the Palestinians. Rather, their reluctant acceptance of the UN plan was only tactical; their true goals were to gain time, establish the Jewish state, build up its armed forces, and then expand to incorporate into Israel as much of ancient or biblical Palestine as they could.

The Palestinians knew of these Zionist intentions, both because of their well-known ideology—"transfer"—and from their behavior in the decades preceding the UN partition. Consequently, their resistance—however unwise as it subsequently proved, in practice, to be—could hardly be described as an unprovoked launching of the conflict. Nonetheless, because "they started it," the Zionist canon holds, they are responsible not only for the 1948 war but, in many versions, the continuation of the Israeli-Palestinian conflict ever since. In any case, I argue that *even if* the "they started it" mythology had been true, it would hardly have justified the violent expulsion of the Palestinians during the 1947–48 period.

The Arab Invasion of Israel. On May 1, 1948, the last British troops and administrators left Palestine, and on the following day the Zionists declared the state of Israel. On May 15, armies from Egypt, Syria, Iraq, and Jordan attacked.[10] In the Israeli mythology, the Arab attack was huge, closely coordinated, and because it was motivated by pure anti-Semitism, there was no chance the war could have been avoided.

The David and Goliath Myth

None of this stands up to serious analysis: in fact, the Arab invasion was small, uncoordinated, riven with conflicting aims, and in all probability could have been avoided if the Israeli leaders were willing to negotiate fair compromises.[11] Even in terms of numbers, the David versus Goliath myth does not work, for none of the Arab armies, individually and even collectively, were strong enough to destroy Israel and "drive the Jews into the sea."

At the onset of the war, the Israeli army's 35,000 troops outnumbered the combined total of 25,000 troops in the invading Arab armies; in the course of the war both sides expanded to 90,000 to 100,000 soldiers.[12] Aside from the fact that the numbers were generally equal, from the outset the Israel Defense Forces (IDF) had technological superiority over the Arab armies, and the Israeli firepower advantage continued to grow throughout the war, especially because the Soviet Union (acting through Czechoslovakia) began supplying modern arms, including military aircraft, to Israel.[13]

As well, the IDF organization and command and control systems were far better than the largely uncoordinated and ill-prepared Arab forces: "It was superior Jewish firepower, manpower, organization, and command and control that determined the outcome of battle," Benny Morris wrote.[14]

Finally, and no less important, the morale and fighting spirit of the Israeli army were much greater than that of the Arab forces—not surprisingly, the Israeli soldiers believed that their very existence depended on victory. By contrast, nearly all accounts of the war agree that the Arab armies were disorganized and dispirited, especially after they started to lose the war.[15]

Israeli historian Tom Segev summed up the evidence: "The bottom line is this: the IDF won because it was stronger than the Arabs of the land of Israel [the Palestinians] and the Arab armies put together."[16] Thus, as Ilan Pappé concluded, the New History "successfully demolished the characterization of the 1948 war as a Jewish David against the Arab Goliath, a myth that was crucial for developing both contempt for Arabs and Palestinians and for cultivating a sense of invincibility of almost metaphysical proportions."[17]

While the myths have certainly been demolished, they continue to play a major role in Israel's unwillingness to negotiate attainable compromise peace settlements with the Palestinians.

That said, regardless of the outcome of the war, at its outset the Israelis could hardly have dismissed the Arab threat or what might have happened had the Arabs won. As an Israeli journalist wrote, the Israelis "could not have known for certain that the invading Arab armies would be poorly coordinated, suspicious of each other, and willing to commit only relatively small forces to 'liberating' Palestine."[18]

Moreover, there is no question that Arab leaders engaged in murderous rhetoric before the war. There were many examples. The secretary general of the Arab League declared, "This will be a war of great destruction and slaughter that will be remembered like the massacres carried out by the Mongols and the Crusaders."[19] Saudi Arabia's King Saud said, "The Arab nations must be prepared to sacrifice up to 10 million [of their peoples] . . . if necessary in order to wipe out Israel. . . . It must be rooted like a cancer."[20] Faris al-Khouri, who at various times had held office as Syria's prime minister, foreign minister, and UN ambassador, said that "Syria, Iraq and Egypt must agree upon a united plan that will enable them to bring about the annihilation of Israel."[21]

All this just three years after the Holocaust. How could it not have had a devastating impact on Israeli attitudes, then and ever since?[22] Even a critic of post-1948 policies as severe as Avi Shlaim wrote: "For the Israelis, it was a war of survival. There can be no doubt that the Arabs would have destroyed the Israeli intruders had they had the power."[23] As well, the 1948 war veteran Uri Avneri, the Israeli "left-wing" peace activist and journalist, wrote: "We, the soldiers, were totally convinced that we were fighting for our existence, for our lives, and the lives of the Jewish population."[24]

In any case, in the early phases of the war, the Egyptian and Syrian armies did advance toward Jewish population areas. They were soon thrown back, but so far as the Israelis knew, that might have been only the first round.[25] As Shlomo Ben-Ami has convincingly pointed out:

> Battlefield strength was never the Zionists' only concern; even more troubling was the fact that the Yishuv [the pre-state Jewish population] was encircled by large, hostile Arab states whose armies could easily retreat, recover, and be ready for the next round. Accounts that focus on the number of troops on the ground ignore the traumatic memory of the destruction of European Jewry, the Yishuv's deep sense of insecurity, and its tendency to see every battle in apocalyptic terms.[26]

While today Israel regularly invokes the Holocaust to excuse its repression of the Palestinians, in 1948 its genuine fears could hardly have been otherwise; indeed, who is to say what would have happened had the Arab states actually conquered Israel?

The Arab State Goals

In reality, though, the Arab state invasion that followed the May 1948 creation of the state of Israel, primarily from Egypt, Syria, and Iraq, was relatively small and poorly coordinated, demonstrating that despite the rhetoric of some fanatics, there was no general Arab determination to destroy Israel, as opposed to much more limited nationalist objectives.

Understanding the timeline of the 1948 war is crucial: contrary to the Israeli mythology, it was not the November 1947 UN support for the creation of a Jewish state that precipitated the Arab attacks, for that did not occur until May 1948 and was principally motivated by several other factors.

First, while none of the Arab states were interested in the establishment of a Palestinian state—that would interfere with their own territorial ambitions in the area—there is no reason to doubt what they said at the time, namely, that they were furious at Zionist massacres and forced expulsion of the Palestinians, which began well before the invasion. Tom Segev put it this way: "The possibility arises that . . . the Arab states attacked Israel—among other reasons—because it had chased out and expelled 400,000 Palestinians."[27]

Moreover, there had been no Arab state intervention in the six months preceding the war—the civil war period between the Jewish and Palestinian peoples, as it is often termed—during which the Zionist forces mainly seized only the areas that the UN had allocated to Israel.[28] The intervention came only after the Zionists began seizing land allocated to the Arabs. Noting that fact, a State Department memorandum of May 4, 1948, concluded that the Israelis "will use every means to obscure the fact that it is their own armed aggression against the Arabs which is the cause of Arab counter-attack."[29]

In any case, the Israeli New Historians agree that the primary cause of the Arab invasion was less that of sympathy for the Palestinians than the result of inter-Arab monarchical and territorial rivalries, especially the fears of other Arab monarchs that King Abdullah of Jordan would seize the West Bank and then use it as a springboard for his long dream of creating a Hashemite kingdom extending over parts of Syria, Lebanon, Egypt, and Iraq.

Avi Shlaim summed up the evidence: there was no Arab plan "directed at strangling the Jewish state at birth," but rather "inter-Arab fears and rivalries."[30] Similarly, Flapan wrote that "although militarily this was a war between Arabs and Jews, politically it was a war between Arabs and Arabs. The issue was not the existence of the Jewish state, because [the Arab leaders] were ready, under certain conditions, to recognize the new realities."[31]

Could the War Have Been Avoided?

Although the Truman administration had strongly supported the UN partition plan, within a few months it began to fear that the impending conflict would open the door to the spread of Soviet influence in the Middle East, especially if the Arab states turned to the Soviets for support against the militarily superior Israel. Consequently, two months before the scheduled creation of the state of Israel in April 1948, the US government proposed to the Security Council that it freeze the partition plan and substitute for it a UN trusteeship over Palestine that would rule until the Zionists and the Palestinians settled their differences.

However, the trusteeship proposal went nowhere. The Zionist leadership rejected it and it met with strong opposition from supporters of the Zionist movement inside the US government; at the same time, many of the Arab leaders distrusted what might become an indefinite new international "mandate." Consequently, the Truman administration soon dropped the trusteeship idea and proposed instead a truce in the ongoing violent Zionist-Palestinian conflict in Palestine—the Arab state armies had not yet entered the conflict—and a temporary postponement of an Israeli declaration of statehood.

Most of the Arab states were prepared to agree to the US proposal, but it failed, thwarted by both the refusal of Israel and Jordan to stop their territorial expansion and by Ben-Gurion's insistence on declaring Israeli statehood as soon as Britain completed its withdrawal from Palestine.[32]

Even so, there had been other lost opportunities either to prevent the 1948 war, or at least bring it to a quick end. As Flapan concluded: "There is a good deal of evidence that Arab leaders and governments were ready to negotiate a solution to the conflict before, during, and after the War of Independence. . . . [T]he efforts of Egypt, Syria, and the Palestinians provided opportunities for peace that were not exploited."[33] These and other lost opportunities for peace are discussed throughout this work.

It is important to look more closely at the policies of the most important Arab states.

Jordan. In fall 1947, a number of meetings occurred between King Abdullah of Jordan and high Zionist leaders. These resulted in a secret agreement under which Abdullah would keep the Arab Legion out of any Arab invasion into the lands designated to Israel by the UN, and Israel would stay out of the West Bank, designated for an Arab state, and East Jerusalem, which was to be internationalized. Because of his ambitions to extend Hashemite rule into the West Bank, Abdullah had no interest in destroying a Jewish state within the UN boundaries; in fact, he preferred a friendly Jewish neighbor to a hostile Palestinian one.[34]

At the same time, the Zionists had no present intentions of seizing the West Bank and Jerusalem, fearing that they lacked the forces to do so and wanting to keep the best Arab army, the Arab Legion, out of the war; further, at that time they did not want to directly challenge US and British policies. Of course, Ben-Gurion and the other Zionist leaders had not abandoned their hopes of establishing a Jewish state in all of historic Palestine, but that could wait until later, once an opportunity arose and Israel was strong enough to take advantage of it. For now, their reasoning appeared to be, better temporary Jordanian rule in the West Bank than a Palestinian state.

Abdullah kept to the secret agreement during the 1948 war; in Benny Morris's words: "Abdaullah's troops kept meticulously to the [agreement]: At no point in May, or thereafter, did the Arab Legion attack the Jewish state's territory," seizing only the northern half of the West Bank and Arab East Jerusalem, which had not been assigned by the UN Partition either to the Zionists or the Palestinians.[35]

To be sure, there were clashes between the Arab Legion and Israeli forces, but they were instigated by Israel, when it attacked areas near Jerusalem that had been assigned to the Arabs. Thus, the Legion's successful defeat of the Israeli attacks were acts of defense, not aggression, and were in strict accord with the pre-war Zionist-Jordanian agreements.

Egypt. The most important Arab state was a reluctant and half-hearted participant in the 1948 war.[36] Before the war began, King Farouk of Egypt made several efforts to explore the possibility of a peace settlement with Israel, provided it would cede part of Gaza and a narrow strip of the Negev Desert to Egypt. Flapan writes: "It is beyond doubt that from Nov. 1947 until 11 May 1948, the Egyptian authorities initiated no steps to prepare for war and staked everything on a last-minute diplomatic solution."[37]

Part of Egypt's motivation was security: it feared further Israeli expansionism and wanted a territorial buffer zone. As it developed, Egypt's fears were well founded, for Ben-Gurion ignored Farouk's overtures and during the war deliberately provoked further clashes with Egyptian armed forces in order to seize all of the Negev and parts of the Sinai that had been allocated by the UN to the Arab state.

Second, Farouk was an archenemy of the Hashemite king Abdullah of Jordan and sought, in Benny Morris's words, "to prevent Jordan from grabbing all the Palestinian Arab areas," as well as "to get hold of chunks of territory" for himself.[38]

Even after the war began, Egypt continued to seek a way out. In early October 1948, knowing the war was lost, Farouk sent secret peace feelers to Israel offering to conclude a separate peace with it and stay out of any future Arab-Israeli wars—but on the condition that Israel cede parts of the Negev and Gaza to Egypt. Ben-Gurion's foreign minister Moshe Sharett and other high officials favored negotiations on this basis but Ben-Gurion rejected the overtures, later writing to Sharett that "Israel will not discuss a peace involving the concession of any piece of territory. The neighboring states do not deserve an inch of Israel's land."[39]

On October 6, Ben-Gurion ordered the IDF to ignore a ceasefire that was then in place (largely because of pressures from the United States and Britain) and drive the Egyptians out of Palestine, excepting only Gaza, where Egypt continued to rule until Israel conquered it in the 1967 Arab-Israeli war.

In short, not only was the 1948 war between Israel and Egypt avoidable on reasonable terms—terms that apparently were acceptable to Sharett and other Zionist officials—but it is highly likely that with Egypt on the sidelines the other Arab armies would not have attacked Israel, that Israel and Egypt would have reached a de facto peace agreement, and that almost certainly there would have been no subsequent 1956, 1967, 1970, and 1973 wars.

Syria. According to historian Moshe Maoz, one of Israel's leading experts on Syria, the Syrian invasion force was small (about 3,000 troops), badly organized, and poorly armed. It was in no position to destroy Israel, nor was that the operational intention of the Syrian leaders. While partly motivated by sympathy with the Palestinians, the primary goals of the Syrian government were to prevent Abdullah's army from seizing all the West Bank, which would cut Syria off from the northern Jordan River and Lake Tiberias, the main sources of fresh water in that region.[40]

During the war, the Syrian army succeeded in capturing a small strip of land on the northeast border of the lake; the status of that tiny strip of land became the central issue in the various secret Syrian-Israeli peace talks that continued in the ensuing decades. Other than the fighting near Lake Tiberias, Maoz writes, "the Syrian army remained by and large inactive during the 1948 war."[41]

Iraq. The literature on the Iraqi invasion is surprisingly thin, but it apparently was motivated by a mix of anger at the Israeli treatment of the Palestinians, ideological and religious objections to the creation of a Jewish state in the heart of the Arab world, and most important, Iraq's own territorial ambitions: "Iraq harbored its own ambition for the unification of the Fertile Crescent under its leadership."[42] As well, Morris writes, Iraq had the more limited goal of capturing Haifa, the port on the Mediterranean Sea through which most of its oil was exported to Europe.[43]

The "Nakba"

Despite the failures of the Israeli leadership to avert war, once the 1948 Arab invasion began, the Israelis of course had to defend themselves. However, the massacres and expulsions of the Palestinians—today widely known as the Nakba (the Catastrophe)—were an entirely different matter.

What Are the Facts?

The Israeli mythology holds that until the Arab invasion, the Zionists, hoping to demonstrate that the Jews and the Arabs could live side by side in the areas designated to be a Jewish state, had tried to persuade the Palestinians not to leave. However, the story goes, the invading Arab armies called on the Palestinians, who had until then largely remained in place, to flee, which most of them voluntarily did.

The facts are otherwise. From the outset of the Zionist movement all the major leaders wanted as few Arabs as possible in a Jewish state; if all other means failed, they were to be "transferred" by one means or another, including, if necessary, by force.

In fact, the forced transfer of the Palestinians began not as a response to the Arab invasion in the spring of 1948, but nearly six months earlier in December 1947, following the proclamation of the UN partition plan. While a number of studies have found no evidence to support the Israeli claim of an Arab propaganda campaign to induce the Palestinians to flee, *well before the Arab invasion* some 300,000 to 400,000 Palestinians (out of a population of about 900,000 at the time of the UN partition) were either forcibly expelled—sometimes by forced marches with only the clothes on their backs—or fled as a result of Israeli psychological warfare, economic pressures, and violence, designed to empty the area that would become Israel of most of its Arab inhabitants.[44]

The timeline is important, because it demonstrates that the large-scale "transfer" was not a result of the Arab state invasion that began on May 15, 1948, but the implementation of the long-intended Zionist policy. As Palestinian-American scholar Walid Khalidi concluded: "It was not the entry of the Arab armies that caused the exodus. It was the exodus that caused the entry of the Arab armies."[45] To be sure, it is possible that the eventual expulsions of about 750,000 Palestinians might have been less extensive and less brutal in the absence of the Arab invasion.

Was the Nakba an Intentional Israeli Policy?

In addition to the forced expulsions, Zionist forces carried out several massacres, some of them even before the May 1948 Arab state invasion. The most notorious of them was the April 8–9 killing of over one hundred Palestinian civilians in the village of Deir Yassin, near Jerusalem. There is a lively debate among Israeli historians over whether Deir Yassin and other massacres reflected deliberate Zionist policy or rather was perpetrated by individual military units, particularly by the Irgun and fanatical "Stern Gang" terrorists who operated independently of the Haganah, the military arm of the Zionist leadership. However, from the point of view of terrorized Palestinians who learned of the massacres, it was entirely irrelevant whether the killings represented official policy or not—either way, they had very good reasons to flee.

That said, if we distinguish between forced expulsions—ethnic cleansing, to use the modern language—and outright murders, there is little doubt that David Ben-Gurion at a minimum knew of and took no action to stop the expulsions. From at least the 1930s, Ben-Gurion intended Israel to be an overwhelmingly Jewish state but assumed that few Arabs would voluntarily leave; therefore, he wrote, "We must expel Arabs and take their places . . . and if we have to use force . . . then we have force at our disposal."[46] These were not empty words; the mainstream historian Michael Bar-Zohar, Ben-Gurion's biographer, writes: "In internal discussions, in instructions to his men, [Ben-Gurion] demonstrated a clear position. It would be better that as few a number as possible of Arabs would remain in the territory of the state."[47]

In 1979, Yitzhak Rabin published his memoirs. During the 1948 war Rabin was a leading Haganah general and commander of a force that violently expelled 50,000 inhabitants of the Palestinian towns of Lydda and Ramle. In a passage that was excised from the Hebrew edition by Israeli government censors, but later published in the *New York Times,* Rabin wrote that when he asked Ben-Gurion what was to be done with the Palestinians, Ben-Gurion "waved his hand in a gesture which said, 'Drive them out.'"[48]

Benny Morris, Ilan Pappé, and other Israeli New Historians wrote extensively about the Nakba and pointed to the evidence of Ben-Gurion's knowledge and at least tacit approval of the expulsions. These findings were later confirmed by the Israeli historian Shay Hazkani. Summarizing his findings in a long article for *Haaretz,* Hazkani wrote:

> Ben-Gurion appeared to have known the facts well. Even though much material about the Palestinian refugees in Israeli archives is still classified, what has been uncovered provides enough information to establish that in many cases senior commanders of the Israel Defense Forces ordered Palestinians to be expelled and their homes blown up. The Israeli military

> not only updated Ben-Gurion about these events but also apparently received his prior authorization, in written or oral form, notably in Lod and Ramle, and in several villages in the north.[49]

In his recent magisterial history of this period, Tom Segev writes that during the 1948 war, if Israeli military commanders and other officials had "doubts about how to treat any given village, they could be helped by the tenor of the messages conveyed by their supreme commander, Ben-Gurion." The overall military plan, Segev and others wrote, included measures that were explicitly designed "to 'break the spirit' of the population of 'enemy cities' ... [including] the option of expelling Arabs from their homes and cutting them off from the essential services ... including water and electricity. Other plans recommended a variety of ways of sowing terror among the Arabs ... including whisper propaganda, a well-known method of causing people to flee."[50]

In his review of the evidence, the former Israeli foreign minister Shlomo Ben-Ami wrote that it showed Ben-Gurion had "personally authorized such orders [of expulsion]."[51] In my view, the evidence supports a stronger conclusion: from the UN partition proclamation through the 1948 war, Ben-Gurion and other Zionist leaders deliberately implemented the long-held Zionist goal of "transfer" by driving hundreds of thousands of Palestinians out of Israel.

To be sure, at the end of the war, about 150,000 to 160,000 Palestinians remained in the expanded Israel and were allowed to remain there, though as a distinctly powerless and unequal minority. The fact that not all the Palestinians fled or were driven out of their homes, lands, and villages—though over 80 percent of them were—is often cited by Zionist apologists as proof that no "ethnic cleansing" took place. However, what that demonstrates is that there was no *genocide*, not that there was no *ethnic cleansing*.

There were a number of motivations: the ideological commitment to create a state that was as Jewish as possible; the intent to suppress Palestinian resistance before the 1948 war and then prevent the Palestinians from supporting the invading Arab armies; and the desire to settle Jewish immigrants in the newly vacated Arab homes, villages, and farmlands.

Further, *after* the war, hundreds of Palestinian villages were either razed to the ground or renamed as "new" towns and villages designated for the incoming Jewish population. As well, Israel methodically destroyed much of the previous Palestinian infrastructure—even mosques—as it sought, in Pappé's words, "to wipe out one nation's history and culture and replace it with a fabricated version of another, from which all traces of the indigenous population were elided."[52]

In 2016 Benjamin Netanyahu declared that he would not remove Jewish settlers in the West Bank as part of a two-state settlement, as that would constitute "ethnic cleansing." Calling that claim "utter nonsense"—for sheer chutzpah it could hardly have been surpassed—in an article entitled "Netanyahu, This Is What Ethnic Cleaning Really Looks Like," Israeli historian Daniel Blatman wrote:

> About half a million Palestinians were cleared by force from the territory where they lived.... The hundreds of communities in which the Arab population lived were razed to the ground or given over for Jewish settlement at the end of the war. Arab property worth tens of millions of Palestinian pounds was stolen and confiscated. Those who tried to return were forcibly expelled or shot. The ethnic cleansing carried out in Palestine in 1948 was one of the most successful of the 20th century.[53]

Was Ethnic Cleansing "Necessary"?

In sum, Israel did not expel the Palestinians because of the Arab attack, as about half of the estimated total of 750,000 had fled or been expelled between the UN partition in November 1947 and the establishment of the state of Israel in May 1948. Nor did they expel the Palestinians because they resisted partition—as the New Historians showed, many of them sought a peace settlement and didn't join the resistance forces. The pre-war expulsion, then, occurred principally because the Zionist leaders wanted a larger Jewish majority in the coming state of Israel, and also because they planned to settle incoming Jews in the former Palestinian homes, farms, and villages.

The central (and only persuasive) Zionist argument is that in light of the history of murderous anti-Semitism in general and, of course, of the Holocaust in particular, the Jewish people had both the right and the need for a Jewish state. However, even accepting that premise (as does this author), there is no avoiding the fact that in 1947 the Jewish people in Palestine faced a very difficult dilemma. As discussed, in December 1947, the area designated by the UN for a Jewish state was estimated to contain about 500,000 Jews and 400,000 Arabs. Understandably, Ben-Gurion told other Zionist leaders that "such a composition does not provide a stable basis for a Jewish state.... [It] does not even give us absolute assurance that control will remain in the hands of the Jewish majority." Even Ilan Pappé, a strong critic of the entire Zionist enterprise, agrees: "The almost equal demographic balance within the allocated Jewish state was such that... Zionism would never have attained any of its principal goals."[54]

Ben-Gurion believed that to secure the stability and security of Israel, the minimum acceptable Jewish majority must be 80 percent. That seems reasonable, and in fact that has been the general population distribution of Israel since 1949. *But does it follow that ethnic cleansing was the only way to achieve that goal?*

Zeev Sternhell, one of Israel's leading political philosophers and a regular columnist for *Haaretz*, essentially makes that argument. Sternhell is perhaps Israel's most prominent and articulate "liberal Zionist," widely defined to mean someone who is a strong critic of Israel's policies and treatment of the Palestinians since 1967 but who accepts the need for a Jewish state and regards Israel's early policies as a tragic necessity.

Sternhell writes: "It was the suffering of the Jews—and not historical right and, it goes without saying, divine promise—that constituted the one moral justification for this act of conquest [and] . . . cruel battle for survival. Over the years, we have killed and evicted and made the lives of Palestinians miserable. But we did it because, in the final reckoning, we had no other choice."[55]

But that is simply not true, for other alternatives were never explored. There were two other possible Israeli policies that would have met the need for a Jewish state but avoided the Nakba. To begin, let us assume that Ben-Gurion was right that Jews needed an 80 percent majority. Assume further that the original UN boundaries were "indefensible" and that the need for national security justified Israeli expansion beyond those boundaries—which in turn meant that Israel somehow had to rid itself of some 700,000 to 750,000 Palestinians to achieve an 80 percent majority within its new and expanded borders after the 1948 war. Even if one accepts those assumptions—shaky as they are—it hardly follows that the only way to have done so was by violent ethnic cleansing.

As mentioned earlier, in 1939 Franklin Roosevelt, who favored the creation of a Jewish state in Palestine, proposed to the British government and American Zionist leaders that the Palestinian Arabs be transferred to neighboring Arab states but generously compensated. He estimated that the total cost would be about $300 million, which he was confident could easily be raised by the United States, the international community, Israel itself, and wealthy Western Jews.

Tragically, nothing came of this idea. If we drop the assumption that Israeli "security" required expansion into the areas designated for an Arab state, then only about 250,000 Arabs—not 750,000—would have to have been "transferred" out of the Jewish state (as designated by the UN) in order to create an 80 percent Jewish majority. *But not necessarily by violence*, let alone by the extensive violence that deserves the name "ethnic cleansing."

How might this have been accomplished? Suppose a generous offer had been made in 1947, let's say as much as $600 million, or double Roosevelt's estimate of what it would take to transfer the Palestinians without violence. That would come to over $6 billion in today's values, a large but still affordable amount, in light of the many possible sources. It seems likely it would have been sufficient to induce a number of the Palestinians who were now caught in the Jewish state to move into Arab areas just a few miles away, with essentially the same geography, climate, history, religion, language, and culture.

Still, in view of the centuries-long Palestinian attachment to their land, homes, and villages, no doubt there would still have been many who continued to refuse to move, but surely it would have been substantially less than 250,000. Those remaining Palestinians could then have been informed that, in due course, with plenty of advance notice, *and with the same compensation*, they would be expelled to the neighboring Arab states with as little coercion as possible. Granted, that would still be an injustice, but radically less of one than the violent expulsion of 750,000 people, many of whom fled in justified fear that they were in danger of being killed, and others who were rounded up in a matter of hours and marched across the border with little but the clothes on their backs.

But now let us go even further and drop the assumption that some significant numbers of Palestinians would have needed to leave Israel for the Jews to have an 80 percent majority. Recall Ben-Gurion's assessment that on the eve of the UN partition there were 500,000 Jews and 400,000 non-Jews (mostly Arab Muslims) in the area allotted for a Jewish state. Other estimates differ only slightly; for example, in his history of Israel, Sachar gives the figures as 538,000 Jews, 397,000 Arabs.[56] Using those figures, then, Jews comprised about 58 percent of the population of the coming Jewish state. However, by the end of 1949, the Jewish population of Israel was about 1 million, and another 450,000 had arrived by the end of 1952.[57] Consequently, within three or four years the total population of an Israel that had remained within its borders and not expelled any Palestinians would have been about 1,850,000, of whom some 1,450,000 would have been Jews—that is, almost the magic 80 percent majority. Moreover, that majority would have continued to grow because during this period Jewish immigration outpaced natural Palestinian growth rates.

In short, had there been no Zionist policy of "transfer" and no expansionism well beyond the UN boundaries, the goal of an 80 percent majority would soon have been reached within a few years, without the need to buy out, let alone expel, *any* of the Arabs. Indeed, Ben-Gurion himself had anticipated that Jewish immigration alone would in time create a large Jewish majority. In 1935, some 60,000 Jewish immigrants arrived in Palestine, leading Ben-Gurion to write to Moshe Sharett saying that "immigration at the rate of 60,000 a year means a Jewish state in all of Palestine."[58]

Had Ben-Gurion and other Zionist leaders decided in 1947 to refrain from expelling the Palestinians and expanding the territory of the new state of Israel beyond the UN partition boundaries, almost certainly there would have been no Arab state invasion in 1948 nor, as I shall later argue, in all likelihood no 1967 or 1973 wars either, which were primarily the result of the Arab states' drive to recover the land they lost in 1948.

It is important to distinguish between the argument that it was necessary to create a Jewish state—even if there was no way to do that without *some* degree of injustice to the Palestinians—and the argument that injustice and harm at the level of the Nakba was unavoidable if the Jewish state was to be created.

Moreover, after the Nakba, the Israelis could have at least mitigated its injustice in a number of ways. To begin with, they should have acknowledged and apologized for the expulsion of the Palestinians and committed themselves to doing everything possible to make up for it, short of disbanding Israel as a Jewish state. For example, they could have said something like this: "We were in a tragic situation forced by necessity to take action that we recognize inflicted grave damage on you. Therefore, we commit ourselves to rectifying this unavoidable injustice in a variety of ways, so long as they don't threaten our basic security and our need for a large Jewish majority."

A number of things could and should have been done. First, the Israelis could have *genuinely* committed themselves to ensure that the Arab (and other non-Jewish) minorities would have political, social, and economic rights equal to those of the Jews.[59] Second, they should have avoided further territorial expansion and expulsion of the Palestinians after 1948, especially the conquest and occupation of East Jerusalem, the West Bank, and Gaza after the 1967 war. Then, they should have agreed to a genuinely viable and independent Palestinian state in those territories, and along with the international community, provided generous development assistance to it.

Had all these things been done, almost certainly the Arab-Israeli or the Israeli-Palestinian conflict would have been resolved long ago, and on terms that ensured the continued existence and security of the Jewish state of Israel.

The 1948 War and Israeli Expansionism

The Zionist movement in general and David Ben-Gurion in particular had long sought to establish a Jewish state in all of "Palestine," which in their view included the West Bank, Gaza, and parts of Jordan, Lebanon, and Syria. After the May 1948 Arab attack began, Ben-Gurion revealed his plans to the IDF's General Staff:

> We should be prepared to go on the offensive with the aim of smashing Lebanon, Transjordan and Syria. . . . The weak point in the Arab coalition is Lebanon [for] the Moslem regime is artificial and easy to undermine. A Christian state should be established, with its southern border on the Litani River. We will make an alliance with it. When we smash the [Arab] Legion's strength and bomb Amman, we will eliminate Transjordan, too, and then Syria will fall. If Egypt still dares to fight on, we shall bomb Port Said, Alexandria, and Cairo. . . . And in this fashion, we will end the war and settle our forefathers' accounts with Egypt, Assyria, and Aram [Transjordan].[60]

Remarkably, Ben-Gurion is here contemplating bombing major Arab cities in "revenge" for acts that may (or may not) have been committed over 2,000 years earlier, by a people who may (or may not) have been the ancestors of the current Palestinian people.

However, his more important motive was less revenge than expansionism. As Ben-Gurion's biographer wrote, the Arab invasion in 1948 gave Ben-Gurion "the pretext for expanding the territory of the Jewish state."[61] As he told his aides, "Before the founding of the state . . . our main interest was self-defense. . . . But now the issue at hand is conquest, not self-defense. As for setting the borders—it's an open-ended matter. In the Bible as well as in history there are all kinds of definitions of the country's borders, so there's no real limit."[62]

Jerusalem and the West Bank

In fact, there were practical limits—at least for the present. Before the war, the Zionists and King Abdullah of Jordan had secretly reached an agreement to avoid war with each other: the Israelis would not oppose a Jordanian takeover of the West Bank as long as Abdullah kept the Arab Legion out of an Israel within its UN-designated boundaries. Nonetheless, once it became clear that Israel would defeat the Arab invasion, a number of its leading generals, including Yigal Allon, at the time the most important one (and in 1970 the deputy prime minister), sought to persuade the government to ignore the previous agreement with Abdullah and allow the Israeli army to take the West Bank and Jerusalem.

For a while, Ben-Gurion seemed to agree with Allon, for in September 1948 he proposed to the Israeli cabinet that the war should be reopened by creating a pretext to attack the Arab Legion, followed by the seizure of extensive parts of the West Bank, possibly including Jerusalem. Moreover, he argued, that would cause the Arabs in the newly conquered territory to flee, "and then we would rule over the entire width of the country up to the Jordan."[63] His proposal evenly split the cabinet (6 for, 6 against), and was therefore dropped; Ben-Gurion described the outcome as a cause for "mourning for generations to come."[64]

On the other hand, a number of Israeli historians point out that Ben-Gurion continued his ambivalence, or inconsistency, about conquering Jerusalem. For example, Avi Shlaim and Anita Shapira wrote that by 1949 Ben-Gurion had become more wary of the consequences of his own September 1948 proposal, especially because of the growing opposition of the United States and Britain to the continuing Israeli expansionism and his own increased concerns that Israel would face "the demography problem of governing hundreds of thousands of Arabs."[65] In an April 1949 speech to the Knesset, Ben-Gurion elaborated: "The IDF can capture the entire territory between the river and the sea. But what sort of country would that give us? . . . We would have a Knesset with an Arab majority. Faced with either a Greater Israel or a Jewish Israel, we choose a Jewish Israel."[66]

When the war ended in March 1949, the UN internationalization plan for Jerusalem was ignored by both Israel and Jordan, which divided the city between them. The rest of the West Bank remained under Jordanian rule, but Ben-Gurion did not accept Jordan's permanent sovereignty over the area. Rather, he evidently considered it to be temporary and reversible—as was made clear in 1956, when he proposed to French and British officials that Jordan itself should be divided: "Jordan has no right to exist and should be partitioned. Eastern Transjordan would be ceded to Iraq [then under a pro-Western monarchy], which would offer to accept and

Map 5.1 Israeli Borders and Armistice Lines, 1949, from Tessler, *A History of the Israeli-Palestinian Conflict*, 2nd ed., 265. Permission granted by Indiana University Press.

resettle the Arab refugees. The territory to the West of the Jordan River should be made an autonomous region of Israel."[67]

By the end of the war Israel had conquered and soon annexed large areas of Palestine that had been assigned by the UN for an Arab state, including most of northern Palestine up to the border with Lebanon, a large segment of the proposed Palestinian state stretching from south of Tel Aviv to West Jerusalem, and the eastern sections of the Negev Desert south of the Gaza Strip—in all, about three-quarters of Palestine under the British Mandate.

As one observer has put it: "So much for [the Arab state of] Palestine."[68]

Egypt

During the war, Egypt advanced into a section of the Negev Desert region of southern Palestine that had been allocated to the Jewish state. The Egyptian government then sent peace feelers to Israel, proposing that an end to the fighting and a peace settlement be reached: Egypt would accept the existence of Israel and refrain from further action against it, in exchange for an Israeli agreement to allow Egypt to keep its territorial gain in the Negev. Moshe Sharett favored exploring this offer, but "Ben-Gurion bluntly brushed it aside. . . . On 6 October, Ben-Gurion presented to the cabinet his proposal for renewing war against Egypt, without even mentioning the Egyptian peace feeler."[69] According to Segev, Ben-Gurion was looking for a pretext that would allow Israel to conquer the Negev,[70] but he had a problem: a UN truce was in effect. In his memoirs, Yitzhak Rabin described how the problem was solved:

> By late August 1948, the Arab armies showed little inclination to renew the war. . . . [W]e intended to capture Beersheba and, if possible, Gaza as well. . . . But there was one catch. To avoid the political handicap of taking the blame for breaking the truce, we had to find some pretext for renewing the fighting. . . . Consequently, we decided to send a supply convoy . . . as a deliberate act of provocation. When the Egyptians opened fire on it, they would provide us with an adequate pretext to renew the fighting.[71]

On October 15, Rabin continued, after Egypt fired a few shots at the convoy, "we had our pretext" and Israel implemented its plan, succeeding not only in expelling the Egyptian forces from the Negev but also seizing a large section of the western Negev region that had previously been allocated to the Arab state. Two months later Rabin's forces were poised to push beyond the Negev into Egypt itself (the western Sinai peninsula); however, facing a British threat that it would militarily intervene if Israel continued attacking the Egyptian army, Ben-Gurion accepted a final ceasefire.[72]

Gaza

The UN partition plan allocated the Gaza Strip to the projected Arab state, but King Farouk of Egypt had his own territorial expansionist goals, so the Egyptian army seized it. Ben-Gurion was of two minds on whether he wanted to expel the Egyptians and incorporate Gaza, with its 60,000 to 80,000 Arab inhabitants, into the Jewish state. In addition, he feared the international consequences if Israeli forces ignored a new ceasefire that had been ordered by the UN. Consequently, in December 1948, Ben-Gurion ordered the IDF to stop its advance toward Gaza—but in his mind that was temporary, for (in Tom Segev's words), "he wanted Gaza, too."[73]

Michael Bar-Zohar, Ben-Gurion's biographer, described the Israeli leader's plans after the final ceasefire, writing that the Arab invasion gave Ben-Gurion "the pretext" he had long sought to expand Israel's territory. However, Bar-Zohar continues:

> When the war ended . . . Ben-Gurion hadn't achieved [all] his territorial dreams." Subsequently, an Israeli writer asked Ben-Gurion, "Why didn't you liberate the entire country?" Ben-Gurion replied: "There was a danger of getting saddled with a hostile Arab majority . . . of entanglements with the United Nations and the big powers, and of the State Treasury collapsing. . . . Now, we have work for two or three generations. As for the rest—we'll see later.

Bar-Zohar then adds, "In his archives, I found abundant proof . . . that he continued to secretly plan the next stage, in which he would achieve his territorial ambitions."[74]

The Consequences of the 1948 War

Regardless of the Zionist policies, behavior, and expansionist ideology that had done much to precipitate war, once the Arab states attacked Israel it had to defend itself. Nonetheless, the war had a number of disastrous consequences.

First, in Simha Flapan's words: "The euphoria of victory gave them [the Israelis] an exaggerated belief in their power. . . . [It] was [seen as] a vindication of Ben-Gurion's doctrine that peace with the Arabs was unattainable."[75]

Second, Flapan continued, in terms of Israel's domestic policies, what followed from the 1948 military victories "was the subordination of foreign policy and socio-economic development to the aim of building up a military deterrent," policies that have continued throughout Israel's history.[76]

Third, the success of Israel's expansion in 1948 seemingly vindicated and fed long-held Israeli expansionist goals that went well beyond the territory conquered in the war. The purpose of Israeli military power was never merely defensive—that is, to provide a "deterrent" against Arab aggression—but also to make possible the expansionist goals that continued to drive future Israeli policies, especially in the 1956, 1967, and 1982 wars, as well as, since 1967, in the Israeli occupation and settlement of the Palestinian territories.

Fourth, as many Israeli writers have pointed out, another consequence of the war was the humiliation of the Arab world, followed by its desire for revenge. It is also important to emphasize, however, that "revenge" was hardly the only explanation of Arab hostility to Israel. During the 1948 war, Count Folke Bernadotte was the UN mediator. In his 1949 report to the General Assembly, Bernadotte said that from the outset of conflict the Arabs feared that "a Jewish state in Palestine will not stay within its defined boundaries, and through population pressure resulting from immigration, encouragement and support from world Jewry, and burgeoning nationalism, a threat will be posed not only to Palestine but the entire Arab Near East."[77]

In fact, the Arabs were right to fear further Israeli expansionism. As Israeli historian Shlomo Sand wrote: "During every round of the national conflict over Palestine, which is the longest running conflict of its kind in the modern era, Zionism has tried to appropriate additional territory."[78]

It was the Palestinians who suffered the greatest consequences of the war, for the area that the UN partition plan had allocated for the creation of a Palestinian state "had disappeared from the map."[79] Israel had conquered most of it, the Egyptian army occupied Gaza, and Jordan had taken control of the West Bank.

Fifth, the expulsion of the Palestinians created the refugee problem that festers to this day and soon led to the emergence of Yasser Arafat's Palestine Liberation Organization (PLO) movement in the refugee camps in Lebanon, Syria, Jordan, and Egypt. Until the late 1970s or early 1980s, the PLO sought the destruction of Israel, by means of guerrilla warfare and terrorism, and the return of the Palestinians to their homelands. Acknowledging no responsibility for the plight of the Palestinians, Israel met the violence with a policy of massive counterviolence, which in turn triggered the four major Arab-Israeli wars of 1956, 1967, 1973, and 1982.

6

Lost Opportunities for Peace, 1949–56

Among the most enduring and potent conventional beliefs about the Arab-Israeli conflict—an article of faith in Israel and widely accepted by the outside world as well—is that until recently most of the Arab states as well as the Palestinians refused to recognize the existence of Israel, rejected all compromise, and sought its destruction. By contrast, it is said, Israel has always been ready and willing to negotiate peace settlements; in Abba Eban's famous epigram, "The Arabs never miss an opportunity to miss an opportunity."

The historical record proves that this myth has it backward: it is Israel, far more than its Arab adversaries, that has been primarily responsible for the many lost opportunities, from 1947 through the present, to end the Arab-Israeli and Israeli-Palestinian conflicts. At one time or another, all the important Arab states and the most important Palestinian leaders—including Yasser Arafat—have been ready to agree to attainable and fair compromise settlements of all the central issues: Israeli security, its legitimate territory and borders, the creation of a Palestinian state, the status of Jerusalem, and the Palestinian refugee issue.

Although after years of avoidable conflict it did eventually reach peace treaties with Egypt and Jordan, Israel has refused to accept reasonable compromises on the issues involving the Palestinians. When the 1948 war ended, David Ben-Gurion, Israel's founding father and first prime minister whose decisions were essentially unchallengeable, firmly believed that no compromise with the Palestinians or with the Arab states was necessary or even desirable. Time was on Israel's side, he believed, telling a US journalist that "I am not in a hurry [to sign peace agreements] and I am prepared to wait ten years. We are under no pressure to do anything."[1] Abba Eban, then Israel's UN ambassador, agreed: "There's no need to run after peace. The armistice is enough for us. If we pursue peace, the Arabs will demand a price of us—borders or refugees or both. Let us wait a few years."[2]

Ben-Gurion concurred. In his view (as paraphrased by Avi Shlaim), "Israel could manage perfectly well without peace with the Arab states and without a solution to the Palestinian refugee problem."[3] In a May 1949 cabinet discussion, he elaborated: "On all of the great questions, time worked to Israel's advantage: borders, refugees, and Jerusalem. . . . With the passage of time the world would get used to Israel's existing borders and forget about UN borders and the UN idea of an independent Palestinian state."[4]

Israel and the Palestinians, 1948–50

At the end of the 1948 war Israel decided to set up some 350 settlements along its borders, "in many cases built on the ruins of abandoned villages," to be populated largely by the newly arrived Jewish immigrants from Europe and the Arab world.[5] For that reason, as well as its "transfer" ideology and security concerns, the Israeli government decided to block the return of the Palestinian refugees—the survivors of the Nakba who had fled into neighboring Arab states—by any means necessary.[6] As Ben-Gurion wrote in his diary in the summer of 1948: the return of the refugees "must be prevented . . . at all costs."[7]

Of course, the "costs" were overwhelmingly borne by the refugees seeking to return to their villages, farms, and properties. In the early years after 1948, most of the refugees were unarmed and nonviolent; dispossessed of their homes and property, poverty stricken and even hungry, they were desperately trying to harvest their crops from the fields and orchards that had been seized by Israel.[8] To be sure, some of them were militants or terrorists—the predecessors of the more organized Palestinian resistance forces, the "Fedayeen" or guerrilla forces of the 1950s—who sought to kill the new owners of their previous properties, or merely any Jews they encountered.[9]

Even when the "infiltrators," as Israel called them, posed no security threats, the government's orders to its soldiers and border police were to shoot them on sight. As a result, in the early years after the war an estimated 3,000 to 5,000 Palestinians were killed.

During these early years, none of the Arab governments supported the refugees' efforts to return to Israel: "There is strong evidence from Arab, British, American, UN, and even Israeli sources to suggest that for the first six years after the war, the Arab governments were opposed to infiltration and tried to curb it."[10] Nonetheless, Israel blamed them and often "retaliated" by attacking Jordanian and Egyptian villages, especially following the few occasions on which armed refugees killed Israeli civilians. Shlaim writes: "Ben-Gurion wanted the IDF to strike hard at civilians across the border in order to demonstrate that no attack on Israeli civilians would go unpunished."[11]

The Truman Administration and the Conflict

As has been discussed, Israel was not interested in reaching a compromise that would allow political settlements with the Arab states or the Palestinians after the 1948 war; instead, in 1949 it negotiated separate military truces or armistice agreements with Lebanon, Syria, Jordan, and Egypt. This was not satisfactory to the US government, which initially pressured Israel to reach permanent peace agreements with the Arab world.

Though Truman had supported the creation of Israel, during the 1948 war and well afterward he refused to allow it to buy American arms. After the war ended, for both moral reasons and US national interests, Truman was anxious to see an overall Arab-Israeli peace settlement. Consequently, as Ben-Gurion's "Iron Wall" intentions became evident, the American government became increasingly disenchanted with Israeli policies.

In particular, Truman was angry at Israel's continued attempts to take over territories allocated by the UN to the proposed Arab state. Well after the Arab attacks of May 1948 had been decisively defeated, Israel continued to advance into Egyptian territory in the Sinai. In December, Ben-Gurion was told that Truman was "deeply disturbed" by Israel's "aggressiveness" and "complete disregard" of the United Nations,[12] and James McDonald, US ambassador to Israel, was instructed to tell the Israeli government that the administration was "not convinced that peace would be had on Israel's terms . . . and we were unwilling to recognize Israel's possession of any territories beyond the November 29th partition line, unless Israel made territorial compensation elsewhere to the Arabs."[13] If Israel did not withdraw from the Egyptian territory, the acting US secretary of state threatened, the United States would "undertake a substantial review of its attitude toward Israel."[14] As Britain was also threatening to "take action" if the Israeli advances into Sinai continued, Ben-Gurion decided to withdraw the Israeli forces.

Nonetheless, throughout 1949 the American government's disenchantment continued to grow; the administration feared that US support for an expansionist Israel would increasingly anger the Arab world and harm US national interests in the region. As well, the administration rejected Israel's policies on the return of Palestinian refugees.

The Lausanne Conference

In the spring of 1949 the Truman administration pressured Israel to agree to an international conference to reach a negotiated settlement of both the Arab-Israeli state conflicts and the Israeli-Palestinian conflict. Since Israel was seeking American and other international support for its drive to validate its legitimacy by gaining admission into the United Nations, it reluctantly agreed to participate.

Accordingly, at the end of April 1949 the conference, under UN auspices but essentially mediated by the United States, met in Lausanne, Switzerland, attended by delegations from Israel, Egypt, Jordan, Lebanon, Syria, and the United States.[15] The main issues that needed to be resolved were the boundaries of an internationally recognized Israel, the status of Jerusalem, and the future of the Palestinian refugees.

If such a conference were to be held today, over seventy years later, the same issues would be on the table, with the addition of a state for the Palestinians. That, in a nutshell, illustrates why the Arab-Israeli/Israeli-Palestinian conflict has been the longest-lasting and most intractable international conflict since the end of World War II.

The first order of business at Lausanne was to agree on a "Protocol," or overall statement of the principles that would guide the conference. On May 12, the Lausanne Protocol was signed by all the delegations, and while the Ben-Gurion government was unwilling to openly boycott it, it was unhappy and had obvious objections to several of its central provisions: Pappé notes that the Protocol "set three principal guidelines for peace in Palestine: recognition of the earlier partition plan and therefore, the existence of Israel, the internationalization of Jerusalem, and the repatriation of Palestinian refugees."[16]

As Pappé and others have pointed out, by agreeing to the Lausanne Protocol and reversing their previous opposition to the UN partition plan, the Arab states had de facto accepted the existence of Israel.[17] Of course, they did so reluctantly, refusing to publicly meet with the Israeli delegation—however, many individual Arab delegates met privately with Israeli delegates. The Israelis were in no mood for compromise on the boundary or any of the other principal issues. As Walter Eytan, the head of the Israeli delegation at Lausanne, later admitted, Israel's purpose was "to begin to undermine the protocol of 12 May, which we had signed only under duress of our struggle for admission to the UN."[18]

The positions of the major actors at Lausanne concerning the most important issues were the following:

The Territorial Issues. The Arab position was that Israel had to return to the UN partition boundaries, and this was supported by the US delegation—Mark Ethridge, the head of the delegation, was "specifically ordered to secure the reversal of a substantial part of the Israeli conquests in 1948–49."[19] However, Israel not only dismissed that out of hand—"no one in Israel . . . was even thinking of conceding territory for peace"[20]—but Eytan told Ethridge that Israel wanted *further* "territorial adjustments" in Lebanon and Syria, so it could exploit the water resources in those regions. In addition, "Eytan also claimed for Israel the whole of the West Bank, asserting that to award the area to Jordan would be to reward its alleged aggression during the late war."[21]

Jerusalem. By accepting the Protocol, all the Lausanne participants had agreed to the internationalization of Jerusalem. The Arab states favored internationalization because they "feared that the alternative would be a Jewish Jerusalem; as well, several Arab leaders were not enthusiastic about the idea of a Hashemite Jerusalem."[22]

In reality, however, Israel had no intention of turning over West Jerusalem, the largely Jewish area that it had conquered in the war, to an international body. On the contrary, Eytan told a UN group that "the integration of the Jewish part of Jerusalem into the economic, political and administrative framework of the state of Israel" had already taken place—meaning, in effect, that West Jerusalem was now part of Israel.[23]

The Refugee Issue. On December 11, 1948, the UN General Assembly had passed Resolution 194, mandating that "the refugees wishing to return to their homes and live at peace with their neighbors should be permitted to do so at the earliest practicable date, and that compensation should be paid for the property of those choosing not to return and for loss of or damage to property which, under principles of international law or in equity, should be made good by the Governments or authorities responsible."

At Lausanne, the Arab states formally demanded that Israel agree to the principle of full repatriation, but in practice their position was more flexible: their only unconditional demand was for the return of the refugees from the areas the UN had designated for an Arab state, as opposed to those from the areas designated for the Jewish state. In the latter case, those refugees who were denied a right to return, or were not interested in doing so, could be offered financial or territorial compensation elsewhere in the Arab world.[24]

Israel rejected the Arab position, falsely claiming that it was the Arab invasion that had created the refugee problem, so the Arab states alone had the responsibility of solving it.

The United States then proposed a compromise: Israel should accept the return of 250,000 refugees, which would bring the Arab population in Israel to about 400,000, roughly the number of Arabs who had lived in the UN-projected Jewish state before they fled or were expelled.[25] If Israel accepted this proposal, the Truman administration promised financial assistance in resettling the remaining refugees in the Arab world.

Under US pressure, the Ben-Gurion government reluctantly made a counteroffer: it would agree to the return of 100,000 refugees, the maximum it could absorb, it argued, without creating an unacceptably large Arab minority within the Jewish state. As a number of scholars have argued, however, even this minimal offer was not serious and was made in the anticipation—as it turned out, correctly—that the Arabs would reject it, both because the number of refugees allowed to return was too small and because it was conditioned on Arab acceptance of Israel's wartime territorial conquests, an obvious deal-breaker.[26]

The Truman Administration Reacts

Mark Ethridge was increasingly angered by Israel's position at Lausanne and began urging the State Department to recommend to Truman that serious pressures be brought to bear on Israel. Acting Secretary of State James Webb and other high State Department officials, including future secretary of state Dean Rusk, agreed with Ethridge's analysis; at the end of May, Webb "strongly urged Truman to make it unambiguously clear that if [Israel] continued to ignore the United States' advice, their American aid would be cut off."[27]

Truman agreed with the assessments of Ethridge and the State Department, and told an American diplomat that "I am rather disgusted with the manner in which the Jews are approaching the refugee problem"; if the Israelis continued to refuse to "conform to the rules" and to ignore US advice, he told several US Jewish leaders, "they were probably going to lose one of their best friends."[28]

Consequently, on May 28, 1949, Truman sent a strong letter to Ben-Gurion, saying that "the Government of the United States was seriously disturbed by the attitude of Israel" and was "deeply concerned" that US policies had "made so little impression on the government of Israel." Israel's "rigid attitude" was liable to cause a rupture at the Lausanne conference, Truman continued. Should Israel continue "to reject the basic principles [of UN Resolution 194] and the friendly advice offered by the U.S. . . . the U.S. Government will regretfully be forced to the conclusion that a revision of its attitude toward Israel has become unavoidable."[29]

Despite Truman's threats, Israel remained adamant; as Ball puts it: "In keeping with its established story, it predictably sought to place all blame on the Arabs and to deny any responsibility for its own conduct."[30] On June 12, Ethridge summarized his views in a long cable to the State Department:

> If there is to be any assessment of blame for a stalemate at Lausanne, Israel must accept primary responsibility. . . . Aside from her general responsibility for refugees, she has particular responsibility for those who have been driven out by terrorism, repression, and forcible ejection.

Further, he wrote, Israel's territorial expansionism and its intransigence on the refugee issue was not only morally wrong but dangerous to Israel's own long-term interest in reaching a peace with its Arab neighbors. He concluded: "There has never been a time . . . when a generous attitude on the part of the Jews would not have unlocked peace."[31]

On June 13, 1949, Truman approved a State Department plan to hold up a pending $50 million Export-Import Bank loan to Israel until Israel changed its position on the refugees. When the Israeli ambassador bitterly complained and took the case to his contacts in the US government, however, Truman soon restored US support for the loan, as well as some technical assistance programs to Israel that had also been held up.[32]

This pattern was to be repeated throughout the history of the Arab-Israeli conflict: when American displeasure, verbal admonitions, and sometimes even real economic and diplomatic pressures were met with Israeli intransigence, it was usually—though not always—the United States that backed down.[33]

Why did Truman retreat? Undoubtedly, the domestic politics of the Israeli issue were a significant factor. Beyond that, though, the onset of the Cold War and the Israeli decision to ally itself with the United States were changing the calculations of the national security establishment about the American national interest. For example, in March 1949, the US Air Force chief of staff wrote:

> Existing Joint Chiefs of Staff policy on this subject appears now to have been overtaken by events. The power balance in the Near and Middle East has been radically altered. . . . [Israel] has demonstrated by force of arms its right to be considered the military power next after Turkey in the Near and Middle East.[34]

As well, in May 1949, reflecting the rapidly changing assessment of the Joint Chiefs, Secretary of Defense Louis Johnson wrote that Israel's "indigenous military forces, which have had some battle experience . . . would be of importance to either the Western Democracies or the USSR in any contest for control of the Eastern Mediterranean–Middle East area."[35]

Why Lausanne Failed

The Lausanne conference came to an end on September 14, 1949. Israeli mythology holds that it failed because none of the Arab states were prepared to accept Israel and make peace with it. It is true that the Arab states had refused to recognize Israel or even to meet in public with its delegates, and so they clearly bear a share of the responsibility for the lost opportunity to have reached a comprehensive settlement of the Arab-Israeli conflict. Nonetheless, most of the New Historians and other Israeli historians hold Israel to be primarily responsible. For example, Simha Flapan concluded that the Arab states' position at Lausanne, as well as other secret proposals they made to Israel, demonstrated that they "were strongly inclined to acquiesce to the existence of a Jewish state," but that the Israeli refusal to accept statehood for the Palestinians proved over the years to be the main source of the turbulence, violence, and bloodshed that came to pass.[36]

Similarly, Benny Morris argues that in claiming that the Arabs have always been "hell-bent on Israel's destruction . . . Ben-Gurion, and successive administrations after his, lied to the Israeli public about the post-1948 peace overtures and about Arab interest in a deal."[37] And while Pappé is critical of the Arabs' refusal "to state publicly what they had promised or even agreed upon privately,"[38] his detailed analysis provides convincing evidence that Israeli intransigence was largely responsible for the Lausanne failure. In fact, while Avi Shlaim had initially been equally critical of the Arab and Israeli positions at Lausanne, he later wrote that Pappé's research supported the conclusion that "it was Israeli rather than Arab inflexibility which stood in the way of a peaceful settlement."[39] While Arab public opinion had hardened after the 1948 war, he wrote, Israel's military victory convinced the leading Arab rulers that they needed to reach peace agreements. As a result, Shlaim continues, "the files of the Israeli Foreign ministry . . . burst at the seams with evidence of Arab peace feelers and Arab readiness to negotiate with Israel from September 1948 on" and their willingness to reach compromises on the key issues of borders and refugees.[40]

A number of UN and US officials reached the same conclusions. For example, George Ball wrote:

> [We had] originally assumed that the conference collapsed because of the Arabs' intransigence and refusal to negotiate directly with Israel. But an examination of the Americans' diplomatic correspondence of the period has demonstrated conclusively that Israel was the party that undercut America's peacemaking efforts.[41]

In fact, the heads of the Israeli delegation to Lausanne, Walter Eytan and Elias Sasson, were far more forthcoming than Ben-Gurion and the Israeli government, and established direct although secret contacts with the Arab delegates. Eytan even proposed that Israel officially recognize the refugees' right to return home, in the expectation that few would want to do so. Sasson also argued that there could be no meaningful talks with the Arab states "without an adequate resolution to the Palestinian refugee problem."[42]

In a remarkable critique of Israel's position at Lausanne, Sasson wrote to the Israeli Foreign Ministry:

> The Jews think they can achieve peace without paying any price, maximal or minimal. They want to achieve (a) Arab surrender of all the areas occupied by Israel; (b) Arab agreement to absorb all the refugees in the neighboring countries; (c) Arab agreement to border modification . . . in the centre, the south and in the Jerusalem area to Israel's exclusive advantage; (d) the relinquishment by the Arabs of their assets and property in Israel in exchange for compensation which would be evaluated by the Jews alone and which would be paid, if at all, over a number of years after the attainment of peace; (e) *de facto* and *de jure* recognition by the Arabs of the state of Israel and its new frontiers; (f) Arab agreement to the immediate establishment of diplomatic and economic relations between their countries and Israel, etc. etc.[43]

In short, the evidence is overwhelming that the failure at Lausanne—as in many other subsequent lost opportunities for peace—was much more the responsibility of Israel than of the Arab states. Carried away by its military victories in 1948—and, indeed, seeking further expansion in the future—Israel felt no need to make concessions on any of the main issues that stood in the way of an early Arab-Israeli peace settlement: territory and boundaries, Jerusalem, and the refugees.

The Early State-to-State Negotiations

After its unwillingness at Lausanne to negotiate a compromise settlement with the Arab world as a whole, Israel rejected a number of opportunities to end its conflicts with its neighboring Arab states. Almost certainly the Arab-Israeli wars of 1956, 1967, and 1973 would have been avoided if Israel had been willing to negotiate peace agreements—as opposed to temporary truces, which in any case were often violated by Israel—with Jordan, Syria, and Egypt.

Lost Opportunities for Peace with Jordan

Before the 1948 war, Israel and Jordan had reached a secret agreement not to go to war with each other. Ben-Gurion and King Abdullah were both opposed to a Palestinian state in the West Bank, Ben-Gurion because he hoped and expected that in the future Israel would expand to incorporate all of historical Palestine into a Jewish state, Abdullah because he wanted the West Bank and East Jerusalem for himself and his Hashemite successors.[44]

The essential terms of the 1947–48 agreements were that the two countries would not fight each other, provided that Israel refrained from sending its forces into East Jerusalem and most of the West Bank and Jordan refrained from joining the Arab state invasion. Though there were some clashes, largely initiated by Israeli military action in the Jerusalem region, the agreement essentially held. It was a close call—as the IDF grew in strength, its leaders pressed Ben-Gurion to allow further Israeli expansion into the West Bank. However, Jordan had a defense alliance with Britain, and when the British government warned that any further Israeli military incursions would lead to British intervention, Ben-Gurion reluctantly overruled the military.

After the 1948 war ended, the secret negotiations continued. Abdullah wanted a formal peace treaty with Israel, but Ben-Gurion refused to give up his expansionist goals. Accordingly, at the end of March 1949, the two sides signed a truce agreement, the main terms of which were Jordanian rule over the West Bank and the largely Arab East Jerusalem, Israeli rule over the largely Jewish West Jerusalem and its environs.[45]

On July 20, 1951, Abdullah was assassinated by an extremist who had been recruited by Palestinian leaders furious at Abdullah's collaboration with Israel. Abdullah was succeeded by his grandson, Hussein bin Talal, who ruled until his death in 1999. King Hussein continued Abdullah's policies toward Israel and the Palestinians, whose drive for an independent Palestinian state—soon to be led by Yasser Arafat and the PLO—was systematically suppressed by the king and his Bedouin army.

Throughout his reign, Hussein regularly met secretly with most of the top Israeli leaders, including Golda Meir, Moshe Dayan, Abba Eban, Yitzhak Rabin, Shimon Peres, and Yitzhak Shamir. There were a number of strains in the Jordanian-Israeli relationship in the early years after the 1948 war, particularly because of Israel's "retaliatory" attacks on Jordanian villages that had allegedly collaborated with Palestinian cross-border attacks on Israel. In fact, Israel knew Jordan was trying to prevent the attacks.

Even so, during the 1950s Ben-Gurion considered invading Jordan and seizing additional territory. An Israeli historian wrote that Ben-Gurion was in the habit of describing the post-1948 borders as "unbearable." In his eyes, Israel's meandering border with the Kingdom of Jordan was especially repugnant. Jordan's hold over the West Bank created a large enclave that bulged into Israel's populated coastal areas.[46]

In an October 1956 meeting with French leaders to plan the Suez War, Ben-Gurion said that "Jordan has no right to exist and should be partitioned. Eastern Transjordan should be ceded to Iraq which would offer to accept and resettle the Arab refugees. The territory to the West of the Jordan should be made an autonomous region of Israel."[47]

Further, declassified Israeli documents have revealed that during the 1956 war there were proposals in the cabinet that Israel invade and occupy not just the West Bank, but Jordan itself. Ben-Gurion then told King Hussein of these proposals and warned that he would approve them if Jordan attacked Israel during the 1956 war. On November 7, 1956, Ben-Gurion reported his decision to his cabinet: "If Syria starts, God bless it. I am not afraid now. If Syria attacks now, it will be erased. *The same applies to Jordan.*"[48]

However, after the 1956 war Ben-Gurion and the other leading Israeli hawks gradually abandoned these expansionist dreams and a de facto peace took hold between the two states. To be sure, Jordan's participation in the 1967 war, though reluctant, minor, and short-lived, for a while created a crisis in Israeli-Jordanian relations. However, it soon passed, and from the end of the war until the formal peace treaty between the two states, their relationship is best described as one of "peaceful coexistence."[49]

Lost Opportunities for Peace with Syria

On several occasions, from the Balfour Declaration through the early twenty-first century, there were opportunities for the Zionist movement and the Israeli government to negotiate political settlements with Syria. Syria came into existence after the collapse of the Ottoman Empire during World War I, initially as a de facto French colony and then in 1923 as a League of Nations Mandate to France, similar to the League Mandate to Britain over Palestine. The French government then decided to allow considerable political autonomy to Syria, whose first semi-independent ruler was the Hashemite King Faisal, the son of Sharif Hussein of Mecca and the brother of King Abdullah of Jordan, all of whom had accepted the Balfour Declaration and chose not to oppose the creation of a Jewish state in Palestine. In January 1919, Faisal and Chaim Weizmann, then the most important Zionist leader and later the head of the World Zionist Organization and the first president of Israel, "signed a historical agreement, which for the first time officially expressed Arab recognition of Jewish nationhood in Palestine."[50]

However, the growing Syrian nationalist movement was ideologically opposed to Zionism and sympathized with Palestinian aspirations. Consequently, Faisal backed away from his support of Zionism, and in any case he soon lost power to the nationalists. In fact, however, the nationalists were considerably more moderate in practice than in their ideological rhetoric, extending only "relatively mild support . . . to their Palestinian comrades."[51] Moshe Maoz sums up attitudes of the leading Syrian nationalist leaders during the 1920–45 period: "Although ideologically they objected to the Zionist venture . . . in practice [they] were periodically ready to acknowledge Jewish national rights (or national home) in parts of Palestine, and negotiate Arab-Jewish accords with Zionist leaders."[52]

In 1946 the French Mandate ended and Syria became completely independent under radical nationalist leadership, thus for the moment—but only for the moment—ending the opportunities for a Syrian-Zionist accord.[53]

The 1948 War and After

Immediately following the war, armistice talks under UN auspices were held between Israel and its Arab neighbors. Since Israel had conquered Egyptian, Jordanian, and Lebanese territories, Israel insisted that the armistice lines must reflect the war's outcome. However, in its negotiations with Syria it—unsurprisingly—took the opposite position, insisting that international law did not allow military conquest to override preexisting territorial rights, as they had been established by the UN partition. Obviously, then, the issue for Israel was not one of "principle" or international law but its demand to return to the pre-war situation in which it had control of the Jordan River and Lake Tiberias.

On July 20, 1949, the Syrian-Israeli armistice was signed. Its most important provisions required Syria to withdraw from the territories it had seized in the war, but established demilitarized zones (DMZs) in the areas bordering the Jordan River and Lake Tiberias (see Map 6.1). According to the truce agreement, neither Israel nor Syria would have political sovereignty over the DMZs and no military forces would be permitted in them, but each side would have access to the river and the lake. The final status of those areas was to be determined when—and if—a formal peace treaty was reached between Israel and Syria.[54]

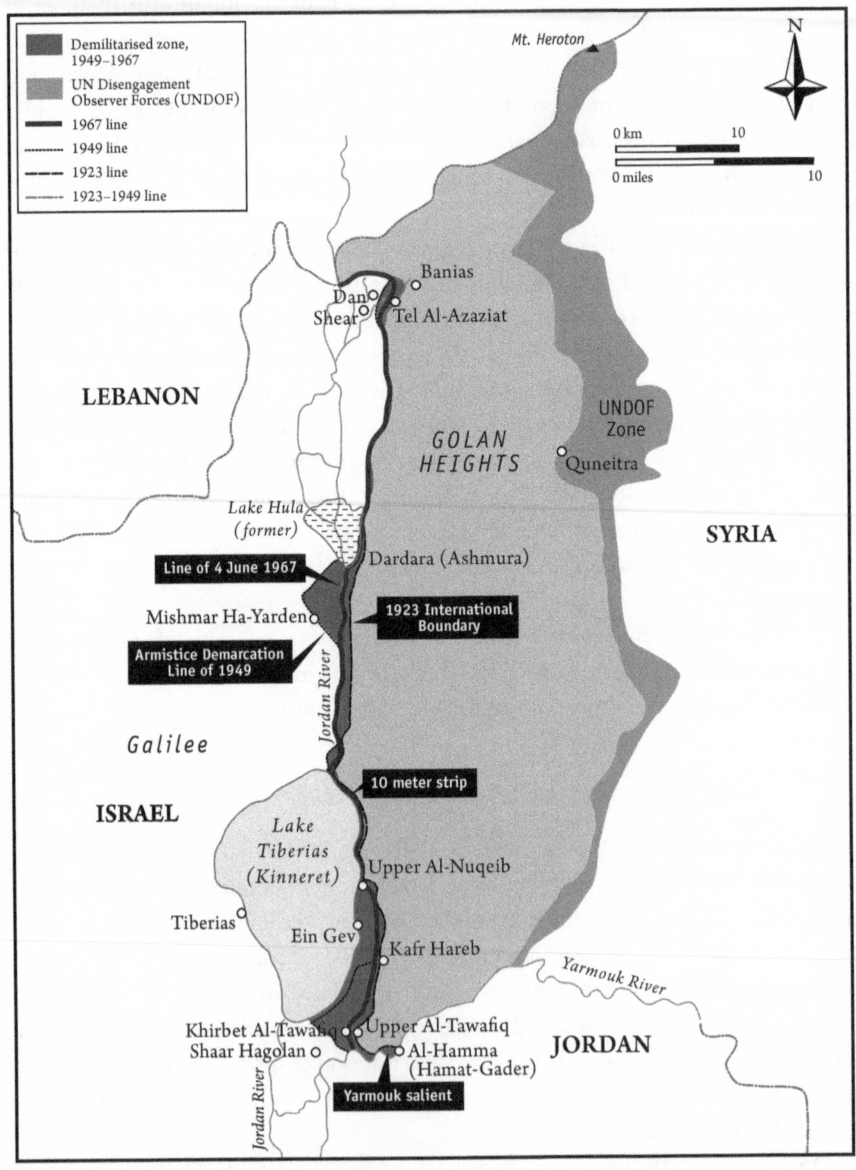

Map 6.1 The Syrian-Israeli Frontiers, from Daniel Kurtzer et al., *Peace Puzzle,* Kindle edition, 67. Permission granted from Cornell University Press.

The Husni Zaim Proposals for a Syrian-Israeli Peace Settlement

On March 30, 1949, a Syrian army colonel, Husni Zaim, overthrew the leftist and nationalist regime of Shukri al-Quwwatli. There have been a number of reports that the CIA encouraged and helped plan the coup, which would certainly fit the widespread pattern of CIA-sponsored right-wing coups in the Middle East during the Cold War.[55]

During the Israeli-Syrian armistice negotiations, Zaim made a remarkable proposal: rather than an armistice there should be a full peace settlement, on the condition that Israel agree to allow Syria to retain the small strips of land that gave it access to the Jordan River and Lake Tiberias. Under Zaim's proposed terms, Syria would agree to permanently resettle some 300,000 to 350,000 Palestinian refugees, about half of those who fled or were driven out of Israel in the 1947–48 period. Moreover, such a peace treaty would include the normalization of diplomatic and economic relations and even of military cooperation.[56]

As established by the scholarship on Syrian policy in this period, Zaim was motivated by the desire to reach a settlement with Israel so that he could get US aid for his ambitious plans for Syrian economic growth. In fact, the Truman administration was impressed with Zaim's proposals as well as his anti-radicalism and anti-communism; in May 1949, Secretary of State Dean Acheson wrote to the US ambassador in Syria that he should support Zaim's "humane and statesmanlike" plan to help solve the Palestinian refugee problem.[57]

Ben-Gurion, however, was not impressed. Despite the urgings of the US government, UN mediator Ralph Bunche, and even some Israeli diplomats—notably UN ambassador Abba Eban, who cabled the foreign ministry asking for "clarifications why we are unimpressed" with the Syrian offer[58]—Ben-Gurion refused even to meet with Zaim as long as Syria would not evacuate its forces from its footholds on the Jordan River and Lake Tiberias.

There were two issues for Ben-Gurion. First, he was unwilling to consider any territorial concessions to the Arabs. Second, he was unwilling to share the waters of the Jordan River and Lake Tiberias. As Foreign Minister Moshe Sharett reported to the Knesset, Zaim's offer was unacceptable because "what is at stake is the water's edge, the shore of Lake Tiberias, the East Bank of the Jordan River. . . . We want to keep these waters within the state's territory and not to make Syria a partner."[59]

Remarkably, though, Zaim then made an even better offer: after a ceasefire based on the existing military lines, Syria would negotiate a peace settlement within three months, but this time it would be based on the *pre-1948 borders,* meaning that he had dropped his demand to retain Syria's newly acquired land on the Jordan River and Lake Tiberias.[60]

Ben-Gurion was still not interested and continued to refuse to meet with the Syrian leader. It is hard to understand why not; Shlaim says that "Ben-Gurion . . . suspected that this might be a diplomatic trap," whatever that might mean. However, Foreign

Minister Sharett now disagreed with Ben-Gurion and pressed him, unsuccessfully, to begin negotiations.[61]

In August 1949, the Zaim government was overthrown by a new military coup. Abed Shishakli, the new Syrian leader, was determined to continue the moderate, pragmatic policies of his predecessor. Accordingly, he banned the fundamentalist, anti-Israeli, and anti-Western Muslim Brotherhood in Syria; sought to end border incidents with Israel; and gave priority to improving relations with both the United States and Israel. In particular, he wanted to strengthen Syria's army and sought US military assistance to do so.

Consequently, Shishakli proposed a modified renewal of Zaim's original offer: Syria would settle its conflict with Israel and increase to 500,000 the number of Palestinians it would absorb, provided that Israel agreed to continued Syrian access to the Jordan River and Lake Tiberias.

The US government again was impressed with the Syrian offers; Acheson told US diplomats that it was in the US interest "to aid Shishakli in his efforts to convene a progressive, stable and pro-western government in Syria."[62] Once again, however, Ben-Gurion refused to consider territorial or water-rights concessions to Syria, even in exchange for peace.[63]

The Armistice Breaks Down

Under the 1949 armistice agreement, brokered by the UN between Syria and Israel, neither country had sovereignty over the three demilitarized zones along their border. Pending a formal peace treaty, normal civilian life in the zones was to be maintained.

For about eighteen months after the armistice came into effect, there were no violent incidents between the Israelis and the Syrians. General Arye Shalev, who headed the Israeli delegation to the UN armistice commission, wrote, "The period of calm that prevailed between Jerusalem and Damascus following the signing of the armistice agreement expressed the two countries' willingness to solve problems through rapprochement."[64]

However, Shalev continued, in early 1951 Israel made "an extreme turnabout," asserting its sovereignty over the DMZs without "putting forward any serious arguments in support of its claim."[65] According to Shalev, the Israeli government knew that its sovereignty claim was weak and would be unacceptable to the UN, so it sought to settle the matter unilaterally, in its typical fashion, by creating "facts on the ground." Shalev summed up this period: "In the first years of the armistice regime it was Israel that tried unilaterally to effect changes in the status quo in the DMZ."[66]

In March 1951, Israel began evicting Arab farmers and razing villages, "to ensure that this Demilitarized Zone is cleansed of Arabs next to the border," in the words of IDF chief of staff Yigael Yadin.[67] Once that was done, Israel began the process of de facto annexation of the DMZs, bringing armed Israeli settlers into the area who began building roads, draining swamps, and planting crops on the previously Arab-owned lands.

Syria responded to the illegal Israeli actions and provocations with limited shelling from its Golan Heights territory overlooking the DMZs. An Israeli journalist who lived on a kibbutz below the Golan wrote that, contrary to the Israeli government's assertions, the Syrians had not engaged in systematic or unprovoked shelling, but had opened fire only when Israel violated the demilitarized zone agreements by carrying out development projects there, especially on former Arab-owned land, or otherwise took actions "that were certain to provoke the Syrians into opening fire."[68] Nonetheless, Israel "retaliated" with far greater force, not only against the Syrian artillery positions but also against Syrian villages, killing many civilians.[69]

In the Israeli mythology, it was the Syrians who were responsible for the conflict over the DMZs. However, one doesn't need the work of the New Historians or the Syrian specialists to set the record straight, in light of the candid assessments of Israeli military participants in the 1950s and 1960s. These included even—or perhaps one should say, especially—Moshe Dayan, who was head of the IDF during much of this period. In a remarkable off-the-record interview that was published after his death, Dayan told an Israeli journalist that Israel had deliberately sought to provoke Syria: Israel had instigated "more than 80 percent" of its clashes with Syria, he admitted:

> It went this way: We would send a tractor to plow someplace . . . in the demilitarized area, and [we] knew in advance that the Syrians would start to shoot. If they didn't shoot, we would tell the tractor to advance farther, until in the end the Syrians would get annoyed and shoot. And then we would use artillery and later the air force also, and that's how it was.

When the Israeli interviewer then protested that Syria was a serious threat to Israel, Dayan responded: "Bullshit . . . Just drop it."[70]

By the early 1950s, the Lake Tiberias demilitarized zone had been effectively partitioned, with Israel establishing control over the west bank of the Jordan River, and Syria retaining control over the northeast corner of the lake and the east bank of the river.[71] However, during the mid-1950s the conflict again escalated. When the Syrians sought to establish their right to fish in Lake Tiberias, shots were exchanged between Israeli and Syrian patrol boats, which in turn led to Israeli raids on Syrian military positions. In one such raid, in December 1955, a force led by Ariel Sharon attacked Syrian positions along the shore of Lake Tiberias and killed fifty men, an action that Shlaim terms "an unprovoked act of aggression" because the Syrians had not been firing on Israeli settlements or even fishing boats, but only at patrol boats that had been deliberately sent close to shore to draw Syrian fire.[72]

This was no isolated incident. According to Mordechai Bar-On, Moshe Dayan's private secretary, several of the raids were *intentionally* disproportionate and destructive. Ben-Gurion and his protege Dayan, writes Bar-On, sought to provoke Egypt (which in 1955 had signed a mutual defense pact with Syria) into providing military support to Syria. If it did, Israel then might have the pretext it sought to embark on a "preventive war" against Egypt—a policy that while initially opposed by a majority of Ben-Gurion's cabinet, was essentially implemented in Israel's 1956 attack on Egypt.[73]

In early 1954, Ben-Gurion and Dayan told Moshe Sharett that if Iraqi forces moved into Syria, as then appeared likely, Israel would create a series of "accomplished facts" by seizing the Golan Heights. Sharett was shocked by this, and in his diaries accuses Dayan of seeking to provoke Syria into attacking Israeli outposts and settlements beneath the Golan Heights so as to justify an Israeli counterstrike, one of "the long chain of false incidents and hostilities we have invented, and the many clashes we have provoked."[74] Sharett records Defense Minister Pinhas Lavon, an ally of Dayan, telling him that an unfolding military coup against the Shishakli government in Syria was "an historical opportunity [that] shouldn't be missed" for Israel to expand into Syria beyond the DMZs.[75]

In September 1980, the Israeli journalist and peace activist Uri Avnery reviewed Sharett's diary entries for this period and noted that "Sharett reveals that Ben-Gurion, Dayan, and Pinhas Lavon requested . . . to exploit the toppling [of Shishakli] . . . by occupying southern Syria and annexing it to Israel. They also requested to buy a Syrian officer who would acquire power in Damascus and establish a pro-Israel puppet government."[76]

Though the plan of Ben-Gurion and his confederates was not put into effect, throughout the 1950s Israel's illegal and provocative policies in the demilitarized zones continued, as it built roads, conducted forward patrols, seized territory, and initiated or escalated firefights.[77] As the conflict continued, the Syrians began supporting Palestinian guerrilla raids on Israel; Israel responded with massive retaliatory raids that often included attacks on local Arab villages. In his autobiography, Abba Eban describes one of these many incidents, in which the Syrians had fired on an Israeli fishing boat in Lake Tiberias. Although no one on the Israeli boat was hurt, the Israeli retaliation killed seventy-three Syrians, which Eban called a disproportionate and "shocking spectacle of carnage."[78]

Even more serious clashes occurred over the waters of the Jordan River and its upstream tributaries. In the early 1960s, Israel began diverting the headwaters of the Jordan River to the Negev to support its agricultural projects there. Syria responded by seeking to divert the tributaries in southern Lebanon and the Golan Heights before their waters could reach the river; Israel then attacked and destroyed the Syrian diversion facilities.

Moshe Maoz has cautiously observed that "it is important to point out the deep sense of fear—justified or not—among many Syrians of what they considered Israeli aggression and expansionism since 1948. . . . Indeed, Israeli leaders, notably Ben-Gurion, hardly attempted to mitigate this Syrian Arab fear, but rather helped to substantiate it, by both words and deeds."[79] In light of the expansionist dreams of Ben-Gurion, Moshe Dayan, and other hawks, as well as actual Israeli behavior, an even stronger conclusion is called for: after the 1948 war and through the 1960s, Israeli intransigence, expansionism, and aggressive behavior were far more responsible for the Syrian-Israeli conflict than was Syria. It is clear that the Syrians were right to fear for the future of the Golan Heights and their access to the Jordan River and Lake Tiberias; indeed, as will be discussed in Chapter 8, they even had some reason to fear for Damascus itself. For decades after the 1956 war the pattern continued, as Israel repeatedly rejected compromise political settlements that were acceptable to Syria and strongly favored by the United States and the international community.

7

Israel, Egypt, the United States, and the 1956 War

Before the 1948 war, King Farouk of Egypt had secretly told Israeli diplomats that he would not participate in the coming Arab attack if Israel would allow Egypt to continue its control over parts of Gaza and a small strip of the Negev Desert. Farouk wanted to maintain these areas as a buffer zone against later Israeli expansion into the Sinai peninsula as well as to prevent his rival, King Abdullah of Jordan, from seizing them.

Foreign Minister Moshe Sharett favored negotiations with Egypt on this basis, but he was overruled by Prime Minister Ben-Gurion, who ordered Israeli forces to break the UN-mediated ceasefire agreements and to seize the Negev and the parts of the Sinai that had been allocated by the partition plan to the Arab state. This was not the first time that the hawkish Ben-Gurion and the relatively dovish Sharett, Israel's most important early leaders, had sharply clashed—and it would not be the last time.[1] Ben-Gurion, who was privately contemptuous of Sharett and considered him to be "cultivating a generation of cowards," almost always prevailed, even during the periods in which Sharett was the prime minister and Ben-Gurion the defense minister.[2]

As well as breaking the truce and seizing territory in Sinai and the Negev, in December 1948 the Israeli forces were about to seize the Gaza Strip from Egypt; however, Ben-Gurion, fearing the international political consequences and possibly even British military intervention, reluctantly called off the impending attack. Nonetheless, Ben-Gurion had not made a permanent decision to forgo seizing Gaza: Michael Bar-Zohar writes that the Israeli archives and Ben-Gurion's diary contain "abundant proof that he continued to secretly plan the next stage, in which he would achieve his territorial ambitions."[3]

As well, Moshe Sharett's diary and other evidence revealed that soon after a nationalist military coup led by Colonel Gamal Abdel Nasser overthrew the Farouk monarchy in 1952, Dayan and other Israeli hawks began planning for the "next stage," which they regarded as "a preventive war." For example, Livia Rokach, a Palestinian journalist who gained access to Sharett's diary, wrote that it revealed "that a major war against Egypt aimed at the territorial conquest of Gaza and the Sinai was on the Israel leadership's agenda at least as early as the autumn of 1953."[4]

There were some tactical differences between Dayan and Ben-Gurion. Dayan argued that as soon as Israel was ready, it should launch a "preventive" attack on Egypt. "In my opinion," he wrote to the defense minister, "we must initiate a major clash between our forces and the Egyptian army as soon as possible."[5] However, Ben-Gurion was not willing to go that far, for he feared British and American reaction to an unprovoked Israeli attack, possibly even British military intervention. Consequently, he instead chose to follow a strategy of increasingly sharp Israel "retaliations" for alleged Egyptian actions, hoping thereby to provoke Egypt into initiating a war.[6]

Another tactical difference between the two hawks was that Ben-Gurion did not want to go to war with Egypt without an alliance with a major Western power, preferably the United States, while Dayan claimed to be uninterested even in a de facto and informal alliance. In a May 1955 speech to Israeli diplomats, he explained why: "We face no danger at all of an Arab advantage of force for the next 8–10 years. . . . The security pact will only handcuff us and deny us the freedom of action which we need in the coming years." Moreover, he continued, the Israeli reprisal policies were psychologically essential: "Without these actions we would have ceased to be a combative people," in which case "we are lost."[7]

Commenting on Dayan's speech in his diary, Moshe Sharett writes:

> The conclusions from Dayan's words are clear. This State has no international obligations. . . . [T]he question of peace is nonexistent. . . . It must live on its sword. . . . Toward this end it may, no—it must—invent dangers and . . . adopt the method of provocation and revenge. . . . And above all—let us hope for a new war with the Arab countries, so that we . . . acquire our space. . . . Ben-Gurion himself said that it would be worthwhile to pay an Arab a million pounds to start a war.[8]

To be sure, the plans of the Israeli hawks do not necessarily demonstrate that their fears of Egyptian aggression were not genuine, or that their motivations were not, in part, defensive—after all, Arab rhetoric, including some of Nasser's, *was* often blood-curdling. In fact, Nasser was not seeking a new war with Israel; nevertheless, whatever the differences between his public rhetoric and his real intentions, one can hardly expect that less than ten years after the Holocaust a Jewish state could or should have simply dismissed Arab threats as mere posturing. While conceding that Ben-Gurion and Dayan might have overestimated the importance of Nasser's aggressive rhetoric that was primarily intended for public consumption, an important book by Israeli colonel Mordechai Bar-On, Dayan's military aide, emphasizes the impact it had on the Israelis: he writes that not only the hawks but other Israeli leaders and the public held "a deep-seated belief in the gravity of the Arabs' intentions to renew hostilities and destroy Israel as soon as they considered themselves capable of so doing."[9]

In light of those understandable fears, there is no question that the deliberate escalations of Ben-Gurion and Dayan were partly motivated by the essentially defensive goal of protecting Israeli security by precipitating a war before Egypt and Syria could reach their full military potential. At the same time, a self-fulfilling prophecy was at work, for there can also be no question that Israeli policies were partly motivated by expansionism. And the Syrian and Egyptian governments knew it—not surprisingly since the Israeli leaders had hardly bothered to disguise their intentions. Whatever the tactical differences between Ben-Gurion and Dayan and other top military leaders—Segev writes, "What is certain is that the IDF's top command advocated a larger Israel and sought to instill that view in the troops"—the differences should not be exaggerated: "Ben-Gurion viewed the Green Line as a temporary border, which is indeed how it had been designated in the armistice agreements. From time to time he pondered ways of correcting it."[10] In short, it is impossible to separate the genuinely defensive fears of the main Israeli leaders from their expansionist ambitions and plans.

The Secret Talks, 1948–55

For a few years between the end of the 1948 war and early 1955, there were a number of secret talks between Nasser's government and Israeli diplomats led by Foreign Minister Sharett. During this period, while Nasser engaged in provocative behavior toward Israel—especially by using Egypt's control over the southern Sinai peninsula to block Israeli shipping through the Straits of Tiran, the gateway to the southern Israeli port of Eilat—he was willing to investigate the chances for a peace settlement and opened up direct and indirect channels with Israeli diplomats, particularly Sharett, who in January 1954 became prime minister.[11] According to Israeli press accounts published in 1961, Egyptian representatives "expressed a willingness to reach a secret agreement with Israel on the normalization of relations without a formal peace agreement."[12] On several occasions, Nasser told Israeli and US officials that while he was interested in peace with Israel, a public agreement would cause him to be seen as a traitor to the Arab world and could lead to his assassination.[13] In light of the assassination of Jordan's King Abdullah in 1951 after he had engaged in peace talks with Israel, Nasser's fears were quite credible—as was further demonstrated in October 1981 when his successor, Anwar Sadat, was assassinated by Egyptian fanatics who opposed the peace treaty he had negotiated with Israel.

During the talks the central issue continued to be over the Negev region. According to Bar-On and others, while Egypt's official negotiating position was that Israel had to return to the UN borders, its real condition—as had been the case in the Lausanne talks—was that Israel must withdraw only its forces from the Negev region south of Beersheba.[14] Nasser's insistence on recovering the Negev was in part motivated by his pan-Arab ambitions and desire to create an unbroken land bridge between Egypt and the rest of the Arab world and in part by his entirely understandable concern that Israel would once again use the Negev to attack the Sinai Peninsula.[15]

Ben-Gurion continued to refuse all territorial compromise in the Negev, even from uninhabited land, despite pressures from Britain and the Eisenhower administration to do so.[16] In December 1955, Ben-Gurion summed up his position in a telegram to Sharett: "Israel will not consider a peace offer involving any territorial concession whatever. The neighboring countries have no right to one inch of Israel's land. . . . We are willing to meet Nasser in any way, but not on the basis of a plan calling for any part of Israeli territory to be torn away for the benefit of her neighbors."[17]

It is true that meeting Nasser's demand for a Negev land bridge to the Arab world would have required Israel to give up not only the land it conquered in 1948 but also parts of the Negev that had been assigned to it by the United Nations. Consequently, as Bar-On notes, "There was a very wide consensus in Israel on the absolute refusal to make significant concessions on territory captured in 1948, certainly not on large sections of the Negev that had been allocated to Israel."[18]

Bar-On does not point out, however, that Israel was just as unwilling to surrender its conquests of Arab territory that had *not* been assigned to it—indeed, it wanted much more. And while Ben-Gurion insisted that the new boundaries with Egypt had to be based on the 1949 armistice agreement, which left Israel in control of almost all the Negev,[19] in its post war conflict with Syria, where the armistice agreements allowed that country to keep the sliver of land on Lake Tiberias that it had seized in the 1948 war, Israel insisted on a return to the pre-war boundaries.

Not for the first time and certainly not the last, Israel claimed to be acting on "principles"—in this case, the sanctity of international agreements—that it ignored when they were in conflict with what it regarded as its national interests. Needless to say, of course, they were hardly alone in such state behaviors.

The "Lavon Affair": Provoking the 1956 War

After becoming prime minister, Sharett continued to hold secret negotiations with Nasser's representatives. However, his efforts to avoid a new war were sabotaged by Dayan, Ben-Gurion, and their key allies, especially Shimon Peres and Pinhas Lavon, who became defense minister in early 1954. In the ensuing years, Tessler writes, "the Defense Department frequently acted in ways that undermined Sharett's effort to maintain a dialogue with Nasser," including intentionally disproportionate "retaliatory" raids that "deliberately extended the scope of strikes authorized by the cabinet in order to embarrass Nasser and exacerbate tensions between Cairo and Jerusalem."[20]

The most important of the Israeli provocations, the so-called Lavon Affair, occurred in the summer of 1954, when members of the Israeli defense and military establishments, supposedly acting under orders from Lavon, plotted to disrupt Western relations with the Nasser regime.[21] A spy ring, consisting of ten Egyptian Jews under the command of Israeli agents, was discovered by Egypt before it could put into effect its plans to place bombs in Egyptian, British, and American civilian institutions in Cairo and Alexandria.[22]

The plotters sought to have the planned attacks blamed on Muslim terrorist groups that the Nasser government allegedly supported or failed to control; Rokach quotes from the instructions given to the spy ring by the head of Israeli military intelligence:

> Our goal is to break the West's confidence in the existing [Egyptian] regime.... The actions should cause arrests, demonstrations, and expression of revenge. The Israeli origin should be totally covered.... The purpose is to prevent economic and military aid from the West to Egypt.[23]

Prime Minister Sharett had not been informed of the plot, since it was known that he would have opposed it. When the plot was revealed by the Nasser government, which hanged two of the plotters, it caused an uproar in Israel. Dayan and Peres were suspected, but they blamed it on Lavon. However, an investigation commission later concluded that Lavon had not given the orders to carry out the Egyptian plot. While exonerating Lavon, though, the commission somehow managed to conclude that it could not fix the true responsibility for the disastrous plot, an odd conclusion in light of their own findings that Dayan and Peres had given false accounts to the investigators as well as their known support of efforts to provoke Egypt into a new war.[24] And in his long discussion of the "Lavon Affair," Segev blandly notes, without comment, that "several newspapers supporting Lavon accused Ben-Gurion himself of having given the order for the operation in Egypt."[25]

Despite the "Lavon Affair," Nasser wanted to continue to explore the possibilities for peace and did not break off ties with Sharett, who he knew was not responsible. However, under great political pressure, especially after the Egyptian hangings, Sharett ended the contacts. Shlaim argues that while it cannot be known whether continued talks would have led to peace, "Nasser offered Israel a chance to talk and . . . this offer was spurned."[26]

In February 1955, Israel killed thirty-seven soldiers in a cross-border attack on an Egyptian military camp in Gaza. Sharett had strongly opposed the attack, knowing it to be a deliberate effort by Ben-Gurion and Dayan to provoke a war with Egypt. In his diary he wrote that he considered the attack to be "wild and foolish . . . in my opinion . . . a criminal act." His diary continued:

> I have thought about a long chain of fabrications and lies that we are to blame for and which cost us lives, and on excesses by our people that have caused the most horrible catastrophes, some of which have had repercussions on the entire course of events and contributed to the security crisis we find ourselves in. I warned against the criminal narrowness of our approach to state security, which leads us to impetuous and wild actions that destroy our political standing on the security front and which severely undermine our position.[27]

As well, he wrote that he had been "meditating on the long chain of false incidents and hostilities we have invited, and on the many clashes we have provoked . . . which brought grave disasters."[28]

Shlaim discussed the consequences of the raid:

> Nasser himself repeatedly described the Gaza raid as a turning point. He claimed that it destroyed his faith in the possibility of a peaceful resolution of the conflict with Israel . . . and forced a change in national priorities from social and economic development to defense, a change that culminated in an arms deal with Czechoslovakia in September of that year.[29]

During the 1956 war, Israel captured Egyptian military records. As discussed by Shlaim, the record proved that until the February 1955 Israeli attack, "the Egyptian military authorities had a consistent and firm policy of curbing Palestinian infiltration . . . and that it was only following the raid that a new policy was put into place, that of organizing the Fedayeen units [Palestinian guerrilla movements] and turning them into an official instrument of warfare against Israel."[30] After the 1956 war, Khalidi writes, "the Egyptian authorities clamped down again."[31]

In October 1955, Egypt signed a mutual defense pact with Syria. Two months later Israeli forces attacked Syrian positions on Lake Tiberias, killing thirty-six soldiers and twelve civilians. Bar-On writes that the attack was "totally out of proportion to the provocations preceding it," shocking Sharett and others, and resulting in a US government decision to postpone any consideration of providing arms to Israel.[32] Bar-On explains why Ben-Gurion (now in his second term as prime minister) had approved such a large raid: Dayan was implementing Ben-Gurion's "policy of escalation . . . [which] should be viewed as a final attempt to provoke Nasser to war."[33]

The US government made another effort to prevent the impending war when Eisenhower sent his personal friend Robert Anderson, a former secretary of defense, to see if a peace agreement could be reached. Nasser told Anderson that in addition to the territorial issue, the Palestinian refugee problem had to be solved by giving the refugees a "free choice" between compensation and repatriation to Israel.[34] However, there is no doubt that the refugee issue was less important to him—as, indeed, has been true of nearly all Arab leaders throughout the conflict—than regaining lost territory.

When Anderson reported his talks with Nasser to the Israeli government, Ben-Gurion said that he would be willing to secretly meet with Nasser to see if a peace agreement could be reached. However, Nasser told Anderson that he feared that the meeting would be discovered, and "he did not want what happened to [King] Abdullah to happen to him."[35]

So, the slide toward war continued. In addition to the deliberately disproportional Israeli "retaliatory" attacks, in the spring of 1956 Ben-Gurion authorized Dayan to carry out letter-bomb assassinations of Egyptian military officials. Several were successful; among those killed were two military officers whom Israel considered to be particularly responsible for cross-border attacks on Israelis. Israelis considered the assassinations to be not only legitimate retaliations but "deterrence" against future ones.[36]

UN secretary general Dag Hammarskjöld disagreed. In a letter to Ben-Gurion he wrote:

> You are convinced that the threat of retaliation has a deterrent effect. I am convinced that it is more of an incitement. . . . You are convinced that acts of retaliation will stop further incidents. I am convinced that they will lead to further incidents. You believe that this way of creating respect for Israel will pave the way for sound coexistence, while I believe your policy will push off coexistence.[37]

In his response, Ben-Gurion dismissed Hammarskjöld's argument, writing in his diary that he "hoped" there would be no further correspondence with the secretary general.

At the end of September Hammarskjöld submitted a report to the Security Council that placed more blame on Israel than on Egypt for the spiraling conflict; Ben-Gurion wrote in his diary that Hammarskjöld, almost universally considered to be one of the period's greatest statesmen, had "revealed himself clearly as an anti-Semite."[38]

The Eisenhower Administration and the Israeli-Egyptian Conflict

In September 1955, the Soviet Union (through its satellite, Czechoslovakia) entered into a major arms deal with Egypt, including the sale of hundreds of jet fighters, bombers, and transport aircraft.[39] In 1948, when Stalin hoped that Israel would be at least neutral in the emerging Cold War, the Soviets had sold arms to Israel. By the early 1950s, however, after Israel had made it clear that it regarded itself as part of the West, the Soviet Union decided to counter Western influence in the Middle East by selling arms to Egypt and Syria.

Even before the Soviet arms deal, in April 1955, the Israeli government had formally asked the United States for arms and a contractual guarantee of Israel's borders, and from that point onward "the demand that the United States guarantee the security of her borders became a formal element of Israel's foreign policy."[40] For example, during this period Israel "raised the idea of either joining NATO or having a bilateral defense pact with the United States," but while Eisenhower and his secretary of state John Foster Dulles privately told Israel that the United States has "a deep interest" in preserving Israel's independence and would therefore "not be indifferent to an armed attack on it," they were not willing to formalize any commitment to Israel as long as the Arab-Israeli conflict remained unsettled.[41]

Despite serious frictions with Israel and his unwillingness to issue written security commitments to it in the existing circumstances, Eisenhower was clearly sympathetic to the country. His biographers and members of his administration agree that he had been deeply moved by what he saw when US armies liberated the concentration camps, and was therefore sensitive to the historical plight of the Jewish people and the consequences of anti-Semitism. To be sure, he had told associates that he was "not even certain that he—in Truman's position—would have supported Israel's birth; but now that it was an accomplished fact, he would have to live with it."[42] Indeed, on several occasions both Eisenhower and his powerful secretary of state, John Foster Dulles, publicly and privately said that while they disagreed with Israel's policies on a number of issues, they felt a moral commitment to Israel's survival and warned Arab leaders that the United States would oppose a war designed to destroy Israel.

Nonetheless, at this point Eisenhower, Dulles, and the State Department believed that it was not in the US national interest to antagonize the Arab world by arming Israel, let alone entering into a formal alliance with it and guaranteeing its borders—and certainly not before a peace agreement that ended the Arab-Israeli conflict had been reached. Bar-On writes that "Eisenhower was unequivocal on the point in his memoirs, declaring that the U.S. administration . . . had concluded that providing Israel with arms would only escalate the Mideast arms race."[43] Dulles elaborated on the point, telling the Senate Foreign Relations Committee that "Israel, due to its much smaller size and population, could not win in an arms race against the Arabs, having access to the Soviet bloc. It would seem that Israel's security could be better assured in the long run through [a peace settlement]."[44]

In an April 1956 statement to congressional leaders, Dulles further explained the government's policies: "The U.S. could not achieve its . . . [national security] objectives if we became a large-scale purveyor of arms to Israel. These actions would precipitate further large-scale Soviet deliveries to the Arab states. . . . A situation like this could lead to World War III."[45]

In any case, alarmed at the scale and purpose of Israel's retaliatory attacks on Egypt and Syria, State Department officials told the Ben-Gurion government of Dulles's "shocked horror" at the raid on Syria.[46] In general, Bar-On wrote, "In the spring of 1956 the American administration was more concerned about possible Israeli aggression than Arab aggression."[47]

As well, Eisenhower and Dulles resented the Israel lobby and its pressures and were determined to resist them. Ben-Zvi quotes a number of comments from Dulles' private papers showing his anger over what he considered to be "the terrific control over the news media and the barrage which the Jews have built up on Congressmen," resulting in the difficulty the administration was having in developing "a foreign policy the Jews don't approve of."[48] And in a private letter to a friend Eisenhower said that "I gave strict orders to the State Department that they should inform Israel that we would handle our affairs exactly as though we didn't have a Jew in America."[49]

It may well be thought that these statements have anti-Semitic overtones, but two points should be kept in mind. First, it is undeniable that the "Israel lobby"—at that time almost exclusively Jewish—had played a major role in the development of American policy toward Israel. Second, both Eisenhower and Dulles repeatedly told Israeli officials that "in principle" the administration would consider a security guarantee to Israel in the context of a peace settlement with the Arab world that would necessarily require Israeli as well as Arab territorial and other compromises.[50]

In any case, despite their concerns about Israel's policies, Eisenhower and Dulles were becoming increasingly alarmed at what they considered to be Nasser's radicalism, and once the Soviets had entered the picture the administration's policies began to shift. It was still not willing to provide heavy US armaments, but it encouraged Israel to seek them elsewhere and welcomed the French government's decision—motivated in part by sympathy with Israel but more importantly by its own interests—to provide them.[51]

The Alliance for War

The Israeli problem, as Ben-Gurion and Dayan saw it, was that while Nasser continued to retaliate against Israeli attacks, he was refusing to engage in the kind of full-scale military actions that would give them the pretext they sought to attack Egypt and get rid of the Egyptian leader. Moreover, they wanted a war before Egypt had fully absorbed the Soviet-bloc heavy arms it had acquired in September 1955. As a result, Ben-Gurion no longer insisted that Israel had to wait for Nasser to start a war and began planning for a full-scale Israeli attack on Egypt in the fall of 1956.

To this end, Israel entered into a secret alliance with Britain and France, both of which also wanted to overthrow Nasser; they saw him as a radical nationalist who threatened their remaining colonial interests in the Middle East. In particular,

Britain was infuriated by Nasser's July 1956 nationalization of the Suez Canal, which until then been jointly owned by Britain and France, and which was the fastest and cheapest shipping route to Europe from the Middle East and Asia, especially for oil shipments.

As for France, aside from its own economic interests in continued Western control over the canal, it was furious at Nasser's support for the nationalist rebellion against the French colony of Algeria. For these and other reasons, including genuine sympathy with Israel, France began arming Israel, even providing crucial assistance to its secret nuclear weapons program.[52]

In the summer of 1956 the three new allies secretly developed their plan to coordinate an invasion of Egypt and overthrow Nasser: Israel would invade Sinai and drive Egyptian forces away from the Suez Canal, aided by British and French attacks on Egyptian military airfields. A few days before the Israeli attack, Ben-Gurion wrote in his diary: "This is a unique opportunity, when two not insignificant powers try to eliminate Nasser, so that we need not stand alone against him as he gains power and conquers all the Arab lands."[53]

Accordingly, on October 29, 1956, Israel attacked and occupied the Gaza Strip and most of the Sinai, and a few days later, on the transparent pretext of "protecting the Suez Canal," British and French troops invaded and occupied the Canal Zone. The declared goals of Israel were to force Nasser to end his support of the Fedayeen, destroy the Palestinian guerrilla bases in Gaza and Sinai, and seize the southern Sinai in order to end Nasser's blockade of Israeli shipping through the narrow Straits of Tiran into the Red Sea and then to Asia. The undeclared goals were at least as important. Ben-Gurion's biographer writes that "Ben-Gurion's territorial ambitions were not limited to Sharm el-Sheikh and the island of Tiran. . . . In effect, he wished to detach the Sinai peninsula from Egypt and annex it to Israel."[54]

A few days before the joint attack, in discussions with the British and French, Ben-Gurion candidly laid out his ambitious goals, which he admitted were "fantastic" but, he thought, achievable:

- An international commission would take over the Suez Canal from Egypt.
- Israel would take permanent control of parts of the Sinai, especially those bordering on the Gulf of Aqaba and the Straits of Tiran. In addition, Ben-Gurion suggested, France and Israel should join forces "to tear from Egypt" parts of the Sinai in which oil deposits had been discovered.[55]
- Jordan, which Ben-Gurion did not consider viable as an independent state, would be broken up: Israel would take control over the West Bank of the Jordan River, and Iraq (still pro-Western at that time) would get the Jordanian territory east of the river, on the condition that it agree to make peace with Israel and resettle the Palestinian refugees there.
- Syria would be partitioned, with Israel annexing part of its territory.[56]

- Lebanon would be divided between Israel and what remained of Syria under its new government.[57] Israel would seize southern Lebanon up to the Litani River, one of the main tributaries of the Jordan River and therefore an important source of fresh water. As well, Israel would use its new position to help turn Lebanon into a Christian state.[58]

Even in Gaza, while continuing his "aversion to annexing the territory," Ben-Gurion evidently did not rule out a "temporary" but indefinite Israeli political and military control that would amount to a de facto annexation. Segev quotes a Ben-Gurion statement to his cabinet—"A temporary regime can last thirty or even fifty years"—and adds that "at times [Ben-Gurion] felt that Israel should retain control of the Gaza regime, even if its population doubled the number of Arabs in Israel."[59]

Avi Shlaim commented that Ben-Gurion's plan for the 1956 war "exposed an appetite for territorial expansion at the expense of the Arabs and expansion in every possible direction: north, east, and south."[60]

US Policies and the 1956 War

In the period preceding the Suez War, the Eisenhower administration—or at least the Central Intelligence Agency (CIA)—may have covertly encouraged Israel to overthrow Nasser. A number of writers have pointed to suggestive evidence; of particular credibility are Sharett's diary entries in early October 1955, which note that after the Soviet-Egyptian arms deal the CIA told Ben-Gurion that "no one would oppose Israel if it struck Egypt once the arms had arrived."[61]

However, even if the administration was prepared to tolerate or even encourage a limited Israeli attack, it did not favor Israel's expansionist goals or the colonialist military interventions of Britain and France. According to Bar-On, Dulles consistently told Britain and France that their conflict with Nasser should not be resolved by force; he cites several sources, including an Eisenhower letter of July 31, 1956, to British prime minister Anthony Eden and French prime minister Guy Mollet: "I have given you my personal conviction, as well as that of my associates, as to the unwisdom even of contemplating the use of military force at this moment."[62]

The evidence suggests that Eisenhower's policies were partly motivated by his opposition to international aggression in general and to an essentially colonial war by Britain and France in particular, but probably more importantly by strategic concerns: the fear that the invasion would result in a powerful radical, nationalist, and anti-Western reaction throughout the Arab world and pave the way for an expansion of Soviet influence in the region.[63]

The War and Its Consequences

On October 29, Israeli forces attacked Sinai and the Gaza Strip, and within a week completely routed the Egyptian forces and seized the entire peninsula. Meanwhile on November 5, British and French paratroopers seized the Suez Canal, as had been prearranged with Israel (see Map 7.1).

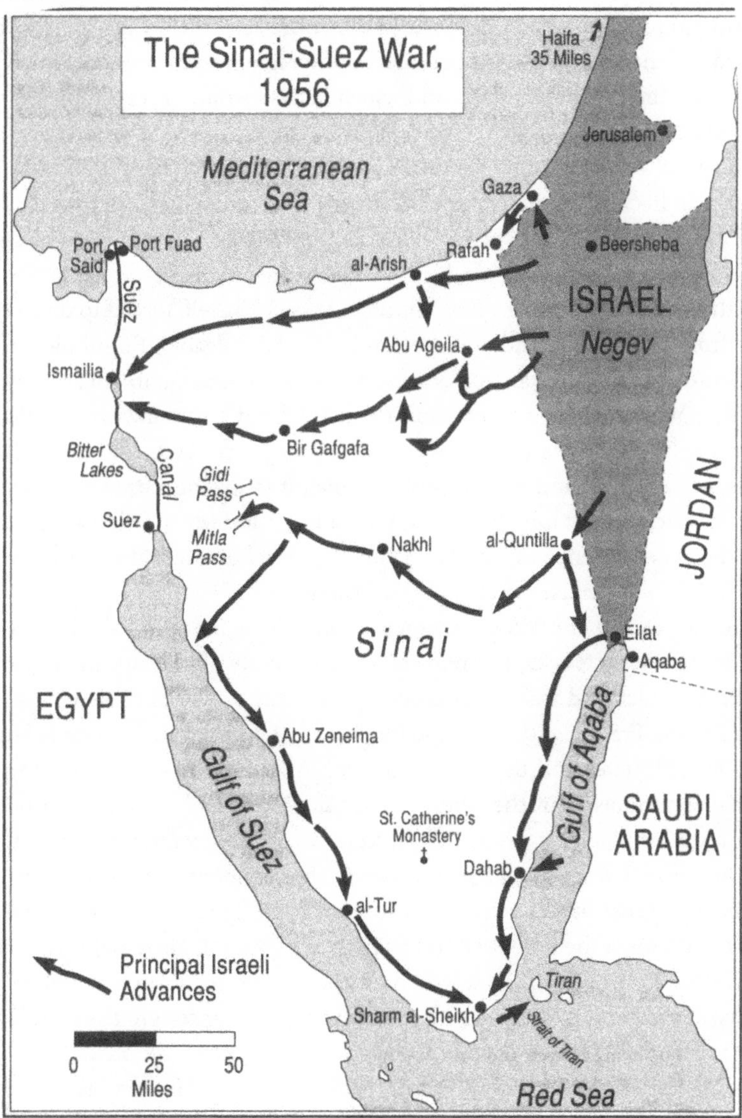

Map 7.1 The Sinai-Suez War, 1956, from Tessler, *A History of the Israeli-Palestinian Conflict,* 2nd ed., 350. Permission granted by Indiana University Press.

On the day before the Israeli attack, Ben-Gurion told his government that there was no chance that Israel could keep most of the Sinai, so its real territorial goals were to retain control of the coastline from Gaza to the Strait of Tiran to ensure the freedom of Israeli shipping. On November 7, Israel agreed to a ceasefire called for by the UN General Assembly but ignored the UN call for a complete withdrawal of all forces from the territories seized during the war and a return to the Israeli-Egyptian 1949 armistice lines. On the same day, a euphoric Ben-Gurion gave a victory speech to the Knesset, stating not only that the armistice agreement was "dead and buried" but also hinting that Israel might annex the entire Sinai peninsula. This would be justified by "the ancient Jewish heritage" in the region, some areas of which he referred to by their Hebrew names and which he said would "revert to being part of the third kingdom of Israel."[64]

The speech—which later even Ben-Gurion admitted had been a mistake, a consequence of his being "too drunk with victory"[65]—shocked and outraged much of the world, including, Abba Eban wrote, "not only Israel's adversaries but also her friends," the most important of which was the United States.[66]

Within twenty-four hours, Ben-Gurion reversed himself, forced to do so by two letters from Eisenhower and Soviet premier Nicolai Bulganin. Eisenhower warned Ben-Gurion that US support of Israel was at stake; Bulganin, in effect, threatened possible Soviet military intervention if Israel did not withdraw, writing that "the Government of Israel is playing with the fate of peace, with the fate of its own people, in a criminal and irresponsible manner. It is sowing hatred for the state of Israel . . . which cannot but affect the future of Israel and which will place a question upon the very existence of Israel as a state. . . . We hope that the Government of Israel will duly understand and appreciate our warning."[67]

Whether or not the US government—or at least the CIA—had encouraged Israel to overthrow Nasser, Eisenhower had apparently not been warned about the impending attack and was taken aback by its scale, by the obvious collusion between Britain, France, and Israel, and by the threat it posed to the national interest of the United States and the West in gaining Arab support for "containing international communism" in the Middle East. As well, Eisenhower was furious over Ben-Gurion's initial refusal to withdraw from Israel's new conquests. Accordingly, a few hours after Ben-Gurion's Knesset speech, the president sent an urgent telegram to him, saying that Israel's refusal to withdraw from Egyptian territory "would seriously undermine the urgent efforts being made by the United Nations to restore peace in the Middle East. . . . It would be a matter of the greatest regret to all my countrymen if Israeli policy on a matter of such grave concern to the world should in any way impair the friendly cooperation between our two countries."

In a meeting with Abba Eban, Acting Secretary of State Herbert Hoover forcibly spelled out the consequences if Israel refused to withdraw: "We both have evidence that the Soviets are exploiting the situation in a way that might endanger world peace. . . . Israel's refusal to withdraw will be interpreted as contempt for American public opinion and will inevitably lead to grave measures, such as ending public and private aid, imposing U.N. sanctions and, finally, expulsion from the U.N."[68]

In effect, Eisenhower was threatening not only to end American governmental assistance to Israel but also to stop private donations from the American Jewish community. These "blunt and powerful threats," Dennis Ross has written, were repeated a few months later when Israel refused to withdraw its forces without formal assurances that the Straits of Tiran would be kept open and Egypt would not be allowed to send its forces back into Gaza.[69]

In view of the Soviet implied threats as well as Eisenhower's anger, Britain and France withdrew their forces from Egypt in December. As well, Ben-Gurion was now resigned to the need to withdraw the Israeli forces from most of Sinai, except for Sharm el-Sheikh on the Strait of Tiran and the Gulf of Aqaba coastline leading to it. While he initially insisted on holding on to Gaza, he changed his mind as a result of continuing US pressures as well as his own unwillingness to assume full responsibility for the hundreds of thousands of residents and Palestinian refugees there.[70]

The remaining issue—Israel's insistence on guaranteed freedom of navigation through the Gulf of Aqaba—was resolved at the end of February 1957 by a US-Israeli compromise: Israel would withdraw from Sharm al-Sheikh and the Gulf of Aqaba coastline but would reserve the right to defend its freedom of navigation if that again became necessary. At the same time, the United States would issue a formal declaration that it viewed the Straits of Tiran as an international waterway, with the understanding that the United States and other nations would intervene if necessary to preserve freedom of passage there.[71]

In Tom Segev's overall judgment, the war was a failure: "The attempt to get rid of Nasser, Israel's principal goal in the war, was quickly revealed as foolish, embarrassing, and ultimately abortive collusion. Nasser emerged as the great victor."[72] Other Israeli historians, however, argue that war did have some benefits for Israel. As summed up by Bar-Zohar and others:

> It opened the Straits of Tiran.
> It brought ten years of peace with Egypt.
> It strengthened the Israeli alliance with France, which for the next ten years continued to provide arms and helped Israel develop a nuclear deterrent.

Because of the renewed demonstration of Israeli military prowess, the Eisenhower administration increasingly regarded Israel as a strategic asset in the Middle East rather than, as had earlier been the case, a liability.[73] For example, in August 1958, Eisenhower told the National Security Council: "If we choose to combat radical Arab nationalism and to hold Persian Gulf oil by force if necessary, a logical corollary would be to support Israel as the only strong pro-Western power left in the Near East."[74] Pursuant to this new assessment of Israel's value, in 1959 the administration provided $100 million in technical and financial assistance to the country, a greater amount than all previous US aid to Israel, and while still reluctant to become Israel's major arms supplier, it did agree to sell it advanced radar equipment and other relatively small military equipment.[75]

Whatever the value of these benefits, there is no doubt that the Israeli attack, especially because of the collaboration with British and French efforts to hold on to some of their colonial positions or influence in the Middle East, intensified the hatred of Israel in the Arab world in general and especially, of course, in Egypt; the result was the 1967 and 1973 wars.

It is worth quoting the overall judgments of Motti Golani and Mordechai Bar-On, two leading historians of the 1956 war, on the war's consequences. After noting some of the Israeli gains from the war, Golani concludes: "In 1948, Egypt had gone to war against Israel very reluctantly. The results of that war, however, sowed in Egypt seeds of animosity toward Israel which hitherto hardly existed. The Sinai War only augmented these. From 1956, Egypt had yet another reason to settle the score with Israel. . . . [T]he Sinai War in fact made the next round almost inevitable."[76]

Bar-On quotes a 1955 Ben-Gurion speech to Israeli army officers: "In both our military preparedness and in the belligerent actions imposed on us, we must never lose sight of the fact that our ultimate goal in our relations with our neighbors is to attain peace and coexistence. . . . After each war we win, we will again face the same problem. . . . We will be confronted by a third round and a fourth." Bar-On then comments: "This was indeed a tragically clear-sighted prediction: Israel was destined to experience a third round, and even two more rounds. The longed-for peace with Egypt was ultimately achieved not by the sword but by reconciliation and compromise."[77]

In fact, an even stronger conclusion is warranted: it is highly likely that *all* of Israel's wars with Egypt, including those of 1948, 1956, 1967, and 1973, would have been avoided if Israel had been willing to forgo its territorial expansionism and reach reasonable and attainable compromise peace settlements with Egypt and its other Arab neighbors.

8

From War to War, 1956–67

The Nuclear Issue

After Israel was created in 1948, Ben-Gurion sought formal and public US security guarantees for the new state, if possible even a military alliance, but both the Truman and Eisenhower administrations refused.[1] After the 1956 war, Ben-Gurion renewed his request for a US security guarantee or at least for major US offensive weaponry. When the Eisenhower administration again turned down the Israeli requests, Ben-Gurion decided that Israel had to have its own nuclear weapons, as the ultimate deterrent against any Arab threat to its survival. By the late 1950s, aided by extensive but secret French assistance, the nuclear weapons development program was well underway with the construction of a nuclear reactor in the Negev city of Dimona.[2]

In late 1960, the Eisenhower administration learned of the Dimona program and raised the issue with Ben-Gurion, who insisted—as other Israeli prime ministers were to do repeatedly during the Kennedy and Johnson administrations—that the reactor was designed solely to produce nuclear energy for peaceful purposes. Most studies of this period are skeptical that the Americans actually believed Israel's denials. If they had, they would have been quite naïve: a post-Holocaust Jewish state was not likely to refrain from seeking the ultimate deterrent against actual or potential threats to its survival.

When the Kennedy administration took office in January 1961, the Israeli requests were renewed. Kennedy was known to be much more sympathetic to Israel than the Eisenhower administration; he had close personal ties with the American Jewish community and had a number of Jewish advisors. As well, he had strong political incentives to be seen as a friend of Israel: the Jewish vote, which went overwhelmingly to him in the 1960 presidential elections, had played an important role in helping him barely defeat Richard Nixon. "You know I was elected by the Jews, I have to do something for them," he told Ben-Gurion in a meeting with the Israeli prime minister in May 1961.[3]

Still, like Truman and Eisenhower before him, Kennedy was not willing to agree to formal and public security guarantees to Israel, telling Israeli foreign minister

Golda Meir that "the United States had global interests, and if it were to exert influence in the Arab Middle East, it needed to cultivate good relations with all nations."[4]

By the time Kennedy took office, the world had learned of the Israeli nuclear development program, especially after documents were leaked to the *New York Times*, which published two major articles on it.[5] Still, the Kennedy administration pressed Israel to refrain from weaponizing the program and to allow US nuclear experts to regularly visit Dimona to verify Israel's assurances that it was not doing so. In May 1961, Ben-Gurion met with Kennedy to discuss the issue. Tom Segev writes: "Ben-Gurion claimed that the project was meant for peaceful purposes. He linked the reactor to a plan to desalinate seawater, but chose his words carefully: 'That is Israel's principal and, for the time, only goal,' he maintained, adding, 'We do not know what will happen in the future.'"[6] And when Kennedy pressed Ben-Gurion to allow US inspections of the Dimona reactor to ensure that it wasn't being used to develop nuclear weapons, the Israeli prime minister refused to allow meaningful inspections. He assured Kennedy: "For the time being," he said, "the only purposes are for peace. . . . But we will see what will happen in the Middle East. It does not depend on us."[7]

These qualifications, of course, made the Israeli assurances all but meaningless, which surely the Americans understood, so the Kennedy and later the Johnson administrations continued to protest the Israeli nuclear program, sometimes quite severely.[8] In the end, however, as Avner Cohen and others have concluded, both administrations decided not to condition continued US support of Israel on an end to the Israeli nuclear program, either because they realized that Israel was going to continue the program regardless of the occasional US threats or that Congress would never support an end to the American commitment to Israel. The Ben-Gurion government was confident that the American government would not go beyond expressions of disapproval.[9]

They were right, of course. To be sure, it is also plausible that Kennedy and Johnson were at least quietly sympathetic to the argument—not an unreasonable one, after all—that Israel needed a nuclear deterrent to assure its survival and would get it one way or another.

In the final analysis, then, Kennedy backed away from creating a US-Israeli crisis over the nuclear issue and started providing Israel with defensive weapons. And in late 1962, while still resisting a formal and public mutual defense treaty with Israel, he privately assured Golda Meir of the US commitment to Israeli security:

> The United States . . . has a special relationship with Israel really comparable only to that which it has with Britain. . . . We are in a position then to make clear to the Arabs that we will maintain our friendship with Israel and our security guarantees [that] . . . in case of an invasion the United States would come to the support of Israel.[10]

In October 1963, despite his continuing unhappiness with Israel's nuclear program, Kennedy reiterated this commitment, writing to Prime Minister Levi Eshkol that "in case of an invasion the United States would come to the support of Israel. . . . This letter in fact constitutes a security guarantee."[11]

From the Nixon administration on, the US government essentially dropped Israeli nuclear weapons as an issue.[12]

The 1967 War

The Myths and the Realities

According to the Israeli mythology, the 1967 war was a purely defensive one, a "war of no choice," forced on Israel by the continuing refusal of the Arabs to agree to a political settlement: the goal of the Arab world in general and of Nasser's Egypt in particular, it was repeatedly said, was to annihilate the Jewish state as soon as they had the capability to do so. As one contemporary purveyor of the myth has put it: "In June 1967 Arab leaders declared their intention to annihilate the Jewish state, and the Jews decided they wouldn't sit still for it. For the crime of self-preservation, Israel remains a nation unforgiven."[13]

Immediately after the war, the mythology continues, Israel offered to return the territories it had conquered during its war for survival, but the Arab world categorically refused to even consider Israel's generous offer. Instead, it is said, it responded with "The Three Noes": no to peace, no to political recognition of Israel, no to any negotiations with it. Thus, the mythology holds, even Israel's overwhelming defeat of Egypt and Syria in the 1967 war—just as had been the case in the 1948 and 1956 wars—not only resulted in no changes in Arab policies but it also strengthened their determination to fight war after war until Israel was finally destroyed. Consequently, it is said, in the last sixty years Israel has repeatedly been forced to fight one "existential" war after another, having no other choice if it was to survive.

As in the case of the other major Israeli mythologies, the facts are very different. In the decade following the 1956 Suez War, the conflict between Israel and Egypt was relatively quiet, as Nasser ended the Egyptian support of Palestinian guerrilla raids against Israel: "For ten years Nasser did not reassemble his forward military deployment along the borders with Israel; he did not send the Fedayun against Israel or resume border incidents; and he did not hamper Israeli shipping in the Straits of Tiran."[14]

Nonetheless, the Israeli hawks were not satisfied, as their expansionist goals continued. In particular, Ben-Gurion and much of the Israeli military establishment now regretted that Israel had refrained from seizing all of Jerusalem and the West Bank from Jordan in the 1948 and 1956 wars. Two of Israel's leading historians, making use of declassified government and military documents of the period, have revealed the thinking of Israel's top political and military leaders during this period.

Ilan Pappé writes: "In order to reevaluate the 1967 war we first need to go back to the war of 1948. The Israeli political and military elite regarded the latter as a missed opportunity: a historical moment in which Israel could, and should, have occupied the whole of historical Palestine from the River Jordan to the Mediterranean Sea."[15] They did not do so because they wanted to ensure that Jordan would not enter the 1948 war, and staying out of Jordan's West Bank was the price that had to be paid.

Nonetheless, Pappé continues, Ben-Gurion described his reluctant decision as one "that future generations would lament."[16] Pappé concludes: "Ever since 1948, important sections of the Jewish cultural, military, and political elites had been looking for an opportunity to rectify this mistake. From the mid-1960s onwards, they carefully planned how to create a greater Israel that would include the West Bank."[17]

In a 2017 book on the 1967 war, based on research in the Israeli archives, the Israeli historian Guy Laron wrote that despite the Jordanian-Israeli agreement during the 1948 war, "the Israelis had been preparing since the 1950s to conquer the West Bank."[18] In October 1955, when Sharett was still prime minister but Ben-Gurion was about to succeed him, Laron continued, Dayan called a meeting of Israel's General Staff "so we can discuss what we want to demand of the [new] government." Israel would have little difficulty in finding a pretext for a strike against Egypt, Dayan argued. The goals of such an attack, he said, should be the following:

> to conquer the Gaza Strip, the demilitarized zones [on the border with Egypt and Syria] and the Tiran Straits . . . And we should think of a triple-stage plan. . . . [I]n the second stage we will reach the Suez Canal; in the third stage we will reach Cairo. . . . As to Jordan, there [is a] two stage [plan]: the first is [to reach] the Hebron line. The second [is to take] the rest [of the territory] up to the Jordan River.[19]

Ben-Gurion continued to describe the post-1948 borders as "unbearable" but was at first hesitant to approve of such a sweeping plan if Israel had to act on its own. However, when it became clear that Britain and France would support an Israeli attack, he "became quite enthusiastic."[20]

Because of the US and Soviet threats, Ben-Gurion's goals could not be attained during the 1956 war. Nonetheless, the Israeli hawks did not abandon them: "The General Staff had never let go of the plan to expand Israel's territory. The contingency plans from 1953, which envisaged the annexation of Sinai, the West Bank, and the Golan Heights, were updated and rewritten in 1957."[21]

In 1963, Levi Eshkol succeeded Ben-Gurion as Israel's prime minister and met with the IDF's General Staff, discovering that they planned to use the next war as an opportunity for further Israeli territorial expansion, including Sinai, the West Bank, and parts of Lebanon.[22]

The Approach to War, 1965–67

At the end of 1965 the head of the Israeli Mossad, Meir Amit, received an invitation to go to Cairo for a secret meeting with Abdel Hakim Amer, deputy commander of the Egyptian armed forces and a close personal friend of Nasser. Amer wanted US economic aid to Egypt, then in the midst of an economic crisis; in return, he promised that Egypt would reduce its anti-Israeli rhetoric and economic boycott, including allowing Israeli goods to pass through the Suez Canal, although only if they were on non-Israeli ships.[23]

Prime Minister Levi Eshkol favored allowing the visit and told the American government about it. However, other high-level Israeli officials opposed the visit, "warning that it was a trap," and Eshkol reluctantly went along. Avi Shlaim concludes that there is no way of telling whether anything would have come out of the meeting of two high-level Egyptian and Israeli officials: "All one can say for certain is that the Egyptians issued an invitation . . . and the Israelis turned it down."[24]

With the possible opening to a peaceful settlement of the Egyptian-Israeli conflict now closed, in late 1966 Nasser decided to allow a few Palestinian raids to resume, but only in a limited manner. Laron writes: "Nasser's leash was tight. . . . PLO sabotage acts remained few and far between."[25]

Throughout 1966 and early 1967, however, Palestinian raids against Israel increased; launched from Jordan and Syria, some of these were directed at Israeli military positions, some against civilians. King Hussein opposed the Palestinian raids, but his forces were not strong enough to prevent all of them. After the radical Ba'ath political party came to power in Syria in February 1966, however, it actively supported and sheltered Palestinian guerrilla attacks on both Israeli military and civilian targets.[26]

While the Fedayeen attacks were limited in scope and did not threaten Israel's "basic security,"[27] there is no doubt that Syrian support of them was highly provocative. On the other hand, it is equally true that the Israeli retaliations sharply escalated the conflict. Moreover, in the decade before the 1967 war, Israel continued to violate the terms of the 1949 armistice, especially by expanding its armed settlements and diverting to Israel water from the Jordan River and its tributaries in Lebanon and Syria.

These actions led to increased Syrian shelling from the Golan Heights of Israeli forces in the DMZ, but according to UN officials at the time, they would not have occurred had it not been for the Israeli provocations. In any case, no Israeli civilians were reported to have been killed by the Syrian artillery in the six months before the 1967 war.[28]

Shlaim sums up the Israeli-Syrian conflict before the 1967 war: "There were three principal sources of tension between Israel and Syria: the demilitarized zones, water, and the activities of the Palestinian guerilla organizations." [29] He concludes that "Israel's strategy of escalation on the Syrian front was probably the single most important factor in dragging the Middle East to war in June 1967, despite the conventional wisdom on the subject that singles out Syrian aggression as the principal cause of war."[30]

If anything, Shlaim understates Israel's responsibility for the 1967 war with Syria, because surely there was a fourth "source of tension" between the two countries: namely, Israeli expansionism directed at Syria, which long pre-dated the escalating conflicts during the 1960s. Ben-Gurion considered the Golan Heights—indeed much of southwestern Syria—to be an integral part of biblical Palestine, belonging by historical right to the Greater Israel that he aspired to bring into existence. To be sure, it was not only Zionist ideology that accounted for Ben-Gurion's expansionist goals in Syria but also Israel's need for access to fresh water sources: some of the tributaries of the Jordan River originated or passed through Syria, and even more important, the Golan Heights commanded the shores of the Jordan River itself as well as the Sea of Galilee. "The possibility of using these rivers freely," Ben-Gurion had written earlier, "was a basic condition for mass settlement in Palestine and for the country's economic independence."[31]

It is clear, then, that the Syrians had good reason to fear for the future of the Golan Heights, although it is undeniable that their own behavior was creating a self-fulfilling prophecy, inevitably adding security concerns to the other motivations for Israeli designs on the area. However, even well before the escalating conflicts of the 1960s, the Israeli hawks had plans to seize the Golan if the opportunity presented itself. In January 1954, for example, Moshe Dayan outlined plans to Moshe Sharett for creating a series of "accomplished facts" by seizing the Golan in certain contingencies. Sharett was shocked by this, and in his diaries he accuses Dayan of seeking to provoke Syria into attacking Israeli outposts and settlements beneath the Golan Heights to justify an eventual Israeli counterstrike to seize the area.

In 1976, Dayan confirmed that Israel had deliberately sought to provoke the Syrians and had instigated more than 80 percent of the clashes with that country. In early 1967, Israel "resumed cultivation of land in the DMZ in a manner calculated to provoke clashes with the Syrians."[32] As the Israeli government expected, Syria reacted with intensified shelling from the Golan Heights, so on April 7 Israel launched 130 warplanes deep into Syria and bombed numerous targets; when Syrian jets rose to meet the attack, six of them were shot down, two of them over the outskirts of Damascus.

At the same time, Prime Minister Eshkol and Chief of Staff Yitzhak Rabin issued a series of warnings that if the Syrian shelling and support of the Palestinian guerrillas continued, Israel might have to take much more drastic action. For example, on May 11 Rabin remarked on an Israeli radio station that "the moment is coming when we will march on Damascus to overthrow the Syrian Government, because it seems that only military operations can discourage the plans for a people's war with which they threaten us."[33] The next day the *New York Times* reported that a highly placed Israeli source, believed to be Prime Minister Eshkol, said that "if Syria continued a campaign of sabotage in Israel it would immediately provoke military action aimed at overthrowing the Syrian regime."[34]

On May 13, the Soviet Union warned Egypt and Syria that its intelligence assessment indicated that Israel was massing troops near the Syrian border and an attack was imminent. In fact, the report was false, as there had been no massing of Israeli forces. The general assessment of historians of the 1967 war is that whether or not the Soviet warnings had deliberately exaggerated the imminence of an Israeli attack, the Syrians had good reason to fear that such an attack was only a matter of time.[35] Indeed, this was the US government's assessment as well: an internal memo of Harold Saunders, then the National Security Council's primary Middle Eastern specialist, stated that "the Soviet advice to the Syrians that the Israelis were planning an attack was not far off."[36]

Thus, the Soviet warnings were an effort to force Egypt to comply with its mutual defense treaty with Syria. While the Soviets were concerned about Syrian support of the Palestinian guerrilla movement, they were determined to protect Syria and Egypt from another military defeat that would not only be a humiliation for Soviet arms and credibility as an ally but might also lead to the collapse of their major Arab allies; the expulsion of the Soviets from Egypt, Syria, and perhaps elsewhere in the Middle East; and the unilateral domination of the area by the United States.[37]

Responding to these reports, Nasser felt that he had no choice but to take action to deter a major Israeli attack on Syria. After the 1956 war he had agreed to allow a UN peacekeeping force to be placed in the Sinai, replacing his own troops. However, as the war approached, King Hussein of Jordan, angrily responding to Egyptian and Syrian accusations that he was essentially collaborating with Israel, taunted Nasser of "hiding behind the skirts" of the UN force. In response, Nasser ordered the UN peacekeeping force out of Sinai, sent 80,000 Egyptian forces into the region, and closed the Strait of Tiran to Israeli shipping, despite his awareness that Israel would regard that as an act of war.[38]

Nonetheless, it is now known that before the Israeli attack, both the US and Israeli governments had concluded that the Egyptian forces in Sinai were deployed defensively and that Nasser had no intention of attacking Israel, only of regaining control of Sinai and Gaza and deterring an Israeli attack on Syria. That is also the overwhelming consensus of historians of the war.

The literature on the Israeli and American intelligence assessments at the time, and the comments of many military and political leaders since then, is extensive.[39] Following are the American assessments:

- In his memoirs, Abba Eban wrote: "The American defense chiefs . . . [gave] a professional view on what the result would be if a conflict broke out between Israel and Egyptian forces. Their studies all pointed toward Israeli success if there was war. *They thought that this would be the case no matter who took the initiative in the air.*"[40]

- On May 25, after Israeli officials told the US government that an Egyptian attack was imminent, President Johnson ordered the CIA and the Defense Department to reassess the situation. Reviewing the supposedly new evidence adduced by Israel, the US analyses rejected the Israeli claim.[41]
- On May 26, Defense Secretary Robert McNamara said the US government believed that Israel "would prevail in a conflict, even if hostilities were initiated by Egypt." General Earl Wheeler, chairman of the Joints Chiefs of Staff, "restated the American view of Israel's military superiority and said that, although we recognize that casualties would be greater than in 1948 and 1956, Israel would prevail. . . . If anything, it was the Israeli army that was pressing to begin hostilities."[42]
- President Johnson summarized the US government's analyses in several meetings with the Israeli ambassador: "If Israel is attacked, our judgment is that the Israelis would lick them. Time would not work against Israel, it would not lose by waiting. . . . During this period there would not be any deterioration in the Israeli military position."[43]

The Israeli views were similar. In fact, many Israeli leaders shared the US assessment that Israel would defeat the Arab forces, even if the Arabs attacked first.

The head of Mossad told McNamara that "there were no differences between the U.S. and the Israelis on the military intelligence picture or its interpretation."[44]

Tom Segev writes that Prime Minister Eshkol was dubious about the need for Israel to go to war but came under heavy military pressure to begin the conflict: "It is doubtful whether he believed Israel's existence was truly in danger, and equally doubtful that he was convinced Egypt would attack. He knew what the army knew: that even if Egypt had attacked, Israel would win."[45] That did not prevent him from trying to mislead Johnson so as to ensure US support, Segev continues, quoting a telegram from Eshkol to an Israeli diplomat stating that some of the Israeli statements were designed "to create an alibi."[46]

Laron writes that despite alarmist Israeli government entreaties to the Johnson administration calling for US military support, "The real Israeli intelligence assessment at the time told a different story. The worst that the Egyptians would do, according to military estimates, was mount a limited air attack on Israeli airfields."[47]

A few months after the war, Chief of Staff Yitzhak Rabin stated the following: "I do not believe that Nasser wanted war. The two divisions he sent into the Sinai . . . would not have been enough to unleash an offensive against Israel. *He knew it and we knew it.*"[48]

In later years, leading Israeli generals concurred that was the case. For example, General Mattityahu Peled, one of Israel's leading generals during the war—and later a severe critic of Israel's role in the Arab-Israeli conflict—wrote that while the Egyptians had 80,000 soldiers in the Sinai, Israel had hundreds of thousands of men poised against them. Therefore, he wrote:

> There was no reason to hide the fact that since 1949 no one dared, or more precisely, no one was able, to threaten the very existence of Israel. . . . To claim that the Egyptian forces concentrated on our borders were capable of threatening Israel's existence . . . insults the intelligence of anyone capable of analyzing [the] situation.[49]

General Ezer Weizman, chief of operations in 1967 and later a prominent right-wing politician, admitted that "there was never a danger of extermination" and hadn't even been considered in any "serious meeting." He then added that it was "a false assumption" that Israel would "wage war only to prevent extermination." At issue was "not our physical security but the realization of our historical and national interests, our Zionist principles."[50]

Similarly, Haim Bar-Lev, deputy chief of staff in 1967, and later a cabinet member, said, "We were not threatened with genocide on the eve of the Six-Day War and we had never thought of such a possibility."[51]

But perhaps the most important, authoritative, and widely quoted rebuttal of the Israeli 1967 myth was provided by Menachem Begin, who shocked the Israeli public when in a 1982 speech to Israel's National Defense College he bluntly stated: "In June 1967, we again [as in the 1956 War] had a choice. The Egyptian Army concentrations in the Sinai approaches did not prove that Nasser was about to attack us. We must be honest with ourselves. We decided to attack him."[52]

The Problem of Arab Rhetoric

Despite the overwhelming evidence of the essentially defensive intentions of Nasser, the fact should not be obscured that the increasingly bloodthirsty rhetoric of the Arab world and of Nasser himself was a major factor in Israel's decision to engage in a preventive war by attacking Egypt first. Carried away by his early success in removing the UN peacekeeping forces and stationing Egyptian forces in the Sinai, Nasser abandoned his usual caution and made increasingly ominous threats that whipped up mass war fever in the Arab world. The examples of bone-chilling Arab threats are many:

- In January 1964, an Arab League summit declared that "the establishment of Israel is the basic threat that the Arab nation in its entirety has agreed to forestall. . . . [T]he existence of Israel is a danger that threatens the Arab nation. . . . Collective Arab military preparations . . . will constitute the ultimate practical means for the final liquidation of Israel."[53]
- A few days before the war, Nasser said, "If we should be attacked this will mean war and our first aim would be the annihilation of Israel."[54] And on May 29 he said that the goal in a war with Israel would be "to restore the situation to what it was in 1948. . . . We are now ready to confront Israel. . . . [T]he issue now at

hand . . . is the rights of the Palestinian people . . . [and reversing] the aggression which took place in Palestine in 1948."[55]

- As well, the PLO leader Ahmed Shukeiry was asked what would happen to the Israeli population after an Arab victory. He responded that those who were born elsewhere would be "repatriated"; as for those who were native Israelis, they would remain in Palestine—"but I estimate that none of them will survive."[56]
- Similarly, on May 31, the president of Iraq said, "The existence of Israel is an error which must be rectified. . . . Our goal is clear—to wipe Israel off the map."[57]

There were many similar Arab threats to "throw the Jews into the sea," and the like. The Egyptian journalist Khaled Diab, reviewing the period, wrote that "there is no doubt that the Israeli public, exposed to a continuous barrage of bombastic radio broadcasts from Cairo promising to put an end to the entire Zionist existence, was terrified in the run up to the war."[58]

It is obvious that Israeli policies and behaviors played a major role in the anger of the Arab world. That said, less than twenty-five years after the Holocaust, a Jewish state could hardly be expected to dismiss murderous threats as mere rhetoric. Even Noam Chomsky, for decades one of Israel's strongest and most perceptive critics, has admitted that "at the time of the war . . . I personally believed that the threat of genocide was real."[59]

The Johnson Administration and the 1967 War

Lyndon Johnson was strongly supportive of the Jewish people. In the late 1930s and early 1940s, as a junior congressman and later Democratic senator from Texas, he had become outraged by evidence of the Holocaust and pressed the State Department to do much more to help the Jews escape from Europe. Throughout his career, many of his closest friends, advisors, and political donors were Jewish. And in his memoirs, he wrote: "I have always had a deep feeling of sympathy for Israel and its people, gallantly building and defending a modern nation against great odds, and against the tragic background of Jewish experience."[60]

To be sure, undoubtedly his genuine beliefs and sympathies were reinforced by political calculations, although in his pre-presidency years there were not many Jews among his Texas constituents. Still, national public opinion was strongly pro-Israel, so there were a number of reasons he did not wish to offend the American Jewish community. According to David Korn, a former US diplomat who had served in Israel for many years, after he became president Johnson told Walworth Barbour, the US ambassador to Israel: "I don't care what happens to Israel, but I care a lot about American Jews. Whatever you do in Israel, keep one eye peeled for the American Jews and do nothing which would get them on my back." Barbour, Korn notes, made that his top priority.[61]

Knowing Johnson's views, Prime Minister Eshkol sought to persuade him to establish a special relationship with Israel and to provide direct US military assistance in case of a major war. Like all former and future presidents, Johnson was not willing to enter into a formal defense alliance with Israel, but he responded that the United States "would not remain idle if Israel is attacked," and for the first time he authorized the sale of offensive weapons to Israel, including tanks and advanced Phantom fighter-bombers.[62] As well, Johnson authorized James Angleton, a high-level CIA official who was strongly pro-Israel, to begin secret collusion with the Mossad.[63]

Nonetheless, during the 1967 crisis, neither the Johnson administration nor US military leaders were willing to be drawn into war on behalf of Israel, especially as the Vietnam War and US involvement in it were escalating. Three days after Nasser sent his forces into the Sinai, Eshkol wrote to Johnson asking him "to reaffirm the American commitment to Israel's security with a view to its implementation should the need arise," pointedly noting "the specific American commitment so often reiterated to us."[64] Three days later, however, Secretary of State Dean Rusk told Eban that a US declaration along the lines of "an attack on you is an attack on us" was not realistic,[65] especially since the US government did not believe that Egypt and Syria would attack Israel, and that even if they did, Israel would win on its own: "Both Rusk and McNamara told [the Israeli government] that their information totally contradicted the claim of an impending Syrian–Egyptian attack. . . . In any case, American intelligence agencies believed that Israel would be the winner, no matter who started the war."[66]

For these reasons, the Johnson administration initially opposed an Israeli preemptive attack on Egypt and Syria, but the administration was not confident it could be prevented if Israel believed its vital interests required it.[67] On June 3, two days before Israel struck, Rusk wrote to US ambassadors to Arab states:

> You should not assume that the United States can order Israel not to fight for what it considers to be its most vital interests. We have used the utmost restraint and, thus far, have been able to hold Israel back. But the "Holy War" psychology of the Arab world is matched by an apocalyptic psychology within Israel. . . . [Unless a political solution is found], Israel will fight and we cannot restrain her.[68]

Similarly, Harold Saunders, the NSC's leading Mideast expert during the war, later wrote that "we were convinced that we just could not move Israel against its will."[69]

Consequently, the administration's main concern was to avoid being drawn into the war if the intelligence reports that Israel would easily win a war against Egypt alone or against all the surrounding Arab countries proved to be wrong. Secretary of State Rusk and Defense Secretary McNamara "took the strong stand that Israel would be on its own if it decided to strike first,"[70] and Johnson himself bluntly told an Israeli envoy that while "Israel was a sovereign Government, and if it decided to act alone, it could of course do so; but in that case everything that happened before and afterwards would be its responsibility and the United States would have no obligation for any consequences that might ensue."[71]

Citing an interview with Harold Saunders, Korn elaborates on Johnson's thinking: "Above all, [Johnson] wanted to avoid assuming responsibility for what he feared could all too easily become a disaster. He did not want to be told that Jews had been slaughtered because of his advice, or to be asked to rescue Israel from imminent destruction because it had followed his directions."[72]

Consequently, Johnson decided not to emulate Eisenhower's pressures on Israel in 1956 and made no threats, not even conditioning the continued delivery of US arms, including offensive arms, on Israel refraining from starting the war. And perhaps most important, he ordered the US Mediterranean fleet to move close to the Syrian shore, signaling that the United States would counter any Soviet military intervention in the war.

The ambiguities of the Johnson administration's position in the lead-up to the 1967 war, especially its decision not to threaten US repercussions if Israel attacked, has prompted debate in the literature over whether Johnson had effectively given Israel "a green light" to start the war. For example, after quoting Johnson's statements that the United States "would have no obligation" in case Israel suffered consequences for its actions, Laron asks: "Was the president threatening Israel or encouraging it to act?"[73]

Put differently, was Johnson telling Israel it had a red light, a yellow light, or a green light? William Quandt's overall assessment of the administration's policy is cautious: while the title of his chapter on the 1967 war is "Yellow Light," his overall conclusion is that although Johnson "had not quite given the Israelis a green light," he effectively "had removed a veto on their actions."[74]

Quandt then raises an interesting issue, and one that has continuing resonance in explaining US policies toward Israel ever since: "If Johnson genuinely had qualms about Israel's resort to force, why did he become such an ardent supporter of Israel once the fighting began? Was he responding to pressures from pro-Israeli opinion in the United States, or to his own sympathy for the Jewish state?"[75] His answer is that both the oil lobby and "the allegedly powerful pro-Israeli interest groups" were unimportant during the crisis:

> He [Johnson] paid no attention to the formal pro-Israel lobby, but he was in constant touch with Americans who were friendly to Israel, some of whom were also key personalities in the Democratic Party. . . . [T]he extremely pro-Israeli tone of American public opinion, coupled with Nasser's hostility, probably did make it easier for Johnson to adopt a policy of unquestioning support for Israel. Lobbying, however, was not a significant factor.[76]

A similar combination of sympathy and political calculation probably explains Johnson's silence over the still-perplexing Israeli attack on the USS *Liberty*, a communication ship in international waters some twenty-five miles off the coast, secretly listening to Israeli and Egyptian transmissions. On June 8, Israeli jets and torpedo boats attacked the *Liberty*, which was displaying large American flags, killing thirty-four crew members.

Since the attack seemed to make no sense, for many years there was considerable debate even over the facts of the case: Why would Israel attack an American ship? Was it deliberate or accidental? Had it mistaken the ship, as it claimed, for an Egyptian warship? For a variety of reasons, including the fact that the ship was displaying a large American flag, the Israeli claim of pilot error was not very plausible and was not believed by almost any senior US officials, including Secretary of State Dean Rusk and CIA director Richard Helms, who noted in his memoirs that based on a variety of evidence a US investigation concluded that "the Israelis knew exactly what they were doing in attacking the *Liberty*."[77]

In an interview some years later, the American historian Douglas Little was told by Walt Rostow, Johnson's national security advisor, that the ship had been "eavesdropping on everybody—the Israelis, the Egyptians," especially to see if Israel intended to attack the Golan Heights. Little concludes: "It seems more than mere coincidence that Dayan sent his troops into the Golan Heights just fifteen hours after the U.S. Navy's electronic eyes and ears had been snuffed out."[78]

Despite the high-level US assessment, as well as his own reported anger over the Israeli attack, Johnson decided not to make an issue over it; George Ball wrote that Johnson "tried vigorously to downplay the matter, limiting itself to 'an elaborate charade' and 'a pro-forma complaint to Israel.'"[79] Evidently, Johnson did not want the "incident" to disrupt the growing US ties to Israel. Ball concluded that "the ultimate lesson of the *Liberty* attack had far more effect on policy in Israel than America. Israel's leaders concluded that nothing they might do would offend the Americans to the point of reprisal. . . . [I]t seemed clear that their American friends would let them get away with almost anything."[80] This may be too strong; a more moderate conclusion would be that the *Liberty* affair was one of many indications over the years that have resulted in Israel feeling free to ignore or merely to placate US disapproval of many of its actions and policies.

The Outcome of the War

On June 5, 1967, after falsely claiming that Egypt had attacked first, the Israeli Air Force bombed and strafed dozens of Egyptian, Jordanian, and Syrian airfields, destroying nearly the entire combat air forces of those states. In the next six days, Israel routed the Egyptian, Jordanian, and Syrian armies and captured the entire Sinai peninsula, the West Bank of the Jordan River, the Gaza Strip, and the Golan Heights.

As a result, Israel took over all the territory that had been allocated for a Palestinian state in the UN partition plan.

The West Bank and Gaza

During the 1956 Suez War, Israel initially had driven the Egyptian forces out of Gaza and briefly considered permanently occupying it, but under fierce pressures from the Eisenhower administration and having his own doubts about whether Israel should be ruling over hundreds of thousands of conquered Palestinians, Ben-Gurion decided against doing so.

As the 1967 war approached, Israeli policymakers again considered whether it would be in Israel's interests to seize the West Bank if war came. According to Segev, six months before the war, a high-level policy analysis concluded that capturing the West Bank would be bad for Israel, on the ground that it "would weaken the relative strength of Israel's Jewish majority, encourage Palestinian nationalism and ultimately lead to violent resistance."[81]

These concerns were particularly relevant to the question of whether Israel should take over Jerusalem if given the opportunity. Yet, in the days before the war, the earlier prescient analyses of the policy planners were ignored; declassified records of Israeli cabinet meetings revealed that, carried away by Israel's overwhelming victory, no cabinet minister questioned why it would now be in Israel's interests to take over both East Jerusalem and the West Bank.[82]

To be sure, in principle, Zionist aspirations had long included the whole of ancient Palestine, including the West Bank and Jerusalem, but most of the earlier Zionist and Israeli leaders, including Herzl and Ben-Gurion, were not religious and doubted the wisdom of seeking Jewish rule over Jerusalem and then having to deal with the unending religious fanaticism and conflicts that had prevailed in the long history of the city.[83]

As well, even though Ben-Gurion had initially supported the Zionist claim to Jerusalem, for a while he apparently changed his mind, for in 1937 he wrote that "to this very day, I still believe nothing but disaster can come from a refusal to partition Jerusalem into two separate municipalities—one Arab, the other Jewish . . . with the Old City converted "into a religious, spiritual, and cultural museum of all the world's religions."[84] As a result, Ben-Gurion was willing to accept either the partition of Jerusalem between Israel and Jordan or, as proposed by the UN partition plan, the internationalization of the city under effective UN control with guaranteed freedom of religion and access to the many religious sites of Christians, Jews, and Muslims alike.[85]

As it turned out, after the 1948 war Israel and Jordan decided to ignore the UN's internationalization plan and partitioned the city between them, with Israel getting the mostly Jewish West Jerusalem and Jordan getting the mostly Arab East Jerusalem—including the Old City. That ended, however, when in the 1967 war

Israel seized and then formally annexed the entire city of Jerusalem and then extended its boundaries to include many outlying areas, leveling three Palestinian villages in them. As well, Israel either bulldozed many Palestinian homes in the Old City or expelled their owners and inhabitants so as to replace them with Jewish settlers.[86] The process of gradually replacing Arab neighborhoods with Jewish ones throughout "Greater Jerusalem" has continued under all Israeli governments since the 1967 war.

Syria and the Golan Heights

In February 1963, the radical nationalist Ba'ath Party overthrew a more moderate Syrian government and seized power. In the next four years it acted—or at least talked—as if it sought a general Arab war to destroy Israel. Moreover, its extremist rhetoric was accompanied by support for cross-border Palestinian guerrilla raids against both military and civilian targets in Israel. Nonetheless, most Israeli historians have concluded that the Syrian government neither sought nor was prepared for a major war.

In particular, that is the conclusion of the most detailed and authoritative study of Syrian policy during this period, by the Israeli historian Eyal Zisser.[87] Zisser's argument is based on the following evidence. First, he shows that both the Syrian government and its military leaders were fully aware that their armed forces would be no match for the IDF, and that they could go no further than supporting Palestinian guerrilla raids. Second, despite its mutual defense treaty with Egypt that called for joint military action, the Syrian government refused to place its forces under Egyptian command. Third, during the unfolding crisis following Nasser's actions in late May, the Syrian forces remained deployed in defensive positions rather than preparing to join an offensive against Israel; indeed, early in the war the government accepted a UN ceasefire and its armed forces "did nothing to prepare for [an Israeli] offensive."[88] Based on this and other evidence, Zisser concludes that the Syrians "took pains to avoid [the war]. . . . They were prepared to stand immobile on the sidelines while Israel pounced on their allies, Egypt and Jordan."[89]

Other Israeli analysts have reached similar conclusions. For example, Itamar Rabinovich—a historian, former Israeli ambassador to the United States, and chief Israeli negotiator with Syria between 1993 and 1996—wrote that Syria was unhappy that Nasser had moved past the brink of war without consulting Syria, and so played only "a very modest role" in the war, limiting to itself to "shelling parts of northern Israel and staging one small land attack."[90] As well, Avi Shlaim wrote that "Syria wanted to stay out of this war."[91]

Nonetheless, most Israeli military leaders wanted to seize the opportunity to take over the Golan Heights, with the surprising initial exception of Defense Minister Dayan, who believed that the Syrians presented no military threat and feared Soviet intervention if Israel attacked the Golan Heights, putting it in a position to threaten

Damascus itself.[92] According to Yitzhak Rabin, Dayan had berated him and Air Force Chief of Staff Ezer Weizman for ordering the April 7 jet attack on Syria: "Have you gone crazy? You're leading the country to war."[93]

During the first few days of the 1967 war, Dayan continued to oppose an Israeli invasion of the Golan Heights, arguing within the government that Syria was no real threat to Israel. However, even though Syria accepted a UN-proposed ceasefire, on June 9 Dayan suddenly changed his mind and gave the order to the IDF to seize the Golan Heights. Years later, Dayan said that his order had been his "greatest mistake," one of the many deliberate Israeli provocations that had led to an unnecessary war with Syria.[94] He attributed this to pressures from the Israeli hawks and from settlers near the Golan Heights who, he charged, "did not even attempt to hide their greed for that land."[95]

In any case and whatever Dayan's shifting views, the Golan Heights had long been coveted by Israel for a number of reasons, including general Zionist expansionist goals, the Golan Heights' command of the Jordan River and its tributaries, perceived security considerations, and, in Zisser's conclusion, "the desire of the decision-makers in Israel . . . to settle accounts with the Syrians for their conduct over the two previous decades of prolonged conflict between the two countries."[96]

As a result, with but few exceptions, the government and military leadership welcomed the opportunity afforded by the war to seize the Golan. The June 9 Israeli attack quickly overwhelmed the Syrian forces, forcing them to retreat. The Israeli forces were then less than forty miles from Damascus, over mostly flat plains, and Syria lacked the ability to stop them if they chose to attack.[97] Fearing just such an Israeli attack, the Soviets warned the United States that they were on the verge of "necessary actions, including military" that could lead to a "grave catastrophe."[98] The Johnson administration responded by warning the Soviets not to intervene, and moved the Sixth Fleet into position to resist any Soviet military action. At the same time, though, Washington warned Israel to end its advances and accept a ceasefire; Israeli compliance with the Soviet and US pressures ended the crisis.[99] Following the Israeli victory, over a hundred Syrian towns and villages in the area were leveled by Israeli bulldozers and some 100,000 to 150,000 Syrians were forced to flee or were expelled into the rest of Syria.[100]

Israel's Postwar Policies

Shortly after the war, both the Mossad and the IDF's Military Intelligence bureau prepared a secret recommendation to the Eshkol government that the government enter into negotiations with the Arabs, offering a return of almost all the conquered territories and the establishment of an independent Palestinian state in the context of an overall peace treaty. As well, there was much support for this proposal in the Shin Bet, including by Meir Amit, its leader.[101]

On June 18, 1967, the cabinet met to decide on Israel's postwar policies toward the Arab states, in particular what to do with the newly conquered territories.[102] It reached the following decisions:

Egypt. In the context of an overall peace settlement, Israel would withdraw from the Sinai—but not from the Gaza Strip—in return for the demilitarization of the Sinai and free navigation for Israeli shipping through the Suez Canal and the Straits of Tiran.

Syria. In exchange for a negotiated peace agreement, Israel offered to withdraw from the Golan Heights, conditioned on (1) the demilitarization of the area, (2) guaranteed access of Israel to the waters of the Jordan River and its tributaries, and (3) a Syrian commitment that its forces would not return to the former demilitarized zones along Lake Tiberias.

The West Bank. No formal policy decision was reached because the cabinet was divided. Dayan, Menachem Begin, and others felt that "Judea and Samaria" were part of the land of Israel, but others "feared that holding on to these heavily populated Arab lands would have grave consequences for the Jewish character of the State of Israel and would be an unending source of conflict between Israel and its Arab neighbors."[103] Even the skeptics of the wisdom of Israeli rule over all the West Bank, however, agreed that the Jordan River would now constitute Israel's border, requiring Israeli control over the mountainous region near the river.

Avi Raz argues that while it may not have been possible to reach peace agreements with Egypt and Syria immediately after the war, it would certainly have been possible to do so with King Hussein, if Israel had been willing to return the West Bank and East Jerusalem to Jordan.[104]

Gaza. Despite Israel's past ambivalence about ruling Gaza, the cabinet "was "adamant about keeping the occupied Gaza strip."[105]

Jerusalem. The cabinet decided to keep all of Jerusalem, including Arab East Jerusalem; Segev comments: "No one asked why, really, Israel should control East Jerusalem, as if this were entirely self-evident."[106] Ten days later, Israel expanded East Jerusalem's borders, annexed it, and began the process, continuing today, of Jewish takeovers of Palestinian homes and properties, making it clear that "the extension of Israeli sovereignty over the Arab part of Jerusalem was meant to last forever."[107]

Since 1967, Israeli governments have portrayed its initial postwar June 18 proposals as demonstrating that Israel's "generosity" is invariably met with Arab intransigence. It is not a convincing argument in light of the following established facts: (1) Egypt and Syria were not offered the return of all their territories; (2) Israel kept *all* of the conquered territories of the West Bank, East Jerusalem, and Gaza; and (3) even the limited offers to Egypt and Syria were soon rescinded.

For these reasons, leading Israeli scholars and American diplomats do not consider the Israeli postwar offers to Egypt and Syria to have been serious, made largely in the expectation that they would be turned down, and designed to defray US pressures for a complete withdrawal.[108]

The Khartoum Conference

After the end of the war, the Egyptian, Jordanian, and Syrian governments gradually disarmed and expelled the Palestinian guerrilla forces that had been based in their countries and had carried out raids inside Israel.[109] Then, at the end of August 1967, King Hussein, the leading Arab moderate political leader, convened an international conference of Arab states to discuss how they should respond to Israel's victory. The Khartoum conference, as it came to be known, was attended by all the leading Arab states except Syria.

At the close of the conference the participants issued a public resolution that has come to be known as "the three noes": "no peace with Israel, no recognition of Israel, no negotiations with it." Unsurprisingly, the three noes were widely taken to mean that there was no chance for an Arab-Israeli settlement and that future wars were inevitable. Despite the unyielding language of the Khartoum resolution, however, Israeli and other scholars have argued that the deeper significance of the conference was that it was dominated by the Arab realists, particularly Hussein and Nasser, who had recognized that they had no military option against Israel: "We have only one way before us by which to regain the West Bank and Jerusalem," Nasser told the delegates: "political action."[110]

In fact, it is now known that the Israeli government, which had obtained the text of the Khartoum debates, was (in Raz's words) "fully aware of this sea change in the Arab attitude.[111] Raz concludes: "Available records show that Israel's policy makers feared Arab moderation. . . . Thus Israel hastened to exploit the three 'nos'" of Khartoum as a pretext to further toughen its political stance."[112]

This is persuasive, especially in light of the overall record of Israel's lost opportunities for peace. Still, it must also be noted that the language of the three noes was a disaster for the cause of peace. As had happened in the past and would occur in the future, Arab public rhetoric made it far harder to understand the Arabs' true intentions.

In the next year, Israeli policymakers became increasingly unhappy with even its conditional and limited June 18 proposals to withdraw from most of the Egyptian and Syrian territories conquered in the 1967 war, and, in a series of decisions, gradually retreated from them.[113] Then, in October 1968, the cabinet approved a secret resolution that explicitly replaced the June 18 proposals and made it clear that Israel would not return to its pre-war borders; in particular, it stated, Gaza would "obviously" be kept, as would the Sinai city of Sharm el-Sheikh near the Strait of Tiran, together with a two-hundred-mile strip of eastern Sinai connecting the area to Israel.[114]

When this decision was communicated to the American government, whose policy had been that most of the West Bank should be returned to Jordan, high government officials were said to be "furious." Citing declassified US government documents, Raz reports that in a meeting with the Israeli ambassador Yitzhak

Rabin, "senior White House officials Walt Rostow and Harold Saunders bluntly said: 'We've told you the U.S. position *ad nauseum*—you have to give the West Bank back, you have to give Hussein a role in Jerusalem. . . . [W]e think [you've] known all along what our position is if [you've] been listening."[115] Raz comments: "Yet the American consternation . . . at overall Israeli policy had no practical follow-up. Instead, Israel was about to receive fifty Phantoms and, by and large, continued to enjoy America's staunch support."[116]

As a result, two Israeli journalists wrote, "The general feeling in postwar Israel, with the added territorial buffers captured in 1967, was that time was on Israel's side." They quote from the personal diary entry of Yaacov Herzog, the deputy director of the Israeli foreign ministry: "There is no feeling here of disappointment or frustration that the Arabs rejected all notions of negotiations for peace. The recognition is growing that the current situation, as long as it continues, is good for us."[117]

Ben-Gurion and the 1967 War

In recent years it has become strikingly common for retired Israeli generals and leaders of the Mossad and Shin Bet to forcefully criticize Israel's policies toward the Arabs and, especially, the Palestinians—even though they had faithfully implemented those policies while they were in office.

In a way, David Ben-Gurion set the precedent. No longer in office in 1967, he strongly opposed the Israeli attacks on both Egypt and Syria, fearing that it would be a long war, that Israeli cities would be bombed, and that there would be thousands of civilian casualties. Segev wrote:

> Contrary to the opinion of the IDF's generals, and most politicians and pundits, and in particular unlike the frightened public, Ben-Gurion opposed an Israeli first strike. He feared that war against Egypt and Syria would lead to the conquest of the West Bank from Jordan—and with it the acquisition of more Arabs. Neither did he see any immediate need to conquer Sinai or the Gaza Strip, nor did he think it would be worthwhile to capture East Jerusalem.[118]

Surprised by Ben-Gurion's opposition to the impending war, Chief of Staff Yitzhak Rabin asked to discuss the issue with him. Later, Rabin candidly related what happened: "The Old Man gave me a dressing down. We have been forced into a very grave situation. I very much doubt whether Nasser wanted to go to war. . . . You have led the state into a grave situation. We must not go to war."[119]

Shortly after the war, Ben-Gurion then issued a public statement, calling for an Israeli withdrawal from the Sinai peninsula in the context of a peace treaty with Egypt that would open the Straits of Tiran and the Suez Canal to Israeli shipping, and

Israeli withdrawal from the Golan Heights in the context of a peace treaty with Syria. As for the West Bank, it should become an "autonomous entity" economically tied to Israel. Perhaps surprisingly, in light of his previous skepticism about the wisdom of incorporating the Arab sections of Jerusalem into Israel, Ben-Gurion now advocated that Israel should remain in it: "From the time of King David it had been the capital of Israel," Segev paraphrased his new view, "and so it would remain forever."[120]

As well, while soon also changing his mind about the Golan Heights, Ben-Gurion said to his biographer, Michael Bar-Zohar, "For a real peace, we should give up all the occupied territories, except for Jerusalem and the Golan Heights." Bar-Zohar comments: "He had dreamed, indeed, of a Greater Israel. Nevertheless, having to choose between a large country and a Jewish majority . . . he chose the Jewish majority."[121]

In 1971, two years before his death, Ben-Gurion further explained his continuing opposition to the decision of the Israeli government not to return to the prewar borders:

> Peace, *real* peace is now the great necessity for us. It is worth almost any sacrifice. . . . Sinai? Sharm el-Sheikh? Gaza? The West Bank? Let them go. Peace is more important than real estate. As for security, militarily defensible borders, while desirable, cannot by themselves guarantee our future. *Real* peace with our neighbors. . . . That is the only true security.[122]

The Aftermath of the 1967 War

The Arab-Israeli State Conflict

In terms of its relations with the Arab states, the long-term consequences of Israel's overwhelming victory in 1967 were mixed. On the one hand, over the next two decades the initial refusal of the major Arab states to enter into negotiations with Israel gradually gave way to realism and pragmatism, especially because from 1969 onward the Arab state leaders assumed that Israel had nuclear weapons and took for granted that Israel would use them to prevent an Arab victory in future wars.[123]

Mohamed Heikal, a leading Egyptian journalist and a confidant of Gamal Abdel Nasser, told a revealing story of an offer by Libya's Muammer el-Qaddafi to fund an attack on Israel if Egypt would provide the troops: Nasser dismissed the offer, telling Qaddafi that there was "a strong probability" that Israel had nuclear weapons.[124] As well, it is known that by the early 1970s Anwar Sadat and Egyptian military leaders recognized that Israel's military superiority, especially its nuclear deterrent, made a war to destroy Israel both unwinnable and suicidal.[125] As a result, the most important Arab states became open to reaching de facto—and eventually formal—peace settlements with Israel. Once again, however, Israeli maximalist positions and intransigence were primarily responsible for the lost opportunities for peace.[126]

The Israeli-Palestinian Conflict

In the early Israeli cabinet discussions on what should be done with the Palestinians in the West Bank and Gaza, three possibilities were debated. The first was simply Israeli annexation, formal or de facto, of those areas, making the Palestinian "problem" exclusively an Israeli one. The second was the "Jordanian option," meaning negotiating a settlement with Jordan that would require Israeli withdrawal from most of the West Bank, thereby turning over the Palestinian issue to Jordan. The third was "the Palestinian option": allowing the creation of a limited or semi-autonomous Palestinian state in the West Bank. Whether such an offer would amount to anything more than a Palestinian "Bantustan" is not clear.

Perhaps surprisingly, a majority of the cabinet ministers, including Dayan and Prime Minister Levi Eshkol, initially favored some kind of "Palestinian option"; at that time few Israeli leaders wanted to establish permanent rule over the Palestinians, especially since even as early as 1967 a "demographic problem" could be foreseen, meaning an eventual Palestinian majority in a "Greater Israel." However, the development of Palestinian nationalism and, especially, the increasing power of the PLO under the then-militant leadership of Yasser Arafat led the top Israeli leadership to abandon the Palestinian option.[127]

At the same time, however, there was growing opposition to the "Jordanian option," initially because of distrust of King Hussein or, conversely, fear that he would lose power to an extremist Islamic or Palestinian movement. In any case, by the 1970s, the growth of militant and even fanatical Jewish settlements in the West Bank resulted in the progressive abandonment of government support for returning the conquered territories to Jordan—either because Israeli political leaders, including Shimon Peres and other Labor Party officials, supported the ever-expanding settler movement or they feared the political consequences of ending it.

US Policies

Shortly after the end of the war, Secretary of State Dean Rusk told a Washington press conference that while the Arabs would have to change their attitudes toward Israel, Israel would have to "face the overwhelming necessity" of reaching a reconciliation with the Arab world. The United States would not play an active role in the conflict, he said; rather, both sides should "sweat" with the problems for a while: "Let's let some of these things ferment for a bit."[128]

In fact, US policy was considerably more activist and one-sided—even though many top officials of the Johnson administration gradually came to believe that the main responsibility for the absence of an Arab-Israeli peace settlement was Israeli rigidity.[129] Nonetheless, the administration expanded military assistance to Israel and deepened its political and diplomatic support of it.

Other than that, behind the scenes the main thrust of the Johnson administration's postwar policy was to support its ally King Hussein of Jordan and to oppose the rise of Palestinian nationalism and militancy. Consequently, the US government made it clear to the Israeli leadership that it strongly opposed the establishment of any kind of Palestinian self-rule in the West Bank, whether as an independent state or some kind of "autonomous" entity; instead, it urged Israel to negotiate a settlement with King Hussein that would turn over the Palestinian problem to Jordan. The US position, Reuven Pedatzur writes, "greatly influenced the position of Israeli policy makers . . . [and] was an important element in the process of Israel's abandoning the Palestinian option."[130]

Of the three policy choices on what to do about the Palestinians in the occupied territories considered by the Israeli government after the end of the 1967 war—the "Palestinian option," the "Jordanian option." or continued Israeli rule—it was the last and initially the least favored of them, amounting to the creeping de facto annexation of the West Bank, that effectively became Israeli policy from 1967 through today.

9

The Cold War and the Arab-Israeli Conflict, 1967–74

During the Cold War, the Arab-Israeli conflict became entangled in the global rivalry between the United States and the Soviet Union. The prevalent view in the United States was that the Soviets sought to exploit the Arab-Israeli conflict in order to drive the West from the Middle East and secure Soviet domination over the area. Soviet expansionism, supposedly, made it impossible to settle the Arab-Israeli conflict on terms that would secure the legitimate security interests of Israel as well as protect the interests of the United States and other Western countries in the region. For these reasons, the United States sought to exclude the Soviet Union from all efforts to reach a negotiated settlement.

The weight of the evidence concerning Soviet goals in the Middle East demonstrates that the dominant American view was based on misperceptions about Soviet interests, objectives, and behavior in the region. As a result of these misperceptions, the Cold War was exacerbated, there were several near-confrontations between the superpowers, and important opportunities to reach a superpower-guaranteed comprehensive settlement of the Arab-Israeli conflict were permanently lost.[1]

What Were the Soviet Objectives?

During the Cold War there were three competing theories of Soviet policy in the Arab-Israeli conflict. US policies were based on the first theory: Soviet Middle Eastern policy was part of a long-range, planned strategy of global expansionism, motivated by some combination of revolutionary ideology and traditional Russian expansionism, especially along Russia's southern periphery.

Taking advantage of the post–World War II "vacuum of power" left by the decline of Western power and the resulting political instability in the Middle East, the theory held, the Soviets moved in: aligned themselves with the emerging radical, nationalist, and anti-colonialist forces in the area: and used the Arab-Israeli conflict as a means of "penetrating" the Middle East. The overall Soviet goals were supposedly to eliminate Western influence, establish Moscow as the dominant power in the area, threaten vital Western communications and sea routes, "outflank" NATO, gain a stranglehold on Middle Eastern oil, and thereby put severe pressure on Western Europe, Japan, and perhaps the United States itself.

In his memoirs, Lyndon Johnson, reflecting the basic viewpoint of every postwar American president from Harry Truman through Ronald Reagan (with the partial exception of Jimmy Carter) put it this way:

> The Soviets used Arab hostility toward Israel . . . to push moderate Arab states toward a more radical course and to provide a Middle East base for expanding its role in the Mediterranean, in Africa, and the areas bordering on the Indian Ocean. . . . The expanding Soviet presence in this strategic region threatened our position in Europe. . . . If they gained control of the areas, the oil and the air space of the vast arc between Morocco and Israel . . . would have been endangered.[2]

The second explanation, common among academic specialists, was that Soviet expansionism was cautious, pragmatic, and to a considerable extent reactive rather than planned. On the one hand, it was typically argued, the Soviets recognized the value of the Arab-Israeli conflict to their goals of eliminating Western influence and expanding their own. On the other hand, after the 1967 war the Soviets also feared the potential of Arab-Israeli wars to precipitate unwanted confrontations with the United States. Therefore, while Moscow took advantage of targets of opportunity when they presented themselves and sought to "probe for soft spots" in the Middle East, it avoided direct attacks on vital Western interests. Its preferred scenario for the Arab-Israeli conflict was to "keep the pot boiling" while ensuring that it didn't boil over, so as to maintain a prolonged state of tension that opened the door to Soviet "penetration" of the Middle East.[3]

The third theory of Soviet behavior—and the one that is most consistent with the evidence and the historical perspective made possible by the passage of time and the end of the Cold War—is that it was best explained in terms other than expansionist objectives, whether motivated by ideological/revolutionary goals or those of traditional Russian imperialism, whether planned or reactive, whether reckless or cautious. Rather, all actual Soviet behavior in the Middle East during the Cold War was best explained as a combination of traditional defensive concerns, the ongoing dynamic of the Cold War or geostrategic rivalry between the United States and the Soviet Union, and Soviet aspirations to be recognized as a superpower equal in influence and prestige to the United States.[4]

Several Soviet objectives were essentially defensive. First, Russia—that is, not just the Soviet Union—had long been concerned with the safety of its southern flank along the 1,800-mile border it shared with the Middle East. In particular, Nikita Khrushchev told Nasser—not implausibly, in light of Western policies—that Soviet policies were designed to prevent "capitalist encirclement" of the Soviet Union.[5] According to Harold Saunders, a former high State Department official specializing in the Arab-Israeli conflict, "The Soviets since the early 1950s had felt threatened by what they saw as a U.S. network of relationships in the Middle East intended to encircle the Soviet Union, contain its influence, and deny it an active presence."[6]

Second, the Soviet Union—again, like Russia before it—sought to secure access to the Mediterranean through the Black Sea and the Straits of the Dardanelles and to protect the sea lanes and lines of communications to Russia. In particular, the Soviets were deeply concerned with the deployment of American aircraft carriers and submarines in the Mediterranean that not only threatened the sea lanes but posed a direct nuclear threat to the Soviet homeland. Thus, the Soviet acquisition of land, sea, and air base rights in the Middle East after the early 1960s can be explained by a desire to monitor US naval forces, develop an anti-submarine warfare capability, and counter the American strategic threat.

Third, the Soviets were also clearly motivated by the desire to be accepted as a superpower equal to the United States: in 1977, Soviet premier Leonid Brezhnev said, "There is no problem anywhere that can be solved without the Soviet Union or in opposition to her." In that light, much Soviet behavior was similar to US behavior. In particular, the Soviet military presence in the Mideast played the same role as the US Mediterranean fleet in American policy—to show the flag, deter intervention against its clients by its superpower rival, and maintain the capability to intervene if necessary to protect a client state threatened by allies or proxies of its adversary.[7]

Finally, like the United States, the Soviets wanted access to Middle Eastern oil in the event that it could no longer produce enough oil at home—as opposed to seeking to seize the oil resources of the Middle East or otherwise deny the West access to them. As the Soviets frequently pointed out at the time, they needed only normal commercial relations for this purpose, not domination, let alone the exclusion of the West.[8] Indeed, in the 1950s Soviet leaders told a radical nationalist regime in Iraq that to avoid precipitating a war, it should reassure the West that it would not threaten its oil supplies.[9]

In light of the overwhelming historical evidence discussed throughout this chapter, Soviet behavior in the Middle East during the Cold War was quite inconsistent with the US government's view that Moscow sought to exploit the Arab-Israeli conflict so as to dominate the region. Rather, the Soviet role in the Arab-Israeli conflict is best explained not in terms of Soviet exploitation of a golden opportunity to expand but rather as a dangerous trap, a quagmire, into which the Soviets were reluctantly drawn and from which for years they sought to escape—provided their security, prestige, and credibility remained intact. The preferred Soviet solution for this predicament was a compromise political settlement of the conflict, presided over and guaranteed by the co-equal superpowers.

How the Soviet Union Was Drawn into the Arab-Israeli Conflict

The initial Soviet role in the Arab-Israeli conflict was one of active support for Israel. In 1948, the Soviet Union supported the creation of Israel, was the first state to recognize its independence, supported its admission into the United Nations, allowed substantial Jewish emigration to Israel from the Soviet Union and Eastern Europe, and, most important, provided Israel with arms through its proxy, Czechoslovakia. Most historians argue that Stalin's purposes in his early support of Israel were to diminish British influence in the Middle East (by supporting the Jewish revolt against British control of Palestine), to win friends in influential circles in the West, and to support a new state whose governing party—the Labor Party—often referred to itself as "socialist."

However, within several years, Soviet support for Israel ended. This shift in policy has been attributed by Soviet and Western scholars to a variety of factors: a rectification of a tactical mistake after Stalin realized he had alienated the Arabs, who were far more numerous and presumptively more powerful than the Israelis; displeasure at the pro-Zionist enthusiasm of Soviet Jewry; disappointment that Israel was clearly not becoming a "socialist" state; and Stalin's own growing anti-Semitism. Whatever role these factors may have played, however, surely at least as relevant was Israel's decision to shift from its initial foreign policy of neutrality in the Cold War to one of alliance with the West and, in particular, support of the United States in the Korean War.[10]

Consequently, by the early 1950s, Soviet support of Israel had ended, though it was not replaced by active support for the Arabs until after 1955. In the mainstream interpretations that guided US policies at the time, Soviet policies were responsible for introducing the Cold War into the Arab-Israeli conflict and creating potential superpower confrontations. However, the historical evidence strongly suggests that the converse is the case: it was the Cold War policies of Israel and United States that brought the Soviet Union into the Middle East and led it to support the Arabs in the Arab-Israeli conflict.

One of the first steps in this process was the Israeli decision to seek arms from the United States in early 1950; although Washington declined direct involvement, it helped facilitate the Israeli arms purchases from Britain and France. Several months later, Ben-Gurion decided to support the West in the Korean War and to abandon nonalignment. Both of these decisions provoked angry denunciation from the Soviet Union.[11]

Also of great importance in accounting for the Soviet shift was the Eisenhower administration's decision in the 1950s to actively extend the containment policy to the Middle East. In 1955, the administration decided to sponsor the "Baghdad Pact," an alliance between Britain, Turkey, Iraq, Iran, and Pakistan, to be organized, armed, and financed by the United States. In effect, the Baghdad Pact sought to extend NATO and the Western alliance system to the Middle East, completing a ring of pro-Western, American-armed states around the entire European, Middle Eastern, and southern Asian periphery of the Soviet Union.

Then, in January 1957, the administration announced what came to be known as "the Eisenhower Doctrine," under which America would provide economic and military assistance to any Middle Eastern state threatened by armed aggression from any state "controlled by international communism." Unsurprisingly, the Soviet Union considered the Baghdad Pact and the Eisenhower Doctrine to threaten its security; it officially stated that "the establishment of foreign military bases on the territory of the countries of the Near and Middle East has a direct bearing on the security of the USSR," and warned that it would be forced to take countermeasures.[12]

Before doing so, though, on several occasions in the mid-1950s, the Soviets proposed to the United States that the Middle East be neutralized and demilitarized by means of arms limitation agreements under which both superpowers would refrain from arming client governments.[13] The US government ignored the Soviet warnings and proposals—as it was repeatedly to do in the next thirty years—and proceeded with its plans to extend the containment doctrine into the Middle East.

The Baghdad Pact and Eisenhower Doctrine were aimed not only at the Soviet Union but also at Egypt under Gamal Abdel Nasser, who was leading the nationalist, anti-colonial, anti-Western revolutionary forces in the area and seeking to destabilize pro-Western governments. He was therefore regarded by the United States as an ally, if not a proxy, of international communism. Under the pact, British power, supported by the United States, would be reintroduced into the Middle East, Egypt would be isolated, and its most bitter Arab enemy, Iraq, then ruled by a pro-British monarch, would be strengthened.

In reaction, Nasser turned to the Soviet Union for military support—motivated, to be sure, not only by the threat posed by the Baghdad Pact but also by his conflict with Israel. The initiative for an Egyptian-Soviet military pact, then, came from Egypt rather than from the Soviet Union; Mohamed Heikal, Nasser's close confidant, writes that "the Soviets had been sucked into the Middle East by events. It was not they who had started [the alliance] . . . but Egypt, who had forced it upon them."[14]

After Nasser threatened to turn to the West if denied Soviet support, the Soviets abandoned their initial reluctance to join an alliance with Egypt and provide it with military assistance. Consequently, in 1955 the Soviets (again acting through their Czech proxy) began providing essentially defensive weapons to Egypt—mainly air defense systems and military advisors—while warning Nasser to avoid provoking a war with Israel that could escalate into a superpower confrontation.[15]

In sum, the growing Soviet influence in the Middle East during the 1950s was a consequence of the Israeli decision to abandon its earlier neutrality in the Cold War as well as of the US decision to extend the containment policy into the region and to provide political, economic, and military support for Israel. Regardless of whether those policies were on balance wise or not, there can be no question that they led the Arab world to seek its own superpower protector and arms supplier, while also providing the Soviets with the motive and opportunity to join forces with the Arabs in an essentially defensive reaction to growing US dominance of the Middle East and the extension of its military power to Russia's southern borders. In short, US and Israeli policies created a convergence of interests between the Soviet Union and Egypt, precipitated rather than contained Soviet interference in the Middle East, and resulted in the two superpowers becoming deeply involved in the Arab-Israeli conflict.

Soviet Proposals for Peace Settlements

From the mid-1950s through the early 1970s, the United States and the Soviet Union may have come close to direct military confrontations—in the 1956 Sinai war, the 1967 war, the 1970 Canal War, and the 1973 "Yom Kippur" war. Yet the historical record suggests that the Soviets were far more alarmed by this than was the United States, for from the 1950s onward they had made a series of serious proposals for an Arab-Israeli peace settlement that were ignored or rejected by the United States.

In 1956, following the Sinai war, the Soviets renewed their earlier proposals for mutual nonintervention in the internal affairs of Middle Eastern states, the renunciation of the use of force, abstention from the creation of conflicting alliances, and "a reciprocal refusal to deliver arms to Middle Eastern countries."[16] The United States refused to discuss the matter.

Then, in the spring of 1957, the Soviet Union suggested a great-power effort to impose peace in the Middle East, and six months later Soviet premier Khrushchev proposed that the Soviets, the United States, Britain, and France guarantee the existing Middle East borders as a basis for peace. Once again, the Eisenhower administration refused even to discuss the matter, telling its allies that it "strongly opposed" Soviet participation "in any way in the formulation of policy in Middle East matters."[17] The evident premise of the US government was that the Soviets had neither legitimate interests nor real power in the area and could therefore be safely ignored. The consequences were that both sides extended their commitments and arms supplies to their Middle East allies, thereby furthering the process of the Cold War polarization of the Arab-Israeli conflict.

From 1967 through 1973, the Soviets followed a dual-track policy in the Arab-Israeli conflict. The first track was the rebuilding of the Egyptian and Syrian armed forces so that they would be capable of deterring or resisting an Israeli attack while becoming strong enough to negotiate a political settlement of the conflict from a position of strength. On the other hand, the Arab states were denied the offensive military capabilities, especially surface-to-surface missiles and modern fighter bombers, that might tempt them into an attack on Israel, particularly within its pre-1967 borders. Harold Saunders, the leading Middle East expert on the National Security Council (NSC) at the time, wrote that "the Soviet Union was continuing its military assistance to its Arab clients, but was doing so with restraint in an effort to avoid actually encouraging its clients to attack Israel."[18]

Moreover, the Soviet advisors and technicians stationed in Egypt and Syria after 1967 retained operational control over the most highly advanced weapons and in other ways acted as a restraint on the indigenous military forces.[19] Indeed, inside accounts of the Egyptian-Soviet alliance discuss Nasser's and later Sadat's anger at Soviet reluctance to provide modern weapons, even for a limited war designed to put pressure on Israel in the occupied territories, let alone for a full-scale attack on the Israeli homeland itself.[20]

The second track of Soviet policy emphasized negotiation to settle the Arab-Israeli conflict. Even earlier, from the outset of their alliance with Egypt and Syria in the 1950s, the Soviets had refused to countenance the elimination of Israel and repeatedly had made that clear to Cairo and Damascus. For example, Khrushchev told Nasser that he must accept the fact that Israel exists rather than pursue the "wholly unreasonable goal" of trying to destroy it.[21] And as discussed earlier, during that period the Soviets made several proposals for the neutralization and demilitarization of the Middle East that were ignored by the West.

During the 1967 war, Soviet premier Alexei Kosygin warned the US government that if Israel did not end its advances in the Golan Heights, the Soviets would take military action. Lyndon Johnson then moved US warships closer to Syria, to signal that the United States would oppose any Soviet intervention—but at the same time he told the Soviets that the United States was pressing Israel to agree to a ceasefire, which in fact took place a few hours later, ending the crisis.

This possible superpower confrontation clearly impressed upon Moscow the necessity of a political settlement of the Arab-Israeli conflict. Following the war, a study of *Pravda's* reporting on Middle Eastern affairs showed that Soviet policy "unequivocally condemned Arab extremism." The study quoted *Pravda*, essentially an arm of the government: "Nobody in the world . . . [can agree to] the annihilation of the state of Israel."[22] And following the 1973 war, Abba Eban wrote that Soviet foreign minister Andrei Gromyko told him that the Soviet Union would "oppose with great force" anyone who sought to deny Israel's existence.[23]

Consequently, even as the Soviets moved to rebuild the Egyptian army, they began pressuring Nasser to accept the existence of Israel and to negotiate an end to the conflict. As a result of this renewed Soviet emphasis on political settlement and the resulting limitations on the arms it was willing to provide Egypt, the Soviet-Egyptian alliance was subject to severe strain, eventually leading to Sadat's decision to break with the Soviets in the early 1970s. As a result, the Soviets moved to maintain their Middle Eastern influence by strengthening their alliance with Syria and forming new ties with Iraq, Libya, South Yemen, and the PLO.

It is particularly instructive to review Soviet policies toward the PLO, which during the 1970s was committed to the destruction of Israel. After Sadat expelled the Soviet military advisors from Egypt in 1972, the Soviets began supporting Yasser Arafat's organization. However, from the outset the Soviets told the PLO that its call for the destruction of Israel was "unsound not only tactically but also as a matter of principle. . . . It is not permissible to talk about eliminating the State of Israel."[24] Consequently, the Soviets consistently opposed Palestinian terrorism and called upon Arafat and other Arab leaders to formally accept UN Resolution 242, which called for a peaceful settlement of the Arab-Israeli conflict.[25]

Superpower Negotiations after the 1967 War

For a brief period after the 1967 war, superpower policy appeared to be converging. Harold Saunders, who participated in the policy debates within the US government and the negotiations with the Soviets, wrote that "the Soviets were willing to support a negotiated peace settlement . . . while the United States for a moment that summer supported total Israeli withdrawal from all the territories occupied in the conflict."[26]

As a result, in the early fall of 1967, US and Soviet negotiators reached an agreement on the basic principles for a settlement, which would be negotiated under the auspices of the United Nations. In November 1967 these principles were adopted by the Security Council in UN Resolution 242, which in the international consensus has remained the basic framework for a peace settlement ever since. The resolution called for "the establishment of a just and lasting peace in the Middle East" based on (among others) the following principles: the withdrawal of Israeli forces from territories conquered in 1967; guarantees of "the territorial inviolability and political independence of every state in the area, through measures including the establishment of demilitarized zones"; freedom of navigation in international waterways; and an unspecified "just settlement of the refugee problem." The deliberately vague nature of this principle indicated that the Palestinian issue was to be treated only as a refugee problem rather than one of self-determination—there was no mention of the creation of a Palestinian state.

Alfred Atherton, a former State Department official who participated in the 1967 negotiations, has remarked that UN Resolution 242 represented "a clear-cut Soviet commitment to a settlement under which the Arabs would for the first time recognize Israel's right to exist."[27] Indeed, because 242 had treated the Palestinian issue only as "a refugee problem," it was an important bone of contention in the Soviet-PLO relationship for many years.

While the leading Arab states initially rejected 242, within a few years they—and the PLO—accepted it, first in principle and eventually officially. However, Israel, which for a brief period after the war had considered accepting the principle of "land for peace" by returning at least some of the occupied territories to Egypt, Syria, and Jordan, soon began the process of consolidating its political, military, and economic control of the occupied territories.

In January 1968, the Soviets presented their own peace plan to the United States and Israel. Based on UN Resolution 242, it called for a political settlement and the end of the war between Israel and the Arab states, an Israeli withdrawal from the occupied territories, the creation of demilitarized zones, and a resolution of the refugee problem.[28] Neither Israel nor the United States was interested in pursuing the Soviet proposal.

In late 1968, the Soviet Union resumed its diplomatic efforts to get a settlement, presenting a proposal to the incoming Nixon administration for the implementation of 242. The proposal sought to meet some of Israel's security concerns and made some concessions toward Israel's insistence on direct negotiations: it called for "contacts" among the belligerents to discuss the details of a settlement, again included provision for the creation of demilitarized zones along Israel's borders and the indefinite stationing of UN peacekeeping forces in those areas, and—perhaps most important—introduced the idea of a formal superpower guarantee of the settlement.[29]

In the next few months there were (in Harold Saunders's words) "persistent Soviet approaches to start a dialogue with the United States to try to advance mediation of an Arab-Israeli settlement."[30] Moscow made still further concessions: the Soviets would support direct negotiations between Israel and its adversaries; Israeli forces would not be required to withdraw from the occupied territories before an overall comprehensive settlement was in place; Palestinian refugees might be resettled with compensation in Arab countries rather than returned to Israel; and the Soviet Union would pressure its clients to accept this framework.[31]

The Nixon Administration and the Arab-Israeli Conflict

Whatever his well-documented anti-Semitic tendencies, on Israel Nixon was torn and often wavered. On the one hand, he often stated his admiration for Israeli anti-communism, "toughness," and military prowess. On the other hand, he sometimes became angry at Israeli intransigence and on several occasions told Kissinger that he was leaning toward responding favorably to the Soviet proposals that the two superpowers impose a comprehensive settlement of the Arab-Israeli conflict.[32]

Throughout his administration, Nixon vacillated on whether to emphasize containment or cooperation with the Soviet Union in the Middle East. William Quandt's explanation is that there was "an apparently unresolved debate within Nixon's mind" on the issue, and then adds, in an obvious capsule summary of what he thought of Kissinger's views, "By contrast, Kissinger had well-developed, *if not well-informed,* views on the Middle East."[33]

In his memoirs, Kissinger writes that after the 1973 war Nixon was convinced "that the Soviet Union and the United States should jointly use the end of the war to impose a comprehensive peace in the Middle East."[34] However, Kissinger continues, he talked him out of it, arguing that "we had never seen one shred of evidence that the Soviets were willing to separate themselves from the hard-line Arab program."[35] This statement, and others equally at variance with the clear evidence that it was false, suggests that the problem was not so much that Kissinger was poorly informed as that he was disingenuous, unwilling to modify his ideological rigidity regardless of the facts and the sustained efforts of the Soviet Union to act in concert with the United States. Whatever the explanation, the consequence was another lost opportunity to defuse the dangerous Cold War in the Middle East and perhaps even settle the Arab-Israeli conflict.

A number of other insider accounts confirm that the Nixon administration—like Nixon himself—was sharply divided on how to deal with the Arab-Israeli conflict in general, and the various Soviet peace proposals in particular.[36] The State Department, including the professionals specializing in the Arab-Israeli conflict and Secretary of State William Rogers, considered the Soviet proposals to be serious and accepted the unavoidability of a Soviet role in a political settlement. As noted, Kissinger emphatically did not: the Soviet position in his judgment "offered no hint of possible compromise," "amounted to blanket support of the hard-line Arabs," and as such was "an obvious nonstarter."[37]

Kissinger's remarkable dismissal of Soviet diplomacy, so at odds not only with the analysis of the State Department specialists but also with the historical record and the plain meaning of Soviet proposals, can only be understood in the context of his overall perspective on Soviet foreign policy. In his view, the Soviets were seizing on the Arab-Israeli conflict to drive the West from the Middle East; therefore, the "principal objective" of US policy was "to keep the Soviet military presence out of the Middle East and to reduce the Soviet political influence as much as possible."[38]

In contrast to Kissinger, Secretary of State William Rogers and high-level officials in the State Department wanted to explore the Soviet proposals. Kissinger allowed them to proceed but cynically admits that he had no intention of following through. Throughout 1969 there were eight months of intensive negotiations between Rogers and Anatoly Dobrynin, the long-term Soviet ambassador to the United States. The outcome of these efforts, in US diplomat David Korn's words, was "a comprehensive and detailed US proposal for a settlement of the Arab-Israeli conflict."[39] At the outset of the negotiations, there were considerable differences between the two sides, but by mid-1970 the Soviets had moved closer to the US position and agreed that there should be a US/Soviet-mediated Israeli-Egyptian agreement in which Egypt would have to accept the existence of Israel and end the state of war between them.

Encouraged by this progress, in December 1969 the secretary of state presented "the Rogers Plan" to Israel, Egypt, and the Soviet Union. The US proposal, based on UN Resolution 242, called for UN-mediated talks between Israel and Egypt to negotiate an agreement based on the following principles: the establishment of a timetable for the withdrawal of Israeli forces from Egyptian territory occupied in 1967; an official end to the state of war between Egypt and Israel; the establishment of secure and recognized borders; the creation of demilitarized zones along the frontier; Israeli freedom of navigation in the Strait of Tiran and the Suez Canal; a "fair settlement" of the refugee problem; and mutual recognition by Israel and Egypt of "each other's sovereignty, political independence, and the right to live in peace within secure boundaries free from threats of force."[40]

There was clearly a close similarity between the evolving Soviet position and the Rogers proposals, and Sadat—who took office after Nasser's death in September 1970—soon came to accept them. In March 1971 he agreed to a detailed UN plan that called for a settlement based on Israeli withdrawal from the Sinai, the establishment of demilitarized zones, the placement of a UN peacekeeping force in southern Sinai, and Israeli freedom of navigation.[41] Then in early 1973, writes Galia Golan, "even as he was planning military action, Sadat abandoned the partial withdrawal idea in favor of a peace agreement with Israel in exchange for a return of Egyptian territory.[42] Similarly, Quandt concludes that Egypt had accepted all of the UN proposals.[43] The State Department was impressed: Galia Golan writes that "the Americans concluded . . . that Sadat had offered Israel a bilateral peace agreement."[44]

Israel, however, continued to refuse to agree even to the principle of withdrawal to the pre-1967 war lines; indeed, in his memoirs, Yitzhak Rabin—then the Israeli ambassador to the United States—admits that he and the Israeli government set out to "launch [in the United States] a public, sharp, and unequivocal campaign against the Rogers Plan"; Rabin even told Kissinger that "I personally shall do everything within the bounds of American law to arouse public opinion against the administration's moves."[45] Rabinovich adds that "Israel reacted sharply, denounced the plan, and launched a massive campaign against it in the Jewish community and on Capitol Hill," which resulted in "Nixon using Kissinger and Rabin to send a back-channel message that he was not entirely supportive of the plan."[46]

Despite this remarkable Israeli intervention in the US policymaking process and its open efforts to sway public opinion, matters might have turned out differently if Nixon had agreed to join with the Soviets in pressuring both sides of the Arab-Israeli conflict. Quandt sums up the outcome, writing that Nixon often spoke to Kissinger "about the need to impose a settlement in concert with the Soviets . . . and was not reluctant to talk of pressuring Israel. But he was neither able nor determined to follow through on these sentiments."[47]

Aside from Nixon's continuing suspicions of Soviet policies and his weakening political position after Watergate, the most important reason that no agreement for joint superpower collaboration was reached was that Kissinger deliberately sabotaged—no other word will do—the negotiations, especially the Rogers Plan. The evidence for this is not in question, as is made clear by the four detailed insider accounts of Atherton, Saunders, Quandt, and Korn, as well as from an otherwise admiring biography of Kissinger.[48] Even more important, in Kissinger's own memoirs he candidly—cynically might be the better term—describes his strategy for undercutting the Rogers Plan by resorting to evasion, delay, and obfuscation, collaborating with Israel rather than pressing it to withdraw from the conquered territories in return for a peace agreement with Egypt. For example, at one point, when it appeared that a Soviet-American agreement could be reached, he reprimanded a State Department official who appeared to be taking the process too seriously: "I told Sisco in mid-February that we did not *want* a quick success."[49] The emphasis is Kissinger's.

The 1970 and 1973 Israeli-Egyptian Wars

With "the peace process" stalemated, in 1970 sporadic exchanges of artillery attacks between Israel and Egypt escalated into what became known as "the Canal War," or "the War of Attrition." In the early stages of the conflict the Soviets turned down Nasser's request for more weapons. By contrast, in September 1969 the United States delivered to Israel a large number of its most advanced jet fighter-bombers, which it then employed for deep penetration bombing raids against military and industrial targets in the Egyptian heartland, including the suburbs of Cairo—in the process, it has been estimated, killing some 10,000 Egyptian civilians.[50] In his book on the Canal War, Lawrence Whetten writes: "One of the major purposes of the raids, Defense Minister Moshe Dayan announced, was to bring home to the Egyptians their military vulnerability and inferiority, and thereby 'topple' Nasser."[51]

In the spring of 1970, Nasser went to Moscow to demand Soviet assistance, threatening otherwise to resign in favor of a new government that would turn from the Soviet Union to the United States.[52] Under these new circumstances the Soviets reluctantly agreed to provide anti-aircraft systems, advisors to operate them, and combat pilots to fly air defense missions in Egyptian planes; however, they continued to refuse to provide their most advanced fighter-bomber aircraft. Although the State Department considered that Israel's behavior was provocative and the Soviet actions clearly defensive, Kissinger dismissed the Soviet motivations as irrelevant, ignoring the many working-level US officials who warned that the Israeli raids were likely to lead to a Soviet response, as Soviet officials were repeatedly warning.[53]

In Kissinger's judgment, the Soviet actions, whatever had precipitated them, "represented a strategic threat that had to be dealt with." The Soviets were using their military presence "to enhance [their] geopolitical influence"—presumably unlike the United States—and therefore had to be "expelled" from the Middle East.[54]

In effect, the Nixon administration simply dismissed the possibility that the Soviets saw themselves as responding to an escalation by the United States and its client, Israel. Rather, the administration saw the increased Soviet military commitment to Egypt as a geopolitical "challenge," to which the United States had to respond.[55] Quandt writes that Nixon and Kissinger not only rebuffed the Soviet bid for cooperation but seized upon the events to "stand up" to Moscow.[56] Consequently, the administration sent more offensive weapons to Israel, while the Soviets continued to furnish only defensive ones to Egypt.[57]

The continuing US arms flow to Israel eliminated any remaining Israeli government incentive to negotiate on the basis of the Rogers Plan principles. Together with Nixon's wavering and inconsistency and Kissinger's adamant opposition to a negotiated settlement that preserved the Soviet role in the Middle East, the best opportunity to have settled the Arab-Israeli conflict some fifty years ago was doomed.[58]

In the late summer of 1970 the United States mediated a ceasefire of the Canal War, which was proving increasingly costly to both Israel and Egypt and which had precipitated several clashes between Israeli pilots and Soviet pilots flying Egyptian aircraft. The Soviet Union then resumed its efforts for a negotiated settlement and continued to deny Egypt military support for a resumption of the war, even though Israel remained adamant and the United States accelerated its delivery of advanced attack aircraft to Israel.[59] In 1971 Soviet officials secretly met with Israeli officials and offered to resume diplomatic relations and guarantee its security in the context of a general settlement based on the restoration of the pre-1967 boundaries. Israel was not interested.[60]

As well, the Nixon administration continued to resist any compromise settlement that was rejected by Israel—which it regarded as a major US "strategic asset" in the Middle East—or that preserved a Soviet role. Nonetheless, the Soviets persisted, and in a May 1972 summit conference Brezhnev warned Nixon and Kissinger of the dangers of a new Arab-Israeli war and urgently called for joint superpower negotiations.[61]

At the conference, Kissinger and Soviet foreign minister Andrei Gromyko agreed upon "general working principles" for an overall negotiated peace settlement: the gradual withdrawal of Israeli forces from the 1967 conquests; security measures, including the establishment of demilitarized zones; the deployment of UN forces at Sharm al-Sheikh; international guarantees with the participation of the United States and the Soviet Union; freedom of Israeli navigation through the Suez Canal and the Strait of Tiran; and a Soviet call for an unspecified "just settlement" of the Palestinian refugee issue.[62] The principles included another Soviet concession to the US and Israeli positions: border rectifications between Israel and its neighbors were possible, it stated, thus omitting the previous qualification that they were to be "minor." In other words, the Soviets were no longer calling for total Israeli withdrawal.

The apparent agreement between Kissinger and Gromyko persuaded the Soviets not to provide further arms to Egypt, which in turn led Sadat to expel the military advisors in an effort to assuage US concerns about Soviet expansionism and induce the Nixon administration to press Israel to agree to the summit principles.[63] However, neither the Soviet concessions or Sadat's actions had any effect on actual US policies—despite Kissinger's private assessment: "You know that the Russians showed restraint; that is why Sadat kicked them out."[64]

As one scholar wrote, "Sadat's expulsion of the Soviets was seen in the United States as the major payoff of a policy of close support for Israel rather than as a possible ground for changing that policy."[65] And instead of exploring the significance of the Soviet concessions, Kissinger simply dismissed them, explaining, "I have never understood why Gromyko accepted them [the new working principles], unless it was exhaustion. . . . In all events, the principles quickly found their way into the overcrowded limbo of aborted Middle East schemes—*as I had intended*."[66]

Just to make sure we don't miss the point, Kissinger adds: "The US-Soviet dialogue on the Middle East remained in abeyance, which was where we wanted it."[67]

The 1973 War

Until the 1973 war, Israel and the United States ignored all indications of both Soviet and Egyptian flexibility. Israel was convinced that the Arabs had no military option and that the diplomatic stalemate worked in its favor, allowing it to "create facts on the ground" by incorporating the Sinai peninsula and the Golan Heights, de facto or formally, into its territory. This policy was supported by the US government, which, despite Nixon's occasional but short-lived interest in cooperating with the Soviet Union to impose a peace settlement, generally shared the Israeli view of the desirability and viability of the status quo. Additionally, the administration's policies were motivated by its view that Israel should not be excessively pressured.

As a result, Egypt and Syria decided to force Israel into negotiations by going to war—but a highly limited war, to be confined to attacks on Israeli military positions in the Sinai and the Golan Heights, in an effort to break the political deadlock and convince Israel that its real security required that it withdraw from the occupied territories.[68]

Neither country, then, had the intention of invading the Israeli homeland; not only did they know that they lacked the military capability to do so but they fully realized that even such a "success" might lead to the Israeli use of nuclear weapons. As noted earlier, in 1969 Nasser had told Qaddafi of Libya that the Arabs could not seek to liquidate Israel because neither superpower would allow it and because Israel almost certainly had nuclear weapons which it would use in such a situation.[69]

In 2017, Israeli historian Dan Sagir wrote that it was clear that Sadat's goals were quite limited: "to break the diplomatic deadlock and draw Israel and the United States into negotiations over Sinai," but to stop well short of appearing to threaten Israel itself. According to high Israeli officials who met with Sadat during his historic November 1977 visit to Israel, Sagir wrote, the Egyptian president told them that Israel's nuclear capability was one of the factors behind his decision to seek a peace settlement. When asked by one Israeli official why he had ordered the Egyptian forces to advance only part way into the Sinai, some 150 miles short of the Israeli border, he answered: "You have nuclear arms. Haven't you heard?"[70]

The Egyptian goal, then, was to cross the Suez Canal, establish its forces on its east bank, advance toward the mountain passes in the Sinai about thirty miles east of the canal, and then stop, judging that once it became clear that Egypt had no intention of threatening the Israeli homeland, the Israeli government would refrain from using nuclear weapons. At the same time, Sadat hoped, the shock of the initial Egyptian military success would force Israel to start negotiations for an overall political settlement.[71]

And he was right, for despite the fact that after their initial military victories the Egyptian army was thrown back across the canal, the Egyptian strategy succeeded: the war was a political success for it did indeed result in a major shock to Israel.

To be sure, it had been a highly dangerous strategy, for as one analyst has written, "At one point [it caused] . . . a teary-eyed Moshe Dayan to predict 'the destruction of the third temple'"[72] and to propose to the Israeli cabinet that Israel start preparing its nuclear weapons and perhaps even somehow "demonstrate" them. Fortunately, Dayan's proposal was rejected by Prime Minister Golda Meir and other high Israeli officials,[73] and once the war was over the Israeli government decided to enter into the long negotiating process that finally resulted in the 1979 Israeli-Egyptian political settlement. In hindsight, even Henry Kissinger came to admire Sadat's strategies, writing that it was an act of statesmanship, one of the few wars "fought to lay the basis for moderation in its aftermath."[74]

Syria's political goals and military actions in the war were also carefully limited. In the opening days of the 1973 war, the Syrian army quickly seized the thinly defended Golan Heights—Israeli forces were then mainly deployed in the Sinai—and were then in a position to invade Israel's Jordan valley and Galilee area. However, even before Israeli reinforcements turned the tide, the Syrian forces stopped at the border; it was later revealed that Assad, fearing a nuclear response by Israel, had issued strict orders to the army leaders that they were not to cross into Israel.[75]

The Superpowers and the 1973 War

The Soviet Union, fearful of being drawn into a confrontation with the United States, had warned both Sadat and Assad not to go to war against Israel, although acknowledging that it could not prevent them from doing so. Of course, the Soviets might have ended their support of Egypt and Syria unless they agreed to the Soviet position, but that would have probably failed and resulted only in a major humiliation and defeat in its Cold War competition with the United States throughout the Middle East.[76]

In a last-ditch effort to save détente and avoid a confrontation with the United States, on September 28, 1973, one week before the outbreak of the war, Soviet foreign secretary Andrei Gromyko met with Nixon and Kissinger in the White House. While not wanting to betray the Soviet allies by telling the United States—and, therefore, Israel as well—about the impending attack, Gromyko hinted at it: "We have a different assessment [from you] of the danger because we feel the possibility could not be excluded that we could all wake up one day [and find that] . . . there is a real conflagration in that area. . . . Is it worth the risk?" As the Israeli journalist who broke the story (based on declassified US documents) concludes: "Nixon and Kissinger failed to take Gromyko's hint, and did not hasten to prevent the war that broke out on October 6."[77]

Still, the Soviets persisted in seeking to join with the United States in an effort to stop the war. On the eve of the war, the Soviets sent another message to the Nixon administration: "We repeatedly pointed in the past to the dangerous situation in that area. . . . We hope to contact you again for possible coordination of positions."[78] Simultaneously, they evacuated their military advisors from Egypt and Syria, and ordered their warships to depart from Egyptian ports, a measure designed to send a message both to the Egyptians and the US government that they wanted no part of a new war.[79]

After the war broke out, while Brezhnev agreed to resupply his allies with small arms and ammunition,[80] the main Soviet effort was to bring about a ceasefire before Egypt and Syria suffered yet another major defeat in its conflicts with Israel.

In the first few days of the war, the Israeli forces suffered heavy losses in men and equipment, resulting in urgent Israeli government requests that the United States institute an emergency airlift to replace the losses. For a few days, Nixon considered delaying a response, in the hope that he could use the new US leverage to pressure Israel into accepting a negotiated peace settlement.[81] On October 9, the fifth day of the war, Nixon and Kissinger met to discuss what to do. Kissinger, who by this time was essentially running US policy as Nixon was fixated on avoiding impeachment, evidently was ambivalent on what to do. On the one hand, declassified US records reveal that in an October 18 phone call with Soviet ambassador Anatoly Dobrynin, Kissinger said, "My nightmare is a victory for either side," and Dobrynin agreed, saying, "It is not only your nightmare."[82]

On the other hand, though, Kissinger told Nixon that it would be a good thing for subsequent peace negotiations if the Israelis "clobbered" the Egyptians. Nixon then acceded to Kissinger's shifting views and authorized a US arms airlift to Israel;

yet, at the same time, Nixon said to Kissinger, "We've got to squeeze the Israelis when this is over. . . . We've got to squeeze them goddamn hard. And that's the way it is going to be done."[83]

But, it turned out that it wasn't.

The American airlift and other factors turned the tide, and by the end of the war Israeli forces had driven the Syrians off the Golan Heights and had advanced to within ten miles of Damascus; at the same time an Israeli tank column, commanded by Ariel Sharon, crossed the Suez Canal, swept aside Egyptian resistance, and was within forty miles of Cairo.

On October 24, an alarmed Brezhnev—perhaps reevaluating the Soviet stakes if the Israelis continued their advances toward Cairo and Damascus—sent an urgent message to Nixon, proposing joint superpower action to enforce a ceasefire but also warning him: "I'll say it straight. If you find it impossible to act jointly with us in this matter we should be faced with the necessity urgently to consider the question of taking appropriate steps unilaterally."[84]

Three Soviet divisions were then placed on alert and a naval force was dispatched to Egypt. Responding to the Soviet threats and troop movements, Nixon and Kissinger then told Brezhnev that they accepted the need for a ceasefire—but that "any Soviet military intervention—regardless of pretext—would be met with American force."[85]

Throughout the war, Kissinger had played a double game. Before the Soviet threats, Benny Morris writes, Kissinger had "virtually egged the Israelis on," even approving their intention to shell the outskirts of Damascus.[86] Kissinger's memoirs make it clear that even after a ceasefire had gone into effect, he privately told the Israelis that he would not complain if they continued to advance awhile longer; indeed he admits—boasts?—that the Soviets understandably "felt tricked by Israel and by us, as the Israelis moved to strangle the [Egyptian] army after the ceasefire."[87] In private, Nixon admitted that the Soviets "had a pretty good beef" about US policies, because his government had been "stringing them along."[88]

Finally, however, Kissinger decided that it would be too risky to continue encouraging the Israelis to keep on with their advances, telling them that "there's a limit beyond which we can't go and one of them is we cannot make Brezhnev look like an idiot." In that case, he warned Israel, the Soviets might have no choice but to send in forces in order to prevent the destruction of the Egyptian army on both sides of the canal.[89] Therefore, Quandt writes, Kissinger told Israel "in no uncertain terms that it must not destroy the surrounded Egyptian army."[90]

Early Postwar Negotiations: More Lost Opportunities for Peace

Following the 1973 war, US-Soviet negotiations were resumed. At the end of the year, each side seemed to make concessions: the Soviets agreed that negotiations would precede Israeli withdrawal and the United States agreed that the Soviets would be equally involved in the Middle East diplomatic process.[91] In fact, as Kissinger admits in his memoirs, Nixon initially was serious about cooperating with the Soviets to impose a settlement, even writing to Kissinger that he was "prepared to pressure the Israelis to the extent required, regardless of the domestic political consequences."[92] However, as he makes clear, Kissinger had no intention of honoring the pledges made to the Soviets, and he evidently talked Nixon out of proceeding as he had described.

To be sure, publicly the United States committed itself to a multilateral approach through an international Geneva Conference to convene at the end of 1973. In his account of this period, Kissinger writes that "Soviet cooperation was necessary to convene Geneva; afterward, we would seek to reduce its role to a minimum. The peace conference could soothe Moscow's nerves."[93]

Moscow was not very "soothed," though, and bitterly complained of its exclusion from the diplomatic process, a clear violation of the 1972 summit conference agreements stipulating that Mideast negotiations would proceed under joint US-Soviet auspices. Harold Saunders wrote: "That subsequent U.S. unilateral mediation denied the Soviets even the appearance of equal involvement remains a source of deep Soviet bitterness over the possibility of cooperation."[94]

The Soviet complaints, Kissinger cheerfully admits, were "perfectly true." The United States took advantage of détente, he continues, to exclude the Soviets: "Our strategy sought to reduce the Soviet role in the Middle East because our respective interests in the area . . . could not be reconciled, at least as long as the Soviet Union identified itself only with a maximum Arab program and did nothing to induce compromise on the part of its clients."[95]

As a result of Kissinger's policies and misrepresentation of the Soviet position (which hardly could be characterized as wedded to "the maximum Arab program," even in his own often stated view inside the US government), together with Nixon's ambivalence about cooperating with the Soviets, the early 1970s became a tragedy of lost opportunities, first to avoid the 1973 war and, that failing, to use the war to bring about a comprehensive settlement of the Arab-Israeli conflict.

To be sure, Kissinger did successfully preside over the Israeli-Egyptian-Syrian negotiations that resulted in the disengagement-of-forces agreements in the Sinai and the Golan Heights, and paved the way for the later Israeli-Egyptian peace settlement. Nevertheless, the step-by-step diplomatic approach favored by Kissinger quickly ran out of steam, for it stopped well short of dealing with the central issues in the conflict, particularly the Palestinian issue. An important 2012 book, coauthored by three former high US diplomats and two leading academic scholars, concluded that because the United States failed to use the opportunity to press for a comprehensive peace settlement, the opportunity for a comprehensive settlement had been lost.[96]

The Ford Administration and the Arab-Israeli Conflict: August 1974–January 1977

Between the end of the October 1973 war and his resignation in autumn 1974, Nixon allowed Kissinger to dominate American policy and to ensure that there would be no US cooperation with the Soviet Union or significant pressures on Israel. In Kissinger's memoirs he writes that in his last days in office Nixon ordered him to "cut off all military deliveries to Israel until it agreed to a comprehensive peace," a step he regretted not having done earlier."[97] Kissinger, of course, did not want to do so, but since Nixon did not return to the subject, he writes, "the relevant papers were prepared but never signed."[98] A few days later President Gerald Ford reversed the order.

Even so, Ford and even Kissinger (now Ford's secretary of state) were increasingly worried that Israeli intransigence was jeopardizing US national interests in the Middle East. Accordingly, in April 1975 Kissinger instituted a US policy review, consulting with the past and present US foreign policy "establishment"—Dean Rusk, McGeorge Bundy, George Ball, Cyrus Vance, Robert McNamara, and other eminences—as well with US ambassadors in the Middle East, his closest aides, and leading academics. The overwhelming consensus of the participants was that (in Quandt's words), "The time for step-by-step diplomacy was past. . . . The Palestinians could no longer be ignored. The Soviets would have to be brought into the negotiations."[99]

Ford and Kissinger were initially cool to these recommendations, distrusting Soviet intentions and fearing a congressional and public backlash if the United States angered the Israeli government. Nonetheless, in the ensuing months they became increasingly angry at the Rabin government's intransigent policies, fearing that if Israel blocked an attainable peace settlement, US interests in the Middle East would be jeopardized. Kissinger now concluded that "step-by-step is dead. We have to consider whether we and the Soviet Union shouldn't make a global approach." Ford appeared to agree, declaring he was now willing to confront the Israelis: "I have no hesitancy to bite the bullet," he told Kissinger.[100]

Accordingly, in a surprisingly strong letter, Ford told Rabin of his "deep disappointment over the position taken by Israel . . . [which would] have far-reaching effects in the area and our relations." As a result, Ford continued, he had ordered "an immediate reassessment of US policy in the area, including our relations with Israel, with a view to assuring that the overall interests of America in the Middle East and globally will be protected."[101]

The threatened "reassessment," however, was stillborn. The Israeli government did not budge, and in the familiar scenario that would be repeated in the future, Rabin mobilized his allies in the US Congress, media, and Jewish community. As a result, two months later a bipartisan group of seventy-six senators wrote to Ford, demanding that there should be no change in US policies. Israel was "a most reliable barrier to the domination of the area by outside parties," the statement said, so it was "imperative that we not permit the military balance to shift against Israel." Therefore, US military assistance to Israel should not be used as leverage, and the administration should be "responsive to Israel's urgent military and economic needs."[102]

The administration capitulated. There would be no changes in US policies toward Israel, and American diplomacy and leverage would be employed only to support limited bilateral deals and partial Israeli withdrawals from the occupied territories, rather than a comprehensive settlement of the conflict. As well, Ford and Kissinger agreed to pay the price that Israel was demanding as a condition for its agreement to partially withdraw from the Sinai: increased military and economic assistance, no US talks with the PLO, a guarantee that the United States would make up any loss of Israeli oil supplies from Arab lands, and a commitment to "make every effort to coordinate with Israel its proposals" and "refrain from putting forth peace plans that Israel would consider unsatisfactory."[103]

The Carter Administration and the Final Cold War Lost Opportunity for Middle East Peace

Despite his anger at what he regarded—correctly—as Israeli intransigence, for moral and religious reasons President Jimmy Carter was deeply committed to protecting the survival, security, and genuine well-being of Israel.

After his presidency, Carter wrote several books describing his commitment to Israel. For example, in his memoirs he wrote:

> In my affinity for Israel I shared the sentiment of most other Southern Baptists. . . . The Judeo-Christian ethic and study of the Bible were bonds between Jews and Christians which have always been part of my life. I also believed very deeply that the Jews who had survived the Holocaust deserved their own nation. . . . I considered this homeland for the Jews to be compatible with the teachings of the Bible, hence ordained by God. These moral and religious beliefs made my commitment to the security of Israel unshakable.[104]

Similarly, in *Palestine Peace Not Apartheid* Carter repeatedly emphasizes his sympathy for Jewish people who, because of their historical persecution and "horrible suffering," have the right and need for a secure state of their own.

Nonetheless, because of his criticism of Israeli policies toward the Palestinians, Carter was frequently accused of being "anti-Semitic." However, a number of leading Israeli officials and writers, themselves highly critical of Israeli policies, wrote that

Carter was not only right but was only saying what Jewish and Israeli critics themselves were saying.[105]

In particular, in a column reviewing *Palestine Peace Not Apartheid*—pointedly entitled "Memoir of a Great Friend"—Tom Segev wrote:

> An Israeli reader won't find anything more in the book than is written in the newspapers here every day. . . . The principal argument is well-founded and backed up by reports from B'Tselem, Peace Now, Israeli newspapers and . . . the *New York Times*. . . . Like many others, Carter points out that the ongoing and systematic violation of the Palestinians' human rights [and] the injustices of the oppression perpetuate the conflict.[106]

In 2009, the Israeli foreign affairs correspondent Akiva Eldar told Carter: "You often sound like you're more concerned about the future of Israel as a Jewish and democratic state than many Israelis." Carter responded:

> I'm deeply concerned about it. I would say that the top priority in my life for international affairs in the last 30 years has been to see Israel as a Jewish state living in security and peace. That's a number-one priority that I have in my life. I've known the history of the Jewish people, the Hebrew people, the Israelites. . . . I'm deeply committed as a Christian to seeing the covenant with Abraham fulfilled.[107]

By mid-1975 it was clear that the incremental step-by-step approach to an Arab-Israeli peace settlement was running out of steam. In November, Harold Saunders told a congressional committee that the Palestinian issue was at the heart of the overall Arab-Israeli conflict and said that the "legitimate interest of the Palestinians must be taken into account in the negotiations of an Arab-Israeli peace."[108] The process of reevaluating the best path to a peace settlement continued when in December 1975, the Brookings Institution published a major study of the Arab-Israeli conflict that attracted wide attention: it called for an Israeli withdrawal to its pre-1967 territory and borders, the creation of a Palestinian state in the West Bank and Gaza, and an Arab state commitment to end its conflict with Israel.

Among the authors of the prestigious report were Zbigniew Brzezinski, who a year later became Carter's national security advisor, and William Quandt, who became the lead Middle East member of the National Security Council. Itamar Rabinovich, a former Israeli ambassador to the United States, later wrote that the Brookings report "was effectively adopted as a blueprint for Carter's Middle East policy."[109]

As well, Carter's secretary of state, Cyrus Vance, agreed with the argument of the Brookings report, in his memoirs writing that "as a practical matter the Soviet Union, with political interests in the region and as a patron of several Arab states, should be accorded a role in negotiations that would help to dissuade it from undermining our efforts."[110] The prospects looked encouraging; in 1975 Soviet foreign secretary Andrei Gromyko reiterated his government's policy: "Israel may get, if she desires, the strictest guarantees with the participation—under an appropriate agreement—of the Soviet Union."[111] Then, in October 1976, Leonid Brezhnev reaffirmed the Soviet aim of seeking a settlement based on the principles of UN Resolution 242 and the Rogers Plan.

As a result, Vance and Gromyko entered into negotiations that culminated in the Joint Soviet-US Communique of October 1, 1977, which called for convening a new international Geneva peace conference, co-chaired by the superpowers, to negotiate a comprehensive settlement of the conflict. The main principles governing the settlement would be these:

1. The "termination of the state of war and establishment of normal peaceful relations on the basis of mutual recognition of the principles of sovereignty, territorial integrity, and political independence."
2. The withdrawal of Israeli forces from "territories"—that is, not necessarily *all* the territories—occupied in the 1967 war.
3. "The establishment of demilitarized zones and the agreed stationing in them of U.N. troops or observers."
4. International guarantees of the borders, with the participation of the United States ("subject to its constitutional processes") and the Soviet Union.
5. The resolution of "the Palestinian question" in consultation with "representatives of the Palestinian people," in a manner that would "insure the legitimate rights of the Palestinian people." Importantly, this formulation did not specify the nature of the "rights" of the Palestinians, did not include any recognition of the PLO as the sole legitimate representative of the Palestinians, and said nothing about the creation of an independent Palestinian state.[112] Even so, under pressure from the Soviets, Arafat and the PLO accepted the declaration as a basis for negotiations with Israel.[113]

As a number of observers of the 1977 joint statement pointed out at the time, the Soviets made most of the compromises, and the principles were essentially a victory for the Carter administration. Yet even this final effort at a superpower-mediated comprehensive settlement failed because Jimmy Carter—not the Soviets—backed away from it.

There were several reasons. First, the Israelis were strongly negative; in fact, it was reported that Defense Minister Moshe Dayan "threatened to mount a campaign within the United States" if Carter pressured Israel.[114] As a result, Carter decided not to use American economic and military aid to pressure Israel. The consequence, George Ball later wrote, was that "the United States unilaterally discarded practically all of its leverage with Jerusalem."[115]

Second, most Arab states were unenthusiastic about a superpower-imposed, or even-mediated, political settlement. Most important, Sadat's November 1977 decision to seek a separate peace with Israel and rely solely on the United States to reach such a bilateral settlement was the kiss of death to prospects of a comprehensive settlement. Thereafter, Carter focused his diplomacy on bringing about a separate Israeli-Egyptian peace.

The third reason for the shift in Carter's policies was that his administration, particularly Brzezinski, increasingly soured on Soviet policies, especially after the Soviet invasion of Afghanistan in late 1979, which not only made pursuing common policies with the Soviets politically impossible but also led to a radical change in Carter's attitudes. "The scales have fallen from my eyes," he famously said.

Thus, in the last two years of the Carter administration the Cold War intensified, leading the administration to return to traditional US policies of basing its Middle East policies on the resistance to "Soviet expansionism." With the inauguration of the Reagan administration and its single-minded emphasis on strengthening the anti-Soviet "strategic partnership" between Israel and the United States, the comprehensive approach came to an end.

Conclusions

During the mid-1970s there were several opportunities to have ended the Arab-Israeli conflict by a peace settlement mediated or even, if necessary, imposed by the superpowers, acting collaboratively. Tragically, the opportunities were squandered, largely because of Israeli intransigence, Henry Kissinger's cynicism and deceitfulness, and American Cold War ideological rigidity.

Throughout this period, Soviet behavior in the Middle East belied the premises on which American policy was based, for there was little evidence that the USSR was following a strategy of expansionism, aggression, or support of indigenous communist groups. Rather, it was seeking regional influence, leverage, and allies—just like the United States. Put differently, like the United States, it was playing the "game of nations" as for centuries it had been played in the Middle East by self-proclaimed great powers.[116]

Even so, the Soviets played the game quite cautiously. For over forty years of involvement in the region, they had provided little support for indigenous communism or revolution, and there had been no direct Soviet military intervention. Even the threat of intervention was rare, coming in the context of the 1956, 1967, and 1973 Arab-Israeli wars, when it appeared that Israeli military successes would endanger the regimes—and perhaps the capitals—of Egypt and Syria, the Soviet Union's major allies in the Middle East. Finally, the Soviets consistently refused to provide the quantity and quality of offensive weapons that might have tempted their allies into attacking Israel, and they used their political influence—not always successfully—to dissuade them from initiating even limited wars designed to regain the territories they had lost in the 1967 war.

Nor was it persuasive that the Soviets sought "to keep the pot boiling" in the Arab-Israeli conflict or to continue a situation of no war, no peace, in order to expand their influence in the Middle East. On the contrary, because of their fear that the conflict could get out of hand and precipitate a superpower confrontation, the Soviets consistently sought to insulate the Middle East from the Cold War and, that failing, to end the conflict by a compromise political settlement.

To be sure, the Soviets were not willing to withdraw from the region and accede to US domination of the Middle East. Motivated by defensive concerns about the security of their southern borders, the drive to achieve recognition as a superpower equal to the United States, and concern about their "credibility"—like the United States in Vietnam—the Soviets supported only those settlement plans in which they would retain their influence in the Middle East, preferably through a co-equal guarantor's role with the United States. Thus they successfully defeated American efforts to exclude them by finding allies—at different times Egypt, Syria, Iraq, Libya, and the PLO—eager to obtain diplomatic, economic, and military assistance.

In sum, even at the height of the Cold War and of Soviet influence in the Middle East, it was the strategic alliance of the United States with Israel that facilitated rather than contained Soviet "penetration"—a word never used to describe the far more extensive US activities in the area—for it gave the Soviets both the motive and the opportunity to acquire allies in the region, in an essentially defensive and reactive effort to balance US influence.

As a consequence of Israeli intransigence and US Cold War ideology, the best opportunity to have reached a comprehensive settlement of the Arab-Israeli conflict, and one that would have ended the danger of escalating into a much wider war, was permanently squandered. Ever since, the tragic consequences of that failure, especially for the Palestinian people, have continued to unfold.

10

Peace with Egypt and Jordan

Egypt

From 1947 onward, Egypt sought to avoid wars with Israel and presented a number of compromise peace offers that persuaded many high Zionist and Israeli officials that they should enter into bilateral peace negotiations.

Before the 1948 war, King Farouk secretly told Israeli diplomats that he would not participate in the Arab attack if Israel allowed Egypt to maintain its control over parts of Gaza and a small strip of the Negev Desert. Foreign Minister Moshe Sharett and other high Zionist leaders favored negotiations on this basis, but they were overruled by David Ben-Gurion.

Had Israel accepted the Egyptian overtures before the war, almost certainly there would have been no 1948 war, for in the absence of the Arab world's largest army, the other Arab states were highly unlikely to have attacked Israel, especially because they were willing to commit only a small number of their military forces to such a war.

During the war Egypt again sent peace feelers to Israel proposing an end to the fighting, followed by a negotiated peace settlement in which Egypt would agree to accept the existence of Israel and refrain from further action against it, if Israel would allow Egypt to retain its small territorial gains in the Negev.

Once again, Sharett and other Israeli leaders favored negotiations to explore the Egyptian proposals, but Ben-Gurion dismissed them outright and ordered Israeli forces to break the UN-mediated ceasefire agreements and seize the Negev and parts of the Sinai that had been allocated by the partition plan to the Arabs.

King Farouk clearly wished to withdraw from the overall Arab-Israeli conflict, provided his territorial conditions were accepted. Had Israel agreed, not only would the war have quickly ended but the subsequent Israeli-Egyptian wars of 1956, 1967, and 1973 would almost certainly have been avoided.

- During the early 1950s, Israel repeatedly sought to provoke Egypt into wars that would provide the pretext and the opportunity to realize traditional Zionist expansionist goals.

- In 1956, Israel collaborated with Britain and France in launching an expansionist war against Egypt.
- In 1965, as the 1967 war approached, Nasser sent out another secret peace feeler, asking for a high-level meeting to discuss the situation. Israel turned it down.[1]
- At the end of 1965, Nasser tried again, inviting the head of Israel's Mossad to meet secretly with the deputy commander of the Egyptian armed forces (and a close friend of the Egyptian leader) to explore the possibility of de-escalating the Israeli-Egyptian conflict. Prime Minister Levi Eshkol favored allowing the visit and told the American government about it. Other high-level Israeli officials, however, opposed it, warning that it was "a trap," so the Egyptian initiative was turned down.[2]
- Israel, not Egypt, initiated the 1967 war. At the time it was widely seen as a justified "preventive war," but now well-established historical evidence shows that was not the case: both US and Israeli intelligence agreed that Nasser, despite his provocations and rhetoric, had no intention of attacking Israel, and in any case he would be easily defeated if he did.
- In 1969, Nasser told Ghadaffi of Libya that Israel's nuclear weapons, together with the opposition of both superpowers to wars designed to destroy Israel, had ended any possibility of such an Arab attack on Israel. Sadat reached the same conclusion, as had leading Egyptian generals.
- In April 1970, Nasser told US officials that he was prepared to recognize Israel if the Palestinian problem could be solved.[3]
- In 1971, Egypt accepted the main principles embodied in UN peace proposals and, more important, the US Rogers Plan: Israeli withdrawal from its 1967 conquests in exchange for peace settlements with the Arabs.
- In 1973, Sadat's decision to engage in a limited attack on Israeli forces along the Suez Canal and in the western sections of the Sinai peninsula was intended not to attack Israel itself, let alone destroy it, but only to break the diplomatic deadlock and convince Israel to withdraw from its conquests of Egyptian territory and reach a peace settlement. Today, there is no serious challenge, even by most Israelis, to this understanding of Sadat's intentions and to the argument that but for Israeli intransigence, the 1973 war would have been averted.

After Israel captured the southern Sinai town of Sharm al-Shaikh in the 1956 war and then refused to withdraw from it during the 1960s and early 1970s, Moshe Dayan had famously said: "I prefer Sharm al-Shaikh without peace to peace without Sharm al-Shaikh." In 1994, Prime Minister Yitzhak Rabin provided the definitive rebuttal to Dayan and other Israeli hawks: in a speech to the Knesset he quoted the Dayan statement and then said, "We responded to the Egyptian president . . . with ridicule and arrogance. . . . It took a bloody war before Jerusalem reached the correct conclusion that peace is preferable to Sharm al-Shaikh."[4]

Jimmy Carter and the Arab-Israeli Conflict

Carter believed that the Arab states were ready for peace if Israel withdrew from the territories it occupied after 1967. On the Palestinian issue he was ambivalent: while he did not favor Palestinian statehood, he believed that they had political rights that could be realized in a Palestinian "homeland," within which they could have "self-rule."[5]

Sadat agreed with Carter's goals: in principle, he sought to end the overall Arab-Israeli conflict and believed it was possible if Israel gave back all its 1967 conquests and agreed to a two-state solution to the Israeli-Palestinian conflict. However, he was not willing to press the Palestinian cause if it conflicted with his main priority of recovering Egypt's lost territories.[6]

The problem was Menachem Begin, whose refusal to even consider withdrawing from the West Bank, Gaza, and the Golan Heights precluded an overall settlement. While he was willing to at least enter into negotiations with Egypt over the Sinai peninsula, he initially insisted that the Israeli settlements that had been established there after the 1973 war would not be removed, a position that came very close to torpedoing even a bilateral Egyptian-Israeli settlement.

In his various memoirs, Carter makes it clear that Begin's intransigence infuriated him. For example, he writes, "It was no secret that he and I had strong private and public disagreements concerning the interpretation of the Camp David accords, the settlements policy in the West Bank and Gaza and his recent invasion of Lebanon . . . [which] had resulted in some personal differences as well."[7] In private, at one point he even described Begin as a "psycho."[8]

It is possible that US military, economic, and diplomatic support of Israel could have given the Carter administration the leverage to induce more flexibility in Begin's policies; on the other hand, however, US pressures might not have worked against an intransigent Begin and perhaps could even have backfired. In any case, Carter was not willing to employ even rhetorical pressures, let alone suggest that the US government might have to reassess its policies toward Israel.[9]

On the contrary, Carter and his vice-president, Walter Mondale, publicly and privately assured Israel—and its supporters in the United States—that it would not use US aid to pressure Israel.[10] American domestic politics, in their view, precluded such pressures; Quandt writes that even before the conference began, "it was clear that domestic political considerations were beginning to affect US policy deliberations" and were responsible for the "watering down" of the administration's initial strong public statements on the need for a comprehensive settlement that included the establishment of a Palestinian homeland.[11]

And just to make sure that American domestic politics would hamstring Carter, Israeli foreign minister Moshe Dayan employed the usual Israeli tactic, threatening to mobilize a campaign in the United States if Israel was pressured by the administration. Carter's national security advisor Zbigniew Brzezinski later called Dayan's threats "blackmail."[12] They worked, though, and not for the first or last time.

The Israeli-Egyptian Peace Treaty

Both Sadat and Carter soon realized that Begin's intransigence made a comprehensive peace impossible, so they had to settle for a bilateral Israeli-Egyptian settlement. In his memoirs, Carter wrote that Israel's announcement of new settlements to be built in the West Bank, in defiance of what Carter believed to be an Israeli promise to refrain from doing so, as well as Begin's refusal to discuss the rights of the Palestinians were "almost insuperable obstacles to peace."[13]

Even to attain a bilateral Israeli-Egyptian settlement, Sadat's bottom-line demand had to be met, namely, that Israel had to withdraw all its forces from the Sinai and "every inch" of it returned to full Egyptian sovereignty. Consequently, Begin's initial insistence on retaining the Israeli settlements, military bases, and even the potentially oil-rich portions of the Sinai had to be overcome.[14]

Carter's leverage was quite limited, as he felt bound by the secret commitments that the Nixon administration had made to Israel to induce it to start withdrawing from the Sinai: to provide it with increased economic and military assistance, to preserve Israel's military superiority over its Arab neighbors, to help Israel replace its Sinai military bases with new ones in the Negev, and to guarantee Israel's oil supply after it withdrew from Sinai.[15]

Consequently, Carter decided that a comprehensive settlement that included recognition of the rights of the Palestinians could not be reached, and when he accepted Israel's conditions for a bilateral Egyptian-Israeli settlement, the Begin government finally agreed to a gradual withdrawal from the Sinai peninsula. Even that concession from Begin would not have been possible unless Egypt and the United States had backed away from insisting on a compromise over the status of Jerusalem. Indeed, Begin even threatened to break up the summit meeting if Carter so much as "set out" the American position on East Jerusalem. Carter was furious, Cyrus Vance wrote, demanding "to know if Israel meant to tell the United States it could not even publicly state its own national position." The issue was resolved when Carter again backed down, agreeing not to go public with the American position.[16]

In March 1979, Egypt and Israel agreed to a formal peace treaty. There is no doubt that the treaty was in important respects a major success: not only did it end the conflict between Egypt and Israel, but it also ensured that there would be no more major wars between Israel and the other leading Arab states. The treaty has been remarkably durable, surviving the assassination of Sadat in 1981; the Israeli invasions of Lebanon in 1978, 1982, and 2006; the rise and fall of the Egyptian regime of Hosni Mubarak; the current military dictatorship of Abdel Fattah el-Sisi—and even the short-lived 2012–13 regime of the Muslim Brotherhood leader, Mohamed Morsi.

On the other hand, the willingness of the Egyptian leadership to reach a separate settlement with Israel—and even, in recent years, to increasingly collaborate with it in repressing the Hamas movement in Gaza and on other Middle Eastern issues—has made it much easier for Israel to continue to refuse legitimate compromise settlements of all the other components of the overall Arab-Israeli conflict.[17]

Above all, it is the Palestinians who have paid the price for Egypt's exit from the Arab-Israeli conflict and Carter's reluctant acquiescence to it. There is no doubt that Carter believed that some kind of just settlement of the Palestinian question was both necessary if the overall Arab-Israeli conflict was to be ended and morally required. That moral theme runs throughout Carter's writings; for example, he wrote: "It was impossible for me to ignore the very serious problems on the West Bank. The continued deprivation of Palestinian rights . . . was contrary to the basic moral and ethical principles of both our countries."[18]

Nonetheless, several factors led to Carter's decision not to push the Palestinian issue. First, Begin threatened to break up the summit over the issue. Second, the US domestic politics of the issue, including strong congressional resistance to concessions to the Palestinians, continued to leave Carter little room to maneuver. Third, he was constrained by the Nixon administration's commitment to Begin that the US government would not recognize or negotiate with the PLO until it ended all violence against Israel, accepted UN Resolution 242, and officially recognized Israel's existence.

Finally, neither Israel nor the United States were under Egyptian pressure to solve the Palestinian issue. In principle, both Nasser and Sadat demanded that Israel end its occupation of the West Bank and Gaza and accept Palestinian political rights—but in practice they were unwilling to give up their goal of regaining the Sinai peninsula, the likely outcome if they had insisted on justice for the Palestinians.

In any case, while Nasser had rhetorically supported the creation of an independent Palestinian state and the "right of return" of the Palestinians to Israel, in practice it was never a high priority for him. For example, in November 1967, Robert Anderson, Lyndon Johnson's "special envoy" to the Middle East, reported to Johnson and Secretary of State Dean Rusk about a conversation on the Palestinian issue he had held with Nasser: when he told Nasser he doubted that Israel would ever agree to allow the return of the Palestinian refugees from the 1948 and 1967 wars, Nasser said: "All right, then let us settle with them by agreeing to pay them compensation."[19]

Similarly, Carter reported that while Sadat initially insisted that "sovereignty in the West Bank and Gaza rests among the people who live there" and that "ultimately" there should be a Palestinian state," Sadat had added that "such a state should not be independent nor have military forces, but should be linked to either Israel or, preferably, Jordan."[20] During the negotiations, the Palestinian issue was supposedly resolved when Begin agreed—for the moment—not to press the Israeli claim to sovereignty over the West Bank and allow the Palestinian residents some form of a vaguely defined "autonomy." As was widely predicted at the time, however, Palestinian "autonomy" turned out to be a sham, as Israel continued its occupation and repression of the Palestinians.[21]

Michael Bar-Zohar summarized the reality of the matter:

> Begin never seriously meant to establish autonomy in the West Bank. . . . [H]e believed that Sadat didn't care about the West Bank and needed the Palestinian chapter of the treaty only as proof of his loyalty to the traditional Arab positions. Once the autonomy agreements had provided him with his fig leaf, Sadat would not lift a finger for the Palestinians. The future was to prove Begin right.[22]

Jordan

Between 1947 and early 1967, a series of secret agreements and general understandings was made between Israeli leaders and King Abdullah and King Hussein of Jordan: essentially, they said that if Israel refrained from attacking the West Bank and Arab East Jerusalem, both then under Jordanian rule, Jordan would stay out of the Arab-Israeli conflict. The agreements generally worked during the 1948 war, though there were some brief clashes when Israeli forces attacked areas that had been allocated to Arab rule. In April 1950, Abdullah annexed the West Bank, preventing the establishment of a Palestinian state there. During the next two decades, a de facto peace between Israel and Jordan generally held; although there were some brief tensions and skirmishes, the two countries remained "the best of enemies," as it has been aptly described.[23]

King Hussein was prepared to go beyond that and reach a formal peace settlement with Israel if it abandoned its aspirations to incorporate the West Bank and East Jerusalem into a "Greater Israel," but Israel refused to do so. Then, in late 1966, the tensions between Israel and Jordan increased, primarily because of the increased Fatah guerrilla raids on Israel originating from bases in Syria and Jordan. Unlike the Syrian government, King Hussein was doing his best to prevent the raids and the Israeli government knew it, but the king's forces could not establish total control over all the West Bank.[24]

Matters came to a head on November 13, 1966, when Israel, following a Palestinian attack that killed three Israeli soldiers, retaliated with a major raid on a West Bank town considered by Israel to be a "guerrilla base." As the Israeli forces blew up houses, Hussein's forces sought unsuccessfully to stop them, and twenty-one of them were killed.[25]

As the slide toward the 1967 war continued in the next few months, Hussein was brought under great pressure to ally Jordan with Egypt and Syria. Consequently, on May 30, Hussein signed a mutual defense pact with Egypt and placed his army under the command of an Egyptian general, fearing that if he tried to stay out of the approaching conflict his regime and perhaps his life would be endangered.[26]

Accordingly, the king secretly notified Israel that he had no choice but to commit some forces to the war, but that their role would be brief and largely symbolic. However, the Jordanian role turned out to be more than merely symbolic, because once his army was placed under Egyptian control Hussein no long had control over its actions; the result was that the army heavily bombed West Jerusalem.[27]

Perhaps for this reason, on the thirtieth anniversary of the 1967 war, Hussein in a speech to his countrymen said that he considered his decision to join the 1967 war to have been a major blunder that he now regretted, blaming it on Muslim militants and the tide of nationalism that had swept through the Middle East, including Jordan.[28]

After the 1967 war, King Hussein made a number of efforts to go beyond the secret and limited agreements. From the end of the war through the late 1980s, a series of regular meetings between the Hussein and Israeli political leaders examined the possibility of reaching a formal peace agreement between Jordan and Israel. Hussein told the Israelis, "I can be the first Arab leader to make peace with Israel or I can give up some part of Arab territory, but I cannot do both."

Consequently, he proposed a compromise settlement that would include strong measures responding to Israeli security concerns: if Israel agreed to Jordanian sovereignty over most of the West Bank, Jordan would agree to some reciprocal exchange of territory, would prevent the creation of a Palestinian state, and would station only small numbers of its own armed forces in the area. The Jerusalem issue, highly important for symbolic and religious reasons to both Israel and the entire Muslim world, would be resolved on the basis of shared sovereignty: Israel over West Jerusalem and Jordan over East Jerusalem.

Israel rejected these proposals, clearly demonstrating that its position was not motivated by genuine security concerns—its security would have been greatly *enhanced* if a friendly state, with its own urgent motivations to suppress Palestinian nationalism, established tight control of a demilitarized West Bank. The real obstacle to peace with Jordan, then, was Israel's ideological or religious insistence that it must have full control and sovereignty over all "Judea and Samaria," including Arab East Jerusalem.

In June 1968, George Ball, then the US ambassador to the United Nations, was asked by Israeli prime minister Levi Eshkol to tell King Hussein that in exchange for peace Israel would return most of the territory it had seized in the 1967 war—but not Jerusalem. Hussein rejected this proposal; Ball writes that "he dared not to cede the Islamic holy city of Jerusalem to Israel."[29]

In a September 1968 meeting with the king, Israel reiterated that any peace settlement would have to leave Israel in control of the Jordan Valley, other parts of the West Bank, and East Jerusalem. It was a nonstarter: the king continued to insist on Jordanian sovereignty over the West Bank and Arab East Jerusalem.[30] Two years later in a 1970 meeting between King Hussein and a delegation led by Prime Minister Golda Meir and Defense Minister Moshe Dayan, the Israelis offered an interim agreement: the Gaza Strip would be transferred to Jordanian rule but Israel would retain its military bases and settlements in the West Bank. The deadlocked Jerusalem issue would "remain open" until a final settlement was reached. Hussein responded that he was ready to reach a full peace agreement if all his territories, including East Jerusalem, were returned, but that he would accept an interim agreement if Israel withdrew its forces from the Jordan River Valley. Israel refused.[31]

In 1972, Hussein made a new offer: if Israel withdrew from the Jordanian territories conquered in 1967 he and the PLO would establish a Jordanian-Palestinian confederation in East Jerusalem and the West Bank, which would relieve Israel of "the Palestinian problem."[32] Israel was still not interested.

Two weeks before the 1973 war, King Hussein secretly visited Israel and warned Golda Meir that Syria and Egypt were planning a limited attack in the Golan Heights and the Sinai peninsula and were pressuring Jordan to join them. The Israeli government and military leaders evidently discounted the warning, for they were caught off guard when Hussein's warnings proved accurate; as a result, Israel suffered heavy casualties and early military defeats.

Even after the war began there was considerable cooperation between Jordan and Israel. After telling Golda Meir that he had no choice but to deploy a small military force to the Golan Heights if he was to preserve his position in the Arab world, the king asked Israel not to attack Jordan. Rather than endanger Hussein's rule, Israel refrained from engaging the Jordanian brigade in the Golan.[33]

After the war ended, Hussein again told Israeli leaders he would agree either to an interim disengagement in the Jordan River Valley—similar to the partial agreements between Israel and Egypt in the Sinai peninsula and Israel and Syria in the Golan Heights—or a full peace treaty, provided he got all his lost territory back.[34]

Remarkably, in 1974 King Hussein went further, suggesting that if Jordanian sovereignty over the West Bank was restored, he would allow Israel to unofficially retain some military bases in strategically important areas. Transcripts of a secret January 1974 meeting between Hussein and Golda Meir show that the king proposed a partial settlement: if Israel agreed to withdraw its forces and settlements from the Jordan River Valley, Jordan would restore its civil administration there but would refrain from reoccupying it with its armed forces. As well, the king said: "The Germans have a military base in Spain. If you agree to the principle to restore our sovereignty over the West Bank, including Jerusalem, we could discuss your request later. But first you must agree to the principle."[35]

For several reasons, Israel again refused to consider the king's proposals. Since the 1967 war ended with Israel in control of the West Bank, Israeli governments—including the Labor administrations of Levi Eshkol and Golda Meir—had been supporting the building of Jewish settlements in parts of the West Bank and Gaza. As well, the security establishment believed that control of the Jordan River Valley was more important to Israeli security than a formal peace with Jordan, reasoning that it needed the area to serve as a forward defense against the still-feared "Arab attack from the east."[36] As a result, over the next twenty years, the continuing secret meetings between King Hussein and Israeli leaders ended in failure: "Israel was still reluctant to pull back from the Jordan River, and Hussein would accept nothing else."[37] However, there were no serious clashes between the two countries, and the state of de facto peace continued.

In 1987, King Hussein and Shimon Peres, then the Israeli foreign minister in the government of Yitzhak Shamir, held secret peace talks in London. Their meeting resulted in what became known as "the London Accord." Uri Savir, a leading Israeli diplomat and close aide to Peres, describes the accord:

> Had it been implemented, it would have changed the face of the Middle East. It mentioned three entities: the State of Israel and Jordan, which were to remain as they are, and a new entity that was supposed to include the West Bank and the Gaza Strip, in the context of a Jordanian-Palestinian federation. . . . Jerusalem would have remained united, with each religion taking responsibility for its own holy sites.[38]

Shamir, one of Israel's most intransigent political leaders throughout its history, vetoed the agreement. Years later, Peres bitterly commented: "Not only did [the proposed agreement] create a path to peace with the Jordanians, it resolved the Palestinian question without requiring Israel to relinquish any of its territory or to change the status of Jerusalem."[39]

Finally, though, by the end of the 1980s the conditions for a formal peace settlement had emerged. First, after the passing from the scene of Ben-Gurion and other early Israeli hawks, most Israeli leaders lost interest in further territorial expansion into Jordan beyond the Jordan River. As well, King Hussein had ended his insistence that Jordan was the legitimate representative of the Palestinians after the Arab League's 1974 decision to recognize the PLO as "the sole legitimate representative of the Palestinian people."

Most important, Hussein had concluded that Jordanian stability and the continuation of the Hashemite monarchy required that he end his rule over the increasingly militant nationalism of the Palestinians in the West Bank. In particular, Israeli analysts have written, the king feared that the West Bank Palestinian uprising against the Israeli occupation (the "Intifada") in 1988 might spread to the Palestinian population of Jordan itself and be directed against him. Alternatively, Israel might expel the West Bank Palestinians into Jordan, thus overwhelming his monarchical rule.

The Israeli-Jordanian Peace Treaty

For these reasons, the king decided to renounce the Jordanian claim to sovereignty over the West Bank, thereby turning over the Palestinian problem to Israel. On

October 26, 1994, an Israeli-Jordanian peace treaty was finally signed.[40] The most important provisions of the agreement focused on security matters, including an end to the state of war and the threat or use of force against each other, as well as cooperative measures to prevent terrorism against either side. Beyond that, the treaty included the normalization of diplomatic relations; an exact demarcation of the borders, including some minor land swaps; the distribution between the two countries of fresh water from the Jordan River and West Bank underground sources; measures covering trade and other economic matters; provisions for environmental, energy, medical, and scientific cooperation; and even measures for developing cultural and tourism exchange.

As for the crucial issue of Jerusalem, Israel maintained its control of the city, although it agreed that the Jordanians would continue their "special responsibilities" in administering the Al-Aqsa mosque and other Islamic religious sites in the Old City.

The peace treaty has held up since, although for several reasons it is now under significant strain, in part because of friction over Israeli "security" measures on the Temple Mount and in part because of growing Jordanian popular anger at the continuing Israeli occupation and repression of the Palestinians. Perhaps the most serious danger, however, is the revival of the past "Jordan is Palestine" strategy of many on the Israeli right.

In its present version, the right-wingers argue that Israel should annex the Jordan River Valley and other sections of the West Bank, which would lead to the flight of many Palestinians into Jordan—or perhaps they could be "transferred" there. That, in turn, would revive the conflict between the radicalized Palestinians and King Hussein's Hashemite monarchy and army. If the monarchy was overthrown, it is reasoned, Jordan would become the Palestinian state and Israel could proceed to annex all of the West Bank, fulfilling the Israeli right's never-abandoned dream of a "Greater Israel."[41]

In early December 2019, Ephraim Halevy, Israel's former head of Mossad and a chief architect of the 1994 peace treaty, said: "I see great danger to the peace treaty. I think that the danger comes not from the Jordanians, but from us, from Israel."[42]

The United States and the Israeli-Jordanian Peace Treaty

The US government did not play a major role in the negotiations that led to the peace treaty.[43] After the 1967 war, the main thrust of US policy was to oppose Palestinian nationalist militancy and support King Hussein, who had become a de facto American ally. Consequently, the US government had made it clear to the Israeli leadership that it strongly opposed the establishment of Palestinian self-rule in the West Bank, whether as an independent state or some kind of "autonomous" entity; instead, it had urged Israel to negotiate a settlement with King Hussein that would turn over the Palestinian problem to Jordan.[44] When the king lost interest in such a settlement, however, the US government agreed to support the Israeli-Jordanian treaty.

Martin Indyk was a former US ambassador to Israel and had held other top positions in a number of US administrations; writing of the Israeli-Jordanian peace settlement, he said:

> The Israeli-Jordan peace treaty was certainly an important milestone in the annals of the Arab-Israeli conflict. It removed one more of Israel's Arab neighbors from the arena of that conflict. . . . The treaty solidified the strategic role of Israel and Jordan in each other's defense. Israelis achieved the warm peace they had craved; Jordan received territory, water, and protection, along with the commitment of the American superpower to the well-being of the Hashemite dynasty.[45]

What Indyk failed to emphasize, however, is that similar to what had happened when Egypt reached its peace settlement with Israel, the Palestinians were essentially abandoned: they had been given no role in the negotiations, no provisions of the treaty covered the Israeli-Palestinian conflict, and the Israeli occupation of the West Bank continued.

11

The Lebanon Wars

From the outset of the Arab-Israeli conflict, the major Israeli leaders, especially David Ben-Gurion and Moshe Dayan, looked for opportunities to seize and annex southern Lebanon and install a friendly Christian government in the rest of the country, one that would reach a peace treaty with Israel and collaborate with it in its conflict with the Palestinians and other Islamic organizations.

In a May 1954 meeting with defense and foreign ministry officials, Ben-Gurion laid out his proposal: "The Israeli army will enter Lebanon, occupy the necessary territory, and create a Christian regime which will ally itself with Israel. The territory from the Litani River southward would be totally annexed to Israel."[1] Sharett dismissed the idea as a "crazy adventure," but Ben-Gurion, back in office on the eve of the 1956 war, asked the French government to support his plan.[2]

Although nothing came of these early proposals, they precisely forecast what Israel sought to do in 1978 and 1982. In March 1978, following a Palestinian guerrilla attack across Israel's northern border, Israeli forces invaded southern Lebanon. At least 1,000 Palestinian and Lebanese civilians were killed, and at least 100,000 people were displaced from homes and villages.[3]

The Israeli attack ended after President Jimmy Carter brought heavy pressure to bear on the government of Menachem Begin. Carter was angered by the attack, partly for moral reasons and partly because it violated the agreement that US military equipment employed by Israel could be used only for defensive purposes. Begin denied that Israel was using US arms in the invasion, but American intelligence concluded otherwise. Carter then demanded that Israel immediately withdraw, warning that an Israeli refusal to do so might "develop into a major problem" in US-Israeli relationships, in which case US military assistance to Israel might be terminated.[4] On this occasion, Begin backed down—but it was hardly the end of Israeli attacks on Lebanon during and after his term in office.

In the next few years, the PLO moved most of its leadership, organization, and guerrilla forces into southern Lebanon; the Lebanese government was not happy about this, accurately foreseeing the likely consequences, but it was too weak to prevent it. In the spring of 1981 Israel repeatedly bombed the PLO bases, and considered mounting another military operation in order to "drive the Palestinian terrorists out of South Lebanon once and for all."[5]

That would have to wait for another opportunity, because at the end of July 1981 the US government brokered a ceasefire between the PLO and Israel. It was accepted by Begin, in part because the IDF was unable to stop Palestinian shelling of northern Israel, and in part because he was convinced that a new war sooner or later was inevitable—and at that time Israel could destroy the PLO in Lebanon.[6]

However, the PLO scrupulously observed the ceasefire in the next year, and it became clear that Arafat was abandoning his original goal of destroying the state of Israel, which he increasingly understood was unattainable. The PLO's real goal, it would soon be explicitly acknowledged, was to establish a Palestinian state in the West Bank and Gaza—that is, as it became known, there would be a "two-state solution." As the changing goals of the PLO became evident, its international isolation waned and the Israeli government feared it would soon face international pressures—perhaps including even from the US government—to negotiate a settlement with the Palestinians.[7]

On June 3, 1982, a Palestinian group that had split off from the PLO in response to Arafat's emerging moderation tried to assassinate the Israeli ambassador to England. Israeli intelligence quickly confirmed that the PLO leadership had not been responsible, but Begin and other hardliners in the cabinet ignored this finding because they had found "the casus belli that [they] . . . had been waiting for."[8]

Therefore, on June 6, Israel launched its long-planned massive attack on Lebanon: 60,000 soldiers, backed by over 800 tanks and supported by heavy air and naval bombing and long-range artillery, advanced well beyond the Palestinian refugee camps and guerrilla strongholds to the outskirts of Beirut.[9] In the two-month course of the war, wrote Mordechai Bar-On, the former chief education officer of the Israeli army, "tens of thousands were killed or wounded by Israel's massive employment of indiscriminate long-range fire power."[10]

During the Israeli planning for the attack, the military told the Begin government that it would be a limited operation, designed to destroy PLO forces in the south of Lebanon and establish an Israeli "security zone" there. However, the effective commander of the operation was Defense Minister Ariel Sharon, who had far more ambitious goals. First, he wanted to kill Arafat and other PLO leaders, principally by bombing and invading their neighborhoods, homes, and offices in Beirut. Second, he wanted to drive the PLO out of Lebanon—two Israeli journalists wrote that "one of the original, albeit unpublished, aims [of the attack] was to rid South Lebanon of its Palestinian population so the PLO would not have a base of operation should it ever attempt to infiltrate the area again."[11] That done, Sharon planned to install Israel's Christian allies in power in Lebanon. At the same time, the remnants of the PLO would be exiled to Jordan, which might become a Palestinian state, thus lessening the pressures on Israel to withdraw from the West Bank and Gaza.[12]

Moreover, in order to achieve these goals, Sharon had to drive Syrian forces who had been supporting the Lebanese government out of the country. Consequently, even though he had assured Begin that the Syrians would be engaged only if they attacked first, Sharon deliberately provoked clashes in order to have the pretext to expel them. In the end, in Sharon's grandiose scheme, the situation both in Lebanon and beyond that into the entire Middle East would be transformed in Israel's favor.[13]

The Syrian forces, who were deployed only in defensive positions pursuant to the Syrian government's decision to stay out of the war even if the PLO were driven out of Lebanon, were no match for the Israelis. By mid-June the Israeli forces had defeated the Lebanese, Palestinian, and Syrian forces. However, Arafat and other PLO leaders escaped and fled the country.

The Reagan Administration and the 1982 Lebanon War

Ronald Reagan was strongly pro-Israel for both moral and strategic reasons. His memoirs and the writings of his biographers and US officials who served in his administration emphasize that Reagan had a long record of opposition to anti-Semitism, had many Jewish friends, and believed that the Jewish people needed and deserved a state of their own.[14]

According to one of his biographers, in 1948 Reagan "rejoiced at the creation of the state of Israel" and later told Israeli prime minister Yitzhak Shamir that his concern for Israel could be traced to World War II when he photographed the Nazi death camps, after which he became concerned for the Jewish people.[15]

In his autobiography Reagan writes:

> No conviction I've ever held has been stronger than my belief that the United States must ensure the survival of Israel. The Holocaust, I believe, left America with a moral responsibility to ensure that . . . [it] never happens again. . . . My dedication to the preservation of Israel was as strong when I left the White House as when I arrived there, even though this tiny ally, with whom we share democracy and many other values, was a source of great concern for me while I was president.[16]

In addition, Reagan supported Israel for the usual Cold War strategic reasons. Samuel W. Lewis, a high State Department official and former US ambassador to Israel, writes that Reagan "looked at Israel through the prism of East-West global confrontation as a natural ally."[17]

In May 1982, while planning the Lebanon invasion, Sharon met with American officials—including Secretary of State Alexander Haig, a strong believer in Israel's importance to US national interests—to inform them of his goals. Some high administration officials, including Secretary of Defense Casper Weinberger and Vice-President George H. W. Bush, were reported to be opposed to the attack, particularly as Sharon's real intentions became clear. Nonetheless the Haig position prevailed: in the judgment of a prominent Israeli historian who has seen the US government documents, they "clearly indicate that an American 'green light' was given for Israel's actions."[18]

However, as reports of how Sharon was conducting the war multiplied, Reagan became increasingly angry at the damage to the civilian population of Lebanon and began strongly pressuring Israel to withdraw from Beirut, even as he continued to support Israel's objective of forcing the PLO to abandon Lebanon.[19]

In early August, Sharon intensified the shelling of the southern suburbs of Beirut, indicating he might be preparing a direct invasion of the city. In his memoirs, George P. Shultz, who had become the secretary of state a few weeks earlier, wrote that Reagan told Foreign Minister Yitzhak Shamir that "if you invade West Beirut, it would have the most grave, most grievous, consequences for our relationship," adding that "should these Israeli practices continue, it will become increasingly difficult to defend the proposition that Israeli use of US arms is for defensive purposes."[20]

When Sharon categorically denied the shelling—even though US representatives on the ground were witnessing it—Reagan wrote to Begin:

> Your actions in Lebanon have seriously undermined our relationship with those Arab governments whose cooperation is essential to protect the Middle East from external threats and to counter forces of Soviet-sponsored radicalism and Islamic fundamentalism now growing in the region. . . . U.S. influence in the Arab world, our ability to achieve our strategic objectives, has been seriously damaged by Israel's actions.[21]

Evidently, Reagan's warnings were motivated by moral as well as strategic concerns. In his autobiography, Reagan writes that the attacks on civilian neighborhoods in Beirut "sickened me and many others in the White House. I told him [Begin] it had to stop or our entire future relationship was endangered. I used the word 'Holocaust' deliberately."[22]

Actually, Shultz and other top leaders of the administration had favored stronger action than Reagan was ready to impose: "Reagan was more hesitant than anyone else about cracking down on the Israelis," Shultz wrote. "I wanted strong pressure on Israel; so did George Bush, Jim Baker, and Ed Meese, but the president would not go along."[23]

Though fuming at Reagan's warnings—a few months earlier Begin told the US ambassador that Israel was not a "vassal state of the United States" or "just another banana republic"[24]—Begin did agree to allow Arafat and the PLO to depart Lebanon.[25]

In mid-August, the Reagan administration unexpectedly proposed an Israeli-Palestinian peace plan that called for an immediate end to new Jewish settlements in the West Bank and Gaza and the eventual end of the occupation of much of the West Bank and Gaza. In his letter to Begin setting out his proposal, Reagan wrote:

> The military losses of the PLO have not diminished the yearning of the Palestinian people for a just solution of their claims. . . . Palestinians feel strongly that their cause is more than a question of refugees. I agree. The Camp David agreement recognized that fact when it spoke of "the legitimate rights of the Palestinian people and their just requirements." . . . The United States will not support the use of any additional land for the purpose of settlements during the transitional period.[26]

However, Begin would not give in on issues that he considered central for both security and ideological reasons, particularly continued Israeli rule over the West Bank. In any case, after the Lebanon crisis ended, the perceived importance of Israel to US national interests in the Middle East again became important to the US government. As a result, Reagan backed away from pressuring Israel on its continuing expansion of Jewish settlements in the occupied territories; on the contrary, he increased military and political assistance to Israel, and agreed to a number of formal agreements establishing US-Israeli military, intelligence, and counterterrorism undertakings.[27]

The Consequences of the 1982 Lebanon War

In the most important book on the 1982 war, two Israeli journalists and commentators argue that the Israeli invasion of Lebanon failed in every important respect: "Of Ariel Sharon's grand design nothing remains." First, the PLO recovered and the Palestinians were not permanently driven out of southern Lebanon. Second, resistance to the Israeli occupation of Gaza and the West Bank intensified rather than ended, for "Israel lacked the wisdom to choose a path of political compromise with the Palestinians."[28]

Third, not only did its Christian allies fail to seize political power in Lebanon, but Israel alienated the Muslim majority, a development that led to the emergence of Hezbollah, the Lebanese Shiite militant party and armed forces, with whom Israel has been in conflict ever since.

Finally, Israel "tarnished its image in world public opinion," created "unprecedented friction between many Jewish communities in the West and Israel," earned itself "the reputation of a country that indulged in overkill to achieve objectives far beyond its legitimate security needs," and failed to learn "the limits of what force can achieve."[29]

To be sure, a counterargument would be that if one discounts the moral issues raised by Israeli behavior in Lebanon—one shouldn't—it is hard to see how, in terms of its conflicts with the Palestinians and the Arab world as a whole, Israel has come up against any "limits of what force can achieve." Indeed, arguably the contrary is the case, at least in terms of hard-nosed realpolitik.

The 1993 War

In May 1983, Israel and Lebanon signed an agreement that formally ended the state of war between them and provided for the gradual withdrawal of the Israeli troops except for a so-called security zone, stretching about 40 to 45 kilometers north of the international border, within which Israeli forces could continue to operate, so as to prevent Hezbollah attacks into northern Israel.

After the agreement, armed clashes between Hezbollah and Israel continued, as the militants tried to use guerrilla warfare to force Israel to withdraw from southern Lebanon. Hezbollah occasionally retaliated against Israeli attacks by firing rockets into northern Israel, but on a much reduced scale. Over the next ten years the tensions gradually eased "and there was a general sense of relief that the nightmare was over."[30]

The emerging uneasy peace was shattered in early 1992, when Israeli forces attacked a convoy carrying Hezbollah secretary general Abbas al Musawi, killing him along with his wife and young child. The new Hezbollah leader, Hassan Nasrallah, then announced that whereas in the past Hezbollah had refrained from targeting Israeli towns even after Lebanese towns had been attacked, the "rules of the game" were now changed.[31] Over the next five days Hezbollah retaliated for the killing of their leader, firing dozens of rockets into northern Israel.

As the situation deteriorated, Israel decided to return to its early strategy, launching a major new attack on Lebanon that went beyond the targeting of Hezbollah forces and installations and included widespread bombing of nonmilitary targets throughout southern Lebanon. The strategy was designed to induce the civilian population to abandon their homes and flee northward, thereby increasing the pressures on the largely helpless Lebanese government to try to curb Hezbollah, which had become at least as powerful as the official Lebanese army.

The IDF, led by Chief of Staff Ehud Barak, carried out the strategy. On July 28, 1993, three days after the Israeli attacks began, Prime Minister Yitzhak Rabin addressed the Knesset, essentially admitting that the Israelis were deliberately attacking Lebanese civilians:

> If there is no security and quiet in our northern communities, there will be no security and quiet for residents of southern Lebanon north of the security zone. We are saddened by the suffering of the Lebanese population

> which is now travelling the roads [in flight]. . . . We may be pained by the sight of Lebanese [civilians] fleeing their homes, but we will tell them: Your government has the option of [empowering] the Lebanese military to prevent Katyusha fire at communities in Israel. Only if fire at the northern communities ceases will you [be able] to return to your homes in southern Lebanon.[32]

On another occasion, Rabin bluntly acknowledged that the Israeli attacks on southern Lebanon were designed "to make it uninhabitable," thus forcing the Lebanese government to suppress Palestinian guerrilla forces there.[33] Rabin did not mention what had precipitated the Hezbollah attacks. However, Daniel Sobelman, an Israeli political scientist, wrote that the Hezbollah attacks on Israel's northern towns came "*mostly after Lebanese civilians had been killed by Israel,* but occasionally also in retaliation for the killing of Hezbollah commanders."[34]

Despite the civilian destruction, the 1993 Israeli attack failed to attain its goals of turning the Lebanese population against Hezbollah and curbing its political and military power. The attacks were temporarily ended when the United States brokered a new agreement that included "unwritten rules" to prevent both sides from deliberately attacking civilian targets. However, the rules were soon broken by both sides, though each side claimed "the other did it first."[35]

"Operation Grapes of Wrath"

Over the next three years the situation continued to deteriorate. In April 1996, Prime Minister Shimon Peres and Ehud Barak, now foreign minister, decided to launch another massive attack on southern Lebanon, calling it "Operation Grapes of Wrath." In the next sixteen days Israel attacked not only Hezbollah forces and Palestinian refugee camps but also homes, businesses, roads, bridges, power stations, water pipelines, and the Beirut international airport—in short, the economic infrastructure of Lebanese society. An estimated one hundred towns and villages were vacated and some 400,000 Lebanese civilians were driven from their homes and forced to flee northward.[36]

The United States and "Operation Grapes of Wrath"

According to Shlaim and Helena Cobban, the Clinton administration had "given Israel the green light to break Hizbullah" and blocked efforts in the United Nations to issue a resolution of condemnation,[37] but as the Lebanese civilian casualties mounted, the administration began urging restraint. On April 27, the US government brokered a ceasefire agreement that incorporated new—but unwritten—rules of the game: each side was prohibited from attacking civilians, but Hezbollah was not prohibited from attacking Israeli military forces inside Lebanon so long as these attacks were not launched from populated areas, and Israel was not prohibited from retaliating against such attacks.[38]

The 2006 Israeli Attack on Lebanon

In the ten years after the 1996 Israeli attack on Lebanon, an uneasy peace generally prevailed. In May 2000 Israel withdrew the last of its forces from its "security zone" in southern Lebanon, following which Hezbollah fired only a few rockets into Israel, although there continued to be occasional border clashes throughout the period.

On July 12, 2006, Hezbollah attacked an Israeli border patrol, seizing two Israeli soldiers who later died of their wounds. Eight more Israeli soldiers were killed when they crossed the border and pursued the attackers. Israel then launched another full-scale air and ground attack on Lebanon, in part for retaliation, in part to strike Hezbollah military targets, especially its growing rocket arsenal; but also, as in its 1993 and 1996 attacks, the intent was to inflict such pain on the Lebanese people that their government would be forced to curb Hezbollah—on the dubious assumption that the government was capable of doing so, if only given sufficient motivation. During the attack, Zeev Schiff, the centrist military correspondent of *Haaretz,* wrote: "If the mass flight of residents continues, the campaign will be seen as a punishment of the Lebanese, and that is a recipe for hatred." It was the Israeli difficulty in preventing Hezbollah from launching missile attacks, he explained, that "gave rise to the idea of encouraging large numbers of civilians to flee northward, toward Beirut, to serve as a source of pressure."[39]

Remarkably, a number of Israeli leaders publicly confirmed Israel's intentions. For example, senior military officers said that "if the kidnapped soldiers were not returned alive and well, the Lebanese civilian infrastructures will regress 20, or even 50 years."[40] Nor were this and similar threats limited to military officials: during the war, at least two cabinet officials publicly threatened to "flatten" Lebanese villages.[41]

These threats were not empty. Shortly after the war ended, the *New York Times* published a major study of the purposes and consequences of the Israeli attack:

> United Nations and independent aid agencies are totaling an enormous tally of damage that includes airports, ports, water and sewage treatment facilities, electrical plants, 80 bridges and 94 roads, more than 25 gas stations, 900 other businesses and 30,000 homes or shops. . . . International aid agencies have documented enormous damage to wells, water mains, pumping stations and water treatment plants, and damage to pipes under destroyed roads. The agencies fear such conditions could lead to diarrhea and cholera. The Red Cross warns that many villages still lack clean water.[42]

At least 1,100 Lebanese people were killed, the vast majority of them civilians.[43] Subsequent international investigations, including by Human Rights Watch and Amnesty International, concluded that, in the attack, Israel had committed a number of war crimes.[44]

Mutual Deterrence: Israel and Hezbollah since 2006

At the time, the 2006 Israeli attack on Lebanon was widely regarded as a failure, even in Israel: Hezbollah's military capabilities were soon restored and since then they have been significantly upgraded, the pro-Western and moderate Lebanese government was badly undermined, and the Lebanese people's outrage at the Israeli attacks resulted, if anything, in *increased* support of Hezbollah.[45]

On the other hand, on a number of occasions Hezbollah leaders have said that they can no longer take actions that might lead to massive Israel retaliation but would seek to maintain a "mutual balance of deterrence" between the two countries.[46] While admitting that Israel could bomb any part of Lebanon, Hezbollah leader Hassan Nasrallah argued that "Israel will now think a thousand times before going to war":

> If you bomb Beirut we will bomb Tel Aviv. . . . If you attack the Rafik al-Hariri International Airport in Beirut, we will attack Ben-Gurion Airport in Tel Aviv. If you bomb our ports—we will bomb your ports. If you attack our refineries, we will bomb your refineries. If you bomb our factories, we will bomb your factories. And if you bomb our power plants—we will bomb your power plants.[47]

In fact, Nasrallah's threats are quite credible, for it is now estimated that Hezbollah has as many as 130,000 rockets and missiles with the range and accuracy to hit most of Israel.[48] As a result, Israeli military leaders have repeatedly acknowledged that Israel is now deterred from major attacks on Hezbollah, including statements by two recent IDF commanders in chief.[49]

Because both sides now acknowledge that a new round of conflict would be devastating to both sides, there have been no major clashes between Israel and Hezbollah since 2006. To be sure, there have been several minor rocket attacks into Israel, probably fired by rogue groups defying Hezbollah's control, but they have done little damage; as a result, Israel's response has been measured, and both sides have been careful not to allow the situation to escalate. In particular, the state of mutual deterrence has survived Israel's two massive attacks on Gaza in 2010 and 2014, during which Hezbollah refused Hamas's requests for armed assistance.[50]

Perhaps more important, the state of no-war, no-peace between Israel and Lebanon has survived Hezbollah's participation in the Syrian civil war. Since 2012,

Hezbollah units have been supporting the regime of Basher Assad in his battle with ISIS and other groups in Syria, often in conjunction with Iranian forces.[51]

This has created a dilemma for Israel. On the one hand (as will be discussed in Chapter 12), Assad, like his father, Hafez Assad, has had no interest in another war with Israel, and after the 1974 Syrian-Israeli truce agreement, both Assads prevented radical Syrian or Palestinian groups from engaging in cross-border attacks on Israel.

On the other hand, today Israel regards Iran as its most dangerous opponent and has carried out a number of air attacks on Iranian forces in Syria and sometimes against Hezbollah forces supporting them—attacks that have been met by Hezbollah with only minor and essentially symbolic retaliations.

As of this writing, the uneasy de facto truce between Israel and Hezbollah has held up, but as long as each side regards the other as an enemy, the no-war, no-peace tacit understanding will remain fragile.

12

The Israeli-Syrian Conflict, 1973–2019

Recapitulating the Israeli-Syrian Conflict, 1947–73

Before turning to a detailed discussion of the Israeli-Syrian conflict from the mid-1970s to today, it may be helpful to summarize Syrian-Israeli relations from the Balfour Declaration through the 1973 war. From the mid-1920s through 1946, Syrian nationalist governments in principle rejected Zionist aspirations for the creation of a Jewish state in Palestine; in practice, however, they were moderate and provided only rhetorical support to the Palestinians.

During 1947–48, Syria's position hardened, and in the 1948 war it joined the Arab state invasion of Israel, though only in a largely symbolic fashion: the Syrian force consisted of about 3,000 poorly armed troops, and in any case the intervention was primarily designed not to destroy the nascent Jewish state but to prevent other Arab states from carving up Palestine and cutting off Syria from the Jordan River and Lake Tiberias, at that time its main sources of fresh water.

In order to preserve its access to these water sources, during the war the Syrian forces seized territory bordering on the Jordan River and Lake Tiberias. In July 1949, Israel and Syria reached an armistice agreement that created demilitarized zones in those areas, within which neither side would have political sovereignty but both would have access to the water sources. In fact, during this period Israel could have reached a political settlement with Syria on very favorable terms, for the moderate and pro-Western governments that were then in power in Damascus offered to end their conflict with Israel and even resettle in their country most of the Palestinian refugees who had fled or been driven out of Israel in 1948, on the condition that Syria would retain its footholds along the river and the lake.

However, Ben-Gurion was not willing to let Syria share those waters and refused even to enter into negotiations with Damascus. Indeed, at this point he had not given up Zionist expansionist goals, including the seizure of southern Syria and the Golan Heights.

In the next few years there were a number of Syrian-Israeli military border clashes, especially in the demilitarized zones: Israeli military leaders, historians, and journalists have established that most of the clashes were initiated or deliberately provoked by Israel, which sought to gradually seize control of the contested areas. The Israeli general with responsibility for the DMZ later wrote: "In the first years of the armistice regime it was Israel that tried unilaterally to effect changes in the status quo in the DMZ." As well, it is worth repeating the candid admission of Moshe Dayan, the head of the Israeli army in the early 1950s, that more than 80 percent of the clashes with the Syrians had been instigated by Israel, so as to create pretexts for seizing more territory and diverting the waters of the Jordan River away from Syria.

Because of its military alliance with Egypt, Syria was reluctantly drawn into the 1967 war, the consequence of which was its defeat and the Israeli seizure of the Golan Heights region of southern Syria. Shortly after the end of the war the Israeli cabinet secretly decided that Israel would withdraw from the Golan provided that it was completely demilitarized and the Syrians would guarantee that they would not interfere with the water resources of the area. However, it soon reversed this policy, especially after Defense Minister Moshe Dayan, who had initially opposed the Israeli conquest of the Golan, now took the position that the IDF should remain in the Golan indefinitely.

In 1973, Syria joined forces with Egypt in seeking to recover the territory they had lost in 1967. In the first few days of the war, the Syrian army defeated the small Israeli forces in the Golan and were then in a position to advance into northern Israel itself. However, under strict orders from Syrian president Hafez Assad—who feared Israeli nuclear retaliation if the Syrian forces continued into Israel—they stopped, well before Israeli reinforcements arrived. The strengthened Israeli forces then again routed the Syrian forces and even seized additional territory in the area.

Assad then decided that Syria could not regain the Golan by military force and therefore had to rely on a negotiated settlement. In particular, in the hopes of persuading the US government to mediate the dispute, he informed the Nixon administration that he now accepted UN Resolution 242, which called for an Israeli withdrawal from the occupied territories in the context of a political settlement that accepted "the right of every State in the area to live in peace within secure and recognized boundaries free from threats or acts of force."

Initially, Assad sought a nonbelligerency agreement with Israel, as opposed to an overall peace settlement, although in a number of statements to the American leaders he emphasized that he was not ruling out a true peace agreement in the future. He put it this way:

> First we must end the state of belligerency. That means the implementation of UN Resolution 242. And the end of belligerency will mean the beginning of a stage of real peace. . . . If the Israelis return to the 1967 frontier and the West Bank and Gaza becomes a Palestinian state, the last obstacle to a final settlement will have been removed.[1]

Though Israel had no intention of acceding to Assad's terms for a full peace treaty, it had no objection to the more modest goal of a de facto end to armed conflict with Syria. Consequently, in May 1974, Israel and Syria signed an "Agreement on Disengagement" in which they agreed to a ceasefire and to "refrain from all military actions against each other." In addition, Israel agreed to withdraw from the parts of the Golan Heights it had seized in 1973—though not from its 1967 Golan conquests. It was also understood—crucially—that the Syrian government would prevent Palestinian or other terrorist attacks on Israel. Since then, it has successfully done so.

Throughout the 1970s, in meetings with US officials, Hafez Assad reiterated his commitment to ending the military conflict with Israel and to gradually moving toward a full peace settlement. This would be followed, he said, by a normalization of diplomatic and economic relations after Israel completely withdrew from the Golan Heights and reached a settlement with the Palestinians. In that event, Assad promised the Americans, he would agree to demilitarize the Golan Heights in an effort to reassure Israel about its security.

Assad maintained this position throughout the 1980s, joining in the 1982 Arab state "Fez Declaration," which called for a peaceful settlement of the Arab-Israeli conflict based on the principles of UN Resolution 242. After Mikhail Gorbachev came to power in the Soviet Union in the mid-1980s and made it clear that there would be no Soviet military support for radical Arab policies toward Israel, the Syrian military option—even for a limited war to regain the Golan Heights—effectively came to an end.[2]

The Israeli-Syrian Negotiations, 1992–2011

In September 1992, the Syrian foreign minister announced that Syria was prepared to sign a "total peace" with Israel in return for full Israeli withdrawal from Arab lands occupied in 1967. After considerable hesitation, Israeli prime minister Yitzhak Rabin agreed to enter into negotiations, telling US officials that in principle he could agree to Syria's demand for a full Israeli withdrawal from the Golan Heights and a return to the pre-1967 borders, provided that Assad accept strict Israeli conditions on other issues in dispute.[3] Three major issues had to be resolved: the precise location of the borders to which Israel would withdraw, the disposition of the water sources of the Golan and Lake Tiberias, and the implications of a bilateral Israeli-Syrian agreement for other issues, especially the Palestinian question.

The Border Issue

In some ways, the border issue was the most complicated one, both because of its symbolic importance to Syria and its connection to Israel's concern over water sources.[4] The dispute over the border had its genesis in the colonial era. After their victory in World War I, Britain and France seized large parts of the defeated Ottoman

Empire—the British took Iraq and Palestine, and the French took Syria and Lebanon. The Anglo-French Agreement of 1923 then drew the Syrian-Palestinian border so that while the Golan Heights would be within the French Mandate (i.e., Syria), both sides of the Jordan River and all of Lake Tiberias would be in Palestine, which then became the British Mandate and later, of course, Israel (see Map 12.1).

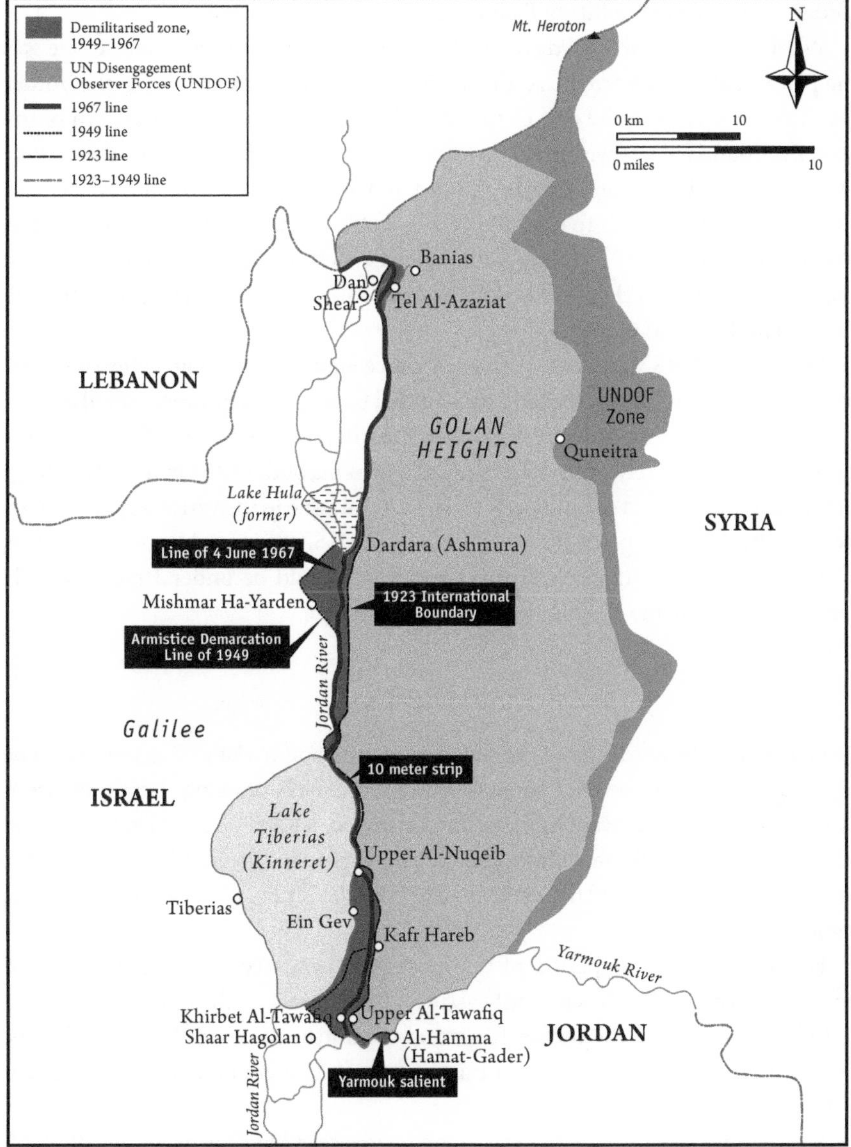

Map 12.1 The Syrian-Israeli Frontiers, from Daniel Kurtzer et al., *Peace Puzzle,* Kindle edition, 67. Permission granted from Cornell University Press.

The 1947 UN partition plan essentially retained those boundaries. However, the 1923 agreement and subsequent British policy during the Mandate distinguished between the issues of who had sovereignty over the Jordan River and Lake Tiberias and the question of water usage, for the agreement stated that "any existing rights over the use of the waters of the Jordan by the inhabitants of Syria shall be maintained unimpaired . . . and the inhabitants of Syria and Lebanon shall have the same fishing and navigation rights on . . . Lake Kinneret [Tiberias] and the River Jordan . . . as the inhabitants of Palestine."[5]

What made it feasible to distinguish between sovereignty and water usage was the placement of the borders. At the northeast corner of Lake Tiberias, the border was only 10 meters to the east of the shoreline; and for several miles north of the lake, the boundary was within 50 to 400 meters of the Jordan River. In accordance with the treaty, Britain and France allowed Syrian villagers to cross the border and use the river and the lake to obtain drinking water, to fish, and to water their cattle. In short, the colonial 1923 treaty—on which Israel still relies to defend its position that Syria has no legal right to a border on Lake Tiberias—gave Syria access to both the Jordan River and the lake.

During the 1948 war, the Syrian army succeeded in advancing some 10 to 400 meters west of the 1923 so-called international border and captured a small strip of land on the northeast border of the lake—thus giving them direct access to the lake instead of having to rely on Israel to uphold the terms of the 1923 treaty.[6] The status of that tiny strip of land continued to be the central issue in the various Syrian-Israeli peace talks that took place between 1948 and 2018, although Menachem Begin's 1981 announcement that the Golan henceforth would be under Israeli law—de facto annexed—made it even more difficult to resolve.

The Water Issue

At first glance, the border issue, involving a piece of land trivial in size, seemed to be essentially a water issue: since some 40 percent of Israel's drinking water came from Lake Tiberias, it didn't want Syria to have access to, let alone control any part of it. Thus, if Israel had withdrawn from the Golan Heights and returned to the pre-1967 lines, Syria's borders would have extended to both the Jordan River and Lake Tiberias itself.

However, during the period of the most promising negotiations, Hafez Assad and other Syrian officials repeatedly assured Israel that if it allowed Syria to return to the eastern bank of the Jordan River and the northeast corner of Lake Tiberias, Syria would agree not to pollute or pump water from them or attempt to interfere with Israel's access to them.

For several reasons, the Syrian assurances were credible. During Syria's 1948–67 presence on the river and the lake it had not interfered with Israel's access to them. In any case, the Banias River, one of the Jordan River's main tributaries, was located entirely within Syrian territory, so that if Syria had wanted to interfere with Israel's water sources, it could easily have done so from there.

The real issue for the Syrians was essentially a symbolic one: throughout the negotiations during the 1990s for an Israeli-Syrian peace treaty, Assad insisted that the issue was neither the trivial amount of territory at stake nor water, but "justice" and "rights," which required the return of "every inch" of Syrian land lost in the 1967 war. He would not reach peace with Israel, he said, until he could once again "dip his feet" into the lake.

Likewise, for the Israelis, the dispute over where the boundary lines should be drawn was equally symbolic. The "original" or "international" borders that placed Lake Tiberias inside Palestine/Israel—that is, those specified in the 1923 treaty and then included in the 1947 UN partition plan—became irrelevant as a result of the Syrian territorial gains in the 1948 war. Consequently, the Israeli position on the lake holds that as a matter of legal and moral principles, nations must not be allowed to benefit by military aggression. However, when it comes to its own military conquests over lands given to the Palestinians in the UN partition, Israel does not mention these "principles."

The Palestinian Issue

From the mid-1970s onward, Assad gradually withdrew, in effect, from the overall Arab-Israeli conflict. Initially his position was that a Syrian-Israeli peace settlement depended on an Israeli withdrawal from all of its conquests in the 1967 war and the creation of a Palestinian state in the West Bank and Gaza. Then, after Egypt negotiated its own settlement with Israel, Assad told Henry Kissinger and later Jimmy Carter that he would be satisfied with an agreement that "restored the rights" of the Palestinians, but that this would not necessarily require the creation of a Palestinian state in the West Bank, as opposed to some form of Jordanian control over that area.

That became moot, however, when Jordan decided to withdraw from the Israeli-Palestinian conflict and reach its own separate peace with Israel. Consequently, Assad's new position was that any solution acceptable to the PLO would be acceptable to him, but he also told the PLO that he would not allow it to undermine the Syrian-Israeli negotiations. In August 1993, Assad told the US government—and therefore, in effect, Israel—that an Israeli-Syrian peace agreement, then seemingly at hand, would not depend on a settlement of the Israeli-Palestinian conflict.[7]

The Rabin-Assad Negotiations

In late 1992, the Assad and Rabin governments entered into intense secret negotiations, which over the course of the next two years resulted in a draft agreement that resolved most of the differences on these issues and greatly narrowed those that remained.[8]

Both sides had made significant concessions. Rabin agreed—in principle—that in the context of full peace, over a three- to five-year period, Israel would withdraw to the pre-June 1967 line rather than insist on a return to the 1923 boundaries. Thus, Assad would attain his most important nationalist or symbolic goals: a repudiation of the colonial boundaries set by Britain and France, the regaining of all the territory lost in the 1967 war, and a Syrian presence on Lake Tiberias.

In exchange, Assad agreed to demilitarize the Golan and share the water sources there with Israel, pledged not to interfere with Israeli access to the Jordan River and Lake Tiberias, and accepted the principle of full normalization of relations in the context of an Israeli withdrawal from the Golan.

What did "full normalization of relations" entail? In January 1994, Assad and President Bill Clinton met in Geneva to discuss the final terms of a settlement. At the close of the conference Assad joined with Clinton in a joint written statement, saying that he had made a "strategic choice" for normal peaceful relations with Israel, including full diplomatic relations, trade, and even tourism.[9] In a post-conference news briefing, Assad added: "We want the peace of the brave, a real peace. . . . If the leaders of Israel have enough courage . . . a new era of security and stability and normal peaceful relations . . . will emerge in the region. . . . We are ready to sign peace now."[10]

Thus, though some details remained to be negotiated, by 1993 an Israeli-Syrian peace agreement was at hand. It failed to materialize, however, because Rabin suspended the talks on the grounds that Israeli public opinion would not simultaneously accept an agreement with the Palestinians (i.e., the Oslo accords of 1993) and one with the Syrians.

In 1994 the peace talks resumed, but Rabin added a new Israeli precondition: any agreement would have to be ratified by a national referendum.[11] This was a major problem for Assad, because if the Israeli public rejected the proposed settlement, Syria would end up with no agreement at all, despite having made painful public concessions. Even so, Assad was willing to continue the negotiations. In the summer of 1995, however, Rabin again broke them off, primarily because domestic Israeli opposition to a withdrawal from the Golan Heights was growing and Rabin was considering calling for early elections.

Shimon Peres and the Negotiations

In his memoirs, Bill Clinton writes that "Rabin had given me a commitment to withdraw from the Golan to the June 4, 1967, borders as long as Israel's concerns were satisfied."[12] After Rabin was assassinated on November 4, 1995, and Foreign Minister Shimon Peres became the acting prime minister of Israel, according to Clinton, Peres reaffirmed that commitment as long as a peace treaty with Syria included measures to ensure Israeli security.

In fact, Assad was ready to accept the demilitarization of the Golan Heights that would be monitored by an international peacekeeping force—either a UN force (as Syria preferred), or a US or US-led force (as Israel preferred).[13] Peres also wanted direct security guarantees from the United States, and Clinton agreed to provide them: "Peres wanted me to sign a security treaty with Israel if it gave up the Golan, an idea that was suggested to me later by Netanyahu and would be advanced again by Barak. I had told them I was willing to do it."[14]

In October 1998, the two sides met in the United States to negotiate the terms of a peace settlement. During the Wye Plantation Talks, as they were called, both Syria and Israel wanted full participation by the Clinton administration. Assad was prepared for a bilateral settlement with Israel, even without any progress toward an Israeli-Palestinian settlement. In exchange for a full Israeli withdrawal to the pre–1967 war line over a two- to three-year period, Syria reiterated that it would agree to a number of joint security measures and normal political and economic relations.[15]

However, Peres began to pull back from the negotiations, which ended in failure when Israel formally "suspended" the talks in March 1996. There were several reasons another opportunity for peace was lost. In the previous few months there had been a series of Palestinian attacks against Israeli civilian targets, resulting in a further hardening of Israeli public opinion; by January 1996, with the national elections looming, more than 75 percent of the public opposed a full Israeli withdrawal from the Golan.[16] As well, Foreign Minister Ehud Barak at this point opposed an Israeli withdrawal from the Golan Heights and began to publicly undercut the negotiations.[17]

Moreover, Peres had decided to attack Hezbollah in Lebanon—1996's "Operation Grapes of Wrath"—and believed it would not be a propitious moment for him to make concessions to Syria. Finally, though Clinton was impressed with Assad's concessions and was enthusiastic about the prospects of Israeli-Syrian peace, he was unwilling to pressure the Israeli government to agree to it.

Peres was widely considered to be Israel's leading advocate for peace. However, the reality was much more complicated. For example, in 2006 the government of Ehud Olmert learned of Assad's statements describing his interest in reopening negotiations for a peace agreement. Peres, then the vice–prime minister, "furiously rejected" the Assad opening and argued against withdrawal from the Golan, asserting that Israel's security required the continuing construction of new settlements in the area. A *Haaretz* columnist commented: "Not peace-shmeace, not Syria-Shmyria. Construction. The Ariel Sharon of the 1980s and the 1990s could not have said it better."[18]

Netanyahu and Syria, Part I

In May 1996, Benjamin Netanyahu was elected prime minister. He initially signaled that he was willing to resume talks with Syria, but when he refused to reaffirm

Rabin's and Peres's conditional commitment to withdraw from the Golan, Assad ruled out the resumption of official Israeli-Syrian talks. Still, there continued to be secret and indirect talks through intermediaries, including the European Union representative Miguel Moritanos and later Netanyahu's personal friend Ron Lauder, a former US ambassador to Israel.

According to Quandt and others, the talks between Lauder and Assad were kept secret from the US government, and while Syrians who were involved in the talks claim that some progress was made, negotiations broke down when Netanyahu refused to provide a map that would "indicate exactly the line to which Israel would withdraw on the Golan in return for peace."[19] While some analysts believe that Netanyahu was seriously considering returning to the Rabin commitment for a complete Israeli withdrawal to the pre-1967 borders, strong public opposition convinced him to back away.

Ehud Barak and the Syrian Negotiations

In the May 1999 Israeli elections, Ehud Barak defeated Netanyahu and became prime minister. Shortly afterward the Israeli-Syrian negotiations were resumed, and in February 2000, Barak told his cabinet that he was bound by Rabin's conditional commitment to withdraw from the Golan.[20] In early 2000, the Clinton administration, which was again mediating the talks, drafted a peace treaty that narrowed the differences between Israel and Syria to essentially symbolic ones.[21] The principles of the draft treaty were basically those that Hafez Assad and Rabin had agreed to eight years earlier: a full Israeli withdrawal from the Golan in return for the Syrian agreement to demilitarize the area and the full normalization of diplomatic and economic relations.

On the water issue, there continued to be some differences. Israel insisted that a final agreement would have to "ensure the continuation of Israel's current use in quantity and quality of all the surface and underground waters in the areas from which Israeli forces will be relocated"—meaning that Israel must continue to have full use of the Jordan River, its tributaries in the Golan, and Lake Tiberias.

Syria responded, probably too vaguely, that the water issue should be "based on the relevant international principles," which apparently implied that Syria must have sovereignty over the Jordan River tributaries in the Golan. Away from the negotiating table, however, Syrian officials stressed that they had no intention of diverting the headwaters of the Jordan River or withdrawing freshwater from Lake Tiberias—a commitment lent credibility by the fact that during the previous nineteen years when the Syrian forces were on the lake, they had refrained from pumping water from it. For Syria, they insisted, the issue was not so much water usage as the national/symbolic one of restoring Syrian sovereignty over "every inch" of land lost in 1967: "Giving up a grain of our soil is treason," Assad said.[22] In his memoirs, American negotiator Martin Indyk explained:

> Insisting on Israel's withdrawal to the June 4 line rather than the international line—a difference of only a few hundred meters—was especially important to Assad because it signaled to the Arab world that he was regaining land taken by conquest; in his mind that represented the difference between dignity and humiliation, patriotism and treason.[23]

There were still some differences on the boundary issue. The draft treaty simply noted Syria's insistence that it must be based on the pre–1967 war lines. Significantly, the Israelis did not flatly reject this, but argued that the boundary must "take into account security and other vital interests of the Parties as well as legal considerations of both sides."

The boundary issue remained unresolved, however, despite Barak's initial admission that the Rabin government had agreed in principle to the Syrian position. There matters stood until Barak repeated the process of Israeli retreats from its previous positions. Facing continued public opposition, Barak backed down. To be sure, that opposition was considerable: "A whole generation of Israelis had grown up believing that the Golan . . . was essential for Israel's security and thus should remain in her hands. . . . Other polls showed that only 13 percent of Israelis were in favor of a full withdrawal from the Golan Heights."[24]

Hafiz Assad died in June 2000 and was succeeded by his son, Bashar Assad. In his first months in office the new Syrian leader on several occasions signaled that he was prepared to restart the negotiations and sign a peace treaty, provided the remaining issues were satisfactorily resolved. Barak insisted, however, that before negotiations could resume, Syria would have to agree to abandon its claim to any part of Lake Tiberias. This position reportedly angered some members of Barak's government, who argued that he "was not responsive enough to the signals that emanated from Damascus following the death of Hafiz Assad," instead giving Syria "the same ultimatum that he gave Arafat: First, announce your willingness to compromise and then . . . we renew the dialogue."[25]

When Barak's demand was rejected by the new Syrian government, he abruptly ended the pre-negotiations process. According to subsequent Israeli reports, Barak had acted unilaterally, without consulting his cabinet. Then, in spring 2001, the Israeli prime minister again rejected signals that Bashar Assad would be willing to pick up the negotiations where they had been broken off a year earlier. And when Bill Clinton told Assad that Barak could not take the political risk of agreeing to a return to the line of June 4, 1967, "a deal that seemed ripe for the making" collapsed.[26]

There is an overwhelming consensus among US and Israeli officials that Hafez Assad (and in all probability Bashar Assad) was prepared for a full peace treaty that would protect Israel's legitimate security and water interests. Consequently, Israel bears the major responsibility for the lost opportunity for peace.

In his memoirs, Bill Clinton wrote:

> The Syrians came to [the negotiations] . . . in a positive and flexible frame of mind, eager to make an agreement. By contrast, Barak, who had pushed hard for the talks, decided, apparently on the basis of polling data . . . to slow-walk the process. . . . I was, to put it mildly, disappointed. . . . It quickly became apparent that Barak still had not authorized anyone on his team to accept June 4, no matter what the Syrians offered.[27]

Strikingly, during the 1990s negotiations, top Israeli military, defense, and intelligence officials strongly supported giving back the Golan Heights in return for a full peace with Syria:

> According to *Haaretz*, "General Staff officers . . . [believed] that a peace deal could be struck after a very short summit meeting." After Barak refused Assad's terms, the story continued, IDF officers now feel at liberty to state explicitly that . . . responsibility for the failure of negotiations with Syria last year is borne by Barak, not Hafez Assad. General Staff officers were willing to assent to Assad's demand that Israel withdraw from the northeast shoreline of Lake Tiberias, and they believed that Barak's intransigent refusal to comply with the Syrian demand reflected a triumph of passing domestic political considerations over permanent security needs.[28]

Barak's senior advisor Gada Baltiansky, told reporters: "I heard senior members of the Israeli delegation saying that an agreement was possible within two or three months. On all the issues—normalization, security, and water—we got more than we'd gotten before. . . . In the negotiations with Syria, there was no creativity, no openness, no readiness to shatter myths—just like in the negotiations with the Palestinians."[29]

In a 2003 Israeli documentary three senior officials who participated in the failed 1999 Israeli-Syrian negotiations said that it was Barak who missed the opportunity, getting cold feet because of domestic opposition. General Uri Sagie, who headed the Israeli negotiating team, said, "It was clear to me and I still hold the view that it was possible to reach an agreement." The documentary also quoted US officials making the same point. For example, Martin Indyk said, "We applied heavy pressure on the Syrians and they made a series of concessions. They expected to hear the magic words, withdrawal to the '67 borders."

Galia Golan summed up the evidence: "The overall verdict not only espoused by Clinton himself but also by most of those involved in the four months of talks under Barak, including and especially Barak's chief negotiator Uri Sagie, was that Barak—not Assad—was the main obstacle to a breakthrough in the Israeli-Syrian talks."[30]

Bill Clinton and the Breakdown of the Negotiations

Clinton shares the blame for the lost opportunity for peace. Though he sought to persuade Barak to accept Assad's overtures—and in his memoirs is critical of Barak's stonewalling—he was unwilling to put any real pressure on the Israeli prime minister and in his public statements he largely blamed Syria for the breakdown of the negotiations.

Even Dennis Ross, Clinton's primary advisor on Israeli matters and almost always inclined to support the Israeli positions, is critical of Barak and Clinton, writing that Barak ruled out making any concessions even as the Syrians moved on every issue, writing, "Why did President Clinton tolerate Barak's posture? Why would he not say to him, If you want my help, and if you want me to continue my efforts, I need you either to directly reaffirm [Rabin's conditional withdrawal offer] . . . or allow me to do it—otherwise you are on your own. That was simply not Bill Clinton. He had great sympathy for Barak's political predicament."[31]

Another key Clinton administration official, Martin Indyk, also makes it clear that he thought the president should have done much more to pressure Barak, pointing out that "there were no suggestions or even hints at a reduction of U.S. aid to Israel or a reduction of other types of support."[32] On the contrary, a recently declassified December 15, 1999, transcript of a telephone conversation between Clinton and Barak reveals the extent to which, in Ahron Bregman words, Clinton was "speaking from Barak's script" when he told him: "I think that the most important thing for you is the Sea of Galilee. If I were in your place I would be concerned that someone [a reference to Syria] could try to poison the water of the Sea of Galilee."[33]

Finally, Quandt argued that Clinton, "rather than simply parrot[ing]" Barak's position, should have presented an American proposal that, in return for Assad's concessions, Israel would withdraw to the June 4, 1967, line "without any gimmicks or ambiguity." Clinton could then "offer to provide American troops for a peacekeeping force on the Golan if both sides requested it . . . consider a bilateral U.S.-Israeli security treaty . . . and offer a generous military support package to help Israel redeploy its forces from Golan."[34]

The Israeli scholar Ahron Bregman concludes:

> The failure of Israel and Syria to reach peace during this period on the basis of a full Israeli withdrawal from the occupied Golan was a missed opportunity and, clearly, the fault lay with Barak. . . . His offer to Assad [was] . . . less than what the late prime minister, Yitzhak Rabin, had proposed before, namely, a full Israeli withdrawal from the Golan Heights and a restoration of the pre-1967 situation, whereby Syria could access the Sea of Galilee.[35]

Ariel Sharon and the Syrian Negotiations

In March 2001, Ariel Sharon was elected prime minister of Israel. In the next few years, Bashar Assad told the Sharon administration and US officials that he wanted to resume talks with Israel without preconditions—meaning that his government would no longer insist that Israel must agree *in advance* that it would return to the lines of June 4, 1967. As well, Syria would not insist that Israel must also agree to reach an agreement with the Palestinians.[36]

Bashar Assad's overtures were rebuffed by Sharon, who on a number of occasions told interviewers that Israeli security prohibited any withdrawal from Golan, even if the Syrians dropped their demand to return to the shoreline of Lake Tiberias, and even in return for full peace. Israeli forces must remain close to Damascus, he said, in order to deter Syrian aggression.[37]

Once again, leading Israeli generals rejected Sharon's security arguments. Chief of Staff Moshe Ya'alon told a *Haaretz* interviewer that he favored negotiations with Assad and that he was ready to cede the Golan Heights to Syria in return for a true peace agreement. However, he said, "Sharon rejected my suggestion outright."[38]

Ehud Olmert and the Syrian Negotiations

After Sharon suffered a major stroke on January 4, 2006, Ehud Olmert became the acting prime minister and was elected to a full term in March 2006. As noted earlier, Olmert initially dismissed the December 2006 Israeli intelligence report that Bashar Assad had "a real desire to reach an agreement with Israel." However, the earlier secret talks had narrowed the gap between the Israeli and Syrian positions on the key issues, and in July 2006, the Israeli and Syrian negotiators reached agreement on the principles that should govern a peace treaty between their countries.[39] The main points are summarized below.

Sovereignty and Borders: Israel would gradually withdraw from the Golan Heights (over a five- to fifteen-year period) to the lines of June 4, 1967, and Syria would hold sovereignty over that territory. However, further negotiations were necessary to establish exactly where those lines were; Syria contended that they extended to the shoreline of the northeast corner of Lake Tiberias—a factual claim that is supported by the judgment of independent experts, including Israelis.

Water. Israel would control the use and disposition of the water in the upper Jordan River and Lake Tiberias. Syria would not interrupt or obstruct the natural flow of water in either quality or quantity in the Jordan River, its tributaries in the Golan Heights, and Lake Tiberias. However, Syrian use of those waters for residential drinking and fishing purposes was guaranteed.

Subsequently, Assad reiterated to former president Jimmy Carter that Syria would not withdraw the drinking water from these sources but that it expected financial assistance for desalination plants and a commitment from Turkey that it would supply Syria with water.[40]

Security. The areas the Israeli forces would vacate would be demilitarized and only a limited Syrian police presence would be deployed. As well, the armed forces of both sides would be limited in the nearby regions, though the Syrians would be required to withdraw to a much greater distance than Israel. An early warning station, manned by the United States, would be established to monitor the agreement.

Another key issue during the negotiations was Syria's ties to Hezbollah, Hamas, and Iran. Israel insisted that Syria commit to breaking those ties; while Syria rejected that as a precondition, senior officials told Israeli journalists that in the context of a peace agreement, Syria would seek to curb militant groups in the region as well as distance itself from Iran.[41] The *Haaretz* diplomatic correspondent wrote: "The Assad family . . . considers itself to be an integral part of the Sunni world, objects to the Shi'a theocratic regime, and is particularly opposed to Iran's policy in Iraq."[42]

Later, in July 2008, the lead Israeli negotiator during the talks said that Syria was willing to cut its close relations with Iran in return for financial and military support from the United States and that Bashar Assad was "increasingly open to a peace deal with Israel which could greatly weaken Iran's influence in the Middle East."[43]

Israeli military and intelligence officials—now including Barak, who became the defense minister in the Olmert government—overwhelmingly and often publicly supported a peace agreement with Syria along the lines of the draft treaty; among those high-level officials were IDF chief of staff Gabi Ashkenazi, and his predecessors as heads of the IDF, Shaul Mofaz, Moshe Ya'alon, and Dan Halutz.[44] Mossad chief Meir Dagan disagreed, but Ilan Mizrahi, former deputy chief of Mossad and the national security advisor to Olmert, argued that Israel should make a deal with Syria because it would "change the security situation in the Middle East." When asked if an Israeli withdrawal from the Golan would be a security threat, he responded: "Our chief of staff doesn't think so. Our head of military intelligence doesn't think so. . . . The best Israeli generals are saying we can negotiate it, so I believe them."[45]

Nonetheless, once again the Israeli government turned down the opportunity to reach a peace agreement; when the Syrians demanded that the talks become official and be conducted at a senior level with the participation of the US government, Olmert refused, and the "unofficial" negotiations ended.[46] There were several reasons. First, surveys continued to show that large majorities of the Israeli public objected to withdrawing from the Golan Heights, even for peace with Syria.[47] Second, Olmert was in the midst of promising negotiations with Palestinian Authority (PA) president Mahmoud Abbas that would require an Israeli withdrawal from the West Bank; he didn't believe that the public could swallow two such reversals of past Israeli policies, especially since the level of national trust in him was declining.[48]

Finally, the Bush administration, furious at what it believed was Assad's "stirring of unrest" in Iraq and his undermining of US policies there, was adamantly opposed to an Israeli-Syrian deal that "would be considered a prize in Damascus." According to a *Haaretz* news story, "When Israeli officials asked Secretary of State Condoleezza Rice about the possibility of exploring the seriousness of Syrian calls for peace talks, she responded: Don't even think about it." And "Jerusalem obeyed," stated the *Haaretz* headline.[49]

Netanyahu and Syria, Part II

In March 2009, Benjamin Netanyahu was elected to his second term as prime minister. In late 2009, John Kerry, then chair of the Senate Committee on Foreign Relations, met with Bashar Assad who told him that he was ready to reopen negotiations with Israel. When Kerry pressed Assad on his support for the Hezbollah in Lebanon, Assad replied that "everything is to be negotiated," which Kerry understood to mean that this policy could change if a peace deal was reached with Israel. When Assad asked Kerry what it would take to convince Israel to reopen negotiations, Kerry advised him to make a secret proposal in the form of a letter to President Obama, which could then be passed on to Netanyahu.[50]

In 2010, Assad sent such a letter to Obama, stating "Syria's willingness to take a number of steps in exchange for the return of the Golan from Israel." The Assad offer was passed to the Israeli government, and as a result, Netanyahu, again at the urging of Barak and other high military and defense officials, authorized secret talks.[51] In January 2011, Netanyahu sent a message to Assad, saying that he would be ready to discuss Syria's demand for a full Israeli withdrawal from the Golan Heights to the June 4, 1967, lines, on the condition that Syria agree to abandon its alliance with Iran and Hezbollah.[52] "The idea," an Israeli participant in the talks told the *New York Times*, "was to see if we could drive a wedge in the radical axis of Iran-Syria-Hezbollah."[53]

The talks, brokered by Obama's chief Middle East advisor Dennis Ross and other US government officials, continued until March 2011. However, neither side was prepared to unambiguously state their bottom lines, for Assad would not go further than a cautious willingness to discuss "Syria's strategic positioning and regional security issues" and Netanyahu refused to commit to a full Israeli withdrawal from the Golan. According to an Israeli official involved in the talks, "Netanyahu did not commit to returning the entire area, but he did not shut the door to the territorial claims of the Syrians. . . . [T]he proposal he suggested was—if I get what I want, the broad context of which was Iran and Hezbollah, I am prepared to discuss their territorial demands."[54]

Israeli-Syrian Relations since the Outbreak of the Syrian Civil War

It is not clear whether this you-go-first dance could have ended successfully if the outbreak of the Syrian civil war in early 2011 had not led Netanyahu to end the talks.

Since then, Israel has followed a dual-track policy toward the Bashar Assad regime. On the one hand, it has repeatedly attacked the forces and weapons sites in Syria of Hezbollah and Iran, two of Assad's major allies in his fight against rebel forces, including ISIS (Islamic State in Iraq and Syria). Yet, in other ways, Israel has operated as "a silent ally of Assad"[55] because it has had no practical alternative to him, especially after the most radical groups became the dominant force in the original rebel coalition and tens of thousands of Jihadists established bases in southern Syria, near the Golan Heights. As well, Assad continued to prevent any attacks on Israel from Syrian territory; in July 2018 Netanyahu said: "We haven't had a problem with the Assad regime. . . . For 40 years, not a single bullet was fired on the Golan Heights."[56]

In March 2019, at Netanyahu's urging, the Trump administration formally recognized Israeli sovereignty over the Golan, almost certainly closing the door to any chance of it being returned to Syria in the context of an overall peace agreement. Thus, once again Israel—this time with the enthusiastic support of the American government—forfeited an opportunity for real peace. In the absence of a peace treaty, it is not difficult to imagine circumstances in which the current no-war, no-peace situation could deteriorate into armed conflict, particularly if Assad continues to accept Iranian military assistance in what remains of the Syrian civil war.

Today Israel considers Iran to be its most dangerous enemy. Yet, but for its fixation on pure symbolism—preventing Syria from having a foothold on a corner of Lake Tiberias—in all likelihood an attainable Israeli-Syrian peace treaty would have included a commitment by the Assads, father and son, not only to refrain from interfering with Israeli access to the Jordan River and the lake but also to curb the Iranian role in Syria.

Perhaps even more than the many other opportunities for peace settlements that have been lost primarily because of Israeli intransigence, the unwillingness of one Israeli government after another to make an almost purely symbolic concession to Syria, one that has been supported by the great majority of its generals and other security analysts, has been an almost unfathomable blow to Israel's own declared national interests.

PART THREE

WAR AND PEACE IN THE ISRAELI-PALESTINIAN CONFLICT

13

The Israeli-Palestinian Conflict, 1917–88

Recapitulating the Zionist-Palestinian Conflict, 1917–48

In the 2,000 years prior to the 1917 Balfour Declaration, except for tiny minorities of Jews and Christians, Palestine was peopled by Arab Muslims, though they were usually ruled by foreign empires: the Romans, the Crusaders, and the Ottoman Turks. Despite that history, the Zionist argument is that even though the Jews were largely expelled from Palestine by the Romans, they never ceased to be the true and only legitimate indigenous people of the land of Palestine. Indeed, throughout those twenty centuries, it is claimed, Palestine continued to be the national home for the Jewish people throughout the world.

At the end of the nineteenth century, however, there were only about 50,000 Jews in Palestine, about 3 percent of the total population and a tiny fraction of the some 10 million global Jewish population, scattered in numerous "homelands" throughout the world. After the development of Zionism, Jewish migration to Palestine increased somewhat, but soon generated resistance by the indigenous peoples.[1] As Palestinian nationalism grew in opposition to both British rule after the Balfour Declaration and the Zionist settlements, major riots occurred in 1920–21, 1929, and the "Arab revolt" of 1936–39.

It is often argued that the Zionists simply didn't recognize that the Arabs constituted the overwhelming majority in the land of Palestine—allegedly regarding it as "a land without a people for a people without a land"—but that was far from being the case. The leading Zionist leaders during the 1930s—Vladimir Jabotinsky, David Ben-Gurion, and even Moshe Sharett, the most dovish of the major leaders—clearly recognized that the overwhelming majority of the indigenous inhabitants of Palestine were unwilling to make way for the establishment of a Jewish state in their land and understandably chose to resist.

The conclusion the Zionists drew was that Palestinian resistance had to be militarily defeated. Of course, they could have made a different choice, namely, to accept the international consensus, from the 1930s until today, that almost all outside observers, leaders, and investigating bodies have reached: that the only fair and legitimate solution to the conflict must be that of partition, the division of the land of Palestine between the Jews and the Palestinians, or in contemporary parlance, "the two-state solution."

To be sure, the Palestinians and the Arab states also initially rejected a two-state compromise, for example, as it was embodied in the 1947 UN partition plan, while for tactical reasons Ben-Gurion and the other Zionist leaders officially "accepted" it—but their fingers were crossed behind their backs, for they planned to expand from the partition borders once they had the power to do so. Which they did.

The Israeli-Palestinian Conflict, 1948–82

For a number of years after the 1948 war there was little organized Palestinian resistance to Israel, as Egypt controlled the Gaza Strip and King Abdullah continued to rule over the West Bank, officially annexing it to Jordan in April 1950.

In 1964, the Palestine Liberation Organization (PLO) was formed to represent the Palestinian nationalist movement; the leading Arab governments had encouraged and played an important early role in the creation of the PLO, partly in order to gain control over it so as to avoid being drawn into war with Israel.[2]

In its early years, however, the PLO was committed to "liberating" all of Palestine, which its 1964 National Charter defined to mean all the territory between the Jordan River and the Mediterranean—meaning, of course, all of the territory that became the state of Israel. In January 1965, the main Palestinian guerrilla organization, Fatah, began launching attacks into Israel from bases in Jordan, Lebanon, and, in particular, Syria. In the next two years, the attacks precipitated increasingly severe Israeli retaliations, culminating in the 1967 war.

Following the war, the Arab defeat intensified the determination of the PLO to free itself from the control of the Arab governments that might reach political settlements with Israel that ignored the plight of the Palestinians.[3] In 1969, Yasser Arafat became the primary leader of the PLO, which in 1974 was designated by an Arab state summit meeting as "the sole legitimate representative of the Palestinian people."

Though himself a practicing Muslim, Arafat was not a zealot and intended the PLO to be a secular national movement rather than a religious one. Even before Arafat came to power, the PLO was primarily secular, had sought to separate religion from politics, and had called for the creation in Palestine of a democratic and secular state. Indeed, many PLO leaders specifically denounced anti-Semitism and emphasized their intention to accept Jews as equal citizens in a new Palestine.

Lost Opportunities for an Israeli-Palestinian Peace Settlement after the 1967 War

The Palestinian issue arose again after the 1967 war, during which Israel captured the West Bank, Gaza, and all of Jerusalem. In the weeks following the war, the Israeli cabinet met a number of times to consider what to do. Three possibilities were considered, the first of which was Israeli annexation, formal or de facto, of the conquered territories. This was quickly rejected, for few Israeli leaders wanted the responsibilities and headaches of establishing permanent rule over the Palestinians, especially since an eventual "demographic problem," meaning the emergence of a Palestinian majority in an expanded or "Greater" Israel, could be foreseen.

The second briefly considered possibility was "the Palestinian option"—allowing the creation of some kind of limited or semi-autonomous Palestinian state in the occupied territories. A large majority of the cabinet ministers, including Defense Minister Moshe Dayan and Prime Minister Levi Eshkol, initially favored some kind of Palestinian option, though there was no agreement on just how much independence the Palestinians would be allowed.[4]

According to Amos Elon, one of Israel's leading journalists during this period, there was a "distinct possibility" that shortly after the 1967 war Israel could have reached a peace settlement with the Palestinians at a time when the PLO was still a "fairly marginal group." During the summer of 1967, Alon wrote, a number of senior Israeli intelligence officers spoke with prominent Palestinian civil and political leaders throughout the West Bank and reported to Dayan that most of them were ready to agree to the establishment of a demilitarized Palestinian state in the West Bank and to sign a separate peace with Israel. However, Dayan buried their report, which was never submitted to the cabinet.[5]

In any case, for several reasons the Israeli government quickly abandoned the Palestinian option. The opposition of the American government was a major factor.[6] On July 30, 1967, Foreign Minister Abba Eban told the Israeli cabinet that the Johnson administration firmly rejected the idea of a Palestinian state and would not provide political or economic support to such a solution for the Israel-Palestinian conflict. Instead, the US government proposed that the Palestinian issue should be decided in negotiations between Israel and Jordan. On hearing Eban's report, Eshkol commented that "Hussein is the darling of the Americans," and therefore Israel could not bypass him in any settlement of the conflict.[7]

In any event, the Israeli government itself became increasingly concerned over growing militant Palestinian nationalism, led by the PLO—which at that point was committed to the destruction of the state of Israel and its replacement by a Palestinian state throughout all of Mandatory Palestine.

The "Jordanian solution," then, was the third opportunity for Israel to have ended its conflict with the Palestinians. Israeli scholarship has conclusively demonstrated that Israel could have reached peace agreements with Jordan at any point from 1948 through the late 1980s, and by so doing could have transferred the Palestinian "problem," in effect, to the Jordanians: until 1988, the Hashemite monarchies of Abdullah and Hussein were no less opposed than Israel to the establishment of an independent Palestinian state in the West Bank and Gaza, over which they claimed their own sovereignty.

Had Israel agreed to accept the Jordanian sovereignty claims, almost all Israeli and other historians of that period agree, Jordan would have stayed out of the 1948 and 1967 wars, suppressed the Palestinian nationalist movement in the West Bank and Gaza, and agreed to a number of measures to meet legitimate Israeli security concerns.

Indeed, no less an authority than Yasser Arafat told his biographer what would have happened if Israel had agreed to withdraw from the West Bank after the 1967 war: King Hussein, he said, would have immediately agreed to a peace treaty with Israel and restored Jordanian sovereignty and military rule in the West Bank. In that case, Arafat continued, "The PLO would have been finished. Absolutely finished."[8]

Nonetheless, after the 1948 war and again after the 1967 war, Israel rejected the Jordanian option. The most important reason, of course, was that the Israelis did not wish to renounce their ambition to create a "Greater Israel," encompassing the West Bank, Jerusalem, and Gaza as well as its expanded territories following the 1948 war. Beyond that, there was growing opposition among Israeli leaders to returning the conquered territories to Jordan—for some, because they distrusted King Hussein; for others, conversely, because they feared that he would lose power to a militant Islamic or Palestinian movement. In any case, by the 1970s the growth of militant Jewish settlements in the West Bank resulted in the progressive abandonment of government support for returning the conquered territories to Jordan—either because Israeli political leaders supported the ever-expanding settler movement or feared the political consequences of opposing it.

The Israeli historian Avi Raz summed up the policy choices facing the Israeli leaders at the end of the 1967 war: either the Palestinian or the Jordanian options would have provided "a historic opportunity to defuse the Palestinian problem which lies at the heart of the decades-long Arab-Zionist conflict." However, he continued, "it chose neither option."[9]

The PLO Evolves

After the 1967 war, UN Resolution 242 ignored the question of Palestinian political rights, particularly the creation of a Palestinian state in the occupied territories, instead calling only for "a just settlement of the refugee problem." For this reason and because at that time the PLO still regarded a Palestinian state in the occupied territories as only the first step toward the full "liberation" of all Palestine, the organization rejected the UN resolution.

In the early 1970s the PLO turned to terrorism, whose main purpose was to call international attention to the Palestinian political cause and ultimately to force Israel to withdraw from the occupied territories. For several years during this period there were numerous PLO bombings and other attacks on Israeli civilian targets both inside and outside Israel, the most notorious of the latter being the killing of eleven Israeli athletes during the 1972 Munich Olympics. While Palestinian terrorism did indeed focus global attention on the Israeli-Palestinian conflict, its methods were not only morally reprehensible but ended by undermining the Palestinian cause and even led to severe criticism from its own supporters.

For example, Rashid Khalidi, a leading Palestinian American historian and activist and informal advisor to the PLO, wrote that the organization's "equivocations and hesitations" with regard to a two-state settlement as well as its "self-defeating" terrorist attacks had resulted only in its exclusion from US and Soviet efforts to bring about a peace settlement.[10]

Similarly, Yezid Sayigh, another prominent Palestinian academician and activist and member of several PLO delegations to international conferences, argued that while Arafat came to genuinely support a two-state compromise with Israel, he undercut the chances for such a settlement by mistakenly believing that diplomacy would have a better chance of success if accompanied by the use of force.[11]

In any case, beginning no later than 1973, the PLO's political position began to give way—albeit ambiguously, tentatively, and inconsistently—to a willingness to seek a compromise political solution with Israel.[12] The first step was the decision by Arafat and the PLO, taken in the wake of international outrage at the attack on the Israeli athletes during the 1972 Olympics, to end attacks on Israel within its pre-1967 boundaries or Jewish targets outside of Israel, though not against attacks within the occupied territories.

The emerging indications of Palestinian pragmatism and hints that a compromise settlement might be acceptable were ignored by the Israeli government. To be sure, Israel could point to the continued terrorism and rejectionism of many in the Palestinian movement, but this argument is best regarded as more the pretext than the reason for its refusal to explore the possibility of a compromise settlement. If Israel had been truly interested in a settlement with the Palestinians it could have specified that it was willing to negotiate with a PLO that accepted the existence of Israel, ended terrorism, and sought only a separate Palestinian state. And in light of growing sentiment within the PLO for a two-state settlement, had it done so almost certainly it would have accelerated the Palestinian movement toward moderation and pragmatism.

The US reaction was somewhat more ambiguous. Declassified White House documents reveal that as early as 1970, State Department officials argued that the Palestinians could not be ignored if a peace settlement was to be reached and urged the Nixon administration to bring them into the peace process;[13] in the next few years the leading government Middle East experts, including National Security Council (NSC) official William Quandt, Assistant Secretary of State Joseph Sisco, and Deputy Assistant Secretary of State Alfred Atherton, continued to argue, as Quandt put it in an internal US government assessment, that "Arafat clearly wishes to move toward a political settlement recognizing, at least implicitly, Israel's right to peaceful existence."[14]

Officially, however, like the Israeli government, the Nixon administration—or more precisely Henry Kissinger—was not interested in opening a dialogue with the PLO, and in September 1975 the administration reached a secret agreement with Israel in which it pledged that the US government would not recognize or negotiate with the PLO until it recognized the right of Israel to exist.[15] In his memoirs, Kissinger acknowledges the emerging indications of changes in PLO policies toward Israel, but says:

> A Palestinian state run by the PLO was certain to be irredentist. Even should it change its professed aims, it would not likely remain moderate for long; the PLO's many extremist factions would see to that. Its Soviet ties, too, would lead it in the direction of becoming a radical state like Libya or South Yemen. . . . To them [the Palestinians], a West Bank ministate could be only an interim step toward their final aims.[16]

In fact, though, Kissinger may not have been quite as inflexible as he implies in his memoirs, for it has now been revealed that with his knowledge and apparent approval, by mid-1973 the PLO had established a secret "back-channel" dialogue with high CIA officials, including director Richard Helms, who along with other CIA experts regarded a quiet dialogue with the PLO as valuable.[17] And indeed, Kissinger authorized the CIA's back-channel officials to convey to Arafat that "if the Palestinians are prepared to participate in a settlement by negotiation, the U.S. would be pleased to hear their ideas."[18]

As a result of these signs of flexibility in the US government, several Israeli and American historians have concluded, Arafat and his close associates in the PLO believed that there was a chance that the door might be opening for US support for a two-state solution but that it would rapidly be closed if terrorism continued.

The disastrous defeat of the Arab states in the 1973 war also played a major role in convincing Arafat of the need for a compromise peace settlement.[19] Arafat's decision to start peace negotiations with Israel led to the June 1974 PLO agreement to adopt a new strategy that called for a struggle for "every part of Palestine *that is liberated*" (emphasis added). Anziska writes that this constituted "an acceptance of a political solution on a limited piece of territory,"[20] the first step, however vague, that opened the door for a Palestinian acceptance of a two-state solution.

Once again, though, Israel dismissed the emerging signs of Palestinian moderation as "nothing new." In the next three years, despite some remaining ambiguities or vagueness in the PLO position as well as the continued violence of radical factions within the movement, it became clearer that the moderate Arafat position was becoming the majority one,[21] as was known to the Israeli government; if the Israelis had been genuinely interested in a peaceful compromise settlement with the Palestinians, they would have seized the opportunity to open negotiations with them.[22]

Despite the Israeli rejectionism, the evidence continued to grow that Arafat and the PLO were serious about a compromise political settlement. For example, in January 1976 the PLO declared its support for a UN Security Council resolution—vetoed by the United States—which called for a two-state settlement based on the pre-June 1967 boundaries; in March 1977 the annual meeting of the Palestinian National Council (affiliated with the PLO) formally declared its desire to participate in negotiations for a political settlement; in October 1977 the PLO welcomed a joint statement of the United States and the Soviet Union that called for an international conference to settle the conflict; and in April 1981 the PLO National Council unanimously passed a resolution endorsing a proposal of Soviet president Brezhnev for peace in the Middle East which called for the establishment of a Palestinian state in the context of "ensuring the security and sovereignty of all states of the region including those of Israel."[23]

The Israeli governments of Menachem Begin and his 1983 successor Yitzhak Shamir ignored the changes in the PLO's policies and opposed even the limited concessions to the cause of Palestinian justice, such as those cautiously advanced by the Reagan administration, as described in the next chapter. Nonetheless, over the next few years the PLO's position continued to evolve: "The notion that a state of Palestine could exist side by side with a state of Israel, near heresy in the 1970s," Anziska writes, "had emerged as the preferred Palestinian position at the close of the 1980s."[24]

Finally, in November 1988, the PLO officially recognized Israel and accepted its right to exist, and therefore would seek only the creation of a Palestinian state in the West Bank and Gaza, with Arab East Jerusalem as its capital. Further, it agreed that the new state would be largely demilitarized, would welcome the stationing of international peacekeeping forces along its borders to ensure demilitarization and peace, and would end terrorism and all forms of attack on Israel from its territory.[25]

In 1989, Herbert Kelman, a renowned Harvard social psychologist and leading scholar on international conflict, arranged a secret meeting between leading PLO and moderate-dovish Israeli politicians and academics.[26] Kelman had a number of conversations with Arafat, and in a widely discussed article concluded that despite his internal hard line, the PLO leader was pragmatic, open, and flexible; was interested in peaceful coexistence with Israel; but was unwilling to state this directly until he was assured that Israel would allow the creation of a Palestinian state. Without such assurances, Arafat emphasized, not only would his political power but even his life would be at risk. Kelman accepted these judgments and argued that mutual concessions could lead to an Israeli-Palestinian peace settlement.[27]

Israel's policies remained unchanged.

14

The Rise and Fall of the Peace Process, 1975–99

Starting in the mid-1970s a number of Arab states began seeking a two-state solution to the Israeli-Palestinian conflict. After the 1973 war it became clear that Egypt under Anwar Sadat and Hosni Mubarak favored such a settlement.

Even Saudi Arabia began moving from the rejectionist camp toward a reluctant but nonetheless increasingly firm recognition that a negotiated settlement was necessary. In May 1975, King Khaled publicly stated that his country was prepared to recognize Israel's right to exist within the 1967 borders, on condition that a Palestinian state was established between Israel and Jordan.[1]

In an August 1981 Arab summit meeting, Saudi crown prince Fahd, who became king a year later, expanded on King Khaled's proposal: Israel should be accepted and recognized by the Arab world if it withdrew from the territories conquered in 1967, dismantled its settlements there, allowed the creation of an independent Palestinian state in the West Bank and Gaza with its capital in East Jerusalem, and gave the refugees from the 1948 and 1967 wars the right to either return to their homes or receive compensation.

Israel ignored the Fahd plan; Shimon Peres was quoted as saying that the plan "threatened Israel's very existence."[2] In reality, as a number of scholars have observed, the Fahd plan was part of the accumulating evidence that the Arab states were ready to accept Israel, provided it withdrew from the West Bank and Gaza.[3]

The Reagan administration also ignored the Fahd plan. Instead, in September 1982, Reagan proposed his own "Reagan Plan" for a peace settlement, saying, "It is clear to me that peace cannot be achieved by the formation of an independent Palestinian state in those territories, nor is it achievable on the basis of Israeli sovereignty or permanent control over the West Bank and Gaza."[4]

Thus, though rejecting the creation of an independent Palestinian state and emphasizing the "ironclad commitment" of the United States to Israeli security, Reagan said that Israeli annexation or permanent control over the occupied territories was "in no way necessary" for the defense of Israel. "The question now," the president continued, "is how to reconcile Israel's legitimate security concerns with the legitimate rights of the Palestinians."[5]

To reconcile this clash of rights, the Reagan Plan proposed a five-year transition period during which the Palestinians would have full autonomy over their internal affairs, followed by a "peaceful and orderly transfer of authority from Israel to the Palestinian inhabitants of the West Bank and Gaza." During this period, Israeli settlement expansion had to end: "The United States will not support the use of any additional land for the purpose of settlements during the transitional period," Reagan said. However, the Palestinians would not be given an independent state but only some kind of unspecified "association" with Jordan.[6]

Unsurprisingly, the Israeli government flatly rejected the Reagan Plan, even as a starting point for negotiations; on the contrary, it announced that it would expand the settlements in the West Bank and Gaza, with a view toward putting more than 1 million Jewish settlers in those areas over the next thirty years.[7]

Because the Reagan Plan opposed the creation of an independent Palestinian state, the PLO was also unhappy; it was even excluded from negotiations looking toward a settlement. Nonetheless, Arafat convinced the PLO not to reject the plan outright, both because it was an improvement over past US policies that had ignored the plight of the Palestinians, and because he was unwilling to offend the US government. Accordingly, as one senior PLO official put it, the PLO's response to the Reagan Plan amounted to "saying yes and no at the same time."[8]

In early September 1982, a week after the Reagan Plan was announced, an Arab state summit met in Fez, Morocco, and adopted the Fahd plan, which had been modified to include Arab recognition of the PLO as "the sole legitimate representative" of the Palestinians. Accordingly, in February 1983, the PLO endorsed the Fez Plan, as it was then called—in fact, Arafat had helped write it—which then became the overall policy, known today as the Arab Peace Initiative (API), which has several times been approved by all the leading Arab states.

Reagan's hope that the PLO could be bypassed in favor of King Hussein—a return, in effect, to the "Jordanian Option"—went nowhere. According to Tessler's analysis, the king rejected the idea for several reasons. First, the Soviet Union was pressuring him to do so. Second, early indications that the PLO might cooperate with the Jordanian monarch were soon dashed by the adamant opposition of the more radical groups within the Palestinian organization. Third, Hussein believed that the Reagan Plan would go nowhere in the absence of American pressure on Israel.[9]

Hussein's misgivings proved correct; the administration even reassured Begin that it would not cut off aid or employ other pressures against it. Indeed, US aid to Israel was increased. Consequently, the Reagan Plan came to an end when in early 1983 both the PLO and Jordan formally declared their opposition to it. As a result, the Reagan administration decided to turn its attention elsewhere, and there were no further US initiatives on the Israeli-Palestinian conflict during Reagan's time in office.[10]

The First Palestinian Intifada

Shortly after the end of the 1967 war, Israel began the process of expanding into and occupying the newly conquered territories in the West Bank, East Jerusalem, and Gaza. In the West Bank, the initial Israeli focus was on the Jordan River Valley, the eastern border area between the West Bank and Jordan. The problem, as the Israelis saw it, was that there were some 250,000 Palestinians living in the region, many of them refugees from the 1948 war and the Nakba. Over the next few years, many of them were either driven from or fled the area because of numerous harsh Israeli actions, such as the seizure of Palestinian lands to build Jewish settlements, the demolition of Palestinian homes, the physical harassment of the local inhabitants, and a number of measures reducing Palestinian access to water, even including the destruction of wells and pipelines.

It is true that in the Jordan River Valley the Israelis had a plausible national security claim, for any invading Arab armies from Jordan, Syria, or Iraq would likely have to pass through the area on their way into the rest of the West Bank and Israel itself. Thus, Israeli military control of the region could provide a forward defense against such attacks. Even so, some Israeli and other military experts questioned the need for Israel to occupy and largely depopulate the low-lying areas of the valley, arguing that it could be defended by purely conventional (non-nuclear) military methods, especially because Israeli forces held the high ground and mountain passes.

Further, whatever the earlier force of the security argument, it became less persuasive as the likelihood of a post-1967 massive attack designed to destroy Israel faded, if only because its adversaries knew or assumed that by the late 1960s Israel had nuclear weapons. Nonetheless, the Israeli occupation of the Jordan River Valley deepened in the ensuing decades.

In any event, there was no legitimate security argument at all for the Israeli seizure of Arab East Jerusalem immediately after the 1967 war and for subsequently settling religious fanatics in the West Bank. The real motivating forces for most of the postwar Israeli expansionism into the West Bank and East Jerusalem were clearly "Greater Israel" nationalism and religious messianism. If anything, as many Israeli security experts pointed out at the time, the "need" to defend the settlers was a security liability.

In December 1987, the first full-scale Palestinian revolt against the Israeli occupation broke out, originating in the Gaza refugee camps and spreading into the West Bank and East Jerusalem. Most analyses of the intifada, as it came to be known, consider it to have been a revolution from below rather than one instituted by the PLO;

for example, Tessler writes that it was "a spontaneous and widespread" reaction to the expanding Israeli settlements in the occupied territories and to the increasingly harsh measures employed by Israel to prevent Palestinian resistance.[11]

The intifada, Morris wrote, "was not an armed rebellion but a massive, persistent campaign of civil resistance, with strikes and commercial shutdowns, accompanied by violent (though unarmed) demonstrations against the occupying forces."[12] To be sure, Morris adds, sometimes Molotov cocktails and knives were used against the occupying forces. Once the PLO gained control of the intifada, however, it prohibited terrorist attacks against civilians; although there were a few such attacks, they were "almost invariably carried out by Hamas or Islamic Jihad."[13]

Shortly after the outbreak of the intifada, Defense Minister Yitzhak Rabin warned that "the first priority of the security forces is to prevent violent demonstrations with force, power and blows. . . . We will make it clear who is running the territories."[14] In addition to the outright shootings, Israel employed the following measures: "mass arrests without trial, torture during interrogation, the assembling of all the men in reoccupied villages . . . in some cases subjecting them to merciless beatings, and the cordoning off of villages as 'secure military areas' . . . and preventing entry and exit for days on end."[15]

According to B'Tselem, the leading Israeli human rights organization, from the start of the intifada until it ended in December 1993, Israel killed more than 1,100 Palestinians; during the same period, about eighty Israeli civilians were killed in the occupied territories or inside Israel itself.[16] In addition to the killings, the IDF's own estimates were that 15,000 to 20,000 Palestinians had been wounded in incidents related to the uprising, and arrests and imprisonments associated with the intifada totaled about 50,000 by the end of its second year.[17]

The Bush Administration and the Madrid Conference

The attitudes and policies toward Israel of George H. W. Bush, Reagan's successor, were similar to those of Eisenhower: ambivalent, alternately seeing Israel as a strategic asset or, in light of US interests in maintaining ties with the Arab world, as a strategic problem.[18]

Soon after Bush took office, Secretary of State James Baker outlined the administration's position on the Israeli-Palestinian conflict: the United States was committed to Israel's security but sought a compromise peace settlement. Israel, he said, must "lay aside the unrealistic vision of a Greater Israel," end the occupation, and grant political rights to the Palestinians. However, these rights did not include the establishment of an independent Palestinian state. Instead, a settlement should be based on "a reasonable middle ground," meaning "self-government for the Palestinians in the West Bank and Gaza in a manner acceptable to the Palestinians, Israel, and Jordan."[19]

The administration emphasized the need for Israel to stop the expansion of its settlements in the occupied territories as the necessary first step toward a peace agreement with the Palestinians. Unsurprisingly, the Israeli government, now led by Yitzhak Shamir, refused to do so; on the contrary it soon announced a new settlement expansion program.

As a result, the Bush administration grew increasingly angry at Israeli intransigence. In a May 1989 speech to—no less—the annual AIPAC conference, Baker said that Israel must "lay aside, once and for all, the unrealistic vision of a greater Israel" and treat the Palestinians "as neighbors who deserve political rights."[20] Then, testifying in June 1990 before a congressional committee, Baker, frustrated by continuing Israeli intransigence, bluntly stated: "The White House number is 202-456-1414. . . . When you are serious about peace, call us."[21]

Despite these strong words, in the ensuing months, US economic and military support continued unchanged. However, the administration's refusal to tie US aid to Israeli policy changes came under internal review, especially after Baker's angry congressional testimony on May 22, 1991:

> Every time I have gone to Israel in connection with the peace process, on each of my trips I have been met with the announcement of new settlement activity. This does violate United States policy. It is the first thing that [the Palestinians and Arab governments] . . . raise when we talk to them. I don't think there is any greater obstacle to peace than settlement activity that continues not only unabated but at an advanced pace.[22]

Emboldened by the defeat of Iraq in the 1990–91 Gulf War and what it saw as the heightened US influence in the Middle East, in 1991 the Bush administration decided it was the right moment to join with the Soviet Union in convening an international conference in an effort to settle the Arab-Israeli conflict. Unsurprisingly, the Shamir government was adamantly opposed to an international effort that would assuredly be critical of its policies. However, the Bush administration was now willing to employ some real leverage after Shamir asked for $10 billion in US loan guarantees. When the administration decided to condition its support on Israeli participation in the negotiating process, Shamir reluctantly agreed to send a delegation to the conference that convened in Madrid in late 1991. Ten years later, Israeli foreign minister Shlomo Ben-Ami candidly explained Shamir's strategy: "Shamir went to Madrid because of U.S. pressure, not out of a desire to make peace with the Palestinians and the Arabs."[23]

Since the Bush administration would not agree to PLO participation in the Madrid conference, Arafat and his organization were also initially opposed to the projected negotiations. However, they reluctantly changed their mind, in part because King Hussein agreed to include Palestinian leaders known to be close to the PLO as part of the Jordanian delegation, and in part because before the conference the American government sent a letter to the Palestinians, saying that "the United States has opposed and will continue to oppose settlement activity in the territories occupied in 1967, which remains an obstacle to peace."[24] Moreover, Baker told the Palestinians that the conference would be held whether or not they participated and warned them that Shamir would use Palestinian rejection as an excuse for his own intransigence. Kurtzer commented: "The Palestinians took seriously Baker's admonition not to 'let the cat die at your doorstep.'"[25]

The Madrid Conference, co-chaired by President Bush and Soviet president Mikhail Gorbachev, convened on October 30, 1991; except for Saudi Arabia, it included representatives of all the major parties to the Arab-Israeli state conflict: Israel, Egypt, Syria, Jordan, and Lebanon.

During the conference, Shamir's attitude remained "defiant" and "truculent,"[26] whereas the Palestinian members of the Jordanian delegation (half of whom were doctors and university professors) were moderate and conciliatory and "agreed to nearly all the American requests on both procedure and substance."[27]

The conference ended in deadlock just two days later. One year later, Shamir famously admitted—or perhaps, better said, boasted—that he had agreed to go to Madrid simply as a stalling tactic: "I would have conducted negotiations on autonomy for 10 years and in the meantime we would have reached half a million people in Judea and Samaria."[28]

US Policies after Madrid

Although some unsuccessful lower-level Israeli-Palestinian talks continued in Washington in 1992, the Bush administration played only a minor role and the talks went nowhere. Though the administration was angry at Israeli intransigence, the backlash in the United States against any serious pressures on Israel, or even any continued verbal condemnations of the ongoing expansion of the Israel settlements, led it to back away, despite its earlier assurances to the Palestinians.[29] Most importantly, the administration continued to reject direct negotiations with the PLO or the creation of a Palestinian state.

In short order, the administration reassured a Jewish Republican group that the United States would not use its aid "to impose our preferences on Israel."[30] On the contrary, the administration continued to support the regular $3 billion aid package to Israel, joined with it on a number of cooperative measures, and after the Gulf War furnished an additional $650 million to help Israel repair the damages caused by the Iraqi missile attack.

Finally, shortly before leaving office in January 1993, the Bush administration agreed to deliver the first $2 billion in loan guarantees on terms so vague and easy that Israel in effect could freely decide how to spend the money.[31]

That there would be no change in US support of Israel became clear shortly after Bill Clinton became president, when he reassured the Rabin government that he would oppose any attempt to reduce US assistance to that country.[32]

The Oslo Accords

Changes in Israeli public opinion and the increasingly firm decision by Arafat and the PLO majority to seek a two-state settlement gradually paved the way for the secret peace negotiations that culminated in the Oslo Accords of September 1993. By the end of 1989, opinion surveys showed that the Israeli public increasingly believed that the government's methods were excessive and that more force would not work. In a way, a stalemate had been reached: the Palestinians could not force Israel to end the occupation, and the Israelis could not force the Palestinians to end their resistance. Consequently, many Israelis were concluding that the occupation had to be brought to an end.[33]

Nonetheless, the intifada and the Israeli repression continued until Yitzhak Rabin succeeded Yitzhak Shamir as prime minister in July 1992. Despite his initial hard-line policies toward the intifada, Rabin gradually became more open to negotiating with the PLO. Daniel Levy, an Israeli diplomat who was a member of the delegations at Oslo and later Camp David, explained why:

> The prime driver of change was the fact that the status quo had ceased to be cost-free for the more powerful party—Israel. The Israeli government was therefore ready to seriously contemplate compromise. And the key factor behind that change was the first Palestinian intifada.[34]

Consequently, in the summer of 1993, Rabin and his foreign minister, Shimon Peres, authorized secret Israeli-PLO negotiations to begin in Oslo. The US government played no role in the negotiations until they culminated in a "Declaration of Principles," signed by Arafat and Rabin on September 13, as a beaming Bill Clinton presided. Neither side had wanted US participation in the negotiations: Israel because it feared American pressures, and the Palestinians, paradoxically, because past experience had convinced them that the American government's policies were not much different from those of Israel.[35]

The Declaration of Principles—also known as Oslo 1—starts with the dramatic statement that "the Government of the State of Israel and the PLO team representing the Palestinian people agree that it is time to put an end to decades of confrontation and conflict, recognize their mutual legitimate and political rights, and strive to live in peaceful coexistence and mutual dignity and security and achieve a just, lasting and comprehensive peace settlement."

The first steps toward that end were to be the establishment of an elected Palestinian "Interim Self-Government Authority," which for the next five years would have authority in the West Bank and Gaza, described as constituting "a single territorial unit, whose integrity will be preserved in the interim period." The Palestinian Authority (PA) would have authority over education, culture, heath, social welfare, taxation, and, especially, internal security, for which it would create "a strong police force." Israel, however, would "continue to carry the responsibility for defending against external threats"—meaning, of course, that Israel would continue to be militarily in control.

At the end of the five-year transitional period, a permanent settlement would be reached, based on Security Council Resolution 242, which called for the withdrawal of Israeli forces from territories conquered in 1967—but which did not specifically call for the creation of an independent Palestinian state. In an unintentionally revealing manner, Rabin argued that turning over "internal security" matters to the PLO was actually good for Israel. Speaking to a Labor Party meeting immediately after Oslo 1, he said that the Palestinian security forces would be able to "deal with Gaza without problems caused by appeals to the High Court of Justice, without problems made by B'Tselem, and without problems from all sorts of bleeding hearts and mothers and fathers."[36]

Within a few months after the establishment of the limited self-rule granted to the Palestinians, Israel agreed to withdraw its armed forces from the Gaza Strip and Jericho, following which there would be further gradual Israeli withdrawals from other areas of the West Bank. However, the Rabin government refused to allow the Declaration of Principles to address the major issues: whether there would be an independent Palestinian state, what would be the borders between such a state and Israel, what would be the status of Jerusalem, how would water resources be shared, what would become of the Jewish settlements in the occupied areas, and to what extent the Palestinian refugees would have "the right of return" to their former homes and villages in Israel. These and all other significant issues, the Oslo 1 accord held, would be negotiated in a final settlement that would be reached during the next five years.

At the conclusion of the Oslo 1 negotiations, Arafat and Rabin exchanged official letters of mutual recognition, but hardly symmetrical ones. Arafat said that (1) "The PLO recognizes the right of the State of Israel to exist in peace and security . . ."; (2) "commits itself to a peaceful resolution of the conflict between the two sides and declares that all outstanding issues relating to permanent status will be resolved through negotiations"; (3) "renounces the use of terrorism and other acts of violence"; and (4) "affirms that those articles of the Palestinian Covenant which deny Israel's right to exist, and which are inconsistent with the commitments of this letter are now inoperative and no longer valid."

Rabin's letter to Arafat, however, committed Israel only "to recognize the PLO as the representative of the Palestinian people and commence negotiations with the PLO within the Middle East peace process."[37]

Why did Arafat and the PLO accept "principles" that effectively conceded some 75 to 80 percent of Palestine to Israel;[38] said nothing about the creation of a Palestinian state in what remained; did not mention the word "occupation"; did not provide for an end even to the construction of new settlements, let alone the withdrawal of the existing ones; committed the Palestinians to end armed resistance to the occupation; made no concessions of the refugee issue; and included no agreement to share water rights on an equitable basis?

A number of prominent Palestinian intellectuals were critical of Arafat's concessions at Oslo on those grounds. For example, Edward Said, a leading Palestinian American intellectual and political activist, argued that Arafat had effectively acquiesced in the consolidation of the Israeli occupation, with Israel having either full control or de facto veto power over everything of consequence.[39] Similarly, Yezid Sayigh, a British Palestinian professor who was a member of several PLO negotiating groups, later wrote that the Oslo agreements obscured the extent of Israeli control over every facet of Palestinian life, including security, trade, travel, land use, water, and more.[40]

Several possible explanations of Arafat's concessions have been suggested. PLO leader Nabil Shaath defended his organization's agreement to the Declaration of Principles on the ground that its language made clear that both sides were considered equal with mutual rights. If things go well, he said, "the sky is the limit. . . . [W]e really have for the first time a chance to implement the Palestinian dream. . . . By creating, now, our own facts on the ground, we can reverse the fact-creating the Israelis have been engaged in so long."[41]

Though those hopes were soon dashed, at the time they were widespread, and not just among the Palestinians. As David Landau, a former high Israeli official, put it, "The natural assumption throughout the region and around the world was that the Oslo process would culminate in the creation of an independent Palestinian state."[42] Thus, Arafat may have been convinced—or gambled—that Rabin or a successor government would eventually agree to such a political settlement.

In any case, as a number of analysts have argued, given the relative weakness of the Palestinians vis-à-vis the Israelis, Arafat had reason to believe that this would be his best and possibly his last chance to create a Palestinian state.[43] Joel Singer, one of the lead Israeli drafters of the Accords, later said that "I think they [the Palestinians] gave in on the assumption that they couldn't convince Israel to freeze [the settlements], preferring to get what they could when, within a few years, they would begin negotiations on a final status agreement."[44] Abu Ala, the lead PLO delegate at Oslo, confirmed Singer's assessment, saying he had been torn between accepting Israel's limited proposals or continuing the struggle, before concluding that the former would be the best route for the Palestinian people.[45]

In the final analysis, it is not clear what other options were available to Arafat. Israel held all the cards and Rabin refused to go any further, telling the US government that his "red lines" were that any agreement "could not touch Jerusalem or the settlements and left responsibility for security in Israel's hands."[46] That left the PLO leader only the hope that the Israeli position would continue to evolve over time, so long as he kept the peace within Palestinian-controlled areas.

Perhaps if Rabin had not been assassinated in 1995, that hope would not have been forlorn. According to David Landau, while Rabin would not publicly commit to the eventual creation of a Palestinian state, in private he recognized that it was inevitable, provided the five-year transitional period demonstrated that the two sides could live together: "Israel officials explained that in Rabin's view, the Israeli public needed to be conditioned gradually to the idea of a Palestinian state."[47]

Oslo 2

On September 28, 1995, two years after the Oslo process began, Israel and the PLO agreed on a 300-page "Interim Agreement" that was designed to implement Oslo 1's Declaration of Principles. Under the terms of the agreement, known as Oslo 2, negotiations for a final settlement were supposed to begin no later than May 1996; however, since no such settlement was ever reached, the Interim Agreement—or, rather, what is left of it—is still in effect.

Oslo 2 specified that Israeli forces were to be withdrawn from Gaza and the leading Palestinian population centers in the West Bank, excluding East Jerusalem. In Gaza, physically separated from the West Bank and with land access to it only through Israeli territory, Israel would retain control over the land containing the Jewish settlements and their environs as well as the roads leading to them—in some estimates actually constituting about 35 percent of the entire Gaza Strip.

The West Bank was divided into three areas, supposedly only temporary until a final agreement was reached.[48] Area A, initially defined to include just 3 percent of the West Bank territory, contained no Israeli settlements but included the eight largest Palestinian cities and their surroundings, and was to be under the governance of the newly created Palestinian Authority (PA). Area B, about 25 percent of the West Bank, containing many small Palestinian villages but no Jewish settlements, was to be administered by the PA but remain under Israeli "security control." Area C comprised the rest of the West Bank—that is, most of it—and was to remain under Israeli rule, though supposedly only until a final settlement was reached. Area C had very few Palestinians but contained all the Jewish settlements, none of which would be removed during the "interim" period (see Map 14.1).

In addition, the entire region was criss-crossed with so-called bypass roads controlled by Israel. They were designed to ensure that Israelis traveling in the area could avoid the Palestinian areas, but they also had the effect of cutting off Palestinian towns and villages from each other. In effect, then, the Palestinians would have only a number of disconnected enclaves or, as many termed them, Bantustans.

Map 14.1 Oslo 2 (Areas A–C).

There was no agreement on Jerusalem, so it was left undecided until the final settlement was negotiated.[49] However, in reality, all of it, including the formerly Arab East Jerusalem and its environs, remained under continuously expanding Israeli settlement and control, leaving little to negotiate.

As well, the Oslo Accords did not eliminate Israeli control of the Palestinian economy, for Israel continued to exercise a variety of trade, custom duties, and currency controls, leaving the PA "dependent on Israeli goodwill for about two-thirds of its revenues."[50]

The agreement on the West Bank water resources also reflected the Israeli dominance of the Oslo process: about 57 percent was allocated to Israel inside the Green Line and 24 percent to the Jewish settlements in the occupied territories, leaving less than 20 percent for the estimated 1.2 million Palestinians in the West Bank and Gaza.[51]

In yet other ways, the Oslo Accords did more to preserve the Israeli occupation than to end it. Prior to 1995, Israel was responsible under international law for the functions assigned to occupying powers by international law: security, the judicial system, the economy, health, education, transportation, and others. After Oslo, Israel was able to transfer those functions to the PA without surrendering what really mattered to it: continuing de facto economic, political, and military control, which was more indirect in some ways but nonetheless quite effective. Thus, as a number of Israeli and Palestinian analysts put it, Oslo "outsourced" the occupation, or "consolidated and improved" it, or "effectively transformed the Palestinian Authority into Israel's security subcontractor."[52]

Within a few days of the signing of Oslo 2, Rabin made it clear that Arafat's and the PLO's hopes that it would lead to a genuinely independent and viable Palestinian state after the next round of negotiations would be dashed. On October 5, Rabin addressed the Israeli Knesset.[53] He was blunt:

> We view the permanent solution in the framework of the State of Israel which will include most of the area of the Land of Israel as it was under the rule of the British Mandate, and alongside it a Palestinian entity which will be a home to most of the Palestinian residents in the Gaza Strip and the West Bank.[54] *We would like this to be an entity which is less than a state* [emphasis added], and which will independently run the lives of the Palestinians under its authority. The borders of the State of Israel, during the permanent solution, will be beyond the lines which existed before the Six-Day War. We will not return to the June 4, 1967 lines.[55]

He then addressed the key issues:

Jerusalem. Jerusalem—now defined to include a major Jewish settlement in the nearby West Bank—would remained the "united" capital of Israel, under sole Israeli sovereignty and control, though Christians and Muslims would have freedom of access to their holy places, predominantly in the Old City of Jerusalem and on the Al-Aqsa mosque.

"Security." The "security border" of Israel, "in the broadest meaning of that term," would be located in the Jordan Valley—meaning that Israel would maintain its military control of the area and, it soon became clear, continue its various means of reducing the numbers of Palestinians living there. Elsewhere in the

West Bank, except for the urban Palestinian centers in Area A, Israel would retain "complete freedom of action in order to implement its security and political objectives."

In Area C, Israeli control was total—but even in Area B, where the PA would rule, sort of, "the IDF forces and the security services will be able to enter any place at any time." In short, Oslo 2 ensured that "Israel will have overall responsibility for the security of Israelis and the war against the terrorist threat" in 97 to 98 percent of the region. Left unmentioned by Rabin was that even in the Palestinian Area A cities, secret Israeli military and intelligence operations—including assassinations—would soon begin.

The Jewish Settlements. As long as the "interim" agreement remained in effect, Rabin said, "not a single settlement will be uprooted." Indeed, the settlements could continue to expand, by "building for natural growth."

Despite Rabin's detailed descriptions of the various Israeli measures and restrictions that would ensure that the Palestinians would end up with, at best, "an entity that is less than a state," the Knesset was bitterly divided, finally approving the Oslo Accords by only a 61-59 vote. That bare majority for even such limited concessions to the Palestinians made it clear that if the accords had been truly designed to pave the way for a two-state peace settlement, they would have been easily defeated.

From Oslo 2 to Camp David, 1995–2000

Though some 65 percent of the Israeli and Palestinian publics initially supported the Oslo agreements, the opposition to them was fierce, and extremists from both sides set out to destroy them. Palestinian terror attacks started almost immediately after Oslo 1's 1993 Declaration of Principles—in the ensuing year, about seventy-five Israeli civilians were killed in bombings and suicide attacks, and in the months following Oslo 2, an estimated one hundred more died in bus, car, and restaurant attacks in Tel Aviv and Jerusalem.[56]

While the Israeli public was understandably outraged at these attacks, Israeli intelligence concluded that Arafat and the PLO were not responsible and had sought to end them but were unable to do so. Summing up the consensus position of the experts, Tessler wrote that the Israelis realized that most of the attacks were being carried out by extremist groups such as Hamas and Islamic Jihad that were seeking to destroy the peace process. Uri Savir, the lead Israeli negotiator throughout the Oslo process, later said that no one in the Israeli delegation doubted that Arafat and the PLO delegations strongly opposed the terrorism, which was directed not only at Israel but at them as well. In reality, he added, the conflict was not between Israel and the Palestinians but between the peace camps of both against the Israeli right wing and Hamas.[57]

Indeed, it would have been entirely self-defeating for Arafat to have encouraged terrorism: in the opinion of many Palestinians who were critical of the one-sided nature of the Oslo Accords, the primary reason Arafat went along with them is that Israel had finally decided it needed to negotiate with the PLO under his leadership, to the exclusion of any other Palestinian organization. For Arafat to have then destroyed the accords could only have resulted not only in Israeli fury and the end of any efforts to negotiate with him, but his delegitimization in the eyes of the international community.

In any case, throughout the Rabin period the PA complied with its obligation to do its best to end terrorism, perhaps excepting a brief period following the Hebron massacre by Baruch Goldstein. And it did so with eventual great (though not total) success, as the Palestinian security forces under Arafat worked hand in hand with Israeli security forces, often in joint patrols, to identify and jail extremists and suspected terrorists, some of them from lists drawn up by the Israelis.

The terrorism of the Islamic extremists was soon matched—and often exceeded—by terrorist attacks by Jewish settlers and religious extremists against Palestinian civilians in the occupied territories. The worst of these attacks occurred on February 25, 1994, when Baruch Goldstein, an American-born settler and religious fanatic, entered a mosque in the city of Hebron in the Palestinian Area A of the West Bank, and opened fire with a machine gun. Before he was beaten to death by the Palestinian worshippers, he had killed twenty-nine of them and wounded another 150.

In the widespread shock that followed the Goldstein massacre, a number of Israelis—including some officials in the Rabin government—urged the prime minister to take advantage of the moment to begin removing the most fanatic settlers, particularly the 400 who had moved into the heart of Hebron. But Rabin refused to do so, even though he had publicly strongly criticized the settlers, saying that they had undermined Israel's security.

Instead, apparently fearing the growing political influence and perhaps even the violence of the settlers, Rabin sent in the army to impose a prolonged curfew and draconian movement restrictions on the *Palestinian* residents of the city. In several columns the Israeli journalist Amira Hass later summed up Rabin's actions:

> Not only were the violent Hebron settlers not punished or evacuated from the city, they were also given a reward. . . . The convenience and welfare of the few Jews were given preference at the expense of the Palestinian majority. . . . [The restrictions] only became worse over time . . . [as] the Palestinian residents were emptied from the city center.[58]

Yossi Beilin, a member of the Rabin and Peres governments who had played a key role in both Oslo 1 and 2, later commented that it was "inconceivable" to him that the settlers were not removed.[59] In fact, under Rabin the growth of the Jewish settlements was greater than it had been under the previous hard-line Likud government of Yitzhak Shamir.

Khalid Elgindy, an advisor to the PA and a member of its negotiation teams during the 2004–9 period, wrote that the Goldstein massacre "set off a chain reaction of extremism violence, and terror that permanently altered the course of the peace process. . . . Hamas shifted its focus from mainly targeting Israeli soldiers and police to deliberate attacks on Israeli civilians."[60] Then, as the cycle of violence escalated, the Rabin government delayed or disregarded a number of the specific provisions of the Oslo Accords. These included the timetables for partial Israeli troop withdrawals; the transfer of tax and custom revenues to the PA; the release of Palestinian prisoners; the building of a Palestinian airfield in Gaza; the detailed provisions for free Palestinian passage between Gaza and the West Bank; the free movement of people, vehicles, and goods within the territories; and the unrestricted access of Palestinians living outside Jerusalem to religious services at the Old City mosques.

The Beilin–Abu Mazen Accord

In the fall of 1995, as the Oslo agreements were falling apart, the most prominent Israeli and Palestinian doves, Yossi Beilin and Mahmoud Abbas (then known as Abu-Mazen), engaged in a series of secret discussions to see if the peace process could be salvaged, reaching an agreement they called "Framework for the Conclusion of a Final-State Agreement between Israel and the Palestine Liberation Organization," better known as the Beilin-Abu Mazen Accord.[61]

The accord was designed to serve as the model for a future two-state settlement. A "demilitarized" Palestinian state would comprise Gaza and about 94 percent of the West Bank; the remaining 6 percent, just across the old Green Line and containing about 75 percent of the Jewish settlers, would be incorporated into Israel. The Palestinians would be compensated for the loss of this relatively small territory with Israeli territory along the borders of Gaza. Israel would withdraw its forces from the territory allocated to Palestine over a three-year period, although it would be allowed to maintain some early-warning facilities and air defense units for an additional five years.

The most difficult issues continued to be Jerusalem and the refugees, though a general framework to resolve them by mutual compromise was reached. West Jerusalem would continue to be part of Israel, which would have its capital there; East Jerusalem would become the capital of the Palestinian state. The especially difficult issue of the Temple Mount / Haram plateau was resolved by giving the Palestinian state "extra-territorial sovereignty" over the Al-Aqsa mosques while ensuring freedom of worship on the plateau for Christians, Jews, and Muslims.

As for the refugee issue, the Israeli delegation refused to accept any responsibility for the creation of the refugee problem, but "acknowledged" that "the war of 1947–49" had caused "moral and material suffering to the Palestinian people," affording them "the right of return *to the Palestinian state*" (emphasis added)—that is, not to Israel. The Israelis agreed to the principle that the refugees were entitled to compensation, though the accord did not say what compensation would be adequate, nor where it would come from.

The Palestinians still maintained that the refugees had a right to return to their homes, but—crucially—accepted that "the prerequisites of the new era of peace and coexistence, as well as the realities that have been created on the ground since 1948 have rendered the implementation of this right impracticable."

Beilin was to present the agreement to Prime Minister Rabin, but before he could do so, on November 4, Rabin was assassinated and was succeeded by Shimon Peres. Beilin, who had been Peres's closest aide for many years, urged the new prime minister to accept and implement the accord. However, Peres refused to do so, as he had still not accepted the idea of an independent Palestinian state: "In off-the-record briefings, Peres clung to an upgraded version of the 'functional autonomy' proposal that he had concocted with Moshe Dayan, which entailed a semi-independent autonomy on the West Bank, linked to Jordan."[62]

Almost in tears as he relates the story in an HBO documentary, Beilin castigates himself for not fighting harder for the comprehensive settlement he had negotiated with Mahmoud Abbas: he should have told Peres, he says, that his refusal to accept the agreements "was the worst mistake of his life."

Far from living up to his reputation as a peacemaker, then, after Rabin's assassination Peres continued the process of undermining the chances that the Oslo Accords would lead to peace. At the very end of his life, Rabin's position on the peace process had been softening, as indicated in some of his public statements that showed empathy with the plight of the Palestinians; there were even indications that he had dropped his opposition to the creation of some kind of Palestinian state. Peres, though, stepped up the process of settlement expansion and road building and continued to oppose Palestinian statehood.[63]

While the accords had not addressed the settlements issue, they did include a commitment that "neither side shall initiate or take any step that will change the status of the West Bank and the Gaza Strip, pending the outcome of the permanent status negotiations." However, the Peres government violated the clear intention of that provision, for it continued to seize Palestinian land and expand the settlements both in the West Bank and East Jerusalem; the number of settlers grew from about 100,000 in 1993 to 150,000 at the end of 1995.[64]

In other ways, Israel under Peres continued to violate the Oslo Accords. For example, the accords specified that the West Bank and Gaza were to be considered as one territorial entity with free Palestinian passage between them—as had been the case earlier. However, Israel used its control of the territory separating Gaza from the West Bank to severely restrict Palestinian movement.

Other Israeli violations of Oslo, especially under Netanyahu, included a range of economic pressures and punishments, a refusal to adhere to the agreements to release prisoners, a decision not to implement the agreed-upon schedule for the Israeli forces to withdraw from several West Bank areas, and various pressures on the Palestinian residents of East Jerusalem designed to convince them to make way for Jewish settlers.[65]

Years later Joel Singer, the co-leader of the Israeli team at Oslo, said that it was a mistake to have refused the Palestinian demand to halt settlement construction: "We fought with the Palestinians, on Rabin's and Peres's orders, against a freeze. If I could do it over, I would say that it is an Israeli interest to freeze the settlements, making it possible to establish an independent [Palestinian] state there." When asked why Rabin and Peres didn't see that, Singer replied, "They needed to garner a majority. After all, the second Oslo Accord barely passed."[66]

It is true that Rabin and Peres had a problem with Israeli public opinion, but as a later study concluded, their actions made the situation much worse and they failed to undertake an education process to convince the public that a peace agreement with the Palestinians could be reached only by means of a two-state settlement.[67]

It is also true, of course, that Palestinian terrorism was a serious violation of the Oslo Accords; however, the Palestinian Authority was not responsible for it. On the contrary, in August 1996 the PLO honored its commitment to revoke its original charter, which had denied the legitimacy of Israel and called for the armed liberation of all of Palestine. As well, by 1996 the PA and its police forces had become increasingly successful in their efforts to end the terrorism of Hamas and other Islamic extremists, even cooperating with the Israeli forces. As a result, there were now far fewer terrorist attacks than in the preceding few years, and from November 1977 to October 2000, no Israelis were killed inside the Green Line.[68]

Because of Arafat's crackdown, the military arm of Hamas was greatly weakened and many of its activists and other extremists were imprisoned.[69] In a June 1999 press conference, Martin Indyk, US assistant secretary of state, stated, "We have always said that the Palestinians have done a good job on some of the issues, particularly on the security cooperation issue and combatting terrorism."[70]

The First Netanyahu Administration and the Peace Process

During the early 1990s Benjamin Netanyahu was one of the main leaders of the Israeli right-wing forces opposing a two-state settlement; in particular, his attacks on Yitzhak Rabin are widely considered in Israel to have played a major role in creating the climate of hate that led to Rabin's assassination.[71]

After defeating Shimon Peres in the May 1996 national elections, Netanyahu moved to destroy the Oslo Accords, especially by rapidly expanding the Jewish settlements in the occupied territories and in East Jerusalem, in the process displacing thousands of Palestinians by seizing land as well as blowing up homes or evicting their occupants.[72] In addition, he reneged on Israel's commitment to continuing the process of troop withdrawal from the West Bank, tightened the Israeli grip on East Jerusalem, expanded the Israeli-controlled roads in the occupied territories, imposed frequent economic closures on Palestinian businesses, and refused to comply with Oslo's provision for continued negotiations for a permanent settlement.

Ron Pundak, an Israeli participant in the Oslo negotiations, later wrote that "Netanyahu sabotaged the peace process relentlessly, and made every effort to delegitimize his Palestinian partners."[73] Indeed, in 2001 Netanyahu himself inadvertently confirmed that he had deliberately sabotaged the accords. The Israeli analyst Akiva Eldar wrote that Netanyahu was secretly recorded as bragging about "the manipulative tactics he had used to undermine the Oslo Accords. By defining the entire Jordan Valley as a military location, he 'actually stopped the Oslo Accord.' He was right. Without this large area, the Palestinians wouldn't have a viable state."[74]

Similarly, two other analysts wrote, in 2001 Netanyahu told a group of settlers that "he was gaming the Oslo process, only pretending to go along with the idea of a two-state solution for the Palestinians. . . . I de facto put an end to the Oslo accords."[75]

The Peace Process and the United States, 1993–99

Bill Clinton took office in January 1993, and over the next eight years he sought to bring about a fair settlement of the Israeli-Palestinian conflict. He failed, however, in part because he refused to confront Israel over the major issues:

The Occupation. The administration did not challenge Israel's contention that the status of the Arab territories conquered in 1967 was "disputed," rather than "occupied," and it refused to condemn Israel for its reported human rights violations in them.[76]

The Settlements. The Bush administration had considered the settlements to be "an obstacle to peace," but that was changed by the Clinton administration to "a complicating factor." As well, it essentially dropped Bush's efforts to ensure that US aid would not be used to finance the building of settlements, looking the other way when Israel routinely evaded the restrictions.[77] At the outset of the Clinton presidency, there were 3,000 Israeli settlers in Gaza and 117,000 in the West Bank; when he left office at the end of 2000 there were 6,700 settlers in Gaza and 200,000 in the West Bank.[78]

Jerusalem. The Bush administration had refused to recognize Israel's unilateral 1967 annexation of East Jerusalem and told the Palestinians that its policies would be based on UN Resolution 242, which it interpreted as requiring Israeli withdrawal from all the conquered territories. The Clinton administration backed away from this commitment when Israel said that its rule over East Jerusalem was non-negotiable.[79]

The Role of the United Nations. The Clinton administration joined with Israel in refusing to allow the United Nations a role in settling the conflict. In particular, during the 1990s, the United States voted against several General Assembly resolutions on the rights of the refugees, asserting that "such resolutions prejudged the outcome of the ongoing peace process. . . . [The refugee issue] should be solved by direct negotiations." Of course, Israel considered the Palestinian demand for the right of refugee return to be non-negotiable, as the US government knew full well.

The Israeli attacks on Lebanon. Unlike Reagan's angry 1982 warnings to Begin that the United States would reevaluate its policies if Israel continued attacking civilians in Beirut, the Clinton administration brought no pressure to bear on Israel to refrain from killing civilians during its 1993 and 1996 attacks on southern Lebanon.

This is not to deny that the Clinton administration was unhappy with some of Israel's policies, particularly under Netanyahu after he took office in June 1996. For example, in an April 1998 conference with American Jewish organizations, Secretary of State Madeleine Albright said: "Don't believe there is a peace process. That is not the situation." Clearly referring primarily to Israeli policies, she added: "There is a real problem and the United States is losing its credibility."[80] A month later, Albright warned Netanyahu that if Israel did not undertake further withdrawals from the West Bank and Gaza, the United States would "reexamine its approach to the peace process."[81]

The Wye Conference

When it became clear that the peace process was once again failing, Clinton decided to hold a summit meeting with Arafat and Netanyahu, which convened at the Wye River Plantation in Maryland in October 1998 and resulted in an agreement that Palestinians would take further steps on security and the Israelis would undertake a series of gradual withdrawals from parts of the occupied territories.

The Palestinians complied with the agreement but Netanyahu did not; after making a few small withdrawals he balked at continuing, charging that the Palestinians were violating the security agreements. He announced that there would be no further implementation of the agreements unless the Palestinians fulfilled additional conditions.[82]

The US government rejected the new Israeli demands, considering the Palestinians to be in compliance with the security agreements. Even Clinton's main Middle East advisor, Dennis Ross, who almost always supported Israeli policies, later wrote that "the Palestinians were working diligently to carry out most of their commitments under Wye, particularly in the area of making arrests and fighting terror."[83]

As well, in April 1999, Clinton wrote to Arafat praising his compliance with the Wye agreements: "The first phase was implemented [by Israel]. Unfortunately, the second and third phases have not been. The Palestinians have implemented many of their commitments for the second phase, and I appreciate your efforts, particularly in the security area where Palestinians are engaged in a serious attempt to fight terror."[84]

Nonetheless, Clinton did not apply any significant pressures on Israel, "making do with noncommittal statements and mild wrist-slapping as new settlements were established by Israel," as the centrist commentator Zeev Schiff wrote.[85] And in January 1999, Israeli Foreign Ministry officials happily noted that there had been no serious reprisals from the US government, reporting that "Clinton has done nothing that remotely parallels Eisenhower's ultimatum to Ben-Gurion to withdraw from the Sinai in 1956, Ford's 'reassessment' during the first Rabin premiership in the mid-70s, Reagan's withholding of F-15s after Israel under Begin bombed the Iraqi nuclear reactor in 1981, or Bush's wrestling over loan guarantees with the Shamir government in 1992."[86]

Why Clinton Failed

A number of factors account for Clinton's failure to press Israel to accept a two-state peace settlement during the post-Oslo period. Part of the reason was that he admired Israel. Like Carter before him, Clinton felt a moral, emotional, and perhaps even religious commitment to Israel. As well, like those of Presidents Kennedy, Johnson, and Carter, many of his personal friends, advisors, and national security appointments were Jewish and strong supporters of Israeli policies. For example, Dennis Ross and Martin Indyk, his leading advisors on the conflict, were closely connected to AIPAC, and one of Vice-President Albert Gore's leading advisors was Martin Peretz, the editor of the *New Republic* and a notoriously uncritical supporter of the Israeli right wing.[87]

Second, Clinton did not challenge the consensus view of the American foreign policy establishment that Israel was an important national security "asset" to US interests in the Middle East—which in the post–Cold War era were defined primarily as the containment of Islamic fundamentalism in general, and Iran in particular—and therefore should not be pushed too hard.

Third, most congress persons were adamantly "pro-Israel," whether out of conviction or political calculation. Consequently, by overwhelming bipartisan majorities, Congress resisted placing pressure on Israel and refused to condition US economic and military aid on more flexible Israeli policies.

Fourth, and perhaps most important, electoral politics in the United States were a major constraint on the enactment of policies that diverged from those of Israel. The outcome of close elections could turn on the Jewish and, increasingly, the Christian evangelist vote; Clinton was known to be particularly concerned about Al Gore's chances in the 2000 presidential race.[88] Further, it has generally been estimated that during the 1990s, Jewish financial contributions accounted for at least 50 percent of Democratic presidential campaign funds.

Finally, Quandt argues, in essence, that Clinton's character contributed to his unwillingness to take on Israel:

> He was intelligent, but not focused . . . flexible, but without a solid core of conviction . . . was inclined toward compromise rather than principled stands . . . [and] was unable to take firm stands with either party, especially the political potent Israelis. Deadlines would come and go, agreements would be broken, and Clinton would find it hard to draw a firm line or to threaten sanctions. Nor would he risk controversy by taking positions that might offend the Israelis in particular.[89]

Quandt writes that in previous Arab-Israeli negotiations, such as those with Egypt in the 1970s, positive outcomes had been facilitated by active US involvement: "Had Clinton looked to those models . . . he might have been more ambitious, less hesitant, less prone to equivocate. . . . [R]esolving the issues in the Israeli-Palestinian conflict required more than friendly persuasion. A real restructuring of incentives through active mediation and the use of carrots and sticks was needed."[90]

Aaron David Miller's assessment was similar. Miller, a high State Department official and a leading advisor to Clinton on the Middle East, writes:

> When it came to Arab-Israeli peacemaking, Bill Clinton was not the son-of-a-bitch he needed to be. . . . Without toughness, the capacity to walk away and impose costs for saying no—it [an Israeli-Palestinian deal] was not going to happen. . . . We needed the president to dish out "tough love" [to the Israelis]. Instead the tough part got dropped.[91]

Remarkably enough, Miller added, Barak's own foreign minister (Shlomo Ben-Ami) regretted that Clinton's failure "to crack heads" had demonstrated to "both sides" that US anger was short-lived.[92]

Even Dennis Ross, widely considered the most "pro-Israel" member of Clinton's team, claimed to be disappointed: "Every time we wanted to be tough on Barak, he'd just call the president and go around us."[93]

Still, the role of Clinton's "character" should not be exaggerated. If not for the continuing broad political support of Israel in US public opinion, Clinton might have been more willing to press Israel when he considered it to be intransigent. As David Hendrickson has commented, "He was politically adept and knew where the path of least resistance lay."[94]

At the US-Israeli-Palestinian summit meeting at Camp David in July 2000, Clinton had another chance to help end the conflict. The Camp David summit, and the follow-up negotiations in the Sinai town of Taba over the next six months, were the most important lost opportunities—and quite possibly the *last* opportunities—to have settled the Israeli-Palestinian conflict. Because of its importance, an analysis of the Camp David/Taba negotiations warrants a full chapter of its own (Chapter 15).

15

Camp David, Taba, and the Clinton Parameters, 2000–2001

Throughout the long history of the Israeli-Palestinian conflict, the most promising Israeli-Palestinian negotiations to reach a comprehensive peace settlement occurred in the Camp David and Taba conferences from the summer of 2000 through early 2001. However, in the end, no settlement was reached—in another and perhaps the most painful lost opportunity for peace.

Camp David

According to the standard mythology, at the Camp David conference in the summer of 2000, Israeli prime minister Ehud Barak offered the Palestinians an independent state in at least 95 percent of the occupied territories but was turned down by Arafat and the PLO, who were happy to "pocket" the Israeli concessions but refused to make compromises of their own, made no counteroffers to the Israeli proposals, and then launched a new, violent, and often terrorist intifada, demonstrating that they had no interest in peace with Israel but rather still sought to destroy Israel and take over all of historic Palestine.

As with the many other mythologies in the Arab-Israeli conflict, this bears little resemblance to reality, as is made clear in the contemporary news accounts in the *New York Times* and *Haaretz*, in later analyses of journalists and historians, and, especially, in the memoirs and writings of many Israeli, Palestinian, and US officials, diplomats, and participants in the 2000–2001 events.[1]

In May 1999, Ehud Barak, head of Israel's Labor Party, defeated Benjamin Netanyahu in the Israeli national elections. Barak had been one of Israel's most decorated war heroes, had served as chief of staff of the Israeli Defense Forces in 1991–95, and then became the Israeli foreign minister in the 1995–96 government of Shimon Peres. During the spring of 2000, Barak asked President Bill Clinton to organize and preside over an Israeli-Palestinian-American peace process that would culminate in a formal peace agreement, to be negotiated in a Camp David summit conference that summer. Clinton agreed to do so, persuaded by Barak's apparent willingness to reach a fair compromise settlement with the Palestinians.

Arafat, however, was not persuaded that Barak was prepared to make significant concessions, so he was reluctant to participate in negotiations that he feared would present him with an unacceptable take-it-or-leave-it ultimatum which he would have to reject, and which would then saddle him with the blame for the failure.

Robert Malley, one of the State Department experts on the Arab-Israeli conflict, later wrote:

> The Palestinians believed the summit was premature, a US-Israeli ploy to pressure them into hastily accepting a flawed deal. Their delegation was deeply divided, popular opposition at home was intense, and Arab countries—kept away from Camp David—were not there either to encourage or to pressure Arafat. There was, too, Arafat's animosity toward Barak, who from the start, he was convinced, had sought to skirt commitments, impose his own timetable and tactics, and generally humiliate, manipulate, and trap the Palestinians.[2]

As well, Dennis Ross later wrote, "I knew that Arafat was coming with a profound sense of gloom and suspicions . . . [believing] that this was a trap Barak was setting to corner him."[3]

Despite the State Department's misgivings, Clinton decided to adhere to Barak's request and pressed Arafat to agree to a summit conference—but he also gave him an apparently iron-clad commitment that he would not blame him if the negotiations failed. Transcripts of the two leaders' discussions reveal that on June 15, 2000, Arafat told Clinton in the White House, "I think Barak has decided to put us in the position of the guilty party, and I need your promise that, wherever we go with the negotiations, you won't shift the blame for failure onto us and won't back us into a corner." Clinton agreed, saying: "I appreciate what you've just told me. . . . I promise you that under no circumstances will I place the blame for failure on you."[4]

With these reassurances and considering it unwise to offend the US president, Arafat reluctantly agreed to go to Camp David, even as he told other PLO leaders: "We're going to face a disaster. We are being set up. They want to take us for a summit. Barak has convinced Clinton. . . . Clinton went along with Barak all the way. . . . [T]hey want to take us to Camp David so they can blame us [for the failure of the peace process]."[5]

In fact, Arafat's fears were well grounded, for after the conference Clinton broke his promise and publicly blamed him for its failure.[6] Moreover, Arafat would have had even more reason to be concerned had he known about a secret letter that Secretary of State Madeleine Albright sent to Netanyahu in November 1998, stating:

> Recognizing the desirability of avoiding putting forward proposals that Israel would consider unsatisfactory, the US will conduct a thorough consultation process with Israel in advance with respect to any ideas the US may wish to offer to the parties for their consideration. This would be particularly true with respect to security issues or territorial aspects related to security.[7]

In effect, Albright had given Israel a veto not only over Palestinian proposals but even those of the US government itself.

US policies aside, Arafat had good reasons to be concerned about negotiating with Barak. To begin, Barak had a long history of adherence to right-wing Zionist ideology—for example, in his insistence on exclusive Jewish sovereignty over Jerusalem, in his oft-repeated references to the West Bank as "Judea and Samaria" and his support for the expansion of the Jewish settlements there, and in his adamant denial of any Israeli moral, legal, or other responsibility for the Palestinian refugees.

Moreover, Barak had a long record of hostility to Arabs in general and the Palestinians in particular. "We live in a bad neighborhood," he often said: "This is not Benelux"; Israel is "a villa in the jungle"; a "vanguard of culture against barbarism"; a "protective wall" for the West.[8] Because of the Arab nature, Barak believed, the Arab-Israeli conflict could not be satisfactorily resolved: "It is because of the character of the Arab discourse that their culture does not contain the concept of compromise. Compromise is apparently a Western concept of settling disputes."[9]

Evidently it had slipped Barak's mind that it was Arab leaders like Anwar Sadat and Hosni Mubarak of Egypt, King Abdullah and King Hussein of Jordan, and even Hafez Assad of Syria who had reached and maintained compromise agreements with Israel.[10]

On the issue of statehood for the Palestinians, Barak had long been a hardliner who repeatedly denigrated or ridiculed the Israeli "left" or "the peace camp," and who by his own admission felt far more at home in the Israeli right wing and even with the religious settlers; at one point he sent his "warm personal greetings" to the fanatical and violent Jewish settlers in Hebron.[11]

Prior to taking office, Barak had opposed the Oslo Accords and worked against any reference to Palestinian statehood in the political platform of the Labor Party. Even though Palestinian terrorism had dramatically declined—a total of three Israeli civilians were killed in terrorist attacks inside Israel during Barak's first year in office—his policies were no different from those of Netanyahu.[12] Indeed, in some ways his actions were even harsher than his predecessor's. The list is instructive:

- He refused to carry out the phased withdrawals of Israeli troops that were required by the Oslo and Wye agreements.

- He did not comply with the agreement that a Palestinian safe-passage would be allowed between Gaza and the West Bank.
- He refused to release Palestinian prisoners in accordance with previous agreements.
- In a number of ways, he expanded Israeli control over "Greater Jerusalem" and refused to implement his promise to withdraw from three Arab villages neighboring Jerusalem and turn them over to the Palestinians.
- He imposed severe economic hardships and worsened Palestinian poverty by repeated business closures, by refusing to implement the Israeli promise to turn over to the Palestinian Authority tax monies that had been collected by Israel in the occupied territories, and by ignoring the agreement that the Palestinians could build a deep-water port in Gaza.
- He authorized the destruction of Palestinian homes in the West Bank to make way for new settler housing.
- He went even beyond Netanyahu's actions (during the latter's first term as prime minister in 1996–99) and expanded the process of settlement expansion and the building of roads the Palestinians were not allowed to use, roads that not only linked the settlements but also cut off the Palestinian population centers from each other, in effect creating a series of enclaves.[13]

Indeed, even as he was meeting with Arafat at Camp David, Barak was preparing a new Israeli government budget for 2001 that included increased subsidies of various kinds to entice Israelis to move into East Jerusalem and the West Bank settlements.[14]

- He used Israeli control over much of the water sources in the occupied territories to ensure that the Jewish settlements had plenty of water, even as the Palestinians suffered severe shortages.
- Not least, he presided over various humiliations that the occupation visited on the Palestinians.[15]

In light of his record, why did Barak agree to seek a settlement of the Israeli-Palestinian conflict, albeit one that heavily favored Israel? The apparent contradiction is explained by the fact that Barak considered himself to be pragmatic, a hardheaded realist who feared that the continuing conflict could eventually undermine Israel's security, if not its very existence. In several interviews Barak explained his decision: "Emotionally, I feel like a right winger, but in my head I'm realistic, pragmatic,"[16] above all fearing where continued wars with the Palestinians and the Arab world could lead:

> Israel is galloping toward disaster. . . . [If] we do not reach a solution and the window of opportunity closes, we will find ourselves in a very sharp

> deterioration. It is impossible to set a timetable. It is impossible to know exactly what the trigger will be. Large-scale terrorist attacks . . . or a fundamentalist wave of operations against us—which the Americans and the rest of the world will be wary of dealing with for fear of their own interests—and with simple nuclear instruments and means of launching in Arab states in the background. . . . Therefore, I understand that we have an interest of a very high order in trying to reach agreements now.[17]

The Negotiations

The Camp David summit negotiations began on July 11, 2000, and continued over the next two weeks. Prior to Camp David, Barak had told the Israeli negotiating team that their goal must not be the creation of a Palestinian state, but only an "entity."[18] Astonishingly, there is no official record of what transpired at Camp David because Barak refused to commit himself in writing to his proposals on the issues under discussion, unless and until he was satisfied with an overall settlement.[19]

Barak's initial diplomatic strategy was to try to convince the Palestinians to agree to the principle of a peace settlement, while postponing for later negotiations the most difficult issues, especially on the final boundaries and Jerusalem. However, the Palestinian delegation rejected this approach, fearing that Barak, like nearly all of his predecessors, was following the strategy of "creating facts on the ground" in order to preempt the future.

As a result, even the participants at Camp David have differing accounts of precisely what Barak offered, especially since there were variations over the course of the negotiations.[20] Here is the range of estimates on the most important issues.

Territory and Borders

Barak refused to turn over all the occupied territories (the West Bank, Gaza, and East Jerusalem, comprising some 22 to 23 percent of the original land of Palestine) to the Palestinian state. There are differences among the participants at Camp David, as well as in later analyses of the negotiations, over the territory that Barak sought either to annex or to retain full military control over; in keeping with his nothing-in-writing strategy, he refused to provide detailed maps that would allow the Palestinians—and, for that matter, the Israeli delegates themselves—to see what, exactly, he was proposing.

For example, Ron Pundak, an Israeli historian, journalist, and diplomat who had played a leading role in the Oslo and later negotiations, wrote that "Barak tried to impose an unbalanced agreement," initially demanding the Israeli annexation of about 12 percent of the West Bank, with no territorial compensation to the Palestinians. In the course of the negotiations, he somewhat improved the terms, but unsurprisingly, in light of the absence of written records and maps, the accounts of other Israeli and Palestinian participants or historians differ somewhat on the exact percentages of the West Bank that Barak demanded at different stages of the negotiations, with numbers ranging from a low of 9 percent to a high of 14 percent.[21]

In a later detailed analysis of the consequences to the Palestinians of Barak's proposals, American political scientist Alexander B. Downes concluded that when the areas that would either be annexed or totally controlled by Israel were totaled up, the Palestinian state would not comprise 95 percent of the West Bank, as repeatedly asserted by Barak. Rather, Downes wrote, "the area of Palestinian sovereignty would comprise no more than 65–75 percent of the West Bank, constricted by access roads and separated by Israeli-held areas into several noncontiguous chunks."[22]

Pundak concluded: "The version presented in retrospect by Israeli spokespersons, claiming that Barak at Camp David offered 95 percent and an additional 5 percent in compensation, or alternatively 97 percent and 3 percent compensation, is an attempt at rewriting history."[23] Whatever the precise numbers, the more crucial point was that even if a Palestinian "state" should emerge from the negotiations, it would be divided into four disconnected areas: Gaza and the three cantons or enclaves ("Areas A–C") in the West Bank.[24]

The Israeli Settlements

Whatever their precise size, the areas Barak proposed to annex to Israel in order to ensure that some 80 percent of the settlers would continue under Israeli sovereignty contained most of the region's scarce water aquifers—one of the reasons that the settlements had been established there in the first place—while the Israeli borderlands that would be given ("swapped") to the Palestinians largely consisted of waterless and infertile desert.

Moreover, the Israeli settlement "blocs" or "clusters," as they were variously called, contained as many as forty small Palestinian villages containing an estimated 80,000 people, who consequently would come under the full control of Israel.[25] What would happen to those people? Since it was most unlikely that Israel would want to incorporate large numbers of additional Arabs into the Jewish state, the Palestinians had good reason to fear that they would be relocated—that is, "transferred"—by one means or another.

Another unanswered question was what would happen to the isolated Jewish settlements outside the settlement blocs in the heavily Palestinian-populated Gaza Strip and West Bank heartland, which presumably would fall under the sovereignty and control of the new Palestinian state. That the Jewish settlers, many if not most of them religious or nationalist right-wingers, would accept such a solution would have been hard to imagine.[26]

Jerusalem

Theodore Herzl, Chaim Weizmann, David Ben-Gurion, and other early nonreligious Zionist leaders had mixed feelings about incorporating Jerusalem into a Jewish state. On the one hand, they hoped to "regain" all of ancient Palestine, including its historic capital; as a result, early statements of Zionist goals and aspirations included the acquisition of Jerusalem.

On the other hand, they had no interest in trying to rule the city's Arab population, mainly located in East Jerusalem, and foresaw the likely consequences of trying to do so. As quoted earlier, Tom Segev wrote: "The Zionist movement has always expressed doubts about Jerusalem. Theodore Herzl agreed to give it up, and the November 1947 partition decision was joyously accepted, even though Jerusalem was not slated to be part of the State of Israel."[27]

That decision had been foreshadowed in 1937, when Ben-Gurion wrote: "To this very day, I still believe nothing but disaster can come from a refusal to partition Jerusalem into two separate municipalities—one Arab, the other Jewish." The Israeli historian Motti Golani explained why Ben-Gurion was not interested in Israeli sovereignty over East Jerusalem, especially the Old City: "He did not want to be burdened with its historical, religious, and political weight."[28]

The Temple Mount, or the Haram al-Sharif as it is known by Muslims, is considered by both religious Jews and Muslims to contain some of the most "holy" sites of their religions—which explains why throughout history, down to today, it has been a flashpoint for violent conflict. To avoid such a conflict not only with the Palestinians but with the entire Muslim world, after Israel conquered the Old City of East Jerusalem in the 1967 war, Moshe Dayan and the Israeli government decided to prevent Jews from ascending to the Temple Mount plateau and establishing a synagogue on what were believed to be the ruins of the ancient Jewish temples: Jewish prayer was banned from the site, except at the Western Wall at the base of the Mount. While the Mount was not formally annexed to Israel, in practice it was considered by Israel to be now under its sovereignty;[29] however, the Al-Aqsa mosque and the Muslim Dome of the Rock were placed under the administrative control of Muslim religious authorities.

In the rest of East Jerusalem, however, Israeli policies were quite different. First, it created or expanded Jewish "neighborhoods," or settlements in what had previously been known as Arab East Jerusalem. Further, it expanded the boundaries of the Jerusalem "metropolitan area," or "Greater Jerusalem," so as to incorporate into the city almost one-fifth of the entire West Bank, which together with new settlements east of the city reached almost to the Palestinian city of Jericho, a short distance from the Jordan River border with Jordan (see Map 15.1).

As well, Israel established a tight system of political and economic control over all Jerusalem, but while the largely impoverished Arab neighborhoods were denied economic assistance and even most city services, Jewish settlers, highly subsidized by

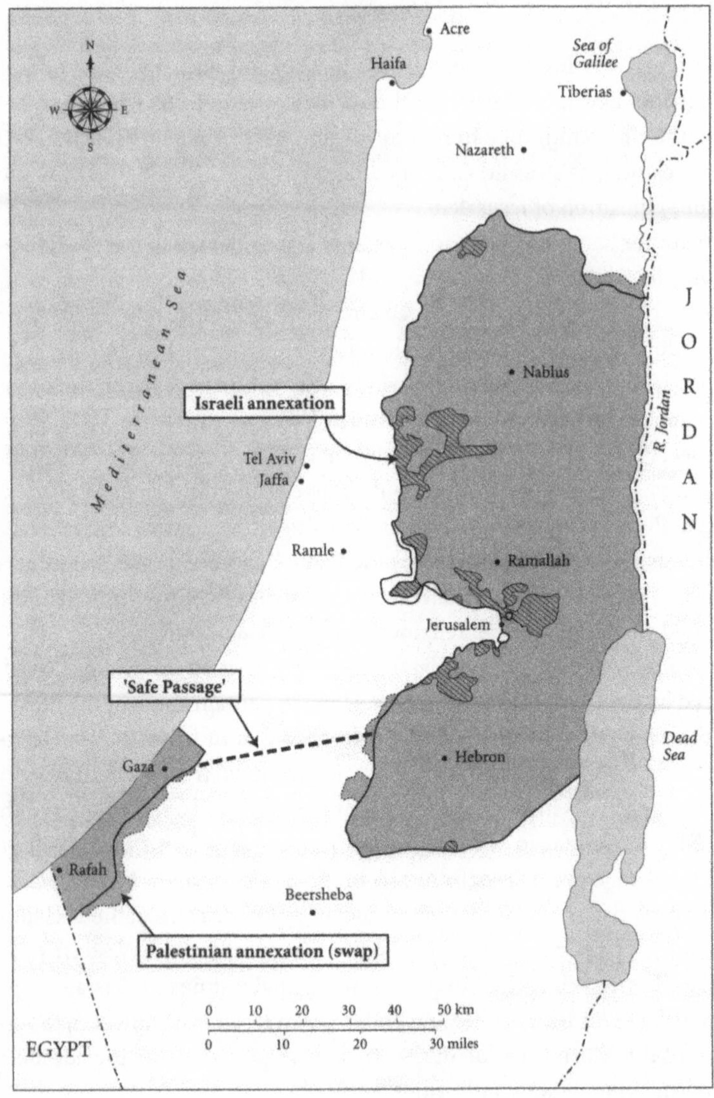

Clinton's peace plan, 2000

Map 15.1 Clinton's Peace Plan, 2000, from Shlomo Ben-Ami, *Scars of War*, 271. Permission granted from Ben-Ami.

the Israeli government, seized Arab property and even existing homes throughout East Jerusalem. While this led to widespread suspicions—and not only among the Palestinians—that the ultimate Israeli goal was to induce as many Arabs as possible to leave East Jerusalem, Israeli governments denied any such intentions and insisted that it was treating both Jews and Arabs alike.

By the end of the 1990s, however, the pretenses had evaporated; even some former Jerusalem city officials and city planners, including the 1971–78 deputy mayor Meron Benvenisti, whose job was to administer East Jerusalem, openly began to admit the true purpose of Israeli policies. As well, in March 1997, a number of current and former Israeli officials told the *New York Times* that "political planning" and "lopsided development strategies" had been employed to ensure Jewish dominance over Jerusalem and to encourage the Palestinians to move out of the city into neighboring West Bank towns.

Even Teddy Kollek, the famous mayor of Jerusalem from 1965 to 1993, who in the past had claimed he did everything he could to help Jerusalem's Arab population, spoke quite differently in a 1990 interview with the Israeli newspaper *Ma'ariv*. The Arabs of East Jerusalem, he bluntly admitted, had become "second and third class citizens," for whom "the mayor [that is, Kollek himself] nurtured nothing and built nothing. For Jewish Jerusalem I did something. . . . For East Jerusalem? Nothing!"

When Barak ran for prime minister during the electoral campaign in spring 1999, he repeatedly asserted that he would never "divide Jerusalem," a standard pledge for Israeli politicians but which did much to tie his hands on the issue and make a compromise highly unlikely.[30] He initially insisted that the Palestinians had to accept the existing "facts on the ground," namely, the enlarged "Greater Jerusalem." In addition, for the first time he demanded that Israel must be formally recognized as holding sovereignty over the Temple Mount as well as what he termed the "sacred basin," or the "Holy of Holies," referring to nearby areas of Jewish religious significance, such as the Jewish Cemetery on the Mount of Olives. Moreover, in defiance of previous Israeli policy, he demanded that Jews be allowed to pray on the Temple Mount (as opposed only to the Western Wall below it), on which a synagogue would be built.

These demands not only outraged Arafat but shocked and angered members of his own administration and the Israeli delegation to Camp David. For example, Matti Steinberg, the advisor on Palestinian affairs to the head of Shin Bet, said: "I never imagined that Barak would demand sovereignty over the whole Temple Mount,"[31] and Ron Pundak wrote that his demand to build a synagogue within the boundaries of the Haram al-Sharif was "an act not contemplated for 2000 years."[32]

As well, Moshe Amirav, Barak's leading Jerusalem expert, wrote that both Arafat and Barak had "committed grave errors" in insisting that their side had to have complete sovereignty on the Temple Mount, but that he found Arafat's position "easier to understand" than Barak's:

> Barak wanted to go down in history as having achieved . . . sovereignty over part of the Temple Mount . . . [but] what Barak didn't understand is that Ben-Gurion actually did everything he could to be rid of the Temple Mount. . . . From Herzl on down, including Weizmann, Dana, and Menachem Begin, all of the leaders of Zionism realized that the Temple Mount was actually a thorn in the side of the Zionist movement.[33]

Sooner or later, Amirav concluded, "Israel will be forced to get rid of the Temple Mount" and recommended that it be turned over to the leading Muslim countries, thus facilitating an Arab-Israeli peace settlement.

Apparently in response to the widespread criticism of his rhetoric and policies on Jerusalem, including from his own delegation, Barak for some time modified his initial position, telling Clinton, "after swearing the president to secrecy,"[34] that he was ready to offer the Palestinians and other Muslim groups "shared custodianship" on the Temple Mount/Haram, "but—crucially—Israel would maintain its sovereignty over the site and the Temple Mount which is buried under it."[35]

In the Old City, Barak now proposed that while the Jewish quarter would remain under Israeli rule, the Palestinians could have sovereignty over the Muslim and Christian Quarters. In the rest of East Jerusalem, the Palestinians would have sovereignty over most—but not all—of the Arab neighborhoods, though they would continue to be largely separated not only from the rest of the Palestinian population centers in the West Bank but even from each other. Moreover, he continued to refuse to allow East Jerusalem to become the capital of the Palestinian state, proposing instead that it be located in the outlying Palestinian village of Abu Dis.

The Palestinian Position. Arafat would not accept any settlement that did not include Palestinian sovereignty on the Temple Mount/Haram plateau, although he was willing to allow Israeli sovereignty over the Western Wall below it. Most analysts believe that Arafat's position reflected his own genuine religious attachment to the Haram, but even if he had been prepared to compromise on the sovereignty issue, it would have been far too dangerous, including to his personal safety. According to a number of accounts, during the discussions on Jerusalem both Arafat and Clinton talked with other Arab leaders to see if they would support a settlement that did not include Palestinian/Muslim sovereignty on the Haram plateau.[36] None of them would do so and warned that if Arafat agreed to any change in the status quo he would be risking his life.

In particular, Egyptian president Hosni Mubarak said that "Arafat did not have the authority to divide Jerusalem and the Old City. This was an all-Arab and all-Muslim matter. . . . Whoever agrees to the partition would be considered a traitor to Arab and Muslim history."[37] And when Arafat told Saudi foreign minister Prince Saud al-Faisal of the pressures he was under from both Israel and the United States, he was warned: "Be careful, you can do everything, but nothing concerning Jerusalem. May God help you."[38]

Later, Arafat reiterated his refusal to agree to any dilution of Palestinian sovereignty on the Haram al-Sharif plateau, adding that "his hands were tied" since not only the leading Arab governments but also "all the muftis in the Arab world have published fatwas forbidding any concession on this Islamic holy place."[39] When Clinton continued to press him on the issue, Arafat was said to have responded: "Do you want to come to my funeral? I will not give up Jerusalem and the holy places."[40]

In the opinion of Edward Walker, the US ambassador to Israel from 1997 to 1999, Arafat was not exaggerating:

> There was no way in hell that Arafat could ever have reached an agreement on Jerusalem. He doesn't represent the Islamic world. He had to have the support of other Arab countries or Islamic countries in order to do so. . . . It was an absolute fact—he would have been assassinated.[41]

The Refugee Issue and the "Right of Return"

The Palestinian Position. Since 1948 the official or public position of Arafat, the PLO, Arafat's successor Mahmoud Abbas, and the Palestinian Authority has been—and, rhetorically at least, still is—that the Palestinian refugees as well as their descendants have the right to return to their lands, homes, and villages. Arafat reiterated that "demand" at Camp David, though he and other Palestinian leaders repeatedly assured the Americans and the Israelis that their real goal was Israeli acceptance only of the "principle" of refugee return, as distinct from implementing that "right" in practice.

For several reasons, it is crucial to distinguish between the principle and the practice. To begin, very few Israelis, including its most adamant internal critics of the treatment of the Palestinians, have ever accepted a literal return, and there is no prospect that they ever will. In any case, the 1948 homes and villages of the Palestinian victims of the Nakba no longer exist. Theoretically, of course, the Palestinians could "return" elsewhere in Israel, but if large numbers were allowed to do so, within a short time there would no longer be a Jewish majority in Israel, thus destroying the very raison d'être of the creation of a Jewish state.

Further, given over a century of mutual violence and hatred, an influx of millions of Palestinians would be a formula for civil and religious warfare.[42] There are no contemporary precedents or models of two peoples long at war with each other suddenly becoming capable of living together in peace and harmony within the confines of one small state—since 1945 alone, Cyprus, Lebanon, Bosnia, Kosovo, Northern Ireland (for decades), and others provide the warning examples.

At least since the 1980s, almost all Palestinian leaders—even, in practice though not in principle, Hamas today—recognize the impossibility of the "right of return" demand, and there is strong evidence that if all other pieces of a peaceful settlement fell into place, the Palestinians would insist only that Israel acknowledge its history in creating the refugee problem and agree to a small, essentially symbolic level of Palestinian "return."

For example, in 1990 Abu Iyad, then one of the most important PLO officials, wrote a widely acclaimed article for an American foreign policy journal, emphasizing that the Palestinians understand that the literal implementation of the right of return is not possible. Negotiations could resolve the matter if Israel accepted "the principle of the right of return *or* compensation," in which case "we shall for our part remain flexible regarding its implementation."[43]

Then, during the Camp David discussions, Ahmed Qurei, a leading Palestinian delegate and later the PA prime minister, told an Israeli magazine:

> We have always said let's approve the principle of the right of return first, and then we can be flexible on the mechanisms. I know the Israelis cannot accept the right of return. But the *principle* should be approved, and then we can talk in details on how to implement it in a way that will be good for both sides.[44]

As well, Arafat himself repeatedly reassured both Clinton and the Israeli delegations of his willingness to separate the principle from practice. For example, quoting from transcripts to which he had access, Enderlin reports that Arafat told Clinton that "we have to find a happy medium between Israel's demographic worries and our own concerns."[45] Enderlin elaborated on the Palestinian position:

> According to several Israeli delegates, the question of the refugees' right of return to Israel was the Palestinians' final card in the negotiation. They were not going to give in on this point until agreements were concluded on all the other pending issues. . . . Arafat repeated that should there be an agreement, he would make sure Israel would not have to confront a demographic problem.[46]

The Israeli Position. The Sher Report characterized the Israeli position as follows:

> On refugees, Israel refused to accept sole responsibility for the creation of the refugee problem and to any right of return, theoretical or actual. Israel did agree to recognize the suffering of the 1948 refugees; to take part in an international effort to bring in a small number of refugees, 20,000 to 40,000, at its discretion based on humanitarian considerations only; and to contribute funds to refugee rehabilitation. Israel's condition was that the "implementation of the final status agreement would bring an end to demands and a solution to the problem."[47]

Other accounts, however, characterize Barak's position in harsher terms, saying that he did not merely reject "sole" Israeli responsibility for the refugee problem but *any* responsibility for it, even ignoring Palestinian position papers that quoted extensively from Israeli memoirs, military documents, and the "New History" scholarship, all definitively demonstrating the extent of Israeli responsibility for the Nakba.

According to Malley and Agha, Barak contemptuously characterized the Palestinian refugees as "salmons"—presumably returning home to die. Malley and

Agha comment: "[The] Palestinian refugees . . . yearning to return to their land somehow is supposed to fade away in roughly eighty years in a manner that the Jewish people never did, even after two thousand years."[48]

Had Barak been willing to acknowledge the historical facts, the way would have been paved for the necessary and obvious compromise on the matter, essentially separating the principle of return from its implementation—just as Arafat and other leading Palestinian officials had been advocating for a number of years.

Camp David Reassessed

After Camp David, a new mythology emerged perpetrated by Barak and his foreign minister Shlomo Ben-Ami, with the support of Dennis Ross, Clinton's secretary of state Madeleine Albright, and to a considerable extent Clinton himself. The mythology holds that at Camp David, Barak made a generous and unprecedented offer to the Palestinians, only to be met by a shocking if not perverse rejection by Arafat who then ordered a violent uprising at just the moment when the chances for peace had never been greater.

For example, shortly after the conclusion of Camp David, Ben-Ami gave a long interview with *Haaretz,* claiming that Arafat did not go to Camp David to reach a compromise settlement but rather treated the negotiations as "a huge camouflage net behind which he sought to undermine the very idea of two states for two nations. . . . Camp David collapsed over the fact that [the Palestinians] refused to get in the game. They refused to make a counterproposal . . . and didn't succeed in conveying . . . that at some point the demands would have an end."[49]

The implied premise of Barak and Ben-Ami was that Arafat thought the Palestinians held all the cards, so that if he held out long enough, he would eventually reach his goal: the destruction of Israel in stages and the takeover of all of historic Palestine. This view became widely accepted in US and Israeli public opinion. My hometown newspaper, the *Buffalo News,* repeated it: "Not only did Arafat turn down the Israeli offer of a Pal period state in 95 percent of the current Pal. territories, he never made a counteroffer, and then launched a second violent intifada."[50]

This and other Camp David mythologies have been rejected, both at the time and in retrospect, by nearly all scholars and knowledgeable journalists and by most Israeli and US officials who participated in the negotiations. In particular, they were challenged in interviews and memoirs by the leading Israeli negotiators, among them Ron Pundak, Yossi Beilin, Oden Era, Shaul Arieli, Yossi Ginosser, Moshe Amirav, and General Amnon Lipkin-Shahak, chief of staff of the IDF in 1995–1998. As well, the mythologies were strongly—and subsequently, publicly—rejected by Israel's leading military intelligence officials, including Ami Ayalon, the 2000 head of Shin Bet, and Matti Steinberg, his chief advisor—and by Amos Malka, head of the IDF's military intelligence bureau, and his second in command, Ephraim Lavie.

Malka summed up the conclusions of his agency, saying that the intelligence assessment was that "it is possible to reach an agreement with Arafat under the following conditions: a Palestinian state with Jerusalem as its capital and sovereignty on the Temple Mount; 97 percent of the West Bank plus exchanges of territory in the ratio of 1:1 with respect to the remaining territory; some kind of formula that includes the acknowledgment of Israel's responsibility for the refugee problem and a willingness to accept 20,000–30,000 refugees."[51] The subsequent negotiations between Olmert and Abbas established tentative agreements that the number of refugees or their descendants that Israel would be willing to admit was somewhere between 10,000 and 50,000, over a three- to five-year period.

Lavie elaborated: "I can unequivocally state that . . . the research division [of the IDF] provided no intelligence foundation for the prevailing concept [that] says Arafat is not interested in anything other than bringing about the destruction of Israel through the right of return."[52]

Similarly, the Shin Bet's Ami Ayalon and the Israeli delegates Lipkin-Shahak, Ginnosat, and Era corroborated the Palestinian contention that the negotiations did not break down over the right of return because Israel knew that Arafat "was holding it as a bargaining chip in exchange for Palestinian sovereignty over the Al-Aqusa mosque." Era is quoted as saying that the Palestinians "continually tried to allay our concerns, saying that fulfillment of the right doesn't entail the return of all the refugees." The problem, Era said, was that the Israeli delegation could not even explore the possibility of a Jerusalem-refugee deal because Barak wouldn't allow them to do so.[53]

Leading State Department experts during this period, including Robert Malley, Aaron David Miller, Daniel Kurtzer, and William Quandt, also rejected the Barak/Ben-Ami argument, which ignored the long history of Palestinian compromises, going back to the 1970s and formalized in 1988 when Arafat and the PLO officially agreed to accept a two-state settlement, in which they would get only 22 to 23 percent of the historic land of Palestine.

The Palestinian negotiators repeatedly pointed this out. For example, in an interview with an Israeli newspaper, Ahmed Qurei (Abu Ala) said:

> We have agreed to settle for the borders of 1967. . . . [W]e get to keep only 22 percent of the historic land of Palestine and you get to hold on to all the rest. We have recognized Israel and agreed to its demands for secure borders, security arrangements. . . . You did not consider this to be a concession on our part. As far as you are concerned, it is all yours, as though we never existed. You pocketed this incredible historical concession and made more demands.[54]

As well, the Palestinians made additional concessions and accepted other compromises. As summarized by Kurtzer: They accepted that the settlement blocs in the West Bank and the Jewish neighborhoods of East Jerusalem and the Jewish Quarter of the Old City would be Israeli; they agreed to allow Israel to continue its early-warning sites in the West Bank; they accepted the principle of territorial swaps that would allow Israel to retain the Palestinian territory it wanted to annex; and they agreed that only a limited number of refugees would be allowed to return to Israel.[55]

Furthermore, while Arafat had made a serious error by initially dismissing the Jewish religious connection to Jerusalem as of little importance and even lacking historical grounds, he soon realized his error. "In practice," Pundak wrote, "the real Palestinian position on this issue during the negotiations was far more moderate and pragmatic,"[56] for by the end of the negotiations Arafat had accepted that Israel would have sovereignty over the Western Wall, the Jewish Quarter of the Old City, and even the previously established Jewish neighborhoods or settlements in or near East Jerusalem.

It is true that while Barak did somewhat modify some of his initial positions at Camp David, a number of Israeli and American officials and historians have written that his proposals fell well short of a genuinely fair settlement that would result in a viable Palestinian state.

For example, in his analysis of the Camp David outcome, Zeev Schiff, the dean of Israel's military/security analysts and a centrist in the Israeli political spectrum, wrote:

> The relentless expansion of the existing settlements and the establishment of new settlements, with a concomitant expropriation of Palestinian land in and around Jerusalem, and elsewhere as well [had resulted in the Palestinians being] shut in from all sides . . . [with] the prospect of being able to establish a viable state fading right before their eyes. They were confronted with an intolerable set of options: to agree to the spreading occupation . . . or set up wretched Bantustans, or launch an uprising.[57]

Pundak agreed with this analysis: "The conclusion is simple. If the full implementation of SC Res. 242 is the fair basis for a permanent-status agreement, Israel's territorial proposal at Camp David was not generous at all. . . . Only an Israeli offer of 100 percent [of the West Bank and Gaza] could have been seen as truly generous."[58] Malley concurred: "The measure of Israel's concession cannot be how far it has moved from its own starting point; it must be how far it has moved toward a fair solution."[59] Similarly, Kurtzer wrote:

> In effect, the Israelis treated the West Bank and Gaza as if they were at best disputed territories and, in the case of east Jerusalem and the annexed suburbs that were incorporated into the Jerusalem municipality, as Israeli territories. . . . Thus when Israel agreed to offer the Palestinians withdrawal

> from 90 percent or more of the West Bank, it was seen by Israelis as a generous offer, whereas the Palestinians saw it as a demand by Israel to keep 10 percent of what was rightfully theirs.[60]

In sum, if the Palestinians had accepted Barak's proposals the result would have been not only that the West Bank would have been separated from the Gaza Strip by Israeli territory, but that each segment of the "state" would be further subdivided into enclaves ("Bantustans," as they have been widely called) by the Israeli settlements, highways, and military positions. As a result, the links between the Palestinian areas could be broken by Israel any time it wished.

Further, the Palestinian state would not be allowed to have its capital in East Jerusalem but only in a small village on its outskirts, would not be allowed to have substantial armed forces, would have little or no control over its water resources, would be denied formal sovereignty over its most important religious sites, and would have no independently controlled border access to neighboring countries. Moreover, with even its internal freedom of movement and commerce subject to continued Israeli closures, the already impoverished Palestinian state would be economically at the mercy of Israel.

The net effect would have been to consolidate and make even more irreversible the Israeli occupation of much of the West Bank and Gaza. Astonishingly, even Barak's foreign minister, Shlomo Ben-Ami, who in his memoirs mostly blamed Arafat for the failure at Camp David, elsewhere admitted that "Camp David might not have been the deal the Palestinians could accept,"[61] and even more forthrightly in a 2006 interview said: "Camp David was not a missed opportunity for the Palestinians, and if I were a Palestinian I would have rejected Camp David, as well."[62]

Ehud Barak and Camp David: What Were His Goals?

At Camp David, Barak refused even to talk with Arafat, let alone negotiate with him, angering Barak's own delegation, many of whom have written or said that the Palestinian leader might have been more flexible had Barak accorded him some respect. Beyond that, Barak's history, ideology, and general contempt for Arabs in general and Arafat in particular caused some of his cabinet ministers to wonder whether he had been seriously seeking a settlement with the Palestinians or rather had been looking for a pretext to "prove" that it was Arafat who had blocked a peace settlement.

In light of his inconsistencies and puzzling behavior at Camp David, it is hard to know whether Barak was cynical and Machiavellian, seeking (as a number of Israeli columnists suggested) to preserve the essence of the Israeli occupation of the West Bank under the guise of negotiating a settlement.[63] Or, perhaps at some level Barak might have genuinely wanted a settlement—given his fears of the eventual consequences to Israel's security in the absence of a settlement—but was so ambivalent and conflicted that he was simply the wrong man for the job.

Had he chosen to do so, Barak could have legitimately described Camp David to the Israeli public as a partial success, the necessary first step toward a settlement of the Israeli-Palestinian conflict.[64] Instead, after the end of the conference Barak all but ensured the Israeli public's rejection of legitimate compromise with the Palestinians—and the subsequent landslide electoral victory of Ariel Sharon—by presenting Camp David not as a step in the right direction, the necessary foundation for a secure peace, but as proof that "the Palestinians are still clinging to the 'phased theory' as a practical plan"—that is, the strategy of destroying Israel in stages.[65]

In the weeks following Camp David, Barak repeatedly and publicly threatened the Palestinians that his "offer" would be Israel's final one, which if not accepted would result in Israel imposing "a unilateral separation," a euphemism for an imposed settlement. Barak told the Israeli public that because Arafat had been offered "everything he asked for," his refusal to agree proved that "we have no Palestinian partner for peace."[66] Malley and Agha commented: "Through his words and actions, Barak helped set in motion the process of delegitimizing the Palestinians and the peace process, thereby enabling Ariel Sharon to deal with them as he saw fit."[67]

In sum, the prevalence of the Camp David mythology perpetrated by Ehud Barak and "pro-Israeli" Clinton administration officials, led by Dennis Ross, was to have dire consequences, undercutting later attempts by the Israeli and US governments and political leaders to reach a fair two-state settlement of the conflict.

The Clinton "Parameters"

Despite his rhetoric, in the months after Camp David, under pressure from members of his own administration and many of the Israeli delegates, Barak reluctantly authorized continued secret negotiations with the Palestinians.[68] However, since both sides continued to maintain their basic positions, no progress was made, especially after the second intifada broke out in September 2000.

As a result, Bill Clinton decided to try further mediation, though by the time he did so, both he and Barak had only a few weeks left in office. On December 23, 2000, the president met with the Israeli and Palestinian negotiators and verbally proposed to them a set of ideas—"the Clinton Parameters," as they came to be known—for a settlement of the conflict.[69]

In his discussions with the delegates of both sides, Clinton made several proposals.

Palestinian Statehood and Territory

Israel would withdraw from the Gaza Strip and the Palestinians would be given sovereignty over "somewhere between 90 and 100 percent of West Bank territory," along with "swaps and other territorial arrangements to compensate for land [close to the Green Line] that Israel annexes for its settlement blocs." A fair solution, in Clinton's view, would provide "between 94 and 96 percent of West Bank territory to the Palestinian state," assuming a land swap of 1 to 3 percent. If these criteria were adopted, the resulting settlement would provide for "80 percent of the settlers in blocs, contiguity of territory for each side, and minimal Israeli annexation, [thus reducing] the number of Palestinians affected" (see Map 15.1).

Security

While the Palestinian state would include—sort of—the Jordan River Valley, in order to accommodate Israeli security concerns about "an Arab attack from the East," Israel would be allowed to maintain a gradually reduced military presence in the region over the next three years. During this period an international peacekeeping force would be gradually introduced to take its place and could not be withdrawn unless both sides consented.

However, even after that three-year period, Israel would be allowed to maintain early-warning radar stations in the West Bank over an additional three years. As well, even though the Palestinian state supposedly would have "sovereignty" in the air spaces over its territory, there would be "special arrangements" that would allow Israel to use them for military purposes.

Palestinian security issues were treated differently. Israel insisted that the Palestinian state must be "demilitarized," but Arafat would agree only to "a state of limited arms." The suggested Clinton compromise was that the state would be "nonmilitarized" but at the same time would be allowed "a strong security force [and] an international force for border security and deterrence purposes." What that would entail, precisely, Clinton left to the two sides to "work out."

Jerusalem

The "general principle" should be that "what is Arab should be Palestinian and what is Jewish should be Israeli," including the Old City, except that some way had to be found to either divide or share "sovereignty" over the Haram/Temple Mount. For example, Clinton proposed that the Palestinians would have sovereignty over the Haram plateau, while the Israelis would maintain sovereignty below the plateau, along with adjoining "sacred" Jewish spaces near it; one alternative, he suggested, would be Jewish sovereignty over "the Western Wall and the holy of holies of which it is a part."

Not only the Palestinians but also Israeli critics considered that the largely secular Barak government was pandering to the Israeli religious political parties and were not happy that even Clinton had adopted the language of Jewish religious extremism. The Palestinians reminded Clinton that Dayan had forbidden Jews from going to the Haram al-Sharif plateau and warned against creating "a religious time bomb and . . . toying with explosives that could ignite the Middle East and Islamic world."[70]

The Refugees and the Right of Return

A formula needed to be found, Clinton said, "that will make clear there is no specific right of return to Israel itself, but that does not negate the aspirations of Palestinian refugees to return to the area."

He then proposed five possible solutions that would be consistent with a two-state solution: a return to the new State of Palestine; a return to areas in Israel that would be transferred to Palestine in the land swap; rehabilitation in Arab countries presently inhabited by the refugees, with priority given to the large Palestinian population in Lebanon; resettlement in third countries; or, finally, admission to Israel—but only at Israel's discretion. To facilitate whichever of these solutions were adopted, Clinton said that the United States would take the lead in the creation of a large international fund for refugee compensation.[71]

Clinton closed with these words:

> I believe this is the outline of a fair and lasting agreement. It gives the Palestinian people the ability to determine their future on their own land, a sovereign and viable state recognized by the international community, al-Quds [the Arabic name for Jerusalem, literally meaning "The Holy One"] as its capital, sovereignty over the Haram, and new lives for the refugees.
>
> It gives the people of Israel a genuine end to the conflict, real security, the preservation of sacred religious ties, the incorporation of 80 percent of the settlers into Israel, and the largest Jewish Jerusalem in history recognized by all as your capital.

Ominously, however, he added that "this is the best I can do," that these were his ideas alone, and that if they were not accepted, "they are not just off the table, they go with me when I leave office."

Nothing was put in writing, it must be emphasized. Dennis Ross explained why:

> Fearing the Arafat style of pocketing any advance and treating it as a point of departure . . . we would not present a formal piece of paper that would exist after the Clinton presidency ended, but would instead have President Clinton present the ideas informally and orally. And lastly, and very much related to the concern about pocketing, we would withdraw the ideas if they were not acceptable to either side.[72]

As a result of their nonwritten status and the inherent lack of specificity in what were only brief statements of general principles, there were many ambiguities that would have to be addressed in any intensive negotiating process that could lead to a highly detailed and comprehensive treaty.

One such ambiguity was that the US government never showed the Palestinians a map of the territorial proposals in the Clinton Parameters, nor specified what areas would be annexed by Israel or what the Palestinians would receive as compensation. Moreover, Dennis Ross later admitted that "we did not know the terrain [or] how each percentage of land might affect particular settlements."[73]

Yet Clinton went along with Ross's insistence that his proposals, "parameters" or not, had to be regarded in effect as a take-it-or-leave-it proposition. In his paraphrase of what Clinton told the Israeli and Arab delegations, Ross writes:

> Negotiations could take place within the parameters, but not on the parameters themselves. If either side could not accept the parameters we would withdraw the ideas, and in any case they would no longer exist once he left office. . . . They would have five days to respond with either a yes or a no. A nonanswer would be taken as a no. A maybe would be taken as a no.[74]

Given the ambiguity and lack of detail in the "parameters," it was inevitable that both sides would respond with counterproposals or at least requests for clarification. What, then, would be considered as "within" or "outside" of the parameters would be determined by the Clinton administration, which given Clinton's dependence on him, effectively meant that Ross himself, at least initially, would be the keeper of the parameters. Thus, when Ahmed Qurei told Ross that Arafat wanted to meet with him before responding to the Clinton proposals, Ross told him, preposterously, that "I will not talk about ideas. The President won't let me. We must have an acceptance first before I can talk about them."[75]

The Palestinian Response

On December 28, five days after Clinton presented his parameters to Israeli and Palestinian negotiators, Arafat wrote to the president with his response. One quite short version of the English-language text of his letter can be found in Clayton Swisher's book *The Truth about Camp David;* however, the Palestinian newspaper *Al-Ayyam* published the original Arabic version, which is considerably more detailed.[76]

Arafat's response to Clinton is extremely important, but it has been widely ignored or misrepresented. For example, as Avi Shlaim has pointed out, the PLO leader's letter is ignored in the memoirs of Clinton and Ross, and in her memoirs, Madeleine Albright claimed that it proved that "the Palestinians had not moved a centimeter."[77] Shlaim commented: "Albright's summary is a travesty."[78]

After praising Clinton for "the historical importance of what you are trying to do," and assuring him "of my will to continue to work with you to reach a peace agreement," Arafat asked the president for his help "in clarifying and explaining the basis of your proposals," and "seeks to explain why [they] do not meet the required conditions for a lasting peace."

There is no question that Arafat's letter was blunt. He began by pointedly noting that "since a map clarifying all the vague issues is not appended to the American proposal," the Palestinians cannot analyze its territorial implications:

> The proposal was phrased in general terms that in some cases lack clarity and specificity. We believe that the Final Settlement Accord should not be merely a document of general political principles . . . [but] a comprehensive agreement that clarifies details, mechanisms, and timetables for ending the Israeli Palestinian conflict. Clarity and detail are necessary, because of our past experiences with vague agreements and from Israel's history of non-compliance with signed agreements. . . . The proposals do not include practical security arrangements between Palestine and Israel nor do they deal with some other issues of great importance to the Palestinian people. The American proposals seem to respond to Israeli demands while ignoring the basic Palestinian requirement: a viable Palestinian state that can survive.

Arafat then addressed the major issues.

Territory. Clinton's territorial proposal, he wrote, "minimizes both the scope of lands to be annexed and the number of Palestinians to be damaged by this annexation," and "gives Israel control over extensive parts of the land." By dividing the West Bank into three separate cantons, disconnected from its international borders and even from each other by Jewish-only roads, he argued, the viability and durability of the state is jeopardized. In particular, "sizeable uninhabited lands in vital areas such as Jerusalem and Bethlehem will be annexed by Israel and this will ruin the geographical contiguity of the Palestinian state. Not only will it limit the Palestinians' freedom of movement, it will also have severe implications on the development of the Palestinian state. Such a vast annexation will inevitably damage Palestinian water rights."

Furthermore, Arafat argued, the territorial exchanges proposed by the Clinton proposals were inequitable in both quantity and quality. First, "the U.S. proposed that Israel annex 2–6 percent of the West Bank and that this annexation will be compensated by Israel only by the equivalent of 1–3 percent." In any case, Arafat contended, the Palestinians "do not need any Israeli lands, with the exception of the safe passage between the West Bank and the Gaza Strip." Yet, on that crucial issue, he continued, the Clinton proposal was silent, nor did it specify the Israeli lands that would serve as compensation for the West Bank areas that would be annexed by Israel.

The second inequity of the Clinton proposals, Arafat said, was this:

> The American territorial proposal disregarded issues of land quality. All the American and Israeli proposals for land exchange in the past referred only to lands adjacent to the Gaza Strip in exchange for valuable lands in the West Bank. In addition to their arid nature, the lands offered to the Palestinians as compensation currently serve for toxic waste disposal. Undoubtedly, we cannot agree to exchange lands valuable for agriculture and development, with garbage sites for toxic waste.
>
> The Palestinian side insists that any compensation for land annexed by Israel will be equal to this land in size and value. We see no other logic. Nevertheless, the American proposal specifically opposes equal size of the swapped lands and disregards the issue of their value or location.

Finally, Arafat rejected Clinton's proposal for continuing Israeli military presence in the Jordan Valley as an infringement on Palestinian sovereignty. Indyk summed up the Palestinian "mind-set":

> From their point of view, all of historic Palestine was rightfully theirs and had been taken away from them by force. In accepting Security Council Resolution 242 they had explicitly recognized Israel's right to control 78 percent of the territories of the Palestine Mandate. Now they argued it was unfair to be expected to bargain over the 22 percent that encompassed the West Bank and Gaza.[79]

The Settlements. For a number of reasons, Arafat wrote, the Palestinians reject "the American use of the 'settlement-blocs' as a principle in the negotiations." The annexation "of 4–6 percent of the land (let alone 10 percent)," he wrote, "would inevitably damage basic Palestinian interests, [for] in the framework of such a formula, the number of displaced Palestinians would increase due to annexation of Arab villages to Israel." As well, Israeli annexation of land adjacent to Jerusalem and Bethlehem would not only "ruin the geographical contiguity of the Palestinian state . . . [and] limit the Palestinians' freedom of movement," but it would "inevitably damage Palestinian water rights" and in other ways "have severe implications on the development of the Palestinian state." Arafat concludes: "It is inconceivable that we accept a proposal punishing the Palestinians and rewarding the illegitimate Israeli settlement policies."

Jerusalem. Palestinian sovereignty over the Haram al-Sharif "in its entirety is indivisible," Arafat wrote.[80] For other reasons Clinton's parameters on the Jerusalem issue were problematic because they did not take into account the manner in which Israeli policies and actions had increasingly resulted in the creation of disconnected Palestinian enclaves throughout the West Bank and, in particular, had progressively narrowed Palestinian access to East Jerusalem. As a result, Arafat continued, Clinton's general principle of "Arab areas to Palestine and Jewish areas to Israel" would result in "the partitioning of Palestinian Jerusalem into several islands detached from one another as well as from the Palestinian state. . . . Any solution that will be acceptable from the Palestinian perspective must include geographical contiguity between the Palestinian areas in Jerusalem on the one hand, and the rest of the Palestinian lands, on the other hand."

While Arafat said he was willing to accept continued Israeli sovereignty over the Western Wall, recent Israeli actions and claims had expanded the definition of the "Wall" in a manner that could infringe on the areas designated for Palestinian sovereignty: "Israel's constant demand for sovereignty over some 'religious sites' in Jerusalem that are not geographically specified and [its] continued refusal to present maps clarifying its demands on Jerusalem," he wrote, "only enhance Palestinian fears."

As well, in recent years there had been a number of occasions in which Israel, citing "security" concerns, had closed Palestinian access to the Haram. With that in mind, Arafat wrote that Jerusalem must be an "open city"—as had been specified in the UN partition plan—in which all peoples have "freedom of movement and worship." However, he concluded, "the American proposal disregards this fundamental principle."

The Refugee Issue. Arafat took a surprisingly hard-line position on the right of refugees to return to Israel—surprisingly, because both he and other high-level Palestinian officials, before, during, and after Camp David, had made it clear that they would settle for a symbolic "return" of only a small number of the refugees.

Rejecting Clinton's proposed alternatives to a full-scale refugee return, Arafat wrote that the proposal "wholly endorses the Israeli position that the Right of Return must be entirely dependent on Israel's discretion." Instead, Arafat insisted, UN Resolution 194 of December 1948 must remain "the basis for a just settlement for the Refugee Problem," and he pointedly noted that the resolution "determines the return of the Palestinian refugees 'to their homes' and not 'to their homeland' or 'historical Palestine.'" He continued: "The essence of the Right of Return is the freedom of choice: the Palestinians should be given the right to choose their place of living, including the homes from which they were expelled. . . . Recognizing the Right of Return and allowing the refugees' freedom of choice are a prerequisite for ending the conflict."

Arafat concluded his long letter to Clinton:

> While we emphasize our commitment to ending the Israeli-Palestinian conflict, we believe that this will be fulfilled only once all the issues that caused the conflict and led to its continuation have been solved. This cannot happen without a comprehensive agreement including detailed mechanisms for solving the core issues of the conflict. . . . Even if we put

> the requirements of international law and justice aside, the American proposals do not present even a pragmatic solution to the conflict, *as long as they are not clarified*[emphasis added]. If real solutions are not found to the actual issues, any formula or text about the end of the conflict will remain void. . . . We cannot accept a proposal that does not include the establishment of a viable Palestinian state and does not guarantee the right of the refugees to return to their homes.

Dennis Ross later characterized Arafat's letter as "stiffing" Clinton with reservations that were essentially "deal-killers."[81] However, it seems persuasive—or even undeniable—that most of Arafat's objections or requests for changes, clarification, or more specific and detailed proposals were reasonable and legitimate. In light of the history of past Israeli violations of apparent agreements—for example, Oslo—he was right to be concerned that every Clinton "idea" could be interpreted by Israel in a manner that effectively undercut his proposed compromises.[82]

Nonetheless, it seems apparent that Arafat made two major errors, the first of which was his insistence on the obviously impossible demand for a literal and unlimited right of return—a demand, moreover, which in reality he had clearly abandoned in the past, and would very quickly do so again. Second, the tone and language of Arafat's letter was surprisingly blunt, even gratuitously so. One can only surmise that he was angry at the continuing American support for Israeli policies.

Still, after first deferring to Ross's insistence that Arafat's reservations were outside the parameters, Clinton finally decided, after several "heated" exchanges with Arafat, to interpret his reply as (in Yossi Beilin's description), "Yes, but—a readiness in principle to adopt the Clinton Plan, together with a number of reservations that did not turn it on its head."[83]

The Israeli Response

On December 30, 2000, Barak responded to Clinton's proposals in a twenty-page letter to the American president. At Barak's request, the letter was kept secret and apparently is still officially classified.[84] Nonetheless, it has been described in detail in Uri Horowitz's long analysis ("Camp David 2") and in both the Sher Report and in Sher's memoir, and it has evidently been seen by other US and Israeli officials or writers.

In the letter, Barak told Clinton that "Israel sees his ideas as a basis for discussion, as long as they are accepted as a basis for discussion by the Palestinians as well,"[85] but then said that "certain elements of the president's ideas differ or run contrary to Israeli positions," including on territory, Jerusalem, security, refugees, and others—in short, on every important issue.[86]

Sher elaborates on what the Barak letter said.

Territory. "Israel's need to include eighty percent of the settlers in the settlement blocs dictates greater [territorial] needs than provided for by the president's ideas."[87]

Security. As well, "further clarification" from Clinton was needed on the status of Palestinians in settlement blocs; the meaning of "safe passage" for the Palestinians; the definition of the Western Wall and "the status of the holy sites in Jerusalem"; the meaning of "non-militarization" of the Palestinian state and the role of the Palestinian security force; the structure, tasks, and leadership of the international force that would gradually replace the Israeli forces in the Jordan River Valley and its relationship with the Israeli force; the control of the airspace; and others.[88]

Jerusalem. The detailed analyses of Horowitz and Sher establish that Israel continued to demand sovereignty over the Temple Mount, which would now include a synagogue; it also insisted on control of "the sacred basin," the area outside the Old City that includes the "City of David" and the Jewish "Tomb of the Prophets." The Palestinians would not have sovereignty over any part of the Temple Mount, though they could continue, perhaps in conjunction with some kind of international commission, to exercise "trusteeship" or "custodianship" over the Islamic mosques on the plateau.

To be sure, Barak did suggest possible alternative arrangements, but when the Palestinians continued to insist on sole Islamic sovereignty on the plateau, Barak retracted his offers. Indyk explains:

> Barak told Albright that since Arafat had rejected the ideas proposed by the president . . . they were now off the table. He wanted Arafat to understand that there was a price to be paid for his refusal of the earlier proposal. Instead of sovereignty over the Muslim and Christian quarters in the Old City, Barak now went back to his old offer of a "sovereign corridor" from the outer suburbs where the Palestinians would have sovereignty through one inner suburb to a "sovereign compound" in the Old City, adjacent to the Haram al-Sharif, where Arafat would have custodianship.[89]

Refugees. Israel agreed that the refugee problem was a regrettable humanitarian issue, Barak stated, and would recognize the right of the Palestinians to return to their own state, but that "no right of return to Israeli territory would prevail." However, he continued, Israel was prepared to admit several hundred refugees annually for a ten- to fifteen-year period, under a family unification program. In a later interview, Barak made it clear that the "family unification program" was not based on any Palestinian rights: "No Israeli prime minister will accept even one refugee on the basis of the right of return."[90]

In any case, three days after his letter to Clinton and even before hearing from Arafat, Barak called the president to warn him that "I do not intend to sign any agreement before the elections," referring to the February 2000 national elections in which he would run against Ariel Sharon.[91] Then, before leaving office, he sent letters to Clinton and Arafat making clear that Israel would not be bound by Clinton's ideas.[92] In any case, by then those ideas would be moot, for Clinton had said that his proposals would expire at the end of his term in January 2001. And in February, the new Bush administration reaffirmed that the Clinton parameters were no longer US policy.

In later years, in an interview with an Israeli historian, Barak explained the true meaning of his supposedly positive response to Clinton's parameters: "Barak admitted, for the first time, that saying 'Yes' to the Clinton parameters was more of a trick to expose Arafat than a genuine acceptance of the proposals." Barak is directly quoted:

> In order not to pass the responsibility [for the failure of the peace process] from Arafat back to us . . . [I convinced my] government to adopt [the plan] . . . and that was part of [my] crusade to fix the fact that what had happened at Camp David was not an [exceptional case] but rather part of Arafat's systematic unwillingness to enter into negotiations over a [peace] settlement.[93]

In sum, while in his memoirs Clinton asserts that Israel's reservations "were within the parameters," but that Arafat's reservations, "unlike Israel's, were outside,"[94] a fairer assessment would be that "both sides were now ignoring the Clinton Parameters."[95]

The Taba Conference

Even though Barak had essentially abandoned the peace process after Camp David, the more dovish members of Barak's government and the Israeli negotiating team were not willing to give up, and in January 2001 they pressured Barak to agree to continued negotiations in Taba, a small Egyptian town bordering on the Israeli city of Eilat.

Shlomo Ben-Ami tells what happened next:

> Barak didn't want to go to Taba. He didn't see any point or purpose in it. But at this stage there was a pistol on the table. The elections were a month away, and there was a minister who told Ehud that if he didn't go to Taba they would denounce him in public for evading his duty to make peace. He had no choice but to go to a meeting for something he himself no longer believed in.[96]

Consequently, Barak reluctantly agreed to let the Israeli doves continue the negotiations, appointing Ben-Ami head of the Israel team that included Yossi Beilin and several other liberal Israeli leaders or officials. Once again, however, there would be no written record, allowing Barak to disavow any agreements he disliked.

However, Arafat's lead negotiators, Ahmed Qurei (Abu Ala), Saeb Erekat, and Yasser Abed Rabbo, were among his closest associates and advisors, suggesting that they were negotiating on his behalf: Israeli military intelligence concluded that "Arafat had identified the practical possibility of reaching a full agreement while Clinton and Barak were still in office, and he was serious about examining that possibility."[97]

Significantly, the American government had no part in the Taba negotiations. It is not clear why—perhaps the incoming Bush administration was not ready or did not want to continue with Clinton's policies or perhaps, simply, it wasn't invited, just as the Clinton administration had not been invited to participate in the Oslo 1 negotiations. Most likely, the Palestinians had had enough of what they regarded, for good reasons, as a one-sided US role in the process.

Indeed, that the US government's "mediation" was indeed often one-sided was later admitted by Aaron David Miller, who wrote that while he often differed with Dennis Ross and Martin Indyk, the most conservative ("pro-Israel") of Clinton's advisors, he joined them in "bringing a clear pro-Israel orientation to our peace process planning. . . . In truth, not a single senior-level official involved with the negotiations was willing or able to present, let alone fight for, the Arab or Palestinian perspective."[98]

Moreover, there is evidence that the Israeli doves were themselves sometimes unhappy with "pro-Israeli" US policies that were to the right of their own, and therefore did not want the American government to disrupt the new negotiations. For example, Ron Pundak later remarked that the American government, as usual, had followed its "traditional approach" in adopting "the position of the Israeli Prime Minister. . . . The American government seemed sometimes to be working for the Israeli Prime Minister."[99]

The departure point for negotiations was the Clinton Parameters, and considerable progress was made, largely because the Israelis moved a considerable distance from Barak's closing position at Camp David and his December response to Clinton's proposals.[100]

Territory. Both sides agreed that the borders between Israel and the Palestinian state would be very near the pre-1967 border between the West Bank and Israel. At Camp David, Barak's best offer (according to Beilin) still left about 8 percent of the West Bank in Israel's hands, and though Barak agreed to some compensating territorial exchanges with the Palestinians, they were highly unequal in both size and land quality.

The Israeli delegation improved on this offer, asking for some 4 to 6 percent of the West Bank, along with more equitable but still somewhat unequal territorial exchanges: while Barak's territorial swap proposals had favored Israel by as much as a 10:1 ratio, the new Israeli proposals reduced the Israeli advantage to a 2:1 ratio.

The Israeli Settlements. The Palestinians made a major concession, agreeing to the Israeli demand to "settlement blocs" inside the areas of the West Bank be annexed to Israel. The blocs would then contain about 80 percent of the settlers. While there were no references to the much smaller settlements that were outside the annexed territory, the Moratinos report said that what was "implied" was that they would now come under Palestinian sovereignty. The Sher Report stated that while no evacuation of settlements was planned for the initial phase of the plan, "at an appropriate time" the settlers would be transferred to one of the settlement blocs or to Israel.

The Security Issues. In this case, the Israeli negotiators made the major concessions, essentially accepting the Clinton Parameters by dropping their demand for Israeli sovereignty over the Jordan River Valley, so long as Israel retained three early-warning stations in the area and could keep their military forces there over a three-year period, only gradually being withdrawn as they were replaced by a US-European peacekeeping force. Ben-Ami explained: "We had arrived at solutions that would preserve our most essential security interests even without sovereignty. It was clear to us that our demand for sovereignty in the Jordan Rift Valley was something the Palestinians could not live with."[101]

According to the Sher Report, the Palestinians still had objections on the security issues: to the demilitarization of the Palestinian state, to the proposed timeline for the Israeli forces to withdraw from the West Bank, and several others. However, Beilin and others believed that these objections would not stand in the way of a peace agreement if the more important issues of the refugees and Jerusalem were resolved.

The Refugees and the Right of Return. There were significant differences, at least of emphasis, on how to describe the outcome of the Taba discussions on this issue. In his summary for Sharon on the state of the issue, Sher wrote that Israel would not accept "sole" responsibility for the refugee issue and rejected any Palestinian right of return, though it might take part, "at its discretion," in an international effort to bring in a small number of refugees on a humanitarian basis.[102]

However, Yossi Beilin, the primary Israeli negotiator on the refugee issue, was more positive; in a 2001 op-ed for the *New York Times*, he wrote: "I can testify that some resolution to the refugee question was within reach at Taba, without in any way compromising the demographically Jewish nature of the state of Israel." The Palestinians had agreed to major compromises on the right of return, he wrote, including a willingness to separate the principle from its implementation, to agree that Israel would be only one of several possible destinations for the refugees; and to accept that the number of refugees returning to Israel would be limited, with Israel having the final say on who would be allowed to "return."[103]

Similarly, in a 2002 *Haaretz* column, Beilin wrote:

> [I am] convinced that it is possible to reach an Israeli-Palestinian agreement without granting the refugees the right of return. We were very close to such a solution at Taba in January 2001. . . . After the Taba talks leaders from the Palestinian Authority began making clear that they would not press for implementation of the right of return.[104]

Other accounts of Taba were less sanguine about the progress made on the issue. In his memoirs, Ben-Ami argues that Beilin was too optimistic,[105] and Shlaim says that the gaps on the refugee issue "were reduced but left behind a good deal of unfinished business."[106] In light of the absence of transcripts or other written records, it is impossible to resolve the differences in these accounts. However, what is certain is that there is a wealth of evidence that even before Taba and certainly ever since, Arafat, Ahmed Qurei, Saeb Erekat, Mahmoud Abbas, and other high Palestinian officials have all repeatedly reassured the Israeli leaders that they have no intention of pressing Israel to admit large numbers of the refugees, let alone their descendants.

Jerusalem. Although both sides continued to have issues with giving concrete meaning to aspects of the Clinton proposals—"What is Jewish is Israeli, what is Arab is Palestinian"—they said they accepted the principle. The major sticking points continued to be over parts of the Old City and, especially, the Temple Mount/Haram. While Israel was willing to consider complex arrangements that split the differences, the Palestinians continued to reject any compromise that did not grant them sovereignty over the Haram. Even Sher's report to Sharon stated, however, that in contrast to Arafat's previous dismissal of Jewish religious claims and feelings, the Palestinians "showed understanding of the sensitivity of the issue for Israel, and a willingness to find a formulation that would balance these feelings with their national needs."

What is the likelihood that the Jerusalem issue could have been resolved if the negotiations had continued? Shlaim is cautious: "On Jerusalem only slight progress was made. Neither side was happy with Clinton's proposals, but the alternative each side proposed was even less appealing to the other side."[107] Beilin's summation of the status of the Jerusalem issue when the conference ended was more upbeat: "The parties' willingness to accept the Clinton Plan was emerging. . . . The matter of sovereignty over the holy places remained open, lingering somewhere between the Clinton proposal and internationalization."[108] As well, Kurtzer ends his summation of the issue on an even more positive note: "Both sides were close to accepting Clinton's ideas regarding Palestinian sovereignty over Haram al-Sharif notwithstanding Palestinian and Israeli reservations."[109]

At the close of the conference, the Israeli and Palestinian negotiators issued a joint communiqué: "The sides declare that they have never been closer to reaching an agreement and it is thus our shared belief that the remaining gaps could be bridged with the resumption of negotiations following the Israeli elections."[110]

A few months later, in a joint *New York Times* op-ed, Yossi Beilin and Yasir Abed Rabbo of the Palestinian delegation wrote that "we can personally testify to have been extremely, even agonizingly close to reaching an agreement. . . . The main missing ingredient was quality time."[111] Similarly, Ahmed Qurei said that if Taba had continued in the same spirit for another two months, there would have been an agreement.[112]

But Barak ended the Taba talks, and in his last few months in office he resumed his previous rigidity on the Israeli-Palestinian conflict, with devastating consequences that continue today. The likely explanations for his behavior were his unresolved ambivalence about the need for compromise and his unwillingness to appear too "leftist" (as that term is defined in Israeli discourse) on the eve of the national elections. To be sure, Barak really did have a domestic politics problem that he would have had to overcome to get public support for a genuinely fair settlement of the conflict. However, rather than attempt to educate the Israeli people, he did the opposite, creating a new mythology about why the peace process had failed and in the process making the conflict even harder to settle than it had been before Camp David.

Thus, Barak not only backtracked from his apparent though short-lived willingness at Camp David to make important concessions to the Palestinians, but his public dismissals of his own delegation's concessions at Taba became increasingly extreme. For example, he told an interviewer that Beilin's suggested compromise on the right of return was a private idea of his own and was "a bad document" that had no validity as an official Israeli position, and he asserted that claims of Beilin, the Palestinians, and the EU's Miguel Moratinos that peace was very close "had no foundation."[113] Of course, maybe what he meant was that they had no foundation because he was going to reject them.

On one occasion Barak went even further, falsely stating in a PBS documentary that because "there was no sense trying to negotiate with Arafat, I did not even allow our people to establish a delegation that sits together with a Palestinian delegation."[114] Indeed, Malley and Agha wrote, "Today he takes pride in having made fewer tangible concessions to the Palestinians than Benjamin Netanyahu."[115]

Bill Clinton and the Camp David/Taba Peace Negotiations

There is no doubt that Clinton was committed to seeking what he believed to be a fair settlement of the Israeli-Palestinian conflict, but for several reasons, he failed. The most important, of course, was that Israel simply was unwilling to end its occupation of the West Bank and allow the Palestinians to have a viable state of their own. Beyond that, though, American domestic politics—the strong support of Israeli policies in public opinion and, especially, in Congress, whether sincere or motivated by political calculations—acted as a major constraint on Clinton's ability to maneuver, especially to credibly threaten Israel with a loss of American support if he believed it was an obstacle to a just settlement.

As well, Clinton had little knowledge of the realities of the Israeli-Palestinian conflict; consequently, in Kurtzer's words, he was "far more in agreement with the Israeli narrative than the Palestinian one."[116] Further, he got little help from his main advisors, especially Dennis Ross, the most important of them, who often served him poorly, especially in their unwillingness to challenge Israeli policies.

In a May 2004 discussion of what had gone wrong, Rob Malley, Aaron Miller, Martin Indyk, and even Ross admitted that the Clinton administration had made many mistakes. In the twenty-five years he was in government, Miller said, there was never "an honest conversation about what the Israelis were actually doing on the ground."[117] Even when Clinton wasn't in agreement with Barak, Miller continued, he backed away from confronting him: "We weren't prepared to impose a cost on the Israelis for their actions." In his memoirs, Miller elaborated: "Had we . . . pushed back when the Israelis went too far, we might have preserved our integrity as a mediator. But we caved to Israeli objections."[118]

Malley and Agha point to one example: "Clinton was furious" when Barak disregarded his commitment to transfer three Jerusalem areas to the Palestinians and on other "questionable tactical judgments," but "in the end the U.S. either gave up or gave in, reluctantly acquiescing in the way Barak did things out of respect for the things he was trying to do."[119]

Finally, Clinton was personally poorly equipped to play the role of a genuine mediator, for he was volatile, self-centered, and had a tendency to personalize policy differences, especially with Yasser Arafat. Thus, in addition to his support of most of Barak's positions at Camp David—sometimes even despite his own reservations—Clinton often berated Arafat and other Palestinian leaders when he was contradicted or merely not complied with.

In their accounts of Clinton's interactions with Arafat and other Palestinian leaders, Swisher, Enderlin, Sher, Ben-Ami, and even Ross all describe Clinton's behavior.

- In an argument with Aba Ala (Ahmed Qurei), the leader of the Palestinian negotiators, "Clinton went postal. . . . Don't make me waste my time. I'm the president of the United States. 'I'm ready to pack my bags and leave. You're obstructing the negotiation. You're not acting in good faith.'" Swisher then quotes Sher: "Aba Ala lost all faith then in the honest, unbiased brokerage of the United States."[120]
- When Arafat refused to accept Israeli sovereignty over the Haram, Clinton "exploded": "Here you go again. You won't have a state, and relations between America and the Palestinians will be over. Congress will vote to stop the aid you've been allocated, and you'll be treated as a terrorist organization. . . . You haven't budged; all you've done is pocket what Barak was giving."[121]
- When Arafat refused to back off from the 1967 borders as the basis for negotiations, "Clinton became boiling mad and started shouting terribly, turned completely red and finally got up and stalked out."[122]
- When Aba Ala maintained that the Israeli settlements were illegal and that the Palestinians needed the 1967 lines, Clinton became "livid," shouted at him that it his position was "outrageous," "not serious," a "mockery," and "a waste of his and everyone else's time."[123]

To be sure, on occasion Clinton also got angry with Barak, at one point saying to him that "he [Clinton] had beaten up on the Palestinians today, but in truth [you] weren't doing a thing in a summit you insisted on having."[124] However, his anger against Barak did not last long, and there was no follow-up. On the contrary, when the negotiations over the Clinton Parameters ended without success, Clinton held a press conference in which he highly praised Barak and said that "the Israeli public should be proud of their Prime Minister."[125] Evidently that was a bit much even for Ross, who in his memoir says: "I marveled at his capacity to put the best face on what Barak had done."[126]

Bregman notes that "there was no similar praise for Arafat," and quotes Malley: "The language was to say that Barak had shown real courage and vision and that Arafat had reiterated his commitment to peace, which was a way of saying that one showed courage and the other showed up."[127]

In effect, then, Clinton had broken his promise to Arafat not to blame him for the failure to reach an Israeli-Palestinian peace settlement. That did not stop him from saying to Arafat: "I am a failure, and you have made me one."[128]

Kurtzer concluded:

> The act of blaming Arafat was hugely consequential for the Palestinians, the Israeli public, and the American role in the coming months and years. . . . The emerging narrative . . . was that Barak had offered Arafat more than any other Israeli leader ever had, maybe even more than the Israeli public was prepared to accept, and Arafat simply pocketed the concessions and gave little in return.[129]

The Arab Peace Initiative

In 2002, the leading Arab states tried again to reach an overall settlement of the Arab-Israeli conflict. The initiative was taken by King Abdullah of Saudi Arabia, who proposed a new version of the 1982 Fahd plan to a summit meeting of the twenty-two member states of the Arab League. The plan was unanimously accepted and became the "Arab Peace Initiative" (API); soon afterward it was also endorsed by the Organization of Islamic Cooperation, representing fifty-seven states, forty of them having a Muslim majority population. The API called for the end of the Arab-Israeli conflict, offering Israel a comprehensive peace agreement that would include not only security provisions but normal relations with the Arab world, on the condition that it withdraw from all the territories occupied in 1967 and accept "the establishment of a sovereign, independent Palestinian state in the West Bank and Gaza Strip, with East Jerusalem as its capital."

Of particular importance, the API did not endorse an unlimited Palestinian "right of return," calling only for "a just solution to the Palestinian refugee problem" in accordance with the UN General Assembly Resolution 194 of December 1948, which had been carefully worded so as to qualify any such right: "Refugees wishing to return to their homes and live in peace with their neighbors should be permitted to do so at the earliest practicable date," with compensation for those who "choose not to return."[130]

As well, King Abdullah let it be known that even the term "full withdrawal" did not necessarily have to be taken literally, for during discussions of his plan with Henry Siegman, he said that his proposal "would allow equal territorial swaps on both sides of the 1967 line to enable Israel to incorporate several settlement blocs . . . [and] also allowed Israel's annexation of Jewish neighborhoods in East Jerusalem and sovereignty over the Western Wall."[131]

Nonetheless, Israel ignored the API, which would have ended both the Arab-Israeli and Israeli-Palestinian conflicts in a manner that would preserve all of Israel's *legitimate* goals and interests.[132]

16

Israeli Occupation and Palestinian Resistance, 2000–2008

International law and just war moral philosophy recognize the right of a people to resist foreign occupation, by political means or nonviolent resistance if possible, by armed uprisings directed against the military forces of the occupier as a last resort. Terrorism, however, defined as attacks on the noncombatant civilians of the occupier, is never legally or morally allowable; moreover, most of the time it doesn't work.

Over the years, Palestinian guerrilla forces, in earlier years the PLO, and more recently Hamas, have often attacked Israeli military forces in hopes of forcing them to withdraw from the occupied territories, such attacks do not constitute "terrorism." Given the huge disparities between the Israeli and Palestinian armed forces, though, all the attacks have failed and there is no prospect of significant change. For that reason, since the 1980s the Palestine Liberation Organization and the Palestinian Authority have essentially abandoned all forms of military resistance. Today, while Hamas in principle continues to adhere to armed resistance, it rarely initiates attacks on Israeli military forces, and never with any success in achieving its political goals.

Armed force having proved futile, the Palestinians repeatedly have sought to resist the occupation of the West Bank and Gaza primarily by means of peaceful marches and demonstrations, although sometimes accompanied by rock-throwing, which should be regarded as primarily symbolic. All these forms of resistance, including those that are entirely nonviolent, have been repressed by Israel, often with deadly force. The facts are not in doubt, and the literature on the issue is extensive; the routine repression of unarmed Palestinian demonstrations—often including Israeli peace groups as well—is regularly reported in the Israeli media. Over the years, hundreds of protesters have been killed, and thousands imprisoned.

In 2008, Meron Benvenisti, a former deputy mayor of Jerusalem, wrote:

> The response of the Israeli authorities to nonviolent protest has been no less severe than their reaction to violent acts. . . . The way to prevent the

> spread of nonviolent resistance is to threaten that it will be met with a violent response, including the use of firearms, in the hope that the threat will be taken seriously, serve as a deterrent. . . . The Israelis have managed to persuade the Palestinians that they have no inhibitions when it comes to using force, even gunfire, against unarmed protesters, and that they make no distinction between violent and nonviolent demonstrations.[1]

In 2013, Yossi Sarid, a longtime political leader, Knesset member, and minister in the Rabin and Peres governments, wrote: "Israel is afraid of a Mahatma Gandhi or Martin Luther King who will suddenly rise up at its gates . . . anyone who preaches civil disobedience is dangerous and must be imprisoned."[2]

In spring 2018, thousands of Gazan residents marched toward the border fence separating Israel from Gaza in a largely but not entirely peaceful protest. Some of them threw stones at the Israeli border guards and some nearby Israeli fields were set on fire by incendiary kites or other devices. To suppress the demonstrations and prevent the marchers from crossing the border, Israeli snipers killed dozens and wounded thousands. A *Haaretz* editorial, entitled "Stop Shooting Gazan Protesters," commented: "The government and the army are sticking to the dangerous policy of shooting live bullets at unarmed demonstrators. They are deliberately refraining from using nonlethal methods, which don't cause permanent disabilities, in order to prevent a few of the demonstrators from crossing the border into Israel."[3]

In short, neither armed nor unarmed resistance has worked. If the Palestinians attack the Israeli occupation forces, the Israeli government usually increases the repression to demonstrate that "violence doesn't work." Then the Israelis see the need to demonstrate that nonviolence and civil disobedience also won't work. And when the Palestinians are quiet, the Israelis typically see no need to end the occupation.

The Second Intifada

Still, there have been periods of significant Palestinian resistance, especially during the second Palestinian intifada. On September 28, 2000, two months after Camp David, Ariel Sharon took a group of his followers and marched to the Temple Mount plateau, an unprecedented action intended to show that Moshe Dayan's prohibitions against Jewish religious worship and shows of force near the mosques were no longer in force.

The day before the march, Arafat asked Ehud Barak to prevent it, but the prime minister refused. The next day the Israeli police fired on unarmed Palestinian protesters, and the second intifada began. In the early days of the intifada there were Palestinian riots and rock-throwing but little armed Palestinian violence; in particular, there were no terrorist attacks on Israeli civilians.[4] Yet the army responded with what two Israeli writers described as "the use of massive firepower . . . as compared to nearly zero losses on the Israeli side. The ratio of victims during the first two weeks of the conflagration stood at twenty to one."[5]

The timeline is crucial, establishing that the intifada did not begin as a violent uprising, let alone a terrorist one: it was not until early November, some four or five weeks later, that the Palestinians retaliated against the violent Israeli repression with suicide attacks and other forms of terrorism, including the bombing of Israeli buses and cafés.

The standard assumption in Israel is that Arafat ordered the intifada to force Israel to make concessions in later negotiations. There is virtually no support for this view in Israeli and American intelligence assessments or in the report of an international fact-finding commission headed by former US senator George Mitchell. The informed consensus view is that the intifada began as a spontaneous reaction to Sharon's provocation, in the context of the Palestinian people's despair over a "peace process" that had done nothing to stop the increasing Israeli repression and expansion and frustration over the failure of Arafat to achieve a Palestinian state by diplomacy and concessions.

For example, the Shin Bet director Ami Ayalon said that the intifada took Arafat and the PLO by surprise and that it was "a result of a Palestinian loss of confidence regarding Israel's readiness to pay the price needed for peace" as well as the erosion in the Palestinians' belief that the PA could establish a regime marred less by corruption and brutality. Ayalon concluded that the intifada "in no way was conceived by Arafat himself" and that it was "a grassroots uprising."[6] His assessment was later confirmed by Shin Bet leaders Avi Dichter and Yuval Diskin.[7]

Israeli military intelligence reached the same conclusion; in 2013 Ephraim Lavie, head of the Palestinian section in the IDF research division, wrote:

> Israeli intelligence had not a scrap of evidence indicating that Arafat had abandoned the negotiating track and had planned and initiated the intifada. This was definitively discounted by internal investigations by Military Intelligence and the Mossad and during interrogations of senior Fatah officials by the Shin Bet. As in the case of the first intifada, this one also broke out at the grassroots level, as a result of anger toward Israel, toward Arafat and toward the Palestinian Authority.[8]

The Mitchell Report concurred: "We have no basis to conclude that there was a deliberate plan by the PA to initiate a campaign of violence" after Camp David. Arafat still wanted to continue the diplomatic negotiation process, Israeli intelligence and other analyses held, but with some 85 percent of the Palestinian public supporting the intifada and the refusal of militants to accept a ceasefire, he had little control over the violence.[9] He was "riding the back of a tiger," it was widely commented, hoping only to hold on to some measure of control.

On the other hand, it is the view of most Israeli and US experts as well as other knowledgeable observers that Arafat and the PA gradually gained control over the intifada but decided not to immediately end it, hoping that it would increase Palestinian negotiating leverage.[10] If that is correct, Arafat initially had some reason to believe that continued resistance might have positive results: for more than fifty years, nearly every concession Israel had made to the Arab states—concessions that ultimately were in Israel's own best interests—had been a consequence primarily of the threat or reality of violence and war, or at least of serious economic consequences.

The pattern was widely noted by Israeli analysts and even, remarkably, by former foreign minister Shlomo Ben-Ami, who wrote that there was ample evidence that Israel might change long-held policies if—but *only* if—threatened with high costs: "Israel is forced to make concessions for peace only under the impact of military pressure and major setbacks. . . . A popular prejudice in Israel about the Arabs is that 'they only understand the language of force.' But this can just as well be said about the Israelis."[11]

For example, Ben-Ami continued, it was "indisputable" that without "the undermining of Israel's myth of invincibility" in the early stages of the 1973 Israeli-Egyptian Sinai war, Israel would have refused to withdraw from the Sinai and there would have been no peace treaty.[12] Similarly, "it took Israel's reverses in the first Intifada and the psychological effects of the Gulf War on the Israeli home front to force Yitzhak Rabin finally to realize that the Palestinian problem is susceptible only to a political solution."[13]

Evidence of the same pattern can be found throughout the earlier history of the Arab-Israeli conflict:

- Following the 1948 war, Israel refrained from occupying the West Bank and withdrew from parts of the Sinai peninsula primarily because of serious American opposition and the threat of British military intervention.
- Following the 1956 war, Ben-Gurion initially intended to incorporate the conquered Sinai peninsula into a Greater Israel, but was forced to withdraw because of the threat of Soviet military intervention and a warning that the United States would cut off all economic assistance.
- In the 1967 and 1973 wars, Israel considered advancing toward Cairo and Damascus but was deterred by US pressures and fear of Soviet intervention.
- After the 1967 war, Israel refused to withdraw from the Sinai—and thereby meet the Egyptian condition for a peace settlement—until the initially successful 1973 Egyptian attack convinced the Israeli government and public opinion that the costs of holding the Sinai were too high.

It is important to note, however, that all of these cases required only that Israel withdraw from its external conquests, as opposed to withdrawing from territories that it regarded—persuasively or not—as its own territory. Terrorism against the Israeli civilian population, such as the spate of Palestinian suicide attacks against urban targets in the later stages of the intifada, has had a very different impact, resulting in the hardening of the Israeli occupation, not a reevaluation of it.

After the February 2001 election of Ariel Sharon as Israeli prime minister—no doubt in good part because of Israeli rage at the recent terrorist attacks in Israeli cities—Arafat came to the conclusion that terrorism had to stop, as he called for "a complete halt to all operations, especially suicidal operations" and warned that "we will punish all those who carry out and mastermind such operations." As a result, the PLO, Hamas, and even Islamic Jihad ended their attacks inside Israel, though they continued to regard attacks on the Israeli settlements in the occupied territories as legitimate targets.[14]

Whether or not those continuing attacks constituted "terrorism," as that term is usually understood, turns on whether the settlers in the occupied territories should be considered "innocent civilians." There are differences of opinion on the question among moral and legal philosophers, though not among most Israelis, very few of whom were prepared to recognize the obvious, namely, that the Palestinian violence was a consequence of the continuing Israeli occupation and violent repression of the intifada, even before the Palestinians responded with undoubted acts of terrorism.

The Israeli Occupation of Gaza

David Ben-Gurion, Moshe Dayan, and other early Zionist leaders had mixed feelings about incorporating Gaza into the coming Jewish state. On the one hand, they considered it to be part of Palestine, so it was included in the early twentieth-century maps of the territory the Zionists intended for their state. On the other hand, they were wary of having to rule over the several hundred thousand Arab inhabitants of Gaza, some 250,000 of whom were embittered refugees who in 1947–48 had fled or been driven from their homes, villages, and lands in the Nakba. Today Gaza has more than 1.8 million Arab inhabitants, some 70 percent of whom are the 1948 refugees and their descendants.

The 1948 war ended before Israel had a chance to conquer Gaza, so the early debate about the desirability of doing so was not resolved. Then, in March 1955, Ben-Gurion proposed to his cabinet that Israel conquer Gaza when the opportunity arose, but a majority was opposed. Nonetheless, in the 1956 war with Egypt, Israel seized the area; however, under heavy pressure from the Eisenhower administration, it decided to withdraw.[15]

During the 1967 war, Israel occupied Gaza and established a number of small Jewish settlements there. Over the years, violent Gazan resistance to Israeli rule grew. In response, in 1991, Israel began imposing a series of punitive economic measures, including periodic widespread business closures. In addition, restrictions were imposed on the free movement of the population, designed to cut off the area from the West Bank—a violation of the Oslo Accords, which specified that the West Bank and Gaza were to be considered as a single territorial unit with free Palestinian movement between them.

As a result of these measures, by 2001 Gaza was suffering from high levels of unemployment and poverty; B'Tselem, the leading Israeli human rights organization, reported that to ensure the safety of the Jewish settlers "Israel imposes sweeping closure, curfew, and siege on millions of people."[16] In addition, Israeli undercover forces, posing as Arabs or foreign journalists, routinely captured or killed Palestinians they regarded as "terrorists."[17]

The Rise of Hamas

Hamas was founded in 1987 by members of the Muslim Brotherhood in the Gaza Strip. Led by the Palestinian religious militant Sheikh Ahmed Yassin, Hamas initially was openly anti-Semitic and called for the destruction of Israel. In August 1988, Hamas adopted its official "Covenant of the Islamic Resistance Movement," which featured standard anti-Semitic notions, many lifted directly from the notorious hoax *Protocols of the Elders of Zion,* such as that the Jews control the world economy and media, were behind communist revolutions everywhere, and were responsible for World War I—and even World War II.[18]

Yet, remarkably, Israeli officials collaborated with Hamas, initially seeing it as a possibly useful counterweight to what they regarded as the far more dangerous nationalist movement led by Arafat.[19] From 1967 through 1989, over 125 new mosques were opened in the occupied territories, with the permission of Israel. As well, in the mid-1980s, Defense Minister Yitzhak Rabin granted permission to Hamas to set up the Islamic University of Gaza, and in other ways "Israel helped Hamas become a leading actor in Palestine."[20]

As Uri Avnery explained: "The Shin Bet had an active interest in the flourishing of the mosques. . . . Turning the Palestinians toward Islam, it was thought, would weaken the PLO. . . . *So everything was done to help the Islamic movement discreetly.*"[21] Years later, Avner Cohen, the Israeli official who was responsible for Gazan religious affairs, wrote: "Hamas, to my great regret, is Israel's creation. . . . Instead of trying to curb Gaza's Islamists from the outset . . . Israel for years tolerated and, in some cases, encouraged them as a counterweight to the secular nationalists."[22]

Matters began to change as a result of the first intifada that began in December 1987. Unwilling to risk clashing with Israel when it was still trying to put down roots among the Palestinian people, Hamas initially refrained from violence; as a result, Israel for a while continued its "relatively tolerant attitude" toward the organization.[23]

However, by September 1988, Israel's policy toward Hamas had hardened, and it began expelling its leaders. Hamas responded with attacks on Israeli soldiers in the occupied territories. In June 1989, Israel declared Hamas to be a terrorist group and a year later it began raiding, searching, and even closing mosques.

According to Matti Steinberg, the former chief advisor on Palestinian affairs to the Shin Bet and one of Israel's leading experts on Hamas, at the time of the intifada Hamas was still carrying out an internal debate over the usefulness of indiscriminate terrorism. Though there were a few such attacks, most of them were committed by Palestinian individuals with no organizational connection to Hamas.

On October 8, 1990, the Israeli police killed seventeen Palestinians in a clash on the Temple Mount/Haram plateau, resulting in a Hamas call for a "jihad against the Zionist enemy everywhere, in all fronts and every means."[24] Meshal and Sela write: "The most tangible result [of the call for jihad] was a sharp rise in spontaneous knifing attacks committed by Palestinian individuals against Israeli civilians, police, and soldiers. The perpetrators of these attacks had no organizational connection with Hamas, though many were clearly susceptible to the Islamic message."[25]

However, after Israel deported 415 Islamic activists to Lebanon in December 1992, Hamas retaliated by ordering two car bomb attacks.[26] Even so, Hamas's internal debate over tactics continued until Baruch Goldstein's February 1994 murder of twenty-nine Palestinians in a Hebron mosque. When Prime Minister Rabin, fearing violent conflict with the Jewish settlers in Hebron, refused to withdraw them in the aftermath of the massacre, Hamas retaliated with suicide bombings in Israel. This turn toward terrorism, Matti Steinberg wrote, "stemmed directly from the Goldstein massacre."[27] He elaborated: "In the Hamas writings there is an explicit prohibition against indiscriminate harm to helpless people. The massacre at the mosque released them from this taboo and introduced a dimension of measure for measure, based on citations from the Koran."[28]

Even so, Mishal and Sela wrote, Hamas did not abandon its policy of "controlled violence," for beginning in 1995 it "repeatedly proposed a conditional ceasefire with Israel, to stop the bloodshed of innocents on both sides." The central condition was a full withdrawal of Israel and its settlements from all the occupied territories.[29]

This condition, of course, had no chance of being accepted. Nonetheless, between August 1995 and February 1996, Hamas and even Islamic Jihad made no terrorist attacks, "a result of the pressure exerted by both Israel and the Palestinian Authority."[30] In early 1996, Hamas publicly announced its willingness to stop the bombings if Israel ended its attempts to assassinate Hamas leaders. The Israeli government ignored the offer; its continued assassinations of Hamas leaders resulted in a new round of terrorist attacks inside Israel in February and March of that year.[31]

Hamas and perhaps some PLO terrorist attacks continued during the second Intifada in 2001–2. On March 27, 2002, a suicide bomber attacked an Israeli hotel, killing forty people. Two days later Israel launched a month-long attack in the West Bank, which it called Operation Defensive Shield, during which it reoccupied the major West Bank population centers. Although its declared purpose was "to systematically dismantle terror infrastructures in the entire region," it was also aimed at curbing the power of the PA and allowing the IDF to carry on military operations throughout the occupied territories that gave it "a free hand to blockade cities, isolate villages, impose curfews, and paralyze the Palestinian economy and social services."[32]

Defensive Shield caused great damage and many deaths in Gaza, as was reported in *Haaretz* at the time and in subsequent reports by B'Tselem and international human rights organizations. Most striking was an interview with four former heads of the Shin Bet, who bluntly said that if the "disgraceful" repression of the Palestinians did not end, a "catastrophe" was inevitable. One of them, Yaakov Perry, said: "We are heading downhill towards near-catastrophe. If nothing happens and we go on living by the sword, we will continue to wallow in the mud and destroy ourselves." All agreed that Israel had to end the occupation, "even if it entailed an inevitable clash with the settlers."

It was significant that the former Shin Bet leaders had decided to speak out in Israel's most widely read newspaper, *Yediot Aharanot,* rather than in, say, *Haaretz,* for they clearly wanted to reach a mass readership rather than just the "leftists." *Yediot* reporters commented: "The gloomy feeling that pervaded this meeting cannot be overstated. It appeared that the four had decided to speak because of the belief that what they say could lead to a turning point [in Israeli policies]."[33]

But it didn't.

Changing Hamas Policies, 1996–2005

Although Israeli policies continued unchanged, Hamas began a gradual, ambivalent, inconsistent, but nonetheless increasingly significant shift in its policies toward terrorism and a de facto acceptance of a two-state settlement. As it did, it began following in the footsteps of Arafat's PLO and especially those of Mahmoud Abbas's Palestinian Authority, as well as of many other radical movements that became more moderate once they gained political power.[34]

- In July 1995, an article in Israel's leading news magazine reported that Hamas was divided between the extremists and pragmatic moderates who say they will accept a two-state settlement.[35]
- In March 1996, Hamas stated that it was taking up arms to combat the Israeli occupation, but it did not repeat its usual call for an Islamic state in all of Palestine; even more significantly, it said that its resistance would "automatically stop when the *occupation* ceases."[36] The statement hinted that Hamas would accept a state in the West Bank, Gaza, and East Jerusalem. There is no record that the Shimon Peres government sought to explore this possible opening with Hamas.
- In September 1997, former Mossad head Ephraim Halevy later revealed, King Hussein of Jordan conveyed an offer from Khaled Meshal, then the chief Hamas leader, to reach an understanding on a ceasefire to last thirty years. Israel not only

ignored the offer, but a few days later, Israeli operatives, acting on orders of Prime Minister Netanyahu, tried to assassinate Meshal in Jordan.[37] The attempt failed, because Hussein threatened to break relations with Israel unless it immediately sent an antidote, which Netanyahu did.

It is true that despite the gradual evolution of Hamas's policies during this period, it carried out a number of terrorist attacks—though they were usually in retaliation for Israeli attacks on Gaza or undercover operations that killed Hamas or other militants in both the West Bank and Gaza. To be sure, the Israeli attacks, and particularly the assassinations, in turn were intended as retaliation for the Hamas attacks, as well as to deter future ones. And so on, ran the cycle of violence.

Yet, at the same time, Hamas policies toward terrorism continued to evolve:

- In January 2004, Sheikh Ahmed Yassin, a founder of Hamas and then its leading religious leader, called for a ten-year truce with Israel if it withdrew to the pre-1967 lines and allowed the establishment of a Palestinian state in the West Bank and Gaza. The *Haaretz* story said that Yassin's comments "appeared to strengthen signs of a big political shift" by Hamas.[38] The Israeli government dismissed the signs of Hamas moderation.
- In February 2004, there were several particularly devastating suicide attacks against Israeli civilians. However, in April the attacks suddenly ended, for though it was not revealed until 2012, Hamas had made a strategic decision to end the bombings and enter into a secret deal with Israel.[39] As a consequence, Israeli casualties in 2004 continued to decline.[40]
- In February 2005, Hamas went public, announcing that it was unilaterally declaring a ceasefire; Israel responded by temporarily suspending its assassinations in Gaza, where the main Hamas leaders were located. However, it continued to target Islamic Jihad activists inside the West Bank, who were not party to the secret deal and who then retaliated with rocket attacks against Israel. Even so, in 2005, Israeli casualties fell by a further 60 percent.[41]

Hamas Takes Over Gaza

Except for occasional retaliations for Israeli assassinations in the West Bank, throughout most of 2005 Hamas continued to observe the de facto truce and emphasized the political process, both with Mahmoud Abbas's Palestinian Authority, its rival for Palestinian political power, and with Israel, should it accept the Hamas overtures for a long-term truce.

In late 2005, the Bush administration pressed Abbas to agree to new elections in the West Bank and Gaza, on the assumption that the PA would easily win. According to Muhammad Dahlan, a high PA official, the Abbas government was less confident than the United States of the outcome but agreed to hold elections when pressed to do so by the American government.

To the shock of the Bush administration, which was touting its commitment to work for democracy and free elections, particularly in the Middle East, the Palestinians voted the wrong way, giving Hamas a majority in the Palestine parliament.

Immediately after the elections, the Bush administration (joined by the European Union, Russia, and the United Nations, the other three members of the short-lived "Middle East Quartet") demanded that Hamas renounce violence, recognize Israel's right to exist, and accept the terms of all previous agreements. "When Hamas refused," David Rose, an informed journalist wrote, "the Quartet shut off the faucet of aid to the Palestinian Authority, depriving it of the means to pay salaries and meet its annual budget of roughly $2 billion."[42]

At the same time, the Bush administration—"suddenly less enamored of Middle Eastern democracy," as Peter Beinart put it[43]—pushed Abbas to ignore the elections, dissolve the parliament, and rule by emergency decree. Abbas was not willing to go that far but agreed to withhold tax and customs revenue from Hamas.

The Sharon government enthusiastically joined in economic pressures against Hamas. The *Haaretz* columnist Gideon Levy described a meeting of Sharon's "Hamas team," headed by Dov Weissglass—he of "the peace process is now on formaldehyde"—and including Israel's top generals, intelligence officials, and diplomats. "Everyone agreed on the need to impose an economic siege on the Palestinian Authority," wrote Levy, "and Weissglass, as usual, provided the punch line: 'It's like an appointment with a dietician. The Palestinians will get a lot thinner, but won't die,' the advisor joked, and the participants reportedly rolled with laughter."[44]

In addition to the economic sanctions, the Bush administration began planning for a coup to overturn the election results. Its chosen instrument was Dahlan, the so-called strongman in the PA's armed forces, who had led previous PA crackdowns on Hamas, had a reputation for political moderation combined with ruthless military effectiveness, and was said to have close ties with George Tenet, director of the CIA. In light of those credentials, Bush met with Dahlan at least three times; the president was quoted as saying that Dahlan was "our guy."[45]

The first step was to increase the military capabilities of Dahlan's forces. According to the Rose account, in November 2006, a US general told Dahlan, "We need you to build up your forces in order to take on Hamas." At Bush's request, the conservative Arab states of Jordan, Egypt, and Saudi Arabia provided the arms—which had been previously supplied to them by the United States.

In June 2007, Dahlan's forces attacked Hamas's forces and government targets in Gaza, but were soundly defeated. Hamas, now stronger than ever, then took full power over Gaza. Since then, in Israel and the United States these events have been typically described as "a coup" when, in fact, it was a response to the *real* coup—the US and PA actions after the wrong side won the Gazan election.

A month later, David Wurmser, Vice-President Cheney's chief Middle East advisor, resigned in protest over the Israeli-American scheme, accusing the Bush administration of "engaging in a dirty war in an effort to provide a corrupt dictatorship [led by Abbas] with victory." According to Rose, Wurmser believed that Hamas had no intention of taking Gaza until Fatah forced its hand: "It looks to me that what happened wasn't so much a coup by Hamas but an attempted coup by Fatah that was pre-empted before it could happen."[46]

Israel and Hamas, 2006–8: More Lost Opportunities for Peace?

In the years following the Hamas victories in Gaza, there were a number of developments that might have opened the door to a peace settlement. As I have argued and will further develop, the evidence is very strong that the PLO was ready to accept a two-state settlement and to make the necessary compromises on the Jerusalem and refugee issues. Hamas's position was much more ambiguous, but the weight of the evidence suggests that it was moving toward a pragmatic, if reluctant, acceptance of the realities of Israeli power and was becoming increasingly amenable to a de facto if not de jure two-state political settlement. If so, it was following in the footsteps of Yasser Arafat's PLO, which had gradually moderated once it had a potential state to run in the West Bank.

According to most studies, Hamas was well aware that its victory in the January 2006 elections was not owing to its religious hostility to Israel but to the hope it would improve social and economic conditions of the Gazan people. At the end of January, the Hamas leader Mahmoud Zahar said that if Israel withdrew from the occupied territories and reestablished the geographic link between Gaza and the West Bank, Hamas would agree to the establishment of an independent Palestinian state in those occupied territories and would "give a long-term hudna [truce]." Over the next ten to fifteen years, he added, Hamas would "see what is the real intention of Israel"; however, he would not say whether the destruction of Israel remained its long-term goal.[47]

Then, a few months after taking office, Gaza prime minister Ismail Haniyeh secretly wrote to President Bush asking him to end the American boycott of Hamas and enter into "direct negotiations with the elected government." *Haaretz* obtained the message and wrote that "Haniyeh laid out the political platform he maintains to this day," quoting him as saying, "We are so concerned about stability and security in the area that we don't mind having a Palestinian state in the 1967 border and offering a truce for many years." The story concluded: "This was not the only covert message from Hamas to senior Bush administration officials. However, Washington did not reply to these messages and maintained its boycott of the Hamas government."[48]

Israel soon assassinated a senior Hamas leader—yet Hamas not only did not retaliate but secretly conveyed a message to the Israeli government that it "would pledge not to carry out any violent actions against Israel and would even prevent other Palestinian organizations from doing so," provided Israel stopped its assassinations and military attacks.[49] Even Islamic Jihad stated that it would refrain from suicide or rocket attacks if Israel ended its attacks.[50] During the next ten months there were no Hamas rocket attacks and very few from Islamic Jihad, apparently as a result of the stringent Hamas restrictions.

In February 2006, Khaled Meshal, head of Hamas's political bureau, said that Hamas would not oppose the Arab Peace Initiative, which offered Israel full recognition and normalized relations in exchange for full Israeli withdrawal from the occupied territories and a solution to the refugee problem.[51] Similarly, in the same month, a Russian newspaper published an interview with Meshal, who said, "If Israel recognizes our rights and pledges to withdraw from all occupied lands, Hamas and the Palestinian people will decide to halt armed resistance."[52]

In response, an Israeli spokesman dismissed the Hamas proposals as "verbal gymnastics. . . . I see no indication that Hamas is moving to accept the international community's benchmarks."[53]

Soon after, Hamas began to go public with its new position. In April 2006, a senior official stated that Hamas was ready to discuss a possible two-state solution,[54] and in May, Gaza prime minister Haniyeh affirmed that the Hamas government would agree to a long-term truce if Israel withdrew to the 1967 lines.

Once again, Israel and its US ally ignored these overtures or contemptuously termed them "tricks."[55] If anything, Israel stepped up its military pressures, killing some 660 Palestinians in 2006, most of them unarmed civilians and up to a third of them minors.[56]

In May 2006, Haniyeh said that the Hamas government was prepared to agree to an extended truce if Israel withdrew to the 1967 lines: "If Israel withdraws to the 1967 borders, peace will prevail and we will implement a hudna [truce] for many years." Another Hamas official added that the ceasefire "will be renewed automatically each time."[57]

In the same month, senior Hamas members imprisoned in Israel joined with PLO prisoners and issued an important "Prisoners' Declaration" which went further than had Haniyeh by calling for the establishment of a Palestinian state "in all the lands occupied *in 1967*" and reserved the use of armed resistance *only in those territories.*[58]

A few months later, Haniyeh in effect incorporated the declaration into the Hamas position, including its crucial distinction between the occupied territories and Israel within its 1967 borders, telling an American scholar: "We have no problem with a sovereign Palestinian state over all of our lands *within the 1967 borders*, living in calm."[59]

In a July 2006 *Washington Post* op-ed column, Haniyeh said that the Palestinians sought to "*reclaim all lands occupied in 1967*," so as to create a state in the *West Bank and Gaza*, with its capital in East Jerusalem.[60]

By the end of 2006, a number of Israeli and American analysts were noting the significant changes in Hamas's positions. For example, Robert Malley and Henry Siegman argued that Israel and the United States needed to drop their refusal to negotiate with Hamas, for otherwise no peace could be reached: "Hamas is prepared to abide by a comprehensive cease-fire, and has proved its ability to implement it when Israel fully reciprocates. . . . It will acquiesce in negotiations between Abbas and Olmert and abide by any agreement ratified by popular referendum."[61]

Israel continued to disregard the changing Hamas positions; in fact, throughout 2007, it stepped up its assassinations and other attacks on militants in Gaza and the West Bank, in the process killing an estimated 360 civilians. According to Israel's official records, the Palestinian rocket attacks killed a total of seven Israeli civilians.[62]

Nonetheless, throughout 2007 and 2008, Hamas's political position continued to evolve. In January 2007, Meshal stated that Hamas would consider recognizing Israel once a Palestinian state was established; *Haaretz* noted that "this is the first time that a Hamas official has raised the possibility of full and official recognition of Israel in the future . . . a fundamental shift in Hamas's position." However, *Haaretz* said, Prime Minister Ehud Olmert "shrugged off" Meshal's statement.[63]

In April 2008, Meshal publicly reiterated that Hamas would accept a Palestinian state in Gaza, the West Bank, and East Jerusalem and would stop attacking civilians if Israel did the same; in mid-June a new truce went into effect.[64] Islamic Jihad said it also would abide by the truce, provided Israel refrained from military actions against its militants in the West Bank.[65] However, Israel continued those actions, leading to several Islamic Jihad retaliatory attacks, although they inflicted few casualties.

According to Hamas, the truce included an understanding that Israel would open the crossing points into Gaza and ease its economic stranglehold; for some time, Israel did allow an increase of goods into Gaza but far less than Hamas had expected. Despite the new tensions, though, Hamas continued to crack down on the Islamic Jihad attacks. *Haaretz* wrote that Hamas leaders have spoken out "vehemently and unequivocally against the [Islamic Jihad] rocket fire . . . [and] have even threatened those who violate the lull with arrest."[66] The *New York Times* reported that Hamas officials had said that "their job was to stop the rocket attacks on Israel not only from its own armed groups but also from others based in Gaza." The *Times* said that the Hamas efforts had been "largely successful" and even included the imprisoning of some who continued to violate the truce.[67]

As a result, Israeli civilian casualties dropped dramatically: from about 680 from 2001 through 2005 to seventeen in 2006, and just seven in 2007. However, over 1,200 Palestinians were killed by Israeli forces from 2005 until just before the major Israeli attack—"Cast Lead"—at the end of December 2008.[68]

In December 2010, Haniyeh said that if Israel agreed to the creation of a Palestinian state in the West Bank and Gaza, Hamas would call for a Palestinian referendum and would accept the results of it, "regardless of whether it differs with [Hamas's] ideology and principles." The *Haaretz* news story said that Haniyeh's statement "signaled a softening of Hamas's long-standing position prohibiting the ceding of any part of the land of what was British-mandated Palestine until 1948."[69]

It is undeniable that in the years following the second intifada, the Hamas position contained ambiguities and apparent inconsistencies. To begin, it was not until 2017 that Hamas officially abandoned its anti-Semitic founding ideology and 1988 Charter, which explicitly stated that it was a religious obligation to eliminate Israel and expel the Jews from Palestine.

Sometimes a Hamas spokesman would make a conciliatory statement or an apparently important new offer, but the next day another spokesman—or even the same one—would appear to back away from its implications. For example, after its Gaza victory, Hamas called for a national unity government with the PLO "for the purpose of ending the occupation and settlements and achieving a complete withdrawal from the lands occupied [by Israel] in 1967, including Jerusalem, so that the region enjoys calm and stability *during this phase*" (emphasis added). Did the organization expect Israel not to notice the rather important qualification?

There were other examples of Hamas inconsistency or ambiguity:

- Hamas statements often called only for a truce rather than a permanent settlement—yet at various times Hamas officials suggested that the truce "would be renewed automatically" and extended indefinitely.[70]
- Sometimes Hamas officials said that they accepted Israel "as a fact" but would "never recognize its legitimacy," but on other occasions they strongly implied that this position had no practical importance and could eventually change.[71]
- Sometimes Hamas says it wants Israel to go back to the 1967 borders, but other times it says that at issue are also the events of 1948, raising the question of whether it accepts the legitimacy of the state of Israel, even within its initial borders. For example, in June 2009, Haniyeh said that Hamas "would support any plan to establish a sovereign Palestinian state in the 1967 borders," but when he asked if that meant Hamas now supported a two-state settlement, he replied "we didn't say that," explaining that "there is no reason not to set up a Palestinian state in the 1967 borders, but that doesn't mean we will give up our rights in the areas of 1948, such as the right of refugees to return to their homes."[72]
- Similarly, sometimes Hamas stressed its commitment to the return of all Palestinian refugees to Israel, perhaps the most difficult obstacle to a permanent settlement, but at other times it downplayed the issue and suggested a compromise could be reached.

And so on. Yet the overall evolution of Hamas's policies was unmistakable. In 2006, two Israeli experts on Hamas summed up their findings: "Hamas' ideology calls for uncompromising activism and focuses on maximalist aims. In practice, however, the movement has adopted a policy that was more pragmatic than dogmatic and more reformist than revolutionary."[73]

Their judgment was supported by former high Israeli officials. For example, in late 2006, Yossi Alpher, a former deputy head of the Mossad, wrote: "Hamas' conditions are almost too good to be true. Refugees and right of return and Jerusalem can wait for some other process; Hamas will suffice with the 1967 borders, more or less, and in return will guarantee peace and quiet for ten, 25 or 30 years of good neighborly relations and confidence-building."[74]

Similarly, in 2009, Ephraim Halevy, former head of Mossad and then the national security advisor to Ariel Sharon, wrote that Hamas militants "have recognized . . . [their] ideological goal is not attainable and will not be in the foreseeable future." Instead, "they are ready and willing to see the establishment of a Palestinian state in the temporary borders of 1967." Halevy concluded, dryly, that "Israel, for reasons of its own, did not want to turn the ceasefire into the start of a diplomatic process with Hamas."[75]

In 2010, Halevy elaborated:

> Now might be the right time to reconsider this policy [of no negotiations with Hamas]. . . . The time has surely come to explore a new relationship with Hamas. Attempts to penalize the group with exclusion have failed; perhaps, the time has come for a strategy that co-opts Hamas. Current policy, after all, sends Hamas the signal that it is doomed to exclusion come what may and forever. But the more that Hamas is permitted inside the tent, the better the prospects of a modest yet historic success.[76]

Ami Ayalon, former head of the Shin Bet, concurred that Hamas's policy was significantly changing:

> They've always wanted, do want and will always want Tel Aviv, Jaffa and Jerusalem, too. Just like we as a collective always wanted, want and will want Jericho, Hebron and Beit El. . . . But the resolution of an existential conflict like the conflict between us and the Palestinians occurs when the dream is separated from the diplomatic plan. And this is what's happening. . . . During the first intifada and the second intifada, an awakening occurred. I, too, woke up very painfully from a dream. And I did so because I came up against a force on the other side. I encountered another reality that I could no longer ignore. And this is also happening in Palestinian society. It is parting with its dream . . . of Greater Palestine.[77]

In sum, a number of factors accounted for the evolution of Hamas thinking during the 2000s, including the realities of governing, especially when most Gazans favored a two-state solution; the fact that most Arab governments—particularly Egypt, Saudi Arabia, Jordan, and probably Syria—also supported a compromise settlement and feared Islamic fundamentalism; the economic sanctions imposed by Israel, the United States, and a number of European states after the 2007 Hamas takeover of Gaza; and, no doubt, the continuing Israeli assassinations and other military pressures and attacks.

In the final analysis, the only way to have resolved the remaining ambiguities in Hamas's policies was by negotiations with the organization as well as with the PA, for no serious peace proposal called on Israel to withdraw from the occupied territories unless and until a reasonable and enforceable political settlement was reached. That the Israeli government refused to explore Hamas's true intentions demonstrated that it was not interested in a potential two-state solution.

17

Israel, the "Siege of Gaza," and Hamas, 2008–14

Ariel Sharon and the Gaza "Disengagement"

In the 1967 war, Israel occupied the Gaza Strip, until then under Egyptian rule, and in 1969 it began establishing small Jewish settlements there. During the 1970s, Ariel Sharon commanded the occupation forces in Gaza, expanding the settlements and ruthlessly crushing Palestinian resistance. Still, only a handful of Israelis were willing to move there; by 2005, there were just 8,000 settlers, in the midst of 1.4 million mostly impoverished Palestinians. However, the settlements took up about 25 percent of the territory of Gaza, 40 percent of the fertile land, and most of the meager water resources.[1] Unsurprisingly, then, the settlements became the target of Palestinian militant attacks, largely led by Hamas, and needed to be defended by thousands of Israeli soldiers.

In March 2001, Sharon defeated Ehud Barak and became prime minister; he was reelected in February 2003 and served in office until January 2006, when he was incapacitated by a stroke and was replaced by Deputy Prime Minister Ehud Olmert. (Sharon remained in a coma until he died eight years later.) During Sharon's first two years in office, there was no change in his policies on the settlements.

By 2003, however, Sharon was having second thoughts about maintaining the Jewish settlements in Gaza, where unlike the West Bank and Jerusalem, Israel had few religious or nationalist claims. As a result, in 2004 he began planning to withdraw the Gaza settlers; in the spring and summer of 2005, the withdrawal was carried out; Sharon also closed four small, isolated settlements in the West Bank.[2]

Whether Sharon's unexpected and uncharacteristic policy shift in Gaza reflected a genuine change in his views on the Israeli-Palestinian conflict or was merely a tactical maneuver has been the subject of debate among Israeli observers. A case can be made for either explanation. A number of Israeli analysts argued that Sharon's intention was only to rid Israel of the burden of defending a handful of Gazan settlers, while retaining its ability to indirectly control the area, and then strengthen its grip on the far more important West Bank, where there were now more than 200,000 settlers.[3] These skeptical interpretations of Sharon's intentions became even more credible as a result of a famous (infamous) statement by Sharon's close advisor, Dov Weissglass:

> The significance is the freezing of the political process. And when you freeze that process you prevent the establishment of a Palestinian state and you prevent a discussion about the refugees, the borders and Jerusalem. . . . We succeeded in removing the issue from the agenda and we educated the world to understand that there is no one to talk to. . . . The disengagement is actually a form of formaldehyde . . . [that is] necessary so that there will not be a political process with the Palestinians. . . . We received a certificate [saying] that (1) There is no one to talk to; (2) As long as there is no one to talk to, the geographic status quo remains intact. . . . And all this with a [US] presidential blessing and the ratification of both houses of Congress.[4]

On the other hand, a case can be made that Sharon's shift was not merely a cynical maneuver. For example, Yossi Sarid, a longtime major figure in Israeli politics and outspoken critic of Israeli policies, but one who maintained ties to Sharon, wrote: "In the middle of his tenure as prime minister, Sharon changed. . . . Suddenly, he got it: The Gaza Strip was a disaster that could only hurt us as its caretaker, as the occupation had no end in sight. . . . Had he not fallen into a coma in January 2006, he may have been remembered as the liberator of Palestine."[5]

Other evidence to support the argument that Sharon was changing his mind about Gaza, and perhaps even about the overall Israeli-Palestinian conflict, includes the following:

- After the 1967 war, Sharon had pushed for the establishment of settlements in the Sinai peninsula, but when Israel agreed to evacuate the Sinai as part of its 1979 peace settlement with Egypt, Sharon presided over their dismantlement. Avnery wrote: "When settlements obstructed his plans, he had no compunction about destroying them. . . . Later he did the same to the settlements in the Gaza Strip."[6]
- In 2002, Sharon started building the Israeli "Separation Wall," a 450-mile barrier that was partly designed to stop Palestinian terrorist attacks but predominantly to wall off from the rest of the West Bank the territory and settlements beyond the old Green Line that Israel intended to keep permanently. According to several informed Israeli analysts, Sharon's plan would incorporate into Israel most of the Jewish settlers who lived in four settlement blocs near Israel's previous borders while avoiding Israeli responsibility for hundreds of thousands of Palestinians who lived in the 90 percent of the West Bank that Sharon was not interested in annexing.[7]

- In May 2003, Sharon addressed the Likud, then his political party: "The idea that it is possible to continue keeping 3.5 million Palestinians under occupation—yes, it is occupation, you might not like the word, but what is happening is occupation—is bad for Israel and bad for the Palestinians, and bad for the Israeli economy. Controlling 3.5 million Palestinians cannot go on forever."[8]
- Similarly, in 2004, he was quoted as saying: "We cannot hold onto Gaza forever. It's impossible over long periods of time to rule in densely populated areas without their having to receive rights in the end."[9]
- In 2005, a cable to the State Department from Daniel Kurtzer, then the US ambassador to Israel, reported that shortly before the Gaza withdrawal, Sharon had held several meetings with US senators Joe Biden and Chuck Hagel, in which he told them that he had no intention of stopping with the Gaza withdrawal, implying that after annexing the major settlement blocs, he would concede other parts of the West Bank to the Palestinians.[10]
- In 2014, *Haaretz* reported that leaked Palestinian documents revealed that after Arafat's death in November 2004 Sharon met several times with Mahmoud Abbas, the new Palestinian president, in an effort to end the intifada, coordinate the Gaza pullout with the Palestinian Authority, and move on to make "a new start between the Israelis and the Palestinians," provided that Palestinian terrorism was ended.[11] As well, Dov Weissglass claimed that Sharon told him that "he saw in the near future a series of significant steps in Judea and Samaria, of withdrawal from isolated settlements."[12]

Whatever Sharon's ultimate intentions in the West Bank, it is crucial to emphasize that even after withdrawing its settlements and armed forces, Israel continued its "indirect" but effective occupation of Gaza. It did so by retaining control over Gaza's borders, airspace, coastline, and territorial waters; by refusing to allow Gaza a functioning airport or seaport; by continuing to control Gaza's electricity, fuel, water, and telecommunications networks; and by its often-exercised control and restrictions over Gazan travel and trade with the outside world through its military checkpoints into and out of the area.[13]

Moreover, some of the "control" measures employed by Israel have been considerably more than indirect: it continues to assassinate Palestinian activists, mostly those in Islamic Jihad but sometimes in Hamas as well, and especially, it has launched several major military attacks on Gaza since 2006.[14]

The Siege of Gaza

The devastating effects on the Palestinian economy and people of what is widely called Israel's "siege of Gaza" have been apparent since at least 2005, even before Hamas's electoral and military victory in Gaza in early 2006 led to the intensification of Israel's punitive policies. In November 2005, an authoritative study of the siege found these outcomes:

> According to the World Bank, Palestinians are currently experiencing the worst economic depression in modern history, caused primarily by the long-standing Israeli restrictions that have dramatically reduced Gaza's levels of trade and virtually cut off its labor force from their jobs inside Israel. This has resulted in unprecedented levels of unemployment of 35 to 40 per cent. Some 65 to 75 per cent of Gazans are impoverished (compared to 30 per cent in 2000); many are hungry. . . . There is no doubt that the destruction wrought by Israel over the last five years—the demolition of homes (some 4600 between 2000 and 2004), schools, roads, factories, workshops, hospitals, mosques and greenhouses, the razing of agricultural fields, the uprooting of trees, the confinement of the population and the denial of access to education and health services as a consequence of Israeli roadblocks and checkpoints—has been ruinous for Palestinians, especially those in the Gaza Strip.[15]

Three years later, a UN report found that the economy of Gaza was on the verge of collapse, with nearly 95 percent of the Gazan factories closed down, unemployment ranging from 45 to 60 percent, and an estimated 80 percent of Gazans below international poverty lines. According to a number of studies, these were among the worst such figures in the world.[16]

In addition to the economic devastation of the siege, the number of Palestinian casualties from Israeli military attacks grew. According to studies by the UN and Israel as well as international human rights organizations, from 2005 through the end of 2008, more than 1,200 individuals were killed, up to half of them civilians and as many as a quarter of them children[17]—though the numbers of Israeli civilians killed by terrorist attacks were steadily dropping; for example, official Israeli figures reported a total of seven civilian deaths in 2007.[18]

In early March 2008, Israel attacked densely populated refugee camps in Gaza, killing 130 Palestinians, more than half of them civilians, including many women and children.[19] A month later, Hamas leader Khaled Meshal announced that Hamas was ready to stop attacking civilians if Israel did the same.[20]

Israel accepted these terms, and in early June, a negotiated six-month truce went into effect. According to Hamas, the truce included an understanding that Israel would open the crossings into Gaza and ease its economic sanctions and blockade. Israel initially did allow some increase of goods to flow into Gaza but by no means enough to lift the siege.[21]

Islamic Jihad said it would abide by the truce, provided Israel refrained from attacking its militants in the West Bank. Israel, however, continued such attacks, leading to several retaliatory attacks on Israel, though they inflicted few casualties and no deaths.

In September and October 2008, only two rockets fell on Israel, neither one from Hamas. Nonetheless, Israel tightened its siege and its assassinations, some of which killed many civilian bystanders. Then, on November 4, Israel attacked a Gazan tunnel, killing six Hamas men. Israel claimed that the tunnel was intended to facilitate Hamas attacks inside Israel; however, the tunnels served a number of purposes, especially by bringing into Gaza food and other goods that were prohibited by the continuing blockade.

For the next ten days, Hamas did not retaliate. However, Israel continued its "targeted assassinations" on Islamic Jihad militants, killing eleven of them. On November 14, Hamas did retaliate, firing rockets into southern Israel and announcing that it would no longer abide by the ceasefire agreement that would expire in December but would be prepared to negotiate a new one if Israel stopped its attacks and eased its siege.[22] A *Haaretz* military correspondent explained Hamas's decision to retaliate: "Hamas has been trying for some time to create a balance of deterrence with Israel. . . . For every large-scale strike on its people, it has responded in recent months with massive rocket barrages. The organization especially wants to see targeted assassinations taken out of the equation."[23]

Throughout this period Hamas continued to crack down on Islamic Jihad rocket attacks: "Hamas leaders have spoken out vehemently and unequivocally against the rocket fire," a columnist wrote, "[and] have even threatened those who violate the lull with arrest."[24] In December 2008, a *New York Times* reporter concluded that Hamas had "imposed its will and even imprisoned some of those who were firing rockets," in a "largely successful" effort to halt all attacks.[25] According to Henry Siegman, "Even Israel's intelligence agencies acknowledged this had been implemented with surprising effectiveness."[26]

The evidence leaves no serious doubt that Hamas wanted to continue the ceasefire. For example, according to an unchallenged story in the *Guardian*, for several years Gershon Baskin, a well-connected Israeli journalist and peace activist, had been secretly meeting with senior members of Hamas, who told him that they wanted to negotiate the conditions for a new ceasefire and the end of the Israeli blockade. Baskin then conveyed these offers to representatives of Ehud Olmert, then the Israeli prime minister. However, according to Baskin the offer was rejected out of hand by Olmert, who said that "Israel did not negotiate with terrorists."[27]

On December 23, 2008, four days before the start of "Cast Lead," the massive Israeli attack on Hamas in Gaza, Israeli Shin Bet chief Yuval Diskin confirmed the Baskin account, telling the Israeli cabinet that Hamas would continue the truce if Israel accepted a ceasefire in both Gaza and the West Bank and ended its blockade.[28] To reiterate, during the six-month period between June and December 2008, not a single Israeli civilian had been killed.

It was not the first time that Hamas had sent secret overtures to Israel. In 2012, the Israeli journalist Shlomo Eldar revealed that in 2006, Hamas leader Khaled Meshal and Shin Bet chief Yuval Diskin had held secret meetings, approved by other senior Hamas leaders, in which Meshal offered a settlement based on a Palestinian state within the 1967 lines. According to Eldar, Diskin took the discussions seriously and reported them to Olmert; however, the prime minister immediately turned the offer down.[29]

In February 2009, the UN Human Rights Council concluded that the six-month ceasefire had been "remarkably effective in shutting down cross-border violence and casualties on both sides . . . demonstrating both the willingness and the capacity of those exerting control in Gaza to eliminate rocket and mortar attacks." However, the report continued, "Israel failed to implement its undertaking to lift the blockade . . . [and] the breakdown of the ceasefire seems to have been mainly a result of Israeli violations . . . [as it] engaged in targeted assassinations and other violent and unlawful provocations . . . most significantly by its air strikes of 4 November 2008, with Hamas then retaliating." The pattern was not new: "From 2000 to 2008, it was found that in 79 percent of the violent interaction incidents, it was Israel that broke the pause in violence."[30]

In 2010, General Shmuel Zakai, a former commander of Israel's forces in Gaza, said that the Israeli government had made a "central error" during the June–November 2008 truce:

> [We failed] to take advantage of the calm to improve, rather than markedly worsen, the economic plight of the Palestinians of the Strip. . . . When you create a tahdiyeh [ceasefire], and the economic pressure on the Strip continues, it is obvious that Hamas will try to reach an improved tahdiyeh, and that their way to achieve this is resumed Quasam fire. . . . You cannot just land blows, leave the Palestinians in Gaza in the economic distress they're in, and expect that Hamas will just sit around and do nothing.[31]

The Israeli Attacks on Gaza, 2009–14

Operation Cast Lead

On December 27, 2008, three days after a rocket and mortar attack on Israel that was part of the tit-for-tat pattern, Israel launched "Operation Cast Lead." The attack, which included a ground invasion as well as air and artillery strikes, resulted in the deaths of about 1400 Palestinians, two-thirds of them noncombatants.[32] A number of investigations, including by Israeli human rights groups, showed that during Cast Lead, Israel systematically attacked the Gazan economic and civil infrastructure, including transportation and communications networks; roads and bridges;

government buildings; industrial facilities and businesses; electric generation plants and power lines; and even sewage plants, water storage tanks, schools, homes and apartment houses, hospitals and ambulances, and various food production systems, including orchards, greenhouses, and fishing boats.[33]

Operation Pillar of Defense

On January 18, 2009, Israel ended Cast Lead and a new ceasefire went into effect. The Israeli blockade or siege of Gaza continued, however, deepening the unemployment and poverty as well as hampering the rebuilding of homes, factories, businesses, and hospitals.[34]

Nonetheless, because it feared another major attack and the possible loss of its support from the Gazan people, for the next three years Hamas continued to enforce the ceasefire, taking firm action, including the use of force and jailing, to prevent extremist groups or even individuals from disrupting the truce. As well, Hamas continued to call for a long-term truce (*hudna*) with Israel, sometimes even describing it as permanent, which would for practical purposes amount to a de facto political two-state settlement:

- At the end of January 2009, senior Hamas officials said they would accept a long-term truce if Israel allowed Gaza's borders to be opened to the rest of the world. "We want to be part of the international community," Hamas leader Ghazi Hamad told journalists.[35]
- Shortly afterward, Khaled Meshal told a Russian diplomat that Hamas would not stand in the way if the PA reached a peace settlement with Israel that was approved by a referendum of the Palestinian people.[36] In short, Hamas would go along with a two-state settlement.
- Clearly responding to indications that Hamas was changing its policies, Amos Yadlin, Israel's chief of military intelligence, said that Hamas was now interested in reaching a peace settlement.[37] Of particular importance was a study published by the U.S. Institute of Peace, a semi-official but independent government organization, which concluded:

> Although peaceful coexistence between Israel and Hamas is clearly not possible under the formulations that comprise Hamas's 1988 charter, Hamas has, in practice, moved well beyond its charter . . . [and has] undergone significant political changes . . . and has sent repeated signals that it may be ready to begin a process of coexisting with Israel.[38]

Instead of seeing the Hamas truce and crackdown on attacks on Israel as an opportunity to enter into negotiations, however, the Israeli government ignored the Hamas overtures and actions and continued the siege of Gaza and assassinations of

Hamas and Islamic activists. In early 2010, an Israeli journalist wrote that although "Hamas has not fired Qassam rockets for more than a year . . . the blockade of the Gaza strip has continued. . . . In Israel's eyes this is something natural that should have no effect on the Palestinians' positions."[39]

Throughout 2011 and most of 2012, retaliatory attacks by Hamas on Israel caused little damage. According to Gershon Baskin, who had continued his discussions with Hamas officials, this was deliberate. While the organization had decided that it could not ignore the Israeli attacks, its responses targeted only open fields.[40]

One of the Hamas officials marked for assassination was Ahmed Jabari, the head of Hamas's military forces in Gaza. Like most other Hamas leaders, Jabari was becoming receptive to negotiations and a compromise peace settlement. The Israeli government knew it; nonetheless it killed him in a targeted air attack on November 12, 2012.

When Hamas retaliated with a barrage of rockets, on November 14 Israel launched its second major attack on Gaza, "Operation Pillar of Defense," which had clearly been long planned. The attack ended a week later and a new ceasefire supposedly went into effect. Though not as destructive as Cast Lead, the attack killed 167 Palestinians, over half of them noncombatants, and further damaged the Gaza economy and civil infrastructure.[41]

One day after the Israeli attack started, *Haaretz* reported that "senior officials in Israel" knew that Hamas might have been on the verge of accepting a permanent truce, "but nevertheless approved the assassination."[42]

On November 17, Baskin went public:

> On the morning that he was killed, Mr. Jabari received a draft proposal for an extended cease-fire with Israel, including mechanisms that would verify intentions and ensure compliance. This draft was agreed upon by me and Hamas's deputy foreign minister, Ghazi Hamad, who received Mr. Jabari's authorization to deal directly with me. . . . Other key Hamas leaders . . . supported a new cease-fire effort because they, like Mr. Jabari, understood the futility of successive rocket attacks against Israel that left no real damage on Israel and dozens of casualties in Gaza. Mr. Jabari was not prepared to give up the strategy of "resistance," meaning fighting Israel, but he saw the need for a new strategy and was prepared to agree to a long-term cease-fire.[43]

After the Israeli attack, more information was revealed about the Israeli government's decision to ignore the evidence of Hamas's efforts to reach a long-term truce: Reuven Pedatzur, *Haaretz*'s military analyst, wrote that the government knew that Jabari was expected to agree to such a truce because Baskin's negotiations had been held "with the knowledge and consent of Defense Minister Ehud Barak . . . and perhaps also

Prime Minister Benjamin Netanyahu." Pedatzur concluded: "Thus the decision to kill Jabari shows that our decision-makers decided a cease-fire would be undesirable for Israel at this time, and that attacking Hamas would be preferable."[44]

In light of the long history of Israel's lost or even deliberately sabotaged potential openings for peace negotiations, Pedatzur's conclusion was entirely warranted.

Operation Protective Edge

After the November 21, 2012, conclusion of Pillar of Defense, a new ceasefire went into effect, which continued for the next eighteen months. During this period, Shin Bet's own records showed that not a single Israeli civilian was killed or injured.[45] Nonetheless, throughout 2013 Israel continued the siege of Gaza, including not only the punitive economic measures but also assassinations and armed incursions, even though Hamas was observing the ceasefire and cracking down even harder on Islamic Jihad and other militants to prevent them from launching rocket or mortar attacks.

On June 12, 2014, three Israeli teenagers were kidnapped from their West Bank settlement and murdered. The Netanyahu government immediately accused Hamas, even though Israeli intelligence knew that Hamas was not responsible and that the attack had been carried out in *defiance* of Hamas's policy of maintaining the ceasefire: the kidnapping was the action of what the Israeli police called "a lone cell."

That did not stop Netanyahu from calling for "vengeance," claiming that "Hamas is responsible and Hamas will pay."[46] Over the next eighteen days, Israeli forces carried out disruptive searches throughout the West Bank, looking for the teenagers (whose bodies were later found) but also seizing the opportunity to invade homes and arrest some 400 Palestinians, most of them members of Hamas.[47]

Hamas reacted by firing rockets into southern Israel, the first such action since the November 2012 ceasefire. Israel then struck the rocket launch sites, Hamas retaliated, and the usual escalation process set in, culminating with hundreds of rockets flying in both directions and another major Israeli ground invasion of Gaza. "Operation Protective Edge" was launched on July 8, 2014, and continued for fifty-one days.

As in Cast Lead in 2009, Israel bombed from the air and fired over 30,000 shells into Gaza, many of them into densely populated areas. Civilian institutions were again struck, including homes, schools, hospitals, industries and workshops, agricultural facilities, roads, water and sewage-treatment plants, and the main Gaza electrical power plant. According to the UN, other international agencies, a Human Rights Watch report, and an investigation by B'Tselem, some 2,100 to 2,200 Palestinians were killed, three-quarters or more of them civilians (including more than 500 children), and about 11,000 were wounded. An estimated 100,000 people were left homeless.

Nonetheless, although the attack, like Cast Lead, had been designed to weaken Hamas's hold on Gaza and turn the people of the area against the organization, it failed. Support for Hamas actually increased. Opinion surveys reported that nearly 80 percent of the Palestinians believed that Hamas had won the war and some 60 percent thought the "gains" were worth the cost.[48]

Were the Israeli Attacks Justified as Self-Defense?

Though Israel paid few costs in terms of the reaction of other states—even the Arab states, some of which had their own issues with Hamas, said little—Israel's treatment of Gaza was strongly criticized by international and Israeli human rights advocates, especially because of its attacks on the civilian infrastructure. Israel retorted that it had acted only in self-defense, in response to the rocket attacks into Israel. A number of the reports tacitly seemed to accept that argument, for the focus of most of them was on Israel's "disproportionate" or "indiscriminate" military methods.

The self-defense argument turned on whether Israel had genuinely ended its occupation of Gaza in 2005, only to suffer continued attacks by organizations dedicated to its destruction, leaving it no choice but to defend itself. The argument is unpersuasive on at least four grounds.

First, Israel had not really withdrawn from Gaza, for it had continued to exercise both direct and indirect control and inflict severe suffering on its inhabitants.

Second, even if Israel had truly ended the occupation and repression of Gaza, it certainly hadn't ended its occupation, settlement, and control over the West Bank and East Jerusalem. According to international law and the Oslo agreements, Gaza and the West Bank constituted a single nation. Consequently, the Palestinian people, including the Gazans, had not lost their right to resist the occupation of the West Bank. To believe otherwise is like believing that if in the 1770s the British had continued to occupy New York but had withdrawn from New Jersey, that state's residents would have no right to continue fighting for overall American independence.

Third, long-term truces with Hamas were readily attainable, at the least. Such measures, however, would have necessitated negotiations with Hamas and left it in power, which in the 2000s Israel was unwilling to accept. Consequently, it had ignored a number of Hamas truce proposals and violated others that it had arranged with the organization.

Fourth, the weight of the evidence suggests that Hamas was not only prepared for extended truces but was moving toward accepting a two-state political settlement. Israel's stated reason for refusing to explore Hamas overtures was that it was wrong to negotiate with terrorists. Of course, its real reason was that it didn't want to make the concessions that would pave the way for a peace settlement, even with Arafat, Abbas, and the Palestinian Authority, let alone with Hamas.

Thus, the Palestinians were put into an impossible dilemma. On the one hand, terrorism—deliberate attacks against innocent noncombatants—is always morally wrong, practically by definition. On the other hand, the overwhelming military superiority of Israel had made nonterrorist Palestinian armed resistance almost impossible and Israel had also either ignored or crushed all forms of nonviolent Palestinian resistance, sometimes by lethal force. Further, most Palestinian terrorism almost certainly would have ended if Israel had ceased to occupy the West Bank and Gaza—after all, even while the occupation *continued*, Hamas had not only observed the truces but enforced them on more radical Palestinian terrorist organizations, except for a relatively few retaliations for far larger Israeli attacks.

In this light, the central question is this: Can a state justly claim the right of self-defense when the terrorism directed against it is a consequence of its repression of another people? In my view, the answer is that such a state does not have a convincing claim of "self-defense" when its victims turn to armed resistance—even when their means, terrorism, are morally wrong.

Consider an analogy. After the end of World War II, the Soviet Union occupied Eastern Europe, installed puppet regimes in the area, and intervened with force to put down legitimate revolutions against them. Suppose the Hungarians and Czechs, clearly lacking any other means of resisting the 1956 and 1968 Soviet invasions, had responded with terrorism, for example, by indiscriminate rocket attacks on Soviet cities. Such attacks would still be morally wrong; on the other hand, we would not be inclined to say that in ruthlessly crushing the revolutions the Soviets were only "defending themselves."

In short, while the Palestinian use of terrorism cannot be defended on either practical or moral grounds, Israel's attacks on Gaza, designed to maintain its illegitimate and illegal control over it, cannot be considered "self-defense." If Israel withdrew from the occupied territories and allowed the Palestinians to build a state of their own, but the Palestinians *still* attacked Israel, *then*—and only then—would Israel have a legitimate claim of self-defense.

18

The Peace Process

Last Gasps, 2001–2016

Bush, Sharon, and the "Road Map," 2001–3

For several reasons, President George W. Bush was strongly inclined to support Israel—at least as he understood what constituted "support": as an evangelical Christian, he shared the "pro-Israel" beliefs of that group; he admired Israel's hard-line policies toward Islamic militancy, especially those of Ariel Sharon; and as had been the case for previous presidents, the domestic politics of Israel-related issues reinforced his own inclinations.

Even so, in his first few months in office Bush clashed with Sharon on several issues, opposing Israel's continuing settlement expansion in the occupied territories as well as its military actions there and, in particular, its assassinations of Palestinian militants. As well, Bush was the first president officially to endorse the creation of a Palestinian state, though with important qualifications.

Shortly before the September 11, 2001, terrorist attacks in the United States on the New York Twin Towers and the Pentagon, Secretary of State Colin Powell was preparing a major policy speech that would announce American support for a Palestinian state, with an American and international peacekeeping force to be stationed along its borders.[1] After 9/11, however, the Bush administration focused on combating Islamic terrorism and saw Israel as its natural and perhaps indispensable ally.

On June 24, 2002, Bush gave a major policy speech on US policies in the Israeli-Palestinian conflict. He gave lip service to the need for Israel to change its policies toward the Palestinians, but his vague and highly conditional support for the creation of a "provisional" Palestinian state put no pressure on Sharon. On the contrary, Bush famously called Sharon "a man of peace" and praised him for "his leadership and commitment to build a better future for the Palestinians."[2]

The emphasis in Bush's speech was on what the Palestinians had to do before they could get a "provisional" state. Not only did they have to end their "terrorism"—and he clearly accepted the Israeli position that any form of armed Palestinian resistance, even when directed against soldiers in the occupied territories, constituted "terrorism"—but they also had to establish a "market economy" and a "working democracy with new and different leadership."

In 1996, Arafat was freely elected by the Palestinians to head the Palestinian Authority. Nonetheless, despite Bush's ostensible support for a "working democracy," Arafat had to go. Only then, Bush made it clear, could the Palestinians "count on American support for the creation of a provisional state of Palestine, meaning one whose borders and certain aspects of its sovereignty will be provisional until resolved as part of a final settlement in the Middle East."[3]

During 2002, European diplomats developed their own peace plan, called "The Road Map for Peace." It was accepted—nominally—by the Bush administration, and in April 2003 it was presented to Israel and the Palestinians as a joint plan of the United States, Russia, the European Union, and the United Nations—"the Quartet," as they came to be known.

The Road Map was officially described as a "performance-based" peace plan "with clear phases, timelines, target dates, and benchmarks aiming at progress through reciprocal steps by the two parties in the political, security, economic, humanitarian, and institutional fields, under the auspices of the Quartet." The final "destination" was to be a comprehensive, two-state settlement of the Israeli-Palestinian conflict, to be reached no later than 2005.

The plan's three "phases" imposed obligations on both sides, which were to be carried out simultaneously—that is, neither side was to wait until it saw what the other was doing before taking its own required steps. Phase One required the Palestinians to "reiterate" Israel's "right to exist," to unconditionally end all violence and "incitement" against the Jewish state, and to "undertake comprehensive political reform in preparation for statehood . . . and free, fair, and open elections."

Simultaneously, Israel was required to announce that it would support the creation of "an independent, viable, sovereign Palestinian state" living in peace and security alongside Israel; would "freeze" all settlement activities; and would "end violence against Palestinians everywhere."

Phase Two was to consist of preparations for the creation of the Palestinian state within "provisional" borders, including negotiations on other important issues—including economic cooperation and development, sharing of water, environmental issues, and the status of refugees. Phase Three was the negotiation of a final two-state settlement that would not only resolve all the major Israeli-Palestinian issues but would also require the acceptance by the Arab states of "full normal relations with Israel and security for all the states in the region in the context of a comprehensive Arab-Israeli peace."

Arafat immediately announced that the Palestinians accepted the Road Map without reservations, not surprising in view of the fact that it imposed no unacceptable obligations on them: they had already agreed to end all terrorism and recognized "the right of Israel to exist," and it embodied the two-state solution that they had sought for at least two decades.

After being elected in March 2001, Sharon had been blunt about his goals, and he had no intention of allowing the Bush administration or the Road Map to change them. In April he said that Israel would not withdraw from most of the West Bank, would continue to occupy the Jordan River Valley and the roads leading to them, would make no concessions on Jerusalem, would "absolutely not" evacuate a single settlement "at any price," and would not cede control of the West Bank water aquifers. In case that wasn't sufficiently clear, over the next year he repeatedly said that the Israeli concessions at Oslo, Camp David, and Taba were no longer valid.[4]

A number of prominent Israeli analysts commented that Sharon's intentions were to torpedo the diplomatic process, continue the Israeli occupation, and limit the Palestinians to a series of enclaves surrounded by the Israeli settlements; some even wrote that Sharon's long-term strategy resembled that of the "Bantustans" created by the South African apartheid regime.[5]

Almost immediately after the promulgation of the Road Map, Sharon concluded that the Bush administration had no intention of pressuring him to comply.[6] As a result, he set out to sabotage it, submitting fourteen "reservations" to it, which in fact amounted to its rejection:

- Despite the Road Map's requirements that both sides must move together to meet their conditions and deadlines, Israel would not comply until the Palestinians had ended all "terror, violence, and incitement," dismantled Hamas, ended all weapons production, and replaced the current PA with "new and different leadership." That is, Arafat had to go, now.
- Any redeployment of Israeli military forces in the West Bank would occur only after "absolute quiet" had been achieved.
- "Attention would be paid not to timelines but to performance benchmarks"—meaning that Israel would have no obligations until it was satisfied with the Palestinian "performance."
- The provisional Palestinian state must be "fully demilitarized, and Israel would have "control over the entry and exit of all persons and cargo, as well as of its air space and electromagnetic spectrum."
- There would be no right of return of Palestinian refugees to Israel.
- Until the final phase, the central issues of a two-state settlement were not even to be discussed, including the status of Jerusalem and the settlements "in Judea, Samaria and Gaza."[7]

Far from starting the process of "freezing" the settlements, Sharon began expanding them even further. In her memoirs Condoleezza Rice wrote:

> I would learn valuable lessons about how frustrating it can be to get the Israelis to actually carry through on promises relating to the Palestinians. The illegal outposts were always *going* to be moved but were never quite moved. Gratuitous "security" roadblocks that kept the Palestinians from moving around in the West Bank were always *going* to be moved but were never quite taken down.[8]

In July 2003, Sharon met with Bush. Sharon was reported to have been delighted with the meeting, because Bush reiterated his support of Israel, downplayed US-Israeli disagreements, and essentially dropped the issue of the settlements. One Israeli commentator wrote: "Sharon will come home completely happy. No outpost removal, no tangible pressure to improve the lives of the Palestinians. In fact, nothing."[9]

In April 2004, Bush revealed that he had sent a letter to Sharon saying that "the realities on the ground and in the region have changed greatly over the last several decades, and any final settlement must take into account those realities," in effect, as an Israeli historian wrote, "rewriting the rules of the peace process."[10] A year later, Bush reiterated that these "realities" dictated that some settlement blocs would end up in Israel as part of a settlement, adding that it was "the American view" that this *should* occur. Israeli officials said that Bush's wording "was very satisfying" to Sharon.[11]

A number of former US diplomats and State Department officials who had played prominent roles in the development of American policies in the Arab-Israeli conflict subsequently criticized Bush's capitulations to Sharon. For example, Martin Indyk wrote that Bush lacked interest in the peace process, and that his blaming of the Palestinians in general and Arafat in particular for the continuation of the conflict "fed the narrative of humiliation in the Muslim world that Osama bin Laden sought to exploit."[12]

Similarly, Aaron David Miller wrote that the Bush administration "was not prepared to get serious [about the Road Map]":

> Increasingly bogged down in the war in Iraq, the administration continued to demonstrate a lack of interest and capacity to deal effectively with the opportunities and crises that beset the Arab-Israeli arena . . . [and did] not even follow up seriously on its own initiatives. The road map quietly expired.[13]

Daniel Kurtzer, US ambassador to Israel during the Bush administration, was even more blunt:

> The Bush team did not believe in active peacemaking. . . . From the outset, the Bush administration did not assess resolving the Arab-Israeli conflict as

> central to American interests in the Middle East. . . . [The administration's] lack of interest in promoting the peace process and weak follow-up when it did get involved made a bad situation worse.[14]

Blunter still was a November 2004 open letter to Bush, signed by eighty-eight retired American diplomats. Its importance and candor merit extensive quotation:

> We are deeply concerned by your April 14 endorsement of Israeli Prime Minister Ariel Sharon's unilateral plan to reject the rights of three million Palestinians . . . [which] undermines the Road Map for peace drawn up by the Quartet, including the U.S. . . . [and] it reverses longstanding American policy in the Middle East. . . . In fact, you and Prime Minister Sharon consistently have excluded Palestinians from peace negotiations.
>
> By closing the door to negotiations with Palestinians and the possibility of a Palestinian state, you have proved that the United States is not an even-handed peace partner. . . . Your unqualified support of Sharon's extrajudicial assassinations, Israel's Berlin Wall–like barrier, its harsh military measures in occupied territories, and now your endorsement of Sharon's unilateral plan are costing our country its credibility, prestige and friends. Nor is this endorsement even in the best interests of the State of Israel.[15]

Haaretz's diplomatic correspondent concurred that Bush was not only harming the Palestinians, but he was also harming Israel: "It is difficult to think of an American president who has caused more damage to Israeli interests than the president who is considered one of the friendliest to Israel of all time. No leader has done more than Bush—by commission as well as omission—to destroy the Palestinian Authority under Yasser Arafat and Mahmoud Abbas."[16]

The Geneva Accord

In 2003, eight years after Yossi Beilin and Mahmoud Abbas negotiated the Beilin–Abu Mazen Accords, they tried again. Building on that agreement as well as on the Oslo agreements of 1993, the Camp David negotiations, the Clinton Parameters of 2000, and the Taba conference in early 2001, they agreed upon the Geneva Accord (GA) in October 2003, a fifty-page set of agreements covering all the major aspects of the conflict.[17] In the increasingly unlikely event that a true compromise two-state settlement should become feasible in the future, the GA is likely to be the model on which it would be based.

While unofficial, the GA was negotiated by high-level teams from both sides. Beilin's team included Amram Mitzna, head of the Labor Party; Avraham Burg, recently the Speaker of the Knesset; a number of retired Israeli generals, including former IDF chief of staff Amnon Lipkin-Shahak; academicians and specialists in the Israeli-Palestinian conflict; and intellectuals and writers, including Amos Oz and David Grossman.

The Palestinian delegation was headed by Yasser Abed Rabbo, a longtime PLO leader known to be close to Yasser Arafat, and it included a number of PA ministers, deputy ministers, and prominent academics. While they did not officially represent the PA, there was no doubt that Arafat had encouraged the negotiating process—Beilin wrote that the negotiators met three times with Arafat, who "expressed tremendous interest in our project and encouraged us to continue."[18]

The GA begins by endorsing "the right of both the Jewish and Palestinian peoples to statehood," the first time that the Palestinians explicitly accepted Israel as a Jewish state. In an important interview, Arafat was asked if he objected to the Jewish character of Israel; his response was that he, the PLO, and the PA on a number of occasions had officially recognized the state of Israel, so "it follows that the citizens of Israel have the right to determine the identity and character of the State of Israel, as long as it remains a democratic state that grants equal rights to others, including its large Arab population."[19] The other main issues in the conflict were to be resolved as delineated below.

Territory and Borders. Israel was required to end the occupation and withdraw from almost all of the territories it had conquered in the 1967 war, including Gaza and about 98 percent of the West Bank, and allow a Palestinian state to be created in those areas. The 2 percent of the West Bank that Israel would annex was adjacent to the 1967 border and contained about 110,000 Jewish settlers within three of the largest settlements that had been built after the 1967 war; the remaining 100,000 Israelis who were scattered in small settlements throughout the West Bank would be moved back into Israel by the Israeli government.

The Palestinians were to be compensated for the loss of the annexed areas by means of a 1:1 "land swap," in which they would get Israeli territory along the 1967 borders near the Gaza Strip. Moreover, the land they would receive would not be desert, as in previous Israeli proposals, but would be suited for agriculture. A corridor would be created between Gaza and the West Bank, so as to link the two territories. The corridor was to be under Israeli "sovereignty" but "under Palestinian administration" and "permanently open."

Security. Each side had "the right to live in peace within secure and recognized boundaries free from the threat or acts of war, terrorism and violence"; each must "refrain from the threat or use of force" against each other; and must refrain from participating in any military organization or alliance that endangers either state—a provision that was designed to prevent the Palestinian state from allying itself with Arab states that might threaten Israel.

To further accommodate Israel's security concerns, the Palestinian state would be largely "nonmilitarized" (the term the Palestinians preferred to "demilitarized"), meaning that it would not be allowed an army or heavy weapons but only police

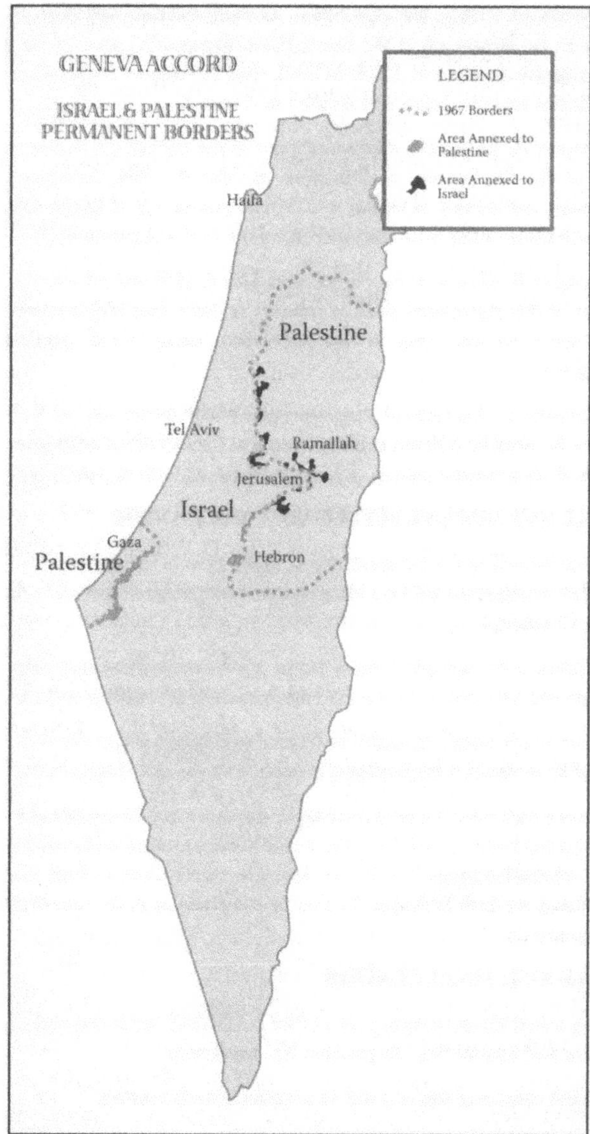

Map 18.1 Geneva Accord, from Yossi Beilin, *Path to Geneva*, 362. Permission granted from Akashic Books.

forces to maintain internal order; all other armed organizations—that is, private militias, Hamas, Islamic Jihad—would be disarmed.

In addition, an international peacekeeping force would replace Israeli forces along the new Israeli-Palestinian borders; to ensure that the international force would be a serious one, American troops would be predominant within it. In theory, the function of the peacekeeping forces was to guarantee the security of both states;

in fact, of course, its real function was to protect Israel from Palestinian incursions, since it would be hard to imagine circumstances in which American troops would be employed in the event of an Israeli armed attack on Palestine.

In other Palestinian concessions, for three years after the GA came into effect Israel would be allowed to continue a "small military presence" in the Jordan River Valley, although it would be at least nominally under the authority of the international force. As well, Israel would keep two early-warning stations in the West Bank.

It should be noted, of course, that the Palestinians would be offered no similar security guarantees, such as the demilitarization of Israel or the stationing of Palestinian forces inside Israel. The huge power disparity between Israel and the Palestinians left the Palestinian negotiators no choice but to accept the inequities.

Water. The issue of how the water resources would be divided or shared was not fully resolved. Some of the Israeli settlements that were to be annexed to Israel had been deliberately built over important aquifers, making it imperative for the Palestinian state to be compensated for their loss, primarily by the building of internationally financed desalination plants. The GA stated that these and other technical economic and legal issues were "professional matters that are being dealt with by teams of experts," which later would submit their results to the Israeli and Palestinian publics.

Jerusalem. Jerusalem would be divided into East Jerusalem and West Jerusalem, which would become the capitals of each state. The line of division would be based on the general principle of the Clinton Parameters: "What is Jewish is Israeli, what is Arab is Palestinian." In some of his earlier remarks, Arafat seemed to be calling into question the Jewish people's historical connection to Jerusalem; however, after the GA became public, he said that the Palestinians "accept Jewish sovereignty over the Wailing Wall and over the Jewish quarter of the Old City . . . because we recognize and respect the Jewish religion and the Jewish historical attachment to Palestine."[20]

Thus, the Palestinians agreed that Israel would keep the Jewish neighborhoods it had established after 1967 within Arab East Jerusalem, and would hold sovereignty over the Jewish Quarter of the Old City and the Western Wall; other religious sites, regarded as holy by Jews, Muslims, and Christians alike, would be under international supervision, with free access to all. The Palestinians would gain sovereignty over the remaining Arab areas of East Jerusalem and, most important, over the mosques on the Temple Mount plateau.

The agreement would be administered and monitored by a multinational and multireligious "International Group," the membership of which would be subject to the approval of both sides.

Refugees. The accord generally followed the Clinton principles. There would be no overall "right of return" to Israel, but some might be allowed to return, "at the sovereign discretion of Israel." Israel agreed to specify the number of refugees it would "consider" admitting; Beilin said that Israel would "probably" admit something like 30,000 refugees.[21] However, the key point was that Israel would have a veto over *any* such arrangements, as was repeatedly emphasized by Beilin and other supporters of the GA in their efforts to gain government and public acceptance of the settlement.

Other than the small number of refugees who might, or might not, be allowed to return to Israel, the refugees would be given the options of remaining in, or returning to, the state of Palestine or locating permanently in any state that would accept them—most likely Lebanon and Jordan, where hundreds of thousands already lived. As well, the refugees would be offered compensation for their property losses in Israel and funds to enable them to resettle elsewhere. The funds would be provided primarily by the international community, though no specifics were offered. The amounts would later be determined by the International Commission.

In summary, it was the unresolved Jerusalem and refugee issues that had blocked the 2000 negotiations from reaching a comprehensive settlement—that is, before the intifada and the election of Sharon ended those negotiations. The Geneva Accord resolved them by means of a trade-off: the Palestinians essentially accepted the Clinton proposals on the refugees, thus giving Israel a de facto veto over any return to Israel, and the Israelis conceded the division of Jerusalem and Palestinian sovereignty over the Haram al-Sharif. The logic of this compromise, Beilin wrote, "will undoubtedly be the basis for any future agreement."[22]

Both Israeli and Palestinian public opinion generally supported the compromise agreement: a variety of polls showed that over 60 percent of each group either supported or at least were not strongly opposed to it. Even on the right of return, long thought to have been a deal-breaker, there had been a major change: 46 percent of the Palestinians (up from only 25 percent in 2003) accepted the principle that most of the refugees would have to choose between resettlement and compensation rather than returning to Israel.[23]

The Outcome of the Geneva Accord

As the intifada escalated in 2003–4, leaders on both sides backed away from the accord. As expected, Sharon furiously dismissed it, and while Arafat had effectively appointed the Palestinian delegation and supported the compromises during the secret negotiations, he was silent after the GA became public. Subsequently he was criticized by Mahmoud Abbas and others for not throwing his support behind it. Some observers argued that the progressive Israeli compromises at Camp David may have led Arafat to decide to wait for even more favorable terms. Others, including Barak, asserted that it failed because Arafat still wanted all of Israel.

However, the most plausible explanation is that Arafat knew the compromises would arouse Palestinian resistance, while Sharon would never accept them. Therefore, Arafat might have reasoned, he had little to gain and everything to lose by endorsing them. Still, a braver and more farsighted leader might have acted differently, but Arafat's failure to do so does not shift to the Palestinians the main responsibility for yet another lost opportunity.

The Arab Peace Initiative Reaffirmed

In March 2007, the 2002 Arab Peace Initiative was unanimously reaffirmed by all twenty-two signatories; indeed, the section on the refugee issue was significantly modified in favor of Israel, for the words "right of return" were omitted and, following the language of the Geneva Accords, the API now stated that there had to be "a just *and agreed* solution" (emphasis added) to the problem.[24] A year later Marwan Muasher, a former Jordanian foreign minister who played a major role in the development of the API, wrote: "For the first time, the Arab world committed itself to an agreed-upon solution to the refugee problem, addressing Israel's concern that Arabs will demand that four million refugees be sent to Israel. . . . Not a single Arab state has withdrawn its support [for such a settlement]."[25]

In short, the Arab states unanimously gave Israel a veto over any refugee plan. Even Iran, considered the most radical Muslim state, had gone along, despite the threatening rhetoric of Mahmoud Ahmadinejad, the country's president from 2005 to 2013. An Israeli journalist wrote: "Since the Arab Peace Initiative was proposed in 2002, Iran hasn't expressed opposition to it. Moreover, the initiative was adopted by the foreign ministers at a summit of the Organization of Islamic Cooperation in 2003, in Tehran of all places."[26]

The Arab Peace Initiative is still on the table, and there is no doubt that the Palestinian Authority, headed by Mahmoud Abbas since Arafat's death in 2004, supports it. To be sure, the PA continues to give lip service to the right of return, but it has repeatedly made clear that it will not allow that issue to become an obstacle to a fair two-state settlement.

Hamas's position has been steadily evolving in the same direction, though not entirely consistently. For example, in 2006 Hamas said it was "ready to consider" the API if Israel accepted it first,[27] but in 2012 its leader Khaled Meshal said that the organization would never recognize Israel or abandon its claim to all of historic Palestine: "Palestine is ours from river to the sea and from the south to the north. There will be no concession on an inch of land," he told a Gazan rally.[28]

Meshal's statement was particularly shocking, since it was not consistent with the other signs of change in Hamas policies, or even with his own previous statements, in which he was far more moderate and supported the end of Palestinian violent resistance if Israel agreed to a two-state solution. Of course, it was hardly irrelevant that Netanyahu had just announced a major expansion of the Israeli settlements in the West Bank.[29]

In any case, a month later Meshal authorized King Abdullah of Jordan to tell President Obama that Hamas had accepted the idea of a two-state solution and welcomed the API and efforts by Mahmoud Abbas to gain international support for this outcome. Saeb Erekat, the PA official in charge of relations with Israel, said that Hamas's policy was now in line with that of the PA.[30]

In 2014, Munib al-Masri, a leading Palestinian official in the West Bank, wrote that Hamas's "readiness to sign off on the 1967 border is not a mere tactical move but reflects deeper strategic calculations."[31] Since then there has been even more evidence (discussed in Chapter 19) that Hamas would not be an obstacle to a two-state settlement, including one that denied any Palestinian "right" of return and allowed Israel to decide how many, if any, refugees it would admit.

Nonetheless, the Netanyahu administrations, in power since 2009, continue to claim that the right-of-return issue makes a two-state settlement impossible. Thus, it has simply ignored the API, much to the disapproval and even amazement of many non-"leftist" Israeli political and military leaders. For example, in 2010 a retired Israeli major general wrote that the "absurd thing is that the Israeli government has never even held a single organized debate of the initiative. Some 22 Arab countries signed a peace initiative that Israel has not only not adopted, but has not even discussed."[32] And in 2017 it was reported that "most of Israel's former defense chiefs . . . consider [the API] a suitable basis for starting negotiations, and many politicians, including former right-wingers, believe we should respond to the proposal."[33]

As a result of the government's ignoring of the API, most Israelis didn't know about it. After a 2013 public opinion poll found that almost 75 percent had never even heard of it, an astonished Carlo Strenger, an Israeli psychologist, wrote:

> The overwhelming majority of Israelis do not know that the Arab world as a whole would accept Israel's existence! But there was also a surprisingly positive finding in this poll. After respondents heard what the initiative entails, they were asked what their position would be were Netanyahu to adopt the Arab League proposal. A full 69% said they would support it![34]

In a subsequent column, Strenger wrote that the unwillingness of the Sharon and Olmert governments to give the API serious consideration was "puzzling," in light of the fact that "for most of its existence, Israel could only dream of an offer that explicitly includes peace, recognition of Israel's right to exist and normalization of its relationship with the Arab world."[35] Yet the explanation of why no Israeli government has been willing to explore the API proposals for a two-state settlement is hardly difficult: no such settlement is possible unless Israel withdraws from its 1967 conquests of the West Bank and East Jerusalem, and no Israeli government, let alone Netanyahu's, has been willing to even consider doing that.[36]

The Olmert-Abbas Negotiations, 2008–9

Ehud Olmert became the acting prime minister in January 2006, following Ariel Sharon's stroke, and was elected prime minister in March. Olmert was a longtime leading member of Likud and had served as mayor of Jerusalem from 1993 through 2003. Prior to becoming prime minister, his views were those typical of hard-line Likud members: he had opposed any Israeli withdrawal from its 1967 territorial conquests and had "hit the roof," Condoleezza Rice says, when the Bush administration statement referred to the Arab Peace Initiative in issuing a call for an international conference to settle the conflict.[37] As well, he had opposed the Oslo Accords and the Camp David compromises, and as mayor of Jerusalem had subscribed to the Likud view that there had to be a "united, undivided Jerusalem under eternal Israeli sovereignty." Acting on those views, he had aggressively expanded the Jewish settlements in and near East Jerusalem, demolished some 300 Palestinian homes, and in a variety of ways sought to marginalize the Palestinian residents.

Moreover, in Olmert's first few months as prime minister, he launched two heavy military attacks that killed hundreds of Palestinian and thousands of Lebanese civilians: in June 2006 against Hamas in Gaza, in retaliation for the kidnapping of an Israeli soldier and the killing of two others, and in southern Lebanon in July, in retaliation for a Hezbollah cross-border raid that resulted in the death of several Israeli soldiers.

In a major surprise, however, in November 2006, Olmert gave a major speech at a memorial service honoring David Ben-Gurion, announcing that he was ready to make a number of compromises—some of them going beyond not just Barak's policies but even those embodied in the 2003 Geneva Accord—in order to reach a two-state peace settlement.

In subsequent interviews, Olmert admitted that his past views were wrong: "I thought that the land from the Jordan River to the [Mediterranean] Sea was all ours, but ultimately, after a long and tortured process, I arrived at the conclusion that we must share with those we live with if we don't want to be a binational state."[38]

In his 2006 speech, Olmert quoted Ben-Gurion's 1948 address to the Knesset, in which he explained why he had not authorized an attempt to seize the West Bank: "When we were faced with the choice between the entire land of Israel without a Jewish State, or a Jewish State without the entire land of Israel, we chose a Jewish State without the entire land of Israel." Then, Olmert continued, Ben-Gurion agreed to withdraw from the Sinai after the 1956 war, opposed the Israeli attacks on Egypt and Syria in 1967, and then called for withdrawal from most of the territories seized by Israel in that war. Olmert then came to his central point:

> Ben-Gurion ruled that in exchange for true peace, Israel must relinquish a vast majority of the territories occupied in the Six Day War. I wholeheartedly identify with the statements made by Ben-Gurion regarding the duty

> of every government in Israel to strive for peace. . . . I would consider it a great sin, not only towards our generation but towards future generations as well, if we did not do everything in our power to reach a mutual understanding with our Arab neighbors, and if future generations had cause to blame the Government of Israel of missing an opportunity for peace.[39]

A two-state peace agreement would be possible, Olmert continued, if the Palestinians end violence, disband "the terrorist organizations," and agree to border modifications. Those modifications, however, must be based on George Bush's 2004 letter to Ariel Sharon, in which the US president said that the "new realities on the ground" had made it unrealistic for there to be a complete return to the pre-1967 Israeli borders. The implication was that the new border must be more or less along Sharon's separation wall and include some West Bank territory beyond the 1967 border, thus allowing Israel to annex its major settlements there.

If the Palestinians accepted these terms, Olmert concluded,

> I will invite Abu Mazen [PA chairman Mahmoud Abbas] to meet with me immediately, in order to conduct a real, open, genuine and serious dialogue between us . . . [resulting in] an independent and viable Palestinian state. . . . We will significantly diminish the number of roadblocks, increase freedom of movement in the territories, facilitate movement of people and goods in both directions, and release Palestinian funds for the purpose of alleviating the humanitarian hardship which many of you suffer. We can assist you in formulating a plan for the economic rehabilitation of the Gaza Strip and areas in Judea and Samaria [the West Bank]. . . . We will agree to the evacuation of many territories and communities which were established therein.

There is no question that Olmert's apparent offers were striking and had apparently opened the door to a peace settlement: "Greater Israel is over," he told a cabinet meeting: "There is no such thing. Anyone who talks like that is deluding himself."[40] Astonishingly, he even said that if Israel did not soon agree to a two-state settlement, "the country is finished."[41]

Leading Israeli commentators initially were impressed—Olmert's plan "is the most dovish, conciliatory and far-reaching of any offered by an Israeli leader in recent years," Meron Benvenisti wrote.[42] However, in the next two years, instead of cutting back Jewish settlement of the West Bank, Olmert continued to expand it; as well, the siege of Gaza continued. The apparent disconnect between Olmert's rhetoric and his behavior was noted by a number of Israeli analysts who initially had been optimistic.[43]

Even so, Olmert had not abandoned his efforts to negotiate a two-state settlement with the Palestinian Authority. Between his 2006 speech and his departure from office at the end of 2008, he and Abbas secretly held some thirty-six meetings, in the course of which he laid out his proposals. There are somewhat different versions of what Olmert was offering, because, as had been the case with Barak at Camp David, he was not willing to put his offers in writing until Abbas accepted them, and refused to show Abbas a map of his territorial proposals.[44] Hardly unreasonably, of course, Abbas was not willing to officially accept Olmert's proposals until he knew their exact nature.[45]

Still, there have been a number of leaks and inside accounts; in particular, the *Guardian*'s 2011 publication of the "Palestine Papers"—based on the WikiLeaks release of some 1,600 Israeli, Palestinian, and US classified documents—revealed the main lines of Olmert's proposals:

Territory and Borders. Olmert proposed to annex 6.3 to 6.8 percent of the West Bank (analyses differ on the precise amount), including all the Jewish neighborhoods that had been established in East Jerusalem and the four main settlements in the West Bank, containing about 75 percent of the settlers. Three of those settlements were near the 1967 borders, but one of them, Ariel, extended well into the heart of the West Bank. In exchange, Olmert offered a territorial swap, in which Israel would give 5.5 percent of its territory to the Palestinians, most of it along the borders of the Gaza Strip. As well, Israel would establish a territorial link or corridor that would connect Gaza and the West Bank, which would nominally remain Israeli territory but would be under Palestinian control.[46]

These offers were portrayed by Olmert as providing for the "establishment of a Palestinian state on territory equivalent in size to the pre-1967 West Bank and Gaza Strip with mutually agreed-upon land swaps that take into account the new realities on the ground."[47] In fact that was a somewhat exaggerated estimate of the size of the Palestinian state; more important, Olmert continued building Israeli roads and bridges in the West Bank—some of them reserved only for Israelis—that would link the settlements and effectively cut the Palestinian state into four sections. As well, almost half the territory Olmert was offering to swap with the Palestinian state was in the Negev Desert.

Security. As in previous Israeli peace proposals, in Olmert's plan the Palestinian state would have no army or air force, though it would be allowed to have a strong police force to protect law and order. Olmert did make a significant concession to the Palestinians by dropping the previous Israeli insistence that Israeli security required its military forces, if not settlements, to remain in the Jordan River Valley. Traditional Israeli defense strategies, he said, were outmoded, for they were "all about tanks and land and controlling territories and this or that hilltop. All these things are worthless. Who thinks seriously that if we sit on another hilltop, on another hundred meters, that this is what will make the difference for the State of Israel's basic security?"[48]

On another occasion he said: "I completely gave up on having an Israeli presence in the Jordan Valley. That was because I could protect the line of the Jordan River through an international military force on the other side of the Jordan River. There was no opposition on the Palestinian side to our having a presence in warning stations along the mountain range."[49]

Jerusalem. Olmert did not mention Jerusalem in his 2006 speech, neither offering a compromise nor repeating the standard Israeli claim that "it will remain Israel's capital forever."[50] However, over the next two years he essentially adopted the Clinton Parameters' proposals on Jerusalem, even explicitly recanting his previous policies, especially during his years as mayor of the city: "I am the first who wanted to enforce Israeli sovereignty on the entire city. I admit it. I am not trying to justify what I did for 35 years. For a large portion of those years, I was unwilling to look at reality in all its depth."[51]

Olmert now proposed to Abbas that Jerusalem be partitioned or "shared," as he preferred to put it. The Israeli areas—predominantly in West Jerusalem but also including some that had been developed in East Jerusalem after the 1967 war—would remain under Israeli sovereignty, while the Palestinians would be given sovereignty over the rest of East Jerusalem.[52] Addressing his shocked Israeli critics, Olmert responded: "Whoever wants to maintain control over the entire city will have to absorb 270,000 Arabs into the borders of Israel proper. This won't do."[53]

Throughout the course of the Arab-Israeli and Israeli-Palestinian conflicts, one of the most explosive issues was the status of the Old City of Jerusalem, especially the Temple Mount/Haram al-Sharif. Olmert now proposed, in essence, that the Old City be internationalized, as had been proposed in the 1947 UN partition plan. The Temple Mount/Haram al-Sharif and other areas of religious significance would be ruled by a joint trusteeship of Israel, Palestine, Saudi Arabia, Jordan, and the United States—though the Haram would continue to be administered by a Muslim commission, as Israel had allowed since the 1967 war.

It was a complicated arrangement, of course, but in terms of Israeli policies it was revolutionary. Even the Geneva Accords had proposed the division of sovereignty of Jerusalem between Israel and Palestine rather than its internationalization.[54]

The Refugees and the "Right of Return." Olmert proposed that an agreement on the refugees would acknowledge their suffering since 1948 but include no language admitting Israeli responsibility for their plight. As for their "return" to Israel, Israel would admit 1,000 refugees per year for a period of five years, but only on a "humanitarian" or "family reunification" basis. Later, Olmert said that if Abbas had proposed an agreement "that would require Israel to absorb 10,000–15,000 refugees over five years, I would have agreed."[55] As well, Olmert agreed to work with international organizations to "generously compensate" refugees for their loss of homes and property.

The Palestinian Response

The two sides were very close on the most important issues. Abbas's proposals would allow Israel to annex its three largest settlement blocs just over the pre-1967 borders, containing over 80 percent of the settlers in the West Bank. On security, Abbas accepted the Palestinian state as "nonmilitarized," with the exact details on the size and armaments of the internal security force to be later negotiated. On Jerusalem, Abbas accepted the main outlines of Olmert's proposals, which were very close to the principles he had agreed to in the Beilin–Abu Mazen and Geneva Accords, including the ceding to Israel of nearly all the Jewish areas of East Jerusalem and its environs. Moreover, it was Abbas's idea to establish a joint committee to administer the "holy sites" in the Old City, thus getting around the symbolic "sovereignty" problem.[56]

As for the "right of return," the Palestinian leaders reaffirmed that they had neither the intention nor the power to undermine the status of Israel as a Jewish state by demanding the "return" of millions of refugees; indeed, there were indications that they would agree to recognize Israel as a Jewish state as long as the rights of the Israeli Arabs were preserved.[57]

Had the negotiations continued, it is highly likely that there would have been an agreement to admit over a five-year period somewhere between 30,000 Palestinian refugees—Olmert's offer—and 100,000, as Abbas proposed.[58] Addressing the issue of whether even the larger number would result in what the Israelis euphemistically call "the demographic problem" (meaning the loss of a large Jewish majority), the Israeli analyst Shaul Arieli pointed out that "the issue is an argument over a symbolic return of refugees which would become demographically negligible" once the 300,000 Palestinians in East Jerusalem became part of the Palestinian state.[59]

The main remaining gaps between Olmert and Abbas concerned the size and borders of the projected Palestinian state, and the status of the settlements deep inside the West Bank heartland. Abbas was willing to accept Israeli annexation of the area just beyond the 1967 borders (comprising 2 percent of the West Bank), which contained the largest Israeli settlements, provided the Palestinians were compensated with territory of the same size and quality.[60] However, there was no agreement on the remaining smaller settlements in the heart of the West Bank.

Both the Israeli and Palestinian negotiators believe that an agreement could have been reached if Olmert had been able to complete his term and been reelected in March 2009. Olmert claimed, "We were very close, more than ever in the past, to complete an agreement on principles that would have led to the end of the conflict between us and the Palestinians."[61] On another occasion he said he could almost "touch the peace deal." While the Palestinians had not accepted his proposals, they had not rejected them either: "And there is a difference. They didn't accept them because the negotiation hadn't ended. . . . If I had remained prime minister for another four to six months, I believe it would have been possible to reach an agreement. The gaps were small."[62]

Palestinian leaders essentially confirmed Olmert's appraisal, believing that despite his past record and, for that matter, the ongoing expansion of the Jewish settlements, Olmert was genuinely willing to compromise. "It's very sad," said

Saed Erekat, Abbas's chief negotiator. "He was serious."[63] After the fact, Abbas was even more positive, telling members of the Knesset that "we didn't strike a deal but reached understandings in many of the core subjects"; if Olmert could have remained in office for "maybe two months more," he continued, a peace agreement would have been reached.[64]

Why then, it is reasonable to ask, didn't Abbas strike while the iron was hot and publicly state that he had accepted the main outlines of Olmert's proposals, with some details to be later resolved? Some have argued that Abbas was playing a waiting game, in the expectation that Israel would soon offer an even better deal. It is true that, between May 2000 and September 2008, Israel negotiators had retreated from their initial demands for about 35 percent of the West Bank to just 6 or 7 percent.[65] Even so, there simply is no evidence that Abbas was following such a risky strategy, and it is particularly unlikely considering that he had a long history of making compromises to bring about a peace settlement.

Indeed, in a 2008 interview on an Arab television network, Abbas said: "The opportunity for the 1947 partition has been lost, and before that the opportunity for the Peel Commission partition was lost. But we do not want to lose another opportunity. That is why we have accepted the 1948 and 1967 partition . . . [even though they] do not include more than 22 percent of historical Palestine."[66]

The most likely explanation for Abbas's failure to accept at least the principles of the Olmert proposals was Olmert's deteriorating political position. For some time he had been investigated by the Israeli police on corruption charges (for which he was later convicted), and for other reasons he had become extremely unpopular—astonishingly, one poll found that only 3 percent of the Israeli public approved of his leadership. As a result, it was becoming increasingly likely that he would soon lose his reelection bid to Benjamin Netanyahu, who almost certainly would jettison or sabotage any agreement negotiated between Olmert and Abbas.

In July 2008, Olmert announced he was resigning as prime minister but would stay on until a successor could be chosen or until the next general elections in March 2009. In effect, then, he was conducting negotiations with Abbas as the lame-duck head of a caretaker government that would probably be replaced by Netanyahu. Condoleezza Rice writes that "Tzipi Livni [Olmert's main advisor on the negotiations] urged me (and, I believe, Abbas), not to enshrine the Olmert proposal. 'He has no standing in Israel,' she said."[67] As well, Yariv Oppenheimer, the director of Peace Now, commented: "Under these circumstances, the Palestinians understood that even if they attain a far-reaching agreement with the Israeli leadership, the likelihood that Olmert would get the approval of the Israeli public and win the battle with the Israeli right wing led by Netanyahu was slim."[68]

Abbas had been placed in a dilemma: on the one hand, he had been offered a better deal than by any previous Israeli prime minister, and one that was not likely to become much better. On the other hand, there would likely be serious repercussions from his Palestinian opponents because of his abandonment of the "right of return" and his willingness to finesse the sovereignty issue on the Temple Mount/Haram al-Sharif.

Nonetheless, a strong case can be made that Abbas should have accepted an agreement with Olmert when that was still on the table, an agreement that, at long last, could have ended the Israeli-Palestinian conflict—and with it, the overall Arab-Israeli conflict as well. By December 2008, however, the issue became moot after Olmert authorized "Operation Cast Lead," the massive Israeli attack on Gaza. In any case, the February 2009 election of Benjamin Netanyahu would have spelled the end, one way or another, of any agreement that had been reached.

Netanyahu—at the time of this writing still in power, following his election in 2009, his reelections in 2013 and 2015, and the negotiated outcome of the inconclusive 2020 elections—opposed all the proposed and actual settlements, not merely with the Palestinians but with the Arab world as a whole. He opposed the peace treaties with Egypt and Jordan, and has ignored the Arab Peace Initiative. As for a compromise peace with the Palestinians, Netanyahu opposed the Oslo Accords, the Camp David and Taba proposals, the Clinton Parameters, and, of course, the Geneva Accords, let alone the additional concessions that Olmert was considering.

Netanyahu is widely regarded as a cynical demagogue who panders to the Israeli right wing in order to maintain his political power. However, Netanyahu is not merely cynical, he is also a lifelong adherent to "Greater Israel" ideology. Thus, he routinely refers to the West Bank as "Judea and Samaria," which in Israeli discourse signals that because the area was part of biblical Israel, it belongs solely to the Jews and contemporary Israel.[69]

In this respect, his views have even been to the right of Ariel Sharon's. For example, in 2002 when the newly elected Sharon began hinting that he might accept a two-state solution, Netanyahu angrily responded that "a Palestinian state means no Jewish state and a Jewish state means no Palestinian state."[70] And in 2005 he resigned from the Sharon administration to protest the withdrawal of Israeli settlers from Gaza.

To be sure, on a few occasions, Netanyahu claimed that he, too, supported a two-state compromise. For example, in a 2011 speech before a joint session of the US Congress, Netanyahu said that "I am willing to make painful compromises. . . . I recognize that in a genuine peace we will be required to give up parts of the ancestral Jewish homeland." However, he offered no specifics on what a Palestinian state would include, except to say that Israel "will not return to the indefensible borders of 1967." As an Israeli analyst pointed out, the kind of "state" that Netanyahu had in mind was "in reality, [only] a series of semiautonomous and demilitarized enclaves, with Israel controlling its borders."[71]

Knowledgeable American officials were not impressed; in a later public letter to Secretary of State John Kerry, Zbigniew Brzezinski and a group of retired American diplomats, government officials, and congresspeople said:

> The terms for a peace accord advanced by Netanyahu's government, whether regarding territory, borders, security, water and other resources, refugees or the location of the Palestinian state's capital, require compromises of Palestinian territory and sovereignty on the Palestinian side of the June 6, 1967, line. They do not reflect any Israeli compromises, much less the "painful compromises" Netanyahu promised in his May 2011 speech before a joint meeting of Congress. Every one of them is on the Palestinian side of that line.[72]

Netanyahu repeatedly claimed that he was prepared to negotiate but that Abbas refused to meet with him. It is true that in recent years Abbas has said that in light of Netanyahu's unwillingness to agree to a fair two-state settlement, there is no longer any point in his continuing to participate in a charade. However, in the first few years after Netanyahu's 2009 election, when Abbas was willing to continue the negotiations, Netanyahu refused to do so. In 2012 Yuval Diskin, the head of the Shin Bet from 2005 to 2011, was interviewed by Akiva Eldar, who wrote:

> Diskin backed Abbas when the latter said Netanyahu had refused to launch real negotiations and never bothered to respond to the Palestinian positions on borders and security. . . . "Don't listen to those stories they're trying to sell you about how Abu Mazen [Abbas] doesn't want to talk," said Diskin. . . . "I was there until a year ago and I know what's happening from up close. This government has no interest in resolving anything with the Palestinians, and this I can say with certainty."[73]

In January 2020, Netanyahu ended all of his pretenses, enthusiastically endorsing the "Trump Peace Plan" (discussed in Chapter 19), which marks the definitive end to any legitimate compromise two-state settlement.

Barack Obama and the Israeli-Palestinian Conflict

Obama took office in January 2009, two months before Netanyahu defeated Olmert and once again became prime minister. A number of observers hoped Obama would use US support as a means to pressure Netanyahu to end the expansion of the settlements and agree to serious negotiations with the Palestinians.

There were several reasons to do so, supporters of such pressures urged. First, they argued, it was in the American national interest to support peace and stability in the Middle East and to minimize friction with the Arab states and publics. Second, US pressures would be good for Israel as well—at least, good for its rational self-interest—and in fact would be supported by a significant number of Israelis who had lost hope for their own government. It was often said that Israel "must be saved from itself," and that the only way to do it was by "tough love" from its most reliable friend.

Many Israeli observers made such arguments. For example, in remarkably candid terms a leading columnist called for US pressures: "The worse thing for Israel now is if the U.S. continues its policy of supporting Israel whatever it does. Israel is now standing on top of a cliff, and a friend, the U.S., must do whatever is necessary to save this friend."[74]

Similarly, another Israeli commentator wrote: "We should hope Obama will help Israel help itself because that is how friendship is measured. So bring us an American president who is not another dreadful 'friend of Israel' who blindly follows the positions of the Jewish lobby and the Israeli government."[75]

In addition to such Israeli support, if Obama had chosen to follow that advice he would have had some important domestic US political cover, for the creation of a viable Palestinian state was gaining important support. In particular, in March 2009, Brent Scowcroft and Zbigniew Brzezinski, respectively national security advisors to Jimmy Carter and the first Bush administration, joined other former government officials and congresspeople to issue a public statement arguing that "it is essential that the Obama administration make Arab-Israeli peace a high national security priority from the beginning," which could only happen if negotiations included "a legitimate, unified, and empowered Palestinian side."

To that end, they argued, George W. Bush's policy of "shutting out Hamas and isolating Gaza" had failed: "There should be a shift from ousting Hamas to modifying its behavior, offering it inducements that will enable its more moderate elements to prevail."[76]

During his electoral campaign Obama had sought to convince Jewish organizations that he was strongly "pro-Israel," even going as far as disavowing the views of Brzezinski and other supporters and advisors, such as Rob Malley, who had urged him to distance himself from the Netanyahu government.[77] Still, once he was elected, there were some initial indications that Obama might be open to pressing Israel to agree to a two-state settlement. For example, in January 2009 he appointed former senator George Mitchell as his chief representative for negotiations on the Israel-Palestinian conflict—Mitchell had headed an international investigation of the intifada in 2001, and his report was critical of Israel's policies and behavior.

As well, the incoming president had praised the Arab Peace Initiative as the basis for a fair settlement and according to some reports privately said that "Israel would be crazy not to accept it." Further, there were indications he intended to press Israel to at least freeze the ongoing expansion of the settlements.

In particular, in what was initially taken to signal a rethinking of American policy in the Middle East, in June 2009 Obama gave a major speech in Cairo that reached out to the Muslim world. In it, he stated his support for a Palestinian state and asserted that "the United States does not accept the legitimacy of continued Israeli settlements."

However, Obama did not say that the settlements were illegal or, most important, call for the removal of the *existing* settlements. As well, in other ways Obama signaled that he was not willing to take on Israel or its US supporters on this crucial issue.[78] For one thing, his choice of Dennis Ross to be his primary advisor on Middle East affairs—Ross was often described as "Israel's lawyer in the American government" or, as one prominent Palestinian official put it, "as more Israeli than the Israelis"—was completely at odds with the Mitchell appointment, indicating that Obama had decided there would be no serious pressures on Israel. As Elgindy put it, after his initial policies condemning the settlements had been ignored by Netanyahu, he "essentially washed his hands of the issue."[79]

In that light, it was not surprising that Obama refused to criticize Israel's Cast Lead military attack at the end of 2008, saying earlier that year, "If somebody was sending rockets into my house . . . I'm going to do everything in my power to stop that and I would expect Israelis to do the same thing." On several occasions during Cast Lead, Defense Minister Ehud Barak quoted Obama's statement.[80]

Then, in January 2009 Obama refused to make any comment on the impending election of Netanyahu—in contrast to the 1992 election campaign when George H. W. Bush made it clear to the Israelis that the United States strongly favored Yitzhak Rabin over Yitzhak Shamir, an intervention that Israeli analysts concluded had a significant role in Rabin's election.

Following Netanyahu's election, the administration decided that there would be no cut in the $30 billion in military aid that had been promised by the Bush administration over the next decade.[81] Then, during the summer of 2009, as Netanyahu increased settlement construction in the occupied territories, especially in East Jerusalem, Obama backed away from his Cairo promise to seek a settlement freeze. On the contrary, in 2011 the United States *vetoed* a UN resolution condemning the settlements. As well, the administration worked to ensure the defeat of Arafat's efforts to have the United Nations declare a symbolic recognition of a Palestinian state in the occupied territories.

Moreover, disregarding the strong recommendation of the Brzezinski-Scowcroft group, the administration revealed that, like the Netanyahu government, it would not negotiate with Hamas, despite Obama's repeated campaign statements about the need to engage in diplomacy with one's adversaries. In fact, Hamas's control over Gaza had actually been solidified by Israeli military attacks, making it still more unlikely that there could be a settlement of the conflict without the participation of the organization.

The Chas Freeman Affair

Obama's unwillingness to take on Israel and its US supporters became even more obvious during the Freeman affair. At the end of February 2009, Dennis Blair, the director of US National Intelligence, named Charles "Chas" W. Freeman Jr., one of the most experienced and respected American diplomats of recent decades, to chair the National Intelligence Council.

However, because Freeman had made a number of unusually candid and forceful statements criticizing Israeli policies, AIPAC and other "pro-Israeli" organizations mounted a fierce public attack on him. The powerful senator Charles Schumer of New York, then the third-ranking Democrat and today the minority leader of the Senate, charged that Freeman had an "irrational hatred of Israel."[82]

Under these pressures, Obama declined to defend Freeman, leaving him dangling in the wind; as a result, Freeman announced that he was no longer willing to serve. He did not go quietly, though, publicly charging that the affair had "conclusively shown" that the Israel lobby was "determined to prevent any view other than its own from being aired, still less to factor in American understanding of trends and events in the Middle East."

There can be no doubt that the Freeman affair is one of the strongest arguments for the power of the lobby. Yet Schumer and other strongly "pro-Israeli" congresspeople did not need to be lobbied to resist the appointment of Freeman, and even Obama had a long record of "pro-Israel" attitudes, friends, and alliances—many of Obama's Jewish friends and allies from Chicago termed him "America's first Jewish president." That said, it could scarcely be denied that the Freeman affair demonstrated that the Israel lobby continued to play a major role in the US policymaking process on the Arab-Israeli conflict.

Finally, in October 2009, the administration rejected out of hand the findings and conclusions of the Goldstone report on Israel's behavior in Cast Lead, and its recommendation that the UN consider taking Israel's "war crimes" to the International Criminal Court. Effectively stopping any international action, Obama's UN representative termed the Goldstone Commission Report "unbalanced, one-sided and basically unacceptable."[83] Israel's ambassador to the United States was pleased, saying that the American position "could have been drafted in Tel Aviv, it was so wonderful."

The Kerry Negotiations

In summer 2014, Secretary of State John Kerry began an effort to negotiate an Israeli-Palestinian settlement. Over the next eight months, until the negotiations broke down in March 2015, Kerry sought to establish a personal relationship with Netanyahu, evidently on the naïve assumption that if he did so, the Israeli prime minister might soften his position on a two-state settlement.

By contrast, Abbas and the Palestinians were treated as distinctly less important. After the breakdown of the negotiations, an Israeli official who participated in the talks was strongly critical of Kerry's failure to treat Abbas seriously:

> "At one point we discovered that throughout the entire period, the Americans didn't actually talk to the Palestinians, only to us," a senior Israeli

> official said. "The result was a crisis of expectations. How many times did *we* [emphasis added] say to them: What about Mahmoud Abbas? Did you talk to him? Does he agree to all these points?" The Americans neglected Mahmoud Abbas throughout this period. A senior official in the US administration who took part in the talks acknowledges that the biggest mistake made by the Americans was in dealing with Abbas. "It's true, we weren't sensitive enough toward him and we didn't understand how he felt," this source says. "In retrospect, we should have behaved differently."[84]

In June 2017, *Haaretz* published the text of Kerry's proposals;[85] astonishingly, to one degree or another all of them backed away from the compromises embodied in the Clinton Parameters, the Taba conference, the Geneva Accord, and especially the Olmert offers to Abbas.

Territory and Borders. As in previous peace plans, Kerry proposed that the borders should be based on the 1967 lines, "with mutually agreed swaps whose size and location will be negotiated." However, he added: "In negotiating the borders, the parties will need to take into account subsequent developments, Israel's security requirements and the goal of minimizing movement of existing populations while avoiding friction." That was a circuitous if not evasive way of saying that the "facts on the ground" that Israel had been creating since 1967 would remain in place.

The Settlements. Not only would all or most of the settlements remain, but when Netanyahu refused to agree even to a three-month freeze on new settlements, Kerry dropped the issue. After the failure of the Kerry negotiations effort, in an interview with Nahum Barnea, a prominent Israeli journalist, the American official quoted above explained why: "The negotiations had to start with a decision to freeze settlement construction. We thought that we couldn't achieve that because of the current makeup of the Israeli government, *so we gave up*." (emphasis added). As well, the official confessed, only after the negotiations broke down did the US government realize that Netanyahu's plans for building new homes for the settlers was "also about expropriating land on a large scale."[86]

Evidently, the Americans were also surprised, somehow, by Netanyahu's position on negotiating with the Palestinians. When the American official was asked by Barnea, "Were you surprised when you discovered that the Israelis don't really care what happens in the negotiations?" He answered, "Yes, we were surprised. It surprised us all along the way."

The Security Issues. Kerry's draft stated that there would be a "full and final" Israeli withdrawal from the territory allotted to the Palestinian state, but it would be phased and gradual. However, rather than setting out an explicit timetable, the Kerry plan said only that the timetable would be negotiated by the two sides. In effect, then, Israel was given a veto on when and where it would remove its military forces. Given Netanyahu's views, it was entirely predictable that he would insist the Israeli forces would indefinitely remain—at the least—in the Jordan River Valley and on the

Palestinian state's border with Jordan. Barnea's analysis was blunt: "Israel demanded complete control over the territories. This told the Palestinians that nothing was going to change. . . . Israel was not willing to agree to time frames—its control of the West Bank would continue forever."[87]

Refugees. Here the Kerry proposals mostly mirrored the previous compromises: there would be no right of return to Israel, only resettlement in the Palestinian state or elsewhere. Kerry was dismissive of Palestinian rights: "The establishment of an independent Palestinian state will provide a national homeland for all Palestinians, including the refugees, and thereby bring an end to the historic Palestinian refugee issue and the assertion of any claims against Israel arising from it." As in previous proposals, some might be admitted on a humanitarian basis, but Kerry's language made it absolutely clear that Israel would not be required to admit *any.* The matter would "be decided by Israel, without obligation, at its sole discretion."[88]

Jerusalem. In an initial draft, the Kerry plan followed the Clinton Parameters in stipulating that a final peace accord would have "to provide for both Israel and Palestine to have their internationally recognized capitals in Jerusalem, with East Jerusalem serving as the Palestinian capital."[89] However, the US proposal postponed until later negotiations the crucial issues of the status of the Old City, sovereignty on the Temple Mount/Haram, and the Jewish settlements in East Jerusalem. When Netanyahu predictably rejected even that formulation, Kerry backed away, in the end merely describing the disagreements and blandly noting that "Israel seeks to have the city of Jerusalem internationally recognized as its capital and the Palestinians seek to have East Jerusalem as the capital of their state."[90]

Prisoner Releases. During the negotiating process, Kerry told the Palestinians that Netanyahu had agreed to a mutual exchange of prisoners. However, Netanyahu failed to fully comply, so the Palestinians demanded that Kerry make good on what he had promised, However, Barnea wrote, "Netanyahu [now] demanded something in return. Kerry persuaded Obama to give him Pollard."

That was Jonathan Pollard, an American government intelligence analyst who was serving a life sentence for passing highly sensitive top-secret documents to Israel, some or all of which were thought to have found their way to the Soviet Union. Pollard had been "controlled" by a high Israeli intelligence officer, and after his conviction he had been awarded Israeli citizenship. When it became known that Obama was considering pardoning Pollard, a number of active and retired high-level officials, including Vice-President Joe Biden, were outraged, leading Obama to cancel the deal.[91]

The Jewish State Demand. Netanyahu was now demanding that the PA recognize Israel as a "Jewish state," not just as part of a final deal but as a precondition for even entering into negotiations. The senior US official told Barnea:

> Abbas refused to recognize Israel as a Jewish state. We couldn't understand why it bothered him so much. For us, the Americans, the Jewish identity

> of Israel is obvious. We wanted to believe that for the Palestinians this was a tactical move—they wanted to get something (in return) and that's why they were saying "no." The more Israel hardened its demands, the more the Palestinian refusal deepened. . . . They suspected there was an effort to get from them approval of the Zionist narrative.[92]

Obviously.

In February 2014, Kerry presented his proposed plan to Abbas. *Haaretz* described the outcome: "When Kerry presented this kind of formula to Abbas, the Palestinian leader became visibly angry, saying he could not put his signature on such a document, according to former US officials."[93] Kerry was said to be "stunned" at the reaction.[94] Likewise, Obama was said to have been "disappointed and frustrated" by Abbas's reaction: "Obama asked Abbas to 'see the big picture' instead of squabbling about this or that detail."[95]

Elgindy explains that Abbas's "non-response" was partly because of his weak domestic political position and partly because he "had reason to doubt Obama's ability to bring Netanyahu on board for the more difficult issues later on." He then quotes Ben Rhodes, one of Obama's closest foreign policy advisors, on the Netanyahu government: "They used us as cover, to make it look like they were in a peace process. They were running a play, killing time, waiting out the administration." Elgindy comments: "Rhodes's revelation seemed to vindicate Abbas's silence in response to Kerry's framework; if even American officials felt they were being played by Netanyahu, why should the Palestinians gamble everything on their ability to get concessions out of the Israeli leader?"[96]

Actually, Abbas continued to make concessions. The American official described them:

> He agreed to a demilitarized state; he agreed to the border outline so 80 percent of settlers would continue living in Israeli territory; he agreed for Israel to keep security sensitive areas (mostly in the Jordan Valley) for five years, and then the United States would take over. . . . He also agreed that the Jewish neighborhoods in East Jerusalem would remain under Israeli sovereignty, and agreed that the return of Palestinians to Israel would depend on Israeli willingness. "Israel won't be flooded with refugees," he promised.[97]

However, Abbas would not make any additional concessions until Israel agreed to specified and fair borders, a timetable for evacuating its forces from the Palestinian territories, and above all, agreement that East Jerusalem would be the capital of the Palestinian state.

Netanyahu rejected all Abbas's conditions, later stating that "I never agreed to return to '67 lines, I never agreed to recognize the right of return and I never agreed to forgo our presence in the Jordan Valley. Never."[98] On the eve of his reelection in March 2015 Netanyahu said that "there would be no Palestinian state on my watch."[99]

In his account of the Kerry negotiations, Barnea concluded: "The last chapter of the American initiative was borderline pathetic." An even harsher judgment might well have been warranted. How was it possible for the Obama administration not to realize that Abbas could never agree to the plan's wholesale retreat from the previous compromise plans? Or that Abbas would agree to the kind of "state" that Netanyahu had in mind? Or that he would accept Netanyahu's demand that East Jerusalem remain under Israeli rule?

Some critics, frustrated by the ineptness of the Kerry mission, correctly argued that there had been no chance of moving Netanyahu unless Kerry had delivered a serious ultimatum: either end the occupation and agree to a two-state settlement or forfeit US support. The problem, however, is that there was no chance that Congress would support such action.

Moreover, it is far from obvious that Israel would have had no choice but to bow to such a US ultimatum—then or now. By the early 2000s, Israel was no longer dependent on US support—as opposed to being happy to accept it, so long as it was unconditional. Even in the all but unimaginable circumstance that Netanyahu had been willing to order a withdrawal of the settlers and military forces from the occupied territories and agree to a viable Palestinian state, with sovereignty over East Jerusalem, he would have faced a revolt, quite possibly a violent revolt, from the settlers and their supporters. Indeed, a number of Israeli analysts feared that even the armed forces, in which settlers and right-wing religious forces were becoming increasingly strong, would refuse to obey such orders.

In light of Netanyahu's known views and the swing to the right of the Israeli public, it is at least as likely that rather than acceding to serious US pressures, the Israelis would conclude that since the whole world was against them anyway, they could do whatever they wished, and to hell with them all. As Ben-Gurion had said: "What matters is not what the goyim say, but what the Jews do." In that frame of mind, what Israel might do, especially in the face of continued Palestinian resistance to the occupation, might be even more violent, morally insupportable, and potentially more dangerous to Middle East peace than what it was already doing.

Under these circumstances, then, perhaps Obama faced an intractable dilemma: if he had sought to engage in the only kind of pressure that had even a chance of working he could not have gotten the necessary legislative approval and at the same time would have jeopardized the chances of getting his domestic programs through a Congress that was controlled by the increasingly "pro-Israel" Republican Party during most of his presidency. Indeed, a number of Democrats would also have been outraged at serious pressures on Israel and might well have joined with the Republicans in holding Obama's domestic policies hostage against such a course of action.

In addition to undercutting Obama's domestic program, pressures on Israel could well have put at risk congressional support for the 2015 US-Iranian agreement over the Iranian nuclear program. In these circumstances, it was understandable that Obama was unwilling to engage in a quixotic and possibly dangerous quest to force Israel to agree to a compromise peace with the Palestinians. Indeed, in 2016, despite Netanyahu's fervent opposition to US policy on Iran, Obama agreed to a ten-year, $38 billion military assistance program to Israel, one of the largest such programs in US history.[100]

So, the president's predicament was real. It is plausible that under the circumstances, Obama was willing to let Kerry see what he could do, but without committing himself to confronting either Israel or Congress in the event his secretary of state failed. Robert Malley, a member of Obama's White House staff during the period, put it this way: "I believe President Obama felt that if the parties were not going to move, and if he could not take the kinds of decisions that would make them move, it was better to do nothing than to perpetuate the illusion that the peace process would lead to peace."[101]

Even so, the administration, in particular John Kerry, at least might have avoided the inconsistencies, the odd proposals, and even the sheer ineptness that characterized some of their rhetoric and policies. The stage was now set for the final abandonment by the Trump administration of a constructive US role in a meaningful Israeli-Palestinian "peace process."

19

The Arab-Israeli and Israeli-Palestinian Conflicts in the Netanyahu/Trump Era, 2017–20

Throughout his political career, Netanyahu has opposed the creation of a Palestinian state: "The Arabs have twenty-two states," he often argued. "They don't need another one." That's like saying to a separatist movement in Europe—say, the Welsh nationalist movement in the United Kingdom—"The Europeans have fifty-one states. They don't need another one."

The West Bank

Ever since Israel captured the West Bank in the 1967 war, its annexation by Israel has been under consideration in Israeli political discourse. In July 1947, Yigal Allon, perhaps the most prominent Israeli general during the 1948 war and later a government minister and high Labor Party official, proposed annexation of the West Bank, in what came to be known as "the Allon Plan." Though never adopted as government policy, the Allon Plan has played a major role in Israeli annexationist sentiment—"an unchanging way of thinking over the years," wrote Shaul Arieli, one of Israel's leading experts on the Israeli-Palestinian conflict.[1]

Until 2019, Netanyahu deflected pressures from the Israeli right wing to annex the West Bank, which would have put a definitive end to the two-state solution. Whether it reflected his own views or his efforts to solidify his alliance with the right wing, during the April 2019 election campaign Netanyahu announced that if reelected he would start annexing much of the West Bank.[2]

Even before Netanyahu began talking about official annexation of the West Bank, he had returned to the traditional Israeli policies of "transfer," though not labeling them as such. Although certainly less violent than the Nakba, as described in the Israeli press Netanyahu's version of transfer sought to expel Palestinians from East Jerusalem, from the expanded "Greater Jerusalem" region, and from "Area C," covering most of the West Bank. The methods included home demolitions as well as preventing the Palestine Authority from constructing new homes, laying new water and electrical lines, building sewage purification facilities, paving roads, or building schools. In addition, in the areas he sought for settlement expansion or annexation, Netanyahu severely limited Palestinian access to fresh water for both drinking and irrigation purposes, and the Israeli Defense Forces or border police tolerated or even sometimes collaborated with settler violence against their Palestinian neighbors and their orchards.[3]

In April 2019, a major analysis clearly based on discussions with the Netanyahu administration concluded that Netanyahu's goal was Israeli control, with or without formal annexation, of about 60 percent of the West Bank, containing all of the Jewish settlements, the Jordan River Valley and the nearby mountainous area, Jerusalem and its surroundings, corridors of territory linking these areas, and the West Bank's main water aquifer, supplying about 40 percent of Israel's drinking water.[4]

In a July 2019 speech at an Israeli settlement in the West Bank, Netanyahu said that his policies were based on several "principles": the West Bank is "our homeland," no settlements would ever be uprooted, Israel would continue to build and develop them, and "Israeli military security forces will continue to rule the entire territory."[5] Since then, Netanyahu has continued the de facto "creeping annexation" process in the West Bank, especially in the Jordan River Valley.

At least until recently, there was no Israeli consensus on the need to formally annex the Jordan River Valley, as opposed to simply regarding it as Israel's "security border," even as it continues to be under nominal Palestinian sovereignty. As well, at the time of this writing (May 2020) there was no strong demand for annexation of the West Bank from the Israeli public; on the contrary; according to a March 2019 poll, only 42 percent of Israelis supported annexation of the West Bank,[6] and a January 2020 poll found that almost half of Jewish Israelis remained opposed.[7]

Perhaps more importantly, serious opposition to formal annexation has developed in Israel, especially from its security establishment. In October 2018 the "Commanders for Israel's Security"—a group including some 220 retired generals and high-ranking members of the Mossad and Shin Bet—warned that even partial annexation could lead to the end of the Palestinian Authority and its security cooperation with Israel, the necessity for a military occupation of the entire West Bank, and the absorption of its 2.6 million Palestinian inhabitants. If that should occur, "the damage to Israel's interests in the security, diplomatic, economic, legal, and domestic spheres will be unprecedented."[8] In April 2020 the Commanders reiterated their opposition to annexation, saying that it could "jeopardize the peace treaty and security cooperation with Jordan, coordination with the Palestinian security forces, and the very Jewish character of the state."[9]

In the United States, there also has been growing opposition to formal Israeli annexation of the West Bank, despite Secretary of State Mike Pompeo's statement that annexing part of the West Bank was "ultimately Israel's decision to make."[10] In

December 2019, the House of Representatives approved a resolution advocating a two-state settlement and expressing opposition to "the unilateral annexation of territory." In particular, even strong supporters of Israel who previously had voiced little or no criticism of the Israeli occupation voted for the resolution.[11] Even Republican stalwarts, like Senator Lindsey Graham, said that they opposed Israeli annexation of the West Bank.

Since 2004, except for incidents in which individual Palestinians have attacked Israelis, the West Bank has been largely quiet, in good part because President Mahmoud Abbas and the PA decided to put down Palestinian terrorism before it undermined any remaining possibility of a two-state solution. As a result, Palestinian security forces, effectively as much under the direction of the Israeli army and intelligence officials as the direction of the PA, have largely ended West Bank terrorism.[12]

As of early 2020, there were some 400,000 Jewish settlers in the West Bank, principally in Area C—where they actually outnumber the Palestinian residents—as well as another 200,000 in East Jerusalem; these numbers will increase as Netanyahu continues to construct housing for many thousands more. In particular, largely because of security concerns over "an invasion from the East," all Israeli governments since the 1967 war have sought to depopulate the Jordan River Valley of its Palestinians. Evidently today's transfer methods are working, for the Palestinian population in the region has declined from 250,000 before 1967 to some 50,000 today—and by some estimates, considerably less.

Elsewhere in the West Bank, and despite the PA's security cooperation with Israel, Netanyahu and the Trump administration have increased economic pressures on the PA in an effort to further undermine its chances of forming the nucleus of an independent state. Among such measures have been major cuts in American aid to the Palestinians and Netanyahu's freeze on the Oslo-mandated tax transfers to the PA, supposedly as punishment for PA subsidies to the families of Palestinian "terrorists" in Israeli prisons.[13]

Gaza

In 2015, a UN study predicted that by 2020 Gaza would become "unfit for human habitation." It attributed the process of "de-development," as it called it, to the continuing Israeli economic blockade and the lasting consequences of Israel's three major military attacks on Gaza since 2009, the last of which (Operation Protective Edge in 2014) had "effectively eliminated what was left of the middle class, sending almost all the population into destitution and dependence on international humanitarian aid."[14]

Since the UN and other reports, the Netanyahu government, fearful that a total economic collapse would force Israel to reoccupy Gaza—a prospect opposed by the armed forces and intelligence services—has allowed increased international economic assistance (principally from Qatar) to reach Gaza, and from time to time has eased the blockade to allow external humanitarian aid, to provide fuel for Gazan industries, and to expand the zone off Gaza in which Gazan fishermen can ply their trade.[15]

On the other hand, during periods in which tensions with Hamas or, more often, Islamic Jihad have increased, Israel again clamped down. As a result, Gazan poverty continues to be extreme. In terms of 2011 purchasing power, 46 percent of Gazans live on $5.50 a day and unemployment is among the highest in the world—the rate is at least 40 percent among young people.[16] Beyond that, electricity is often scarce and unreliable; unpolluted fresh water sources are declining, with an estimated 95 percent of the available water unsafe to drink; raw sewage flows into the ocean, devastating the fishing industry, one of Gaza's most important sources of food and income; and the medical situation is deteriorating as drugs are in short supply, hospitals are closing, and doctors and other professionals are leaving in what has been termed "a massive brain drain or human capital flight."[17]

The Netanyahu administration continues to claim that a continuing economic blockade is necessary to deter terrorism. Aside from the probability that deliberate impoverization creates as much terrorism as it deters, it is clear that the blockade or siege also has other goals: to keep Hamas dependent on occasional Israeli forbearance and to maintain Israel's effective control over Gaza—but without the need for a major war and a possible military occupation of the area.

Israel, then, wants to avert a total collapse of the Gazan economy. As a result, the Israeli army and intelligence services are increasingly in favor of easing the economic blockade; in June 2018, *Haaretz* reported that "senior military officers have asserted repeatedly that the dangerous situation in Gaza stems first and foremost from the ignominious poverty, severe unemployment, terrible overcrowding, and lack of basic services. All of these are generating frustration and rage among the residents. . . . Hamas is in distress and cannot cope with the economic burden of running the Strip."[18]

A year later it was reported that "the Shin Bet continues to support easing of the blockade; even the prime minister recognizes the need for at least an economic solution that will reduce the potential threat from Gaza, and was persuaded to allow an influx of millions of dollars to Gaza."[19] And as of the end of 2019, the IDF was continuing to support a deal on Gaza that would improve its economy and lessen the risks of Hamas attacks against Israel.[20]

Perhaps most importantly, Netanyahu wants to make Gaza's separation from the West Bank permanent, thereby making a two-state settlement even more unattainable. To this end, the Netanyahu government as well as leading military officials have evidently concluded that so long as Hamas ends attacks on Israel from Gaza, Israel should not let it collapse.[21] On the other hand, Israel increases its economic pressures against both Hamas and the PA in the West Bank whenever they may be close to reconciling, which would strengthen their political position should serious negotiations with Israel take place. And as long as the Palestinians remain divided, Israel can continue to claim there's no one who can speak for all of them, therefore no one with whom to negotiate.

If that sounds like an updated version of Catch-22, that's because it is.

Hamas Today

In view of the recent changes in Israeli policies toward Hamas, it is evident that a significant, if limited, convergence of interests between the two sides has emerged: Hamas cannot achieve its practical goals of ending the military attacks and economic blockade, of consolidating its power over Gaza, and of remaining independent of the PA in the West Bank until it ends all attacks on Israel from Gaza and definitively and unambiguously gives up hope of "liberating" all Palestine from Israel.

Hamas leaders have often publicly stated that they want no new wars with Israel. For example, following a brief exchange of fire, Yahya Sinwar, the main Hamas leader in Gaza, called for a ceasefire with Israel that could lead to "a historic opportunity for change. . . . A new war is in no one's interest, certainly not our interest. Who really wants to confront a nuclear superpower with four slingshots? War doesn't achieve anything."[22] In November 2019, a *Haaretz* commentator wrote: "In April 2018, Sinwar made what now seems a strategic decision to stop launching rockets at Israel and not respond militarily [to Israeli attacks]."[23]

As a result, there have been no major armed conflicts between Israel and Hamas in the last few years. In August 2018, *Haaretz*'s military correspondent wrote:

> Israel is not looking for a war in the Strip. Israel's political leadership is concerned about the consequences of sending infantry and tank divisions into the heart of a densely populated area in Gaza and is bothered by projections over losses among its forces, asking itself if at the end of such a war, the situation would necessarily be better than it is now. . . . [As well] the IDF has long stated that there is no military solution to the Gaza problem.[24]

Israeli leaders have sometimes explicitly acknowledged Hamas's efforts to avoid a new war, as when in 2016 Defense Minister Moshe Ya'alon said that since the Israeli attack on Gaza in 2014, Hamas had "not fired a single rocket, nor even a single bullet" from Gaza and that the few rockets that had been fired were sent by small Palestinian factions.[25] To be sure, since then there have been military clashes between Israel and Hamas, but they have been relatively brief and followed by periods of calm, as neither side has sought an escalation.

Potentially the greatest danger of a prolonged armed clash that neither Israel nor Hamas wants would be an escalation of the periodic border clashes between Gazan protest marchers and Israeli soldiers. Since late 2018, following Israeli refusals to implement tentative agreements with Hamas to ease the blockade, Hamas has sometimes allowed mostly unarmed Gazan protesters to advance toward the fence separating Gaza from Israel; some of them sought to breach the fence separating Gaza from southern Israel or sent incendiary balloons across the border, leading Israeli snipers to kill or wound hundreds. However, when things have threatened to get out of hand and risk another full-scale Israeli attack on Gaza, Hamas has quickly clamped down on the protesters and confiscated their weapons. Indeed, it even issued a religious fatwa prohibiting any individual armed attacks on Israel, *including on its soldiers*.[26] As a result, as of May 2020 the border had been quiet for a number of months; a high Israeli official told a *Haaretz* columnist that the quiet was a result of "a silent agreement between Israel and Hamas and Islamic Jihad . . . to maintain it."[27]

Hamas's New Charter

Hamas clearly has recognized the need to moderate not only its practical goals and behavior but also its ideology. As early as 2009, Hamas began moving away from its 1988 Charter, which was openly anti-Semitic and called for the violent destruction of Israel. In May of that year, Hamas leader Khaled Meshal said that the charter should be ignored because circumstances had changed. "We are shaped by our experiences," he said, clearly implying that the extremist Hamas goals were unattainable and now irrelevant.[28]

In the next few years Meshal and other Hamas leaders reiterated that the charter no longer described the practical goals of the organization. Finally, in May 2017 the more pragmatic Hamas leaders overcame the opposition of the hardliners and a new charter was issued. There were still ambiguities and apparent inconsistencies, but there was a clear change: the new charter downplayed the religious fundamentalism of the original one, dropped the anti-Semitic language, and stated that the Islamist movement was not at war with the Jewish people but only with "Zionism" and the Israeli occupation of Palestine.

Most importantly, while continuing to assert that it would not recognize the "Zionist entity," that "armed struggle" for the liberation of all Palestine remained "a legitimate right and duty," and that the Palestinian people had the right to return to Israel, Hamas again suggested that it could accept a two-state settlement. The key passage stated:

> Hamas considers the establishment of a fully sovereign and independent Palestinian state, with Jerusalem as its capital *along the lines of the 4th of June 1967* [emphasis added], with the return of the refugees and the displaced

> to their homes from which they were expelled, to be a formula of national consensus.[29]

Still, ambiguities remain: on the one hand Hamas seems to accept an Israel that returns to its pre-1967 war boundaries—that is, a two-state solution—but on the other hand, it continues to demand the right of the refugees to return to their original homes inside Israel. That doesn't cohere; however, an Israeli government seriously interested in a political settlement would have treated the new charter, as well as other indications of moderating Hamas policies, as the basis for exploratory talks.

Hardly surprisingly, though, Netanyahu immediately tore up a copy of the new charter in front of television cameras, while his spokesman said that "Hamas is attempting to fool the world, but it will not succeed."

During the last year, reports have claimed that Israel and Hamas are on the verge of a deal, negotiated with Egyptian mediation, in which Hamas will end all military attacks from Gaza and Israel will ease—though not end—its economic pressures and allow increased international economic support, principally from the oil-rich Persian Gulf states, to flow into Gaza.[30] In particular, Israeli military and security leaders continue to see Hamas as a stabilizing factor in Gaza, especially because of its strong opposition to Islamic Jihad. Consequently, they now favor agreeing to the Hamas proposals for a long-term truce and substantially easing the Israeli economic blockade.[31] So far, though, the deal has not materialized, reportedly because the Netanyahu government has only partially, and inconsistently, moved in that direction, presumably because of both ideological and electoral considerations.[32]

If such a deal should be reached and a long-term or even a permanent truce is negotiated in Gaza, it actually would be a further blow to an overall Israeli-Palestinian peace settlement: it would leave the West Bank and the PA out in the cold, as intended by both Hamas and the Netanyahu government. For that reason, and because of other political conflicts between Hamas and the PLO, Mahmoud Abbas and other PA leaders have been strongly opposed to a limited deal that leaves Hamas, tacitly backed by Israel, in power in Gaza.

In some ways Israeli policies toward the Islamic movements in the occupied territories have come full circle. From the 1960s through the late 1980s Israeli governments often tolerated and sometimes even helped Palestinian Islamic movements, rather than deal with the more moderate Palestinian nationalists led by Arafat and the PLO. A number of Israeli scholars, journalists, and former officials have discussed the matter. As quoted earlier, a high Israeli official who implemented these policies later admitted: "Hamas, to my great regret, is Israel's creation. . . . Instead of trying to curb Gaza's Islamists from the outset . . . Israel for years tolerated and, in some cases, encouraged them as a counterweight to the secular nationalists."[33]

Consider the irony, if not the perversity, of Israel's policies. In order to kill any chances for a two-state settlement, Israel today is more willing to negotiate with Hamas than with the PA: in effect, then, it favors a group with a history of violence and religious fundamentalism whose willingness to support a formal two-state settlement is at best lukewarm, rather than to compromise with the far more secular and moderate Abbas and the PA, whose long-held and repeatedly demonstrated commitment to nonviolence and compromise is not open to question.

Even before the Trump Plan, Netanyahu had almost certainly killed the chances of a genuine two-state settlement. Ten years ago, various polls found that up to two-thirds of both the Israeli and Palestinian publics supported such a settlement (depending on how the question was asked), but in June 2018 a new poll found that less than half of the relevant publics did so.[34] And in March 2019 another poll found that only 34 percent of the Israeli public supported the two-state solution, whereas 42 percent favored partial or complete annexation of the West Bank.[35]

As a result, during the 2019 and 2020 Israeli electoral campaigns none of the significant political parties called for an end to the Israeli occupation and peace negotiations with either the PA or Hamas. If anything, the future looks even bleaker, as post-election surveys and analyses found that the younger generation of Israeli voters were far more likely to support Netanyahu than were their elders: voters from eighteen to twenty-four years old preferred Netanyahu to his main opponent, former IDF chief Benny Gantz (himself hardly a dove) by the astonishing margin of 65 percent to 16 percent.[36]

For many years—and even more so today—despairing Israeli liberals have hoped that pressures from the "international community" could force changes in Israeli policy. Even if such pressures had materialized, though, they might well have resulted in even more hard-line attitudes and policies. In any case, the issue is moot, for where would such pressures come from?

The Arab World

Not from the Arab world. Even in the early stages of the Israeli-Palestinian conflict, from the mid-1930s to the 1960s, most of the Arab states subordinated the Palestinians to their own goals.[37] Today, none of the leading Arab states have the interest or capacity to pressure Israel to agree to a two-state settlement, whether because of lack of interest in the fate of the Palestinians or even outright hostility to them, as well as because of their unwillingness to cross Israel and the United States.[38] More specifically, consider the position of the leading Arab states:

Egypt. Egyptian governments have never been willing to commit to a Palestinian state, choosing to give priority to ending their bilateral conflict with Israel. In addition, today Egypt is engaged in an ongoing struggle with local Islamic radicals, as a result of which it is openly collaborating with Israel's punitive economic measures against Hamas to ensure that it remains too weak to assist its Egyptian counterparts. In particular, the military dictatorship of Abdel Fattah el-Sisi is supporting the Israeli siege of Gaza by its tight controls over the goods it allows Hamas to import and export over its Sinai border with Gaza; in January 2019, el-Sisi confirmed that Egypt and Israel now had a wide range of military cooperation.[39]

Jordan. Recently tensions between Israel and Jordan have been growing, among other reasons because of the indications that the Netanyahu government is still considering annexing the Jordan River Valley, which King Abdullah fears would lead to an influx of unwanted Palestinians into his country. Still, all indications are that—as in the case of Egypt—Jordan has no intention of jeopardizing its peace treaty with Israel and risking a crushing military defeat. Moreover, Abdullah has his own reasons to oppose Islamic fundamentalism, which if it took root in Jordan would almost certainly spell the end of the Hashemite monarchy.

Syria. The Assad regime is occupied with the civil war, and even if, as seems likely, it regains full control, almost certainly it will continue its decades-long policies of avoiding war with a far stronger Israel. Indeed, even Israel's annexation of the Golan Heights led to no Syrian military response: if the loss of its own territory did not cause it to confront Israel, then certainly the plight of the Palestinians will not do so.

Saudi Arabia and the Gulf States. The conservative autocracies that rule these states fear Iranian expansionism and revolutionary messianism as well as Hamas and Hezbollah Islamic fundamentalism. As a result, they not only have no interest in taking on Israel over the Palestinian cause, they are increasingly close to a de facto political and military alliance with the Jewish state over "the common threat of Iran."[40]

As a result of these developments in the Arab world, "for the most part, the Palestinian issue has fallen off the agenda."[41] Or worse: Muhammad Shehada, a Palestinian columnist for *Haaretz*, writes that during a brief clash between Israel and Hezbollah forces in Lebanon, over Hezbollah's military collaboration with Iran, "for the first time in the Israeli-Arab conflict, significant Arab officials (and mouthpieces for Arab regimes) openly and unabashedly took Israel's side over their fellow Arabs, while others fell silent. One word has changed it all: Iran."[42]

The West

The countries of Western Europe, in the past much more critical than the United States of Israeli policies, have given up seriously pressing for a two-state settlement, in part because they recognize the futility of doing so, in part because of their unwillingness to confront both Netanyahu and Trump, and in part because their increasingly powerful internal right-wing political competitors are "pro-Israel."

The plight of the BDS (Boycott, Divestment, and Sanctions) movement, once widely considered to have real potential for exerting serious pressures on Israel, illustrates the futility of relying on outsiders to force Israel to agree to a two-state settlement. Founded in 2005 by Palestinian intellectuals and initially attracting support around the world, BDS called on businesses, universities, civic bodies, and international institutions to boycott, divest from, or impose sanctions on Israel until it ended the occupation, recognized and protected the rights of the Israeli Arabs to full equality, and agreed to the Palestinian refugee right to return to their pre-1948 homes and properties.[43]

However, even many critics of Israeli policies balked at the demand for a full right of return, which had no chance of being implemented and drove away many who otherwise would have supported it. For example, Noam Chomsky, one of the most prominent early supporters of outside pressures on Israel, wrote that while there was "near-universal international support" for a two-state settlement, "there is virtually no meaningful support" for the right of return,[44] let alone the end of Israel as a Jewish state, which is implied by an unlimited right of Palestinian return.

As a result, after some initial enthusiasm by critics of Israel, including Israeli dissidents, the BDS movement has had little success. As early as 2016, the signs were emerging: "No reduction in aid to Israel or in commercial cooperation is on the agenda in either the European Union or the United States. Even the EU's decision to label products from the settlements isn't really causing damage.... Last year, foreign investment in Israel totaled some $285 billion, three times its level in 2005, the year the BDS movement began operations."[45]

That trend has continued, and today BDS has little significant support in either the Arab or the Western world. Indeed, in what might be a final blow to its relevance, in May 2019 the German parliament resolved to not cooperate with BDS, which it termed "anti-Semitic."[46]

Trump and Israel

Since the 2016 election of Donald Trump, the US government no longer is seeking or even supporting a two-state solution; it simply supports what Netanyahu and the Israeli right wing want.

Since he became president in January 2017, Trump has taken the following actions:

- Appointed David Friedman as ambassador to Israel, Jason Greenblatt as Middle East advisor, and Jared Kushner as his senior NSC advisor; behind the scenes the billionaire Sheldon Adelson is reported to be highly influential. All were far right wingers with no diplomatic or foreign policy experience and no claim to expertise in the Middle East; moreover they were increasingly at odds with the changing views of much of the American Jewish community.

- Broken with seventy years of American foreign policy and defied nearly the entire international community by moving the US embassy from Tel Aviv to Jerusalem and officially recognizing the city as Israel's "undivided" capital—thereby effectively denying the Palestinians the right to establish their capital in East Jerusalem. That step alone makes a two-state settlement impossible.
- Closed the PLO's offices in Washington and the US consulate in Jerusalem, which had functioned as an unofficial diplomatic mission to the Palestinians, thereby eliminating almost all negotiations with the PLO.
- Supported the Netanyahu government's official annexation of the Golan Heights, which almost certainly has made impossible a future Israeli-Syrian peace treaty.
- Ended all US economic assistance to the Palestinians in both the West Bank and Gaza, including its programs that had annually provided $200 million support for Palestinian development projects in the West Bank and $25 million for East Jerusalem hospitals. In addition, the administration cut off all US funding for the UN Relief and Works Agency (UNRWA), the main UN agency for economic and social assistance to the impoverished Palestinians.[47]
- Rejected for the first time the overwhelming consensus in the UN and among international law experts that the Israeli occupation of the West Bank is illegal and that Israel had no legal right to build settlements there. The State Department dropped the term "occupied" from its longtime description of the status of the West Bank, and the administration announced in November 2019 that the US government no longer considered the Israeli settlements to be illegal.[48] A number of Israeli analysts pointed out that the American declaration could open the door to Israeli annexation of its West Bank settlements.[49]

The Trump Plan

On January 28, 2020, the long-expected "Trump Peace Plan" was announced.[50] Under its terms, the so-called deal of the century, Israel would be allowed to annex the Jordan River Valley and all of the West Bank's Jewish settlements—altogether some 30 percent of the entire territory. The Palestinians, for their part, would receive a "state" comprising non-contiguous separated enclaves in the rest of the West Bank, as well as some territory in the Negev desert, adjacent to the Gaza Strip, along Israel's southern border. The Palestinian leadership immediately rejected the plan, correctly charging that it was heavily biased in Israel's favor. The Trump Plan would be better described as the Netanyahu Plan.[51] In books and speeches over the last thirty years, Netanyahu has described his vision of a peace settlement with the Palestinians, beginning with his insistence that they must accept Israel as "the nation-state of the Jewish People"[52]—that is, not merely "a Jewish state." (The difference is significant, as discussed in Chapter 20.) The Trump Plan follows Netanyahu in stating, several times, that "the State of Israel has a legitimate desire to be the nation-state of the Jewish people and for that status to be recognized throughout the world."

Further, the plan adopts the patronizing, if not contemptuous, tone that Netanyahu and other Israeli rightists typically adopt toward the Palestinians. For example, the Trump Plan's architect, Jared Kushner, said: "They [the Palestinians] are proving through their reaction that they are not ready to have a state; the hope is that, over time, they can become capable of governing."

Worse, the plan dismisses established historical facts about the Israeli-Palestinian conflict. For example, it proclaims that the history of the conflict is irrelevant: "Reciting past narratives about the conflict is unproductive." However, since the plan adopts the Israeli mythologies throughout, what Trump and Netanyahu really mean is that the *Palestinian* "narrative," which in fact is far more persuasive than the Israeli one, is irrelevant.

Arguing that Israel's actions are always purely defensive, and that "Israel is not a threat to the region whatsoever," the plan dismisses the history of Israeli expansionism and military attacks on neighboring states. For example, it asserts that Syria and Lebanon are "extremely hostile" to Israel but fails to mention the history of major Israeli military attacks on those nations, or the seizure of their territories, such as the Golan Heights, which Israel has annexed. And on Iran, Trump echoes Netanyahu, asserting that Iran's missiles, especially if they carry nuclear warheads, are designed "to wipe the State of Israel off the map."[53] Furthermore, it is claimed, Iran seeks to "encircle" Israel, using Lebanon, Syria, and Gaza to establish a "land bridge" that "stretches from the Iran-Iraq border to the Mediterranean Sea."[54]

The plan repeatedly states that the West Bank and Gaza potentially pose "existential threats" to Israel's security and even its very existence. It cites missile attacks on Israel from those areas, without mentioning the Israeli occupation, economic siege, military attacks, and repeated assassinations as possible causes of those attacks.

The Trump Plan has a long section in which the United States pledges to create a $50 billion international fund (most of it from Arab countries and, according to a number of reports, none from the United States) for the economic, political, and social "development" of a new state of Palestine—all contingent, however, on full Palestinian compliance with a long list of US and Israeli conditions. Further ensuring that the economic component of Trump's proposal plan has no chance of Palestinian acceptance, the Trump Plan insists, in ridiculous detail, on the creation of a business-friendly capitalist economy that embodies right-wing Republican economics.

Trump's economic plan for Palestine therefore can be disregarded, so the focus should be on its political and military components.

Territory. "Israel needs defensive borders," the plan asserts, which requires further expansion into Palestinian lands and the annexation of all the Jewish settlements in the West Bank, even the most isolated ones deep in Palestinian territory. All past peace plans envisaged only, at most, Israeli annexation of its relatively large "settlement blocs" just over the 1967 borders, but not the small isolated Jewish settlements scattered throughout the rest of the West Bank.

In particular, except for the Palestinian city of Jericho, the plan supports the annexation of the Jordan River Valley, which Israel claims is essential to its security as the first line of defense against what it often calls "an invasion from the east," meaning a coalition of Iranian, Iraqi, and Syrian forces large enough to invade and conquer Israel. Aside from the extreme unlikelihood that such an Arab coalition could ever come into existence, the plan ignores the fact that Israel has hundreds of nuclear weapons, which have deterred even far less risky Arab intrusions into Israel.[55]

The plan also includes some "territorial swaps." As in past peace plans, as compensation for the Palestinians' loss of territory in the West Bank, some largely uninhabited Israeli territory in the Negev Desert close to the Gaza Strip will become part of the Palestinian state. In addition, another proposed "swap," contemplated in no previous peace plan but representing a long-held goal of Netanyahu and other prominent Israeli rightists, would remove a number of towns and villages in central Israel, containing some 200,000 Israeli Arabs, and "transfer" them into the projected Palestinian state. In effect, the "swap" is just a new form of Israeli transfer, with no provision for the affected population, most of them citizens of Israel, to reject the proposal and remain in place as Israeli citizens.[56]

The plan does not affect the major Palestinian cities and allows their towns and villages in the areas that will be annexed to Israel to remain in place, linked to each other by roads, railroads, or tunnels. However, they will be small islands or enclaves, completely surrounded by Israeli territory and under its military control: "Bantustans," as many Israeli critics term them. Israel would retain complete control of the air space over Palestine—the Palestinians would have no airport of their own—and Israel would continue its military control over the territorial waters near Gaza.

To be sure, the plan calls on Israel to allow the Palestinians the use of its ports at Haifa and Ashdod, but it leaves it to Israel to decide when, if, how, under what conditions, and for how long the Palestinians will actually be afforded that "privilege" (see Map 19.1).

Security. The Trump Plan is based on the premise that the Palestinians have no need for protection against foreign states, and certainly not from Israel. By contrast, the stated premise is that Israel's security has always been under attack and remains so today:

> The State of Israel suffers from extraordinary geographic and geostrategic challenges. Simply put the State of Israel has no margin for error. As dangerous as Gaza, run by Hamas, is to the State of Israel's security, a similar regime controlling the West Bank would pose an existential threat to the State of Israel.[57]

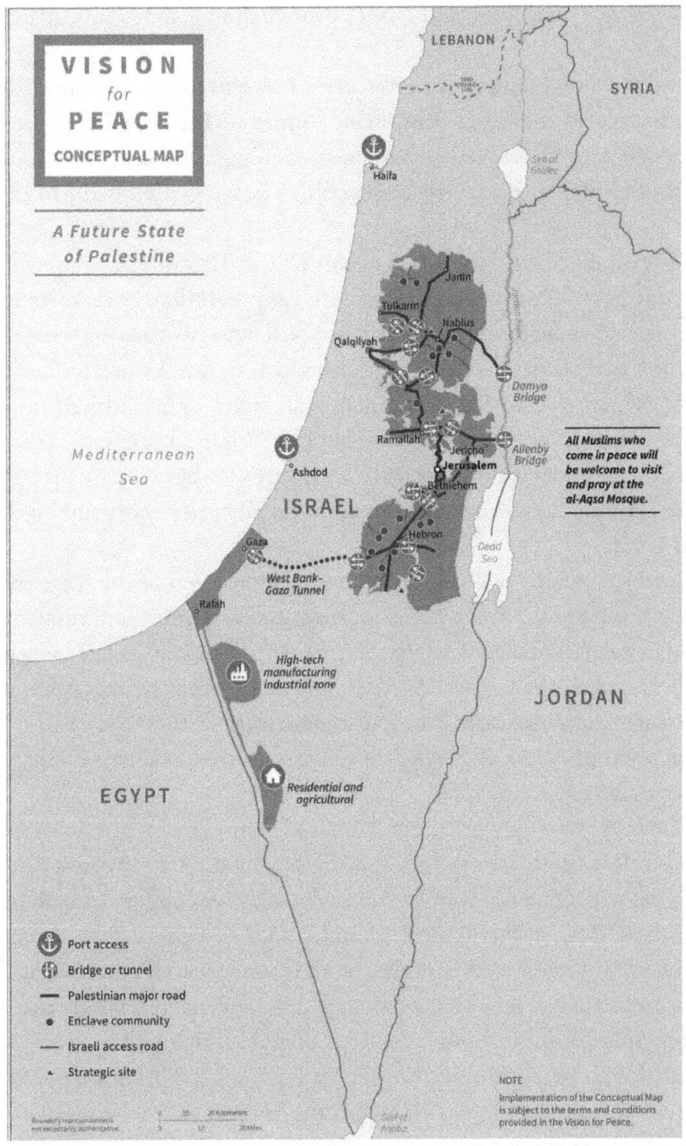

Map 19.1 "Vision for Peace Conceptual Map" of "A Future State of Palestine."

No analysis accompanies this assessment which, as I have argued, is wildly overstated, in light of the PA's long-held adherence to nonviolence in the West Bank, Israel's formal peace treaties with Egypt and Jordan, the clear decisions by Syria and Saudi Arabia to avoid threatening behavior toward Israel, the fragmentation of Iraq and its lack of capability or interest in threatening Israel, the remoteness of an "existential" threat from Iran, and Israel's overwhelming conventional and nuclear superiority.

Nonetheless, the Trump Plan gives carte blanche to any measures that Israel deems necessary to meet the Palestinian "threat": "The security portion of this Vision was developed based on our best understanding of the security" requirements of the State of Israel, as presented by successive Israeli governments to the United States."[58]

Key provisions of the security section of the Trump Plan require that the territory under Palestinian control will be fully demilitarized, so as to ensure Israel's "ironclad security. The Palestinians will have no army or heavy weapons and will not have control over its airspace or territorial waters. The only "security forces" allowed to the Palestinian state are a lightly armed military, essentially a police force sufficient to ensure its "internal security." And if Israel becomes dissatisfied with the "security" measures undertaken by the Palestinian authorities, it will have the right to restore its "security footprint" in the West Bank and Gaza.

Jerusalem. Jerusalem "will remain the sovereign capital of the State of Israel."[59] While religious freedom for all faiths must continue, politically Jerusalem will not be divided or even shared between Israel and the Palestinians, as had been proposed by the Clinton plan, the Geneva Accords, and every other serious peace proposal. The Palestinian state can have its capital principally in the small, run-down, and dangerous town of Abu Dis,[60] which it will be allowed to rename "Al Quds," the Arabic name for Jerusalem.

Described as an East Jerusalem "suburb," Abu Dis is not even physically connected to Jerusalem, from which it is divided by the Israeli Wall or "separation barrier." Israel will retain full control and its declared sovereignty over all Jerusalem, including the Old City, the Temple Mount, and the Western Wall. As at present, a Muslim commission would continue to administer the Haram al Sharif and the Islamic mosques, where Israel has conceded "religious sovereignty" to the Muslims, even as it retains full control and indeed has often blocked Arab access to it.

In short, for all practical purposes the Palestinians will have no political rights in Jerusalem and their religious rights on the Haram will be subject to periodic closures and other restrictions.

Gaza. The Trump Plan states that "the people of Gaza have suffered for too long under the repressive rule of Hamas," and attributes the desperate plight of the Gazan people to their being "held hostage by Hamas, Palestinian Islamic Jihad (PIJ) and other terrorist organizations committed to Israel's destruction.[61] The plan blames Hamas for Gaza's massive unemployment, widespread poverty, and drastic shortages of electricity and potable water.

The dishonesty is breathtaking. There is no mention of the fact that Hamas came to power in 2006 as the result of free elections that the United States and the PLO tried to violently overturn; there is no mention of the continuing Israeli blockade or siege that began even before Hamas came to power and that has had devastating effects on the Palestinian people; there is no mention of the fact that with few minor exceptions, Hamas has sought long-term ceasefires and ended most of its own attacks on Israeli territory as well as actively sought to prevent Islamic Jihad attacks; and there is no mention of Hamas's efforts to get the Israeli government to end its siege in return for the end of Gazan attacks on Israel.

Refugees and the "Right of Return." According to the Trump Plan, "The Arab-Israeli conflict created both a Palestinian and Jewish refugee problem. Nearly the same number of Jews and Arabs were displaced by the Arab/Israeli conflict."[62] Therefore, its argument is that Israel has no legal or moral responsibility for the Palestinian refugees—it took care of its fellow Jews in its own country, so the Palestinians must also take care of their fellow Palestinians in their own country. Indeed, the plan says, not only the Palestinians but also the Israelis deserve compensation for the costs of absorbing refugees.

The alleged symmetry is false. It is true that many Jews left the Arab world and emigrated to Israel, but there was no Arab Nakba against their Jewish citizens: few were driven out or killed, and most left voluntarily because they became uncomfortable or fearful of the future or because they voluntarily chose to emigrate to a Jewish state. In fact, many emigrated not because they were pressured by Arab governments but because they were pressured by the *Israeli* government to do so, especially in Iraq.[63]

In any case, even if the Jews had been ruthlessly driven out of the Arab states, only those states would have a moral responsibility for compensation. But there is no serious dispute over the fact that the Israelis were responsible for the Nakba against the Palestinians.

Another problem with Trump's treatment of the refugee issue is truly startling. Every previous peace plan, even those rejecting a right of return of the Palestinians to Israel, had held that they had the right to return to a Palestinian state. However, the Trump Plan no longer provides even that right, for it states:

> *The rights of Palestinian refugees to immigrate to the State of Palestine shall be limited in accordance with agreed security arrangements....* The rate of movement of refugees from outside Gaza and the West Bank into the State of Palestine shall be agreed to by the parties and regulated by various factors, including economic forces and incentive structures, such that the rate of entry does not outpace or overwhelm the development of infrastructure and the economy of the State of Palestine, *or increased security risks to the State of Israel.*[64]

Palestinian Foreign Relations. The Palestinians are prohibited from joining in defense alliances with other states and may not join any international organization without

Israel's consent. In particular, the Palestinians are prohibited from bringing war crimes charges against Israel to the International Criminal Court.

Over the next four years, all the above conditions must be met to the satisfaction of Israel and, by clear implication, the United States. If not, Israel will have the right to "reverse the process," ending the Palestinian chances of gaining even the highly restricted "statehood" envisaged by the Trump-Netanyahu Plan.

How Should the Palestinians React?

Naturally enough, both the PA in the West Bank and Hamas in Gaza have angrily rejected the Trump Plan in its entirety, but they will be more alone than ever in their struggle for justice. The Netanyahu government, Israel's general population, and even Benny Gantz, Netanyahu's opponent in the March 2020 Israeli elections, announced their support for the Trump Plan, including the annexation at least of the Jordan River Valley.[65] Most European countries have, at most, expressed mild disapproval of the plan; the European Union actually stated that it welcomed Trump's efforts toward a "viable two-state solution."[66]

As for the Arab states, most of them clearly intend to largely ignore the Trump Plan. The Arab League confined itself to a brief statement calling the plan "unfair"; an Arab scholar described this statement as "purely formalistic, declarative, and insignificant."[67] Similarly a few states, like Jordan, have mildly criticized the plan but clearly intend to do nothing more. And others, including Saudi Arabia and the United Arab Emirates, have stated that they view the plan as a "serious initiative" that addresses the main issues.

With Europe and the Arab states remaining on the sidelines, radical changes in US policy are the only remaining Palestinian hope for serious outside pressures on Israel. The only prospect of new US policies rests on a Democratic sweep of the 2020 presidential and congressional elections—at the time of this writing, most polls show that some 60 to 70 percent of Democratic voters are disenchanted with Netanyahu's policies and an even larger number with those of Trump.[68] Even if such a sweep should occur, though, the likelihood that a new US government would seriously pressure Israel to reach a genuine two-state settlement with the Palestinians would be low, as would the likelihood that such pressure would overcome Israeli intransigence, at least for the foreseeable future.

In short, more than ever before, the Palestinians are all alone, and their plight is highly likely to get even worse. In that light, there may be a case for them to not simply dismiss the Trump Plan in its entirety. Moreover, if justice can ever be attained—or, more realistically, greater justice than now prevails—a change may be necessary in the goals and methods of the Palestinians. This issue is discussed in Chapter 20, Summary and Conclusions.

20

Summary and Conclusions

Note to Readers

The first section of this chapter summarizes the arguments of the book and the evidence that supports them. For those who have read through all the previous chapters, this summary may be too long and repetitious, so you may wish to skim or bypass it and go on to the second part ("Is There Any Solution?"), where I discuss possible solutions to the Israeli-Palestinian conflict. For those who have not read or only skimmed the main body, this summary is important—but please bear in mind that the detailed evidence on which the arguments of this book are based can only be found in the previous chapters.

Israeli Mythology

The Arab-Israeli and Israeli-Palestinian conflicts have led to many myths that have been decisively refuted by serious historical inquiry but are still widely believed, especially in Israel and the United States, with devastating consequences for the cause of peace. The most important of these is, "The Arabs never miss an opportunity to miss an opportunity," as Abba Eban famously put it in 1973.

Eban was wrong about the history of the conflict, wrong about the failure to settle it in the 1970s, and wrong in his often repeated assessment. The reality is closer to the converse. While the Arab states and the Palestinians have certainly contributed to the conflict, it is Israel—almost always supported by its key ally, the United States—that has been mostly responsible for the tragedy.

The main purpose of this book has been to examine this and other Israeli mythologies, not merely for the sake of historical truth but also because the conflict is unlikely to be settled as long the mythologies continue to prevail in Israel and the United States.

Since 1947, Israel has fought eight to ten wars against the Arab states and the Palestinians (depending on what counts as a "war" as opposed to lesser-scale "armed conflicts"). None of them, probably not even the 1948 war, was unavoidable. Israel's independence and security could have been protected had it accepted reasonable compromises on the four crucial issues: a partition of the historic land of Palestine; Palestinian independence and sovereignty in the land allotted to them in the 1947 UN partition plan, including Arab East Jerusalem; the return of most of the territory captured from the Arab states in the various wars; and a small-scale symbolic "return" to Israel of some 10,000 to 20,000 Palestinian refugees (or their descendants) from the 1948 war.

Throughout most of the conflict, all the key Arab states and the most important Palestinian leaders were, or soon became, willing to reach peace with Israel if it accepted these compromises. Had it done so, there would have been few if any wars, justice would have prevailed, and Israel's independence and security would have been greatly enhanced.

The Israeli Narrative

In the Israeli narrative, the stories the Israelis tell themselves to justify their policies and actions, the Arabs bear the responsibility for the Arab-Israeli and Israeli-Palestinian conflicts. Throughout history, the narrative holds, the Zionists in the pre-state era and then the Jewish state of Israel were willing to share or partition the historic land of Palestine. They agreed, it is said, to the 1937 Peel and the 1947 UN partition plans, but both were rejected by the Palestinians and the leading Arab states, who then launched a war of annihilation against the newly established state.

Despite the Arab attack and subsequent Palestinian terrorism, the narrative continues, after the war Israel continued to seek fair compromise settlements with the Arab states and the Palestinian people, but the Arabs refused to negotiate and provoked the later Arab-Israeli wars of 1956, 1967, and 1970–73, leaving Israel no choice—"Ein Breira," in the Hebrew phrase—but to defend itself. After their repeated defeats, Egypt and Jordan finally decided to reach peace settlements with Israel. However, the rest of the Arab world, particularly the Palestinians, continued to seek the destruction of the Jewish state, primarily by terrorist attacks against its homeland.

While there are some elements of truth in this narrative, most of it does not stand up to historical examination. This book undertakes that examination, and is divided into three general sections: on the origins and early years of the Arab-Israeli conflict, on the Arab-Israeli state conflict from 1948 through today, and on the Israeli-Palestinian conflict from 1917 through today.

In each chapter, the role of the United States is examined. The book begins with an overall analysis of US policies, focusing especially on the question of what accounts for the remarkable, often nearly unconditional US support for Israel. I argued that these policies are best explained by a number of factors, including (1) moral and religious values and beliefs ("the Judeo-Christian heritage") and pro-democracy; (2) public and elite opinion that is strongly "pro-Israeli"; (3) the evolution of perceived US strategic and national interests in the Middle East—the containment of the Soviet Union and "international communism" during the Cold War and resistance to Islamic expansionism and terrorism in the Middle East since then; and (4) the power of the "Israel lobby."

Because the last explanation has been the subject of much disagreement, I analyzed it in considerable detail, concluding that while the power of the lobby over Mideast policy is real and often unmistakably demonstrated, it can also be exaggerated, as has been shown by its defeat on some major issues.

In the final analysis, then, it is the convergence of a number of factors, all working in the same direction and not balanced by strong countervailing forces, that explains US policies toward the Arab-Israeli conflict since 1948 and through today.

Zionism and the Conflict

Zionism has played a strong role in the origins and perpetuation of the conflict. The central argument is that while there was clearly a strong reason for the creation of a Jewish state as a refuge against murderous anti-Semitism, which has occurred repeatedly throughout history, Zionist ideology was also based on weak and even intellectually indefensible arguments that still block the most promising possibilities for peaceful settlement of the Israeli-Palestinian conflict.

The first such argument was that the Jews had a permanent right to sovereignty over all of historic or biblical Palestine, and for that reason no other place would do as the location for a Jewish state. That was a tragic error, for the insistence on Palestine—even when other sites for a Jewish state were still being considered—was based on erroneous religious, archaeological, and biblically based stories that have long been shown by Israeli and other historians and archaeologists to have little or no factual foundation.

Even if the ancient stories and religiously based claims had a strong factual basis, they would be irrelevant. There is no dispute over the facts that for 2,000 years Jews constituted only a tiny minority in Palestine. Consequently, even if 2,000 years ago—that is, before the Roman "expulsion" of the Jews—there had been a reasonable argument for Jewish sovereignty in Palestine, a (metaphorical) "statute of limitations" for that claim had long ago expired. As I argued, there is scarcely any place on earth that at one time or another has not been conquered, subjugated, and populated by other peoples; yet nowhere is the argument for permanent sovereignty of the "original" inhabitants—itself an impossibly murky concept—accepted, whether in law, moral reasoning, or plain common sense.

With the crucial exception of the argument for existential necessity, the twentieth-century arguments for Zionism were also unpersuasive. The argument that the 1917 British Balfour Declaration gave the Jews the right to a Jewish state in Palestine is unpersuasive, both because the promise was for a Jewish "homeland" rather than a state, and more fundamentally because colonial states—or even the

League of Nations, itself dominated by the colonial West—had no moral right to dispose of their imperialist "possessions" as they pleased, particularly over the opposition of most of the inhabitants of these places.

Consequently, the only persuasive argument for the creation of the state of Israel in Palestine—but one that could reasonably be seen as sufficient—was that by 1948 there was no longer any other place to put it. Hence the tragedy: had the Zionists jettisoned all their unpersuasive arguments that Palestine belonged, forever, to the Jewish people, they would have been far more likely to have recognized the injustices done to the Palestinians, then and after. And, in that case, they would have been much more likely to accept the moral and security necessity to compromise with them, as well as with the neighboring Arab states.

After reviewing Zionism and its consequences, I examined the onset of the Israeli-Palestinian conflict during the 1917–47 period, and argued that because the Zionists wanted to ensure a large Jewish majority in the coming state of Israel, their leaders repeatedly discussed the means by which most of the Palestinians could be expelled or induced to flee; the euphemism they employed was "transfer." The scholarship on "transfer"—especially by Israeli historians—leaves no doubt about its importance in the thinking of every major Zionist leader before and after the creation of Israel.

To be sure, many non-Israeli or non-Jewish political leaders and writers also believed that some form of transfer was a necessity for the creation of a Jewish state in a partitioned Palestine. Included among them were the 1937 British Peel Commission; US president Franklin D. Roosevelt; Reinhold Niebuhr, the celebrated American liberal theologian and moral philosopher—and even some Arab monarchs who were indifferent to the Palestinians. However, none of them believed that massive violence was an acceptable method to accomplish this otherwise defensible goal.

Despite the Israeli mythology, the evidence is irrefutable that Ben-Gurion and other Zionist leaders were not willing to compromise over Palestine and therefore "accepted" the 1947 UN partition plan only as a temporary tactic to gain time until Israel was strong enough to take over all of Palestine, which in the early Zionist program had been defined to include Jerusalem, the West Bank, Gaza, southern Lebanon, the Golan Heights, and large sections of Jordan beyond the Jordan River.

Indeed, because the Zionists hardly concealed their true objectives, the Palestinian rejection of partition was a function not only of their anger that their land would have been taken away by the UN plan but also of their legitimate fear that Israel would later seize opportunities to take even more.

That said, in practice the Palestinian rejection of partition backfired, in part because if they had accepted it, it would have been harder for the Israelis to immediately seize more land than the UN plan had allocated to them, and in part because their rejection gave rise to the Israeli argument—mostly tacit but sometimes overt—that because the Palestinians rejected a compromise settlement in 1947, their treatment by Israel since then is legitimate: as they sowed, so have they reaped, is the implicit argument.

This argument lacks force at every level: in logic, in law, and in common morality. The Palestinian "mistake" (if indeed it was a mistake) in 1947, the argument implies, justifies their ongoing punishment, even though since the 1980s the main Palestinian leaders (increasingly including Hamas, de facto though not yet officially) have been willing to accept a two-state peace settlement. Yet the argument based on the alleged original Palestinian culpability for the conflict has been widely accepted among Israelis, and it contributes to their unwillingness to compromise now.

The Israeli-Arab State Conflicts

The second part of the book focuses on the Israeli-Arab state conflicts, beginning with an analysis of the 1948 war. Though it is still widely accepted in Israel and the United States, no serious scholars and historians—least of all Israeli ones—subscribe to the dominant Israeli narrative, as summarized by Avi Shlaim:

> Seven Arab states sent their armies into Palestine with the firm intention of strangling the Jewish state at birth. . . . [Then] hundreds of thousands of Palestinians fled to neighboring states, mainly in response to orders from their leaders and despite Jewish pleas to stay and demonstrate that peaceful coexistence was possible.[1]

As Shlaim and many other Israeli historians have shown:

- The David and Goliath story is false. The Arab invasion was small, uncoordinated, and the consequence more of rival monarchical claims to parts of Palestine than of the goal of driving the Israelis into the sea. Moreover, even in the early days of the war Israel had more troops in the field than the Arab invaders, superior military technology, better leadership, and greater motivation—and all of these gaps continued to grow throughout the war.
- It is false that the war was unavoidable. Jordan and Egypt both sought agreements with Israel to avert war, based on certain minor territorial compromises. Israel agreed to Jordanian king Abdullah's terms, and although there still were some military clashes between the two sides, especially in the Jerusalem region, a full-scale war was avoided. On the other hand, Israel rejected Egyptian king Farouk's request for a territorial buffer zone between the two states and deliberately provoked clashes in order to seize more Egyptian territory. Syria played only a minor role in the war, and its goals had much more to do with preventing territorial gains by its Jordanian rival than with destroying Israel, which it had neither the capability nor the intention of doing.

- It is false, as the standard Israeli claim holds, that there would have been no killing and expulsions of hundreds of thousands of Palestinians if the Arab states had not invaded Israel in May 1948. In fact, the Israelis had already expelled over 200,000 Palestinians *before* the invasion. Indeed, the Arab leaders at the time pointed to that fact as justifying a decision to intervene and save their fellow Arabs from further deaths and expulsions. Many Israeli and other historians agree that the Arab governments had to take into account the outrage of their own people at the Israeli behavior.

Nevertheless, it is undeniable that much of the Arab rhetoric—"throwing Israel into the sea," and the like—was murderous and could hardly be ignored by a people who had just lost 6 million of their fellow Jews in the Holocaust. Therefore, even though the invasion was partly a consequence of their own behavior, the Israelis had the need and the right to defend their state.

On the other hand, they did far more than "defend" themselves, for they also took advantage of the Arab attack to seize large areas of Palestine that the UN plan had designated for an Arab state, thus taking the first steps toward the long-held Zionist goal of Jewish rule over not only all of Palestine, but neighboring areas in Egypt, Lebanon, Syria, and Jordan.

Finally, the legitimate goal of self-defense cannot possibly justify the Nakba. It is no longer a matter of serious dispute that in the 1947–48 period—beginning well before the Arab invasion in May 1948—some 700,000 to 750,000 Palestinians were expelled from or fled their villages and homes in Israel in fear of their lives—an entirely justifiable fear, in light of massacres carried out by Zionist forces.

While Israeli historians still argue about whether the Nakba was the intended or explicit "policy" of the Israeli government, no one doubts that the indisputable desire of Ben-Gurion and other Zionist leaders to ensure a large Jewish majority in Israel had a great deal to do with it.

To be sure, a strong case can be made that a heavily Jewish majority in the state of Israel was a historically justifiable goal, but it by no means follows that ethnic cleansing—as we would call it today—was the only way to bring that about. In Chapter 5 a number of possible alternative means of achieving that goal were discussed—such as economic incentives , compulsory but largely nonviolent exchanges of population (as recommended by the Peel Commission), or simply waiting for a few years until the expanding Jewish population, by itself, created a near 80 per cent Jewish majority—that were ignored by the Zionist and Israeli leadership.

The book continues with an examination of the period from the end of the 1948 war through the 1956 war, when Israeli unwillingness to make fair territorial compromises with Jordan, Egypt, and Syria, based principally on a return of Arab lands captured in 1948, prevented peace settlements with the leading Arab states and resulted in the unnecessary wars of 1956 and 1967.

The 1956 War

Before the 1956 war, Israel rejected overtures from the Egyptian government to end the conflict if Israel agreed to Egyptian control over Gaza and small neighboring areas of the Negev Desert, which King Farouk wanted as a defensive buffer zone against feared expansionism by Jordan and Israel itself. However, at that time Ben-Gurion still had not abandoned his occasional hopes that Israel could take over Gaza, and as a result Israel engaged in a series of provocative actions against Egyptian forces. The purpose of these actions was both expansionist and defensive: Israel wanted to create a pretext to seize Gaza, but it also saw an attack as a "preventive war," designed to deal a heavy blow to Egypt and Syria before they could build up their forces and again attack Israel. Therefore, it is impossible to separate the genuinely defensive fears of Israeli leaders from their expansionist ambitions and plans.

Between 1954 and 1956 the new Egyptian government led by Gamal Abdel Nasser secretly offered compromise peace proposals to Israel. The Israeli prime minister, Moshe Sharett, long the leading dove among the early Israeli leaders, sought to avoid a new war and favored negotiations with Nasser, but he was undercut by Ben-Gurion and Moshe Dayan, who continued their efforts to provoke a new war with Egypt.

They were aided in these efforts by the still-imperialist Britain and France, which had their own reasons to seek the overthrow of Nasser, the most important nationalist and anti-colonial Middle East leader. In the summer of 1956, therefore, they reached a secret agreement with Israel for a tripartite invasion of Egypt, in the course of which not only would Nasser be overthrown but Israel could implement its long-held expansionist goals in the Sinai peninsula, the West Bank, southern Lebanon, and the Golan Heights.

The subsequent October 1956 joint attack of the allies easily succeeded, and Israel quickly seized the Sinai peninsula, including the Gaza Strip. However, under heavy pressures from the Eisenhower administration and the threat of Soviet military intervention, Israel was forced to withdraw from the Egyptian territories it had conquered. Because of the indecisive outcome of the war—Nasser still in power and Israel's goals unrealized—the stage was set for the next round.

The 1967 War

The mythology holds that Israel's surprise attack against Egyptian, Syrian, and Jordanian airfields in June 1967 was a defensive "pre-emptive" one, forced on Israel by an imminent Egyptian attack on Israeli forces in the Sinai peninsula as well as by threatening Syrian rhetoric over the Golan Heights. No serious study today would support that mythology: the evidence is that despite Nasser's provocations, especially his demand that UN peacekeeping forces withdraw from Sinai, he had no intention of initiating a war because he knew that Egypt would almost certainly be defeated again. Both US and Israeli intelligence analyses concluded—entirely correctly, as was shortly revealed—that the Egyptian forces (and those of its reluctant ally, Syria) were in defensive positions, and that if war did come it would end with an overwhelming Israeli victory.

Just the same, Israel decided to attack Egypt's forces in the Sinai, and a few days later the Syrian forces in the Golan Heights. In part, it was reacting to Nasser's irresponsible and bellicose rhetoric and threats, but the primary reason, most historians agree, was that Israel was again seeking a pretext to deliver another blow to Egypt, especially Nasser, as well as to further expand into the Sinai and the Golan Heights, and this was its opportunity. None other than Menachem Begin bluntly revealed the truth: "In June 1967, we again [as in the 1956 war] had a choice. The Egyptian army concentrations in the Sinai approaches did not prove that Nasser was about to attack us. We must be honest with ourselves. We decided to attack him."

To be sure, Nasser's reckless moves and threatening rhetoric made it much easier for the Israelis to claim that they had no choice.

Within six days, Israel seized new territory in the Sinai, the Golan Heights, the West Bank, and all of Jerusalem—as had been their objective from early Zionist days. After the war the Israeli government decided it would keep most of their conquests, returning only part of the Sinai. Had it decided differently, the evidence is overwhelming that it could have quickly reached peace settlements with Egypt, Syria, and Jordan. Another opportunity to have ended Arab-Israeli conflict had been lost.

The Cold War and the Israeli-Arab State Conflicts

In some ways, the extension of the Cold War into the Middle East, with the Soviets supporting the Arabs and the United States supporting Israel, worsened the conflict and made it potentially more dangerous, as on several occasions, especially during the 1973 Israeli-Egyptian war, the superpowers may have come close to directly confronting each other. But because neither superpower wanted such a war, during the 1970s there were several opportunities for them to impose a settlement on Israel and its Arab enemies. That these opportunities were squandered is almost entirely the responsibility of the Nixon administration, especially of Henry Kissinger.

The prevalent view in the United States was that the Soviets sought to exploit the Arab-Israeli conflict in order to drive the West from the Middle East and secure their own domination over the area. For this reason, the US government sought to exclude the Soviet Union from all efforts to reach a negotiated settlement. However, Soviet goals were misperceived, for the evidence is that they were best explained not in terms of Soviet expansionism or support of communist revolutions, but by a combination of traditional *Russian* defensive concerns about hostile states on or near their southern borders and by the dynamics of the Cold War rivalry with the United States.

Thus, the Soviets sought to counterbalance the US ties with Israel and the growing American power in the Middle East by their alliances with Egypt and Syria. At the same time, however, they feared—with good reason—that future Arab-Israeli wars, in which each side was armed and supported by its superpower ally, could end in a direct superpower military confrontation. Therefore, they repeatedly sought a political settlement of the conflict, with the United States and the Soviet Union acting as co-equals in ensuring the peace.

On several occasions, Nixon and a number of high State Department officials gave serious consideration to such a settlement, but eventually the president was persuaded by Kissinger that the US goal in the Middle East must continue to be the "containment" of the Soviet Union—indeed as much as possible to eliminate its influence in the region. Therefore Kissinger, by his own admission, deliberately sabotaged peace proposals that would have continued the Soviet role in the Middle East.

Israel and Egypt

Meanwhile, the conflict between Israel and Egypt (and, to a lesser extent, with Syria) continued, each state armed and assisted by its superpower ally, and then escalated into the major 1973 war. Precipitated by Israel's refusal to withdraw from the Egyptian and Syrian territories it had conquered in 1967, the 1973 war again came uncomfortably close to a direct superpower confrontation.

As a result, the Soviets again sought to convince the United States to join with them in a joint superpower-imposed Arab-Israeli peace settlement—but the Soviets were again rebuffed, initially by the Nixon administration and then even by the Carter administration, which bowed to Israeli intransigence.

After the election of Ronald Reagan in 1980, US cooperation with the Soviets that would have preserved their role in the Middle East became unthinkable. The result was tragic: several opportunities to have ended the Arab-Israeli conflict were squandered, largely because of Israeli intransigence and American Cold War ideological rigidity.

Even so, the deadlock between Israel and Egypt, and to a lesser extent with Jordan, began to break up, primarily because Nasser's successor Anwar Sadat decided to reach a separate peace; his dramatic 1977 visit to Israel convinced the Israelis of his sincerity and that the few costs of a peace treaty would be outweighed by its benefits. Consequently, Israel agreed to return the Sinai—though not Gaza—to Egypt, in exchange for the 1979 peace treaty that resulted in Egypt's withdrawal from the Arab-Israeli conflict.

Israel and Jordan

After the 1967 war, King Hussein of Jordan sought to reach a separate peace with Israel, on the condition that Jerusalem and the West Bank were returned to

Jordanian rule. Israel repeatedly rebuffed Hussein, even after he made a number of concessions to alleged Israeli security concerns—among them to withdraw all but a few of his forces from the area, to allow Israel to retain military bases there, and to continue his efforts to suppress the PLO. Israel's rejections of these overtures demonstrated that the real obstacle to a settlement with Jordan was less "security" concerns than its ideological or religious insistence that it must have full control and sovereignty over all of "Judea and Samaria," including Arab East Jerusalem.

Had Israel been willing to give up the West Bank to Jordan as well as Gaza to Jordan or Egypt, it would have ended the Israeli-Palestinian conflict, transferring the Palestinian "problem" to those countries. Its unwillingness to do so was one of the greatest lost opportunities for peace between Israel and the entire Arab world.

However, by the early 1990s, Hussein had decided that holding on to the West Bank and Jerusalem was not worth its costs, which were not only the possibility of war with Israel but the growing threat to his rule by militant Palestinian nationalism in his kingdom. Consequently, he decided to renounce the Jordanian claim to the West Bank. As a result, the last obstacles to peace were overcome, resulting in the 1994 Israeli-Jordan treaty which, as in the case of the Israeli-Egyptian settlement, has been maintained ever since.

Israel and Lebanon

From the outset of the Arab-Israeli conflict the major Israeli leaders, especially Ben-Gurion and Dayan, looked for opportunities to invade Lebanon in order to annex its southern region and install a friendly Christian government in the rest of the country, one that would accept the Israeli conquests and collaborate with Israel in its conflict with the Palestinians and other Islamic organizations.

One of Ben-Gurion's goals in the 1956 war was to create the conditions in which his Lebanon ambitions could be realized. While that failed, by the 1970s the growing conflict between Israel and the PLO, which was then largely based in Lebanon, had broadened Israel's concerns beyond expansionism, for there now were security concerns.

In 1978, Israel attacked and defeated PLO forces in southern Lebanon, withdrawing only under pressure from the Carter administration. In the next two or three years, Israeli-PLO attacks and counterattacks resumed, though at a lesser level. However, by the early 1980s, Yasser Arafat was in the process of abandoning his original goal of destroying the state of Israel, which he now concluded was unattainable, in favor of establishing a Palestinian state in the West Bank and Gaza. As a result, the PLO was scrupulously observing a ceasefire with Israel that had gone into effect in 1981.

For just that reason, though, Prime Minister Menachem Begin and Defense Minister Ariel Sharon worried that the growing PLO moderation would increase the pressure on Israel to accept the creation of a Palestinian state. To prevent that, in 1982 they seized upon a pretext to again invade Lebanon and attack the PLO, this time on a far larger scale than in previous conflicts. The attacks resulted in tens of thousands of Lebanese civilian casualties; however, the PLO forces in southern Lebanon, still led by Arafat, who escaped Israeli efforts to kill him, were soon reconstituted.

Moreover, the Israeli attack led to the creation of Hezbollah, the militant Islamic movement that after the 1982 war became the dominant military force in Lebanon. During the 1990s, armed clashes between Israel and Hezbollah continued, resulting in Israeli invasions of southern Lebanon in 1993, 1996, and 2006, all of them again resulting in heavy casualties in the Lebanese civilian population.

None of these attacks resulted in serious damage to Hezbollah's dominant political role in Lebanon or to its military power, though, particularly its rocket forces, which have continued to grow. However, since the end of the 2006, the borders have been quiet, as a state of mutual deterrence—often explicitly acknowledged by both sides—has prevailed; both Israel and Hezbollah now generally realize that a new conflict would be as inconclusive as the previous ones, yet even more damaging to both of them.

Still, the dangers of a new war may not have passed, and recently may even be growing because of Hezbollah's direct or indirect support of the Iranian forces that back the Assad regime in Syria's civil war. Israel has frequently attacked Hezbollah's military forces in Syria, and while no escalation into open Israeli-Hezbollah war has yet occurred, the possibility that it will do so continues to exist.

Israel and Syria

In the early years of the Syrian-Israeli conflict, Israel repeatedly rejected opportunities to reach peace agreements with Syria, because they required Israel to give up its dreams of annexing southern Syria, especially the Golan Heights. In 1920, the Zionists rejected an opportunity to reach a negotiated settlement with the Syrian monarchy of King Faisal, who accepted the Balfour Declaration and chose not to oppose the creation of a Jewish state in Palestine. After a nationalist movement took control of the government, the new leaders rejected Faisal's policies and joined in the Arab attack on Israel in 1948. However, Syria sent only a small and largely symbolic force of some 3,000 men, whose goal was not to destroy Israel, which it had no capability of doing; its purpose primarily was to prevent its Jordanian rival from seizing control over the waters of the Jordan River and Lake Tiberias.

After the war, Israel repeatedly violated the terms of its 1949 truce agreement with Syria, encroaching on the agreed-upon demilitarized zones along the Jordan River and on occasion deliberately provoking armed clashes so as to justify its violation of the truce and create pretexts for seizing the Golan Heights. In 1949, two Syrian governments proposed formal peace agreements with Israel, provided Syria could keep the Golan Heights and its access to the Jordan River and Lake Tiberias. The Truman administration urged Israel to enter into negotiations with Syria on that basis, but Ben-Gurion refused.

It is worth repeating Dayan's later admission, published only after his death, that during the 1940s and 1950s, Israel had been deliberately provoking the Syrians so that it could seize the Golan Heights. When an interviewer protested that Syria was a serious threat to Israel, Dayan responded: "Bullshit. . . . Just drop it."

During 1966, Israel continued to provoke clashes with the Syrian army; as a result, as well as because of its military alliance with Egypt, Syria was drawn into the 1967 war, though again only marginally. This gave Israel the opportunity and justification it had long sought to seize the Golan Heights. Syria sought to recover the area when it joined with Egypt during the 1973 war, but its forces were again routed and Israel seized additional territory in or near the Golan.

Syrian president Hafez Assad then decided that his country could not regain the Golan by military action but only by a negotiated settlement with Israel. From 1973 until his death in 2000, Assad repeatedly offered to end Syria's conflict with Israel, to prevent any attacks from Syrian territory by Palestinian or other Islamic guerrilla forces, and even to fully normalize relations with Israel by means of a formal peace treaty, provided that Israel withdrew from the Golan and allowed Syrian forces to retain a small strip of land bordering on Lake Tiberias.

During this period there were intensive secret negotiations between Syria and Israel, many of them mediated by the US government, which urged Israel to accept Assad's terms. Israeli prime ministers Rabin, Peres, Barak, Olmert, and perhaps even Netanyahu came very close to agreeing to such a peace settlement, especially because most Israeli military leaders believed that Israeli security would be better served by a peace pact than by continuing to hold on to the Golan Heights. However, on the brink of success the Israeli governments backed away, mostly because of expected resistance from the Israeli right wing.

Hafez Assad was succeeded by his son, Bashar Assad, who reaffirmed to the Israeli and US governments his willingness to sign a peace treaty with Israel on the same conditions as had his father. Once again the Israeli military and the US government urged the Israeli governments of Olmert, Sharon, and Netanyahu to accept the Syrian offers, but they continued to refuse to do so.

Netanyahu ended the talks after the outbreak of the Syrian civil war in 2011; as well, with the support of the Trump administration, the first US government to formally recognize Israeli sovereignty over the Golan Heights, he made it clear that Israel had no intention of ever returning the area to Syria. Thus, over forty years of peace negotiations have failed, overwhelmingly because of Israeli intransigence.

The Israeli-Palestinian Conflict

The third part of this book focused on the Israeli-Palestinian conflict. During the 1960s the PLO and Yasser Arafat became the leaders of Palestinian nationalism and in the early years sought to "liberate" all of Palestine, carrying out terrorist attacks against

Israel. After the 1967 war, the Israeli government briefly considered but rejected a two-state solution—effectively, partition—so the conflict continued. Nonetheless, by the mid-1970s, especially after Israel's rout of Egypt and Syria, Arafat and the PLO became more pragmatic; recognizing that they had no chance of defeating Israel, they gradually moved toward acceptance of the two-state principle, finally agreeing officially in 1988 to end the conflict in return for the creation of a largely demilitarized Palestinian state in the West Bank and Gaza, with East Jerusalem as its capital. Supported by the Nixon and Reagan administrations, Israel refused the Arafat-PLO offers.

Starting in the mid-1970s, a number of Arab states began seeking a two-state solution to the Israeli-Palestinian conflict. After the 1973 war it was clear that Egypt under Anwar Sadat and Hosni Mubarak favored such a settlement, and within a decade Saudi Arabia joined with them, offering to accept Israel within its pre-1967 borders once it had permitted the creation of a Palestinian state in the occupied territories. And in 2002 an Arab League summit conference, attended by twenty-two Arab states, *unanimously* adopted the Saudi proposals, soon to be known as the Arab Peace Initiative (API). In March 2007, not only did all twenty-two of the signatories unanimously reaffirm the API, but they also dropped any mention of a "right of return" and substituted language that made it clear that Israel would have a veto over how many Palestinian refugees, if any, it would admit.

To this day, most observers of the conflict are astonished that Israel has never been willing to acknowledge the API, especially its 2007 version, let alone agree to negotiate a settlement based on its principles.

The next major peace effort was the Oslo Accords of September 1993, the product of intensive secret negotiations between representatives of Israel and, in effect, the PLO. The accords mandated a series of gradual Israeli withdrawals from the occupied territories and the initiation of a number of steps toward Palestinian self-government which, if all went well over a five-year period, were expected by both negotiating teams to result in the creation of a fully independent Palestinian state. However, the accords soon broke down because of violations by both sides; however, the greater responsibility was Israel's.

As it became clear that the Oslo process was not likely to lead to a two-state settlement, Palestinian terrorism, mostly by Hamas and other Islamic extremists, was resumed. However, Arafat and the PLO had sought to prevent that terrorism, and in any case its resumption was hardly unconnected to Israel's policies: Israeli prime minister Yitzhak Rabin not only refused to withdraw the settlers from the West Bank, but he actually increased them. As well, he insisted on retaining sole Israeli control of Jerusalem and in a number of other ways demonstrated he was not ready to accept a Palestinian state.

Bill Clinton took office in January 1993, and in the next eight years he sought to bring about a two-state solution, actively mediating peace talks between Israel and the Palestinians, which culminated in the intensive and months-long talks in 2000, known as the Camp David/Taba negotiations.

However, those failed as well. A dispute continues among observers and participants in the negotiations over the responsibility for their failure. Both sides made mistakes, Israeli prime minister Barak principally because of his ambivalence about compromising with the Palestinians, particularly over sharing Jerusalem, and Arafat because he was not willing to officially abandon the Palestinian demand for an unlimited right of return to Israel.

However, Barak bears the greater responsibility for the collapse of the peace talks in early 2001. The most important issues on the table were the territory and borders of a Palestinian state in the West Bank and Gaza, the status of the Israeli settlements in those areas, the sharing of Jerusalem, and the refugee right of return. Initially Barak had agreed to the principle of a two-state settlement, and some of his verbal territorial proposals were more forthcoming than previous Israeli positions. However, he was still conflicted over whether Israel should allow the creation of a Palestinian state. Consequently, when some of his initial offers were rejected by Arafat, his position hardened, especially over the refugee and Jerusalem issues.

Though he was not always consistent, Arafat and the other leading PLO officials—especially Mahmoud Abbas after his 2004 assumption of the leadership of the PLO and the PA after Arafat's death—were willing to compromise over the refugees: if Israel acknowledged some responsibility for the creation of the refugee problem (the Nakba), the Palestinians would drop their demand for a complete "right of return." For example, according to an authoritative analysis, in his secret 2008 discussions with Israeli prime minister Ehud Olmert, Abbas asked Israel to gradually accept 100,000 refugees over a five-year period. Olmert countered with an offer to accept 30,000 refugees over a ten-year period.[2] The relatively small difference in numbers suggests that the issue was bridgeable, as was concluded by peace negotiators on both sides.

The Jerusalem issue, however, was harder, for there was and remains no possibility that Arafat and the Arab world could accept Israeli rule over Arab East Jerusalem—or what's left of it, after over fifty years of Israeli takeovers of Palestinian homes and neighborhoods. Above all, the Palestinians and, for that matter, the entire Arab and Muslim world will never agree to Israeli sovereignty over the mosques on the Temple Mount/Haram plateau.

After it became clear that Israel and the Palestinians could not reach an agreement on their own, Clinton made his own proposals, which sought to bridge the differences on the major issues. Though in the end he blamed Arafat for the breakdown of the process, Clinton had also been critical of Barak's rigidity and inconsistency. Many officials in his administration and in the State Department urged him to use US leverage, especially its military and economic assistance to Israel, to seriously press Barak to be more forthcoming. The president, however, refused, and after some additional progress at the Taba negotiations at the end of 2000, the election of Ariel Sharon in early 2001 made a continuation of the peace process impossible.

The breakdown of the peace process in 2001 led to an increase in Palestinian resistance to the occupation. Hamas grew increasingly powerful and in 2007 took over Gaza as the result both of its victory in free elections and its defeat of a coup attempt led by the PA and supported by the US government. That, in turn, led to an intensification of the Israeli blockade or siege of Palestine.

The siege is largely still in effect today. Together with four highly destructive attacks on Gaza and Hamas in 2002, 2008, 2012, and 2014 (and many other smaller ones) that killed thousands of Gazan civilians, the siege has wrecked the Gazan economy and reduced most of the population to poverty.

Nonetheless, whether despite the Israeli repression or because of it, during the 2000s, Hamas began a gradual and inconsistent but nonetheless increasingly significant shift in its policies toward terrorism and the possibility of a de facto two-state settlement. As evidence of the Hamas changes mounted, a number of former high Israeli officials, including retired generals and previous heads of the Mossad and Shin Bet, began urging the government to explore Hamas's willingness to reach a compromise settlement.

The Sharon administration refused. It was willing to withdraw the isolated Jewish settlements from Gaza, which it did in 2005, but it then intensified its repressive measures and military actions against Hamas and the Gazan population. Still, leading Israeli and Palestinian doves continued to work on the main issues that needed to be resolved if a two-state solution were ever to become a reality. In 2003, the result of their unofficial but high-level negotiations was made public. Known as the Geneva Accords (GA), the agreement called for the end of the Israeli occupation of the West Bank and Gaza and the creation of an independent but largely demilitarized Palestinian state.

The fifty-page agreement included compromises on all the major issues: the territory and borders of the Palestinian state, the Jewish settlements in those areas, the sharing of water resources, the division of Jerusalem, and the Palestinian refugee problem. The latter two issues, the most contentious ones in all previous negotiations, were resolved on the basis of a trade-off: the Palestinians agreed to give Israel a de facto veto over refugee return, and the Israelis agreed to divide Jerusalem and give the Palestinians sovereignty over the remaining Arab sections of East Jerusalem and the Muslim religious sites in the Old City.

It is widely understood that the Geneva Accord would be the foundation for any future two-state settlement—in the (highly) unlikely event that it should become a realistic possibility—and while Sharon denounced it, according to many leaked documents and Israeli reports, Olmert and Abbas essentially accepted the GA principles and main provisions. However, before a formal agreement could be negotiated, the increasingly unpopular Olmert lost his political power and was succeeded by Benjamin Netanyahu.

Yet another opportunity for peace had been lost. The Obama administration made several efforts to revive the two-state solution, but they were doomed to fail by Netanyahu's intransigence and Obama's unwillingness to threaten Netanyahu with meaningful pressure, probably because Obama realized that doing so would have jeopardized his domestic political power and policy programs and might have failed anyway.

The 2016 election of Donald Trump and his complete support of Netanyahu and the Israeli right wing, together with the expanding Israeli control over, settlement in, and creeping annexations of the West Bank and Jerusalem, have almost certainly spelled the end of the two-state solution to the Israeli-Palestinian conflict.

What Has Gone So Wrong?

There are several explanations for why things have gone so wrong. The history of anti-Semitism in general and, of course, the Holocaust in particular obviously explain much of Israeli psychology. In the early years of Jewish statehood, Arab rhetoric was often murderous—and among Arab extremists, still is—cementing the Israelis' view of themselves as a beleaguered minority and permanent victims in a hostile world.

In addition, as Colonel Mordechai Bar-On, a former IDF chief of education, observed: while the Palestinian hostility to Zionism was understandable, the Arab state invasion of 1948, however limited in its intentions and capabilities, was lastingly traumatic for the Israeli people, who had little knowledge of, or interest in, the Palestinian narrative. In 1996, Bar-On wrote:

> Israelis have been revisiting the events of the 1948 war for the past fifty years, not only because they were branded with the personal memories of the generation that lived through them . . . but primarily because they still occupy a major segment of the collective memory that constitutes' Israel's mental space and identity. . . . [The events] imprinted on [our] collective memory a sense of weakness and vulnerability that subsequent victories could not eradicate.[3]

So, yes, up to a point the attitudes of most Israelis toward the Arabs in general and the Palestinians in particular are understandable. Yet they have persisted long after it should have become clear to them that their own behavior has had a great deal to do with the conflict. In particular, most Israelis, amazingly, fail to see any connection between Arab hostility and their own early expansionism and, especially, the decades of the occupation and repression of the Palestinians.

The Israeli historian Avi Raz, now teaching at Oxford, quotes a 1969 Israeli song, which he says "appropriately captured the Israeli collective spirit":

> The whole world is against us,
> Never mind, we'll overcome.

And everybody who's against us
Let him go to hell.[4]

The continuing influence of the Israeli historical myths on most Israelis, including the vast majority of its politicians, is another explanation for Israeli behavior. For a tragically brief period, the Israeli "New History" promised to correct the myths. The implications of this historiography were profound, for it conclusively demonstrated that the narrative of Israeli innocence and fanatical, monolithic Arab/Palestinian determination to destroy Israel was false.

From the late 1980s through the early 2000s the New History seemed poised to have a significant impact on Israel—not merely on historical scholarship but in the Israeli school system, where the major New History works became part of the curriculum. However, with the sharp turn to the right throughout Israel since 2000, the New History has to a great extent been dropped from the school curriculum, and the dominant mythology has reemerged in most of Israeli politics and society, though certainly not among the overwhelming majority of Israeli scholars. Ilan Pappé, one of the leading New Historians, along with Benny Morris and Avi Shlaim, writes: "From the vantage point of 2013 . . . the saddest and in many ways most disappointing aspect of [the New History] . . . is its almost complete lack of influence on the education system in Israel."[5]

Consequently, blinded by Zionist ideology and the past Jewish history of victimization, today the Israelis continue to be either largely ignorant of, or indifferent to, their own history and its implications for the continuing conflict with the Palestinians, as the discredited mythology has once again become dominant in Israeli politics, society, and public discourse.

A more general explanation for why Israel, a state founded not only to ensure the survival of the Jewish people but to serve as a moral exemplar to the world—"a light unto the nations"—has failed to do so is to be found in its unconstrained power. As the nineteenth-century British historian and politician Lord Acton famously observed, "Power tends to corrupt, and absolute power corrupts absolutely." Since 1957, Israel has exercised, if not absolute, then certainly great power over the Palestinians. In 2018, an Israeli columnist wrote: "The Holocaust is not responsible for our disengagement from Western liberalism. What is responsible for this disengagement is the transition from the ruled to the rulers. Power went to our heads."[6]

Where Do Things Stand Now?

Throughout this work I have emphasized the Israeli responsibility for both the origins and the continuation of the hundred-year Israeli-Palestinian conflict. The Palestinians, of course, share in that responsibility, in part because of their early refusal to accept the Peel and UN partition plans to divide the land of Palestine into Jewish and Arab states, and in part because until relatively recently their primary leaders and organizations—principally, Arafat, the PLO, and Hamas—turned to violence as their main form of resistance.

It is true, of course, that the Israelis have suppressed—often violently—all forms of Palestinian resistance, including nonviolent resistance. Perhaps if the Palestinians had eschewed armed resistance from the outset of the conflict—especially terrorism—it is possible that the Israelis would have been responsive to a two-state solution of the conflict. While that is unknowable, there is no doubt that terrorism has utterly failed, resulting only in a hardened Israeli resistance to a political compromise peace settlement.[7]

As a consequence of both Israeli intransigence and the continuation of terrorism by Palestinian Islamic extremists (though on a far lesser scale than in the past), the prospects have never been worse for a two-state solution that would require Israel to withdraw its settlers and military forces from the West Bank and East Jerusalem.

Until about 2018, Israeli public opinion polls usually indicated that a majority accepted the general principle of two states for two peoples, though even that was misleading, since there was no Israeli majority for the kind of concessions necessary to bring about such a settlement—for example, an equal division of Jerusalem. In any case, an Israeli majority supporting a single solution no longer exists, even for the principle of a two-state settlement. For example, a March 2019 poll showed that only 34 percent supported a two-state solution, whereas 42 percent favored some form of annexation of the West Bank.[8]

In light of these and similar findings, even if a future Israeli government wanted to revive the two-state solution, according to many Israeli experts it would be risking civil war. For example, Menachem Klein, an Israeli political scientist and former advisor to Ehud Barak, writes that because "almost the entire state is invested in [the settlements] . . . any solution to the Israeli-Palestinian conflict is likely to lead to an armed revolt against the legitimate government, or even a civil war in some form. . . . The possibility that a revolt or civil war will break out is not hypothetical: It is in the air and exists in the consciousness of the decision-makers."[9]

In particular, many Israeli political analysts are worried about the future role of the army in the event that a future Israeli government seeks to revive a two-state settlement: the growing influx of the settlers as well as religious fundamentalists into the army, including at high levels of the officer corps, raises the question of whether the army could be relied on to remove the West Bank settlements or to put down a right-wing uprising.[10]

In any case, all the indications are that the *standard* two-state solution is dead. What, then, are the prospects for the Palestinians in the foreseeable future? Since they have no workable options, Israel may simply seek to maintain the status quo, meaning the direct occupation of the West Bank, with or without de facto or formal annexation, and a continued "indirect occupation," as it has been termed, of Gaza.

A second option, favored by some despairing Israeli dissidents and their supporters in the United States and elsewhere in the West, is a "one-state" or "binational" solution, meaning the creation of a single democratic Israeli-Palestinian state and society.

The third option would be—*must* be, I will argue—a renewed effort to reach some kind of *limited* two-state settlement, one that admittedly would be far less fair to the Palestinians than all previous two-state plans—but nonetheless better than no settlement at all.

Maintaining the Status Quo

To be sure, if moral considerations are ignored, it can be argued that living by the sword has worked for Israel. Its military power clearly induced the PLO to abandon its hopes of defeating Israel and led the Arab states either to reach a political settlement with Israel (Egypt in the 1970s, Jordan in the 1980s, and recently, Saudi Arabia—de facto if not formally), or at least to refrain from major military attacks against it (Syria, Lebanon, and Iraq). In a 2019 book, Israel's former deputy national security advisor Chuck Freilich concluded that Israel's security situation was a "dizzying success":

> We aren't under any existential threats; there's no immediate nuclear threat. The friction with the Arab states has decreased considerably. With some of them, the conflict has basically ended and been replaced by a commonalty of interests.[11]

As well, Israel's overwhelming military power and its repeatedly demonstrated will to employ it ruthlessly have quashed any meaningful Palestinian resistance. For a number of years, the PA in the West Bank has actively collaborated with Israeli military and intelligence organizations to prevent Hamas and Islamic Jihad from launching armed attacks or terrorism against Israel. Moreover, as I have argued, the weight of the evidence indicates that Hamas has increasingly recognized the futility of any effort to destroy Israel and will now settle for retaining its power in Gaza, increasingly with the tacit acceptance of Israel.

Nonetheless, it is not difficult to imagine changed circumstances that could once again threaten Israel's security. For one thing, the Arab "street," as it is often termed, does not share the attitudes toward Israel of their rulers—all of them monarchs or autocrats, possibly vulnerable to a renewed Arab Spring. In that case, populist Arab states might support, or at least tolerate, Islamic fundamentalist terrorism or guerrilla warfare against Israel or, at a minimum, end their collaboration with Israel's occupation and suppression of the Palestinian people.

Israeli governments have long cited "security" as the reason they need to maintain occupation of Arab territories—but when Israel withdrew from Lebanon and Egyptian territory, the attacks against it ended. It is unlikely that an Israeli withdrawal from the Palestinian territories would have a different result—and if it did, there would be little to prevent Israel from reinvading and occupying those territories. Moreover, in those circumstances repression of any continuing Palestinian violence would have a legitimacy that it currently lacks. For these reasons, Israel has a security problem with the Palestinians only in the same way that colonial powers had "security problems" with nationalist uprisings that eventually forced them to withdraw.

For these reasons, many retired Israeli military and intelligence officials are increasingly making public their continuing concern—often in strikingly blunt terms—that the Israeli occupation could once again threaten Israeli security:

- In 2013, in a dramatic and widely viewed Israeli documentary, *The Gatekeepers*, six former heads of the Shin Bet forcefully opposed the continuation of the Israeli occupation of the West Bank as inconsistent not only with Israeli security, but because they believed (in the words of Dror Moreh, the maker of the documentary) that "Israel's occupation is eating away at the country's political and moral substance." Moreh also claimed that most current members of the Israeli security establishment privately had come to the same conclusion.[12]
- In 2014, more than 100 retired Israeli generals, Mossad directors, and national police commissioners sent a letter to Netanyahu urging him to reach peace with the Palestinians: "We're on a steep slope to an increasingly polarized society and moral decline, due to the need to keep millions of people under occupation on claims that are presented as security-related."[13]
- In 2015, former Shin Bet leader Admiral Ami Ayalon and the retired chief of police General Alik Ron published a statement in *Haaretz* in support of Breaking the Silence, an organization of former military combatants who opposed the occupation; "I too am breaking the silence," they said.[14]
- In 2016, six former IDF chiefs of staff, five former directors of Shin Bet, and five former heads of Mossad signed a full-page ad in the *New York Times* entitled "Separation into Two States Is Essential for Israel's Security."[15]
- In 2018, a report by retired military and intelligence officials warned that annexation would cause "unprecedented damage" to Israel's national security.
- In April 2019, Admiral Ayalon said: "We are doing everything in order to create a virtual reality in which Palestinians cannot exist. It is not a just war. It will be catastrophe if we should win. It is the end of our Zionist dream."[16]

- In 2020 the same group, led by former high generals, Mossad directors, and Shin Bet directors, reiterated their strong opposition to annexation, arguing that it would undermine the peace treaties with both Jordan and Egypt, could destabilize King Abdullah's government in Jordan, and endanger continued PA military cooperation with Israel. "Risking all that for annexation of territory over which Israel already has full security control makes no sense," they concluded.[17] Even Moshe Ya'alon, one of the most hawkish former IDF chiefs, said that large-scale annexation would be "a grave mistake."[18]

The Nuclear Danger

In 2011, a group of retired security officers issued a long report arguing that while Israel no longer had to worry about conventional attacks from Arab states and could therefore withdraw from much of the occupied territories in the context of peace agreements, the threat to Israeli security of long-range missiles and weapons of mass destruction was increasing.[19]

It is astonishing that the Israelis evidently pay so little attention to the problem. The global spread of nuclear weapons is irreversible, so surely the greatest danger to Israel—and the only truly "existential" one—is an attack by non-state terrorist groups that might not be deterred by the threat of Israel nuclear retaliation, whether precisely because they are fanatics or because their very lack of statehood and dispersion throughout the Arab world—and even beyond—leads them to think, whether correctly or not, that they are invulnerable to retaliation.

It is true that this nightmare scenario has been predicted for many years, but the fact that it hasn't yet occurred hardly means that the danger is past. In effect, Israel is betting that it can continue to suppress the Palestinians, even at the cost of enraging their supporters throughout the Arab and Muslim world indefinitely. As the American historian Peter Viereck once said: "Reality is that which, when you don't believe in it, doesn't go away." In that light, the Israelis should realize that even if there were no other reasons, their long-term security—perhaps their very existence—requires a peaceful settlement with the Palestinians.

The Moral Argument

Aside from the long-range security considerations, the moral case for a fair settlement with the Palestinians should be self-evident to a state that proudly promised to serve as "a light unto the nations." Defenders of Israeli behavior often bitterly claim that Israel is the victim of Western moral "double standards," arguing that many far worse offenders against human rights—Russia, China, Syria, and Iran are often cited—receive much less criticism or opprobrium.[20]

A variation of this defense is that Israel is just an ordinary state, "a nation like all other nations," and as such should not be held to higher standards than all the others. However, while it is obvious that there are many more states in the world, or just in the Middle East, with worse human rights records, Israel is certainly the worst in the West. It's a long way from "a light unto the nations" to "better than Syria."

There are many problems with the "double standards" argument. It is hardly the case that the human rights violations of the leading world or Middle East autocracies are underreported in the West. Moreover, none of those states claim that they serve as beacons of enlightenment or that they have "the world's most moral army." As none other than Abba Eban once admitted, "The world is only comparing us to the standard we set for ourselves."[21]

Put differently, little is expected from non-Western autocracies, and in any case, not only do Westerners have little or no influence on them, but criticism of their human rights records has often backfired and led to even harsher violations, as has been the case with the Soviet Union in the past and possibly with China and Syria today. By contrast, in the case of Israel, which proudly proclaims its adherence to "Western civilization," there has been the expectation—or, at least, the hope—that criticism would matter. So far, however, it must be admitted that Western criticism of Israeli policies and behaviors has had little effect, and today probably less than ever.

Indeed, Israel is much more often the *beneficiary* than the victim of moral double standards, at least in the United States and the West, a point often made by Israeli dissidents. For example, the Israeli journalist Larry Derfner writes: "If you look at the serious, painful punishments the world metes out to oppressor nations, Israel is not being singled out, it's being let off the hook."[22]

Derfner goes on to compare the heavy sanctions against Iran with the absence of them against Israel. He might have added that far from facing sanctions, Israel is the recipient of great US largesse, creating a moral obligation for this country to end its complicity with Israeli human rights abuses and instead use its influence and leverage with Israel on behalf of Palestinian human and political rights. Needless to say, America has no such moral obligations to, say, China or Syria.

There are a number of reasons for the moral free pass granted Israel in the West, beginning with what has been called "Holocaust guilt," the widespread sense of shame in the West that so little was done to prevent the Holocaust and the resulting "never again" determination to support the creation of a strong Jewish state. Indeed, in part because of ignorance or disregard of Israel's record of dispossession, occupation, and repression of the Palestinians, for many years Israel was, as Zeev Sternhell has put it, "the favored child of the international community."[23]

As well, of course, foreign policy considerations contributed to the unwillingness of Western states, especially the United States, to seriously criticize Israel's human rights record: during the Cold War Israel was regarded as a strong ally against communism in the Middle East and since then in "the war against Islamic terrorism."

Finally, although this may now be changing somewhat, in the United States domestic political considerations nearly always mitigate against serious and sustained criticism of Israeli policies, let alone meaningful pressures against them.

Although this book has not discussed the effect on Israel itself of its policies toward the Palestinians, harm to its own democracy, society, and proclaimed values was surely inevitable, as has long been predicted by its internal critics. Today the situation is worse than it has ever been, to the despair of Israeli liberals. Since going into detail is beyond the scope of the book, perhaps a single quote will convey the point. In a 2014 op-ed column entitled "American Jewish Leaders Fiddle While Israeli Democracy Burns," the Israeli journalist Chemi Shalev summed up the situation:

> American Jewish leaders must be fully aware of the evil winds blowing in the Israeli public arena; of the rising intolerance, racism and xenophobia; of the efforts inside and outside the Knesset to stifle free speech and to inhibit freedom of the press; of the spreading use of violence and intimidation to instill fear among those who would stray from the government-inspired right wing line; of the ongoing delegitimization of liberal values and human rights and the organizations that safeguard them; of the increasingly vile and abusive language used in the public sphere and on social media against divergent views; of the growing official and unofficial intolerance and incitement directed at Israel's Arab minority.[24]

In the last five years the situation has only gotten worse. In February 2020 former prime minister Ehud Barak warned that "Israeli democracy is at the height of a political collapse."[25]

The "One-State Solution"

The collapse of hopes for a two-state solution has led a number of observers, including some Israeli and Palestinian intellectuals and their supporters elsewhere, to call for its replacement with a binational state. Such a state might not only be the last chance for the Palestinians to get justice and relief from Israeli occupation and repression, it is argued, but the merger of the Israelis and the Palestinians into a single democratic state with equal rights for all its citizens would be morally superior to the enforced separation—"divorce," as it has been called—of two hostile peoples.

The idea is not a new one: in the pre-state era, some leading Jewish intellectuals, including Martin Buber, Judah Magnes, and Hannah Arendt, argued that the state of Israel should be a democratic and binational one, with full equality between the Jews and the Palestinian Arabs—who at that time would have been nearly equal in numbers within the projected boundaries of the new state. However, this view attracted little support among the pre- state Jewish population and lost its influence after the creation of the state of Israel in 1948 and the escalation of the Arab-Israeli and Israeli-Palestinian conflicts.

Though attractive in principle, the merger of the Israelis and the Palestinians into a peaceful democracy with equal power and rights for each people is less likely—better said, more utopian—than ever. In the first instance, it has little popular and even intellectual support among both the Israelis and the Palestinians.

Not only have repeated Israeli polls shown that the vast majority of the Jewish public, for historical, cultural, or religious reasons, want to live in a Jewish state, not in a binational state on co-equal terms with the Palestinians,[26] but many leading Israeli opponents of current Israeli policies are also dismissive of the feasibility and even desirability of a binational solution. For example, Menachem Klein writes:

> The one-state solution doesn't remove the possibility of the outbreak of civil war. Instead of a struggle between the State of Israel and a rebel Jewish group, within one state the struggle would be between two ethnic-religious-linguistic collectives. . . . The Jewish ethnic group would not agree to give up its privileges for the creation of an egalitarian regime between Jews and Palestinian Arabs. . . . One state is a guaranteed prescription for an ongoing civil war, similar to what happened in the Balkans with the breakup of Yugoslavia, or in Lebanon.[27]

Yossi Sarid, an Israeli political activist, government official, and Labor and Meretz Party leader, who was outspoken in his criticisms of Israeli policies toward the Palestinians, wrote that "the dream of one state for two peoples is a nightmare to both. If we couldn't integrate Israel's one million Arabs, how will we live together with five million?"[28]

Amos Oz: "If anyone would have proposed that in 1945 Germany and Poland immediately become a binational state they would put him in a madhouse. How can anyone in Israel or elsewhere think that Israelis and the Palestinians can simply jump into a honeymoon bed together? After generations of hatred, we need a divorce, a fair divorce."[29]

Support for a binational solution is not much greater among the Palestinians, where only about one-third of the general public is in favor.[30] Ghassan Khatib, a prominent Palestinian political leader, PA minister, and member of the two-state negotiating teams in the 1990s, wrote:

> The reality created by Israel rendered the one-state idea a utopian dream. . . . The vast majority of the public, according to public opinion polls, and the majority of the [Palestinian] political elite consider the idea of a bi-national state a dangerous alternative strategy.[31]

In a 2011 article, Ghada Karmi, a Palestinian academician and prominent intellectual, reported that only 20 percent of the Palestinian public supported a binational state, ensuring that for the indefinite future, "it is likely to remain an idealistic dream."[32]

Yasser Abed Rabbo, a former long-term PLO leader, peace negotiator with Israel, and PA minister, bluntly dismissed the binational idea as a fantasy: "Do these 'one-state solution' people imagine that if Israelis do not accept the return of a few hundred thousand refugees to Israel . . . that they will accept adding over three and a half million Palestinians . . . as voters in the coming Knesset?"[33]

Today, the population figures make the binational dream even more unrealistic. As of 2019, there were about 7 million Palestinians and Israeli Arabs in Israel, the West Bank, and Gaza, and about the same number of Jewish Israelis. At least in the past—though that may be changing—most demographic estimates were that the Arabs had a higher birth rate than the Jewish Israelis, meaning that they might soon become a majority.[34] If most Israelis reject a co-equal binational state, how could they be expected to accept the prospect of becoming a minority?

In short, the binational solution is a utopian fantasy. And in the current circumstances, if it was tried it could end in disaster, as has been the case in a number of other attempts to create stable binational states, such as the civil war that followed efforts to create a binational Greek-Turkish state in Cyprus in the 1970s; the many periods of violent Muslim-Christian conflict within Lebanon; the breakup of Yugoslavia and the ensuing nationalist or religious wars of the 1990s; the ongoing Hindu-Muslim communal violence in India, and the unending tribal or religious intrastate conflicts in Africa since the end of the colonial era.

The Jewish State Issue

In 2014, Netanyahu introduced a new demand—the Palestinians must recognize Israel as a Jewish state, not just as the outcome of a peace settlement, but as a precondition before negotiations could begin. Moreover, he and his ally Donald Trump have upped the ante even further, as they now demand Palestinian recognition of Israel "as the nation-state of the Jewish people." The difference is significant: Israel today has less than 7 million Jews, whereas the core Jewish population in the rest of the world is over 8 million, including some 7 million in the United States alone. The intended implication of the "nation-state of the Jews" formulation is that all Jews outside of Israel must be regarded—and regard themselves—as a "diaspora," yearning to return to their true home, Israel.

The disconnect between the diaspora concept and reality is startling. If anything, the converse is the case; for example, though the figures are not precise, some studies have estimated that since 1948, only about 150,000 American Jews have relocated to Israel, whereas estimates of the number of Israelis who have moved to the United States range between 500,000 to 1 million. If I may interject a personal note, as a member of the American Jewish community, I have yet to meet who thinks of him- or herself as part of a "diaspora," yearning to "return" to their real homeland.

The importance of the Jewish state demand, even in its more modest version, as an obstacle to a two-state settlement warrants a more detailed discussion. In May 2011, Netanyahu said, "It's time for President Abbas to stand up before his people and say, 'I will accept a Jewish state,'" a demand that has been repeatedly reiterated by Netanyahu—and now by Trump—since then.

There has been some ambiguity over how the Jewish state demand is to be understood. Is it an Israeli precondition before negotiations for a two-state settlement can even begin, or only a necessary outcome of such negotiations? The weight of the evidence suggests that Netanyahu and most members of his coalition intend it as a precondition, and that is certainly how the Palestinian political leaders have interpreted it.

Although the UN partition plan specifically called for the creation of an independent "Jewish state," alongside an "Arab state," for more than fifty years after the creation of Israel, its leaders did not make formal Arab recognition of Israel as a Jewish state a central demand in the negotiations for peace settlements. Consequently, Israel signed peace treaties with Egypt in 1979 and with Jordan in 1994 without asking or receiving official Arab recognition of Israel as a Jewish state. Indeed, even in negotiations with the Palestinians, there was no such demand included in the Oslo negotiations of 1992–93 or at the 2000 Camp David and Taba negotiations.

The issue apparently arose for the first time in 2002, when Sharon declared that a peace agreement with the Palestinians must include "references to Israel's right to exist as a Jewish state and to the waiver of any right of return for Palestinian refugees to the State of Israel."[35] In 2007, Israeli prime minister Ehud Olmert reportedly took the same position.[36]

Nonetheless, neither Sharon nor Olmert had made the Jewish state demand a central issue, or insisted that the Palestinians explicitly accept the demand as a precondition for a two-state settlement. For these reasons, Netanyahu's demand is best understood as a cynical ploy to raise yet another obstacle to a two-state agreement.[37]

That said, it does not necessarily follow that the Palestinians are wise to reject out of hand the Jewish state demand, for it has now become a major issue not only for Netanyahu—who in any case would almost surely find other grounds to reject a serious two-state settlement—but for the Israeli general public, which, in theory at least, might under certain circumstances accept some kind of Palestinian state.

To be sure, in light of Israeli policies and the irreversible situation on the ground, it is hard to imagine any circumstances in which the international consensus two-state solution could again become feasible. However, it is at least conceivable that under certain circumstances, beginning with a future election of an Israeli centrist government (the chances that a "leftist" government can be elected in the foreseeable future are nonexistent), Israel might allow the Palestinians to have a more limited state.

Before that can happen, the Palestinians must forthrightly accept that Israel is and will remain a Jewish state, generally understood to mean a state in which Jews are a large majority and have political sovereignty, whose armed forces and other security institutions are overwhelmingly Jewish—that is, predominantly Jewish in culture and religion—and that allows, as a matter of right, unlimited Jewish immigration.

It was understandable that the Palestinians rejected Netanyahu's demand that they formally recognize Israel as a Jewish state as a precondition to even begin negotiations for a two-state settlement. There were several reasons for their decision. First, it is obvious that Netanyahu's demand was a pretext for avoiding such negotiations, and that if the Palestinians accepted it he would find other pretexts. Second, the Palestinians feared that defining Israel as a Jewish state would prejudice the political and civil rights of the Israeli Arab citizens, some 21 percent of the population. As well, they feared that formal Palestinian recognition of Israel as a Jewish state would make even more unlikely the implementation of a "right of return" for Palestinian refugees.

These are significant arguments. Even so, the Palestinian leadership has erred in continuing to refuse the Jewish state demand, if for no other reason than that, once Netanyahu raised the issue, an overwhelming majority of the Jewish Israelis have supported it, if not necessarily as a precondition but certainly as a necessary outcome of peace negotiations.

In any case, aside from the practical considerations, there is a strong argument, on the merits, for Israel to continue as a Jewish state, at least until dramatically changed circumstances make possible the implementation of the utopian binational or "state of all its citizens" concept. To begin, though it has often been argued that democracy does not allow for discrimination between different groups, it is not difficult to show that in reality there are many other basically democratic states that, in one way or another, privilege their ethnic or religious majorities; the literature on the subject cites Greece, Ireland, the Slovak Republic, Slovenia, and in some respects even France and other Western democracies.[38] Since even genuine democracies often, in one way or another, privilege some of its people over others, the extent to which there are departures from the ideal of full and equal rights for everyone matters a great deal.

It is also relevant that the UN Partition plan explicitly divided Palestine into "Arab and Jewish states," and that from the time of its creation, Israel has been recognized by most of the world as a Jewish state. In the past, even many Palestinian leaders, including Yasser Arafat, also did so, and there are many indications that despite their public statements, the private position of many of the current Palestinian leaders is much more flexible.

For example, in a 2002 *New York Times* op-ed, Arafat strongly implied that there could be Palestinian recognition of a Jewish state in the context of a two-state agreement.[39] In the 2003 Geneva Accords, Arafat said that so long as the Israelis granted equal rights to the Israeli Arabs, they had the right to "determine the identity" of their state. In 2004, Arafat told *Haaretz* that he "definitely" understood and accepted that Israel must continue to be a Jewish state: "[The Palestinians] accepted that openly and officially in 1988 at our Palestine National Council . . . and they remain completely committed to it."[40]

To be sure, Arafat—characteristically—was inconsistent, sometimes contradicting himself by saying he would *not* recognize Israel as a Jewish state. As well, Mahmoud Abbas, despite his unmistakable commitment to a two-state settlement, has sometimes publicly rejected the Jewish state demand, but at the same time left himself an out:

> The "Jewish state." What is a "Jewish state"? We call it, the "State of Israel." You can call yourselves whatever you want. . . . It's not my job to define it, to provide a definition for the state and what it contains. You can call yourselves the Zionist Republic, the Hebrew, the National, the Socialist [Republic], call it whatever you like.[41]

Other high Palestinian officials have gone further than Abbas; for example, in 2010, Yasser Abed Rabbo, secretary general of the PLO, bluntly stated that in the context of a two-state settlement, Palestine would offer "recognition of Israel under any formula,"[42] and in 2011 the prominent PLO and PA negotiator Saeb Erekat told Israeli negotiators that "if you want to call your state the Jewish state of Israel . . . call it what you want," and he told his own staff that the matter was "a non issue."[43] Thus, there are good reasons to believe that the moderate Palestinian leadership would recognize Israel as a Jewish state as a final component in an overall Israeli-Palestinian two-state settlement.

The Anti-Semitism Problem

The most important reason for Israel to continue as a Jewish state is the persistence and recently the apparent intensification of anti-Semitism in the world, even in Europe, where an increasing number of Jews are considering emigration to Israel, the United States, or Canada.[44] Even in the United States, the recent individual attacks on Jews is worrisome—though both public authorities and the general public have unreservedly condemned them and instituted measures to prevent further attacks and protect Jewish synagogues and other potential targets. Nonetheless, though present-day anti-Semitism remains far short of threatening the lives of global Jewry, in light of past history, particularly but not limited to the Holocaust, it can never be said that murderous anti-Semitism is a thing of the past. Consequently, there is no basis for the claim that there is no longer a need for a Jewish state. As the American political philosopher Alan Wolfe has put it:

> Jews [can] never succumb to any illusion of security the Diaspora seemingly offers. . . . Jews must keep their mental suitcases constantly packed. It is only a matter of time before societies long known for their record of anti-Semitism, especially those in Eastern Europe such as Hungary, Ukraine, and Russia, return to their pattern of hating the Jews.[45]

None of this to deny what ought to be obvious: that Israel's treatment of the Palestinians has had a lot to do with growing anti-Semitism, especially among Muslims in the Middle East and Europe. Still, while it is likely that a fair peace settlement with the Palestinians would do a lot to mitigate the problem, in the meantime Israel can hardly be expected to agree to give up its status as a Jewish state that can serve as a refuge for Jews wishing to emigrate there.

The Right of Return Issue

The Israeli political philosopher Zeev Sternhell writes:

> If I were a Palestinian . . . I would instantly agree to Benjamin Netanyahu's demand to recognize Israel as the nation-state of the Jewish people. . . . At the same time I would loudly declare that I relinquish the right of return of Palestinian refugees, since only delusional people really believe that they will one day return to Haifa, Ramle or Tiberias.[46]

His argument is persuasive. As I have discussed, for all practical purposes most Palestinian leaders have already abandoned the right of return demand, except perhaps for a symbolic return of a few thousand refugees. The Israeli political leaders know this, so the right of return "issue" is just another pretext for them to avoid a settlement with the Palestinians—not so much a lost opportunity as a deliberately discarded one. Nonetheless, while it is understandable that Palestinian leaders have not been willing to publicly and unambiguously drop the right of return demand, they must do so and candidly explain why to the Palestinian people if there is to be a chance for even a greatly modified two-state settlement.

Paradoxical as it may be, the Israelis evidently need Palestinian reassurances, for they fear that their country is becoming "delegitimized"—its very existence supposedly threatened by a coordinated and deliberate "international campaign." Of course this concern is entirely misplaced: most Israelis are blind to the consequences of their country's policies and actions and simply deny the obvious, namely, that it is not the "existence" of Israel but its occupation and repression of the Palestinians that is regarded as illegitimate. Yet, for historical and psychological reasons, the Israeli fears are real, so they are genuine obstacles to peace. In that light, Palestinian formal recognition of Israel as a "Jewish state" and its dropping of the essentially symbolic "right of return" demand that has no chance of being accepted is essential to pave the way toward a revival of a peace process.

The Israeli Arabs

Finally, what of the argument that the continuation of Israel as a Jewish state, formally accepted as such by the Palestinians, would prejudice the rights of the Israeli Arab minority? So long as the current 21 percent Arab minority does not become far larger, there is no inherent inconsistency between Israel as a Jewish state and equal civil, political, and economic rights for the Israeli Arabs. In fact, the Israeli Declaration of Independence—explicitly creating a Jewish state—promised to "ensure complete equality of social and political rights to all its inhabitants irrespective of religion [or] race . . . [and] guarantee freedom of religion, conscience, language, education and culture."

Of course, that promise has been broken, for in a variety of ways the Israeli Arabs have always been treated as second-class citizens. Even the Israelis have acknowledged this, and over the years their leaders have repeatedly committed themselves to end this injustice, only to renege. Consequently, it could be argued that even if Israel agreed to full equality for the Palestinian and other minorities in a Jewish state, there would be no guarantee that it would honor its new commitments and no means of enforcement if it didn't.

True, but it stands to reason that the rights of the Israeli Arabs would have a greater chance of being realized if a peace settlement included a formal commitment by Israel that it will grant and enforce full citizenship and equality to them. And in the context of real peace between the Israeli and Palestinian people, there would be a much greater likelihood that Israel would honor its own declared principles and formal guarantees.

Yet an uncomfortable question remains: What if the current Israeli Arab minority became much larger, perhaps because its birth rates continue, as in the past, to be higher than that of the Israeli Jews? And how much higher would it have to be to challenge Jewish predominance in an Israeli democracy? Perhaps surprisingly, Moshe Arens, long one of Israel's most prominent right-wing political leaders, has addressed this issue in an interesting and forthright manner:

> Most Israelis are determined to assure the state's Jewish character . . . while respecting its Arab citizens. We insist on continuing the mission that the Jewish state has set for itself of providing a haven for those Jews throughout the world who may need one. What happened during the Holocaust can never be allowed to happen again. This requires a substantial Jewish majority.
>
> How big a majority? That's a question that needs to be pondered. Is the present 80 percent Jewish majority sufficient? Would a reduction to a

> 70 percent Jewish majority be a catastrophe? Is it solely a question of numbers or is it also a function of the degree to which Israel's minority population has been integrated into Israeli society?[47]

In fact, the differentials between the Jewish and Arab populations of Israel have changed very little since late 1948, as the Jews have continued to maintain the roughly 80 percent majority that the founders of Israel thought necessary to ensure that Israel would be a Jewish state. As well, there is increasing evidence that the birth rate differential that many Israelis feared is disappearing, at least as of 2013, when according to Israeli government statistics, the Israeli Arab birthrate was only slightly higher than the Jewish birthrate. As well, most demographers think that today the differential has further declined. Moreover, if global anti-Semitism worsens, the immigration of Jews into Israel would almost certainly increase, and if a Palestinian state, even a small one, is created, it is likely that some of the Israeli Arabs—or "Palestinian Israelis," as they are often called—would relocate to it. In short, the hypothetical problem—or dilemma—of an ever-growing Arab population in a state that wanted to preserve a large Jewish majority while remaining a democracy for all its citizens is highly unlikely to occur.

In the final analysis, it has become tragically necessary to separate the Jewish state demand, in principle, from the kind of Jewish state Israel has become. Zionism's drive to create a state for the Jewish people was designed to serve two purposes. The most fundamental was to provide a refuge that would ensure the well-being and security of the Jewish people, wherever they were endangered by the ever-recurring historical cycles of murderous global anti-Semitism—most recently, of course, the Holocaust. But beyond that, the Jewish state of Israel was to be a moral exemplar for all mankind, the famous "light unto the nations."

If only. As Henry Siegman, a former national director of the American Jewish Congress, eloquently put it: "Israel's problem is not the Palestinian or Arab refusal to recognize it as a Jewish state. It is, rather, the increasing difficulty of Jews familiar with Jewish values to recognize it as a Jewish state."[48] In that light, it is tempting to conclude that while there may continue to be a strong case for a Jewish state, *this* one won't do: meaning, of course, not that Israel should "cease to exist," whatever that is supposed to mean, but only that Israel's behavior continues to undercut the argument that a Jewish state is still a good idea.

A Palestinian Ministate: A Possible Solution?

The Trump Plan (or as I have termed it, the Trump-Netanyahu Plan) is the final nail in the coffin of the international consensus two-state settlement. As well, there is no chance for a democratic binational one-state solution. The Israelis will not agree to either, and there will be no significant outside pressures on them to do so, whether from the United States, Western Europe, or the Arab states. And even if there were such pressures, they would likely fail, as they always have in the past. Likewise, Palestinian nonviolent protest and resistance would fail, and violent resistance, terrorist or not, would be ruthlessly crushed.

Whether formally or de facto, it is likely that whether under Netanyahu or Gantz or any other electable leader, Israel will annex the Jordan River Valley, except for the Palestinian city of Jericho. And even if Israel does not formally annex much of the rest of the West Bank, the most likely prospect in the near future will be the continuation of its traditional strategy—and, it must be admitted, so far a successful one—of creating irreversible "facts on the ground," also known as "creeping" or de facto annexation. Moreover, the strategy is all too likely to be accompanied by a "transfer" process—already in fact underway—as Israel continues in a variety of ways to deliberately make the lives of the Palestinians so unpleasant that increasing numbers of them, especially in the Jordan River Valley, give up and relocate elsewhere. For those who remain, unless an alternative solution is found, it is probable that the Palestinians will become increasingly marginalized and confined to impoverished and beleaguered Gaza and West Bank "Bantustans."

For this reason, it may not be wise for the Palestinians to reject the Trump Plan in its entirety, for it just possibly could open the door for the creation of a Palestinian ministate. Clearly the creation of such a state would be morally and in many other ways far inferior to a true two-state settlement; nonetheless, it would have a good chance of being better than the unending misery that otherwise the Palestinians are likely to face.

The territory that could comprise a Palestinian state would be principally in Gaza and the Oslo-designated "Area A" of the West Bank. Though that area comprises only about 18 percent of the West Bank, it includes the eight largest Palestinian population centers and their nearby surroundings, which together contain most of the 2.7 million to 2.8 million Palestinians in the West Bank.

To be sure, the creation of a Palestinian state in Area A and Gaza would leave Israel free to annex the Jewish settlements in the rest of the West Bank. However, as I have argued, that is going to happen in one form or another, if indeed it hasn't already, in practice, occurred. In that light, the end of futile Palestinian resistance to that inevitable outcome could make it more likely that Netanyahu or at least a more centrist Israeli government could support the creation of a Palestinian ministate.

Perhaps one could think of this as a "Luxembourg solution." The prosperity and security of Luxembourg—and even that of the yet smaller European "microstates" of Lichtenstein, San Remo, and Andorra—provide a model for very small states that can become prosperous, democratic, and safe, so long as they are not perceived as threatening to the far larger states that surround them; for example, the obviously defenseless Luxembourg is wedged between Germany, France, and Belgium.

Although the general principles that could guide such a solution to the Israeli-Palestinian conflict can only be briefly sketched out here, the Luxembourg model illuminates the conditions in which ministates can work:

First, instead of having the capacity to defend themselves, the European ministates must rely on the lack of interest of nearby far stronger states in taking them over. A Palestinian ministate could meet that condition, for even if Israel formally or de facto annexes Area C, constituting 60 percent of the West Bank, almost certainly it will continue to have no interest—far from it—in annexing the approximately 4.8 million Palestinians in Gaza and the major Palestinian cities in the West Bank.[49]

Second, as is the case with Luxembourg, the ministate must not be seen as threatening to its neighbors. The necessary precondition for a Palestinian ministate to be accepted by Israel, then, is its renunciation of all forms of violence, radicalism, and intransigence, including by Hamas and other Islamic fundamentalist groups. And if those groups fail or refuse to do so, they must be excluded from political power and brought firmly under the control of the Palestine government, with or without Israel's help.

Those are not utopian conditions, at least in the case of Hamas, for there is strong evidence that the leading Palestinian Islamic organization has become increasingly resigned to either some kind of two-state solution or, alternatively, to limiting its rule to Gaza. Indeed, there is also increasing evidence that Israel is ready to accept the continuation of Hamas rule in Gaza, so long as it ends attacks on Israel from its territory. In any case, Israel would hardly have to "trust" the Palestinians not to return to violence at a later point—any more than Germany, Belgium, and France have to "trust" Luxembourg—for within a few days Israel could end Palestinian independence and resume the occupation.

Third, the ministate must be economically viable. Though it is lacking mineral resources, Luxembourg—thanks largely to the thriving banking and trading services that it provides to Western Europe—is regarded as one of the most prosperous states in the world.[50] The other European ministates are almost equally prosperous.

It is often said that the Palestinian people are a literate, well-educated, and industrious people with a talent for entrepreneurship—or would be, if given any chance to develop their economy. If so, a ministate, despite its grave limitations, just might be an opportunity for them to do so. Undoubtedly it would require substantial international economic assistance at the outset, but there is every reason to expect that this would be forthcoming from a world that would welcome the end to the Israeli-Palestinian conflict. Note, for example, that the Trump Plan calls for a $50 billion economic development program for the Palestinians, if the kind of settlement it envisages materializes.

It must be admitted that there are significant problems with the Palestinian ministate solution that European ministates did not have to face. First, the lack of geographical contiguity between sections of the state would have to be ameliorated in one way or another; at present, the Palestinian cities in the West Bank are not connected to each other or to East Jerusalem, and Gaza is not connected to any part of the West Bank. Still, the distances are quite small and manageable—provided that Israel refrains from interfering with the roads, rail lines, and small corridors that the Trump Plan proposes as a means of connecting all Palestinian territories to each other.

That may seem to be a utopian condition, and in the context of continued Israeli-Palestinian conflict, it surely would be. However, if the Palestinians adhere to the main conditions demanded by Israel—a demilitarized state under the firm political control of a moderate government resigned to a ministate solution, a definitive Palestinian rejection of a refugee "right of return" to Israel, and the disarmament of Hamas and other rejectionist Palestinian organizations—it is hard to see why Israel would have an incentive to break the agreement and return to occupation, repression, and ongoing violence.

Moreover, the Israelis would have significant economic and other incentives *not* to disrupt such an agreement. Not only would a return to occupation be highly costly in the broadest sense of that word—a fact that explains the reluctance of the Israeli military to resume major attacks on Gaza—but a modern Palestinian economy would benefit Israel as well, through trade, mutual investment, joint development projects, and other ways.

Finally—and probably the most difficult problem—there would have to be an agreement on the location of the Palestinian capital. The Trump Plan's proposal that the town of Abu Dis—which no longer is even physically connected to East Jerusalem—be accepted by the Palestinians as their capital has no chance of being accepted. However, if every other issue were resolved, and a more reasonable government is elected in Israel, perhaps the Israelis would agree to some variation of previous proposed settlements, such as "shared sovereignty" of the Old City. Lest that seem far-fetched, it is well to remember that such a Jerusalem solution was a central part of Prime Minister Ehud Olmert's 2008 peace plan.

It is sometimes argued that the Palestinian people would never accept such a truncated state. Maybe not now, and not unless the Jerusalem issues can be resolved, but if it were, the Palestinian leaders could then put the matter to a referendum and state something like this: "If we accept the plan, we will get a state of our own, with control over our religious sites and our capital in part of East Jerusalem; the unlimited right of all Palestinian refugees to return to their own state within the historic land of Palestine; the end of Israeli attacks and economic blockades or other sanctions; and international assistance in developing our economy. But if we reject it, the opportunity may never come again, and we will face an indefinite future of Israeli occupation, repression, violence, poverty, and forced or voluntary exile."

All of that said, and even if the central issues can be resolved, it is obvious that a Palestinian ministate in noncontiguous areas of the West Bank would be inferior in every way to the kind of two-state solution embodied in the international consensus and would constitute yet another injustice to the Palestinian people. However, the key issue is, compared to what? It can only be recommended because the probable real-world alternatives are much worse.[51]

Finally, I am painfully aware not only that the Palestinians may reject the argument I have made here, and indeed resent what might be seen as patronization—and from an American Jew, no less. Yet, I'd like to hope it will be seen as a good-faith effort to at least introduce into political discourse a possible alternative to the otherwise bleak prospect for the future of the Palestinian people.

Israel and the US National Interest

The nearly unconditional American support for Israel is explained by a number of factors: the widespread belief in the United States that the history of Western anti-Semitism has made it a moral obligation; political affinities, especially the belief that Americans have both the national interest and the moral obligation to support "the only democracy in the Middle East"; shared religious beliefs, or "the Judeo-Christian heritage"; admiration for Israel's military prowess; shared anti-communism during the Cold War; the joint struggle against Islamic radicalism and terrorism in the post–Cold War era; and finally, domestic politics, especially the influence and power of the Israel lobby in the United States.[52]

The interplay of a number of these factors, especially the moral and religious beliefs and electoral considerations, greatly influenced President Harry Truman to support the creation of Israel. He took this stance despite the opposition of most of the foreign and defense policy officials in the US government who believed that supporting Israel was not in the nation's interest, as it would almost certainly antagonize the Arabs; the fear was that the Arab countries might turn away from the United States and toward the Soviet Union for military support in the Arab-Israeli conflict, and also possibly decrease US access to Middle Eastern oil, then crucial to the American economy.

These arguments, based strictly on the perceived national interests at stake, were not so much rebutted as they were overridden by Truman. In any case, as the Cold War intensified and the Ben-Gurion government decided to end its early neutrality and align itself with the United States and the West, Israel came to be seen as a "strategic asset," crucial to the goals of containing possible Soviet expansionism in the Middle East.

In fact, the growing US ties with Israel actually opened the door to the spread of Soviet influence, as the leading Arab states, especially Egypt, turned to the Soviets for military assistance to offset the rising power of Israel. Rather than containing Soviet "penetration" of the Middle East, then, US support of Israel and its growing power in the region gave the Soviets both the motive and the opportunity to acquire its own allies in the region, in an essentially defensive and reactive effort to balance US influence. Put differently, if the United States had not decided to support Israel in the Arab-Israeli conflict, it likely would have had no need for a strategic ally in the Middle East.

As for the oil issue, it is true that the potential conflict between US support of Israel and access to Arab oil did not materialize, except for the leaky Saudi "oil embargo" that was briefly imposed on the United States after the 1973 Israeli-Egyptian war. Even so, had the United States remained neutral in the Arab-Israeli conflict, there would have been no risk at all to its access to Middle Eastern oil.

Since the end of the Cold War, the most important American national interests in the Middle East have been the maintenance of regional stability, the containment of Islamic fundamentalist expansionism, and—above all—the avoidance of international terrorism as well as interstate war in an environment in which weapons of mass destruction and the means to deliver them are rapidly spreading. American support of, or collaboration with, current Israeli policies toward the Palestinians undercuts all these interrelated interests.

Today, though, the oil issue is far less important. As a result of numerous factors—among them the expansion of American domestic oil production and the increasing turn toward to natural gas and other energy sources—the United States today not only has little need for Middle Eastern oil (or, for that matter, imported oil from anywhere), but has become a net *exporter* of oil.[53] These trends are expected to continue in the foreseeable future.

The stability and terrorism issues, however, are another matter. Although the rise of Islamic fundamentalist fanaticism and terrorism has had much more to do with Arab poverty as well as the corruption and authoritarian misrule of Arab leaders, it is exacerbated by populist rage at Israel and the United States and has thus endangered this country, as demonstrated in the 9/11 attacks on the World Trade Center and the Pentagon.

Israel and its supporters frequently deny that 9/11 had anything to do with US support of Israel—George Bush said that its cause was that "they hated our values"—but there is now a wealth of evidence on the motivations of Islamic terrorists to attack the United States:

- Osama Bin Laden repeatedly stated that the 9/11 attacks in 2001 were primarily motivated by US support of Israel as, for example, in a 2009 video message addressed to the American people: "This is my message to you: a reminder of the reasons behind 9/11 and the wars and the repercussions that followed. . . . Are your security, your blood, your children . . . dearer to you than the security of the Israelis?"[54]
- As well, Khalid Sheikh Muhammed, described by the US 9/11 Investigation Commission as "the principal architect of the attacks," told his American captors that his hatred of the United States "stemmed from . . . his violent disagreement with U.S. foreign policy favoring Israel."[55]

- In 2010 General David Petraeus, then head of the US Central Command in the Middle East, told the Senate Armed Forces Committee that the Israeli occupation was fomenting anti-American sentiment throughout the Islamic world and hindering the development of America's partnership with Arab governments. Similarly Petraeus's successor, General James Mattis, publicly stated: "I paid a military security price every day as a commander of CENTCOM because the Americans were seen as biased in support of Israel, and that [alienates] all the moderate Arabs who want to be with us because they can't come out publicly in support of people who don't show respect for the Arab Palestinians."[56]

To be sure, one could acknowledge the painfully obvious connection between the US-Israeli alliance and anti-American Arab and Islamic rage but still argue that US support for Israel should continue on the grounds that the military power of Israel is a strategic asset that offsets its political liabilities. However, in practice, Israel's vaunted military strength has proven to be of little or no value to the United States. For example, when this country went to war against Iraq in 1991 and 2003, it not only didn't need but actively discouraged a direct Israeli military contribution. The policy assumption was that the military value of whatever assistance Israel could provide would be far outweighed by its political costs, particularly in terms of gaining the support or at least acquiescence of America's major Arab allies in the Middle East.

The only truly vital national interests of the United States in the Middle East today are to avoid either being drawn into regional conflicts or becoming a target for terrorist attacks, especially weapons of mass destruction attacks, on our own country. Both of those interests are harmed, not furthered, by US support of Israel in its continuing conflict with the Palestinians.

The Moral Issues

Aside from the national interest of the United States in settling the Israeli-Palestinian conflict, moral considerations should play a major role in determining US policies. The moral argument for continued US support for the existence and basic security of Israel is still strong, of course, but Israel today faces no such "existential" threat, except perhaps from a nuclear attack by Islamic fanatics—a possible threat that would be greatly lessened by an Israeli-Palestinian peace settlement.

In light of the absence of overriding national interests, considerations of morality and justice should be at the heart of US policies toward the Palestinians, who have paid, and continue to pay, a very high price for the creation of Israel. Some of that price—though hardly all—may have been unavoidable at the outset of the conflict, but since then the conflict could have been resolved had it not been for Israeli intransigence, in collaboration with the United States. Consequently, more than seventy years of strong support for Israel has created for the United States a compelling obligation to now counterbalance unconstrained Israeli power and level the playing field.

In short, for reasons of both the national interest—avoiding Middle East wars or terrorist attacks on the American homeland—and justice, the United States should make its support of Israel political conditional on Israeli acceptance of some kind of limited Palestinian state, perhaps something along the lines of what I have called a "Luxembourg solution."

US Pressure

The American government has a variety of means that might be used as leverage over Israeli policies. US political, diplomatic, economic, and military support of Israel has been crucial to that country since its creation. Economic assistance began in 1948 and was gradually increased until it ended in 2008, when Israel agreed it no longer needed it. Since then, however, Israel has continued to benefit from US laws specifically designed to encourage private financial support—for example, the granting of "nonprofit" status to pro-Israeli US organizations, making contributions to them tax deductible.

US military assistance to Israel has been even more important, and it continues today. Beginning in 1959 at a relatively low level, it was greatly increased by the Nixon administration in 1974 and the Reagan administration in the early 1980s. Currently, Israel gets $3.8 billion annually, in a program begun by the Obama administration in 2016 and scheduled to continue until 2026, an amount that accounts for about a fifth of Israel's defense budget.[57]

As in the case of economic assistance, the real value of US military support of Israel is much higher, in the first instance because the American government is committed to maintaining Israel's technological military superiority over the Arab states; for just one example, in the Middle East only Israel is allowed to buy the most advanced US fighter jets. Beyond that, the United States holds regular joint military exercises with Israel, and the two countries work closely together on military planning, research, and intelligence.

Altogether, the various direct forms of US economic and military aid to Israel are estimated to total over $140 billion, making that country the largest recipient of US foreign aid since World War II.[58]

The extent to which US support of Israel in the past provided leverage over Israeli policies is another matter. There is no question that when the US government was serious about forcing changes in those policies, it was often successful:

- In late 1948, after Truman threatened a wholesale reassessment if Israel didn't stop its advances into Egypt's Sinai peninsula, Ben-Gurion agreed to withdraw the Israeli forces.

- In 1948 and early 1949, under heavy US pressure, Israel withdrew from parts of the Sinai and southern Lebanon.
- In 1953, after major Israeli raids against Jordan and violations of the demilitarized zones separating Syria from Israel, Eisenhower threatened to suspend all US aid to Israel if it didn't desist. Israel complied.
- In the 1956 war, Israel invaded Sinai and intended to permanently occupy much of the area, but it hastily withdrew its forces in the face of Soviet threats of military intervention and Eisenhower's threats to end all US aid.
- In the 1967 war, US pressures forced Israel to accept a ceasefire and refrain from further advances into Syria.
- During the 1970–73 exchanges of fire between Israel and Egypt along the Suez Canal, Israel began bombing populated areas of Egypt far from the canal—but ended the so-called deep penetration raids, which might have led to Soviet intervention and a direct superpower confrontation, when the Nixon administration began suspending arms deliveries to Israel.
- Similarly, in the 1973 Arab-Israeli war, Israel agreed to a ceasefire and halted its advance into Egypt only after the Nixon administration threatened to end the American military airlift to Israel and to fly in food, water, and medicine to surrounded Egyptian forces.
- In 1975, Israel agreed to a partial withdrawal from the Sinai only after Ford combined promises of new American aid with the threat of a major shift in US policy if Israel refused to do so.
- In 1978, Jimmy Carter wrote a letter to Menachem Begin warning of a suspension of US aid if Israel continued with its invasion of South Lebanon; Begin withdrew the Israeli troops.
- In 1979, the Carter administration used carrot-and-stick policies to induce Begin to agree to the complete withdrawal of Israel from the Sinai in exchange for a peace treaty with Egypt.
- In July 1981, suspensions of some US military aid deliveries, this time augmented by pressures from American Jewish leaders and close supporters of Israel in Congress, convinced Begin to end the bombing of civilians in Beirut and accept a ceasefire in Lebanon or face a major shift in American attitudes toward Israel.
- A year later, the Israelis discarded their planned ground assault against PLO forces in Beirut after strong Reagan administration and congressional warnings threatened the end of the policy of unconditional US aid to Israel.

Nonetheless, it is important to understand that US pressures have been successful only when Israel sought to overturn the territorial status quo or when its military attacks caused extensive civilian damage. By contrast, US pressures have been ineffective whenever Israel has believed—however dubiously—that its truly vital national interests were at stake, particularly in its opposition to a two-state solution. In 1977 the Israeli foreign minister put it this way:

> If the U.S. insists on a Palestinian state . . . any Israeli Government would reject it. If we have to make the choice . . . we would rather have problems with the U.S. than agree to a Palestinian state which we seriously think would eventually bring the destruction of Israel.[59]

In any case, when Israel makes it clear that it will resist American pressures regardless of the consequences, the pressures are typically weak, unsustained, and quickly abandoned. For example, Israel used *its* leverage in Congress to force President Ford to back down from his 1975 threat to "reassess" American policy unless Israel withdrew from the occupied territories. And in the late 1990s, while Bill Clinton was often angered by Israeli intransigence in peace negotiations, he refused to use American aid as leverage, even when being urged to do so by some members of his administration. According to Aaron Miller, a former State Department official specializing in the Arab-Israeli conflict during this period, the US government never held "an honest conversation about what the Israelis were actually doing on the ground. Nor were we prepared to impose, at least in the last seven or eight years, a cost on the Israelis for their actions."[60]

Finally, after initial indications that Obama intended to change the near unconditional US support of Israel in its policies toward the Palestinians, he backed down when it became clear that he would face strong congressional resistance that could jeopardize his domestic program.

This history has often convinced Israeli governments that it can ignore American pressures or mobilize congressional and public opposition to them, causing the US government to back down. For example, Moshe Dayan once said: "Our American friends offer us money, arms, and advice. We take the money, we take the arms, and we decline the advice."[61] More recently, when Netanyahu was asked in 2012 whether his policies would jeopardize relations with the United States, not realizing he was being recorded he responded: "I know what America is. America is something that can be easily moved. They won't get in our way."[62]

While that has not always been true, as demonstrated by the instances in which US pressures succeeded, there is next to no chance that the American government—especially, of course, the Trump administration, but probably even a Democratic successor—would adopt serious pressures in an effort to force Israel to end the occupation, withdraw the settlers, and accept a Palestinian state in most of the West Bank and Gaza—that is, the standard two-state solution. And even if such pressures were applied, it is hard to imagine they would succeed.

On the other hand, however, pressures to require Israel to accept a Palestinian *ministate* in the West Bank and Gaza—one that would allow Israel to keep all its settlements and maintain overall political and military control over most of the West Bank—might be successful, as long as the Palestinians agree to drop the right of return, publicly accept Israel as a Jewish state, and end all violence against it.

In such circumstances, there would be several reasons to be hopeful about the prospects for a settlement. To begin, there is little American support for an Israeli annexation of most of the West Bank, even from mainstream Democrats who have always supported whatever policies an Israeli government followed—and recently even from a few prominent Republicans as well as from the usual conservative, "pro-Israeli" quarters.[63]

As well, should a new US administration and Congress come to power in 2021 and give serious consideration to employing US leverage if Israel continues to refuse to consider any form of Palestinian statehood, it would have strong support from a number of prominent Israelis.

Over forty years ago, George Ball, one of America's leading foreign policy statesmen, wrote a famous article calling on the United States to "Save Israel in Spite of Herself."[64] Israel's hard-line policies were jeopardizing the chances for real peace, Ball argued, requiring the United States to act against Israeli government policies—but on behalf of true Israeli interests. Many Israeli analysts, including a number of past military leaders and government officials, agreed with Ball and decried the failure or refusal of the American government to use its leverage to prevent Israel from destroying itself, especially by its constant settlement expansions in the West Bank. Here are a few examples:

- In a December 30, 1982, op-ed in the *New York Times*, Major General Mattityahu Peled, retired, a member of the Israeli General Staff in the 1967 war, wrote that lavish US military aid was making the IDF far too strong, even jeopardizing civilian control, and said that he and other retired military men would welcome US pressures on behalf of a two-state settlement.
- In the same period, Max Frankel, the editorial page editor of the *New York Times*, wrote a number of columns reporting that opposition Labor Party leaders had "privately indicated to him that they wanted the United States to exert pressure on Begin's government and hasten its end by reducing the level of economic assistance."[65]
- In September 1997, during Netanyahu's first prime ministership, he rejected a plea by US secretary of state Albright that Israel freeze settlement expansion; the Israeli columnist Yoel Marcus wrote that Albright had "left her stick at home," allowing "Bibi to win this round . . . to the frustration of many moderate Israelis who had hoped that Ms. Albright would apply pressure on both Mr. Arafat and Mr. Netanyahu." Indeed, even the Israeli president, Ezer Weizman—another former leading Israeli general—urged Secretary of State Albright to be firm with both Arafat and Netanyahu and "bang some heads together."[66]
- In September 2002, former foreign minister Shlomo Ben-Ami and retired deputy chief of staff General Amnon Shahak sent a letter to President Bush saying that the peace process was deadlocked and called on the US government to "move

beyond its traditional roles as a mediator . . . to develop in detail a solution and vigorously encourage both sides [to agree to it]."[67]

Other prominent Israelis have not bothered with euphemisms like "vigorously encourage." For example, David Landau, the editor of the English-language edition of *Haaretz*, wrote:

> The US must "save Israel in spite of itself. . . . He [Bush] must firmly state that Israeli occupation compromises the national interests of the United States. To save Israel in spite of itself? Yes . . . on our own we will never extricate ourselves. . . . [U]nless the United States pulls us out by the scruff of the neck we will continue to wallow in the mire.[68]

By the early 2000s, Zeev Sternhell wrote that it was the standard view among Israeli liberals that the United States and the international community had to impose a peace settlement, since neither the Israelis nor the Palestinians could reach one by themselves.[69]

Even Israeli governments have sometimes privately welcomed US pressures, hoping that it would help them resist domestic opposition and let them do what they really wanted to do. In 1976, Malcolm Toon, for many years one of America's most important diplomats and then the US ambassador to Israel, sent a telegram to Secretary of State Henry Kissinger. The "easiest course" for Israeli governments, he wrote, was to give in to popular pressures against Israeli concessions:

> In the absence of counterpressure it will always be easier for an Israeli prime minister and government to yield on issues which seem to have popular support, even though they violate international wishes and complicate the overall peacemaking process. I have come to the conclusion that effective counterpressure to the temptation of the Israeli government to give in . . . can only come from the U.S.[70]

Toon's assessment has sometimes been borne out. A common example often cited by historians is that despite domestic opposition, by citing US pressures the Rabin government was able to agree to the 1993 Oslo Accords, which in fact it believed to be in Israeli interests.[71] As well, in 2007 some Israeli leaders argued that US pressures on behalf of Israeli prime minister Ehud Olmert's peace proposals might have enabled him to continue to push them, rather than abandon them in the face of domestic opposition. A former Israeli negotiator commented: "A smart American administration" should understand that it is very difficult for an Israeli prime minister to overcome strong domestic opposition to conciliatory policies, so that "sometimes they need to be able to say, 'Washington is holding my feet to the fire on this.'"[72]

American Jews and Israel

It is time for true friends of Israel, especially the American Jewish community to withdraw our support from an increasingly right-wing and illiberal Israel and encourage an after-Trump US government to use its leverage, including both carrots and sticks, to bring about changes in Israeli policies—and not only for the cause of justice for the Palestinians but also to support the beleaguered forces of enlightenment in Israel itself.

In view of the domestic political realities in the United States, in the absence of Jewish support there would be little chance that Congress would go along with pressures on Israel. To be sure, regardless of the Jewish position, the Christian religious right might well continue to oppose pressures, but its influence would be far less if the Democrats come to power in 2021 and, especially, if American Jews abandoned their past near-unconditional support of Israel. In any case, while there may be little the Jewish community can do about the Christian right, it is morally obligated to take responsibility for its own actions.

In the past, for a number of reasons it was all but unimaginable that most of the American Jewish community, especially its organized leadership, would publicly criticize Israel, let alone support US government pressures against it. Although it has become increasingly uneasy about what Israel has become, the community fears strengthening the hand of anti-Semites who do not care about Israel's best interests—or, for that matter, those of the Palestinians. But beyond that, the Jewish community has largely accepted the mythology of the Arab-Israeli conflict, despite its decisive refutation by Israeli historians, writers, and even retired political and military leaders. A continued refusal to face facts does not serve the true interests of Israel, and it amounts to an abdication of the liberal and humanistic values that the Jewish people are supposed to represent.

Another obstacle to change has been that most American Jews until recently accepted the argument that only Israel knows its best interests, as was insisted by Menachem Begin in 1980, who admonished US Jewish leaders: "Please refrain from proffering advice, at least in public, within earshot of our enemies—we and our children and grandchildren are the ones who live in Israel."[73]

But the argument that nations know their best interests has often been proven to be a fallacy. Nations regularly fail to act in their best interests. The examples abound, but to name but two: Did the United States act in its best interests when it went to war against Vietnam in the 1960s and invaded Iraq in 2003?

In fact, prominent Israeli liberals have frequently decried the failure of American Jewry to use its influence to pressure Israel to end the occupation and repression of the Palestinians and agree to a just settlement of the conflict. For example, in 1981 the famous Israel writer Amos Elon said that because of the community's influence in blocking US government pressure on Israel, "on the whole, the impact of American Jews on Israel has been destructive."[74] As recently as 2011, the Israeli political psychologist Daniel Bar-Tal returned from a year in the United States, during which he frequently met with Jewish leaders, most of whom identified as liberals. Interviewed in *Haaretz* about his experience, he said:

> When I arrived in the United States, I assumed I would find a receptive audience in the Jewish community, and a willingness to discuss the processes taking place in Israeli society. To my great regret, in most of those communities I found paralysis. The most progressive Jewish circles—those who demonstrate against any American injustice, protest the undermining of human rights in Iran and Sudan and of freedom of speech in China and Russia—turn blind, deaf and dumb when it comes to the lack of social justice, or oppression and discrimination, in Israel. They don't want to know what's happening, and for the most part refuse to conduct a rational discussion about the deterioration of Israeli society.[75]

In the last few years, however, there are signs that continued unthinking and unconditional support of Israel's policies, especially its occupation and repression of the Palestinians, is being rethought in the American Jewish community, the Democratic Party, and even in Congress. There is now considerable evidence that the US Jewish community, particularly its younger generation and college students, is becoming far more critical of Israel.[76] And even the Jewish community as a whole—as liberal as ever and disenchanted with Trump, Netanyahu, the settlements, and the occupation—is disengaging from Israel.[77]

There are many examples:

- During the 2018 midterm congressional elections, Jewish voters were asked in a J Street poll to name their two most important issues; only 4 percent named Israel.[78]
- In a February 2019 poll, only 43 percent of Democrats said they were partial to Israel.[79]
- A spring 2019 poll found that 57 percent of Democrats support "economic sanctions" or "something harsher" in response to settlement growth.[80]
- An October 2019 poll showed that 71 percent of Democrats believed that the US government "should not provide unrestricted financial and military assistance" to Israel.[81]
- In November 2019, more than 100 Democratic House representatives sent a letter to Trump opposing his decision to end the US policy that for decades has condemned Israeli settlements as illegal. The letter asserted that Trump's

policies had "discredited the United States as an honest broker between Israel and the Palestinian Authority." The *Haaretz* story discussing the letter concluded that it was "the latest example of the growing opposition within the Democratic Party to the alliance between President Trump and Prime Minister Benjamin Netanyahu, particularly on the issue of settlements."[82]

- Two weeks later, 221 of the 233 Democratic House members—including strong Israel supporters who until then had almost never criticized Israeli policies—voted for a resolution advocating a two-state solution and expressing opposition to "unilateral annexation of territory."[83]
- A February 2020 poll revealed that Netanyahu's alliance with Trump and his treatment of the Palestinians is leading to a growing disenchantment with Israel among American Jews, over half of whom were critical of "some" or "many" Israeli policies. As a result, nearly one-third of the respondents said they were "not very" or "not at all" attached to Israel.[84]
- In early 2020, most of the leading Democratic presidential candidates were criticizing the Netanyahu government for his settlement policies, opposition to the Iran nuclear deal, and support for annexation. Incredibly, half of Democrats today either support the Boycott, Divestment, and Sanctions (BDS) movement, or do not oppose it.[85]

The changing attitudes of the Jewish community are almost certainly having a wider impact in America, especially in the Democratic Party. Three years ago, Hillary Clinton argued that Obama had been too *hard* on Israel and that, if elected, she would "vigorously oppose any attempt to outside parties to impose a solution."[86] Her obvious political calculations might be different today: while during the Democratic presidential campaign Joe Biden continued to consider it "outrageous" to use US aid to pressure Israel, Elizabeth Warren, Bernie Sanders, and Pete Buttigieg all indicated they were open to considering doing so. In the words of Philip Gorden, a former US assistant secretary of state and White House coordinator for Middle East affairs, there is now "a debate that would have been unheard of a few years ago."[87]

If these trends continue, the convergence of attitudes between an increasingly critical American Jewish community and congressional Democrats could become a major force in bringing about changes in US policies toward Israel, especially, of course, if a Democrat is elected to the presidency in 2020. And such changes might help check the growing right-wing extremism in Israel as well as help provide at least a modicum of justice to the Palestinians.

A US-Israeli Security Treaty?

To help bring about a political settlement between Israel and the Palestinians, it is worth considering not only what the US government can do to pressure

Israel—"sticks"—but also how it can add positive incentives and measures of support, or "carrots." In particular, in the context of a settlement of the Israeli-Palestinian conflict, the United States and Israel could reexamine the question of whether their close relationship should be institutionalized in a formal "mutual defense" alliance, in which the United States commits itself to come to the assistance of Israel if its security is jeopardized by Arab attacks.

The issue of the desirability of such a security treaty, from the point of view of both sides, has been on the table in US-Israeli discussions since 1948.[88] It is well established that since the country's creation most Israeli prime ministers and other leaders have sought security guarantees from the United States, though some military leaders who have gone on to be prime ministers, like Moshe Dayan, Yitzhak Rabin, and (if and when he becomes prime minister under the rotation agreement with Netanyahu) Benny Gantz today, have opposed it because they feared excessive dependence on the United States and wanted to preserve unconstrained Israeli political and military freedom of action.[89] Of course, they also believed, in Avner Yaniv's words, "that in any case [Israel] . . . had all the essentials of a security alliance anyway, because of close US military and strategic cooperation."[90]

Nonetheless, the historical record makes it clear that the dominant Israeli view has been that it would benefit from the formalization of the alliance, and that many US political leaders have given serious consideration to such an alliance in the context of peace agreements:

- In the early 1950s, David Ben-Gurion sought either to join NATO or reach a defense treaty with the United States.[91] President Eisenhower and Secretary of State John Foster Dulles were not willing to do so as long as the Arab-Israeli conflict remained unsettled,[92] but privately they told Israel that the United States had "a deep interest" in preserving Israel's independence and would therefore "not be indifferent to an armed attack on it."[93] As well, according to Abba Eban's memoirs, Dulles "held out the possibility" of a US-Israel "security treaty" in the context of an Arab-Israeli peace settlement.
- After John Kennedy took office, Ben-Gurion renewed his request for a US treaty commitment to Israel's security. While Kennedy was moving toward considering Israel to be a strategic asset for US policies in the Middle East, he was not willing to go that far; however, he privately assured Israeli foreign minister Golda Meir that "in case of an invasion the United States would come to the support of Israel."[94] As well, in October 1963, Kennedy wrote to Prime Minister Levi Eshkol that the two states were "de facto allies . . . in case of invasion the United States would come to the support of Israel. . . . This letter in fact constitutes a security guarantee."[95]

- In August 1971, Senator J. William Fulbright, the powerful and highly influential chair of the Senate Foreign Relations Committee, called for a US-Israeli mutual defense treaty in the context of an overall Arab-Israeli peace settlement.[96]
- Richard Nixon considered the possibility of some form of US-Israeli military ties or formal political alignment after a peace treaty was signed. Years later, Nixon claimed to believe that despite the absence of a formal alliance, the United States and Israel "are bound together by an even stronger moral commitment. . . . [N]o American President will ever let Israel go down the tube."[97]
- During the Carter administration, Secretary of State Cyrus Vance, Defense Secretary Harold Brown, and National Security Advisor Zbigniew Brzezinski all suggested to the president the possibility of a defense treaty with Israel as part of an overall settlement.[98] According to Carter's memoirs, Menachem Begin wanted such an alliance, and even Egypt's Anwar Sadat "encouraged the idea." However, Carter rejected it on the grounds that such an American commitment to Israel would be "a serious mistake" as "it would make it impossible [for us] to mediate between Israel and the Arab nations."[99]
- In April 1986, Shimon Peres tried again to get the United States to join a mutual defense pact, but though President Reagan increased various forms of strategic cooperation with Israel, he was not prepared to go that far.
- In 2000, Barak renewed the Israeli request, asking President Clinton to join with Israel in a mutual defense agreement, which would also commit the United States to respond to an Arab nuclear attack against Israel with its own nuclear forces.[100] Clinton assured Barak that he would give serious consideration to some kind of bilateral defense treaty if an Israeli-Palestinian peace settlement was reached, though it is not clear whether it would include the nuclear commitment that Barak sought.[101] The collapse of the Camp David peace process made the issue moot.
- According to Daniel Kurtzer, former US ambassador to Israel, "[George W.] Bush reportedly assured Sharon in private that the United States would protect Israel by force if needed—much to Sharon's astonishment and pleasant surprise."[102]
- In the last few years, Netanyahu and Trump, with the support of leading Republican senators such as Lindsey Graham, have discussed the possibility of a defense alliance between the United States and Israel. For example, in a September 2019 official public statement, Netanyahu wrote to Trump that he "looked forward to our meeting . . . to advance a historical Defense Treaty between the United States and Israel."[103] In a Twitter message Trump indicated support for such a possible treaty.[104]

In light of this history, there would be every reason to expect strong political support in the United States to formalizing and extending the existing de facto American military commitment to the security of Israel, provided it was not unconditional and presented to Congress and the American public as a necessary component of a comprehensive Arab-Israeli and Israeli-Palestinian peace settlement that would come into effect only upon the conclusion of such a settlement. Moreover, any such defense pact must specify that the United States would intervene militarily *only* if—in the judgment of the American government—Israel faced an overwhelming threat to its homeland as a result of unprovoked or massive Arab or Iranian aggression that it could not repel on its own without having to resort to nuclear weapons.[105]

To be sure, the likelihood that such a contingency could arise is very small. Nonetheless, Israeli military and other security experts continue to plan against a massive Arab invasion, and therefore there is every reason to expect that most of them would support a limited mutual defense treaty with the United States. Moreover, because fears of annihilation are still widespread among many Israelis, security guarantees from the United States would be psychologically very important and could well increase the likelihood that Israel would accept a mini Palestinian state along the lines of the kind proposed here.

A Final Word

Could the Israeli-Palestinian conflict have been averted, or at least settled long ago? The weakest part of Zionist ideology has always been its claim to Jewish sovereignty over the entire land of Israel, whether based on religious fundamentalism, long discredited biblical fables that would be irrelevant even if they had been true, or the twentieth-century Balfour Declaration. What the Zionist movement should have done was rest its case for the creation of a Jewish state in Palestine on historical necessity, particularly but not only because of the Holocaust and the absence after it of a practical alternative to the land of Palestine.

In 1948, the Israelis could have said to the Palestinians: "We are in a tragic situation, forced by necessity to take action that we recognize diminishes your rights and creates real harm. Therefore, we commit ourselves to rectifying this unavoidable injustice in a variety of ways, so long as they don't threaten our basic security, our right to exist." Had they acted in that spirit, they would not have driven the Palestinians out of their land and there would have been no Nakba.

Even after the Nakba, a settlement could have been reached long ago—and certainly since the 1980s when the PLO abandoned its hope of destroying Israel and formally and publicly accepted a two-state settlement—had Israel agreed to share Jerusalem with the Palestinians and refrained from attacking, occupying, and settling the West Bank.

Today, many Israelis and their supporters fear that Israel would be "delegitimized" if it abandoned Zionist mythology and their other disproven historical narratives. But this fear is groundless. Since 1948, the only argument necessary to the Zionist case has been the *existential* one: new human realities have been created, Israel exists, and it has a right to survive. Moreover, there is no basis to conclude that the historical conditions that created Zionism—murderous anti-Semitism—have permanently disappeared from the world scene; on the contrary, though still relatively minor in its scope, anti-Semitism has recently reemerged, even in the West. Therefore, the case for a Jewish state that can serve as a refuge for endangered world Jewry remains strong.

In fact, this argument is accepted, formally or de facto, not only by the general international community but by an increasing number of Arab states and even by some Palestinian political leaders and intellectuals. Consequently, an Israeli acknowledgment of past injustices and acceptance, at long last, of some kind of compromise peace settlement with the Palestinians would have the effect of *legitimizing* rather than delegitimizing Israel among all but the most fanatical Palestinians, who in any event have been marginalized by the mainstream Palestinian leadership and even increasingly by Hamas.

Tragically, however, the Israelis have never been willing to acknowledge their role in the origins and dynamics of the Arab-Israeli conflict, have never been willing to acknowledge their moral responsibility for the plight of the Palestinians, and have missed, ignored, or even deliberately undercut a number of opportunities to settle both the Israeli-Palestinian and the larger Arab-Israeli conflict. Blinded by Zionist ideology and their other national mythologies, as well as by the genuine history of Jewish victimization, Israel has failed to realize that in *this* conflict it is Israel that is the oppressor and the Palestinians who are the victims.

If there ever is to be an at least minimally just solution to the Israeli-Palestinian conflict, whether it takes the form of some kind of two-state settlement or a binational democratic single state, the most important prerequisite, indeed the sine qua non, must be an Israeli recognition that their historical narrative of the conflict is largely mythological and that they have incurred an overwhelming moral obligation and an enlightened national self-interest to reach a peace settlement with the Palestinian people.

NOTES

Introduction

1. Sand, *Invention,* Kindle 282.
2. Ravid, "State Archives to Stay Classified for 20 More Years."
3. The most important repository of US government records including previously classified foreign policy documents, *Foreign Relations of the United States,* currently extends only through the end of the Carter administration in 1981.

Chapter 1

1. For a major study discussing the various factors explaining US policy toward Israel, see Kaplan, *Our American Israel.*
2. Israelis and American Jews who are happy to collaborate with Christian fundamentalists downplay the fundamentalist belief that following Armageddon the Jews will be required to choose between converting or forever perishing in hell.
3. Rabkin, *Modern Israel,* Kindle location 350.
4. Moreover, the support of Israel by most American Christians goes well beyond religious convictions. As Peter Beinart, one of the most perceptive analysts of US policies toward Israel, succinctly explains: "Secular conservatives are almost as pro-Israel as their fervently religious counterparts. The contrast between Israel and 'Islamic terrorism' is key. Since the United States became a world power, conservatives have tended to define America's mission as leading the West against some global, existential, civilizational foe. First it was the Nazis; then it was the communists; now it is 'radical Islam' " (Beinart, "For the American Right, Israel Embodies the Values that Obama's U.S. No Longer Does").
5. Quoted in Gendzier, *Dying to Forget,* Kindle 277–78.
6. At least half of *The Israel Lobby* is devoted to an extensive and highly persuasive analysis of the *substance* of US policies in the Middle East and toward Israel, but unfortunately Mearsheimer and Walt's insightful critique has not had nearly the impact it should, primarily because of the controversy over their argument about the policy *process,* namely, the power of the Israel lobby.
7. Allin and Simon disagree with this assessment, writing that the pro-Israeli attitudes of Democratic administrations in the 1948–2000 period "did not depend on a perception of Israel as a strategic partner; in fact, [they were] adopted despite a broad assessment that

U.S. support for Israel was a strategic liability" (*Our Separate Ways*, 6). However, this is a minority view among both historians and former US officials.

8. Mearsheimer and Walt, *Israel Lobby*, 65.
9. Mearsheimer and Walt prefer a broader definition, defining the lobby as a "loose coalition of individuals and organizations that actively work to shape U.S. foreign policy in a pro-Israel direction" (Mearsheimer and Walt, *Israel Lobby*, 112). However, in my view this definition is problematic, for it makes empirical testing of their theory difficult. I develop this argument in my critique of the *Israel Lobby:* Slater, "The Two Books of Mearsheimer and Walt." Mearsheimer and Walt responded to my critique in "Is It Love or the Lobby? Explaining America's Special Relationship with Israel."
10. The importance of the waning of US anti-Semitism is emphasized by Tivnan, *The Lobby;* Goldberg, *Jewish Power*; and Koplow, "Value Judgment." See also the remarkable public opinion survey by the highly regarded Pew Research Center, which found that Jews—2 percent of the national population—were the most popular religious group in America ("Pew Survey Finds Jews to Be America's Favorite Religious Group").
11. Cited in Wright, *Thirteen Days*, Kindle location 132.
12. Kyle, *Suez*.
13. Melman and Raviv, *Friends in Deed*, 100.
14. To be sure, perhaps they were still partially motivated by electoral considerations—for example, by not wanting their party to lose even more Jewish votes in the future. Even so, the weight of the evidence suggests that their support of Israel was largely based on moral considerations and/or on Israel's hard-line anti-communist and anti-Islamic terrorism policies.
15. These figures are widely cited. For example, see Goldberg, *Jewish Power*, xxi; and Guttman, "Courting the Jewish Vote May Not Be Worth It."
16. Cited in Bruck, "Friends of Israel."
17. Rice, *No Higher Honor*, 134.
18. The absence of countervailing interest group power is emphasized in Bruck, "Friends of Israel." As well, Stephen Walt quotes Bill Clinton's assertion that AIPAC was "better than anyone else lobbying in this town" and former representative Lee Hamilton as saying that "there's no lobby group that matches it. . . . They're in a class by themselves" (Walt, "Whiff of Desperation").
19. For a discussion of the reasons for the American public's early strong support of Israel, emphasizing the importance of the movie *Exodus*, and other pro-Israeli movies, books, and newspaper reports, see Little, *American Orientialism*, 29–31.
20. Over the years there have been myriad polls, surveys, and studies of US public opinion toward Israel. One of the most systematic and thorough is Koplow, *Value Judgment*. Although Israel may now be losing support among Democrats, until very recently most studies and surveys showed that nearly two-thirds of Americans were more sympathetic to Israel than to the Palestinians. See "Poll: Americans Sympathize with Israel More than with Palestinians."
21. Rabinovich, *Rabin*, Kindle 115.
22. The Ford "reassessment" and its outcome are discussed by Tillman, *U.S. in the Middle East*, 66–67; Spiegel, *Other Arab-Israeli Conflict*, 294–301; and Tivnan, *The Lobby*, 89.
23. The Percy case is widely discussed in the literature on the Israel lobby. For a brief summary, see Stolberg, "Concerns Raised over Power Wielded by a Pro-Israel Lobbying Giant."
24. Goldberg, *Jewish Power*, 269.
25. Mearsheimer and Walt, "Is It Love or the Lobby," 67–68. In the next sentence in this passage, Mearsheimer and Walt write: "Slater does not answer that question." Later in this chapter, I attempt to do so.
26. Landler, "Questions Emerge about Pro-Israel Groups' Prowess."
27. Landler, "Questions Emerge about Pro-Israel Groups' Prowess."
28. Davis, "Influential Pro-Israel Group Suffers a Stinging Political Defeat." See also Elgindy, *Blind Spot*, Kindle 7.

29. To be sure, in *The Israel Lobby* and in other of their works, Mearsheimer and Walt argue that pro-Israeli opinions are a function of the power of the lobby in the mass media, which ensures that serious criticism of Israel is muted. There is no way to test this argument, but given the depth of political support of Israel in the United States since 1948, it is open to question.
30. For a recent discussion of the declining power of AIPAC, particularly because of the growing unpopularity of the Netanyahu government in the American Jewish community, see Pfeffer, "Bibi Killed AIPAC Long before Bernie Came Along."

Chapter 2

1. Though there were earlier Zionist writers, they had little political influence and did not result in the creation of a Jewish nationalist movement. It was Herzl who "put Zionism on the map," in the words of Sachar, *History of Israel*, 64.
2. See Elon, *Herzl*. Professor Carlo Strenger of Tel Aviv University wrote that Herzl "promoted a country in which Jewish religion has no formal standing at all. . . . [Herzl] takes pride in the treacherous notion that the Nation-state of the Jews gives completely equal rights to all citizens, including Arabs, and is cosmopolitan in nature . . . multi-cultural and multi-lingual" (Strenger, "Meet the Worst Anti-Zionist of Them All"). Indeed, according to one Israeli writer, Herzl envisaged the possibility that the Jews *and* the Arabs could form an enlightened state but would have to join together to defeat the forces of religious Jewish extremism. Michael, "In Classic Occupier Fashion, Israel Has Hit Rock Bottom, and Now It's Too Late."
3. Sand, "How Israel Went from Atheist Zionism to Jewish State."
4. Theodore Herzl, quoted in *Haaretz*, November 3, 2003.
5. Excerpts from Herzl, *Der Judenstaat*, https://www.jewishvirtuallibrary.org/excerpts-from-quot-the-jewish-state-quot.
6. Herzl, "Zion and the Jewish National Idea," 185.
7. Shlaim, *Iron Wall*, Kindle 1.
8. Herzl, *The Jewish State*, cited by Uri Avnery in his weekly blog, May 29, 2014.
9. Vital, *Zionism*, 283. Ilan Pappé writes: "It was Herzl who sanctified Palestine by defining Jewish nationalism as Zionism, irrevocably connected to settling Palestine (Zion)" (Pappé, *History*, Kindle location 1351).
10. Quoted in O'Brien, *Siege*, 95.
11. Quoted in Pfeffer, *Bibi*, Kindle 10.
12. Quoted in Hacohen, "Ben-Gurion and the Second World War," 255.
13. Both quotations are Steven L. Spiegel's paraphrase of Roosevelt's offer and Saud's response. Spiegel, *Other Arab-Israeli Conflict*, 13. For another discussion of the Roosevelt-Saud exchange, see Sachar, 254–55.
14. Quoted in Haddad, "Arab Peace Efforts and the Solution of the Arab-Israel Problem," 179–80.
15. Cf. the comment by the *Haaretz* columnist Ari Caspi: "Had the world been guided by notions of historical justice, the Jewish state would have been established on the ruins of Berlin. But that was unthinkable. We wanted Zion." Caspi, "Running Out of Time."
16. Bar-Tal, *Intractable Conflicts*, 438–39.
17. Cited in the major contemporary work on the dangers of national narratives by the Oxford historian Margaret MacMillan, *Dangerous Games*, 82. Note also the observation of the MIT political scientist, Stephen Van Evera: "Human organizations of all sorts, from families to villages to nations, infuse themselves with myths and so are deluded about themselves and their neighbors. They almost never understand their own past in truthful terms" (Manuscript, November 2003).
18. Bar-Tal, *Intractable Conflicts*, 63, 141.
19. Cited in Bar-Tal, *Intractable Conflicts*, 167. On the Zionist arguments based on ancient religious and territorial claims, in addition to Bar-Tal and the books already cited, see Sand, *Invention of Israel*, especially Kindle 206–10.

20. Sand, *Invention of Israel*, 206.
21. Bar-Tal, "How Israeli Politicians Took Peace with the Palestinians off the Table."
22. Bar-Tal implies that this narrative was no longer "hegemonic" in Israel after the early 1970s. Among other factors, he probably has in mind the rise of "the New Israeli History" in the subsequent decade or two. However, the current dominance of the Israeli right wing has ended or marginalized the teaching of the New History in the Israeli school system; consequently, the old narrative is arguably even more dominant in Israel today than it was in the decades after the establishment of the state.
23. Quoted by Bar-Tal, *Intractable Conflicts*, 167.
24. Avnery, "In Their Shoes." Avnery was a passionate Zionist and was even a member of the extremist Irgun forces, fighting in Israel's 1948 "war of independence." After that war, however, Avnery became one of the most courageous and celebrated critics of its policies toward the Palestinians.
25. Pappé put it this way: the Palestinians "need to avoid dwarfing or eliminating the role of the Holocaust in Jewish national identity and collective memory. . . . [T]here was a European injustice inflicted upon the Jews that can be recognized as a first link in the chain of victimization." He then cites a powerful passage from Edward Said making the same point: "We cannot fail to connect the horrific history of anti-Semitic massacres to the establishment of Israel" ("The Visible and Invisible in the Israeli-Palestinian Conflict," 292, 294).
26. In 2000, the leading scholarly journal in the field, *Biblical Archaeology Review*, devoted an entire issue to summarizing the scholarship that demonstrated that most of the biblical narrative was mere mythology for which there was little to no evidence: "The Search for History in the Bible." Since then, the evidence against standard biblical history—much of it compiled by prominent Israeli historians and archaeologists—has continued to mount. Among the leading works see Finkelstein and Silberman, *The Bible Unearthed;* Sand, *Invention of the Jewish People;* and Sand, *The Invention of the Land of Israel.* Summarizing his findings, Sand writes: "There is not one study by a historian who specializes in antiquity that recounts that 'exile'" (Sand, "The Twisted Logic of the Jewish 'Historic Right' to Israel").
27. Quoted in the Israeli magazine *Jerusalem Report*, September 11, 2000.
28. Hasson, "Is the Bible a True Story?"
29. To be sure, during the Roman Empire, Herod was appointed "King of the Jews" in Palestine. However, the state of "Judea," ruled by Herod, was essentially a vassal of Rome, lacking true sovereignty.
30. Sachar, *History of Israel*, 18.
31. Haber, "No, Rivkele, The Jews Weren't Driven into Exile by the Romans."
32. All population figures during this period are general estimates. The figures cited here are drawn largely from Tessler, *History*, 20–21; Sachar, *History of Israel*, 18–24; Jewish Virtual Library, http://www.jewishvirtuallibrary.org/jewish-and-non-jewish-population-of-israel-palestine-1517-present.
33. Lewy, *Religion and Revolution*, 91, quoted in Tessler, *History*, 16.
34. The "right of return" issue is discussed in Chapters 15, 18, 19, and 20.
35. Cf. the argument of Hurst Hannum, a Tufts University professor of international law: "Nearly every state in the world was founded directly or indirectly on conquest. . . . One might note that those who claim a right to independence based on historical arguments tend to choose the historical period that would give them the greatest amount of territory, that is, the period in which they themselves were successful conquerors" (Hannum, "The Specter of Secession," 15).
36. St. Fleur, "Fate of Ancient Canaanites Seen in DNA Analysis."
37. Quoted in Bowersock, "The Many Lives of Palestine."
38. Pappé, *History*, 68.
39. Morris, "Derisionist History."

40. Quoted by Chomsky, *Fateful Triangle*, Kindle 96, and Rabkin, *Modern Israel*, Kindle location 1288.
41. Quoted in Morris, *Righteous Victims*, 99. On Churchill's respect for the Jewish people and belief that a Jewish homeland would advance civilization, see Makovsky, *Churchill's Promised Land*.
42. Both statements quoted by Arieli, "Those Undermining the Jewish State." Arieli concludes: "The recognition of the natural right of the Jewish people to self-determination drew its strength from the international community's recognition of the Jews, dispersed across the world, as one nation. In other words, as a group with a common national history, language and culture, not just as a religious community that believes in the Old Testament."
43. Quoted in Segev, *State at Any Cost*, Kindle, 78.
44. Diab, "The Arab World's Missed Opportunities." For a similar argument by a prominent Palestinian-American analyst, see Rashid Khalidi's criticism of "the reductionist view of Zionism as no more than a colonial enterprise." To be sure, he continues that Zionism was and is colonial in terms of its relationship to the indigenous Arab population of Palestine, but adds that "Palestinians fail to understand, or refuse to recognize, however, that Zionism also served as the national movement of the nascent Israeli polity being constructed at their expense" (Khalidi, *Iron Cage*, 498).
45. As argued by Daniel Blatman, a professor of Holocaust and genocide studies at the Hebrew University of Jerusalem, who writes: "In 1967 Israel relaunched the war of settler colonialism against the Palestinian people. It's different from the 1948 version, which was the war of the settlers for the establishment of the national structure that they were building. The leaders of the current war of settler colonialism do not have the goal of ensuring a haven for persecuted Jews and refugees of genocide, as was the case in 1948" (Blatman, "The Banality of Evil Revisited").
46. "Zionism Is Not Racism, but Zionists Can Be Racists."
47. To be sure, even after the Holocaust some Jewish non-Zionists continued to oppose the creation of a Jewish state, some because they preferred assimilation in the United States and Western Europe and feared being charged with "dual loyalties," and some because of a principled opposition to nationalism and ethnic states.
48. It is true that in November 1941 the dominant Palestinian leader, Amin al-Husseini (Grand Mufti of Jerusalem) met with Hitler and other high Nazi officials, seeking to enlist their support against the Zionists. Some have even charged that he urged Hitler to carry out the Holocaust, though historians disagree on what exactly was said in those meetings. In any case, the scholarship on this issue confirms common sense, namely, that there is no evidence that history would have been different if the Mufti had refrained from his suggestion. The episode is discussed in Segev, *One Palestine Complete*, Kindle 463.
49. These issues will be discussed in a number of places throughout the book, beginning with the discussion of alternatives to the Nakba, in Chapter 5.

Chapter 3

1. There are no universally accepted statistics on the population distribution of Palestine in this period. The figures here are a rough average of the estimates of the leading writers on the history of Palestine. For two examples, see Pappé, *Ten Myths*, Kindle locations 145–49, and Thrall, *Only Language*, Kindle 77–78.
2. This figure is widely cited in the scholarship on David Ben-Gurion and the Zionist movement. For example, in December 1947, Ben-Gurion—the de facto leader of the Zionist movement and later the first prime minister of the state of Israel—told other Zionist leaders that "only a state with at least 80 percent Jews is a viable and stable state." Quoted from Ben-Gurion's writings in Pappé, *Ethnic Cleansing*, 48.
3. Rokach, *Sacred Terrorism*, Kindle locations 27–29.
4. Manchester, *The Last Lion*, Kindle location 13183.

5. Flapan, *Zionism,* 144. For other discussions of the Zionist territorial goals, see Shlaim, *Iron Wall,* 171–78, 184–85; Segev, *One Palestine,* Kindle 117–18; Teveth, *Ben-Gurion,* Kindle locations 9957–59. Teveth was Ben-Gurion's authorized biographer.
6. Cited, among many others, by Avnery, *1948,* Kindle location 231.
7. Widely cited, for example, by Remnick, "Newt, the Jews, and an 'Invented' People.'"
8. Flapan, *Zionism,* 11–12.
9. Morris, "A New Exodus for the Middle East?" This is a summary of the voluminous archival evidence developed by Morris in a number of his major works, including *Birth of the Palestinian Refugee Problem Revisited* and *Righteous Victims.* Other major works on transfer include Shlaim, *Israel and Palestine,* especially 54–61; Shahak, "A History of the Concept of 'Transfer' in Zionism"; Pappé, *The Ethnic Cleansing of Palestine*; and Flapan, *Birth,* especially 103–6. See also the frank appraisal of Shlomo Ben-Ami, a Labor Party activist and minister of Internal Security and then foreign minister of Israel, who wrote, "The idea of population transfers had a long and solid pedigree in Zionist thought" (Ben-Ami, "A War to Start All Wars"). A number of Palestinian writers have discussed the concept of transfer in Zionist thought—and action. The most important is Masalha, *Expulsion of the Palestinians.*
10. Segev, *State at Any Cost,* Kindle 268.
11. Quoted in Masalha, *Expulsion,* Kindle locations 688–89. Masalha cites a number of other Weizmann statements or writings in which he supports the expulsion of Palestinians.
12. Quoted by Flapan, *Zionism,* 82, and Morris, "Refabricating 1948," 86.
13. Quoted in Gans, *A Political Theory,* 248.
14. Segev, *One Palestine,* Kindle 405.
15. Teveth, *Ben-Gurion,* 188, 189.
16. Bar-Zohar, *Ben-Gurion,* 91–92. As this passage has been translated from the Hebrew by a number of different scholars, there are minor variations, but there is no doubt that Ben-Gurion was saying that the Zionists would use force if it proved necessary.
17. Quoted in Teveth, *Burning Ground,* Kindle location 12809. Emphasis in original.
18. Morris, *Righteous Victims,* 144.
19. Quoted in Morris, "A New Exodus for the Middle East?"
20. Morris, *Righteous Victims,* 169.
21. Segev's description of Ben-Gurion's thinking, *State at Any Cost,* Kindle 268.
22. Quoted in Masalha, *Expulsion,* Kindle location 3914. On Sharett's emphasis on the use of peaceful means of transfer, see Raz, "Israel's First Ruling Party Thought about Palestinian Citizens."
23. As Masalha put it: "Yishuv leaders continued to assert that there was nothing 'immoral' about the concept. . . . [T]he uprooting and transfer of the population to Transjordan, Iraq, or any other part of the Arab world would merely constitute a relocation from one Arab district to another" (*Expulsion,* Kindle location 790).
24. Quoted in Flapan, *Zionism,* 83.
25. Shapira, *Ben-Gurion,* Kindle 84–85. Benny Morris cites other similar statements made by Ben-Gurion, for example: "Thankfully, the Arab people [in Palestine] have large, empty areas [outside Palestine]." Brackets in the original, Morris, "Refabricating 1948," 86.
26. Quoted in Masalha, *Expulsion,* Kindle location 473–74.
27. Quoted in Melman, "Father of Indecision."
28. Flapan, *Zionism,* 83, emphasis in original.
29. This Zionist argument is discussed in Masalha, *Expulsion,* Kindle location 790; Morris, *Birth Revisited,* 41–43; and Gorenberg, *Unmaking of Israel,* 46.
30. The commission cited the 1923 Greek-Turkish population exchange as a relevant precedent. The full text of the Peel Commission report can be found at https://www.jewishvirtuallibrary.org/jsource/History/peel1.html. Discussions of the Peel report can be found in Chowers, "Peel Back Time"; Masalha, *Expulsion*; and Morris, *Birth Revisited,* 44–46. Masalha and Segev note that the Peel Commission recommendation would have required the 225,000 Arabs be

transferred out of the areas it earmarked for the Jewish state, but only some 1,250 Jews out of the proposed Arab state areas (Masalha, Kindle location 1314; Segev, *State at Any Cost,* Kindle 264).

31. Segev, *State at Any Cost,* Kindle 263–64.
32. First quote, Morris, *Birth,* 48; second, Masalha, *Expulsion,* Kindle location 2433.
33. Elgindy, *Blind Spot,* Kindle 32.
34. Judis, *Genesis,* 213.
35. Grose, *Israel in the Mind of America,* 138, 142.
36. Quoted in Allin and Simnon, *Our Separate Ways,* 25.
37. Grose, *Israel,* 139.
38. Grose, *Israel,* 149.
39. Grose, *Israel,* 140, 156.
40. Grose, *Israel,* 156–57. On Roosevelt's policies, see also Hahn, *Caught in the Middle East,* especially 15–19.
41. Morris, *Birth,* 59, and Morris, "A New Exodus for the Middle East?"
42. This period is covered in detail by Morris, *Righteous Victims,* 2001 expanded edition; he summarizes his main points on 679–85. See also Tessler, *History,* Kindle 233–40.
43. Segev, *One Palestine,* Kindle 274, 378. Yossi Melman states that the Zionist land purchasers often cheated the landowners—themselves often corrupt—securing the land by "bribery, deceit, and intimidation" (*The New Israelis,* 44). For other discussions of the role of Jewish land purchases in the intensifying Palestinian resistance, see Cohen, *Origins and Evolution of the Arab-Zionist Conflict,* and Gill, "The Original 'No': Why the Arabs Rejected Zionism, and Why It Matters." Natasha Gill, a professor at Barnard, writes: "The Palestinian Arabs said No to the idea that in the 20th century a people who last lived in Palestine in large numbers over 2,000 years ago could claim, on the basis of a religious text, rights to the land where the current inhabitants had been living for a millennium and a half. . . . They did not base their rejection on a denial of Jewish historical and religious ties to the Holy Land. . . . What they said No to was the idea that the Jews' *humanitarian* plight granted them special *political* and *national* rights in *Palestine,* and that those Jewish rights should trump Arab rights. The Arabs said No to the idea that they should pay the price for longstanding Christian persecution of the Jews."
44. Eban, *Personal Witness,* 49, 50.
45. Discussed, among other histories, in Tessler, *History,* Kindle 253–54.
46. Flapan, *Zionism,* 273.
47. Christison, *Perceptions,* 2.
48. Beit-Hallahmi, *Original Sins,* 73.
49. Flapan, *Birth of Israel.*
50. Flapan, *Birth of Israel,* 72, 78–79.
51. Flapan, *Birth of Israel,* 73–74.
52. Heydemann, "Revisionism and the Reconstruction of Israeli History," 13–14.
53. The major work on Jabotinsky and the Iron Wall strategy is Shlaim, *Iron Wall.*
54. Quoted in Gans, *Political Theory,* 256, and Pfeffer, *Bibi,* Kindle 18–19.
55. Quoted in O'Malley, *Two-State Delusion,* Kindle 176.
56. Flapan, *Zionism,* 113–14.
57. Teveth, *Ben-Gurion,* 15–26.
58. Segev, *State at Any Cost,* Kindle 254.
59. Teveth, *Ben-Gurion,* 165.
60. Teveth, *Burning Ground,* Kindle 11349, 11427.289.
61. Quoted in Teveth, *Ben-Gurion,* 143.
62. Quoted in Nahum Goldmann, *The Jewish Paradox,* 121.
63. Flapan, *Zionism,* 141–42.
64. Flapan, *Zionism,* 142.
65. Teveth, *Burning Ground,* Kindle location 11305.

66. Flapan, *Zionism*, 148–49.
67. Flapan, *Zionism*, 153.
68. Quoted in the Israeli newspaper *Yediot Aharanot*, October 17, 1969.
69. Quoted, among many other places, in Shalev, "Moshe Dayan's Enduring Gaza Eulogy."
70. Flapan, *Zionism*, 117.
71. Quoted from many sources in Suarez, *State of Terror*, 29.
72. This quote is an amalgam of two slightly different translations of Ha'am's 1891 report, from Sand, *Invention of the Land of Israel*, 198–99, and Thrall, "Feeling Good about Feeling Bad." Among many other works, cultural Zionism is examined in Vital, *Zionism: The Formative Years*, especially 24–35.
73. Quoted in Shlaim, *Iron Wall*, Kindle 813.
74. Teveth, *Ben Gurion*, 159.

Chapter 4

1. On the evolution of British policy, from the Balfour Declaration through the decision to withdraw from Palestine, see Khalidi, *Blind Spot*.
2. Under Secretary of State Sumner Welles later wrote that "every form of pressure, direct and indirect" was employed to get the two-thirds majority. Quoted in Suarez, *State of Terror*, 235. See also Elgindy, *Blind Spot*, Kindle 40–41.
3. Bar-Zohar, *Facing a Cruel Mirror*, 18. As well, Benny Morris notes Ben-Gurion's repeated statements that partition "would serve merely as the springboard for future Jewish *conquest* of the whole land: Palestine was to be taken over in stages" (Morris, *Righteous Victims*, 681). Morris pointedly adds: "Half a century later, many Zionists would accuse Yasser Arafat of secretly harboring much the same thoughts and plans." Chaim Weizman, Ben-Gurion's protégés Moshe Dayan and Ariel Sharon, and many other Zionist leaders shared his view, as has been documented by a number of Israeli scholars. For a map of the Zionist vision, see Flapan, *Birth*, 17.
4. Ben-Gurion's letter has been widely cited. See Shlaim, *Iron Wall*, Kindle 22; Bar-Zohar, *Facing a Cruel Mirror*, 16; Teveth, *Ben-Gurion*, 188.
5. Quoted in Segev, *State at Any Cost*, Kindle 267. See also Elgindy, *Blind Spot*: "During the war, Ben-Gurion had confided to his followers that no aspect of partition would be considered final, "not with regard to the regime, not with regard to borders, and not with regard to international agreements" (Kindle 54).
6. Ben-Ami, *Scars of War*, 34.
7. See Chapter 5.
8. Khalidi, "A Palestinian Perspective on the Arab-Israeli Conflict," 40. Chaim Gans, one of Israel's leading political philosophers, agrees that "the Palestinians were made to pay an unfair price," arguing that while the partition plan was just in principle, the Palestinians, who were the only ones being asked to pay the price of the creation of the Jewish state, had justification for opposing it: "The constant reiteration of the fact of the Palestinians' refusal to accept the Partition Plan, in an effort to make them responsible for the completely unfair costs we extract from them for the conflict, is to close our eyes to the great injustices that we are carrying out." Gans, "Palestinians Were Made to Pay an Unfair Price."
9. Bailey, *Four Arab-Israeli Wars*, 41–42. Because of his positions on the conflict, Bernadotte was later assassinated by an extremist Jewish group.
10. Flapan, *Zionism*, 285. However, Eli Podeh, an Israeli historian, argues that while it was true that some Palestinian leaders were prepared to compromise, they fell silent, or were intimidated into silence, by the vehement opposition of al-Husseini (Podeh, "The UN Vote on the Partition of Palestine; the Palestinians' Biggest Missed Opportunity").
11. George M. Haddad, an Arab writer, put it this way: "Israel evidently felt that the war of 1948 released it from [the partition]. . . . Israeli logic seemed to imply that because the Palestinian Arabs resisted the invasion of their country and failed, they lost the right to live in their

country. . . . That the Palestinian leaders refused the partition of their country in 1947 does not mean that the Palestinian people should be deprived forever of a state in a much smaller part of their country" (Haddad, "Arab Peace Efforts and the Solution of the Arab-Israel Problem," 189, 238).

12. Thrall, *Only Language They Understand,* Kindle 69.
13. Quoted in O'Malley, *Two-State Delusion,* Kindle 75, and Podeh, "The UN Vote on the Partition of Palestine."
14. Quoted in Arieli, "Zionism Doesn't Need 'Divine Promise' to Justify Jewish Nation-State."
15. Elgindy, *Blind Spot,* Kindle 21.
16. Joseph Lelyveld writes, "The president's self-assigned mission was to smooth the way for a Jewish homeland in Palestine. . . . [He remarked] that he considered himself a Zionist" (*His Final Battle: The Last Months of Franklin Roosevelt,* Kindle location 5466).
17. For example, Peter Hahn argues that while Roosevelt "was not averse to accelerated Jewish immigration to Palestine, and refused to rule out . . . a prospective Jewish state in Palestine . . . [he] consistently elevated national security imperatives over his political interests in satisfying Zionists" (Hahn, *Caught in the Middle East,* 19). Similarly, Benny Morris writes that while "the plight of European Jewry may have weighed heavily on the side of Zionism, American global interests . . . as perceived by most of [the State and Defense Department officials] . . . militated in the other direction. The officials worried about the continued supply of oil, American bases, [and] . . . countering Soviet influence and power" (Morris, *1948,* 24). On Roosevelt's "philo-Semitism," but his failure to support large-scale Jewish immigration into the United States, see Allin and Simon, *Our Separate Ways,* 12–14.
18. Quoted in many works, including Grose, *Israel in the Mind of America,* 150.
19. Grose, *Israel in the Mind of America,* 153.
20. Quoted in Grose, *Israel in the Mind of America,* 113.
21. Grose, *Israel in the Mind of America,* 113.
22. A number of studies of this period discuss the internal disputes within the administration and, in particular, the Kennan analysis. One of the most extensive is Neff, "Palestine, Truman and America's Strategic Balance."
23. Quoted in many works, including Perry, "Petraeus Wasn't the First." Perry adds, "Put more simply, Marshall believed that Truman was sacrificing American security for American votes." In a 1991 article, Clark Clifford and Richard Holbrooke discussed the Truman-Marshall meeting and the president's subsequent decision to recognize Israel, despite the opposition of Marshall and the other high government officials: "Serving the President: The Truman Years." A similar account can be found in Leffler, *Preponderance of Power,* 240–42.
24. On the influence of the Holocaust in Truman's decision to go against his primary national security advisors and recognize Israel, see Pappé, *Idea of Israel,* Kindle 118. Clark Clifford tells this story: in 1961, Ben-Gurion told Truman that his support for Israel "had given him an immortal place in Jewish history." On hearing these words, Ben-Gurion recounted, Truman wept with joy. Quoted by Clifford and Holbrooke, "Serving the President: The Truman Years," 71.
25. The importance of domestic politics—whether or not it was the most important consideration—is discussed in two major works on Truman and Israel: Cohen, *Truman and Israel,* and Judis, *Genesis.*
26. Grose, *Israel in the Mind of America,* 262.
27. Cohen, *Truman and Israel,* 89.
28. For a full discussion of the State Department's failed effort to establish a UN Trusteeship instead of a Jewish state in Palestine, see Judis, *Genesis,* 288–306, and Pappé, *History,* Kindle 120. On Truman's overall policies, see Allin and Simon, *Separate Ways,* 14–19.

Chapter 5

1. Quoting Avi Shlaim's characterization of the Israeli narrative, from his "The Debate about 1948."
2. The most important works of the new Israeli historiography are Bar-Joseph, *Best of Enemies*; Bar-Zohar, *Facing a Cruel Mirror;* Beit-Hallahmi, *Original Sins*; Flapan, *Birth of Israel*; various works by Benny Morris, including *Birth of the Palestinian Refugee Problem, 1948 and After*, and "The New Historiography: Israel Confronts Its Past"; various works by Ilan Pappé, including *Making of the Arab-Israeli Conflict* and others; Segev, *1949: The First Israelis*, and *1967*; Shlaim, *Collusion across the Jordan*, and *Iron Wall*. A number of non-Israeli scholars also made major contributions, including Hirst, *The Gun and the Olive Branch;* Khouri, *Arab-Israeli Dilemma*; Palumbo, *The Palestinian Catastrophe*; and Tessler, *A History of the Israeli-Palestinian Conflict*.
3. Nir Baram, interview of Benny Morris. To be sure, Morris subsequently made a sharp turn to the right, arguing essentially that the Israeli crimes he had earlier described were necessary if Israel was to survive. More important, however, he did not attempt to retract or refute the *facts* that he—and many others—had revealed.
4. For a review of the origins of the New History, see Silberstein, *New Perspectives on Israeli History*.
5. The most important pre–New History works included Gabbay's account of the expulsion of the Palestinians, *A Political Study of the Arab-Jewish Conflict;* Hirst, *The Gun and the Olive Branch*; Palumbo, *The Palestinian Catastrophe*; Sheffer, *Moshe Sharett*. As well, there are a number of accounts, memoirs, and barely fictional novels or short stories by Israeli participants in the expulsion of the Palestinians during the war. See especially the English translations of Avnery, *1948*, and Yizhar, *Khirbet Khizeh*. Commenting on Yizhar's firsthand account of "the expulsion of innocent Palestinian villagers by soldiers of the new Jewish state," David Shulman of Hebrew University pointedly noted, "His story for many years was a canonical text in Israeli high schools (not anymore)" (Shulman, "A Hero in His Own Words"). For a full discussion of the largely ignored pre–New History works on the expulsion of the Palestinians, see Beinin, "Forgetfulness for Memory: The Limits of the New Israeli History." For a contemporary discussion of the overlooked importance of the Gabbay book, especially in its revelations about Ben-Gurion's goals and policies, see the Israeli historian Shay Hazkani "Catastrophic Thinking: Did Ben-Gurion Try to Rewrite History?," 3.
6. Flapan, *Birth*, 72–73.
7. Flapan, *Birth*, 73–74.
8. From an internal Zionist document, quoting Ben-Gurion's statement to Moshe Sharett, Flapan, *Birth*, 73–74.
9. Heydemann, "Revision and Reconstruction of Israeli History," 13–14.
10. Some of the accounts of the Arab invasion include Lebanon as one of the participants. However, according to Benny Morris, "At the last minute Lebanon refused to join the invasion" (Morris, *1948*, 189).
11. The literature on the Arab invasion is extensive. Among many others, it includes the works of the New Historians, particularly Morris, Shlaim, Segev, and Flapan.
12. These numbers are generally accepted by historians of the 1948 war. See, among others, Pappé, *History*, Kindle locations 2907–10; Waxman, *The Israeli-Palestinian Conflict*, 66–68; Segev, *State at Any Cost*, Kindle 457.
13. The reasons for early Soviet support for Israel are examined in a later chapter.
14. Morris, *1948 and After*, 15.
15. A possible exception was Jordan's British-commanded Arab Legion, the best of the Arab armies; however, it only had about 7,000 men and, more importantly, the Arab Legion did not invade the areas designated by the UN Partition to Israel, fighting only to resist Israeli attacks in territory designated for an Arab state.
16. Segev, "Review of Benny Morris."
17. Pappé, *The Idea of Israel*, Kindle 292.

18. Pfeffer, *Bibi*, Kindle 44. In an email to me, Pappé argues that while the general public was terrified, the political and military leadership were not, because they knew that the Arab armies were weak and disorganized.
19. Quoted by Bergman, *Rise and Kill First*, Kindle 25.
20. Cohen, *Israel and the Arab World*, 313.
21. Cohen, *Israel and the Arab World*, 314.
22. Similarly, Allin and Simon conclude that the "Arab propaganda of extermination" obviously influenced Israeli behavior, especially in the Nakba (*Our Separate Ways*, 20). Pappé also notes the impact of some of the Arab rhetoric on Israeli behavior (*A History of Modern Palestine*, Kindle location 3492).
23. Shlaim, *War and Peace in the Middle East*, 23.
24. Avnery, *A Soldier's Tale*, Kindle location 263. See also Mordechai Bar-On, former chief education officer of the IDF, historian, and Knesset member: "Our perceptions [of Arab aggression] were not invented; they stemmed from the recurrent, very real experiences of this generation. . . . [W]hat choice did . . . [we] have but to fight back?" (*Remembering 1948*, 34).
25. A personal experience: while I was a Fulbright lecturer at Haifa University in 1989, I was invited to the home of one of my colleagues who lived in a kibbutz near Lake Tiberius. The lead tank in the Syrian advance—still there—was stopped just outside the front gate. That was bound to make an impression.
26. Ben-Ami, "A War to Start All Wars," 151.
27. Segev, "Review of Benny Morris, *1948: A History of the First Arab-Israeli War*." See also the comment by the Israeli historian Ami Gluska, who points out that the Arab League emphasized the purpose of the invasion as not to eliminate the Jewish state but "to save the Palestinians who were suffering at the hand of the Jews. . . . In particular they mentioned the Deir Yassin massacre" (Gluska, "The Old Man's 'Day of Horrors'"). It is evident from Gluska's column that he is not merely reporting what the Arab League said but strongly implying that it had a basis in fact.
28. For a discussion of the 1947–48 civil war period, see Rabinovich, *Rabin*, Kindle 18.
29. Quoted in Neff, *Fallen Pillars*, 65.
30. Shlaim, *Collusion*, 204, 211. On Syria's limited objectives, principally of countering Jordanian territorial expansion, see Landis, "Syria in the 1948 Palestine War: Fighting King Abdullah's Greater Syrian Plan."
31. Flapan, *Birth*, 150.
32. Flapan discusses in great detail the failure of the trusteeship and truce plans in *Birth*, 155–86.
33. Flapan, *Birth*, 203.
34. The secret negotiations and agreements have been widely described by Israeli historians. In addition to the various works of Benny Morris and Avi Shlaim, see Bar-Joseph, *Best of Enemies*, and Garfinkle, *Israel and Jordan*.
35. Morris, "Refabricating 1948," 89.
36. The ensuing passages are based on various works of the New Historians, particular those by Morris, Shlaim, Flapan, and Pappé. An important additional work is Rabinovich, *The Road Not Taken*. Rabinovich, a historian who is also a high member of the Israeli centrist establishment, a former ambassador of Israel to the United States, and rector of Tel Aviv University, takes some pains to distinguish himself from the New Historians. Yet his analysis of these events in no way challenges their analyses.
37. Flapan, *Zionism and the Palestinians*, 341.
38. Morris, "Looking Back," 48.
39. Morris, *Righteous Victims*, 265.
40. The centrality of the water issue is emphasized by Ma'oz in his *Syria and Israel*, as well as by other Israeli historians and participants in the Israeli-Syrian conflict. See especially the major work by Aryeh Shalev, *Israel and Syria*. Shalev was an Israeli general who was his country's representative to the Mixed Armistice Commission that was created to oversee the armistice

signed by Syria and Israel in 1949. As discussed in Chapter 6, Shalev is quite critical of Israeli provocations of Syria, especially over the water issue.

41. Maoz, *Syria and Israel*, 19.
42. Karsh, *The Arab-Israeli Conflict*, Kindle location 414.
43. Morris, *1948*, 188.
44. There is no serious dispute among Israeli, Palestinian, or other historians about the central facts of the Nakba. All of the leading Israeli New Historians—particularly Morris, Shlaim, Pappé, and Flapan—extensively examined the issue and revealed the facts. Other accounts have reached the same conclusions. For example, see Ben-Ami, "A War to Start All Wars"; Rashid Khalidi, "The Palestinians and 1948"; Walid Khalidi, "Why Did the Palestinians Leave, Revisited"; Masalha, *Expulsion of the Palestinians*; Raz, *Bride and the Dowry*. Reviewing the evidence marshaled by Morris and others, Tom Segev concluded that "most of the Arabs in the country, approximately 400,000, were chased out and expelled during the first stage of the war. In other words, before the Arab armies invaded the country" (*Haaretz*, July 18, 2010). Other estimates have varied concerning the number of Palestinians who fled or were expelled before the May 1948 Arab state attack; Morris estimated the number to be 250,000–300,000 (*The Birth of the Palestinian Refugee Problem Revisited*, 262); Tessler puts it at 300,000 (*A History of the Israeli-Palestinian Conflict*, 279); Pappé's estimate is 380,000 (*The Making of the Arab-Israeli Conflict*, 96). In another recent review of the evidence, the Israeli historian Daniel Blatman estimates the number to be about 500,000 (Blatman, "Netanyahu, This Is What Ethnic Cleansing Really Looks Like"). Whatever the exact number, even Israeli "Old Historians" now admit that during the 1948 war, the Israeli armed forces drove out many of the Palestinians, though they emphasized the action as a military "necessity." For example, see Anita Shapira, *Israel: A History*, 167–68. In July 2019, the Israeli government sought to cover up the extensive documentary evidence in its state archives that revealed detailed evidence about the extent of the Nakba—even the evidence that had already been published by newspapers and Israeli historians. A *Haaretz* investigation of the attempted cover-up concluded: "Since early last decade, Defense Ministry teams have scoured local archives and removed troves of historic documents to conceal proof of the Nakba, including Israeli eyewitness reports at the time" (Shezaf, "Burying the Nakba: How Israel Systematically Hides Evidence of 1948 Expulsion of Arabs").
45. Walid Khalidi, "Why Did the Palestinians Leave, Revisited," 48.
46. Ben-Gurion, 1937 letter to his son, quoted in Morris, *The Birth of the Palestinian Refugee Problem*, 25.
47. Bar-Zohar, *Ben-Gurion*, 703.
48. Shipler, "Israel Bars Rabin from Relating '48 Eviction of Arabs."
49. Hazkani, "Catastrophic Thinking: Did Ben-Gurion Try to Rewrite History?"
50. Segev, *State at Any Cost*, Kindle 420.
51. Ben-Ami, "A War to Start All Wars," 152.
52. Pappé, *Ethnic Cleansing*, 216.
53. Blatman, "Netanyahu, This Is What Ethnic Cleaning Really Looks Like."
54. Pappé, *Ethnic Cleansing*, 35.
55. Sternhell, "Post-Zionist Settlement."
56. Sachar, *A History of Israel*, 292.
57. These figures are drawn from the detailed population study undertaken by the Jewish Agency: Jonathan Kaplan, *The Mass Migration of the 1950s*, April 27, 2015. See also Anshel Pfeffer: "The armistice agreements signed between Israel and its neighbors in 1949 left around 160,000 Arabs within the new state's borders, and for the first time in nearly 1,900 years there was a Jewish majority in the land. This population was soon bolstered by hundreds of thousands of Holocaust refugees and Sephardi Jews fleeing Arab countries. Israel's population would double in its first five years" (Pfeffer, *Bibi*, 44).

58. Ben-Gurion's letter to Sharett is quoted in Teveth, *Ben-Gurion*, 168. Citing this figure and Ben-Gurion's letter, Rashid Khalidi writes: "David Ben-Gurion realized that the massive wave of immigration to Palestine sparked by the Nazis' rise to power in the early 1930s finally provided the critical demographic mass that would soon make it possible for the Zionist movement to achieve absolute Jewish hegemony and sovereignty over the entire country" (Rashid Khalidi, *Iron Cage*, Kindle location 804).
59. In principle, Israel already does this; the practice is very different.
60. Bar-Zohar, *Ben-Gurion*, 166.
61. Bar-Zohar, *Facing a Cruel Mirror*, 17.
62. Quoted in Segev, *1949*, 6.
63. From a letter of Ben-Gurion to a journalist friend, quoted in Bar-Joseph, *Best of Enemies*, 115.
64. Shlaim, *Iron Wall*, 39.
65. Shapira, *Israel*, 280. Pappé also points to Ben-Gurion's ambivalence and inconsistency about whether Israel should seize the West Bank and East Jerusalem. Some Israeli historians, Pappé writes, believed he voted for the 1948 action only because he knew it would be defeated (email from Pappé to this author).
66. Goodman, *Catch-67*, Kindle location 876.
67. Quoted by many Israeli historians. For example, see Melman and Raviv, *Behind the Uprising*, 53.
68. Wright, *Thirteen Days*, Kindle location 1629.
69. Shlaim, *Iron Wall*, 39.
70. Segev, *State at Any Cost*, Kindle 443.
71. Rabin, *Memoirs*, 37.
72. Rabin, *Memoirs*, 40–41, 345–47.
73. Segev, "Gaza without Gazans: History of an Israeli Fantasy."
74. Bar-Zohar, *Facing a Cruel Mirror*, 17–18.
75. Flapan, *Zionism*, 343.
76. Flapan, *Zionism*, 343.
77. Quoted in Bailey, *Four Arab-Israeli Wars*, 41–42.
78. Sand, *Invention of the Land of Israel*, Kindle 258.
79. Tessler, *History*, Kindle 278–79, quoting a Palestinian writer. See also Pfeffer, *Bibi*, 49.

Chapter 6

1. Quoted in Shlaim, *Israel and Palestine*, 73.
2. Quoted in Pappé, *The Making of the Arab-Israeli Conflict*, 240.
3. Shlaim, *Israel and Palestine*, 76.
4. The quote is Shlaim's paraphrase of Ben-Gurion's statement to the cabinet, *Iron Wall*, Kindle 54.
5. Levy, *Trial and Error*, 63–64.
6. Israel's policies and actions in this period are described in the works of Morris, Pappé, Shlaim, and many other Israeli historians. More recently, declassified documents from the Israeli state archives "reveal how Israel prevented Arabs from returning to villages they had left in 1948—chiefly, by razing structures and planting dense forests" (Berger, "Declassified: Israel Made Sure Arabs Couldn't Return to Their Villages").
7. Quoted in Flapan, *The Birth of Israel*, 105.
8. See Morris, *Israel's Border Wars*, 35–37.
9. Pappé, *A History of Modern Palestine*, Kindle 148; Bergman, *Rise and Kill First*, Kindle 39–40.
10. Shlaim, *Iron Wall*, Kindle 87.
11. Shlaim, *Iron Wall*, 91. By 1955 the situation had changed somewhat: Segev writes that "most of the infiltrators and attackers who penetrated Israel from the Gaza strip were refugees, as were the fedayun ('those who sacrifice themselves') guerrillas, some of whom operated under the direction of the Egyptian army" (Segev, *State at Any Cost*, Kindle 558).

12. Morris, *1948, History,* 366, quoting a cable from an Israeli representative in Washington to Foreign Minister Moshe Sharett. As well, Morris relates, the State Department also criticized Israel's "threatening" attitude toward Jordan.
13. McDonald, *My Mission,* Kindle 54.
14. The cable is quoted by Ross, *Doomed to Succeed,* Kindle location 394. For another discussion of Truman's growing "exasperation" with Israel's territorial claims, see Leffler, *Preponderance of Power,* 245.
15. The literature on the Lausanne Conference is extensive. Among the best works are Pappé, *The Making of the Arab-Israeli Conflict,* 203–43; Shlaim, *Iron Wall,* Kindle 59–62; and Caplan, "A Tale of Two Cities: The Rhodes and Lausanne Conferences, 1949," 5–34.
16. Pappé, *The Idea of Israel,* Kindle 204.
17. See especially Pappé, *The Making of the Arab-Israeli Conflict,* 209–11.
18. Pappé, *The Making of the Arab-Israeli Conflict,* 212.
19. Ball and Ball, *Passionate Attachment,* 36. George Ball was one of the most important American diplomats and statesmen in the twentieth century, holding many top foreign policy positions during his long career. He is perhaps best known for his powerful opposition to the Vietnam War while he was under secretary of state in the Kennedy and Johnson administrations. Douglas Ball is his son.
20. Pappé, *The Making of the Arab-Israeli Conflict,* 210.
21. Ball and Ball, *Passionate Attachment,* 36.
22. Pappé, *The Making of the Arab-Israeli Conflict,* 221.
23. Quoted in Pappé, *The Making of the Arab-Israeli Conflict,* 221. For greater detail on the Jerusalem issue at Lausanne, see Caplan, "A Tale of Two Cities."
24. This paragraph is a close paraphrase of Flapan, *The Birth of Israel,* 224–25.
25. Morris, *Birth Revisited,* 574. On the Truman administration's policies toward the refugee problem during this period, see Landis, "Early U.S. Policy."
26. See Pappé, *The Making of the Arab-Israeli Conflict,* 231–33; Shiffer, "The 1949 Israeli Offer to Repatriate 100,000 Palestinian Refugees"; Morris, *Birth Revisited,* 573–77; Ball and Ball, *Passionate Attachment,* 35–37.
27. As quoted in Ball and Ball, *Passionate Attachment,* 37.
28. Quoted in Spiegel, *The Other Arab-Israeli Conflict,* 46, citing a declassified US document.
29. Truman's letter is quoted in Caplan, "A Tale of Two Cities," 20–21, and summarized in Ball and Ball, *Passionate Attachment,* 37–38.
30. Ball and Ball, *Passionate Attachment,* 39.
31. All quotes are directly from the Ethridge cable of June 12, 1949, as cited in Ball and Ball, *Passionate Attachment,* 39–40, and Morris, *Birth Revisited,* 571.
32. Leffler, *Preponderance,* 288, citing official US government documents. See also Pappé, *The Making of the Arab-Israeli Conflict,* 221, and Ball and Ball, *Passionate Attachment,* 40–41.
33. Commenting on the episode, George Ball wrote: "The flaccid manner in which Washington responded became a stylized practice: to take a strong, principled position, then retreat from principle in the face of Israeli opposition" (Ball and Ball, *Passionate Attachment,* 37).
34. Gendizer, *Dying to Forget,* quoting from a March 1949 memorandum, Kindle 277.
35. Gendizer, *Dying to Forget,* quoting from a May 16, 1949, memorandum of the secretary of defense, Kindle 283–84.
36. Flapan, *The Birth of Israel,* 232.
37. Morris, *Righteous Victims,* 268.
38. Pappé, *The Making of the Arab-Israeli Conflict,* 242.
39. Shlaim, *Israel and Palestine,* 61.
40. Shlaim, *Iron Wall,* Kindle 51.
41. Ball and Ball, *Passionate Attachment,* 34.
42. Flapan, *The Birth of Israel,* 215, citing declassified Eytan and Sasson reports to Foreign Minister Sharett during the conference.

43. Quoted in Shlaim, *Israel and Palestine*, 72. The remarkable Sasson report is also widely quoted by other Israeli historians.
44. The following section is largely based on these works: Bar-Joseph, *The Best of Enemies;* Flapan, *The Birth of Israel*; Garfinkle, *Israel and Jordan*; Melman and Raviv, *Behind the Uprisings;* Morris, *Righteous Victims*; Pappé, *The Making of the Arab-Israeli Conflict*; Rabinovich, *The Road Not Taken*; Raz, *Bride and Dowry;* Shlaim, *Collusion across the Jordan* and *The Iron Wall.*
45. The most extensive analysis of the armistice negotiations is Pappé, *The Making of the Arab-Israeli Conflict*, 180–91.
46. Laron, *Six-Day War,* Kindle 107.
47. Ben-Gurion's statement has been widely quoted. For example, see Melman and Raviv, *Behind the Uprisings*, 53. At the same meeting with the French leaders, according to Flapan, Ben-Gurion "also proposed that Israel annex southern Lebanon up to the Litani River, with a Christian state established in the rest of the country" (Flapan, *The Birth of Israel*, 51).
48. Quoted in *Haaretz*, January 12, 2001, emphasis added.
49. Raz, *Bride and Dowry,* 16.
50. Maoz, *Syria and Israel*, 2. Maoz, a professor of Middle East studies at the Hebrew University of Jerusalem, is considered Israel's preeminent expert on Syrian-Israeli relations.
51. Maoz, *Syria and Israel*, 6.
52. Maoz, *Syria and Israel*, 11–12.
53. Maoz, *Syria and Israel*, 13.
54. Two of the most important—and revealing—sources for the Israeli-Syrian conflict after the armistice were written by Israeli general Aryeh Shalev, *The Israel-Syria Armistice Regime,* and *Israel and Syria.* General Shalev was Israel's representative on the Syria-Israel Armistice Commission, created to administer the armistice. Similar accounts include Drysdale and Hinnebusch, *Syria and the Middle East Peace Process*; Maoz, *Syria and Israel;* Neff, "Israel-Syria: Conflict at the Jordan River, 1949–67"; and Rabinovich, *The Road Not Taken.*
55. On the probable role of the CIA—which is to say, the Truman administration—in the Zaim coup, see Rabinovich, *The Road Not Taken*, citing a book by the former high CIA official Miles Copeland, *The Game of Nations*, 42. The scholar Douglas Little cites documentary evidence supporting Copeland's role in the coup: "Covert War and Covert Action: The United States and Syria, 1945–1958," 55–56.
56. The most important discussions of the Zaim proposal are Maoz, *Syria and Israel,* 20–26; Morris, *1948, History,* 389–91; Landis, "Early U.S. Policy"; Shlaim, *Israel and Palestine*, 62–76; Rabinovich, *The Road Not Taken*, 65–110; Segev, *1949*, 16–18.
57. Acheson's now-declassified cable is quoted by Rabinovich, *The Road Not Taken,* 90–91.
58. Rabinovich, *The Road Not Taken,* 75.
59. Quoted from the Israeli archives by Israeli journalist Hirsh Goodman in the February 10, 1994, issue of *The Jerusalem Report.*
60. Shlaim, *Iron Wall,* Kindle 47–49
61. Shlaim, *Iron Wall,* Kindle 48.
62. From a cable of December 14, 1951, quoted in Shalev, *Armistice Regime,* 95.
63. On the Shishakli offers and Israel's response, see Maoz, *Syria and Israeli,* 28–31.
64. Shalev, *Armistice Regime,* 86.
65. Shalev, *Armistice Regime,* 99.
66. Shalev, *Israel and Syria,* 45.
67. Shalev, *Armistice Regime,* 77, citing Yadin.
68. Shapiro, "What Price Peace with Syria?," 4.
69. On the Israeli "retaliations" against Syrian villages, see Maoz, *Syria and Israel,* 28, and Shlaim, *Iron Wall,* Kindle 71–72.
70. Dayan's 1976 interview is quoted in Shlaim, *Iron Wall,* Kindle 251; the "bullshit" remark is quoted in an article by Tel Aviv University professor Tanya Reinhart, "Evil Unleashed," 17.
71. Hof, "The Line of June 4, 1967," 2.

72. Shlaim, *Iron Wall,* Kindle 158.
73. Bar-On, *The Gates of Gaza,* 64. On the pattern of deliberate Israeli violations of the demilitarized zone (DMZ) agreements designed to provoke a Syrian response so that Israel could retaliate with massive force, see also Maoz, *Syria and Israel,* 47–48, and Yaniv, "Syria and Israel," 157–58.
74. Quoted from a Sharett diary entry in early 1954, Rokach, *Israel's Sacred Terrorism,* 4.
75. Rokach, *Israel's Sacred Terrorism,* Sharett diary entry of February 25, 1954, 17.
76. The Avnery article is translated and published in Rokach, *Israel's Sacred Terrorism,* 56.
77. See Levy, *Trial and Error,* and Maoz, *Syria and Israel,* 45–52.
78. Eban, *Autobiography,* 198.
79. Maoz, *Syria and Israel,* 32–33. On the reasonableness of Syrian fears, see also Shalev, *Israel and Syria,* 128–29.

Chapter 7

1. On the conflict between Ben-Gurion and Sharett, see Pappé, *A History of Modern Palestine,* Kindle 162.
2. Bar-Zohar, *Ben-Gurion,* 218.
3. Bar-Zohar, *Facing a Cruel Mirror,* 18.
4. Rokach, *Sacred Terrorism,* 3. The quote is Rokach's paraphrase of Sharett's Hebrew-language diary. Bar-Zohar writes that in March 1955, when Sharett was prime minster, Ben-Gurion proposed to the Israeli cabinet that the Egyptians be driven out of Gaza; however, his proposal was rejected, in good part because of opposition to incorporating such a large Arab minority into Israel's population (Bar-Zohar, *Ben-Gurion,* 219–20).
5. Quoted in Shapira, *Ben-Gurion,* Kindle 208.
6. See Bar-On, *Gates of Gaza,* 42–47. Golani writes that convincing Ben-Gurion to agree to this strategy "was not overly difficult, since he believed that war was inevitable in the long term and preferred to have Israel initiate rather than respond to it" (Golani, *In Search of a War,* 193).
7. The speech is quoted in Sharett's diary entry of May 26, 1955, recorded in Rokach, *Sacred Terrorism,* 41.
8. Rokach, *Sacred Terrorism,* 41.
9. Bar-On, *Gates of Gaza,* 23.
10. Segev, *State at Any Cost,* Kindle 564.
11. A number of Israeli historians have discussed Nasser's overtures. For example, see Pappé, *Biggest Prison,* Kindle 539–49.
12. The Israeli press reports and the terms of an informal peace agreement are discussed in Tessler, *A History of the Israeli-Palestinian Conflict,* Kindle 339. See also Bar-On, *Gates of Gaza,* 100–101.
13. Bar-On, *Gates of Gaza,* 102, 106, 109.
14. Bar-On, *Gates of Gaza,* 102. See also Segev, *State at Any Cost,* Kindle 568.
15. Bar-On, *Gates of Gaza,* 87, 99–100.
16. Bar-On discusses the British and American support of returning some of the Negev to Egypt, writing that "[Secretary of State] Dulles had always believed that a final settlement might involve adjustments in the border that could result in the loss of some acres for Israel" (Bar-On, *Gates of Gaza,* 97).
17. Quoted in Bar-On, *Gates of Gaza,* 89.
18. Bar-On, *Gates of Gaza,* 112.
19. See Map 6.1 in Chapter 6.
20. Tessler, *A History of the Israeli-Palestinian Conflict,* Kindle 341.
21. For a full discussion of "the Lavon affair," see Segev, *State at Any Cost,* 537–44, 621–26.
22. Yossi Melman, one of Israel's leading journalists for many years, writes that consideration was also given to poisoning Egyptian wells—as had also been considered for German water systems after the end of World War II. Both plans were abandoned, Melman reports, but Israeli

military intelligence collaborated with drug dealers in Sinai and Lebanon. See Melman, "Counterfeit Egyptian Money, Stamps, and Poisoned Wells: When Young Israel Stirred the Water of the Nile."

23. Rokach, *Sacred Terrorism,* 34.
24. Segev writes that "it is inconceivable" that the Israeli plotters would have planned the Egyptian bombings on their own initiative: "If [they] had not received the order from Lavon, [they] received it from Dayan" (*State at Any Cost,* Kindle 543).
25. Segev, *State at Any Cost,* Kindle 626.
26. Shlaim, *Iron Wall,* Kindle 129.
27. Quoting from the diary entries, Segev, *State at Any Cost,* Kindle 572.
28. Quoted from Sharett's diary, Rokach, *Sacred Terrorism,* 4.
29. Shlaim, *Iron Wall,* Kindle 133. On Nasser's decision to support the Fedayeen after the Israel raid in February, see also Bar-Zohar, *Ben-Gurion,* 218.
30. Shlaim, *Iron Wall,* Kindle 136–37. For another discussion of the evidence of Egyptian suppression of Palestinian infiltration or armed attacks against Israel, see Rokach, *Sacred Terrorism,* 61–62. In his major history of Israeli terrorism, the Israeli journalist and historian Ronen Bergman writes that some 1,000 Israeli civilians were murdered by Fedayeen infiltrators between 1951 and 1955. *Rise and Kill First,* Kindle 39. It is likely that most of the attacks did not occur until Nasser ended his policy of curbing the Fedayeen after Israel's February 1955 raid.
31. Khalidi, *Iron Cage,* Kindle location 5105.
32. Bar-On, *Gates of Gaza,* 57, 59.
33. Bar-On, *Gates of Gaza,* 64.
34. Bar-Zohar, *Ben-Gurion,* 224.
35. Bar-Zohar, *Ben-Gurion,* 225.
36. Bergman, *Rise and Kill First,* Kindle 49–51.
37. Quoted in Bar-On, *Gates of Gaza,* 211.
38. Bar-On, *Gates of Gaza,* 212.
39. For details, see Golani, *Israel in Search of a War,* 12–13.
40. Bialer, *Between East and West,* 66–67.
41. First quote, Allin and Simon, *Our Separate Ways,* 122; second and third quotes, Ben-Zvi, *Decade of Transition,* 71, quoting from a US government document. In his memoirs, Abba Eban writes that Dulles did not exclude the possibility of a US-Israel "security treaty" in the context of an Arab-Israeli peace settlement.
42. Raviv and Melman, *Friends Indeed,* 72.
43. Bar-On, *Gates of Gaza,* 61.
44. Bar-On, *Gates of Gaza,* 145–46.
45. Quoted in Ben-Zvi, *The United States and Israel,* 53. Making use of declassified documents from this period, Ben-Zvi quotes many other similar statements from Dulles and Eisenhower.
46. Quoted in Bar-On, *Gates of Gaza,* 61.
47. Bar-On, *Gates of Gaza,* 151.
48. From a transcript of a Dulles telephone conversation with other US officials (Ben-Zvi, *United States and Israel,* 73).
49. Ben-Zvi, *United States and Israel,* 56.
50. Eban, *Personal Witness,* 245.
51. A number of works on this period discuss the growing US encouragement of an Israeli-France arms agreement. In his autobiography, Eban discusses his conversations with Dulles, who made it clear not only that "he had no objection to other countries giving Israel arms," but that "actually, he would rather have liked this to happen" (Eban, *Abba Eban: An Autobiography,* 197). See also Rokach, *State of Terror,* 48.
52. The French role in the development of Israel's nuclear weapons has been widely described. For example, see Pappé, *A History of Modern Palestine,* 162.
53. Ben-Gurion's diary entry of October 24, 1956, quoted in Bar-On, *Gates of Gaza,* 247.

54. Bar-Zohar, *Ben-Gurion*, 242.
55. Quoted from Ben-Gurion's diary, in Shlaim, *Iron Wall*, Kindle 186.
56. Segev, *State at Any Cost*, citing Ben-Gurion's diary, Kindle 579.
57. Bar-Zohar, *Ben-Gurion*, 236.
58. For a detailed discussion of these Israeli goals, see Shlaim, *Iron Wall*, Kindle 180–83. Shlaim's account, in turn, is based on Ben-Gurion's diaries, on the memoirs of Israeli participants in the events, and especially, he says, on the "copious notes" kept by Mordechai Bar-On, the secretary to the Israeli delegation that met with Britain and France.
59. Segev, *State at Any Cost*, Kindle 587.
60. Shlaim, *Iron Wall*, Kindle 190.
61. Bar-On, *Gates of Gaza*, 4, and Rokach, *Sacred Terrorism*, 47.
62. Bar-On, *Gates of Gaza*, 181.
63. Eisenhower's motivations are discussed in Raviv and Melman, *Friends Indeed*, 78, 81–82, and in an authoritative article by Alfred Atherton, a former high State Department official and US ambassador to Egypt: "The Soviet Role in the Middle East."
64. Ben-Gurion's speech is quoted in Bar-On, *Gates of Gaza*, 270, and Shapira, *Ben-Gurion*, 210–12. As well, Bar-Zohar writes that "Ben-Gurion's words displayed clear intentions of annexing Sinai and the islands in the Gulf of Akaba" (Bar-Zohar, *Ben-Gurion*, 249).
65. Quoted by Eban, *Abba Eban: An Autobiography*, 230, and Bar-Zohar, *Ben-Gurion*, 253.
66. Eban, *Abba Eban: An Autobiography*, 229.
67. Quoted by Bar-On, *Gates of Gaza*, 269.
68. Eisenhower's letter and Hoover's blunt threats are quoted in Bar-On, *Gates of Gaza*, 269–70, and Bar-Zohar, *Ben-Gurion*, 250–51.
69. Ross, *Doomed to Succeed*, Kindle location 837.
70. Shapira, *Ben-Gurion*, 212; Bar-On, *Gates of Gaza*, 300.
71. Bar-On, *Gates of Gaza*, 301, 313.
72. Segev, *State at Any Cost*, Kindle 598.
73. Golani, *Israel in Search of a War*, 196–97; see also Ben-Zvi, *Decade of Transition*.
74. Cited in Ben-Zvi, *Decade of Transition*, 81.
75. Little, *American Orientalism*, 94, citing US government documents.
76. Golani, *Israel in Search of a War*, 198.
77. Bar-On, *Gates of Gaza*, 323.

Chapter 8

1. Segev, *State at Any Cost*, Kindle 643.
2. The literature on the Israeli nuclear weapons program is extensive. The works of the Israeli political scientist Avner Cohen are considered the most authoritative; he has written extensively on the issue for many years, particularly in two works: the article "Stumbling into Opacity: The United States, Israel, and the Atom, 1960–63," and his major book, *Israel and the Bomb*. Two other major studies reviewing the history of Israel's nuclear deterrent and US policy are Or Rabinowitz and Nicholas L. Miller, "Keeping the Bombs in the Basement: U.S. Nonproliferation Policy toward Israel, South Africa, and Pakistan," and Galen Jackson, "The U.S., the Israeli Nuclear Program, and Nonproliferation."
3. Quoting Ben-Gurion's account of his meeting with Kennedy, in Raviv and Melman, *Friends Indeed*, 100.
4. Ball and Ball, *Passionate Attachment*, paraphrasing Kennedy's explanation to Golda Meir, 51.
5. Smith, "U.S. Assumes the Israelis Have A-Bomb or Its Parts," and Finney, "US Hears Israel Moves toward A-Bomb Potential."
6. Segev, *State at Any Cost*, Kindle 629.
7. Quoted in Cohen and Barr, "How a Standoff with the U.S. Almost Blew Up Israel's Nuclear Program."

8. For example, in May 1963, Kennedy sent Ben-Gurion a letter warning that despite the "deep commitment to the security of Israel," US support "would be seriously jeopardized in the public opinion in this country and in the West as a whole if it should be thought that this Government was unable to obtain reliable information on a subject as vital to peace as this question of the character of Israel's effort in the nuclear field" (quoted in Ross, *Doomed to Succeed,* Kindle 1569–76).
9. See Bass, *Support Any Friend,* 195, quoting a declassified US government document.
10. Quoted in Laron, *Six-Day War,* Kindle 204, and Ross, *Doomed to Succeed,* Kindle location 1531.
11. Maoz, *Syria and Israel,* 86. See also Clarke, "Entanglement: The Commitment to Israel," 218.
12. Christison, *Perceptions of Palestine,* 133.
13. Stephens, "Six Days and Fifty Years of War."
14. Bar-On, *Gates of Gaza,* 314.
15. Pappé, *Ten Myths,* Kindle locations 1012–24.
16. Pappé, *Ten Myths,* Kindle location 1210.
17. Pappé, *Ten Myths,* Kindle location 1218.
18. Laron, *Six-Day War,* Kindle 269.
19. Laron, *Six-Day War,* Kindle 107–8.
20. Laron, *Six-Day War,* Kindle 108.
21. Laron, *Six-Day War,* Kindle 108–9.
22. Laron, *Six-Day War,* Kindle 106.
23. Shlaim, *Iron Wall,* Kindle 239.
24. Shlaim, *Iron Wall,* Kindle 241.
25. Laron, *Six-Day War,* Kindle 77.
26. On the attacks, see Shlaim, *Iron Wall,* Kindle 249, and Maoz, *Syria and Israel,* 88–89.
27. Shlaim, *Iron Wall,* Kindle 249.
28. Neff, "Israel-Syria: Conflict at the Jordan River, 1949–1967," 26–40.
29. Shlaim, *Iron Wall,* Kindle 243. See also Maoz, *Syria and Israel,* 88–91.
30. Shlaim, *Iron Wall,* Kindle 250.
31. Ben-Gurion, *Talks with Arab Leaders,* 7, 10–11.
32. Shlaim, *Iron Wall,* Kindle 249. See also Segev, *1967,* 209.
33. Quoted in Rubenberg, *Israel and the American National Interest,* 105. Similar threatening statements by Rabin and other high Israeli officials are quoted in Shlaim, *Iron Wall,* Kindle 251; Maoz, *Israel and Syria,* 98–99; and Brecher, *Decisions in Israel's Foreign Policy,* 358–61.
34. Quoted in Jabber and Kolkowicz, "Arab-Israeli Wars," 419–20.
35. See Tessler, *A History of the Israeli-Palestinian Conflict,* 385–87, and Aronson, *Conflict and Bargaining in the Middle East,* 62.
36. The declassified memo is quoted by Neff, *Warriors for Jerusalem,* 59.
37. In his book *Conflict and Bargaining,* Aronson quotes from an article by Abba Eban that makes these points (388).
38. The quotations are from Allin and Simon, *Our Separate Ways,* 33. For Egyptian insider works that confirm these accounts of Soviet policy, see Heikal, *Sphinx and the Commissar,* and Anwar Sadat's memoirs, *In Search of Identity.*
39. On Nasser's defensive intentions, see Parker, *Politics of Miscalculation*; Safran, *From War to War;* Khouri, *Arab-Israeli Dilemma*; and Tessler, *A History of the Israeli-Palestinian Conflict.*
40. Eban, *Abba Eban: An Autobiography,* 352 (emphasis added).
41. Shalom, "Looking Back at the June 1967 Middle East War," 3.
42. All quotes are from declassified State Department documents, as cited in Shalom, "Looking Back," and Ryan, *The Myth of Annihilation and the Six-Day War,* 42–43.
43. Johnson, *Vantage Point,* 293.
44. Shalom, "Looking Back," 3.
45. Segev, *1967,* 334.
46. Segev, *1967,* 257.

47. Laron, *Six-Day War,* Kindle 207. For another discussion of the confidence of Israeli military and intelligence leaders that Israel would easily win the coming war, see Bronner, *Stuck.*
48. From a *Le Monde* interview with Rabin on February 29, 1968 (emphasis added), quoted in Rubenberg, *Israel,* 104.
49. From a 1972 Israeli newspaper interview with Peled, quoted by Rubenberg, *Israel,* 104.
50. Quoted in Ryan, "Myth of Annihilation," 40.
51. Quoted in Ryan, "Myth of Annihilation," 39.
52. Quoted in the "Excerpts from Begin's Speech at National Defense College," *New York Times,* August 21, 1982.
53. Quoted by Shlaim, *Iron Wall,* Kindle 244.
54. Quoted by Laron, *Six-Day War,* Kindle 216. To be sure, Laron notes that the threat was in the context of a war initiated by Israel.
55. Quoted in Eban, *Abba Eban: An Autobiography,* 379–80.
56. Eban, *Abba Eban: An Autobiography,* 81–82.
57. Quoted by Tessler, *A History of the Israeli-Palestinian Conflict,* Kindle 393.
58. Diab, "Israel's Missed Opportunities."
59. Chomsky, *Middle East Illusions,* 99.
60. Johnson, *Vantage Point,* 297. Other historians who discuss Johnson's strong pro-Israel leanings include Elgindy, *Blind Spot,* Kindle 69, and Christison, *Perceptions of Palestine,* 109.
61. Korn, *Stalemate,* 15–16.
62. Bar-Siman Tov, *Israel,* 156. See also Safran, *Embattled Ally,* 431.
63. Taylor, *The Superpowers and the Middle East* 75.
64. Quoted in Laron, *Six-Day War,* Kindle 205.
65. Quoted in Laron, *Six-Day War,* Kindle 210.
66. Quoted in Laron, *Six-Day War,* Kindle 210.
67. Quandt, *Peace Process,* 25–30.
68. Quandt, *Peace Process,* 440.
69. Quoted in Gorenberg, *Accidental Empire,* 53.
70. Quandt, *Peace Process,* 34
71. Quoted in Laron, *Six-Day War,* Kindle 213.
72. Korn, *Stalemate,* 18.
73. Korn, *Stalemate,* 18.
74. Quandt, *Peace Process,* 42.
75. Quandt, *Peace Process,* 42.
76. Quandt, *Peace Process,* 51.
77. Quoted in Rubenberg, *Encyclopedia of the Israeli-Palestinian* Conflict, Vol. 2, 887. On Rusk's views, see Parker, *Miscalculation,* 110.
78. Little, *American Orientalism,* 242.
79. Ball and Ball, *Passionate Attachment,* 57–58. In his memoirs, Johnson says only that the *Liberty* was "attacked in error" (*Vantage Point,* 300); other accounts suggest that he knew, or suspected, otherwise.
80. Ball and Ball, *Passionate Attachment,* 58.
81. Segev, "What If Israel Had Turned Back?" Similarly, Lawrence Wright wrote, "From the Israeli perspective, the war really had no design beyond the elimination of the Egyptian threat, but it opened up opportunities. . . . In that dizzying, unaccountable, almost thoughtless moment, the decision to seize the West Bank was made" (Wright, *Thirteen Days,* Kindle 2510).
82. Segev, "What If Israel Had Turned Back."
83. For example, Tom Segev wrote: "It is widely believed that control of Jerusalem expresses the essence of the Zionist dream. The truth is that the Zionist movement has always expressed doubts about Jerusalem. Theodor Herzl agreed to give it up, and the November 1947 partition decision was joyously accepted, even though Jerusalem was not slated to be part of the State of Israel" (Segev, "Everyone Thinks Jerusalem Is Lost," *Haaretz,* November 10, 2008).

84. Quoted in Dan Margalit, *Haaretz,* December 25, 2001.
85. For extensive details on the earlier positions of Ben-Gurion and other Zionist leaders, see Golani, "Zionism without Zion: The Jerusalem Question, 1947–1949."
86. For a detailed discussion, see Klein, *Jerusalem.* On the three leveled Palestinian villages, see Sand, *Invention of Land of Israel,* Kindle 243. In addition to the expulsion of thousands of Palestinians from Jerusalem, some 200,000 to 300,000 fled from the newly conquered territory, "some of them under duress," as Benny Morris has put it (*Righteous Victims,* 683).
87. Zisser, "June 1967—Israel's Capture of the Golan Heights."
88. Zisser, "June 1967—Israel's Capture of the Golan Heights," 179.
89. Zisser, "June 1967—Israel's Capture of the Golan Heights," 172.
90. Rabinovich, *Brink of Peace,* 21
91. Shlaim, *Iron Wall,* Kindle 262.
92. Dayan's views, and subsequent change of mind, are discussed in detail in Shlaim, *Iron Wall,* 246–50; see also Zisser, "June 1967—Israel's Capture of the Golan Heights"; Segev, *1967,* 387. In his biography of Rabin, Rabinovich writes that Dayan also feared that an Israeli attack on Syria would force Nasser to respond to avoid another humiliation by Israel and that would threaten both his domestic power and his leadership in the Arab world; in fact, Dayan predicted that Nasser would block Israeli shipping in the Straits of Tiran, forcing Israel to act (Rabinovich, *Yitzhak Rabin,* Kindle 61).
93. Quoted in several accounts, including Zisser, "June 1967—Israel's Capture of the Golan Heights," 176–77.
94. From Dayan's interview with an Israeli journalist in the Israeli newspaper *Yediot Aharanot,* April 27, 1997; quoted in Shlaim, *Iron Wall,* Kindle 250. The affair is also discussed in Zisser, "June 1967—Israel's Capture of the Golan Heights," 169.
95. Quoted in Zisser, "June 1967—Israel's Capture of the Golan Heights," 169.
96. Zisser, "June 1967—Israel's Capture of the Golan Heights," 187.
97. Zisser, "June 1967—Israel's Capture of the Golan Heights," 190.
98. Bar-Siman-Tov, *Israel,* 142.
99. According to the memoirs of both Dayan and Rabin, the Israeli intention was not to attack Damascus but to put pressure on Syria to end its support of Palestinian guerrillas. In his memoirs, Rabin wrote that even though Israel was now in a position to invade Damascus without much difficulty, it understood that even with the Golan territory they already had conquered there would be great political pressure to return it (117–19). On Johnson's response to the Soviet threat, see his memoir, *Vantage Point,* 302.
100. The Israeli expulsion of Syrian villagers in the Golan Heights, forthrightly called "ethnic cleansing" by the Israeli historian Ahron Bregman, is discussed in his book *Cursed Victory,* Kindle 73–74. See also Fogelman, "The Disinherited."
101. Zertal and Eldar, *Lords of the Land,* 7, and Bergman, *Rise and Kill First,* Kindle 114–15.
102. The relevant government documents and minutes have been declassified and widely discussed by Israeli scholars. See especially Segev, "Origins of the Occupation"; Aronson, *Conflict and Bargaining in the Middle East,* 86; Korn, *Stalemate,* 13–15.
103. Korn, *Stalemate,* 14. See also Segev, "Origins of the Occupation": "Some of the ministers were conscious that the populated territories endangered Israel's future as a Jewish state. Justice Minister Shapira argued that the West Bank should be returned to Jordan: "Otherwise, the whole Zionist project is finished and we'll be a ghetto here." But not one of the ministers thought to warn the government at the outset that it would not be a good idea to occupy the West Bank.
104. Raz, *Bride and the Dowry,* 2.
105. Raz, *Bride and the Dowry,* 44.
106. Segev, "Origins of the Occupation."
107. Raz, *Bride and the Dowry,* 54.
108. For example, see Laron, *Six-Day War,* Kindle 285; Raz, *Bride and the Dowry,* 46–47; Korn, *Stalemate,* 14.

109. Most of them relocated to southern Lebanon, setting the stage for the 1978 and 1982 Israeli attacks on them.
110. Quoted in Tessler, *A History of the Israeli-Palestinian Conflict,* Kindle 409. Tessler writes that despite rhetoric, "the meeting was dominated by the more moderate Arab leaders, and there were repeated statements about the need for political compromise. . . . There were no calls for the destruction of Israel" (410). Similarly, Raz writes that Nasser told other Egyptian leaders that while "I cannot negotiate now, but this doesn't mean that I am not going to negotiate forever." Raz concludes: "The three noes notwithstanding, the Arab leaders . . . realized at Khartoum that . . . they should seek a political settlement" (*Bride and the Dowry,* 137).
111. Raz, *Bride and the Dowry,* 138.
112. Raz, *Bride and the Dowry,* 138.
113. Raz, *Bride and the Dowry,* 259.
114. Korn, *Stalemate,* 72; Raz, *Bride and the Dowry,* 258–59.
115. Raz, *Bride and the Dowry.*
116. Raz, *Bride and the Dowry* , 259–60.
117. Melman and Raviv, *Behind the Uprising,* 92.
118. Quoting from Ben-Gurion's diary entry of May 21, *State at Any Cost,* Kindle 654. On Ben-Gurion's opposition to the war, see also Bar-Zohar, *Ben-Gurion,* 312.
119. Rabin, *Memoirs,* 75–76.
120. Segev, *State at Any Cost,* Kindle 656–57.
121. Bar-Zohar, *Facing a Cruel Mirror,* 21. On the importance to Ben-Gurion of ensuring a Jewish majority in a democratic Israel, see Sokatch, "Netanyahu Won the Election, Will He Now Dismantle Israel's Democracy?"
122. Ben-Gurion, as told to an interviewer, cited in Fred J. Khouri, "United Nations Peace Efforts," 98.
123. Yaniv, *Deterrence without the Bomb;* Maoz, "The Mixed Blessing of Israel's Nuclear Policy."
124. Heikal, *Road to Ramadan,* 76.
125. For the evidence of the thinking of Sadat and the Egyptian military, see Feldman, *Israeli Nuclear Deterrence,* 56–61, 87–88.
126. For works by prominent Israeli historians emphasizing not the only lost opportunities for peace after the 1967 war but the pernicious effects of the Israeli occupation on Israeli society as well as, of course, on the Palestinians, see Sand, *Land of Israel*: "It was the 1967 war that finally ensnared Israel in a honeyed but bloody trap from which it has proved incapable of extricating itself" (Kindle 258). Ahron Bregman, in his aptly named book, *Cursed Victory:* "The true tragedy of the Arab-Israeli conflict . . . is one of lost opportunities" (Kindle location 314). Benny Morris: "The unleashed currents within Israeli society that militated against yielding occupied territory and against compromise. Expansionism, fueled by fundamentalist messianism and primal nationalist greed, took hold of a growing minority, both religious and secular, getting its cue, and eventually creeping support, from the government itself" (Morris, *Righteous Victims,* 330–31).
127. The best and most detailed study of the early postwar discussions in the Israeli cabinet, based on the minutes of the relevant cabinet meetings, is a long article by the Israeli political scientist and military analyst Pedatzur, "Coming Back Full Circle."
128. Quoted in Neff, *Warriors for Jerusalem,* 270.
129. Little, *American Orientalism,* 283–84.
130. Pedatzur, "Coming Back Full Circle," 290.

Chapter 9

1. Much of this chapter is drawn (and updated) from my article, Slater, "The Superpowers and an Arab-Israeli Political Settlement."

2. Johnson, *Vantage Point*, 288.
3. During the Cold War, typical statements of this view included Aspaturian, "Soviet Policy in the Middle East"; Freedman, "Moscow and a Middle East Peace Settlement"; Hunter, "Seeking Middle East Peace"; Jabber and Kolkowicz, "The Arab-Israeli Wars of 1967 and 1973"; Kolkowicz, "Soviet Policy in the Middle East"; and Rubinstein, "The Soviet Union's Imperial Policy in the Middle East."
4. This is the general perspective of many scholarly studies, including Brown, *International Politics and the Middle East*; Breslauer, "Soviet Policy in the Middle East, 1967–1972"; Breslauer, "On Collaborative Competition"; Evron, *The Middle East*; Golan, *Yom Kippur and After*; Kass, *Soviet Involvement in the Middle East*; MacFarlane, "The Soviet View"; Marantz and Steinberg, *Superpower Involvement in the Middle East*; MacFarlane, "The Middle East in Soviet Strategy"; McGuire, *Military Objectives in Soviet Foreign Policy*; and Tillman, *The United States and the Middle East*, chapter 6.
5. As quoted by Heikal, *Sphinx and the Commissar*, 91.
6. Saunders, "Regulating Soviet-U.S. Competition," 552.
7. As argued, among many others, by Robert Harkavy, "Strategic Access, Bases and Arms Transfers."
8. On this point see the chapter by Evgeni M. Primakov, the former Soviet foreign minister: "Soviet Policy towards the Arab-Israeli Conflict."
9. Heikal, *Sphinx*, 98.
10. Brecher, *Decisions*, 113–15.
11. For a brief summary of these decisions and their consequences, see Safran, *Embattled Ally*, 338–40.
12. Soviet statement of April 1955, quoted in Karsh, *The Soviet Union and Syria*, 1.
13. For a brief summary of these Soviet proposals, see Klinghoffer, *Israel and the Soviet Union*, 39.
14. Heikal, *Sphinx*, 65.
15. Heikal, *Sphinx*, 197, 276. See also Laqueur, *Soviet Union and the Middle East*, 190, and Ra'anan, *The USSR Arms the Third World*, 172.
16. The quote is from a Soviet note, discussed in Jabber, *Not by War Alone*, 41.
17. As quoted from a declassified 1957 State Department document, cited in Hahn, *Caught in the Middle East*, 231. See also Walt, *The Origins of Alliances*, Kindle location 4246, and Heikal, *Sphinx*, 76–77.
18. Saunders, "Regulating Soviet-U.S. Competition," 561.
19. The scholarship on Soviet arms sales to the Arab countries is virtually unanimous that the various limitations imposed by the Soviets reflected an overall policy of not providing arms that would give Egypt or Syria an offensive capability. Among numerous works in this vein, see Glassman, *Arms for the Arabs*; Breslauer, "Soviet Policy in the Middle East"; and Halliday, *Soviet Policy in the Arc of Crisis*. For a fuller list of sources, see footnote 26 in Slater, "The Superpowers and an Arab-Israeli Political Settlement."
20. See Heikal, *Sphinx*, 193–202, and Sadat, *In Search of Identity*, 219–21, 225–31. A recent article quotes from a declassified CIA analysis, "[The Soviets] were wary of Syria's provocative actions along the Israeli border, and apparently have attempted quietly to discourage . . . actual hostilities in the area" (Jackson, "Who Killed Détente?," 140).
21. Talbott, *Khrushchev Remembers*, 345. In his own memoirs, Sadat writes that the Soviet Union never tried to conceal from Egypt its support for Israel's right to exist, and he repeatedly emphasized that he strongly opposed an Egyptian attack on Israel (Sadat, *In Search of Identity*, 297).
22. The first quote is the conclusion of the Soviet scholar Ilana Kass, in *Soviet Involvement*, 50. The second quote is from Kass's translation of the *Pravda* statement, 50.
23. Eban, *Personal Witness*, 551.
24. The Soviet statement is quoted in Golan, *Soviet Union and the PLO*, 51. My argument here is based primarily on that book and similar analyses in Kuniholm, "The Soviet Attitude to the

Palestine Problem"; Yaniv, *Dilemmas of Security;* and from the memoirs of Sadat and Heikal, both of whom quote statements of Soviet premier Leonid Brezhnev in which he pressed Arafat to accept a two-state settlement of the Israeli-Palestinian conflict.

25. Sadat discusses Brezhnev's position in *Search for Identity*, 297.
26. Saunders, "Regulating Soviet-U.S. Competition," 552. Other accounts of the post-1967 negotiations reach the same conclusion; for further citations, see Slater, "The Superpowers and an Arab-Israeli Political Settlement," note 31.
27. Atherton, "The Soviet Role in the Middle East," 692.
28. The Soviet proposal is discussed in Klinghoffer, *Israel and the Soviet Union*, 63.
29. For discussions of this Soviet proposal, see Breslauer, "Soviet Policy in the Middle East," 72–73, and Kass, *Soviet Involvement in the Middle East*, 71–72.
30. Saunders, "Regulating Soviet-U.S. Competition," 555.
31. Whetten, *The Canal War*, 75–76; Breslauer, "Soviet Policy in the Middle East," 85.
32. Quandt, *Peace Process*, 1st ed., note 36, 345.
33. Quandt, *Peace Process*, 3rd ed., 59 (emphasis added).
34. Kissinger, *Years of Upheaval*, 550.
35. Kissinger, *Years of Upheaval*, 551.
36. Among these accounts are Atherton, "The Soviet Role in the Middle East"; Garthoff, *Detente and Confrontation*; Quandt, *Decade of Decisions*; and Saunders, "Regulating Soviet-U.S. Competition." All of them stress the profound differences between Kissinger and the State Department on how to respond to the Arab-Israeli conflict in general and the Soviet role in particular.
37. Kissinger, *White House Years*, 346, 349; Kissinger, *Years of Upheaval*, 600.
38. From a 1973 Kissinger memo, cited in Jackson, "Who Killed Détente?," 157.
39. Korn, *Stalemate*, 155.
40. Quoted in Quandt, *Decade of Decisions*, 89–90.
41. Golan, *Israeli Peacemaking*, Kindle 30.
42. Golan, *Israeli Peacemaking*, Kindle 30.
43. Quandt, *Peace Process*, 3rd ed., 89.
44. Golan, *Israeli Peacemaking*, 30.
45. Rabin, *Memoirs*, 161–62.
46. Rabinovich, *Yitzhak Rabin*, Kindle 78.
47. Quandt, *Peace Process*, 1st ed., 545, 550. For further evidence on Nixon's willingness to consider serious pressures on Israel (based on declassified documents), see Jackson, "Who Killed Détente?," 155.
48. Isaacson, *Kissinger.*
49. Kissinger, *White House Years*, Kindle location 7452.
50. This is the generally accepted figure. See Levy, "So Stupid, Beautiful and Pure."
51. Whetten, *Canal War*, 90.
52. Heikal, *Sphinx*, 253. See also Sadat, *Identity*, and Rabinovich, *Yitzhak Rabin*, 83.
53. Saunders, "Regulating Soviet-U.S. Competition," 556; Quandt, *Decade of Decisions*, 95.
54. Kissinger, *White House Years*, 579–80.
55. Atherton, "Soviet Role"; Breslauer, "Soviet Policy."
56. Quandt, *Decade of Decisions*, 108–9.
57. Whetten, *Canal War*, 94.
58. Quandt writes: "The Rogers-Kissinger feud, and Nixon's own ambivalence, meant that the Rogers Plan never really had a chance of succeeding" (*Peace Process*, 3rd ed., 69).
59. Saunders, "Regulating Soviet-U.S. Competition," 557.
60. As later reported by the Israeli journalist Moshe Zak, in *Jerusalem Post*, February 17, 1989.
61. Garthoff, *Détente and Cooperation*, chapter 11.
62. Quandt, *Peace Process*, 1st ed., 134–35.
63. Quandt, *Decade of Decisions*, 150–51.
64. Jackson, "Who Killed Détente?," quoting from a declassified US government document, 145.

65. Safran, *Embattled Ally*, 469. See also Sella, "Changes in Soviet Political-Military Policy in the Middle East."
66. Kissinger, *White House Years*, 1294 (emphasis added).
67. Kissinger, *White House Years*, 1300.
68. For a summary of the Arab goals, see Shlaim, *Iron Wall*, Kindle 324.
69. Heikal, *Road to Ramadan*, 76–77.
70. Sagir, "How the Fear of Israeli Nukes Helped Seal the Egypt Peace Deal." The article is a summary of Sagir's Hebrew University PhD dissertation, "Israel's Nuclear Deterrence Posture and Its Effects on the Arab-Israeli Conflict—1967–2017."
71. The literature on the 1973 war is extensive, and there is no dispute over the limited purposes of the Egyptian attack. For representative discussions, see Kipnis, *1973*; Shlaim, *Iron Wall*; Wright, *Thirteen Days in September*; Heikal, "Egyptian Foreign Policy"; and Korn, *Stalemate.*
72. Thrall, *Only Language They Understand*, Kindle 28.
73. See Green, "This Day in Jewish History 1973," and Cohen, "When Israel Stepped Back from the Brink."
74. Kissinger, *Years of Upheaval*, 460.
75. The main sources for this account of Syrian purposes and actions, particularly concerning Assad's orders to his army, are Aronson, *Conflict and Bargaining*, 177–79; Wakebridge, "The Syrian Side of the Hill"; Maoz, "Syrian-Israeli Relations and the Middle East Peace Process"; Drysdale and Hinnebusch, *Syria;* Seale, *Asad of Syria.*
76. For further discussion of the Soviet position, see Saunders, "Regulating Soviet-U.S. Competition," 562–64; Drysdale and Hinnebusch, *Syria;* and Daigle, *The Limits of Détente.* Citing post–Cold War Russian scholarship on the 1973 war, Daigle writes: "Soviet leaders fully expected a 'certain and speedy defeat' of the Arabs, and did not want to be forced to intervene. . . . 'It should be clear,' Brezhnev told his colleagues . . . ' that Soviet involvement on behalf of the Arabs would mean a world war' " (300).
77. Oren, "Soviet Envoy Warned Nixon and Kissinger against Mideast War."
78. Oren, "Soviet Envoy Warned Nixon and Kissinger against Mideast War."
79. Jabbar and Kolkowicz, "The Arab-Israeli Wars," 442.
80. Daigle, *Limits*, 300.
81. Ross, *Doomed to Succeed*, chapter 5, "Nixon and Ford."
82. The transcript of the phone call is discussed in Green, "Declassified."
83. Kipnis, *1973*, quoting from a telephone conversation between Nixon and Kissinger, 226.
84. Daigle, *Limits of Détente*, 320, quoting the declassified Brezhnev message.
85. Kissinger, *Years of Upheaval*, 510.
86. Morris, *Righteous Victims*, 435.
87. Kissinger, *Years of Upheaval*, 587. Patrick Tyler commented that declassified US records "indicate with remarkable clarity how Kissinger had been engaged, far beyond any instructions from Nixon, in undermining the cease-fire in order to allow Israel to destroy or force the surrender of the Egyptian third Army. The sustained level of Kissinger's deceit . . . is striking" (Tyler, *World of Trouble*, 171).
88. From a declassified US government memo, cited and quoted in Jackson, "Who Killed Détente?," 147.
89. Daigle, *Limits*, 319, citing US declassified records.
90. Quandt, *Decade of Decisions*, 197–98. For Kissinger's strategy of warning the Soviets against intervening but at the same time pressuring Israel to stop, see Saunders, "Regulating Soviet-U.S. Competition," 562.
91. Saunders, "Regulating Soviet-U.S. Competition," 564.
92. Kissinger, *Years of Upheaval*, 550–51.
93. Kissinger, *Years of Upheaval*, 755.
94. Saunders, "Regulating Soviet-U.S. Competition," 564. See also the account of another high-level US participant in the post-1973 diplomacy: Atherton, "Soviet Role in the Middle East," 698–702.

95. Kissinger, *Years of Upheaval*, 943–44. See also Kissinger's admission that the United States "has squeezed [the Soviets] in the Middle East in an unbelievable way" and "pushed them out" of the region. . . . Brezhnev's colleagues can say he was taken to the cleaners." Quoting a declassified government memo, in Jackson, "Who Killed Détente?," 159.
96. Kurtzer, Lasensky, Quandt, Spiegel, and Telhami, *The Peace Puzzle*. Daniel Kurtzer is a former US ambassador to Israel, Scott Lasensky and William Quandt were high NSC and State Department Middle East officials, and Steven Spiegel and Shibley Telhami are longtime academic specialists on US policy and the Arab-Israeli conflict.
97. Kissinger, *Years of Upheaval*, 1205.
98. Kissinger, *Years of Upheaval*, 1205. Kissinger's account is also discussed by Kissinger's biographer Walter Isaacson, in *Kissinger*, 596, and in a declassified memo from Nixon to Kissinger and Defense Secretary James Schlesinger (Jackson, "Who Killed Détente?," 155).
99. Quandt, *Decade of Decisions*, 270.
100. Quoted in a major article by the American political scientist Galen Jackson in "The Showdown That Wasn't."
101. Quoted from declassified US documents, Jackson, "The Showdown That Wasn't," 143.
102. Jackson, "The Showdown That Wasn't," 155. In his discussion of the Israeli demands and the Ford/Kissinger response, George Ball concludes: "Rabin's package represented, in effect, nothing less than an effort to euchre the United States into agreeing to the Israeli annexation of Gaza, Jerusalem, the West Bank, the Golan and, possibly, parts of the Sinai. . . . As such, these transactions strongly resembled a non-too-subtle system of extortion" (Ball and Ball, *Passionate Attachment*, 82–83).
103. For a full discussion, see Thrall, *The Only Language*, 6–7.
104. Carter, *Keeping Faith*, 274.
105. For example, see the statement by Yossi Beilin, the Labor Party leader and close aide to Shimon Peres: "There is nothing in the criticism that Carter has for Israel that has not been said by Israelis themselves." Quoted in *Jewish Forward*, January 19, 2007.
106. Segev, "Memoir of a Great Friend."
107. Eldar, "Include Hamas in Israel-Palestine Peace Talks."
108. Eldar, "Include Hamas in Israel-Palestine Peace Talks."
109. Rabinovich, *Yitzhak Rabin*, 136.
110. Vance, *Hard Choices*, 164.
111. Quoted in Sheehan, *The Arabs, Israelis and Kissinger*, 207.
112. The text of the October 1 statement is printed in Quandt, *Middle East*, Appendix B, 447–48.
113. On Soviet pressures on the PLO to move toward peace with Israel, see Tessler, *A History of the Israeli-Palestinian Conflict*, Kindle 721.
114. Bass, *Support Any Friend*, 171.
115. Ball and Ball, *Passionate Attachment*, 86.
116. For assessments stressing the factors of Soviet prestige and credibility rather than expansionism, see Garthoff, *Detente and Confrontation*; Golan, *Soviet Union*; MacFarlane, "The Middle East in Soviet Strategy"; Spechler, "Soviet Policies toward Third World Conflicts"; and Walt, *Origins of Alliances*.

Chapter 10

1. Shlaim, *Iron Wall*, Kindle 239–40.
2. Shlaim, *Iron Wall*, Kindle 239–40.
3. Little, *American Orientalism*, citing declassified US documents, 287.
4. Quoted by Voice of Israel Radio, October 4, 1994.
5. Carter, *Keeping Faith*, 311–12; Anziska, *Preventing Palestine*, Kindle 115–16.
6. Anziska quotes William Quandt, the NSC's leading Middle East specialist during the Carter administration, as saying that Sadat "could not continue to insist on much for the Palestinians, at least not at the expense of recovering Egyptian territory" (*Preventing Palestine*, Kindle 123).

7. Carter, *Blood of Abraham*, 50–51.
8. Shlaim, *War and Peace*, 52.
9. Quandt writes: "Carter had no stomach for a confrontation with Israel" (*Camp David*, 317).
10. Quandt, *Camp David*, 70–71; Ball and Ball, *Passionate Attachment*, 86–87.
11. Quandt, *Camp David*, 77.
12. On Dayan's threats, see the memoir by former high US State Department official Aaron David Miller, *The Much Too Promised Land*, 171. On Brzezinski's comment, see Thrall, *Only Language They Understand*, Kindle 19.
13. Carter, *Keeping Faith*, 292–93. In his book on the Camp David negotiations, Quandt discusses Begin's reneging on his promise to Carter (Quandt, *Camp David*, 247–48).
14. Carter discusses Sadat's position in *Keeping Faith*, 339.
15. Bregman, *Cursed Victory*, Kindle 97.
16. Vance, *Hard Choices*, 225–26.
17. A leading Middle East scholar put it this way: "The Egyptian-Israeli peace treaty solved the least problematical aspect of the Arab-Israeli dispute. It had no linkage with the other dimensions of the conflict and totally overlooked the crucial Palestinian issue" (Alan Taylor, *Superpowers and the Middle East*, 97–98).
18. Carter, *Keeping Faith*, 277.
19. Quoted in Oren, "First in War, Last in Peace."
20. Carter, *Keeping Faith*, 352.
21. Bregman, *Cursed Victory*, Kindle 117–18.
22. Bar-Zohar, *Facing a Cruel Mirror*, 81.
23. Cf. Bar-Joseph, *Best of Enemies*. This section is based on that book and Raz, *Bride and the Dowry*, esp. 16–17; Melman and Raviv, *Behind the Uprising*; Pappé, *Ten Myths*; Parker, *Politics of Miscalculation*, 40–41.
24. Melman and Raviv, *Behind the Uprising*, 77–78.
25. Melman and Raviv, *Behind the Uprising*, 76.
26. Raz, *Bride and the Dowry*, 16. See also Melman and Raviv, *Behind the Uprising*: "The Arab world was going to war against Israel, and that left Hussein with a dilemma: either join the conflict and risk the loss of the West Bank, or refuse to join and lose the confidence and support of his people . . . leading to the loss of his entire kingdom" (79).
27. However, Pappé points out that the Jordanian role was more than merely symbolic; because his army was commanded by an Egyptian general, West Jerusalem was bombed. Pappé, *Ten Myths*, Kindle 1338–46.
28. "King Says Jordan Erred in 1967."
29. Ball and Ball, *Passionate Attachment*, 60.
30. Golan, a longtime political leader, government official, and political science professor at Hebrew University, concludes: "While cognizant that peace with Jordan was possible, the Israeli leadership was not willing to budge on these two demands, so peace with Jordan was rejected in favor of holding onto parts of the territory" (Golan, *Israeli Peacemaking*, Kindle 14).
31. The meeting is described by Bar-Zohar, *Cruel Mirror*, 43–44.
32. Elon, "Look over Jordan."
33. The Hussein warnings and Israeli-Jordanian relations during the 1973 war have been widely reported. In particular, see Melman and Raviv, *Behind the Uprisings*, 121; *New York Times*, January 28, 1994; Adet, "Jordan and Israel Cooperated during Yom Kippur War, Documents Reveal." The Adet story is based on Israeli scholarship after the relevant documents were declassified.
34. Bar-Zohar, *Cruel Mirror*, 59. See also Golan, *Israeli Peacemaking*, Kindle 95.
35. Moshe Zak, *Jerusalem Post*, October 12, 1991.
36. Golan, *Israeli Peacemaking*, Kindle 96. See also Rabinovich, *Yitzhak Rabin*, Kindle 111.
37. Quandt, *Peace Process*, 1993 edition, 225.
38. Savir, "Bring Back the Oslo Accords."
39. Quoted in a review of Peres's memoirs, in David Shulman, "A Hero in His Own Words."

40. The text of the treaty is available online at http://www.mfa.gov.il/mfa/foreignpolicy/peace/guide/pages/israel-jordan%20peace%20treaty.aspx. As well, the treaty and the negotiations are described in detail in Shlaim, *Iron Wall,* Kindle 556–64, and Golan, *Israeli Peacemaking,* Kindle 105–9.
41. For a discussion of these recent developments, see Alpher, "Israeli Right Wants End to Peace with Jordan."
42. Quoted in Nir, "Israel's Campaign to Destabilize Jordan." See also "Jordan-Israel Ties Strained by Detentions"; Kardoosh, "Jordanians Now See Israel as an Implacable Enemy, Despite 25 Years of Peace."
43. Golan, *Israeli Peacemaking,* Kindle 107.
44. On these US policies, see Pedatzur, "Coming Back Full Circle," 290; Hart, *Arafat,* 532–33.
45. Indyk, *Innocent Abroad,* Kindle 140–41.

Chapter 11

1. Rokach, *Israel's Sacred Terrorism,* 3rd ed., 26.
2. Flapan, *Birth,* 51.
3. Anziska, *Preventing Palestine,* Kindle 117–18.
4. Quoted and discussed in Thrall, *Only Language,* Kindle 17.
5. Schiff and Ehud Ya'ari, *Israel's Lebanon War,* 35, 37.
6. Schiff and Ehud Ya'ari, *Israel's Lebanon War,* 37.
7. One of Israel's leading foreign policy analysts wrote that his interviews with high Israeli officials confirmed that a major motive of the 1982 Israeli attack was the "danger" that the PLO was moving toward acceptance of UN Resolution 242, which would meet the US government's condition for entering into negotiations with it. Yaniv, *Dilemmas of Security,* 301.
8. Shlaim, *Iron Wall,* Kindle 414.
9. The ensuing discussion of the 1982 war is based on the accounts in Landau, *Arik,* Kindle locations 3866–4522; Oren, "With Ariel Sharon Gone, Israel Reveals the Truth about the 1982 Lebanon War"; Rabinovich, *War for Lebanon;* Randal, *Going All the Way;* Rubenberg, *Israel,* 254–28; Schiff and Yaari, *Israel's Lebanon War;* Shlaim, *Iron Wall,* Kindle 405–30; Tessler, *History,* Kindle 568–99.
10. Bar-On, "The Palestinian Aspects of the War in Lebanon," quoted in Chomsky, *Fateful Triangle,* Kindle 295. These figures are widely accepted in the literature on the 1982 war.
11. Schiff and Ya'ari, *Israel's Lebanon War,* 240.
12. Bar-Zohar, *Cruel Mirror,* 114–15.
13. Shlaim, *Iron Wall,* Kindle 407; on Sharon's plans, see also Schiff and Yaari, *Israel's Lebanon* 112–15, 118, 133; Tessler, *A History of the Israeli-Palestinian Conflict,* Kindle 573–82.
14. On Reagan's deep-rooted support of the Jewish people and the state of Israel, see Reagan, *An American Life;* Lou Cannon, *President Reagan: The Role of a Lifetime* (New York: Public Affairs, 1991); Goldberg, *Jewish Power,* 213–15; Ross, *Doomed to Succeed,* Kindle locations 4005–26.
15. Cannon, *President Reagan,* 487.
16. Reagan, *An American Life,* 410.
17. Samuel W. Lewis, "The United States and Israel: Constancy and Change," 228.
18. Anziska, *Preventing Palestine,* Kindle 200–201.
19. Rabinovich, *War for Lebanon,* 146. See also Ben-Zvi, *The United States and Israel,* 139–42.
20. Shultz, *Turmoil and Triumph,* Kindle location 1101.
21. Anziska, *Preventing Palestine,* Kindle 205.
22. Reagan, *American Life,* 427–28.
23. Shultz, *Turmoil,* Kindle location 1218.
24. Quoted in many places, including in Landau, *Arik,* Kindle location 3709. Begin later admitted that Reagan "spoke to me in terms of an ultimatum," as quoted by Amir Oren, "1982 Memo Shows Israel Learned Little from First Lebanon War."

25. For another account of Reagan's threats and Begin's response, see Ben-Zvi, *Alliance Politics and the Limits of Influence.*
26. Quoted in Landau, *Arik,* Kindle location 4191–207.
27. Ross, *Doomed to Succeed,* Kindle 4026–35. For an overall assessment of the Reagan era and US policies toward Israel, see Quandt, *Peace Process,* 285–90.
28. Schiff and Yaari, *Israel's Lebanon War,* 306, 308.
29. Schiff and Yaari, *Israel's Lebanon War,* 218, 308.
30. Shlaim, *Iron Wall,* Kindle 440.
31. Sobelman, "Learning to Deter," 164.
32. The English translation of the text of Rabin's speech can be found on this Israeli Foreign Ministry website: http://mfa.gov.il/MFA/ForeignPolicy/MFADocuments/Yearbook9/Pages/93%20Statement%20in%20the%20Knesset%20by%20Prime%20Minister%20Rabi.aspx.
33. The Rabin statement is quoted by the Israeli political philosopher Igor Primoretz, in his book *Terrorism: A Philosophical Investigation,* 42.
34. Sobelman, "Learning to Deter," 165, emphasis added.
35. Shlaim, *Iron Wall,* Kindle 580.
36. Avi Shlaim summed up the purpose of the Israeli attacks: "The Israeli military planners . . . wanted to stampede the bulk of the civilian population from south to north Lebanon in order to clear the areas for a massive strike against Hizbullah and to impose . . . a change in the 1993 rules of the game. . . . The idea was to put pressure on the civilians of southern Lebanon, for them to pressure the government of Lebanon, for it to pressure the Syrian government [which was supporting Hezbollah] to curb Hizbullah and grant immunity to the IDF in southern Lebanon" (*Iron Wall,* Kindle 581).
37. *Shlaim, Iron Wall,* Kindle 581; Cobban, *Israeli-Syrian Peace Talks,* 162.
38. On the ceasefire agreement, see the *New York Times,* April 27, 1993; Shlaim, *Iron Wall,* Kindle 580; Sobelman, *Learning to Deter,* 163.
39. Schiff, "A Strategic Mistake."
40. Harel, "Israel Prepares for Widespread Military Escalation."
41. Quoted by Segev, "Ten Theses for the Committee's Examination."
42. Worth and Kifner, "The Destruction: Lebanese and Aid Groups Find Dangers in the Rubble."
43. This general figure has been reported in many subsequent news stories and investigations by international human rights organizations. See especially "Civilian Casualties in Lebanon during the 2006 War," Human Rights Watch, September 5, 2007.
44. "Amnesty: Israel Committed War Crimes in Lebanon Campaign"; Kifner, "Human Rights Group Accuses Israel of War Crimes."
45. At the time, Zeev Schiff, the longtime centrist defense analyst for *Haaretz,* accurately predicted that Hezbollah would emerge from the conflict both politically and militarily stronger: "by encouraging large numbers of civilians to flee . . . to serve as a source of pressure," Israel was making "a strategic mistake," because such methods had led to the creation of Hezbollah in Lebanon and Hamas in the Palestinian occupied territories (Schiff, "A Strategic Mistake," *Haaretz,* July 20, 2006).
46. The post-2006 Hezbollah policies are discussed in Sobelman, *Learning to Deter,* 154.
47. Sobelman, *Learning to Deter,* 186.
48. Sobelman, *Learning to Deter,* 174; Harel, "Hundreds of Rockets and Mass Evacuations: IDF Lays Out What War with Hezbollah Will Look Like.".
49. In 2010, Gadi Eisenkot said that "a pattern of mutual deterrence" now existed between Hezbollah and Israel (quoted in Sobelman, *Learning to Deter,* 153); and in 2013 Benny Gantz admitted that "if Hezbollah chooses to hit a specific target anywhere in Israel, it knows how to do it" (quoted in Sobelman, *Learning to Deter,* 192).
50. Pfeffer, "Hezbollah Refused Hamas Request to Bomb Israel in the Gaza War."
51. Lebanon and Iran are largely Shiite, and both oppose the extremist Sunni forces of ISIS. While Assad is Alawite, he and his father have long supported Hezbollah in Lebanon.

Chapter 12

1. Quoted in Maoz, *Syria*, 145.
2. According to the *New York Times*, Gorbachev told the Syrian leader in 1987 that Moscow would not support a military solution to the Syrian conflict with Israel. The level of Soviet arms shipments to Syria, most of them defensive, had already dropped by more than 50 percent during Gorbachev's tenure, the news story reported, and further reductions were in store. Consequently, the Soviets told Assad, the Syrians must drop their objective of reaching military parity with Israel in favor of seeking "a reasonable defense sufficiency" (*New York Times*, November 28, 1989).
3. Cobban, *Israeli-Syrian Peace Talks*, 63.
4. The next two sections, on borders and water, are drawn from Hof, "The Line of June 4, 1967"; Bregman, *Elusive Peace;* Golan, *Israeli Peacemaking;* Quandt, "Israeli-Syrian Negotiations of the 1990s"; Shalev, *Israel and Syria*; Maoz, *Syria and Israel*.
5. The Anglo-French Treaty of 1923, quoted in Eldar, "Bordering on the Ridiculous"; Hof, "The Line of June 4, 1967."
6. Golan, *Israeli-Syrian Peace Talks*, Kindle 65.
7. Kurtzer, *Peace Puzzle*, Kindle 73. As early as mid-1974, Henry Kissinger writes, Assad "informed the PLO that its demand for the destruction of Israel was incompatible with the negotiating process as well as with UN resolutions that Syria recently accepted" (*Years of Upheaval*, 1133).
8. The most important sources on the secret negotiations in the early 1990s are Cobban, *Israeli-Syrian Talks*; Hinnebusch, "Does Syria Want Peace?"; Kurtzer et al., *The Peace Puzzle*, 59–104; Rabinovich, *Israeli-Syrian Negotiations*; and Seale, "The Syria-Israel Negotiations: Who Is Telling the Truth?"
9. Golan, *Israeli Peacemaking*, Kindle 69.
10. Cobban, *Israeli-Syrian Talks*, 61.
11. Rabinovich, *Yitzhak Rabin*, Kindle 195.
12. Clinton, *My Life*, 883.
13. Cobban, *Israeli-Syrian Talks*, 93.
14. Clinton, *My Life*, 883. Rabinovich confirms that Clinton told Rabin that the United States would provide a peacekeeping force in the Golan and guarantee the stability of the agreement (Rabinovich, *Yitzhak Rabin*, Kindle 182).
15. Cobban, *Israeli-Syrian Talks*, 10.
16. Golan, *Israeli Peacemaking*, Kindle 74.
17. For details, see Cobban, *Israeli-Syrian Talks*, 136–38.
18. Verter, "Not Peace-Shmeace. Not Syria-Shmyria."
19. Quandt, "Israeli-Syrian Negotiations of the 1990s," 84. On Netanyahu and the Syrian negotiations, see also Golan, *Israeli Peacemaking*, Kindle 77–79; Cobban, *Israeli-Syrian Talks*, 194–95; Pfeffer, *Bibi*, Kindle 254–57; Shlaim, *Iron Wall*, Kindle 656.
20. Benn, "Barak: Past PMs Set Syria Talks on '67 Lines."
21. The draft treaty was published in *Haaretz* on January 13, 2000, and analyzed by Akiva Eledar, "A Framework for Peace between Israel and Syria." Unless otherwise noted, quotations in the following three paragraphs are taken from the draft treaty.
22. Quoted in Indyk, *Innocent Abroad*, Kindle location 2113.
23. Indyk, *Innocent Abroad*, Kindle location 2133.
24. Bregman, *Elusive Peace*, Kindle location 900.
25. Benziman, "Reading Barak's Body Language."
26. Quandt, "Clinton and the Arab-Israeli Conflict," 26, 30. On Barak's abandonment of the negotiations, see also Swisher, *Camp David*, 77–89; Golan, *Israeli Peacemaking*, Kindle 79–86.
27. Clinton, *My Life*, 886–87.
28. Oren, "IDF to Tell Sharon to Show Restraint This Month."
29. Quoted in Oren, "IDF to Tell Sharon to Show Restraint This Month."

30. Golan, *Israeli Peacemaking*, Kindle 80. On Barak's abandonment of the negotiations, see also Swisher, *Camp David*, 77–89.
31. *Doomed to Succeed*, Kindle location 6283.
32. Golan summarizes Indyk's position in *Israeli Peacemaking*, Kindle 85.
33. Bregman, *Cursed Victory*, 208.
34. Quandt, "Israeli-Syrian Negotiations of the 1990s," 94–95, 100.
35. Bregman, *Cursed Victory*, Kindle 215–16.
36. Indyk, "Assad Offering to Make Peace with Israel."
37. As reported in *Haaretz*, November 9, 2005.
38. As quoted in Shavit, "No Way to Go to War." On the rejection by other leading Israeli generals of Sharon's security arguments for holding on to the Golan, see *Haaretz*, May 13, 2003.
39. For the text of the agreements, see *Haaretz*, May 13, 2003.
40. Eldar, "Small Piece of Land Could Scupper Israel-Syria Talks."
41. Eldar, "Small Piece of Land Could Scupper Israel-Syria Talks"; see also Golan, *Israeli Peace Making*, Kindle 175.
42. Eldar, "Israelis, Syrian Reach Secret Understandings."
43. "Former Top Israeli Diplomat Says Syria Ready to Cut Iran Ties."
44. Among other stories, see Oren, "This Time, the IDF Favors Syrian Peace Deal"; Harel, "Too Many Question Marks"; "Ex-IDF Chief: Golan Heights Not Indispensable."
45. Quoted in Noe, "Is This Lebanon's Final Revolution?"
46. Eldar, "Small Piece of Land."
47. Galili, "Poll: More Israelis Object to Golan Accord than to Jerusalem Deal."
48. Harel, "Too Many Question Marks." See also Golan, *Israeli Peacemaking*, Kindle 175.
49. Schiff et al., "U.S. Hardens Line on Israel-Syria Talks, J'lem Obeys."
50. Tibon, "Kerry Reveals Details of Assad's Secret Letter to Netanyahu in 2010."
51. Kershner, "Secret Israel-Peace Talks Involved Golan Heights."
52. Ravid, "Netanyahu Told Assad: I'm Ready to Discuss Golan Withdrawal, If You Cut Iran, Hezbollah Ties."
53. Kershner, "Secret Israel-Peace Talks Involved Golan Heights."
54. Ravid, "Netanyahu Told Assad." For another analysis of Netanyahu's position before 2011, stressing that despite the application of Israeli law to the Golan in 1981, Netanyahu was serious about returning it to Syria in the context of an overall peace agreement that also ended Syria's alliance with Iran, see Misgav, "Some Golan Loyalist Bibi Is."
55. Benn, "Assad's Israeli Friend"; see also Harel, "Between a Ruthless Dictator and Global Jihad, Israel, U.S. Prefer Assad."
56. Halbfinger, "Israeli Leader Says Russia Agreed to Restrain Iran in Syria."

Chapter 13

1. The Israeli historian Yakov Rabkin has described the developments:

   > The first Jewish immigrants, at the end of the 19th century, settled on the land in a random and disparate manner, employing Arab workers on their farms. Unlike them, those who migrated to Palestine in the early 20th century practiced a concentrated form of colonization: they set up exclusively Jewish settlements, which entailed the displacement of local populations. The accent placed on the establishment of ethnically homogenous settlements could not but have created resistance.

   Rabkin, *What Is Modern Israel?*, Kindle location 1293.
2. Tessler, *A History of the Israeli-Palestinian Conflict*, Kindle 373–74. See also Quandt, "Political and Military Dimensions of Contemporary Palestinian Nationalism," and Indyk, *Innocent Abroad*: "From the initial establishment of the PLO in 1964, it had been used as a pawn by Arab states that would give it rhetorical support but act in their own interests" (Indyk, *Innocent Abroad*, Kindle Location 1444).

3. Quandt, "Political and Military Dimensions," 50, 150.
4. Making use of declassified documentation, the internal Israeli deliberations are analyzed in Pedatzur, "Coming Back Full Circle." Pedatzur was the senior security analyst for *Haaretz*—Israel's most important and prestigious newspaper, the country's equivalent of the *New York Times*—and a lecturer in the Department of Political Science at Tel Aviv University.
5. Elon, "Israelis and Palestinians: What Went Wrong." It is likely, Elon wrote, that in any case the cabinet would have rejected the plan.
6. According to Pedatzur, "One of the major obstacles in the way of implementing the Palestinian option was the policy of . . . the Johnson Administration [which] had a great deal of influence on the position of the policymakers in Israel" ("Coming Back Full Circle," 290).
7. Pedatzur, "Coming Back Full Circle."
8. Quoted in Hart, *Arafat,* 357. See also Shlaim, *Iron Wall,* Kindle 317.
9. Raz, *Bride and the Dowry,* 2.
10. Rashid Khalidi, "The Palestine Liberation Organization," 275–76.
11. Sayigh, "Arafat and the Anatomy of a Revolt."
12. On this process, see Khalidi, *Iron Cage,* especially Kindle location 3718, and Bergman, *Rise and Kill First,* Kindle 1919–92.
13. Chamberlain, "When It Pays to Talk to Terrorists."
14. Quandt memorandum of August 1974, quoted in Chamberlain, *Global Offensive,* 239–40.
15. As discussed, among many other histories of this period, in Elgindy, *Blind Spot,* Kindle 94.
16. Kissinger, *Years of Upheaval,* 626.
17. The secret dialogues are described in Bird, *The Good Spy,* Kindle location 2400–530.
18. Kissinger's memo is quoted in Bird, *The Good Spy,* location 2503. In Bird's view, "Kissinger was, in fact, inviting the PLO to the negotiating table . . . [and] conceding that the Palestinians had a right to some kind of 'political self-expression.'" See also Judis, "Who Bears More Responsibility for the War in Gaza," and Bergman, *Rise and Kill First,* 216–17.
19. In a recent major work, historian Seth Anziska writes that the 1973 war "launched a new phase in the PLO's struggle, oriented toward partition and the acknowledgment of Israel's presence. In the aftermath of the October War, the PLO sought a place within the comprehensive diplomatic negotiations, which required political compromise and the eventual embrace of a state on far less territory than historic Palestine" (Anziska, *Preventing Palestine,* Kindle 25). Similarly, Bird writes: "By mid-1974 the PLO was rapidly moving away from a strategy of armed struggle and morphing into a political movement seeking international legitimacy" based on a two-state solution (Bird, *The Good Spy,* Kindle location 2560–75). For similar assessments of the importance of the 1974 PLO program, see Hart, *Arafat,* 10–11; Weinberger, "The Palestinian National Security Debate"; Nofal, "Yasir Arafat: A Mixed Legacy"; Tessler, *A History of the Israeli-Palestinian Conflict,* Kindle 483–84; and Elgindy, *Blind Spot,* Kindle 88.
20. Anziska, *Preventing Palestine,* 25.
21. The PLO under Arafat was actually an umbrella organization that included a number of Palestinian resistance groups. The most important of them was Fatah, a guerrilla movement that was more militant than the PLO as a whole and still held to a strategy of "stages," in which the creation of a Palestinian state in the occupied territories was just the first step toward the "liberation" of all Palestine. However, the weight of the evidence is that Arafat's evolving acceptance of a two-state settlement as the only feasible PLO strategy came to prevail in the organization as a whole. The distinctions between Fatah and the PLO are discussed in Tessler, *A History of the Israeli-Palestinian Conflict,* 373–78, and elsewhere.
22. In correspondence with this author, Ilan Pappé points out that it would have been easier for Israel to reach an agreement with the Palestinians in the West Bank and Gaza than with the Palestinian refugees, where Palestinian nationalism was intensifying. Even so, it was Arafat's and the PLO's position that over time continued to become the dominant one.
23. These and other examples of the evolving Arafat/PLO position are discussed by the American scholar Rubenberg in "The US-PLO Dialogue."

24. Anziska, *Preventing Palestine,* Kindle 260.
25. The 1988 PLO decisions are discussed in Tessler, *A History of the Israeli-Palestinian Conflict,* Kindle 721–23; Anziska, *Preventing Palestine,* Kindle 260–62; Quandt, *Peace Process,* 281–85.
26. The meeting was discussed by *New York Times* columnist Anthony Lewis, who participated in the conference and wrote about it in his column, "Abroad at Home: 'We Don't Have Time.'"
27. Kelman, "Talk with Arafat."

Chapter 14

1. *Haaretz,* May 26, 1975. See also Moshe Maoz, "The Israeli-Saudi Common Interest," *Haaretz,* August 3, 2008.
2. *Haaretz,* August 10, 1981.
3. Among other discussions, see Tessler, *A History of the Israeli-Palestinian Conflict,* Kindle 537–38.
4. Quoted in Anziska, *Preventing Palestine,* Kindle 211.
5. Reagan's remarks are quoted in Anziska, *Preventing Palestine,* Kindle 209–10, and in Shultz, *Turmoil and Triumph,* Kindle location 2001–2.
6. The full text of the Reagan Plan can be found on many internet sites, including https://ecf.org.il/issues/issue/158.
7. Tessler, *A History of the Israeli-Palestinian Conflict,* Kindle 604–5.
8. Quoted in Chomsky, *Fateful Triangle,* Kindle 392. Chomsky cites several *New York Times* news stories in September 1982, but doesn't directly cite the source of the quote. On Arafat's reaction to the Reagan Plan, see Hart, *Arafat,* 460–61; Tessler, *A History of the Israeli-Palestinian Conflict,* Kindle 621–22; Chomsky, *Fateful Triangle,* Kindle 391.
9. Tessler, *A History of the Israeli-Palestinian Conflict,* Kindle 618–20.
10. The most complete discussion of the Reagan and Fez Plans is in Tessler, *A History of the Israeli-Palestinian Conflict,* Kindle 600–622.
11. Tessler, *A History of the Israeli-Palestinian Conflict,* Kindle 674. However, others argue that Arafat may have come to believe that the intifada increased his bargaining leverage in political negotiations with Israel. For example, see Zoughbie, *Indecision,* 11.
12. Morris, *Righteous Victims,* 561.
13. Morris, *Righteous Victims,* 583.
14. Quoted in Pappé, *Biggest Prison on Earth,* Kindle locations 3175–80.
15. Pappé, *History of Modern Palestine,* Kindle 233.
16. Cited in Morris, *Righteous Victims,* 596.
17. Tessler, *A History of the Israeli-Palestinian Conflict,* Kindle 703.
18. Allin and Simon, *Our Separate Ways,* 51.
19. Text of Baker speech of May 22, 1989, in State Department document, http://mfa.gov.il/MFA/ForeignPolicy/MFADocuments/Yearbook8/Pages/59 %20Statement %20to %20AIPAC %20by %20Secretary %20of %20State %20Baker-.aspx.
20. Christison, *Perceptions,* Kindle location 3713.
21. Quoted in Tessler, *A History of the Israeli-Palestinian Conflict,* Kindle 736.
22. Quoted and discussed in Kurtzer, *Peace Puzzle,* Kindle 23–24.
23. Kurtzer, *Peace Puzzle,* Kindle 28.
24. Quoted in Khalidi, *The Iron Cage,* Kindle location 3790.
25. Kurtzer, *Peace Puzzle,* Kindle 26. On the role of the PLO and its influence behind the scenes, see Tessler, *A History of the Israeli-Palestinian Conflict,* Kindle 752–56, and Anziska, *Preventing Palestine,* Kindle 270.
26. Anziska, *Preventing Palestine,* Kindle 272.
27. Shlaim, *Israel and Palestine,* 163.
28. Shlaim, *Iron Wall,* Kindle 516.
29. Khalidi, *Iron Cage,* Kindle locations 3775–90.

30. Quoted in *Jerusalem Post,* March 31, 1992, and *Washington Report on Middle East Affairs,* February 1993.
31. *Washington Report on Middle East Affairs,* February 1993.
32. *New York Times,* March 16, 1993.
33. Shalev, "The Miracle of Occupation Nation." See also Benny Morris's conclusion: "The Intifada ended in a stalemate, with the Palestinians unable to eject the Israelis from the territories and the Israelis unable to stop the violence. . . . As a result, both sides soon fundamentally revised their policies" (*Righteous Victims,* 596).
34. "The Oslo Accords Are Dead, but There Is Still a Path to Peace," 8.
35. Indyk, *Innocent Abroad,* Kindle location 1380; Shaath, "The Oslo Agreement." At the time of Oslo, Shaath was the foreign minister of the Palestine Authority.
36. Quoted in Chomsky, *Fateful Triangle,* Kindle 621.
37. For a full discussion of the two letters, see Klein, "The Oslo Agreements Twenty Years Later—What Remained."
38. Some years later Shimon Peres, defending his support of the Oslo agreements, boasted: "Before Oslo, the Palestinian state's size should have been according to the 1947 UN map [about 44 percent of Palestine]. In Oslo, Arafat moved from the 1947 map to the 1967 one. He gave up on 22 percent of the West Bank. I don't know any Arab leader who would give up 2 or 3 percent. He gave up 22 percent." Quoted in Siegman, "Can Kerry Rescue a Two-State Peace Accord?"
39. Interview with Edward Said, winter 1995, 61.
40. Yezid Sayigh, "Arafat and the Anatomy of a Revolt," 47–60.
41. Interview with Nabil Shaath, "The Oslo Agreement." Interestingly, the quoted words from page 13 of the original version of the interview were later deleted from the archived issues of the journal—evidently because Shaath's optimism or exaggerations would soon prove to be embarrassing.
42. Landau, *Arik,* Kindle location 5990.
43. Cygielman, "No, Oslo Is Not Dead."
44. From an interview with Singer, in Levy, "I Believed in the Oslo Accords for Years, but It Was Merely a Deception."
45. *Oslo Diaries,* HBO Documentary, September 2018.
46. Indyk, *Innocent Abroad,* Kindle location 1380.
47. Landau, *Arik,* Kindle 5992.
48. For a summary of how the West Bank was divided, see Rabinovich, *Rabin,* Kindle 210–11.
49. Both Rabin and Peres opposed any sharing of sovereignty in Jerusalem. As revealed in recently declassified documents, Peres told a leading Palestinian moderate that "There is no precedent for dual sovereignty over one city. You won't be able to deny us our only capital, Jerusalem." Quoted in Ofer Adeeret, "Deal or No Deal," *Haaretz,* March 13, 2020.
50. Ehrenreich, *The Way to the Spring,* Kindle 70.
51. *Report on Israeli Settlement of the Occupied Territories.*
52. In order of the quoted phrases: Ehrenreich, *Way to the Spring,* Kindle 7; interview with Edward Said, *Journal of Palestine Studies,* Winter 1995, 61; Buttu, "Success in Oslo," 84. Said and Buttu were prominent Palestinian critics of the PLO; their assessment was shared by many Israeli critics of the Israeli occupation.
53. The text of the Rabin speech can be found on the website of the Israel Ministry of Foreign Affairs, http://www.mfa.gov.il/mfa/mfa-archive/1995/pages/pm %20rabin percent20in %20knesset- %20ratification %20of %20interim %20agree.aspx.
54. Indyk writes: "Most Israelis agreed with Rabin's bluntly expressed sentiment that Gaza could sink into the sea. For all he cared, Arafat was welcome to it" (*Innocent Abroad,* Kindle location 1483).
55. For a slightly different translation of some passages of Rabin's address, see Rabinovich, *Rabin,* Kindle 212–13.

56. Tessler, *A History of the Israeli-Palestinian Conflict*, Kindle 775–76.
57. Interview with Savir, *Oslo Diaries.*
58. In particular, see Hass, "Setting the Record Straight on Yitzhak Rabin."
59. *Oslo Diaries*, HBO documentary,
60. Elgindly, *Blind Spot*, Kindle 143.
61. The Beilin-Abu Mazen accords are discussed in detail in Beilin, *Path to Geneva.*
62. Shalev, "Oslo Accords and Recognition of PLO Are the Walking Dead."
63. In March 1997, Yossi Beilin said that whereas Rabin had envisaged a limited Palestinian state in Gaza and the West Bank, Peres wanted Palestinian sovereignty to be limited to Gaza, with some kind of joint Israeli, Jordanian, and Palestinian rule over the West Bank (Beilin interview in *Ha'aretz*, March 7, 1997). Similarly, Yossi Sarid, head of Israel's moderate left Meretz political party, said that Peres's plan for the West Bank was "little different from Ariel Sharon's" and amounted to mere "cantonization." Quoted in Report of the American Academy of Arts and Sciences, *Israeli-Palestinian Security*, 1995, https://www.amacad.org/publication/israeli-palestinian-security-issues-permanent-status-negotiations.
64. For details, see Tessler, *A History of the Israeli-Palestinian Conflict*, Kindle 771–75.
65. For a discussion of these Israeli violations of the Oslo Accords, see "Settlements or Peace."
66. Quoted in Levy, "I Believed in the Oslo Accords for Years, but It Was Merely a Deception."
67. Kelman, "Building a Sustainable Peace." Kelman was a Harvard University professor of social ethics.
68. Golan, *Israel and Palestine*, 28; Buttu, "Success in Oslo," 76.
69. Makovsky, "Middle East Peace through Partition," 38.
70. Cited in Buttu, "Success in Oslo," 77.
71. The *Haaretz* columnist Chemi Shalev later wrote, "The left has never absolved Netanyahu of his sinful fanning of right wing fury after the 1993 signing of the Oslo Accords or of exploiting the ensuing wave of Palestinian terror attacks for political gain" (Shalev, "Netanyahu's Current Politics Reopen 23-Year-Old Wound of Rabin's Assassination").
72. For details, see Tessler, *A History of the Israeli-Palestinian Conflict*, Kindle 786–89; Klein, "The Oslo Agreements Twenty Years Later"; and PLO Negotiations Affairs Department, "Oslo Process: Twenty Years of Oslo."
73. Pundak, "From Oslo to Taba: What Went Wrong?," 31–45.
74. Eldar, "Israel's New Politics and the Fate of Palestine."
75. Hirsh and Lynch, "The Long Game of Benjamin Netanyahu."
76. The occupation and the Israeli human rights violations are examined in detail in Chapter 16.
77. Neff, "Clinton Places US Policy at Israel's Bidding," 15–16.
78. Bregman, *Cursed Victory*, Kindle 248.
79. Neff, "The Clinton Administration and UN Resolution 242."
80. As reported in the *New York Times*, April 1, 1998.
81. Quoted in Quandt, "Clinton and the Arab-Israeli Conflict," 27.
82. Quandt, "Clinton and the Arab-Israeli Conflict," 28.
83. Quoted in Tessler, *A History of the Israeli-Palestinian Conflict*, Kindle 794.
84. Enderlin, *Shattered Dreams*, 108.
85. Zeev Schiff, *Haaretz*, November 24, 2000.
86. *Jerusalem Report*, January 4, 1999, 19.
87. On the background and role of Clinton's advisors, see Hadar, "Thawing the American-Israeli Chill."
88. Quandt, "Clinton and the Arab-Israeli Conflict," 38.
89. Quandt, "Clinton and the Arab-Israeli Conflict," 37.
90. Quandt, "Clinton and the Arab-Israeli Conflict," 39.
91. Miller, *Much Too Promised Land*, 309, 311.
92. Quoted in Miller, *Much Too Promised Land*, 311.

93. Miller famously accused the Clinton team of acting as "Israel's lawyer in the American government." Miller himself was a member of that team, but it is widely believed that Ross was the main target of his comment.
94. From a comment of Hendrickson to me.

Chapter 15

1. The literature on the Camp David / Taba period is extensive and is cited throughout this chapter. There are two major books based on transcripts, written documents, and interviews with the participants: Enderlin, *Shattered Dreams*, and Clayton E. Swisher, *The Truth about Camp David*. As well, many of the leading Israeli and American diplomats have written their memoirs or articles on the negotiations, and there are a number of scholarly accounts, including my own article, "What Went Wrong? The Collapse of the Israeli-Palestinian Process." See also Malley and Agha, "Camp David: The Tragedy of Errors." Robert Malley was a member of the State Department team of experts that advised Bill Clinton during the negotiations, and Hussein Agha is a senior associate at Oxford University.
2. Malley, "Israel and the Arafat Question."
3. Ross, *The Missing Peace*, 649.
4. Enderlin, *Shattered Dreams*, 164. Charles Enderlin was a French journalist who subsequently obtained the transcripts. Clinton's promise to Arafat is also reported in Bregman, *Elusive Peace*, Kindle location 1673. Ahron Bregman, an Israeli historian, cites his interviews with leading participants in the Camp David negotiations.
5. Bregman, *Elusive Peace*, Kindle location 1744; Enderlin, *Shattered Dreams*, 171.
6. Malley and Agha, "Camp David: The Tragedy of Errors."
7. Quoted in Bregman, *Cursed Victory*, Kindle 228.
8. Israeli journalist Hass, "Barak's Jargon Is Identical to That of Gush Emunim." Gush Emunim is in the far-right religious fanatical group.
9. Ari Shavit, "Interview with Ehud Barak," February 2, 2001.
10. Though not in a formal or written commitment, in the 1970s Assad promised the Israeli government that in exchange for an Israeli withdrawal from part of the Golan Heights, he would prevent all Palestinian or other guerrilla organizations from using Syrian territory as a base for attacks on Israel. Since then, both Hafez and Bashar Assad have rigorously held to that commitment.
11. Hass, "Barak's Jargon."
12. Johnson, *Chronology of Terrorist Attacks in Israel*, johnstonarchive.net/terrorism, 2018. Other sources, such as the Jewish Virtual Library, report higher numbers but count attacks on Israeli soldiers in the occupied territories as "terrorist."
13. During the six months prior to Camp David, Barak authorized the expansion of settlements at a pace that exceeded both the earlier Shamir and Netanyahu governments (Samet, "Settler's Friends in High Places"). In Barak's final year in office, nearly 2,000 new housing units were constructed, the highest number since Ariel Sharon had served as housing and construction minister in 1992 (*Haaretz*, March 5, 2001).
14. *Haaretz*, February 27, 2001.
15. For an extensive discussion of these actions by the Barak government before Camp David, see Pundak, "From Oslo to Taba: What Went Wrong." Ron Pundak was a leading Israeli negotiator at the Oslo conferences.
16. Interview with Jeffrey Goldberg, "Arafat's Gift," January 29, 2001, 66.
17. Barak first pointed to the looming nuclear danger as requiring an Arab-Israeli settlement in the *Jerusalem Post*, September 24, 1999. The quote above is from Shavit, "Interview with Ehud Barak."

18. Eldar, "They Just Can't Hear Each Other." In a 2003 speech, Ron Pundak cited Barak's continued use of the term "entity" rather than "state"—like Rabin before him—as one of many indications that could lead the Palestinians to believe that Israel was not serious in seeking a peace settlement.
19. In his memoirs, Yossi Beilin, who served in Barak's government and was a leading Israeli peace negotiator, wrote that Barak avoided written records so "he could recant what he did not like" (Beilin, *The Path to Geneva*, 288). See also Golan, *Israeli Peacemaking*, 147: "There was no formal record kept beyond individual note taking, and no formal written proposals. Thus, it is not easy to determine the exact or necessarily final positions of either side."
20. William Quandt wrote that "verbal understandings had a way of dissolving when the Americans tried to translate them into concrete terms. . . . [A]s a result, it was hard to know at the end, what if anything, had been agreed upon" (Quandt, "Clinton and the Arab-Israeli Conflict," 33). See also Eldar, "On the Basis of the Nonexistent Camp David Understandings."
21. Cf. Arieli, "Netanyahu's 'Map' Is a Non-Starter"; Horowitz, "Camp David 2 and President Clinton's Bridging Proposals"; Bregman, *Elusive Peace*, Kindle location 2158; Tessler, *A History of the Israeli-Palestinian Conflict*, Kindle 801.
22. Downes, "The Holy Land Divided," 101.
23. Pundak, "From Oslo to Taba," 40.
24. See Map 14.1, Chapter 14.
25. This is the estimate of the Israeli analyst Baskin, "What Went Wrong"; other estimates were even higher. According to Malley and Agha, even Bill Clinton's later compromise proposals would have left "tens of thousands" of Palestinians within the settlement cluster boundaries (Malley and Agha, "Reply to Ehud Barak").
26. In December 2007, *Haaretz* published an Israeli document, signed by Gilead Sher, one of Barak's closest advisors, entitled "The Status of the Diplomatic Process with the Palestinians: Points to Update the Incoming Prime Minister" (hereafter: Sher Report). Summarizing the Israeli plan, Sher wrote: "No evacuation of settlements was planned for the initial phase of the plan. At an appropriate time, it stated, isolated settlements outside the blocs or security zones would be transferred to one of the settlement blocs or to Israel." The Sher Report is discussed in Ravid, "Document Shows Progress on Core Issues at Camp David Summit."
27. "Everyone Thinks That Jerusalem Is Lost."
28. Golani, "Zionism without Zion: The Jerusalem Question, 1947–1949."
29. On the technical/legal question of who is "sovereign" on the Temple Mount, see Lustick, "Has Israel Annexed East Jerusalem?" While Lustick argued that Israel refrained from officially annexing East Jerusalem, he cautioned that he is not arguing that the "legal niceties" are the same as the actual "political outcomes."
30. David Landau, a prominent Israeli journalist and one-time editor of *Haaretz*, wrote that like the "religious zealotry in the Muslim world on the issue of Jerusalem," Barak and Foreign Minister Ben-Ami "were influenced by the religious fundamentalism on the Israeli side regarding the Temple Mount . . . [taking] a position at Camp David that made a pragmatic compromise on Jerusalem effectively unattainable" (Landau, *Arik*, Kindle location 7076).
31. Quoted by Eldar, "The Road to Hell."
32. Pundak, "Oslo to Taba," 42.
33. Dayan, "Barak Began Referring to 'Holy of Holies,'" 2.
34. Indyk, *Innocent*, Kindle location 5339.
35. Bregman, *Cursed Victory*, Kindle 237.
36. Among such accounts, see the authoritative discussion by the State Department's Aaron David Miller, in his memoirs, *Much Too Promised Land*, 305–7.
37. Quoted in O'Malley, *Two-State Delusion*, Kindle 93. See also Indyk, *Innocent Abroad*, Kindle locations 4982 and 5371.
38. Bregman, *Cursed Victory*, Kindle 242.

39. Enderlin, *Shattered Dreams*, 276. Similarly, Bregman writes that Arafat "felt that he was in no position to budge an inch over the holy sites as it affected the broader Muslim community, not only the Palestinians. Land mattered to him far less than emotional and Islamic values and, quite clearly, there was no way he could have signed off on any solution to Jerusalem which was less than full sovereignty over the Haram without Arab support, particularly from Saudi Arabia, Egypt and Jordan" (Bregman, *Cursed Victory*, Kindle 243).
40. Bregman, *Cursed Victory*, Kindle 242. Other accounts have Arafat as "yelling" this to Clinton.
41. Quoted in an interview with Swisher, *Truth about Camp David*, 306.
42. Estimates differ on how many refugees and their descendants are still alive, especially because there is no consensus on how to define "descendants." According to some, there are now 6 million such refugees.
43. Iyad, "Lowering the Sword," 103 (emphasis added).
44. Iyad, *Jerusalem Report*, July 16, 2001, 15 (emphasis in original).
45. Enderlin, *Shattered Dreams*, 164.
46. Enderlin, *Shattered Dreams*, 252.
47. Ravid, "Document Shows Progress."
48. Malley and Agha, "Camp David and After."
49. Quoted in Shavit, "End of a Journey," and in a continuation of his interview with Barak (Shavit, "Interview with Ehud Barak"), February 2, 2001.
50. Editorial, *Buffalo News*, May 4, 2002.
51. Quoted in Eldar, "Popular Misconceptions."
52. Stern, "Following the Stretch from Concept to Dogma to Axiom."
53. Akiva Eldar, *Haaretz*, September 18, 2001.
54. *Ma'ariv*, October 28, 2001.
55. Kurtzer et al., *Peace Puzzle*, Kindle 126.
56. Pundak, "From Oslo to Taba," 43.
57. *Haaretz*, November 24, 2000.
58. From a 2003 Ron Pundak speech, "Camp David II: Israel's Misconceived Approach." Cited in Norman Finkelstein, "The Camp David II Negotiations," *Journal of Palestine Studies*, Winter 2007.
59. Malley op-ed, *New York Times*, July 7, 2001.
60. Kurtzer et al., *Peace Puzzle*, Kindle 118.
61. Ben-Ami, *Scars of War*, 270.
62. Widely quoted, including in Maoz, *Defending the Holy Land*, 476.
63. For example, Meron Benvenisti wrote that many Israeli supporters of a two-state settlement "held that the new arrangements . . . would replace direct Israeli control with a form of indirect Israeli control, through the Palestinian Authority . . . and thereby continue its occupation of Palestinian territory." *Haaretz*, March 8, 2001.
64. Kurtzer makes that case, writing that if Camp David "had been seen in historical perspective simply as one important round of negotiations, rather than as an end-all summit, it would have been assessed as a remarkably successful episode, where historic compromises were put on the table, and issues that were considered taboo in the past, such as Jerusalem and refugees, were discussed" (*Peace Puzzle*, Kindle 153). Similarly, while arguing that it was not true that Camp David came close to settling the Israeli-Palestinian conflict, Indyk argues that "important progress" had been made because "complex final status issues were discussed seriously for the first time" and both sides had made significant concessions. He concludes: "If Camp David had been billed and organized as a preliminary summit, it might have been treated as a great success rather than a miserable failure" (*Innocent Abroad*, Kindle location 5597).
65. Barak, as quoted in Shavit, "Interview with Ehud Barak," February 2, 2001.
66. Ten years later an Israeli study found that many of the Israelis who moved rightward in the years following Camp David cite Barak's statement that "We have no Palestinian partner for

peace" (Eldar, "Where Was Barak When Israel and the Palestinians Were Working Out a Peace Deal?").

67. Malley and Agha, "Camp David and After."
68. As reported in *Haaretz* interviews with Shlomo Ben-Ami and in Sher, *Israeli-Palestinian Peace Negotiations,* 122.
69. The Clinton Parameters are widely discussed in the literature. For a highly detailed analysis see Horowitz, "Camp David 2."
70. As reported by the Palestinian journalist and delegate Akram Hanieh, "The Camp David Papers," 83.
71. As discussed in Horowitz, "Camp David 2," and Ross, *The Missing Peace,* 743.
72. Ross, *The Missing Peace,* 749–50.
73. Quoted in Malley, "Israel and the Arafat Question."
74. Ross, *The Missing Peace,* 751.
75. Ross, *The Missing Peace,* 754.
76. Swisher, *The Truth about Camp David,* 399–401; the Arabic version was translated into English by the Middle East Media Research Institute and published in the institute's journal, *Memri:* "Arafat's Letter of Reservations to President Clinton," Special Dispatch, no. 170, January 3, 2001, https://www.memri.org/reports/arafats-letter-reservations-president-clinton.
77. Albright, *Madam Secretary,* 497.
78. Shlaim, *Iron Wall,* Kindle 700.
79. Indyk, *Innocent Abroad,* Kindle location 5140.
80. Quoting from Arafat's letter, Indyk, *Innocent Abroad,* Kindle location 6052.
81. Ross, *The Missing Peace,* 755, 756.
82. Shlaim commented: "Far from rejecting anything, the letter raises perfectly legitimate questions" about the crucial matters: "It is difficult to see how Arafat could have committed his movement to Clinton's guidelines without having the clearest understanding of the terms" (Shlaim, *Iron Wall,* Kindle 700). See also Swisher's assessment: "As with any other important binding document affecting the fate of nations, it would have been unconscionable for either the Palestinians or the Israelis to make any commitment to Clinton's guidelines without having the clearest understanding of all the terms presented. In this regard, Arafat's request was not only not obstructionist but the minimal fulfillment of his critical responsibilities as Palestinian leader (Swisher, *Truth about Camp David,* 401).
83. Beilin, *Path to Geneva,* 242.
84. Shlaim, *Iron Wall,* Kindle 697.
85. Quoted in Ravid, "Government to Clinton in 2000."
86. The issues are summarized in the memoirs of Sher, *Israel-Palestinian Peace Negotiations,* 206–7.
87. Sher, *Israel-Palestinian Peace Negotiations,* 206.
88. Sher, *Israel-Palestinian Peace Negotiations,* 206–07.
89. Indyk, *Innocent Abroad,* Kindle location 5509.
90. Interview with Shavit, "Continuation of Eyes Wide Shut," *Haaretz,* September 4, 2002.
91. Bregman, *Elusive Peace,* Kindle location 2780.
92. Ravid, "Government to Clinton."
93. Bregman, quoting Barak in his interview with him on March 9, 2005, *Elusive Peace,* Kindle location 2780.
94. Clinton, *My Life,* 938, 947.
95. Indyk, *Innocent Abroad,* Kindle location 6109. Similarly, while throughout his two books on the Israeli-Palestinian conflict Bregman is highly critical of Israel, in his discussion of the Palestinian response to the Clinton Parameters, he writes that "there is little doubt that . . . in December 2000, Arafat missed an opportunity to have an independent Palestine with Arab East Jerusalem as its capital and . . . Palestinian sovereignty over the Haram al-Sharif," and quotes Arafat's advisor Mohammed Rashid as admitting that "we have made a strategic mistake in not accepting the Clinton proposals" (Bregman, *Cursed Victory,* Kindle 263).

96. Shavit," Interview with Ehud Barak," September 14, 2001. Yossi Beilin's comment is blander: "Taba was the last-ditch effort to reach a solution before the elections, and Barak was willing to give it a chance" (Beilin, *Path to Geneva*, 227).
97. Eldar, "They Just Can't Hear Each Other."
98. Miller, *Much Too Promised Land*, 243.
99. Pundak, "From Oslo to Taba," 41.
100. Though there was no official record, the Taba process is discussed in the memoirs of Ben-Ami, Sher, and especially Yossi Beilin. As well, participants generally agree that the most accurate and detailed account was provided in a report to the European Union by Miguel Moratinos, the EU's emissary to the Middle East, who had been invited as an observer to the conference. Moratino's report to the EU was published in *Haaretz*, February 15, 2002. On the accuracy of Moratino's unofficial account, see Kurtzer, *Peace Puzzle*, Kindle 150.
101. Shavit, "End of a Journey."
102. Ravid, "Document Shows Progress."
103. Beilin, op-ed, *New York Times*, April 18, 2001.
104. Beilin, "What Really Happened at Taba," *Haaretz*, July 15, 2002.
105. Ben-Ami, *Scars of War*, 275.
106. Shlaim, *Iron Wall*, Kindle 706.
107. Shlaim, *The Iron Wall*, Kindle 704–5.
108. Beilin, *Path to Geneva*, 246.
109. Kurtzer et al., *Peace Puzzle*, Kindle 277.
110. Quoted in Tessler, *A History of the Israeli-Palestinian Conflict*, Kindle 817, and Maoz, *Defending the Holy Land*, 470.
111. Beilin and Rabbo, "A Mideast Partnership Can Still Work."
112. *Jerusalem Report*, July 16, 2001.
113. Quoted in Ari Shavit, "Reality Bites," 12.
114. Quoted in Swisher, *Truth about Camp* David, 403.
115. Malley and Agha, "Camp David and After—Continued."
116. Kurtzer et al., *Peace Puzzle*, 147.
117. The discussion was reported in Eldar, "Learning from Past Mistakes."
118. Miller, *Much Too Promised Land*, 302.
119. Malley and Agha, "Tragedy of Errors," *New York Review*, August 9, 2001.
120. Quoted in Swisher, *Truth about Camp David*, 274–5.
121. Enderlin, *Shattered Dreams*, 253.
122. Ben-Ami, as told to Shavit, "End of a Journey."
123. Ross, *The Missing Peace*, 668.
124. Ross, *The Missing Peace*, 671.
125. Bregman, *Elusive Peace*, Kindle location 2401.
126. Ross, *The Missing Peace*, 711.
127. Bregman, *Elusive Peace*, Kindle location 2401.
128. Clinton, *My Life*, 944.
129. Kurtzer et al., *Peace Puzzle*, Kindle 143. Two Israeli historians reached similar conclusions about the consequences of Clinton's role in the failed 2000 peace process. Shlaim wrote that while Clinton had genuinely sought a solution in the Israeli-Palestinian conflict, "by tilting so unashamedly toward Israel he contributed to the failure of this quest." By acting "like a spin doctor for Barak," Shlaim continued, he "propagated Barak's narrative . . . in order to help Barak get reelected." The problem was, Shlaim concluded, "this narrative was seriously flawed" (Shlaim, *Iron Wall*, Kindle 702). In the same vein, Bregman concluded that "Clinton's eagerness to please and inability to stand his ground, particularly with Barak, turned out to be a serious liability in a summit where only hard pressure on the Palestinians and the Israelis could have led to success. What was needed from the American president was not empathy but unsentimental toughness and leadership" (Bregman, *Cursed Victory*, Kindle 230).

130. The text of the Arab Peace Initiative was printed in the *New York Times,* March 29, 2002.
131. Siegman, "Prime Minister Netanyahu and the Arab Peace Initiative." Saudi officials confirmed that Siegman's account accurately reflected Abdullah's views.
132. A *Haaretz* columnist commented: "The Arab League/Saudi proposal, astonishingly, was greeted with almost complete silence in Israel, despite the fact that it was an historic proposal. As expected, Sharon contemptuously rejected it, but the Israeli press hardly discussed it. If two years ago we were all echoing Barak that 'the real face of the Palestinians has been exposed,' what can be learned about Israel's real face if it is now the one to refuse the proposal?" (Aviv Lavie, *Haaretz,* April 4, 2002). Other Haaretz columnists have expressed their astonishment at the continuing indifference of Israel to the API. For example, see Strenger, "Why Israel Does Not Engage with the Saudi Initiative." In 2008, the former Jordanian foreign minister and first ambassador to Israel wrote that the unanimous peace offer of the Arab League still stood but was "not related to seriously by the two players whose support and endorsement were crucial to its implementation. Neither Israel nor the United States responded with more than lip service" (Muasher, "The Initiative Still Stands").

Chapter 16

1. Benvenisti, "An Explosive, Dangerous Balance."
2. Sarid, "If Not with a Stone, Then with What?," *Haaretz,* April 12, 2013.
3. Editorial, "Stop Shooting Gazan Protesters."
4. There are many analyses of the intifada, in particular the Israeli killing of Palestinians even before they turned to terrorism. For examples, see Bregman, *Cursed Victory,* Kindle 248–51; Zertal and Eldar, *Lords of the Land,* 407–15; and Tessler, *A History of the Israeli-Palestinian Conflict,* Kindle 808–11.
5. Zertal and Eldar, *Lords of the Land,* 413.
6. Quoted in *Haaretz,* September 18, 2001.
7. Eldar, "Military Intelligence: Never Expected Hamas Victory in 2006."
8. Lavie and Steinberg, "Worrisome Findings on Decision Making." Steinberg was an advisor to the Shin-Bet director.
9. *New York Times,* September 28, 2001.
10. For one such assessment, see Kurtzer: "Although the Intifada was primarily spontaneous, Arafat embraced it . . . probably believing that a measure of violence could be employed as a complement to negotiations in order to persuade the Israelis that there were consequences for not reaching an agreement" (Kurtzer et al., *Peace Puzzle,* Kindle 144, 147). See also Indyk, *Innocent Abroad,* Kindle location 6841, and Sayigh, "Arafat and the Anatomy of a Revolt." See Elgindy's assessment that Arafat "cynically used violence and calculated chaos during the Intifada" to show his relevance, but it backfired, as did Hamas terrorism against Israeli civilians (Elgindy, *Blind Spot,* Kindle 253).
11. Ben-Ami, *Scars of War,* 314, 188.
12. Ben-Ami, *Scars of War,* 52.
13. Ben-Ami, *Scars of War,* 52.
14. Bregman, *Elusive Peace,* Kindle location 3103–17.
15. Tom Segev, "Gaza without Gazans."
16. The statement was published in *Tikkun,* vol. 16, no. 2, 2001. See also Roy, "A Dubai on the Mediterranean."
17. As early as 1991 these activities became publicly known, when an Israeli television program discussed them in some detail. See *New York Times,* June 24, 1991.
18. An English translation of the Hamas Charter is printed in *MEMRI,* the journal of the Middle East Media Research Institute, February 14, 2006. For discussions, see Tessler, *A History of the Israeli-Palestinian Conflict,* Kindle 696–98, and Avineri, "What to Speak with Hamas About."

19. The leading scholarly work on Hamas is Mishal and Sela, *The Palestinian Hamas*. Both authors are prominent Israeli academicians. Unless otherwise cited, this section is based largely on their work on Hamas's early years.
20. Drucker, "Hamas Has Proven Israel Only Understands Force."
21. Avnery, "Shukran, Israel" (emphasis added). Shukran is Arabic for "Thank you."
22. "How Israel Helped Spawn Hamas," interview with Avner Cohen, January 24, 2009. On Israel's early efforts to employ Hamas as a counterweight to what it initially regarded as the more dangerous nationalism of the PLO, see Khalidi, *Iron Cage*, Kindle location 316, and Bregman, *Cursed Victory*, Kindle 137.
23. Mishal and Sela, *Palestinian Hamas*, 55–56.
24. Quoted in Mishal and Sela, *Palestinian Hamas*, 57.
25. Mishal and Sela, *Palestinian Hamas*, 57.
26. Mishal and Sela, *Palestinian Hamas*, 65–66.
27. Eldar, "Evacuate Jewish Hebron."
28. Quoted in Zertal and Eldar, *Lords of the Land*, 123.
29. Mishal and Sela, *Palestinian Hamas*, 71–72.
30. Mishal and Sela, *Palestinian Hamas*, 73–74.
31. Mishal and Sela, *Palestinian Hamas*, 75. The details of these events are discussed in Gambill, "The Balance of Terror," 51–56.
32. The quotes and general discussion are from Shlaim, *Iron Wall*, Kindle 741–47. For other discussions, see Montell, "Operation Defensive Shield," and Rynhold and Waxman, "Ideological Change and Israel's Disengagement from Gaza."
33. The story originally appeared in *Yediot Aharanot* on November 14, 2003, entitled "Ex-Shin Bet Heads Warn of 'Catastrophe' without Peace Deal." The English translation of the interviews was published in the Winter 2004 issue of the *Journal of Palestine Studies*.
34. On the history of the moderating influence of governance on radical movements, and its particular application to Hamas, see Shlaim, "How Israel Brought Gaza to the Brink of Humanitarian Catastrophe."
35. *Jerusalem Report*, July 27, 1995.
36. *New York Times*, March 14, 1996 (emphasis added).
37. The offer and the Israeli response were made public by ex-Mossad chief Ephraim Halevy, in an interview with the *Haaretz* columnist Zeev Schiff, "Hamas Offered 30-Year Ceasefire in 1997," March 30, 2006.
38. "Hamas Proposes a 10-Year Truce for Israeli Pullback."
39. Shlaim, *Iron Wall*, Kindle 772.
40. Rynhold and Waxman, "Ideological Change," 29.
41. Rynhold and Waxman, "Ideological Change," 29.
42. Rose, "The Gaza Bombshell." Rose's article is the most complete account of the Israeli and American efforts to subvert Hamas's electoral victory in 2006. Rose gained access to US government classified documents covering these events, and interviewed a number of Bush administration officials, who confirmed the accuracy of his account. The accuracy of the Rose article has not been challenged, and it has been widely cited in other US and Israeli accounts of this period.
43. Beinart, "Gaza Myths and Facts: What American Jewish Leaders Won't Tell You."
44. Levy, "As the Hamas Team Laughs."
45. Rose, "Gaza Bombshell."
46. Rose, "Gaza Bombshell."
47. Regular, "Hamas Hints at Long-Term Truce in Return for 1967 Borders."
48. Ravid, "In 2006 Letter to Bush, Haniyeh Offered Compromise with Israel."
49. Schiff, "Hamas Says Ready for Two-State Solution."
50. As reported in *Haaretz*, January 17, 2006, and in the *New York Times*, November 24, 2006.
51. Rubinstein, "Don't Boycott the Palestinians."

52. Regular, "Hamas Rounds Up Weapons."
53. *Haaretz*, February 26, 2006.
54. Schiff, "Hamas Says Ready for Two-State Solution."
55. Issacharoff, "PM Dismisses Meshal Comments That Israel's Existence Is a Reality."
56. "B'Tselem: Israeli Security Forces Killed 660 Palestinians in 2006"; Issacharoff, "57 Unarmed Palestinian Minors Killed by IDF since June."
57. Rubinstein, "Hamas PM Haniyeh: Retreat to 1967 Borders Will Bring Peace."
58. Regular, "Hamas, Fatah Prisoners Agree to Two-State Solution in Joint Draft" (emphases added). Citing an analysis by the Palestinian political scientist Khalid Shikaki, Zoughbi writes that the document "essentially committed Hamas to a more moderate position that explicitly embraced a Palestinian state along the 1967 borders" (Zoughbi, *Indecision Points*, 110).
59. Atran, "Is Hamas Ready to Deal?," emphasis added.
60. Haniyeh, "Aggression under False Pretenses," emphasis added.
61. Malley and Siegman, "The Hamas Factor."
62. "B'Tselem: Israeli Security Forces Killed 650 Palestinians in 2006"; Issacharoff, "57 Unarmed Palestinian Minors Killed by IDF since June"; El-Khodary and Kershner, "Gaza Is Tense as It Tallies Casualties."
63. Bar'el, "Meshal Declaration Basic Shift in Hamas's Position," and Issacharoff, "PM Dismisses Meshal's Comments That Israel Is a Reality."
64. Khoury, "Meshal: Shalit Still Alive," 8.
65. Kershner, "Rockets Hit Israel, Breaking Hamas Truce."
66. Yakobson, "Not Israel's Policemen."
67. Bronner, "Truce in Gaza Ends, but May Be Revived by Necessity."
68. "B'Tselem: Israeli Security Forces Killed 660 Palestinians during 2006"; El-Khodary and Kershner, "Gaza Is Tense"; Issacharoff, "B'Tselem's End-of-Year Report."
69. "Hamas Vows to Honor Palestinian Referendum on Peace with Israel."
70. Rubinstein, "Hamas PM Haniyeh: Retreat to 1967 Borders Will Bring Peace."
71. An assessment of the British news magazine *The Economist* put it this way: "Some of the religious zealots may well believe in the obnoxious charter. Others, including Meshal and Haniyeh, try to brush it off and then, if pressed, dangle it as an item for negotiation, much as Fatah used the dropping of the PLO's charter, which equally rejected Israel's existence, as a bargaining tool" ("Will the Relationship Change? Yes It Can").
72. Issacharoff, "Ex-President Carter Urges Obama to Remove Hamas from U.S. Terror List."
73. Mishal and Sela, *Palestinian Hamas*, xxiv.
74. "Problematic Options," *bitterlemons*, November 20, 2006.
75. From an Israeli newspaper column by Halevy, quoted in Siegman, "Israel's Lies."
76. "Why Not Hamas?"
77. Ari Shavit, interview with Ami Ayalon, "Clearly Speaking," *Haaretz*, February 9, 2006.

Chapter 17

1. Shlaim, "How Israel Brought Gaza to the Brink of Humanitarian Catastrophe."
2. For a detailed discussion of the Gazan withdrawal, see Tessler, *A History of the Israeli-Palestinian Conflict*, Kindle 833–37, and Shlaim, *Iron Wall*, Kindle 774–77, 782–87.
3. For these arguments, see Pappé, *Ten Myths*, Kindle location 1922–28; Burg, "End of an Era"; and Zertal and Eldar, *Lords of the Land*, 446.
4. Quoted in Shlaim, *Iron Wall*, 786–87.
5. Sarid, "My Travels with Ariel Sharon."
6. Avnery, "The Imperator."
7. Amirav, "Time Is Ripe for Borders"; Arieli, "Netanyahu Could Learn from Sharon's Realistic Approach to Zionism"; Benn, "Sharon's Vision."
8. Alon, "Irate Likud MKs Put PM on the Defensive."

9. Arieli, "Netanyahu Could Learn from Sharon's Realistic Approach to Zionism."
10. This and other documents were released by WikiLeaks and were analyzed in Ravid, "Sharon Was Planning Diplomatic Moves Beyond Gaza."
11. Ravid, "Sharon Was Planning Diplomatic Moves Beyond Gaza." Ravid concluded that the cables "show that in fact, even before the Gaza withdrawal, Sharon was planning his next big diplomatic move."
12. Quoted in Arieli, "Netanyahu Could Learn."
13. These and other measures are discussed in Bregman, *Cursed Victory*, Kindle 300–302.
14. In a column pointedly entitled "So What Have We Done to Them?," Nehemia Shtrasler, a *Haaretz* columnist, wrote: "We are told that we have withdrawn from Gaza and for some reason they are still shooting. Immediately after the withdrawal, quiet was in fact maintained. . . . Quassams were not fired and the truce was honored. But then Israel said that . . . in the West Bank it would continue to pursue Islamic Jihad activists. The IDF embarked on extensive assassination operations in the West Bank, and then the Jihad in Gaza declared it would not abandon its people there and would retaliate. . . . [T]he firing on [southern Israel] was renewed . . . and the IDF responded with assassinations."
15. Roy, "A Dubai on the Mediterranean." Roy is a Harvard professor (and the daughter of Auschwitz survivors) and is considered to be the preeminent academic specialist on the siege of Gaza. Her major work is *The Gaza Strip: The Political Economy of De-Development*.
16. During this period, a number of UN and international human rights groups as well as individuals reported on the consequences of the Israeli economic and military actions against Gaza. Among these were Amnesty International, Human Rights Watch, the Red Cross, Physicians for Human Rights, CARE, Oxfam, Israeli human rights organizations, academics, and journalists. The reports, as well as the details of the Israeli siege, are discussed in Slater, "Just War Moral Philosophy and the 2008–09 Israeli Campaign in Gaza."
17. Among many other places, the studies were cited in Erlanger, "Israel's Dilemma in Response to Rockets," and Bronner and Tavernise, "In Shattered Gaza Town, Roots of Seething Split."
18. El-Khodary and Kershner, "Gaza Is Tense as It Tallies Casualties."
19. "Rights Group: Close to Half of Palestinian Fatalities in IDF Operation Were Civilians."
20. Khoury, "Meshal: Shalit Still Alive."
21. Bronner, "Truce in Gaza Ends."
22. Bronner and El-Khodary, "Hamas Fires Rockets into Israel."
23. Harel, "Hamas Response: Calculated Escalation."
24. Yakobsen, "Not Israel's Policemen."
25. Bronner, "Truce in Gaza Ends."
26. Siegman, "Israel's Lies."
27. Beaumont, "Olmert Rejected Palestinian Attempts to Set Up Talks."
28. According to the British journalist Johann Hari, Diskin's report was revealed in Israeli newspaper stories. Hari's account, never denied, is "The True Story behind This War Is Not the One Israel Is Telling."
29. The Eldar book, published only in Hebrew, is discussed in O'Malley, *The Two-State Delusion*, Kindle 121.
30. "Human Rights Situation in Palestine and Other Occupied Arab Territories."
31. Interview with General Shmuel Zakai, quoted in Bradley Burston, "Can the First Gaza War Be Stopped Before It Starts?"
32. These figures were the most commonly used ones in the various reports. Importantly, even the Israeli army's own analyses estimated that two-thirds of the Palestinians killed in Cast Lead were civilians. See Pedatzur, "The War That Wasn't."
33. For full discussion and citations of the various reports, see Slater, "Just War."
34. For example, B'Tselem reported: "In the Gaza Strip, Israel's siege continues. The almost total prohibition on the import of raw materials and on exports has led to the collapse of the economy and the closing of most of the factories and workshops in Gaza. The restrictions

on import of building materials have prevented the reconstruction of buildings that Israel destroyed during Operation Cast Lead. Poverty and deprivation, which were widespread before the operation, have worsened still further" (see its report, "Human Rights Review," January 1, 2009, to April 30, 2010). Another extensive report was the joint statement of Amnesty International UK, Oxfam, and fourteen other European church and physicians' organizations. In February 2010, Sara Roy summed up the findings of B'Tselem and the international organizations, in "Gaza: Treading on Shards," *Nation*, February 10, 2010.

35. "Hamas: We Will Accept Long-Term Truce If Gaza Borders Opened."
36. Ravid and Issacharoff, "Hamas: We Won't Stand in Way of PA-Israel Deal."
37. Ravid, "MI Chief: Obama Mideast Policy Threatens Israel."
38. Scham and Abu-Irshaid, "Hamas: Ideological Rigidity and Political Flexibility." Scham was a professor of Jewish studies at the University of Maryland; Abu-Irshaid, founder and editor-in-chief of *Al-Meezan*, an Arab-language newspaper published in the United States.
39. Bar'el, "Let's Calm Down on Syria and Hezbollah."
40. Hasson, "Israeli Peace Activist."
41. B'Tselem Report, "Human Rights Violations during Operation Pillar of Defense." The report is discussed in Cohen, "B'Tselem: More Than 50 percent of Palestinians Killed in Israel's Last Gaza Operation Were Civilians."
42. Hasson, "Israeli Peace Activist."
43. Baskin, "Israel's Short-Sighted Assassination." The offer has sometimes been described as a "permanent" truce, other times as a "long-term" truce. The discrepancy may be explained by the fact that Hamas officials often said that a "long-term" truce could become permanent.
44. Pedatzur, "Why Did Israel Kill Jabari?"
45. Cited in Ehrenreich, *Way to the Spring*, Kindle 345. See also Nathan Thrall's analysis: "Israeli officials were impressed . . . [but] convinced themselves that the quiet on Gaza's border was primarily the result of their own deterrence and Palestinian self-interest. Israel therefore saw little incentive in upholding its end of the deal. Its forces made regular incursions into Gaza . . . [and] the end of the closure never came. . . . Yet Hamas largely continued to maintain the cease-fire to Israel's satisfaction. . . . In 2013, fewer rockets were launched from Gaza than in any year since 2003" (Thrall, *Only Language They Understand*, Kindle 157).
46. Quoted in Blumenthal, *The 51-Day War*, Kindle location 232.
47. O'Malley, *Two-State Delusion*, Kindle 155.
48. The surveys are reviewed in O'Malley, *Two-State Delusion*, 161–62.

Chapter 18

1. These and other policies during the first year of the Bush administration are discussed in Rynhold, "Behind the Rhetoric: President Bush and U.S. Policy on the Israeli-Palestinian Conflict"; on Powell's intended speech, see Perlez, "Before Attacks, US Was Ready to Say It Backed Palestinian State."
2. Bush's description of Sharon was greeted with widespread astonishment and ridicule. In her memoirs, even Condoleezza Rice, Bush's secretary of state, is critical (*No Higher Honor*, 140).
3. The text of Bush's 2002 speech can be found at https://www.theguardian.com/world/2002/jun/25/israel.usa.
4. As quoted in *Haaretz*, September 9, 2002, and Viorst, "Road Map to Nowhere."
5. For examples, see Sharon's biographer Uzi Benjamin, in "Sharon's Work," *Haaretz*, December 15, 2002; Yossi Alpher, former Mossad deputy director, in "Issue Brief," March 31, 2003; and Avi Primor, a former foreign ministry deputy director, who wrote, "For those who desire to keep the West Bank and Gaza, to expand the settlements without annexing the Palestinian population, and who understand that transfer is impractical, the original South African model is particularly tempting" (Primor, "Sharon's South African Strategy").

6. On the administration's decision to "set aside" the Road Map, see *New York Times*, May 9, 2003. On Sharon's realization that he could now ignore the Road Map without facing serious US pressures, see Samet, "The Convoy Is Passing."
7. The text of Sharon's fourteen "reservations" was published in *Haaretz* on May 27, 2003.
8. Rice, *No Higher Honor*, 219.
9. *New York Times*, July 30, 2019; Samet, "Pleading for the Right to Babble."
10. Bregman, *Elusive Peace*, Kindle location 5141.
11. *New York Times*, April 14, 2005.
12. Indyk, *Innocent Abroad*, Kindle location 6323.
13. Miller, *Much Too Promised Land*, 354.
14. Kurtzer et al., *Peace Puzzle*, Kindle 235, 237, 239.
15. The text of the letter is printed in the *New York Review*, November 18, 2004.
16. Eldar, "With Friends Like These . . ."
17. The text of the highly detailed, fifty-page agreement is in Beilin, *Path to Geneva*, Appendix Five. It can also be accessed at https://www.jewishvirtuallibrary.org/the-beilin-abu-mazen-document.
18. Beilin, *Path to Geneva*, 256.
19. The interview is discussed in Eldar, "Arafat Recognizes Jewish Ties to Zion."
20. Eldar, "Arafat Recognizes Jewish Ties to Zion," interview with Henry Siegman of the Council on Foreign Relations.
21. *Tikkun*, January/February 2004
22. Beilin, *Path to Geneva*, 265.
23. *Haaretz*, January 17, 2005.
24. Eldar, "What Arab Initiative?," 7.
25. Muasher, "The Initiative Still Stands." Other prominent Israeli writers who emphasize the lost opportunity include Eldar, "Arab Peace Initiative Is Another Missed Opportunity for Israel," and Maoz, "The Israeli-Saudi Common Interest."
26. Bar-Joseph, "The Iranian Threat and the Arab Peace Initiative."
27. "Hamas: We'll Consider 2002 Arab Peace Plan Only If Israel Accepts It First."
28. Avi Issacharoff, "Hundreds of Thousands Mark Hamas' 25th Anniversary in Gaza Rally," *Haaretz*, Dec. 8, 2012.
29. Siegman, "Meshal's Folly."
30. Bar'el, "Meshal Says Hamas Accepts a Two-State Solution."
31. "United: The Palestinians Have Endorsed 1967 Borders for Peace."
32. Sharoni, "Investigating Israeli Refusal." Four years later, *Haaretz* reported that "no Israeli government has held a single discussion [of the API]" (June 15, 2014).
33. Bar-Joseph, "The Iranian Threat and the Arab Peace Initiative." Uri Bar-Joseph is a professor of political science at Haifa University.
34. Strenger, "Get Arab Leaders to Recognize Israel." To be sure, in reality there was zero chance of Netanyahu accepting the API, let alone the increasingly right-wing Knesset, so the matter remained strictly hypothetical.
35. Strenger, "Why Israel Does Not Engage with the Saudi Initiative."
36. Rice writes that the Israelis didn't see the API "as a basis for anything" (Rice, *No Higher Honor*, 604).
37. Rice, *No Higher Honor*, 605.
38. Quoted in Ravid, "PM at Final Cabinet Meeting: Greater Israel Is No More."
39. Quoted in Benn, "PM Speech Intended to Promote West Bank Withdrawal."
40. As reported in *Haaretz*, September 15, 2008.
41. Quoted by Eldar, "Talking Like Meretz, Behaving Like the Likud."
42. "Plan or Spin?"
43. For examples, see Eldar, "Talking Like Meretz," and Levy, "Believing Olmert."
44. Rice, *No Higher Honor*, 723.

45. In a major *New York Times* analysis of the Olmert-Abbas negotiations, Bernard Avishai wrote: "Sources say that there was never a document, formal or informal, presented to Abbas. Everything was offered orally and provisionally, and with the specific proviso that Olmert's ideas were not endorsed either by Foreign Minister Livni or Defense Minister Barak" (May 4, 2009). As well, a *Jerusalem Post* analyst wrote: "Throughout all the talks with Abbas Olmert refused to have anything written down and there were no formal joint minutes at those meetings. There were, in fact, no detailed and systematic negotiations. In his final meeting with Abbas, Olmert described the offer and Abbas had to take notes on what the offer contained" (Baskin, "Encountering Peace").
46. These provisions of the Palestine Papers were summarized in the *Jerusalem Post,* January 24, 2011. For a detailed analysis of the Olmert-Abbas negotiations, see Elgindy, *Blind Spot*, Kindle 193–96.
47. "Peace Now or Never."
48. Bronner, "Olmert Says Israel Must Leave West Bank."
49. Issacharoff, "Olmert: I Am Still Waiting for Abbas to Call"; Avishai, "A Plan for Peace That Could Still Be."
50. Benn and Ravid, "Olmert Offered to Withdraw from 93% of West Bank."
51. Bronner, "Olmert Says Israel Must Leave West Bank."
52. Arieli, "Bridging the Gap."
53. Olmert, "The Time Has Come to Say These Things."
54. As discussed in Benn, "My Ideas Will Prevail."
55. As told to Issacharoff, "Olmert: I Am Still Waiting for Abbas to Call." Shaul Arieli's analysis of the Olmert-Abbas talks had different numbers: "Olmert thought absorbing 30,000 refugees over 10 years could get both sides to agree. Abbas sought to increase that number to 100,000" (Arieli, "Bridging the Gap").
56. Ravid, "Palestinians Agreed to Cede Nearly All Jewish Areas of East Jerusalem."
57. Avishai, "A Plan for Peace That Still Could Be"; Ravid, "Palestinians Agreed to Cede."
58. Ravid, "Palestinians Agreed to Cede."
59. Arieli, "Palestinian Critics Shouldn't Be So Hasty to Dismiss Abbas."
60. Ravid and Issacharoff, "Abbas Challenges Mitchell."
61. Avishai, "A Plan for Peace."
62. Winer, "Olmert Says Jerusalem Has Never Really Been United."
63. Quoted in Peraino, "Olmert's Lament."
64. Ravid, "Abbas: Palestinians, Israel Were Two Months Away from Inking Peace Deal."
65. Thrall, "What Future for Israel?," citing Herzog, "Minding the Gaps."
66. Quoted in Arieli, "The Palestinian Question."
67. Rice, *No Higher Honor*, 723.
68. *bitterlemons,* June 29, 2009.
69. On Netanyahu as an ideologue, see Pfeffer, "2010–2019: The Decade in Which All Israelis Became Netanyahu."
70. Quoted in Pfeffer, "Benjamin Netanyahu the Undertaker of the Two-State Solution."
71. Pfeffer, "Benjamin Netanyahu the Undertaker of the Two-State Solution."
72. *New York Times*, April 9, 2014.
73. Eldar, "Again That Guy with His Peace Talk," *Haaretz*, November 5, 2012.
74. Akiva Eldar, in a February 11, 2009, interview with the American Jewish peace organization, J Street.
75. Gideon Levy, *Haaretz*, July 24, 2008.
76. The text of the statement, "A Last Chance for a Two-State Israel-Palestine Agreement: A Bipartisan Statement on US/Middle East Peacemaking," appeared in the *Daily Kos*, May 7, 2009; it was also discussed in Cohen, "The Fierce Urgency of Peace."
77. Kamiya, "Obama's Middle East Moment of Truth."
78. For a detailed review of Obama's policies on the Israeli settlements and other issues, see Elgindy, *Blind Spot*, Kindle 12–13, 200–215.

79. Elgindy, *Blind Spot*, Kindle 209.
80. Quoted by Hass, "Where Even Emergency Generators Break Down."
81. As reported by Sullivan, "The Daily Dish" (blog), March 13, 2009.
82. Mazzetti and Cooper, "Israel Stance Was Undoing of Nominee for Intelligence Post."
83. Carey, "Goldstone Reports."
84. Quoted in Ravid, "The Secret Fruits of the Peace Talks."
85. Tibon, "Obama's Detailed Plan for Mideast Peace Revealed."
86. Barnea didn't identify the US official, but it is widely assumed to be Martin Indyk. The interview was published in the Israeli Hebrew-language newspaper *Yedioth Ahronoth*, May 2, 2014. The English language translation of the interview was published in *Journal of Palestine Studies*, Summer 2014, 183–87.
87. *Yedioth Ahronoth*, May 2, 2014.
88. Tibon, "Obama's Detailed Plan."
89. Elgindy's summary of published accounts on the initial Kerry Plan is in *Blind Spot*, Kindle 230.
90. Tibon, "Obama's Detailed Plan."
91. The outrage at the projected release of Pollard is further explained by the fact that the stolen documents were said to have revealed the names of thousands of people who had cooperated with the US intelligence agencies and were feared to have reached other countries, including the Soviet Union.
92. Barnea interview, *Yedioth Ahronoth*, May 2, 2014. For a detailed discussion of the Jewish state demand and the Palestinian response, see Chapter 20, "Summary and Conclusions."
93. Tibon, "Obama's Detailed Plan."
94. Ravid, "The Secret Fruits of the Peace Talks."
95. Tibon, "Obama's Detailed Plan."
96. Elgindy, *Blind Spot*, Kindle 232.
97. Barnea interview, *Yedioth Ahronoth*, May 2, 2014.
98. "Netanyahu Agreed to Withdraw to '67 Lines, Document Confirms."
99. *Times of Israel*, March 16, 2015.
100. Elgindy, *Blind Spot*, Kindle 13; Beinart, "It's Time to End America's Blank Check Military Aid to Israel." 9.
101. Quoted by Elgindy, from his correspondence with Malley, in *Blind Spot*, Kindle 243.

Chapter 19

1. Hagar Shezaf, "Annexation for Dummies," *Haaretz*, January 26, 2020.
2. For a discussion of Netanyahu's statement, see Halbfinger, "Netanyahu Vows to Start Annexing West Bank."
3. Among many Israeli reports, see the summary of the transfer methods employed by Netanyahu in Hass, "Israel Has Created Ten Methods for Deportation."
4. Pfeffer, "After Almost 20 Years, Netanyahu May Finally Realize His Vision for 'Durable Peace.'"
5. Berger and Landau, "At West Bank Event, Netanyahu Promises No More Settlers." See also Halbfinger, "Netanyahu, Facing Tough Israel Election."
6. In 2019, Yossi Kuperwasser, a central member of the Israeli security establishment, wrote: "The vast majority of the Israeli public does not support annexation, not even of the entire Area C (full civil and security control), and Israel has no intention of annexing areas densely population by Palestinians (Areas A and B), or imposing Israeli law on them" ("Kushner's Objective: An Economic Carrot to Change the Palestinian Narrative").
7. Judah Ari Gross, "Nearly Half of Jewish Israelis Oppose Unilateral West Bank Annexation," *Times of Israel*, January 29, 2020.
8. Commanders for Israel's Security, "Ramifications of West Bank Annexation: Security and Beyond."

9. Judy Maltz, "Netanyahu Can Now Push Through His Annexation Plan for the West Bank—But Will He?," *Haaretz,* May 4, 2020.
10. Amir Tibon, "Pompeo Says Annexing West Bank Is Israel's Decision to Make," *Haaretz,* April 22, 2020.
11. Shalev, "House Resolution on Annexation Is a Wakeup Call for Israel and Netanyahu."
12. For a discussion see the book by the Israeli journalist Larry Derfner, *No Country for Jewish Liberals,* Kindle 10.
13. The Oslo Accord stipulated that the Israeli government could collect taxes from the areas of the West Bank under its control but was required to turn them over to the PA. For a discussion, see Rosenberg, "The Palestinian Authority Is Collapsing, and Annexation Could Follow."
14. "Gaza Could Become 'Uninhabitable' by 2020, UN Report Warns," 5.
15. On the growing opposition in the Israeli military, including by Chief of Staff Aviv Kochavi, as well as Shin Bet and other security services, see Harel, "Even after Weekend Violence, Israel and Hamas Moving toward Long-Term Gaza Calm."
16. The continuing deterioration of life in Gaza was summarized in a report in early 2018: Harel, "Gazan Economy, Infrastructure on Verge of Collapse, Israeli Security Officials Say." The later statistics are discussed in Peretz, "The Fighting Is Over, but Gaza's Economic Problems Remain"; Peretz, "Hamas Seeks Concession from Israel in Gaza"; and George Zeidan, "Fauda Isn't Just Ignorant, Dishonest and Sadly Absurd; It's Anti-Palestinian Incitement," *Haaretz,* April 22, 2020.
17. Shehada, " How Turkey Has Become the Palestinian Promised Land." See also Shalev, "Gaza Emigration Ploy Suggests Netanyahu Hell-Bent on Torching Israel's Image Abroad."
18. Harel, "Gazan Economy, Infrastructure on Verge of Collapse, Israeli Security Officials Say." For the continuing support of the IDF for a deal on Gaza that will improve its economy, see the *Haaretz* editorial, "Gaza Deal Is in Israeli Interests," December 31, 2019.
19. "End the Blockade, Aid Gaza's Economy," *Haaretz* editorial, November 14, 2019.
20. "Gaza Deal Is in Israeli Interest," *Haaretz* editorial, December 31, 2019.
21. Khoury and Landau, "Israel-Qatar Deal to Transfer Funds to Hamas Officials Underway." For similar analyses, see Shehada, "Hamas Desperate for a Deal with Israel," and Hass, "Israel-Hamas Now Negotiating": "Israel considers the Gaza Strip a separate political entity from the West Bank and is working to perpetuate the separation."
22. Kershner, "As Tensions Rise with Israel, Hamas Chief Calls for Cease-Fire in Gaza."
23. Pfeffer, "Netanyahu and Hamas Chief in Gaza Have Emerged as Unlikely Allies."
24. See Harel, "Israel's Groundhog Day in Gaza"; Harel, "End the Blockade, Aid Gaza's Economy." Another columnist wrote: "The one thing that Netanyahu seeks to avoid above all else is a re-occupation of the Gaza Strip. He is rightfully concerned about the potential loss of Israeli life in what may turn out to be a deadly anti-guerilla campaign in densely populated areas" (Shalev, "Gaza Flare-up Imperils Netanyahu's Cynical Cohabitation with Hamas"). For a similar analysis, see Halbfinger, "Why Do Israel and Gaza Keep Fighting?"
25. Harel, "Israeli Military Keen to Lower the Sound of War Drums."
26. Harel, "Hamas Takes Extraordinary Step to Quell Gaza's 'Angry Youth.' "
27. Yossi Melman, "Stars Align for an Israeli-Hamas Deal, But the Road Is Long," *Haaretz,* April 14, 2020.
28. El-Khodary and Bronner, "Addressing U.S., Hamas Says It Grounded Rockets."
29. Quoted in Hroub, "A Newer Hamas? The Revised Charter." Other accounts include Walsh, "Hamas Leaders Play Final Hand: Trying to Lift Group's Pariah Status," and Khoury, "Hamas Presents New Charter Supporting Palestinian State along 1967 Borders."
30. For details, see Halbfinger and Kershner, "Israel-Gaza Clashes Intensify and Death Toll Rises"; Khoury and Landau, "Israel-Qatar Deal to Transfer Funds to Hamas Officials Underway"; and Halbfinger, "Tensions Ease in Gaza, Allowing Money and Fuel to Roll In since Last Month."
31. See a series of analyses by Amos Harel, the *Haaretz* military correspondent: "Israeli Military Keen to Lower the Sound of War Drums"; "Israel Now Sees a Rare Opportunity

for Long-Term Quiet in Gaza"; and "Israeli Army Concerned New Election Will Torpedo Possible Israel-Hamas Deal."

32. For a discussion of the factors that have blocked an Israeli-Hamas deal, see Melman, "Stars Align."
33. Cohen, "How Israel Helped Spawn Hamas."
34. Maltz, "Solutions to the Israeli-Palestinian Conflict." See also Thrall, "How the Battle over Israel and Anti-Semitism Is Fracturing American Politics."
35. Alpher, "A Lottery to Pick the Next Israeli Victims of West Bank Annexation Policy."
36. Ashkenazy and Efron, "Israel's Future Saviors Wear IDF Uniforms."
37. For a general discussion, Khalidi, *The Iron Cage*, Kindle locations 2433–48.
38. "The Arab kings and dictators have little interest in the Palestinian cause, beyond paying it lip service," wrote the *Haaretz* columnist Anshel Pfeffer ("And What If the Trump Plan Should Work After All"). See also the comment by the Gazan intellectual and writer Muhammad Shehada: "The long Arab exploitation, repression, and undermining of the Palestinian cause has . . . contributed significantly to impeding Palestinian statehood" ("For Arab Regimes, Palestine Is Old News. Now, It's All about Iran," *Haaretz*, February 27, 2019).
39. "Egypt's Sissi Confirms Unprecedented Military Cooperation with Israel."
40. For summaries of the recent developments in the Arab world, see Goodman, *Catch-67*, Kindle location 1841; Thrall, *Only Language They Understand*, Kindle location 103–5; Derfner, *No Country*, 247–48; Hubbard, "In Netanyahu's Win, Arabs See Another Nail in the Coffin of a Palestinian State"; Halbfinger, "Arab Thinkers Call to Engage with Israel and Abandon Boycotts," 9.
41. Khaled Elgindy, quoted in Hubbard, "Little Outrage in Arab World over Netanyahu's Vow to Annex West Bank."
42. Shehada, "The Arab World Just Handed Netanyahu Its Most Powerful Weapon."
43. Among many other places, the BDS movement is discussed in Shafir, *Half Century of Occupation*, 213–17.
44. Chomsky, "On Israel-Palestine and BDS."
45. Bar-el, "Israel Has Never Been So Secure or Prosperous, but Don't Thank Netanyahu."
46. Levy, "Germany, Shame on You and Your Anti-BDS Resolution."
47. Among other sources, see Harel, "Israel-Hamas Deal Stalls"; Harel, "U.S. Ends Aid to West Bank, Gaza at Palestinian Authority's Request"; Harel, "Final Salvo Campaign Shows Direction He'll Take if He Wins"; Singh, "How to Make Trump's Israeli-Palestinian Peace Plan Work."
48. Jakes and Halbfinger, "In Shift, U.S. Says Israeli Settlements in West Bank Do Not Violate International Law."
49. For example, see Bar'el, "It's Open Season on Land Theft"; Bar'el, "Trump's Poisoned Gift to Israel." The *Haaretz* columnist Gideon Levy wrote: "The settlements are legal. There is no occupation, there is not a Palestinian people, there are no human rights or international law. We can move on to the next stage—annexation and transfer. American will allow these too" (Levy, "New U.S. Stance on Israeli Settlements Is Akin to 'Thou Shalt Murder'").
50. *Peace to Prosperity: A Vision to Improve the Lives of the Palestinian and Israeli People.* https://www.whitehouse.gov/peacetoprosperity/.
51. For an analysis comparing the Trump Plan with Netanyahu's proposals, see Levy, "Don't Call It a Peace Plan." Levy was a member of the Israeli delegations to Oslo and Taba and a lead drafter of the Geneva Accord.
52. For example, in Netanyahu, *A Place among Nations*, and in a major speech at Bar-Ilan University, June 14, 2009; full text in the *Jerusalem Post*. For a review of the Trump Plan's "translations of Netanyahu's ideas into a highly detailed document," see Benn, "Trump Fulfills Netanyahu's Diplomatic Vision."
53. Here the Trump Plan alludes to the ambiguous and now discounted 2005 rhetoric of former Iranian president Ahmadinejad, not repeated by any of his successors.

54. *Peace to Prosperity,* 13.
55. On a personal note, in 1990 I interviewed Yossi Alpher, then deputy head of the Jaffee Center for Strategic Studies, Israel's most prestigious center for security studies. The Jaffee organization had recently published a detailed analysis of the importance of the Jordan Valley to Israel's defense against "the threat from the East." However, it did not mention the war-avoiding and, if necessary, the war-fighting role of Israel's nuclear weapons, since Israel was still unwilling to concede that it had had nuclear weapons for at least twenty years. When I pointed out to Alpher that the study's silence on the nuclear dimension made its strategic analysis largely meaningless, he more or less conceded the point, saying to me: "As you know, we are prohibited from discussing Israeli nuclear weapons, why don't you write about their importance?"
56. For discussions, see Tibon and Landau, "Netanyahu Suggested to U.S. Moving Israeli Arabs to Future Palestinian State, Sources Say." And Shezaf, "Land Swap in South, Population Swap in North: Israel and Palestine According to Trump."
57. *Peace to Prosperity,* 11–12.
58. *Peace to Prosperity,* 48
59. *Peace to Prosperity,* 21.
60. The unsuitability of Abu Dis as a Palestinian capital is described in an uncharacteristically blistering article by Isabel Kershner and David M. Halbfinger, the two leading *New York Times* journalists in Israel: "Capital in Trump Mideast Plan Makes 'a Joke' of Palestinian Aspirations."
61. *Peace to Prosperity,* 14, 29.
62. *Peace to Prosperity,* 35.
63. There are a number of studies of Israel's severe pressures on Iraqi Jews to emigrate to Israel. For example, see Tessler, *A History of the Israeli-Palestinian Conflict,* 310–11.
64. *Peace to Prosperity,* 37, emphasis.
65. Landau, "Gantz Vows to Annex Jordan Valley." If Netanyahu continues as prime minister, whether in rotation with Gantz or not, he will now be freer than ever to annex the Jordan Valley and other parts of the West Bank. However, the fact that he can does not necessarily mean that he will, as the other constraints against annexation remain in place. For analyses, see Judy Maltz, "Netanyahu Can Now Push Through His Annexation Plan for the West Bank—But Will He?," *Haaretz,* May 4, 2020, and Anshel Pfeffer, "Why Netanyahu Will Never Annex West Bank Settlements and the Jordan Valley."
66. "European Union Welcomes Trump 'Efforts' toward Two-State Solution."
67. Assi, "How the Arabs Have Betrayed Palestine—Again."
68. Tibon, "Most Americans Hold Negative View of Israeli Government, Pew Survey Shows."

Chapter 20

1. Shlaim, "The Debate about 1948."
2. Arieli, "Bridging the Gap."
3. Bar-On, *Remembering 1948,* 28, 38–39.
4. Raz, *Bride and the Dowry,* 285.
5. "Conversations with Ilan Pappé."
6. Klein, "The New Israeli Is Frankenstein's Monster."
7. For criticisms of Palestinian violence throughout the course of the conflict by leading Palestinian scholars and activists, see Khalidi, *The Iron Cage,* and Sayigh, "Arafat and the Anatomy of Revolt."
8. Kraft, "42 Percent of Israelis Back West Bank Annexation, including Two-State Supporters."
9. Klein, "Any Solution to the Israeli-Palestinian Conflict Will Lead to Civil War." He explains: "This does not refer only to the ideological investment [in the settlements] and the transfer of settlers. . . . It's also about jobs for hundreds of thousands or millions of Israelis. The existence of an independent Palestinian state in the West Bank and Gaza Strip would require

far more than a political decision or the evacuation of about 100,000 settlers: It would require a total change in direction by the State of Israel."

10. For an analysis, see Levy, "The Theocratization of the Israeli Military."
11. Quoted in Amos Harel, "What Israel Needs Is Strategic Patience, There Are No More Existential Threats." See also Nathan Thrall's earlier assessment: "In 2016 Israel faced no threat of conventional war from any Arab state" (*Only Language They Understand*, Kindle 104).
12. Quoted in Carlo Strenger, "Keepers at the Gates of Our Democracy."
13. As cited by J. J. Goldberg, *The Forward*.
14. "Two New Israeli Defense Brass Join in Support for Breaking the Silence."
15. "Separation into Two States Is Essential for Israel's Security."
16. Quoted in a *Haaretz* editorial, "Mr. Netanyahu's Next Test."
17. Ami Ayalon, Tomair Pardo, and Gadi Shamni, "Netanyahu's Annexation Plan Is a Threat to Israel's National Security," *Foreign Policy*, April 23, 2020.
18. Quoted in Guy Ziv, "Call Yourself a Friend?" *Haaretz*, May 6, 2020.
19. Eldar, "Mideast Peace Can Provide All the Security Israel Needs."
20. The argument is a standard and oft-repeated one in most of Israeli political discourse and in other pro-Israel circles. For example, that is the central argument of Dershowitz, *Case for Israel*.
21. Quoted in Friedman, *From Beirut to Jerusalem*, 439.
22. Quoted from the Israeli dissident publication, +972, December 27, 2013.
23. Sternhell, "Subversive Action against the Jewish People."
24. Chemi Shalev, "American Jewish Leaders Fiddle While Israeli Democracy Burns."
25. Barak, "Last Chance to Save Israeli Democracy," *Haaretz*, February 27, 2020.
26. According to a *Haaretz* study, the binational state has never received more than 20 percent support among Israelis (Maltz, "Special Project on the Two-State Settlement").
27. Klein, *Any Solution*.
28. Sarid, "Sober Up, President Rivlin, from Your Good Intentions."
29. Quoted in Sarid, "Sober Up, President Rivlin, from Your Good Intentions."
30. Maltz, "Special Project."
31. *Bitterlemons*, August 18, 2008.
32. Karmi, "The One-State Solution."
33. Quoted in a 2004 interview with him in *Tikkun*.
34. Morris, "Gideon Levy Is Wrong about the Past, the Present, and I Believe the Future as Well."
35. Quoted in Kuperwasser and Lipner, "Why the PA Must Recognize a Jewish State," 5.
36. Zreik, "Why the 'Jewish State' Now?"
37. For two of the many analyses that stress Netanyahu's seizure on the issue as a way of preventing a two-state solution that he opposes under any conditions, see Zreik, "Why the 'Jewish State' Now?" and Alpher, "A Popular but Problematic Position." Yossi Alpher, former senior official in the Mossad, concluded: "Netanyahu seems to be using the Jewish state demand more as a way of browbeating the Palestinians than as a legitimate means of explaining to Palestinians and their backers the problematic nature of their own positions. . . . This explains the widespread suspicion that the prime minister grasped onto the Jewish state demand as a convenient deal-breaker."
38. For summaries of the arguments, see Strenger, "Is the Law of Return Inherently Racist?" and Wolfe, "Israel's Moral Peril."
39. Arafat, "The Palestinian Vision of Peace."
40. Landau and Eldar, "A Jewish State? 'Definitely.'"
41. Abbas speech of April 27, 2009; accessed from http://www.discoverthenetworks.org/individualProfile.asp?indid=801, January 31, 2012.
42. Beker, "US Jews and Israel versus Barack Obama."
43. As reported in *Haaretz*, January 25, 2011.
44. There have been a number of studies pointing to rising anti-Semitism in the West. For example, see Kingsley, "Anti-Semitism Is Back"; Kingsley, "The Old Scourge of Anti-Semitism

Rises Anew in Europe"; Maltz, "Growing Number of U.S. Jews Support Evacuation of All West Bank Settlements." Several other news stories reported that over half of French and American Jews felt less safe than they did a year ago.

45. Wolfe, *At Home in Exile,* 4.
46. Sternhell, "If I Were a Palestinian."
47. Arens, "Demographic Bogey."
48. Siegman, "Is Israel's Legitimacy under Challenge?"
49. In June 2019, a leading Israeli journalist, in an apparently authoritative analysis, wrote: "Netanyahu doesn't seek to extend Israeli sovereignty over the entire territory. . . . He has no desire to rule directly over the Palestinians and would prefer to see them accepting limited autonomy over disjointed enclaves of Gaza and parts of the West Bank instead. For now, he is content to preserve Israel's rule of Area C—the 60 percent of the West Bank under full Israeli civil and security control. Sovereignty can wait, if necessary, for another generation. . . . Netanyahu would prefer not to provoke another intifada or jeopardize the ties he is building with the Saudis and other Arab regimes by annexing parts of the West Bank anytime soon" (Pfeffer, "With Annexationist Comment, Friedman Just Made Netanyahu's Life More Difficult"). In May 2020, Pfeffer repeated his analysis, which is shared by many Israeli political commentators, that despite his electoral rhetoric, Netanyahu has never really been willing to risk the consequences of outright annexation, and now that it appears likely he will remain in power for at least 18 months, if not longer, he now will no longer need to appease the settlers and the extremist Israeli rightwingers. Pfeffer, "Why Israel Will Never Annex."
50. For a detailed analysis, see Mehmet, "Growth and Equity in Microstates: Does Size Matter in Development?"
51. In his book *Catch-67,* the Israeli analyst Micah Goodman proposes a variation of the ministate idea, though he does not call it that, and in other ways it significantly differs from the one discussed here: while Israel would maintain control over Area C, the plan would require it to withdraw from Areas A and B. Such an arrangement, he writes, would give the Palestinians only an "almost" state, and the Israeli residents of Area C would be "almost" citizens of Israel. But in that case, it is not clear why either the Palestinians or the Israelis would accept it.

    Further, the Palestinians would not be required to recognize Israel and "would be expected neither to forgo the return of refugees, nor to reconcile themselves to alien sovereignty over Islamic soil, nor even to agree to end the conflict permanently or renounce all their claims" (Goodman, *Catch-67*, Kindle location 1825). However, in that case why would Israel agree?

    In a brief but intriguing passage, Martin Indyk writes that in 1993, Shimon Peres outlined to Arafat a "vision of a Gaza that would become the Middle East's Singapore." Arafat did not reject that idea, and implied that if the Palestinian choice was "between Soweto and Singapore," it might be acceptable if it would have to have "American support in all aspects of their development" (Indyk, *Innocent Abroad,* Kindle location 1274). Obviously, nothing came of the Peres-Arafat exchange, but it did demonstrate that even the Palestinians' most important leader did not reject the ministate concept out of hand.
52. These factors are more fully discussed in Chapter 1.
53. The literature on the steadily declining US dependence on Middle East oil is extensive. A good summary is Reed, "The Oil Market Shows It Can Take a Punch." A different issue, of course, is whether it's actually a good thing that the United States is producing more oil, but that's beyond the scope of this book.
54. Issacharoff, ""Osama Bin Laden Blames Israel for America's Mideast Problems."
55. As summarized by the 9/11 Commission, reported in Stephen Walt, *ForeignPolicy.com,* November 9, 2011.
56. Quoted in Madar, "Washington's Military Aid to Israel."
57. Rosenberg, "American Aid Will Be the Death of Israel."

58. For an overview of US economic and military support of Israel, direct and indirect, public and private, see Koplow, "Value Judgment: Why Do Americans Support Israel?" and a report by the Congressional Research Service, "U.S. Foreign Aid to Israel."
59. Quoted in Ben-Zvi, *United States and Israel,* 116.
60. Roy, "A Dubai on the Mediterranean."
61. Quoted in Shlaim, *Iron Wall,* Kindle 320.
62. Quoted in Eldar, "Israel's New Politics and the Fate of Palestine."
63. For example, Daniel Pipes, a prominent American right-wing political commentator and long a near-unconditional supporter of Israeli policies, including its occupation of the West Bank, recently wrote a remarkable op-ed for the *New York Times,* giving six reasons why Israel should not annex *any* of the West Bank. Among those reasons, he argued, are to avoid "radicalizing the Israeli Left and harming the Zionist goal of a Jewish state"; to stop alienating American Jews and Democrats and the European states; to prevent a break with Saudi Arabia and other Sunni Arab states; to avoid the destabilization of Jordan; and to avoid provoking a new Palestinian intifada. Daniel Pipes, "Annexing the West Bank Would Hurt Israel," *New York Times,* May 7, 2020.
64. "How to Save Israel in Spite of Herself."
65. Quoting the paraphrased Frankel columns in Christison, *Perceptions,* 222.
66. Quoted in *New York Times,* September 11, 1997.
67. Quoted in Eldar, "Two Plus Two Are Always Four—Or Are They?"
68. Landau, "Good News from the Rubble."
69. Sternhell, "An Imposed Solution Is the Only Option." Recently Sternhell has repeated his call for "all means of [US] pressure to be utilized" against Israel's settlement policies (*Haaretz,* December 30, 2019).
70. The Toon cable is discussed in Amir Oren, "Reflections on a Tortured Part of the World, *Haaretz,* April 9, 2010.
71. Chamberlain, *Global Offensive,* 265.
72. Daniel Levy, quoted in Cooper, "Rice's Way: Restraint in Quest for Peace."
73. As quoted in the *New York Times,* July 25, 1980.
74. Quoted in the *New York Review,* August 13, 1981.
75. Eldar, "Electricity in the Air."
76. For example, see Beinart, *Crisis of Zionism,* 171; Mayer, "Why Young Jews and Democrats Are Waving Goodbye to AIPAC"; Maltz, "Young American Jews Increasingly Turning Away from Israel"; Ziri, "2020 Candidates' Stand on Israel Is Lowest Priority for U.S. Jews, Poll Shows"; Maltz, "Growing Number of U.S. Jews Support Evacuation of All West Bank Settlements, Survey Finds."
77. Shalev, "2010–2019, the Decade That Devoured the Ties between Israel and U.S. Jews."
78. Kampeas, "Why Israel Isn't a Top Consideration for American Jewish Voters."
79. "Criticize Israel? For Democratic Voters, It's Now Fair Game."
80. Beinart, "Democratic Party Split."
81. Beinart, "Democratic Party Split."
82. Tibon, "House Democrats Chide State Department for Settlement Policy Reversal."
83. Shalev, "House Resolution on Annexation Is a Wake-Up Call for Israel and Netanyahu." Shalev commented that the resolution "highlighted the growing gap between the party and not only Netanyahu, but also Israel's right wing as a whole . . . [and] marks a clear-cut victory for the left-leaning lobby J Street, which supported the resolution, over its main rival AIPAC."
84. Maltz, "Netanyahu's Embrace of Trump Is Driving U.S. Jews Away from Israel, Survey Shows."
85. Maltz, "Netanyahu's Embrace of Trump Is Driving U.S. Jews Away from Israel, Survey Shows."
86. Quoted in Beinart, "Democratic Party Split over Military Aid to Israel."
87. Gordon and Goldenberg, "Sign Up for Trump's Peace Plan, Sign Away Israel's Special Status in America."

88. For the best summary of the discussions, together with an argument for the desirability of a mutual defense pact in the context of an overall peace settlement, see Allin and Simon, *Separate Ways,* 222–28.
89. On Gantz's opposition, see Freilich, "Israel Needs a Mutual Defense Treaty with America—Now."
90. Yaniv, *Deterrence without the Bomb,* 13.
91. Allin and Simon, *Separate Ways,* 223; Schiff, "The Pact That Ben-Gurion Wanted"; Freilich, "Israel Needs a Mutual Defense Treaty."
92. In 1956, Dulles publicly said that "the United States never seriously considered making an alliance as long as no arrangement between Israel and the Arabs had been settled." Quoted in Bialer, *Between East and West,* 274.
93. Quoted from US government documents, in Ben-Zvi, *Decade of Transition,* 71.
94. Quoted in Laron, *Six-Day War,* Kindle 204, and Ross, *Doomed to Succeed,* Kindle location 1531.
95. Maoz, *Syria and Israel,* 86; Clarke, "Entanglement: The Commitment to Israel," 218.
96. Whetten, *Canal War,* 116.
97. From a 1992 letter of Nixon to the Israeli journalists Dan Raviv and Yossi Melman, quoted in Raviv and Melman, *Friends in Deed,* 460.
98. On the suggestions of Vance, Brown, and Brzezinski, see Brzezinski, *Power and Principle,* 249, 280; Quandt, *Camp David,* 242.
99. Carter, *Keeping the Faith,* 355.
100. Bregman quotes from the notes of Barak's chief of staff: "The Prime Minister asked Clinton for . . . a Defense pact [between Israel and the US] which would cover a non-conventional missile attack and a full conventional attack . . . [i.e. a non-conventional weapon attack on Israel would be met with an equivalent attack by the US]," *Cursed Victory,* Kindle 235. See also Allin and Simon, *Our Separate Ways,* 223–24, and Schiff, "Pact Ben-Gurion Wanted."
101. Benn, "At Camp David, Barak and Clinton Agreed on a Nuclear Defense Treaty"; Freilich, "A Mutual Defense Treaty."
102. Kurtzer et al., *Peace Puzzle,* 157.
103. There have been a number of reports in *Haaretz* on the Netanyahu-Trump discussions of a mutual defense treaty. See "Trump's Peace Plan"; Tibon and Harel, "Netanyahu, Trump in Intensive Talks for Dramatic Diplomatic Gesture"; Tibon, "Trump, Netanyahu Discuss Iran, Annexing Jordan Valley"; Freilich, "Israel Needs a Mutual Defense Treaty with America—Now."
104. *New York Times,* September 18, 2019.
105. Retired US admiral James Stavridis, a former commander of NATO, recently proposed a carefully limited and narrow US-Israeli mutual defense treaty. Unlike NATO and other US defense treaties, which "state unequivocally that an attack on one is an attack on all," he writes, his proposal "would cover only a defined set of exceptional circumstances that would place either country in extreme peril." In particular, it would commit the United States to come to the aid of Israel only if "Israel's strategic and economic viability" was threatened, especially by nuclear threats or major land attacks by Iran or a coalition of Arab states. Stavridis, "For a Narrow U.S.-Israel Defense Pact."

SELECT BIBLIOGRAPHY

Adet, Ofer. "Jordan and Israel Cooperated during Yom Kippur War, Documents Reveal." *Haaretz*, September 12, 2013.

Allen, Harry S., and Ivan Volges. *Israel, the Middle East, and U.S. Interests*. New York: Praeger, 1983.

Allin, Dana H., and Steven N. Simon. *Our Separate Ways: The Struggle for the Future of the U.S.-Israel Alliance*. New York: Public Affairs, 2016.

Alon, Gideon. "Irate Likud MKs Put PM on the Defensive." *Haaretz*, May 27, 2003.

Alpher, Rogel. "Israeli Right Wants End to Peace with Jordan." *Haaretz*, December 22, 2019.

Alpher, Rogel. "A Lottery to Pick the Next Israeli Victims of West Bank Annexation Policy." *Haaretz*, March 31, 2019.

Alpher, Yossi. "Issue Brief." March 31, 2003.

Alpher, Yossi. "A Popular but Problematic Position." *bitterlemons*, October 25, 2010.

Amirav, Moshe. "Time Is Ripe for Borders." *Haaretz*, April 9, 2006.

"Amnesty: Israel Committed War Crimes in Lebanon Campaign." *Haaretz*, August 23, 2006.

Anziska, Seth. *Preventing Palestine: A Political History from Camp David to Oslo*. Princeton, NJ: Princeton University Press, 2018.

Arab Peace Initiative (text). *New York Times*, March 29, 2002.

Arafat, Yasser. "The Palestinian Vision of Peace." *New York Times*, February 3, 2002.

"Arafat's Gift," interview with Jeffrey Goldberg. *New Yorker*, January 29, 2001.

"Arafat's Letter of Reservations to President Clinton," Special Dispatch, no. 170, January 3, 2001. *Memri*, January 3, 2001.

Arens, Moshe. "Demographic Bogey." *Haaretz*, September 14, 2010.

Arieli, Shaul. "Bridging the Gap." *Haaretz*, April 10, 2009.

Arieli, Shaul. "Palestinian Critics Shouldn't Be So Hasty to Dismiss Abbas." *Haaretz*, January 29, 2011.

Arieli, Shaul. "Netanyahu's 'Map' Is a Non-Starter." *Haaretz*, June 3, 2013.

Arieli, Shaul. "Netanyahu Could Learn from Sharon's Realistic Approach to Zionism." *Haaretz*, February 4, 2014.

Arieli, Shaul. "The Palestinian Question." *Haaretz*, April 17, 2016.

Arieli, Shaul. "Those Undermining the Jewish State." *Haaretz*, August 25, 2016.

Arieli, Shaul. "Zionism Doesn't Need 'Divine Promise' to Justify Jewish Nation-State." *Haaretz*, October 22, 2017.

Aronson, Shlomo. *Conflict and Bargaining in the Middle East*. Baltimore: Johns Hopkins University Press, 1978.

Ashkenazy, Amit, and Noah Efron. "Israel's Future Saviors Wear IDF Uniforms." *Haaretz*, April 18, 2019.

Aspaturian, Vernon V. "Soviet Policy in the Middle East." In *Israel, the Middle East, and U.S. Interests,* edited by Harry S. Allen and Ivan Volgyes. New York: Praeger, 1983.

Assi, Seraj. "How the Arabs Have Betrayed Palestine—Again." *Haaretz,* February 3, 2020.

Atherton, Alfred. "The Soviet Role in the Middle East." *Middle East Journal* 39 (Autumn 1985).

Atran, Scott. "Is Hamas Ready to Deal?" *New York Times,* August 17, 2006.

Avineri, Shlomo. "What to Speak with Hamas About." *Haaretz,* April 6, 2009.

Avishai, Bernard. "A Plan for Peace That Could Still Be." *New York Times,* February 12, 2011.

Avnery, Uri. *1948: A Soldier's Tale.* London: One World Publications, 2008.

Avnery, Uri. "Shukran, Israel." *Haaretz,* December 31, 2011.

Avnery, Uri. "In Their Shoes." *Haaretz,* April 6, 2013.

Bailey, Sydney D. *Four Arab-Israeli Wars and the Peace Process.* London: Macmillan, 1990.

Ball, George W., and Douglas B. Ball. *The Passionate Attachment: America's Involvement with Israel, 1947 to the Present.* New York: W. W. Norton, 1992.

Baram, Nir. Interview of Benny Morris. *Haaretz,* February 9, 2007.

Bar'el, Zvi. "Meshal Declaration Basic Shift in Hamas's Position." *Haaretz,* January 11, 2007.

Bar'el, Zvi. "Let's Calm Down on Syria and Hezbollah." *Haaretz,* February 28, 2010.

Bar'el, Zvi. "Meshal Says Hamas Accepts a Two-State Solution." *Haaretz,* January 30, 2013.

Bar-el, Zvi. "Israel Has Never Been So Secure or Prosperous, but Don't Thank Netanyahu." *Haaretz,* August 24, 2016.

Bar'el, Zvi. "It's Open Season on Land Theft." *Haaretz,* November 20, 2019.

Bar'el, Zvi. "Trump's Poisoned Gift to Israel." *Haaretz* editorial, November 20, 2019.

Bar-Joseph, Uri. *The Best of Enemies: Israel and Transjordan in the War of 1948.* London: Frank Cass, 1987.

Bar-Joseph, Uri. "The Iranian Threat and the Arab Peace Initiative." *Haaretz,* October 9, 2017.

Bar-On, Mordechai. *The Gates of Gaza: Israel's Road to Suez and Back, 1955–57.* London: Palgrave Macmillan, 1995.

Bar-On, Mordechai. *Remembering 1948.* Ann Arbor: University of Michigan Press, 1996.

Bar-Simon Tov, Yaacov. *Israel, the Superpowers, and the War in the Middle East.* New York: Praeger, 1987.

Bar-Tal, Daniel. *Intractable Conflicts: Socio-Psychological Foundations and Dynamics.* Cambridge: Cambridge University Press, 2013.

Bar-Tal, Daniel. "How Israeli Politicians Took Peace with the Palestinians off the Table." *Haaretz,* September 11, 2016.

Bar-Zohar, Michael. *Ben-Gurion: A Biography.* New York: Delacorte Press, 1977.

Bar-Zohar, Michael. *Facing a Cruel Mirror.* New York: Charles Scribner's Sons, 1990.

Baskin, Gershon. "What Went Wrong?" Jerusalem: Israeli-Palestinian Center for Research and Information, May 22, 2001.

Baskin, Gershon. "Encountering Peace." *Jerusalem Post,* September 29, 2009.

Baskin, Gershon. "Israel's Short-Sighted Assassination." *New York Times,* November 17, 2012.

Bass, Warren. *Support Any Friend: Kennedy's Middle East and the Making of the U.S.-Israel Alliance.* New York: Oxford University Press, 2003.

Beaumont, Peter. "Olmert Rejected Palestinian Attempts to Set Up Talks through Go-Between before Gaza Invasion." *The Guardian,* March 1, 2009.

Beilin, Yossi. Op-ed for the *New York Times,* April 18, 2001.

Beilin,Yossi. "What Really Happened at Taba." *Haaretz,* July 15, 2002.

Beilin, Yossi. *The Path to Geneva: The Quest for a Permanent Agreement, 1996–2004.* New York: RDV Books, 2004.

Beilin, Yossi, and Yasir Abed Rabbo. "A Mideast Partnership Can Still Work," joint op-ed. *New York Times,* August 1, 2001.

Beinart, Peter. *The Crisis of Zionism.* New York: Henry Holt, 2012.

Beinart, Peter. "Gaza Myths and Facts: What American Jewish Leaders Won't Tell You." *Haaretz,* July 30, 2014.

Beinart, Peter. "For the American Right, Israel Embodies the Values That Obama's U.S. No Longer Does." *Haaretz*, April 30, 2015.

Beinart, Peter. "Democratic Party Split over Military Aid to Israel." *Forward*, October 30, 2019.

Beinart, Peter. "It's Time to End America's Blank-Check Military Aid to Israel." *Forward*, May 23, 2019.

Beinin, Joel. "Forgetfulness for Memory: The Limits of the New Israeli History." *Journal of Palestine Studies* 34, no. 2 (Winter 2005).

Beit-Hallahmi, Benny. *Original Sins: Reflections on the History of Zionism and Israel*. London: Pluto Press, 1992.

Beker, Avi. "US Jews and Israel versus Barack Obama." *Haaretz*, October 17, 2010.

Ben-Ami, Shlomo. *Scars of War, Wounds of Peace: The Israel-Arab Tragedy*. New York: Oxford University Press, 2006.

Ben-Ami, Shlomo. "A War to Start All Wars." *Foreign Affairs*, September–October 2008.

Ben-Gurion, David. *My Talks with Arab Leaders*. Jerusalem: Keter Books, 1972.

Benjamin, Uzi. "Sharon's Work." *Haaretz*, December 15, 2002.

Benn, Aluf. "Barak: Past PMs Set Syria Talks on '67 Lines." *Haaretz*, February 28, 2000.

Benn, Aluf. "At Camp David, Barak and Clinton Agreed on a Nuclear Defense Treaty." *Haaretz*, July 17, 2002.

Benn, Aluf. "Sharon's Vision." *Haaretz*, April 26, 2005.

Benn, Aluf. "PM Speech Intended to Promote West Bank Withdrawal." *Haaretz*, November 28, 2006.

Benn, Aluf. "My Ideas Will Prevail." *Haaretz*, June 26, 2009.

Benn, Aluf. "Assad's Israeli Friend." *Haaretz*, March 28, 2013.

Benn, Aluf. "Trump Fulfills Netanyahu's Diplomatic Vision." *Haaretz*, January 30, 2020.

Benn, Aluf, and Barak Ravid. "Olmert Offered to Withdraw from 93% of West Bank." *Haaretz*, June 22, 2009.

Benvenisti, Meron. "An Explosive, Dangerous Balance." *Haaretz*, March 1, 2008.

Benziman, Uri. "Reading Barak's Body Language." *Haaretz*, September 22, 2000.

Ben-Zvi, Abraham. *Alliance Politics and the Limits of Influence: The Case of the US and Israel, 1975–1981*. Tel Aviv: Jaffee Center for Strategic Studies, 1984.

Ben-Zvi, Abraham. *The United States and Israel*. New York: Columbia University Press, 1993.

Ben-Zvi, Abraham. *Decade of Transition. Eisenhower, Kennedy, and the Origins of the American-Israel Alliance*. New York: Columbia University Press, 1998.

Berger, Yotam. "Declassified: Israel Made Sure Arabs Couldn't Return to Their Villages." *Haaretz*, May 27, 2019.

Berger, Yotam, and Noa Landau. "At West Bank Event, Netanyahu Promises No More Settlers, Arabs Will Be Evicted." *Haaretz*, July 10, 2019.

Bergman, Ronen. *Rise and Kill First: The Secret History of Israel's Targeted Assassinations*. New York: Random House, 2018.

Bialer, Uri. *Between East and West: Israel's Foreign Policy Orientation, 1948–1956*. Cambridge: Cambridge University Press, 1990.

Bird, Kai. *The Good Spy: The Life and Death of Robert Ames*. New York: Crown, 2014.

Blatman, Daniel. "The Banality of Evil Revisited: To Each Society Their Own Evils." *Haaretz*, August 21, 2016.

Blatman, Daniel. "Netanyahu, This Is What Ethnic Cleansing Really Looks Like." *Haaretz*, October 3, 2016.

Blumenthal, Max. *The 51-Day War: Ruin and Resistance in Gaza*. New York: Nation Books, 2016.

Bowersock, G. W. "The Many Lives of Palestine." *New York Review*, April 18, 2019.

Brecher, Michael. *Decisions in Israel's Foreign Policy*. London: Oxford University Press, 1974.

Bregman, Ahron. *Elusive Peace: How the Holy Land Defeated America*. London: Penguin Books, 2005.

Bregman, Ahron. *Cursed Victory. Israel and the Occupied Territories: A History*. New York: Pegasus Books, 2014.

Breslauer, George W. "Soviet Policy in the Middle East, 1967–1972." In *Managing U.S.-Soviet Rivalry*, edited by Alexander A. George. Boulder, CO: Westview Press, 1983.

Breslauer, George W. "On Collaborative Competition." In *Soviet Strategy in the Middle East*, edited by George W. Breslauer. Boston: Unwin Hyman, 1990.

Breslauer, George W., ed. *Soviet Strategy in the Middle East*. Boston: Unwin Hyman, 1990.

Bronner, Ethan. "Olmert Says Israel Must Leave West Bank." *New York Times*, September 30, 2008.

Bronner, Ethan. "Truce in Gaza Ends, but May Be Revived by Necessity." *New York Times*, December 19, 2008.

Bronner, Ethan, and Taghreed El-Khodary. "Hamas Fires Rockets into Israel." *New York Times*, November 15, 2008.

Bronner, Ethan, and Sabrina Tavernise. "In Shattered Gaza Town, Roots of Seething Split." *New York Times*, February 4, 2009.

Brown, L. Carl. *International Politics and the Middle East*. Princeton, NJ: Princeton University Press, 1984.

Bruck, Connie. "Friends of Israel." *New Yorker*, September 1, 2014.

Brzezinski, Zbigniew. *Power and Principle: Memoirs of the National Security Advisor, 1977–1981*. New York: Farrar, Straus and Giroux, 1983.

B'Tselem. "Human Rights Review." January 1, 2009, to April 30, 2010.

"B'Tselem: Israeli Security Forces Killed 660 Palestinians in 2006." *Haaretz*, December 31, 2006.

Burg, Avraham. "End of an Era." *Haaretz*, August 5, 2005.

Burston, Bradley. "Can the First Gaza War Be Stopped before It Starts?" *Haaretz*, December 22, 2010.

Buttu, Diana. "Success in Oslo: The Bantustanisation of Palestinian Territories." In *After Zionism: One State for Israel and Palestine*, edited by Anthony Lowenstein and Ahmed Moor. London: Saqi Books, 2012.

Caplan, Neil. "A Tale of Two Cities: The Rhodes and Lausanne Conferences, 1949." *Journal of Palestine Studies* 21, no. 3 (Spring 1992).

Carey, Roane. "Goldstone Reports." *The Nation*, October 12, 2009.

Carter, Jimmy. *Keeping Faith: Memoirs of a President*. New York: Bantam Books, 1982.

Carter, Jimmy. *Blood of Abraham: Insights into the Middle East*. Boston: Houghton Mifflin, 1985.

Caspi, Ari. "Running Out of Time." *Haaretz*, June 7, 2001.

Chamberlain, Paul Thomas. *The Global Offensive: The US, the PLO, and the Making of the Post–Cold War Order*. New York: Oxford University Press, 2012.

Chamberlain, Paul Thomas. "When It Pays to Talk to Terrorists." *New York Times*, September 4, 2012.

Chomsky, Noam. *Middle East Illusions*. Lanham, MD: Rowman and Littlefield, 2003.

Chomsky, Noam. "On Israel-Palestine and BDS." *Nation*, July 2, 2014.

Chomsky, Noam. *The Fateful Triangle*. Updated ed. Chicago: Haymarket Books, 2015.

Chowers, Eyal. "Peel Back Time: Should Israelis Revisit the Partition Plan of 1937?" *Haaretz*, September 6, 2012.

Christison, Kathleen. *Perceptions of Palestine: Their Influence on U.S. Middle East Policy*. Berkeley: University of California Press, 1999.

"Civilian Casualties in Lebanon during the 2006 War." Human Rights Watch, September 5, 2007.

Clarke, Duncan L. "Entanglement: The Commitment to Israel." In *The Arab-Israeli Conflict*, edited by Yehuda Lukacs and Abdalla M. Battah. Boulder, CO: Westview, 1988.

Clifford, Clark, and Richard Holbrooke. "Serving the President: The Truman Years." *New Yorker*, March 25, 1991.

Clinton, Bill. *My Life*. New York: Alfred A. Knopf, 2004.

Cobban, Helen. *The Israeli-Syrian Peace Talks: 1991–96 and Beyond*. Washington, DC: US Institute of Peace, 2000.

Cohen, Aharon. *Israel and the Arab World*. Boston: Beacon Press, 1976.

Cohen, Avner. "Stumbling into Opacity: The United States, Israel, and the Atom, 1960–63." *Security Studies* 4, no. 2 (Winter 1994/95).
Cohen, Avner. *Israel and the Bomb*. New York: Columbia University Press, 1999.
Cohen, Avner. "How Israel Helped Spawn Hamas." *Wall Street Journal*, January 24, 2009.
Cohen, Avner. "When Israel Stepped Back from the Brink." *New York Times*, October 3, 2013.
Cohen, Avner, and William Barr. "How a Standoff with the U.S. Almost Blew Up Israel's Nuclear Program." *Haaretz*, May 3, 2019.
Cohen, Gili. "B'Tselem: More Than 50 Percent of Palestinians Killed in Israel's Last Gaza Operation Were Civilians." *Haaretz*, May 9, 2013.
Cohen, Michael J. *The Origins and Evolution of the Arab-Zionist Conflict*. Berkeley: University of California Press, 1987.
Cohen, Michael J. *Truman and Israel*. Berkeley: University of California Press, 1990.
Cohen, Roger. "The Fierce Urgency of Peace." *New York Times*, March 26, 2009.
Commanders for Israel's Security. "Ramifications of West Bank Annexation: Security and Beyond," October 2018.
Congressional Research Service. "U.S. Foreign Aid to Israel." April 20, 2018.
"Conversations with Ilan Pappé." *Logos*, Winter 2004.
Cooper, Helene. "Rice's Way: Restraint in Quest for Peace." *New York Times*, November 29, 2007.
Copeland, Miles. *The Game of Nations*. London: Weidenfeld and Nicolson, 1969.
"Criticize Israel? For Democratic Voters, It's Now Fair Game." *New York Times*, November 2, 2019.
Cygielman, Victor. "No, Oslo Is Not Dead." *Palestine-Israel Journal of Politics, Economics and Culture* 5 (Winter 1995).
Daigle, Craig. *The Limits of Détente: The United States, the Soviet Union, and the Arab-Israeli Conflict, 1969–1973*. New Haven, CT: Yale University Press, 2012.
Davis, Julie Hirschfeld. "Influential Pro-Israel Group Suffers a Stinging Political Defeat." *New York Times*, September 11, 2015.
Dayan, Aryeh. "Barak Began Referring to 'Holy of Holies.'" *Haaretz*, December 9, 2002.
Derfner, Larry. *No Country for Jewish Liberals*. Washington, DC: Just World Books, 2016.
Dershowitz, Alan. *The Case for Israel*. New York: John Wiley, 2003.
Diab, Khaled. "The Arab World's Missed Opportunities." *Haaretz*, November 4, 2012.
Diab, Khaled. "Israel's Missed Opportunities." *Haaretz*, October 22, 2012.
Diskin, Johann Hari. "The True Story behind This War Is Not the One Israel Is Telling." *The Independent*, January 15, 2009.
Downes, Alexander B. "The Holy Land Divided: Defending Partition as a Solution to Ethnic Wars." *Security Studies* 10, no. 4 (Summer 2001).
Drucker, Raviv. "Hamas Has Proven Israel Only Understands Force." *Haaretz*, August 22, 2018.
Drysdale, Alisdair, and Raymond A. Hinnebusch. *Syria and the Middle East Peace Process*. New York: Council on Foreign Relations, 1991.
Eban, Abba. *Abba Eban: An Autobiography*. New York: Random House, 1977.
Eban, Abba. *Personal Witness: Israel through My Eyes*. New York: G. P. Putnam's Sons, 1992.
Editorial, *Buffalo News*, May 4, 2002.
"Egypt's Sissi Confirms Unprecedented Military Cooperation with Israel." *Haaretz*, January 4, 2009.
Ehrenreich, Ben. *The Way to the Spring: Life and Death in Palestine*. New York: Penguin Books, 2017.
Eldar, Akiva. "Bordering on the Ridiculous." *Haaretz*, May 4, 2000.
Eldar, Akiva. "A Framework for Peace between Israel and Syria." *Haaretz*, January 13, 2000.
Eldar, Akiva. *Haaretz*, September 18, 2001.
Eldar, Akiva. "On the Basis of the Nonexistent Camp David Understandings." *Haaretz*, November 16, 2001.
Eldar, Akiva. "Two Plus Two Are Always Four—Or Are They?" *Haaretz*, September 12, 2002.
Eldar, Akiva. "Arafat Recognizes Jewish Ties to Zion." *Haaretz*, December 11, 2003.

Eldar, Akiva. "They Just Can't Hear Each Other." *Haaretz*, March 11, 2003.
Eldar, Akiva. "Learning from Past Mistakes." *Haaretz*, May 2, 2004.
Eldar, Akiva. "Popular Misconceptions." *Haaretz*, June 11, 2004.
Eldar, Akiva. "Israelis, Syrians Reach Secret Understandings." *Haaretz*, January 16, 2007.
Eldar, Akiva. "What Arab Initiative?" *Haaretz*, March 6, 2007.
Eldar, Akiva. "With Friends Like These . . ." *Haaretz*, June 25, 2007.
Eldar, Akiva. "Evacuate Jewish Hebron." *Haaretz*, November 3, 2008.
Eldar, Akiva. "The Road to Hell." *Haaretz*, June 20, 2008.
Eldar, Akiva. "Small Piece of Land Could Scupper Israel-Syria Talks." *Haaretz*, May 22, 2008.
Eldar, Akiva. "Talking Like Meretz, Behaving Like the Likud." *Haaretz*, March 17, 2008.
Eldar, Akiva. "Military Intelligence: Never Expected Hamas Victory in 2006." *Haaretz*, January 9, 2009.
Eldar, Akiva. "Arab Peace Initiative Is Another Missed Opportunity for Israel." *Haaretz*, March 28, 2011.
Eldar, Akiva. "Electricity in the Air." *Haaretz*, August 12, 2011.
Eldar, Akiva. "Mideast Peace Can Provide All the Security Israel Needs." *Haaretz*, September 27, 2011.
Eldar, Akiva. "Where Was Barak When Israel and the Palestinians Were Working Out a Peace Deal?" *Haaretz*, January 25, 2011.
Eldar, Akiva. "Israel's New Politics and the Fate of Palestine." *National Interest*, July–August 2012.
Elgindy, Khaled. *Blind Spot: America and the Palestinians from Balfour to Trump*. Washington, DC: Brookings Institution Press, 2019.
El-Khodary, Taghreed, and Ethan Bronner. "Addressing U.S., Hamas Says It Grounded Rockets." *New York Times*, May 5, 2009.
El-Khodary, Taghreed, and Isabel Kershner. "Gaza Is Tense as It Tallies Casualties." *New York Times*, January 2, 2008.
Elon, Amos. *Herzl*. New York: Holt, Rinehart and Winston, 1975.
Elon, Amos. "Look over Jordan." *New York Review*, April 21, 1994.
Elon, Amos. "Israelis and Palestinians: What Went Wrong." *New York Review of Books*, December 19, 2002.
"End the Blockade, Aid Gaza's Economy." *Haaretz* editorial, November 14, 2019.
Enderlin, Charles. *Shattered Dreams: The Failure of the Peace Process in the Middle East, 1995–2002*. New York: Other Press, 2002.
Erlanger, Steven. "Israel's Dilemma in Response to Rockets." *New York Times*, December 19, 2007.
Ernst, Morris L. *So Far, So Good*. New York: Harper & Brothers, 1948.
"European Union Welcomes Trump 'Efforts' toward Two-State Solution." *Haaretz*, January 29, 2020.
"Everyone Thinks That Jerusalem Is Lost." *Haaretz*, November 12, 2008.
Evron, Yair. *The Middle East: Nations, Superpowers, and Wars*. New York: Praeger, 1973.
"Ex-IDF Chief: Golan Heights Not Indispensable." *Haaretz*, May 23, 2008.
"Ex-Shin Bet Heads Warn of 'Catastrophe' without Peace Deal." *Yediot Aharanot*, November 14, 2003.
Feldman, Shai. *Israeli Nuclear Deterrence*. New York: Columbia University Press, 1982.
Finkelstein, Israel, and Neil Asher Silberman. *The Bible Unearthed: Archaeology's New Vision of Ancient Israel and the Origin of Its Sacred Texts*. New York: Free Press, 2001.
Finney, John W. "US Hears Israel Moves toward A-Bomb Potential." *New York Times*, December 19, 1960.
Flapan, Simha. *Zionism and the Palestinians*. London: Croom Helm, 1979.
Flapan, Simha. *The Birth of Israel*. New York: Pantheon, 1987.
Fogelman, Shay. "The Disinherited." *Haaretz*, July 30, 2010.
"Former Top Israeli Diplomat Says Syria Ready to Cut Iran Ties." *Haaretz*, July 6, 2008.

Frankel, Jonathan, ed. *Jews and Messianism in the Modern Era*. New York: Oxford University Press, 1991.

Freedman, Robert O. "Moscow and a Middle East Peace Settlement." *Washington Quarterly* 8 (Summer 1985).

Freilich, Chuck. "Israel Needs a Mutual Defense Treaty with America—Now." *Haaretz*, December 5, 2019.

Friedman, Thomas. *From Beirut to Jerusalem*. New York: Farrar, Straus and Giroux, 1989.

Gabbay, Rony. *A Political Study of the Arab-Jewish Conflict: The Arab Refugee Problem*. Geneva: Libraire E. Droz, 1959.

Galili, Lily. "Poll: More Israelis Object to Golan Accord than to Jerusalem Deal." *Haaretz*, May 22, 2008.

Gambill, Gary C. "The Balance of Terror." *Journal of Palestine Studies* 29, no. 1 (Autumn 1998).

Gans, Chaim. *A Just Zionism: On the Morality of the Jewish State*. New York: Oxford University Press, 2008.

Gans, Chaim. "Palestinians Were Made to Pay an Unfair Price." *Haaretz*, June 27, 2009.

Garfinkle, Adam. *Israel and Jordan in the Shadow of War*. New York: St. Martins Press, 1992.

Garthoff, Raymond. *Détente and Confrontation*. Washington, DC: Brookings Institution Press, 1985.

"Gaza Could Become 'Uninhabitable' by 2020, UN Report Warns." *Haaretz*, September 2, 2015.

"Gaza Deal Is in Israeli Interests." *Haaretz*, editorial, December 31, 2019.

Gendizer, Irene L. *Dying to Forget: Oil, Power, Palestine, and the Foundations of U.S. Policy in the Middle East*. New York: Columbia University Press, 2015.

Gill, Natasha. "The Original 'No': Why the Arabs Rejected Zionism, and Why It Matters." *Middle East Policy Council*, June 19, 2013.

Glassman, John D. *Arms for the Arabs: The Soviet Union and War in the Middle East*. Baltimore: Johns Hopkins University Press, 1975.

Gluska, Ami. "The Old Man's 'Day of Horrors.'" *Haaretz*, June 3, 2011.

Golan, Galia. *Yom Kippur and After*. New York: Cambridge University Press, 1977.

Golan, Galia. *The Soviet Union and the Palestine Liberation Organization*. New York: Praeger, 1980.

Golan, Galia. *Israeli Peacemaking since 1967*. New York: Routledge, 2015.

Golani, Motti. "Zionism without Zion: The Jerusalem Question, 1947–1949." *Journal of Israeli History* 16, no. 1 (1995).

Golani, Motti. *Israel in Search of a War: The Sinai Campaign, 1955–1956*. Portland, OR: Sussex Academic Press, 1998.

Goldberg, J. J. *Jewish Power: Inside the American Jewish Establishment*. New York: Perseus Books, 1996.

Goldberg, J. J. *The Forward*, November 3, 2014.

Goldmann, Nahum. *The Jewish Paradox*. London: Weidenfeld and Nicolson, 1978.

Goodman, Micah. *Catch-67: The Left, the Right, and the Legacy of the Six-Day War*. New Haven, CT: Yale University Press, 2018.

Gorenberg, Gershon. *The Accidental Empire: Israel and the Birth of the Settlements*. New York: Henry Holt, 2006.

Gorenberg, Gershon. *The Unmaking of Israel*. New York: HarperCollins, 2011.

Gordon, Philip, and Ilan Goldenberg. "Sign Up for Trump's Peace Plan, Sign Away Israel's Special Status in America." *Haaretz*, February 2, 2020.

Green, David B. "This Day in Jewish History 1973: Moshe Dayan Allegedly Suggests Israel Demonstrate Its Nuclear Capacity." *Haaretz*, October 7, 2016.

Green, David B. "Declassified." *Haaretz*, August 12, 2019.

Grodzinsky, Yosef. *In the Shadow of the Holocaust*. Monroe, ME: Common Courage Press, 2004.

Grose, Peter. *Israel in the Mind of America*. New York: Knopf, 1983.

Guttman, Nathan. "Courting the Jewish Vote May Not Be Worth It." *Haaretz*, September 1, 2003.

Haber, Jerry. "No, Rivkele, the Jews Weren't Driven into Exile by the Romans." *Magnes Zionist* (blog), July 29, 2007.

Hacohen, Dvora. "Ben-Gurion and the Second World War: Plans for Mass Immigration to Palestine." In *Jews and Messianism in the Modern Era,* edited by Jonathan Frankel. New York: Oxford University Press, 1991.

Hadar, Leon. "Thawing the American-Israeli Chill." *Journal of Palestine Studies* 22, no. 2 (Winter 1993).

Haddad, George M. "Arab Peace Efforts and the Solution of the Arab-Israel Problem." In *Elusive Peace in the Middle East,* edited by Malcom Kerr. Albany: State University of New York Press, 1975.

Hahn, Peter L. *Caught in the Middle East: U.S. Policy toward the Arab-Israeli Conflict, 1945–1961.* Chapel Hill: University of North Carolina Press, 2004.

Halbfinger, David M. "Israeli Leader Says Russia Agreed to Restrain Iran in Syria." *New York Times,* July 13, 2018.

Halbfinger, David M. "Tensions Ease in Gaza, Allowing Money and Fuel to Roll In since Last Month." *New York Times,* November 1, 2018.

Halbfinger, David. "Arab Thinkers Call to Engage with Israel and Abandon Boycotts." *New York Times,* November 21, 2019.

Halbfinger, David M. "Netanyahu, Facing Tough Israel Election, Pledges to Annex Much of West Bank." *New York Times,* September 10, 2019.

Halbfinger, David. "Netanyahu Vows to Start Annexing West Bank, in Bid to Rally the Right." *New York Times,* April 7, 2019.

Halbfinger, David M. "Why Do Israel and Gaza Keep Fighting? Because It's in Their Leaders' Interests." *New York Times,* May 7, 2019.

Halbfinger, David M., and Isabel Kershner. "Israel-Gaza Clashes Intensify and Death Toll Rises." *New York Times,* May 5, 2019.

Halliday, Fred. *Soviet Policy in the Arc of Crisis.* Washington, DC: Institute for Policy Studies, 1981.

"Hamas Proposes a 10-Year Truce for Israeli Pullback." *Haaretz,* January 26, 2004.

"Hamas: We'll Consider 2002 Arab Peace Plan Only If Israel Accepts It First." *Haaretz,* May 3, 2006.

"Hamas: We Will Accept Long-Term Truce If Gaza Borders Opened." *Haaretz,* January 29, 2009.

"Hamas Vows to Honor Palestinian Referendum on Peace with Israel." *Haaretz,* December 1, 2010.

Hanieh, Akram. "The Camp David Papers." *Journal of Palestine Studies* 30, no. 2 (Winter 2001).

Haniyeh, Ismail. "Aggression under False Pretenses." *Washington Post,* July 11, 2006.

Hannum, Hurst. "The Specter of Secession." *Foreign Affairs* 77, no. 2 (March/April 1998).

Harel, Amos. "Israel Prepares for Widespread Military Escalation." *Haaretz,* July 12, 2006.

Harel, Amos. "Gazan Economy, Infrastructure on Verge of Collapse, Israeli Security Officials Say." *Haaretz,* January 15, 2008.

Harel, Amos. "Hamas Response: Calculated Escalation." *Haaretz,* February 27, 2008.

Harel, Amos. "Too Many Question Marks." *Haaretz,* May 22, 2008.

Harel, Amos. "Between a Ruthless Dictator and Global Jihad, Israel, U.S. Prefer Assad." *Haaretz,* January 23, 2014.

Harel, Amos. "Israeli Military Keen to Lower the Sound of War Drums." *Haaretz,* February 2, 2016.

Harel, Amos. "Gazan Economy, Infrastructure on Verge of Collapse, Israeli Security Officials Say." *Haaretz,* January 15, 2018.

Harel, Amos. "Hundreds of Rockets and Mass Evacuations: IDF Lays Out What War with Hezbollah Will Look Like." *Haaretz,* August 1, 2018.

Harel, Amos. "Israel's Groundhog Day in Gaza." *Haaretz,* August 9, 2018.

Harel, Amos. "Israel-Hamas Deal Stalls." *Haaretz,* September 16, 2018.

Harel, Amos. "End the Blockade, Aid Gaza's Economy." *Haaretz* editorial, November 14, 2019.

Harel, Amos. "Even after Weekend Violence, Israel and Hamas Moving toward Long-Term Gaza Calm." *Haaretz,* December 2, 2019.

Harel, Amos. "Final Salvo Campaign Shows Direction He'll Take If He Wins." *Haaretz,* April 9, 2019.

Harel, Amos. "Hamas Takes Extraordinary Step to Quell Gaza's 'Angry Youth.'" *Haaretz,* August 30, 2019.

Harel, Amos. "Israeli Army Concerned New Election Will Torpedo Possible Israel-Hamas Deal." *Haaretz*, December 12, 2019.

Harel, Amos. "Israeli Military Keen to Lower the Sound of War Drums." *Haaretz*, November 25, 2019.

Harel, Amos. "Israel Now Sees a Rare Opportunity for Long-Term Quiet in Gaza." *Haaretz*, November 25, 2019.

Harel, Amos. "U.S. Ends Aid to West Bank, Gaza at Palestinian Authority's Request." *Haaretz*, February 1, 2019.

Harel, Amos. "What Israel Needs Is Strategic Patience, There Are No More Existential Threats." *Haaretz*, December 22, 2019.

Harkabi, Yehoshat. *Israel's Fateful Hour.* New York: HarperCollins, 1989.

Harkavy, Robert. "Strategic Access, Bases and Arms Transfers." In *Great Power Intervention in the Middle East*, edited by Milton Leitenberg and Gabriel Sheffer. Elmsford, NJ: Pergamon Press, 1979.

Hart, Alan. *Arafat: A Political Biography.* Bloomington: Indiana University Press, 1989.

Hass, Amira. "Barak's Jargon Is Identical to That of Gush Emunim." *Haaretz*, December 21, 1999.

Hass, Amira. "Where Even Emergency Generators Break Down." *Haaretz*, January 5, 2009.

Hass, Amira. "Setting the Record Straight on Yitzhak Rabin." *Haaretz*, November 6, 2017.

Hass, Amira. "Israel-Hamas Now Negotiating." *Haaretz*, April 4, 2019.

Hass, Amira. "Israel Has Created Ten Methods for Deportation." *Haaretz*, August 4, 2019.

Hasson, Nir. "Israeli Peace Activist: Hamas Leader Jabari Killed Amid Talks on Long-Term Truce." *Haaretz*, November 15, 2012.

Hasson, Nir. "Is the Bible a True Story?" *Haaretz*, October 27, 2017.

Hazkani, Shay. "Catastrophic Thinking: Did Ben-Gurion Try to Rewrite History?" *Haaretz*, May 16, 2013.

Heikal, Mohamed. *The Road to Ramadan.* New York: Quadrangle Press, 1975.

Heikal, Mohamed. "Egyptian Foreign Policy." *Foreign Affairs*, July 1978.

Heikal, Mohamed. *The Sphinx and the Commissar: The Rise and Fall of Soviet Influence in the Middle East.* New York: Harper and Row, 1978.

Herzog, Michael. "Minding the Gaps: Territorial Issues in Israeli-Palestinian Peacemaking." *Washington Institute for Near-East Policy*, December 2011.

Herzl, Theodor. *The Jewish State.* Austria, 1896.

Herzl, Theodore. *Der Judenstaat.* Vienna: Verlags-Buchhandlung, 1896.

Herzl, Theodore. "Zion and the Jewish National Idea." In *Zionism Reconsidered.* London: Macmillan, 1970.

Heydemann, Steven. "Revision and Reconstruction of Israeli History." In *Critical Essays on Israeli Society, Politics, and Culture*, Vol. 2, edited by Ian S. Lustick and Barry Rubin. Albany: State University of New York Press, 1991.

Hinnebusch, Raymond A. "Does Syria Want Peace?" Interview with Syrian Ambassador Walid A-Moualem. *Journal of Palestine Studies* 26, no. 2 (Winter 1997).

Hirsh, Michael, and Colum Lynch. "The Long Game of Benjamin Netanyahu." *Foreign Policy*, April 9, 2019.

Hirst, David. *The Gun and the Olive Branch.* London: I. B. Tauris, 1988.

Hof, Frederick. "The Line of June 4, 1967." *Middle East Institute* 14, no. 5 (September–October 1999).

Horowitz, Uri. "Camp David 2 and President Clinton's Bridging Proposals." *Strategic Assessments* 3, no. 4 (January 2001).

"How Israel Helped Spawn Hamas." Interview with Avner Cohen. *Wall Street Journal*, January 24, 2009.

"How to Save Israel in Spite of Herself." *Foreign Affairs* 55, no. 3 (April 1977).

Hroub, Khaled. "A Newer Hamas? The Revised Charter." *Journal of Palestine Studies* 46, no. 4 (Summer 2017).

Hubbard, Ben. "Little Outrage in Arab World over Netanyahu's Vow to Annex West Bank." *New York Times*, September 10, 2019.
Hubbard, Ben. "In Netanyahu's Win, Arabs See Another Nail in the Coffin of a Palestinian State." *New York Times*, April 11, 2019.
"Human Rights Situation in Palestine and Other Occupied Arab Territories." Geneva: Human Rights Council, February 11, 2009.
Hunter, Robert A. "Seeking Middle East Peace." *Foreign Policy* 73 (Winter 1988–89).
Indyk, Martin. "Assad Offering to Make Peace with Israel." *Haaretz*, October 7, 2004.
Indyk, Martin. *Innocent Abroad: An Intimate Account of American Peace Diplomacy in the Middle East*. New York: Simon and Schuster, 2009.
Issacharoff, Avi. "57 Unarmed Palestinian Minors Killed by IDF since June." *Haaretz*, November 8, 2006.
Issacharoff, Avi. "B'Tselem's End-of-Year Report: Number of Palestinians Killed by IDF Dropped Sharply in '07." *Haaretz*, December 31, 2007.
Issacharoff, Avi. "PM Dismisses Meshal's Comments That Israel Is a Reality." *Haaretz*, January 11, 2007.
Issacharoff, Avi. "Ex-President Carter Urges Obama to Remove Hamas from U.S. Terror List." *Haaretz*, June 17, 2009.
Issacharoff, Avi. "Osama Bin Laden Blames Israel for America's Mideast Problems." *Haaretz*, September 15, 2009.
Issacharoff, Avi. "Olmert: I Am Still Waiting for Abbas to Call." *Tower Magazine*, May 24, 2013.
Isaacson, Walter. *Kissinger: A Biography*. New York: Simon and Schuster, 1992.
Iyad, Abu. *Jerusalem Report*, July 16, 2001.
Iyad, Abu. "Lowering the Sword." *Foreign Policy* 78 (Spring 1990).
Jabber, Paul. *Not by War Alone*. Berkeley: University of California Press, 1981.
Jabber, Paul, and Roman Kolkowicz. "The Arab-Israeli Wars of 1967 and 1973." In *Diplomacy of Power*, edited by Steven S. Kaplan. Washington, DC: Brookings Institution, 1981.
Jackson, Galen. "The Showdown That Wasn't." *International Security* 39, no. 4 (Spring 2015).
Jackson, Galen. "The U.S., the Israeli Nuclear Program, and Nonproliferation." *Security Studies* 28, no. 2 (April–May 2019).
Jackson, Galen. "Who Killed Détente? The Superpowers and the Cold War in the Middle East, 1969–77." *International Security* (Winter 2019/20).
Jakes, Lara, and David M. Halbfinger. "In Shift, U.S. Says Israeli Settlements in West Bank Do Not Violate International Law." *New York Times*, November 19, 2009.
Johnson, Lyndon. *The Vantage Point*. New York: Holt, Rinehart and Winston, 1971.
Johnson, William Robert. *Chronology of Terrorist Attacks in Israel*. johnstonarchive.net/terrorism, 2018.
"Jordan-Israel Ties Strained by Detentions." *New York Times*, October 31, 2019.
Judis, John B. "Who Bears More Responsibility for the War in Gaza." *New Republic*, July 25, 2014.
Judis, John J. *Genesis: Truman, American Jews, and the Origins of the Arab/Israeli Conflict*. New York: Farrar, Straus and Giroux, 2015.
Kamiya, Gary. "Obama's Middle East Moment of Truth." *Salon*, March 17, 2009.
Kampeas, Ron. "Why Israel Isn't a Top Consideration for American Jewish Voters." *Haaretz*, December 5, 2019.
Kaplan, Jonathan. "The Mass Migration of the 1950s." The Jewish Agency for Israel, April 27, 2015. http://archive.jewishagency.org/society-and-politics/content/36566.
Kardoosh, Marwan. "Jordanians Now See Israel as an Implacable Enemy, Despite 25 Years of Peace." *Haaretz*, November 3, 2019.
Karmi, Ghada. "The One-State Solution." *Journal of Palestine Studies* 40, no. 2 (Winter 2011).
Karsh, Efraim. *The Soviet Union and Syria*. London: Royal Institute of International Affairs, 1988.
Karsh, Efraim. *The Arab-Israeli Conflict: The Palestine War 1948*. London: Osprey Press, 2014.
Kass, Ilana. *Soviet Involvement in the Middle East*. Boulder, CO: Westview Press, 1978.

Kelman, Herbert. "Talk with Arafat." *Foreign Policy* 49 (Winter 1982–83).

Kelman, Herbert C. "Building a Sustainable Peace: The Limits of Pragmatism in the Israeli-Palestinian Negotiations." *Journal of Palestine Studies* 27, no. 1 (Autumn 1998).

Kerr, Malcolm H., ed. *The Elusive Peace in the Middle East.* Albany: State University of New York Press, 1975.

Kershner, Isabel. "Rockets Hit Israel, Breaking Hamas Truce." *New York Times,* June 25, 2008.

Kershner, Isabel. "Secret Israel Peace Talks Involved Golan Heights." *New York Times,* October 13, 2012.

Kershner, Isabel. "As Tensions Rise with Israel, Hamas Chief Calls for Cease-Fire in Gaza." *New York Times,* October 5, 2018.

Kershner, Isabel, and David M. Halbfinger. "Capital in Trump Mideast Plan Makes 'a Joke' of Palestinian Aspirations." *New York Times,* February 1, 2020.

Khalidi, Rashid. "The Palestine Liberation Organization." In *The Middle East: Ten Years after Camp David,* edited by William B. Quandt. Washington, DC: Brookings Institution Press, 1988.

Khalidi, Rashid. *The Iron Cage. The Story of the Palestinian Struggle for Statehood.* Boston: Beacon Press, 2007.

Khalidi, Rashid. "The Palestinians and 1948." In *The War for Palestine: Rewriting the History of 1948,* 2nd ed., edited by Eugene L. Rogan and Avi Shlaim. New York: Cambridge University Press, 2007.

Khalidi, Walid. "A Palestinian Perspective on the Arab-Israeli Conflict." *Journal of Palestine Studies* 14, no. 4 (Summer 1985).

Khalidi, Walid. "Why Did the Palestinians Leave, Revisited." *Journal of Palestine Studies* 34, no. 2 (Winter 2005).

Khouri, Fred J. "United Nations Peace Efforts." In *Elusive Peace in the Middle East,* edited by Malcolm Kerr. Albany: State University of New York Press, 1975.

Khouri, Fred. *The Arab-Israeli Dilemma.* Syracuse, NY: Syracuse University Press, 1985.

Khoury, Jack. "Meshal: Shalit Still Alive." *Haaretz,* April 1, 2008.

Khoury, Jack. "Hamas Presents New Charter Supporting Palestinian State along 1967 Borders." *Haaretz,* May 2, 2017.

Khoury, Jack, and Noa Landau. "Israel-Qatar Deal to Transfer Funds to Hamas Officials Underway." *Haaretz,* October 31, 2018.

Kifner, John. "Human Rights Group Accuses Israel of War Crimes." *New York Times,* August 24, 2006.

"King Says Jordan Erred in 1967." *New York Times,* June 6, 1967.

Kingsley, Patrick. "Anti-Semitism Is Back." *New York Times,* April 4, 2019.

Kingsley, Patrick. "The Old Scourge of Anti-Semitism Rises Anew in Europe." *New York Times,* May 26, 2019.

Kipnis, Yigal. *1973: The Road to War.* Washington, DC: Just World Books, 2013.

Kissinger, Henry. *Years of Upheaval.* Boston: Little, Brown, 1982.

Kissinger, Henry. *The White House Years.* New York: Simon and Schuster, 2011.

Klein, Menachem. *Jerusalem: The Contested City.* New York: New York University Press, 2001.

Klein, Menachem. "The Oslo Agreements Twenty Years Later—What Remained." *Oslo Newsletter,* September 12, 2013.

Klein, Menachem. "Any Solution to the Israeli-Palestinian Conflict Will Lead to Civil War." *Haaretz,* June 14, 2019.

Klein, Yossi. "The New Israeli Is Frankenstein's Monster." *Haaretz,* January 25, 2018.

Klinghoffer, Arthur J. *Israel and the Soviet Union.* Boulder, CO: Westview Press, 1985.

Kolkowicz, Roman. "Soviet Policy in the Middle East." In *The USSR and the Middle East,* edited by Michael Confino and Shimon Shamir. New York: John Wiley, 1973.

Koplow, Michael J. "Value Judgment: Why Do Americans Support Israel?" *Security Studies* 20, no. 2 (April 2011).

Korn, David. *Stalemate: The War of Attrition and Great Power Diplomacy in the Middle East, 1967–70.* Boulder, CO: Westview, 1992.

Kraft, Dina. "42 Percent of Israelis Back West Bank Annexation, including Two-State Supporters." *Haaretz*, March 25, 2019.

Kuniholm, Bruce. "The Soviet Attitude to the Palestine Problem: From the Records of the Syrian Communist Party, 1971–72." *Journal of Palestine Studies* 2 (Autumn 1972).

Kuperwasser, Yossi. "Kushner's Objective: An Economic Carrot to Change the Palestinian Narrative." *Haaretz*, August 9, 2019.

Kuperwasser, Yosef, and Shalom Lipner. "Why the PA Must Recognize a Jewish State." *Foreign Affairs* 90, no. 6 (November–December 2011).

Kurtzer, Daniel, Scott B. Lasensky, William B. Quandt, Steven L. Spiegel, and Shibley Z. Telhami, eds. *The Peace Puzzle: America's Quest for Arab-Israeli Peace, 1989–2011*. Ithaca, NY: Cornell University Press, 2012.

Kyle, Keith. *Suez: Britain's End of Empire in the Middle East.* London: Weidenfeld and Nicolson, 1991.

Landau, David. "Good News from the Rubble." *Haaretz*, October 4, 2002.

Landau, David M. *Arik: The Life of Ariel Sharon*. New York: Alfred A. Knopf, 2013.

Landau David, and Akiva Eldar. "A Jewish State? 'Definitely.'" *Haaretz*, June 18, 2004.

Landau, Noa. "Gantz Vows to Annex Jordan Valley." *Haaretz*, January 22, 2020.

Landis, Joshua. "Early U.S. Policy toward Palestinian Refugees: The Syria Option." In *The Palestinian Refugees: Old Problems—New Solutions*, edited by Joseph Ginat and Edward J. Perkins. Norman: University of Oklahoma Press, 2001.

Landis, Joshua. "Syria in the 1948 Palestine War: Fighting King Abdullah's Greater Syrian Plan." In *Rewriting the Palestine War: 1948 and the History of the Arab-Israeli Conflict*, edited by Eugene Rogan and Avi Shlaim. Cambridge: Cambridge University Press, 2001.

Landler, Mark. "Questions Emerge about Pro-Israel Groups' Prowess." *New York Times*, February 4, 2014.

Laqueur, Walter. *The Soviet Union and the Middle East.* New York: Praeger, 1959.

Laron, Guy. *The Six-Day War: The Breaking of the Middle East*. New Haven, CT: Yale University Press, 2017.

"A Last Chance for a Two-State Israel-Palestine Agreement: A Bipartisan Statement on US/Middle East Peacemaking." *Daily Kos*, May 7, 2009.

Lavie, Ephraim, and Matti Steinberg. "Worrisome Findings on Decision Making." *Haaretz*, February 27, 2013.

Leffler, Melvin P. *A Preponderance of Power: National Security, the Truman Administration, and the Cold War.* Palo Alto, CA: Stanford University Press, 1992.

Leitenberg, Milton, and Gabriel Sheffer, eds. *Great Power Intervention in the Middle East*. Elmsford, NJ: Pergamon Press, 1979.

Lelyveld, Joseph. *His Final Battle: The Last Months of Franklin Roosevelt*. New York: Knopf Doubleday, 2017.

Lesch, Ann M., and Ian S. Lustick, eds. *Exile and Return*. Philadelphia: University of Pennsylvania Press, 2005.

Levy, Daniel. "Don't Call It a Peace Plan." *American Prospect*, January 30, 2020.

Levy, Gideon. "As the Hamas Team Laughs." *Haaretz*, February 19, 2006.

Levy, Gideon. "Believing Olmert." *Haaretz*, January 13, 2008.

Levy, Gideon. "I Believed in the Oslo Accords for Years, but It Was Merely a Deception" (interview with Joel Singer), *Haaretz*, September 9, 2018.

Levy, Gideon. "Germany, Shame on You and Your Anti-BDS Resolution." *Haaretz*, May 19, 2019.

Levy, Gideon. "New U.S. Stance on Israeli Settlements Is Akin to 'Thou Shalt Murder.'" *Haaretz*, November 21, 2019.

Levy, Yagil. "The Theocratization of the Israeli Military." *Armed Forces and Society* 40, no. 2 (2014).

Lewis, Anthony. "Abroad at Home: 'We Don't Have Time.'" *New York Times*, June 4, 1989.

Lewy, Guenter. *Religion and Revolution*. New York: Oxford University Press, 1974.

Little, Douglas. "Covert War and Covert Action: The United States and Syria, 1945–1958." *Middle East Journal* 44, no. 1 (Winter 1990).

Lowenstein, Anthony, and Ahmed Moor. *After Zionism: One State for Israel and Palestine.* London: Saqi Books, 2012.

Levy, Gideon. "So Stupid, Beautiful and Pure." *Haaretz*, October 30, 2016.

Levy, Yagil. *Trial and Error: Israel's Route from War to De-Escalation.* Albany: State University of New York Press, 1997.

Lewis, Samuel W. "The United States and Israel: Constancy and Change." In *The Middle East: Ten Years after Camp David*, edited by William B. Quandt. Washington, DC: Brookings Institution Press, 1988.

Little, Douglas. *American Orientalism: The United States and the Middle East since 1945.* 3rd ed. Chapel Hill: University of North Carolina Press, 2008.

Lustick, Ian S., ed., *Critical Essays on Israeli Society, Politics, and Culture.* Albany: State University of New York Press, 1991.

Lustick, Ian S. "Has Israel Annexed East Jerusalem?" *Middle East Policy Council Journal* 5, no. 1 (January 1997).

MacFarlane, S. N. "The Middle East in Soviet Strategy." In *The Middle East in Global Strategy*, edited by Aurel Braun. Boulder, CO: Westview Press, 1987.

MacMillan, Margaret. *Dangerous Games: The Uses and Abuses of History.* New York: Modern Library, 2009.

Madar, Chase. "Washington's Military Aid to Israel." *Huffington Post*, February 10, 2014.

Makovsky, David. "Middle East Peace through Partition." *Foreign Affairs* 80, no. 2 (March/April 2001).

Makovsky, Michael. *Churchill's Promised Land: Zionism and Statecraft.* New Haven, CT: Yale University Press, 2007.

Malley, Robert. "Israel and the Arafat Question." *New York Review*, October 7, 2004.

Malley, Robert, and Hussein Agha. "Camp David: The Tragedy of Errors." *New York Review*, August 9, 2001.

Malley, Robert, and Hussein Agha, "Camp David and After: An Exchange." *New York Review*, June 13, 2002.

Malley, Robert, and Hussein Agha. "Camp David and After—Continued." *New York Review*, June 27, 2002.

Malley, Robert, and Hussein Agha. "Tragedy of Errors." *New York Review*, August 9, 2001.

Malley, Robert, and Henry Siegman. "The Hamas Factor." *International Herald Tribune*, December 27, 2006.

Maltz, Judy. "Young American Jews Increasingly Turning Away from Israel." *Haaretz*, January 22, 2018.

Maltz, Judy. "Growing Number of U.S. Jews Support Evacuation of All West Bank Settlements." *Haaretz*, June 3, 2019.

Maltz, Judy. "Solutions to the Israeli-Palestinian Conflict." *Haaretz*, March 25, 2019.

Maltz, Judy. "Special Project on the Two-State Settlement." *Haaretz*, March 25, 2019.

Maltz, Judy. "Netanyahu's Embrace of Trump Is Driving U.S. Jews Away from Israel, Survey Shows." *Haaretz*, February 4, 2020.

Manchester, William. *The Last Lion*, Vol. 1: *Winston Spencer Churchill, Visions of Glory, 1874–1932.* Boston: Little, Brown, 1983.

Mansour, Camille. *Beyond Alliance: Israel in U.S. Foreign Policy.* Washington, DC: Institute for Palestine Studies, 1994.

Maoz, Moshe. "Syrian-Israeli Relations and the Middle East Peace Process." *Jerusalem Journal of International Relations* 14, no. 3 (1992).

Maoz, Moshe. *Syria and Israel: From War to Peace-Making.* New York: Oxford University Press, 1995.

Maoz, Moshe. "The Israeli-Saudi Common Interest." *Haaretz*, August 3, 2008.

Maoz, Zeev. "The Mixed Blessing of Israel's Nuclear Policy." *International Security* (Fall 2003).

Maoz, Zeev. *Defending the Holy Land*. Ann Arbor: University of Michigan Press, 2006.
Marantz, Paul, and Selma S. Steinberg. *Superpower Involvement in the Middle East*. Boulder, CO: Westview Press, 1985.
Margalit, Dan. *Haaretz*, December 25, 2001.
Masalha, Nur. *Expulsion of the Palestinians: The Concept of "Transfer" in Zionist Political Thought, 1882–1948*. Washington, DC: Institute for Palestine Studies, 1992.
Mayer, Emily. "Why Young Jews and Democrats Are Waving Goodbye to AIPAC." *Haaretz*, March 6, 2018.
Mazzetti, Mark, and Helene Cooper. "Israel Stance Was Undoing of Nominee for Intelligence Post." *New York Times*, March 12, 2009.
McDonald, James G. *My Mission in Israel, 1948–1951*. New York: Simon and Schuster, 1951.
McGuire, Michael. *Military Objectives in Soviet Foreign Policy*. Washington, DC: Brookings Institution Press, 1987.
Mearsheimer, John, and Stephen Walt. *The Israel Lobby and U.S. Foreign Policy*. New York: Farrar, Straus and Giroux, 2007.
Mearsheimer, John, and Stephen Walt. "Is It Love or the Lobby? Explaining America's Special Relationship with Israel." *Security Studies* (January–March 2009).
Mehmet, Ozay. "Growth and Equity in Microstates: Does Size Matter in Development?" *International Journal of Social Economics* 29, no. 2 (2002).
Melman, Yossi. *The New Israelis*. New York: Birch Lane Press, 1992.
Melman, Yossi. "Father of Indecision." *Haaretz*, May 3, 2002.
Melman, Yossi, and Dan Raviv. *Behind the Uprisings: Israel and Transjordan in the War of 1948*. London: Frank Cass, 1987.
Michael, B. "In Classic Occupier Fashion, Israel Has Hit Rock Bottom." *Haaretz*, February 27, 2020.
Miller, Aaron David. *The Much Too Promised Land: America's Elusive Search for Arab-Israeli Peace*. New York: Bantam Books, 2008.
Misgav, Uri. "Some Golan Loyalist Bibi Is." *Haaretz*, June 20, 2019.
Mishal, Shaul, and Avraham Sela. *The Palestinian Hamas*. New York: Columbia University Press, 2006.
Montell, Jessica. "Operation Defensive Shield." *Tikkun*, July/August 2002.
Morris, Benny. *The Birth of the Palestinian Refugee Problem, 1947–1949*. Cambridge: Cambridge University Press, 1987.
Morris, Benny. *The Birth of the Palestinian Refugee Problem Revisited*. Cambridge: Cambridge University Press, 1988.
Morris, Benny. "The New Historiography: Israel Confronts Its Past." *Tikkun*, November–December 1988.
Morris, Benny. *1948 and After: Israel and the Palestinians*. New York: Oxford University Press, 1990.
Morris, Benny. *Israel's Border Wars, 1949–1956*. New York: Oxford University Press, 1993.
Morris, Benny. "Looking Back." *Tikkun*, March–April 1998.
Morris, Benny. "Refabricating 1948." *Journal of Palestine Studies* 27, no. 2 (Winter 1998).
Morris, Benny. *Righteous Victims: A History of the Zionist-Arab Conflict, 1881–2001*. New York: Vintage Books, 2001.
Morris, Benny. "A New Exodus for the Middle East?" *The Guardian*, October 3, 2002.
Morris, Benny, ed. *Making Israel*. Ann Arbor: University of Michigan Press, 2007.
Morris, Benny. *1948: A History of the First Arab-Israeli War*. New Haven, CT: Yale University Press, 2008.
Morris, Benny. "Derisionist History." *New Republic*, November 28, 2009.
Morris, Benny. "Gideon Levy Is Wrong about the Past, the Present, and I Believe the Future as Well." *Haaretz*, January 21, 2019.
"Mr. Netanyahu's Next Test." *Haaretz* editorial, April 12, 2019.
Muasher, Marwan. "The Initiative Still Stands." *Haaretz*, August 15, 2008.
Neff, Donald. *Warriors for Jerusalem*. New York: Simon and Schuster, 1984.

Neff, Donald. "Palestine, Truman and America's Strategic Balance." *American-Arab Affairs* (Summer 1988).

Neff, Donald. "The Clinton Administration and UN Resolution 242." *Washington Report on Middle East Affairs*, September–October 1993.

Neff, Donald. "Israel-Syria: Conflict at the Jordan River, 1949–1967." *Journal of Palestine Studies* 23, no. 4 (Summer 1994).

Neff, Donald. "Clinton Places US Policy at Israel's Bidding." *Middle East International* 31 (March 1995).

Neff, Donald. *Fallen Pillars: U.S. Policy toward Palestine and Israel since 1945*. Washington, DC: Institute for Palestine Studies, 1995.

Netanyahu, Benjamin. *A Place among Nations*. New York: Bantam Books, 1993.

"Netanyahu Agreed to Withdraw to '67 Lines, Document Confirms." *Haaretz*, March 8, 2015.

New York Times. "Excerpts from Begin's Speech at National Defense College." August 21, 1982.

Nir, Ori. "Israel's Campaign to Destabilize Jordan." *Haaretz*, December 10, 2019.

Noe, Nicholas. "Is This Lebanon's Final Revolution?" *New York Times*, January 27, 2011.

Nofal, Mamdouh. "Yasir Arafat: A Mixed Legacy." *Journal of Palestine Studies* 35, no. 2 (Winter 2006).

O'Brien, Conor Cruise. *The Siege: The Saga of Israel and Zionism*. New York: Simon and Schuster, 1986.

Olmert, Ehud. "The Time Has Come to Say These Things." *New York Review*, December 4, 2008.

O'Malley, Padraig. *The Two-State Delusion*. New York: Viking Press, 2015.

Oren, Amir. "IDF to Tell Sharon to Show Restraint This Month." *Haaretz*, March 9, 2001.

Oren, Amir. "This Time, the IDF Favors Syrian Peace Deal." *Haaretz*, November 20, 2007.

Oren, Amir. "First in War, Last in Peace." *Haaretz*, May 1, 2009.

Oren, Amir. "1982 Memo Shows Israel Learned Little from First Lebanon War." *Haaretz*, July 12, 2009.

Oren, Amir. "Reflections on a Tortured Part of the World." *Haaretz*, April 9, 2010.

Oren, Amir. "Soviet Envoy Warned Nixon and Kissinger against Mideast War in 1973, Documents Reveal." *Haaretz*, December 30, 2011.

Oren, Amir. "With Ariel Sharon Gone, Israel Reveals the Truth about the 1982 Lebanon War." *Haaretz*, September 17, 2017.

Organski, A. F. K. *The $36 Billion Bargain: Strategy and Politics in U.S. Assistance to Israel*. New York: Columbia University Press, 1990.

"The Oslo Accords Are Dead, but There Is Still a Path to Peace." *Foreign Policy*, September 13, 2018.

Oslo Diaries. HBO Documentary, September 2018.

Palumbo, Michael. *The Palestinian Catastrophe*. London: Faber and Faber, 1987.

Pappé, Ilan. *The Making of the Arab-Israeli Conflict*. London: I. B. Tauris, 1992.

Pappé, Ilan. "The Visible and Invisible in the Israeli-Palestinian Conflict." In *Exile and Return*, edited by Ann M. Lesch and Ian S. Lustick. Philadelphia: University of Pennsylvania Press, 2005.

Pappé, Ilan. *The Ethnic Cleansing of Palestine*. Oxford: One World Press, 2006.

Pappé, Ilan. *A History of Modern Palestine*. Cambridge: Cambridge University Press, 2006.

Pappé, Ilan. *The Idea of Israel*. London: Verso, 2014.

Pappé, Ilan. *The Biggest Prison on Earth: A History of the Occupied Territories*. London: Oneworld Publications, 2017.

Pappé, Ilan. *Ten Myths about Israel*. London: Verso, 2017.

Parker, Richard B. *The Politics of Miscalculation in the Middle East*. Bloomington: Indiana University Press, 1993.

"Peace Now or Never." *New York Times*, September 22, 2011.

Pedatzur, Reuven. "Coming Back Full Circle: The Palestinian Option in 1967." *Middle East Journal* 49, no. 2 (Spring 1995).

Pedatzur, Reuven. "The War That Wasn't." *Haaretz*, January 25, 2009.

Pedatzur, Reuven. "Why Did Israel Kill Jabari?" *Haaretz*, December 4, 2012.

Peraino, Kevin. "Olmert's Lament." *Newsweek*, June 13, 2009.

Peres, Shimon, interview. *Haaretz*, March 7, 1997.

Peretz, Sami. "The Fighting Is Over, but Gaza's Economic Problems Remain." *Haaretz*, May 7, 2019.

Peretz. Sami. "Hamas Seeks Concession from Israel in Gaza." *Haaretz*, November 13, 2019.

Perlez, Jane. "Before Attacks, US Was Ready to Say It Backed Palestinian State." *New York Times*, October 2, 2001.

Perry, Mark. "Petraeus Wasn't the First." *Foreign Policy.com*, April 1, 2010.

"Pew Survey Finds Jews to Be America's Favorite Religious Group." *Haaretz*, July 7, 2014.

Pfeffer, Anshel. "Plan or Spin?" *Haaretz*, November 30, 2006.

Pfeffer, Anshel. "Netanyahu and Hamas Chief in Gaza Have Emerged as Unlikely Allies." *Haaretz*, November 14, 2009.

Pfeffer, Anshel. "Hezbollah Refused Hamas Request to Bomb Israel in the Gaza War." *Haaretz*, November 10, 2010.

Pfeffer, Anshel. *Bibi: The Turbulent Life and Times of Benjamin Netanyahu*. New York: Basic Books, 2018.

Pfeffer, Anshel. "After Almost 20 Years, Netanyahu May Finally Realize His Vision for 'Durable Peace.'" *Haaretz*, April 18, 2019.

Pfeffer, Anshel. "With Annexationist Comment, Friedman Just Made Netanyahu's Life More Difficult." *Haaretz*, June 11, 2019.

Pfeffer, Anshel. "Benjamin Netanyahu, the Undertaker of the Two-State Solution." *Haaretz*, April 1, 2019.

Pfeffer, Anshel. "2010–2019: The Decade in Which All Israelis Became Netanyahu." *Haaretz*, December 30, 2019.

Pfeffer, Anshel. "Why Netanyahu Will Never Annex West Bank Settlements and the Jordan Valley. *Haaretz," May* 7, 2020.

PLO Negotiations Affairs Department. "Oslo Process: Twenty Years of Oslo." *Journal of Palestine Studies* 43, no. 2 (Winter 2014).

Podeh, Eli. "The UN Vote on the Partition of Palestine: The Palestinians' Biggest Missed Opportunity." *Haaretz*, November 30, 2017.

"Poll: Americans Sympathize with Israel More Than with Palestinians." *Haaretz*, August 29, 2014.

Primakov, Evgeni M. "Soviet Policy towards the Arab-Israeli Conflict." In *The Middle East: Ten Years after Camp David*, edited by William B. Quandt. Washington, DC: Brookings Institution Press, 1988.

Primor, Avi. "Sharon's South African Strategy." *Haaretz*, September 18, 2002.

Primoretz, Igor. *Terrorism: A Philosophical Investigation*. Cambridge: Polity Press, 2013.

"Problematic Options," *bitterlemons*, November 20, 2006.

Pundak, Ron. "From Oslo to Taba: What Went Wrong?" *Survival* 43, no. 3 (Autumn 2001).

Quandt, William B. "Political and Military Dimensions of Contemporary Palestinian Nationalism." In *The Politics of Palestinian Nationalism*, edited by William B. Quandt, Fuad Jabber, and Ann Mosely Lesch. Berkeley: University of California Press, 1973.

Quandt, William B. *Decade of Decisions: American Policy toward the Arab-Israeli Conflict, 1967–1977*. Berkeley: University of California Press, 1977.

Quandt, William B. *Camp David: Peacemaking and Politics*. Washington, DC: Brookings Institution Press, 1986.

Quandt, William B. *The Middle East: Ten Years after Camp David*. Washington, DC: Brookings Institution Press, 1988.

Quandt, William B. "Clinton and the Arab-Israeli Conflict: The Limits of Incrementalism." *Journal of Palestine Studies*, 30 no. 2 (Winter 2001).

Quandt, William B. *Peace Process: American Diplomacy and the Arab-Israeli Conflict since 1967*. 3rd ed. Washington, DC: Brookings Institution Press, 2005.

Quandt, William B. "Israeli-Syrian Negotiations of the 1990s." In *The Peace Puzzle: America's Quest for Arab-Israeli Peace, 1989–2011*, edited by Daniel Kurtzer, Scott B. Lasensky, William B. Quandt, Steven L. Spiegel, and Shibley Z. Telhami. Ithaca, NY: Cornell University Press, 2012.

Quandt, William B., Fuad Jabber, and Ann Mosely Lesch. *The Politics of Palestinian Nationalism*. Berkeley: University of California Press, 1973.

Ra'anan, Uri. *The USSR Arms the Third World*. Cambridge, MA: MIT Press, 1980.

Rabin, Yitzhak. *The Rabin Memoirs*. Boston: Little, Brown, 1979.

Rabinovich, Itamar. *The War for Lebanon, 1970–1983*. Ithaca, NY: Cornell University Press, 1984.

Rabinovich, Itamar. *The Road Not Taken: Early Arab-Israeli Negotiations*. New York: Oxford University Press, 1991.

Rabinovich, Itamar. *The Brink of Peace*. Princeton, NJ: Princeton University Press, 1998.

Rabinovich, Itamar. *Yitzhak Rabin, Soldier, Leader, Statesman*. New Haven, CT: Yale University Press, 2017.

Rabinowitz, Or, and Nicholas L. Miller. "Keeping the Bombs in the Basement: U.S. Nonproliferation Policy toward Israel, South Africa, and Pakistan." *International Security* 40, no. 1 (Summer 2015).

Rabkin, Yakov M. *What Is Modern Israel?* London: Pluto Press, 2016.

Randal, Jonathan. *Going All the Way: Christian Warlords, Israeli Adventurers, and the War in Lebanon*. New York: Vintage Books, 1984.

Ravid, Barak. "Document Shows Progress on Core Issues at Camp David Summit." *Haaretz*, December 13, 2007.

Ravid, Barak. "Government to Clinton in 2000." *Haaretz*, December 13, 2007.

Ravid, Barak. "PM at Final Cabinet Meeting: Greater Israel Is No More." *Haaretz*, September 15, 2008.

Ravid, Barak. "In 2006 Letter to Bush, Haniyeh Offered Compromise with Israel." *Haaretz*, November 14, 2008.

Ravid, Barak. "MI Chief: Obama Mideast Policy Threatens Israel." *Haaretz*, April 19, 2009.

Ravid, Barak. "State Archives to Stay Classified for 20 More Years." *Haaretz*, July 28, 2010.

Ravid, Barak, "Palestinians Agreed to Cede Nearly All Jewish Areas of East Jerusalem." *Haaretz*, January 24, 2011.

Ravid, Barak. "Abbas: Palestinians, Israel Were Two Months Away from Inking Peace Deal." *Haaretz*, October 14, 2012.

Ravid, Barak. "Netanyahu Told Assad: I'm Ready to Discuss Golan Withdrawal if You Cut Iran, Hezbollah Ties." *Haaretz*, October 12, 2012.

Ravid, Barak. "The Secret Fruits of the Peace Talks, a Future Point of Departure." *Haaretz*, July 5, 2014.

Ravid, Barik. "Sharon Was Planning Diplomatic Moves beyond Gaza, Lead Documents Reveal." *Haaretz*, January 14, 2014.

Ravid, Barak, and Avi Issacharoff. "Hamas: We Won't Stand in Way of PA-Israel Deal." *Haaretz*, July 22, 2009.

Ravid, Barak, and Avi Issacharoff. "Abbas Challenges Mitchell." *Haaretz*, May 23, 2010.

Raviv, Dan, and Yossi Melman. *Friends in Deed: Inside the U.S. Israeli Alliance*. New York: Hyperion Press, 1994.

Raz, Adam. "Israel's First Ruling Party Thought about Palestinian Citizens." *Haaretz*, January 13, 2018.

Raz, Avi. *Bride and the Dowry: Israel, Jordan, and the Palestinians in the Aftermath of the June 1967 War*. New Haven, CT: Yale University Press, 2012.

Reagan, Ronald. *An American Life*. New York: Simon and Schuster, 1990.

Reed, Stanley. "The Oil Market Shows It Can Take a Punch." *New York Times*. June 21, 2019.

Regular, Arnon. "Hamas, Fatah Prisoners Agree to Two-State Solution in Joint Draft." *Haaretz*, May 11, 2006.

Regular, Arnon. "Hamas Hints at Long-Term Truce in Return for 1967 Borders." *Haaretz*, January 30, 2006.

Regular, Arnon. "Hamas Rounds Up Weapons." *Haaretz*, February 14, 2006.

Reinhart, Tanya. "Evil Unleashed," *Tikkun* 17, no. 2 (March–April 2002).

Remnick, David. "Newt, the Jews, and an 'Invented' People.'" *New Yorker*, December 11, 2011.

Report on Israeli Settlement of the Occupied Territories. Washington, DC: November-December 1998.

Rice, Condoleezza. *No Higher Honor: A Memoir of My Years in Washington.* New York: Crown, 2011.

"Rights Group: Close to Half of Palestinian Fatalities in IDF Operation Were Civilians." *Haaretz*, March 4, 2008.

Rokach, Lidia. *Israel's Sacred Terrorism.* Belmont, MA: Association of Arab-American University Graduates, 1980.

Rose, David. "The Gaza Bombshell." *Vanity Fair*, April 2018.

Rosenberg, David. "American Aid Will Be the Death of Israel." *Haaretz*, September 29, 2014.

Rosenberg, David. "The Palestinian Authority Is Collapsing, and Annexation Could Follow." *Haaretz*, April 30, 2019.

Ross, Dennis. *The Missing Peace: The Inside Story of the Fight for Middle East Peace.* New York: Farrar, Straus and Giroux, 2004.

Ross, Dennis. *Doomed to Succeed: The U.S.-Israel Relationship from Truman to Obama.* New York: Farrar, Straus and Giroux, 2015.

Roy, Sara. "A Dubai on the Mediterranean." *London Review of Books*, November 3, 2005.

Roy, Sara. "Gaza: Treading on Shards." *The Nation*, February 10, 2010.

Roy, Sara. *The Gaza Strip: The Political Economy of De-Development.* Washington, DC: Institute for Palestine Studies, 2016.

Rubenberg, Cheryl A. *Israel and the American National Interest.* Urbana: University of Illinois Press, 1986.

Rubenberg, Cheryl A. "The US-PLO Dialogue." *Arab Studies Quarterly* 11, no. 4 (Fall 1989).

Rubenberg, Cheryl A. *Encyclopedia of the Israeli-Palestinian Conflict.* Boulder, CO: Lynne Rienner, 2010.

Rubinstein, Alvin Z. "The Soviet Union's Imperial Policy in the Middle East." *Middle East Review* 15 (Fall/Winter 1982–1983).

Rubinstein, Danny. "Don't Boycott the Palestinians." *Haaretz*, February 13, 2006.

Rubinstein, Danny. "Hamas PM Haniyeh: Retreat to 1967 Borders Will Bring Peace." *Haaretz*, May 23, 2006.

Ryan, Joseph L. *The Myth of Annihilation and the Six-Day War.* New York: Carnegie Council, 1973.

Rynhold, Jonathan. "Behind the Rhetoric: President Bush and U.S. Policy on the Israeli-Palestinian Conflict." *American Diplomacy* 10, no. 4 (November 2005).

Rynhold, Jonathan, and Dov Waxman. "Ideological Change and Israel's Disengagement from Gaza." *Political Science Quarterly* 123, no. 1 (Spring 2008).

Sachar, Howard M. *A History of Israel.* New York: Knopf, 1989.

Sadat. Anwar. *In Search of Identity.* New York: Harper and Row, 1977.

Safran, Nadav. *From War to War: The Arab-Israeli Confrontation, 1948–1967.* New York: Pegasus, 1969.

Safran, Nadav. *Israel: The Embattled Ally.* Cambridge, MA: Harvard University Press, 1981.

Sagir, Dan. "How the Fear of Israeli Nukes Helped Seal the Egypt Peace Deal." *Haaretz*, November 26, 2017.

Said, Edward, interview. *Journal of Palestine Studies* 24, no. 2 (Winter 1995).

Said, Edward, interview. *Palestine-Israel Journal of Politics, Economics and Culture* 5 (Winter 1995).

Samet, Gideon. "Settler's Friends in High Places." *Haaretz*, April 9, 2000.

Samet, Gideon. "The Convoy Is Passing." *Haaretz*, May 2, 2003.

Samet, Gideon. "Pleading for the Right to Babble." *Haaretz*, July 30, 2003.

Sand, Shlomo. *1948: The First Israelis.* New York: Free Press, 1986.

Sand, Shlomo. *The Seventh Million: The Israelis and the Holocaust.* New York: Hill and Wang, 1993.

Sand, Shlomo. *One Palestine Complete: Jews and Arabs under the British Mandate.* New York: Henry Holt, 2000.

Sand, Shlomo. *1967: Israel, the War, and the Year That Transformed the Middle East.* New York: Henry Holt, 2005.

Sand, Shlomo. "The Twisted Logic of the Jewish 'Historic Right' to Israel." *Haaretz*, November 14, 2008.

Sand, Shlomo. *The Invention of the Jewish People*. London: Verso Press, 2009.

Sand, Shlomo. *The Invention of the Land of Israel*. London: Verso Press, 2012.

Sand, Shlomo. "How Israel Went from Atheist Zionism to Jewish State." *Haaretz*, January 22, 2017.

Sand, Shlomo. *A State at Any Cost: The Life of David Ben-Gurion*. New York: Farrar, Straus and Giroux, 2019.

Sarid, Yossi. "If Not with a Stone, Then with What?" *Haaretz*, April 12, 2013.

Sarid, Yossi. "My Travels with Ariel Sharon." *Haaretz*, January 10, 2014.

Sarid, Yossi. "Sober Up, President Rivlin, from Your Good Intentions." *Haaretz*, December 5, 2014.

Saunders, Harold. "Regulating Soviet-U.S. Competition and Cooperation in the Arab-Israeli Arena." In *U.S.-Soviet Security Cooperation*, edited by Alexander A. George et al. New York: Oxford University Press, 1988.

Saurez, Thomas. *State of Terror*. Northampton, MA: Olive Branch Press, 2017.

Savir, Uri. "Bring Back the Oslo Accords." *Haaretz*, August 30, 2007.

Sayigh, Yezid. "Arafat and the Anatomy of a Revolt." *Survival* 43, no. 3 (January 2001).

Scham, Paul, and Osama Abu-Irshaid. *Hamas: Ideological Rigidity and Political Flexibility*. Washington, DC: US Institute of Peace, 2009.

Schiff, Zeev. "The Pact That Ben-Gurion Wanted." *Haaretz*, February 14, 2000.

Schiff, Zeev. "Hamas Offered 30-Year Ceasefire in 1997." Interview with Ephraim Halevy. *Haaretz*, March 30, 2006.

Schiff, Zeev. "Hamas Says Ready for Two-State Solution." *Haaretz*, April 7, 2006.

Schiff, Zeev. "A Strategic Mistake." *Haaretz*, July 20, 2006.

Schiff, Zeev, Amos Harel, and Yoav Stern. "U.S. Hardens Line on Israel-Syria Talks, J'lem Obeys." *Haaretz*, February 23, 2007.

Schiff, Zeev, and Ehud Ya'ari. *Israel's Lebanon War*. New York: Simon and Schuster, 1984.

Schoenbaum, David. *The United States and the State of Israel*. New York: Oxford University Press, 1993.

Seale, Patrick. *Asad of Syria*. London: I. B. Tauris, 1988.

Seale, Patrick. "The Syria-Israel Negotiations: Who Is Telling the Truth?" *Journal of Palestine Studies* 24, no. 2 (Winter 2000).

"The Search for History in the Bible." *Biblical Archeology Review*, special issue 26 (March/April 2000).

Segev, Tom. 1949: *The First Israelis*. New York: The Free Press, 1986.

Segev, Tom, *The Seventh Million: The Israelis and the Holocaust*. New York: Hill and Wang, 1993.

Segev, Tom. *One Palestine Complete. Jews and Arabs Under the British Mandate*. New York: Macmillan, 2000.

Segev, Tom. 1967. *Israel, the War, and the Year That Transformed the Middle East*. Metropolitan Books. Henry Hold and Co, 2005.

Segev, Tom. "Origins of the Occupation." *Haaretz*, January 6, 2006.

Segev, Tom, "Memoir of a Great Friend," *Haaretz*, Dec. 13, 2006.

Segev, Tom. "Ten Theses for the Committee's Examination." *Haaretz*, August 18, 2006.

Segev, Tom. "What If Israel Had Turned Back?" *New York Times*, June 5, 2007.

Segev, Tom. "Everyone Thinks Jerusalem Is Lost." *Haaretz*, November 10, 2008.

Segev, Tom. Review of Benny Morris. *Haaretz*, July 18, 2010.

Segev, Tom. "Gaza without Gazans: History of an Israeli Fantasy." *Haaretz*, November 23, 2012.

Segev, Tom. *A State at Any Cost; The Life of David Ben-Gurion*. New York: Farrar, Straus and Giroux, 2019.

Sella, Amnon. "Changes in Soviet Political-Military Policy in the Middle East." In *The Limits to Power*, edited by Yaavoc Ro'i. New York: St. Martin's Press, 1979.

"Separation into Two States Is Essential for Israel's Security." *New York Times*, February 4, 2016.

"Settlements or Peace." *Palestine-Israel Journal* 7, no. 3 (2000).

Shaath, Nabil. "The Oslo Agreement." *Journal of Palestine Studies* 23, no. 1 (Autumn 1993).

Shafir, Gershon. *Land, Labor, and the Origins of the Israeli-Palestinian Conflict*. Berkeley: University of California Press, 1996.

Shafir, Gershon. *A Half Century of Occupation; Israel, Palestine, and the World's Most Intractable Conflict*. Oakland: University of California Press, 2017.

Shahak, Israel. "A History of the Concept of 'Transfer' in Zionism." *Journal of Palestine Studies* 18, no. 3 (Spring 1989).

Shalev, Arye. *The Israel-Syria Armistice Regime, 1949–1955*. Tel Aviv: Jaffee Center for Strategic Studies, Tel Aviv University, 1993.

Shalev, Arye. *Israel and Syria: Peace and Security on the Golan*. Tel Aviv: Jaffee Center for Strategic Studies, Tel Aviv University, 1994.

Shalev, Chemi. "Oslo Accords and Recognition of PLO Are the Walking Dead Netanyahu Refuses to Bury." *Haaretz*, September 14, 2008.

Shalev, Chemi. "American Jewish Leaders Fiddle While Israeli Democracy Burns." *Haaretz*, August 19, 2014.

Shalev, Chemi. "Moshe Dayan's Enduring Gaza Eulogy." *Haaretz*, July 20, 2014.

Shalev, Chemi. "The Miracle of Occupation Nation." *Haaretz*, May 2, 2017.

Shalom, Stephen R. "Looking Back at the June 1967 Middle East War." *New Politics* 16, no. 3 (Summer 2017).

Shalev, Chemi. "Netanyahu's Current Politics Reopen 23-Year-Old Wound of Rabin's Assassination." *Haaretz*, October 24, 2018.

Shalev, Chemi. "Gaza Emigration Ploy Suggests Netanyahu Hell-Bent on Torching Israel's Image Abroad." *Haaretz*, August 21, 2019.

Shalev, Chemi. "Gaza Flare-Up Imperils Netanyahu's Cynical Cohabitation with Hamas." *Haaretz*, May 6, 2019.

Shalev, Chemi. "House Resolution on Annexation Is a Wakeup Call for Israel and Netenyahu." *Haaretz*, December 8, 2019.

Shalev, Chemi. "2010–2019, the Decade That Devoured the Ties between Israel and U.S. Jews." *Haaretz*, December 30, 2019.

Shapira, Anita. *Israel: A History*. Waltham, MA: Brandeis University Press, 2012.

Shapira, Anita. *Ben-Gurion: Father of Modern Israel*. New Haven, CT: Yale University Press, 2014.

Shapiro, Allen E. "What Price Peace with Syria?" *Jerusalem Post*, July 26, 1990.

Sharoni, Nati. "Investigating Israeli Refusal." *Haaretz*, July 5, 2010.

Shavit, Ari. "End of a Journey." *Haaretz*, September 14, 2001.

Shavit, Ari. "Interview with Barak." *Haaretz*, September 14, 2001.

Shavit, Ari. "Interview with Ehud Barak." *Haaretz*, February 2, 2001.

Shavit, Ari. "Continuation of Eyes Wide Shut." *Haaretz*, September 4, 2002.

Shavit, Ari. "Reality Bites." *Haaretz Magazine*, September 6, 2002.

Shavit, Ari. "Clearly Speaking." Interview with Shin Bet director Ami Ayalon. *Haaretz*, February 9, 2006.

Shavit, Ari. "No Way to Go to War." *Haaretz*, September 15, 2006.

Shavit, Ari. *My Promised Land: The Triumph and Tragedy of Israel*. New York: Spiegel and Grau, 2015.

Sheehan, Edward R. F. *The Arabs, Israelis, and Kissinger*. New York: Thomas Y. Crowell, 1976.

Sheffer, Gabriel. *Moshe Sharett: Biography of a Political Moderate*. New York: Oxford University Press, 1996.

Shehada, Muhammad. "Hamas Desperate for a Deal with Israel." *Haaretz*, August 21, 2018.

Shehada, Muhammad. "How Turkey Has Become the Palestinian Promised Land." *Haaretz*, July 10, 2018.

Shehada, Muhammad. "For Arab Regimes, Palestine Is Old News. Now, It's All about Iran." *Haaretz*, February 27, 2019.

Shehada, Muhammad. "The Arab World Just Handed Netanyahu Its Most Powerful Weapon." *Haaretz*, September 4, 2019.

Sher, Gilead. *The Israeli-Palestinian Peace Negotiations: Within Reach*. New York: Routledge, 2006.

Sher, Gilead. "The Status of the Diplomatic Process with the Palestinians: Points to Update the Incoming Prime Minister." *Haaretz*, December 2007.

Shezaf, Hagar. "Burying the Nakba: How Israel Systematically Hides Evidence of 1948 Expulsion of Arabs." *Haaretz*, July 4, 2019.

Shezaf, Hagar. "Land Swap in South, Population Swap in North: Israel and Palestine According to Trump." *Haaretz*, January 20, 2020.

Shiffer, Varda. "The 1949 Israeli Offer to Repatriate 100,000 Palestinian Refugees." *Middle East Focus* (Fall 1986).

Shipler, David K. "Israel Bars Rabin from Relating '48 Eviction of Arabs." *New York Times*, October 23, 1979.

Shlaim, Avi. *Collusion across the Jordan*. New York: Columbia University Press, 1988.

Shlaim, Avi. *War and Peace in the Middle East*. New York: Viking Press, 1994.

Shlaim, Avi. "The Debate about 1948." *International Journal of Middle East Studies* 27, no. 3 (1995).

Shlaim, Avi. "How Israel Brought Gaza to the Brink of Humanitarian Catastrophe." *Haaretz*, January 7, 2009.

Shlaim, Avi. *Iron Wall: Israel and the Arab World*. New York: W. W. Norton, 2014.

Shlaim, Avi. "How Israel Brought Gaza to the Brink of Humanitarian Catastrophe." *Guardian*, April 20, 2018.

Shlaim, Avi. *Israel and Palestine*. London: Verso, 2009.

Shtrasler, Nehemia. "So What Have We Done to Them?" *Haaretz*, December 18, 2007.

Shulman, David. "A Hero in His Own Words." *New York Review*, December 7, 2017.

Shultz, George P. *Turmoil and Triumph: My Years as Secretary of State*. New York: Charles Scribner's Sons, 1993.

Siegman, Henry. "Israel's Lies." *London Review of Books*, January 29, 2009.

Siegman, Henry. "Is Israel's Legitimacy under Challenge?" *Haaretz*, August 16, 2010.

Siegman, Henry. "Meshal's Folly." *Haaretz*, December 14, 2012.

Siegman, Henry. "Can Kerry Rescue a Two-State Peace Accord?" *Huffington Post*, April 2, 2013.

Siegman, Henry. "Prime Minister Netanyahu and the Arab Peace Initiative." *National Interest*, July 5, 2016.

Silberstein, Laurence J., ed. *New Perspectives on Israeli History*. New York: New York University Press, 1991.

Singh, Michael. "How to Make Trump's Israeli-Palestinian Peace Plan Work." *New York Times*, April 2, 2019.

Slater, Jerome. "The Superpowers and an Arab-Israeli Political Settlement." *Political Science Quarterly* (Winter 1990–91).

Slater, Jerome. "What Went Wrong? The Collapse of the Israeli-Palestinian Process." *Political Science Quarterly* 116, no. 2 (Summer 2001).

Slater, Jerome. "The Two Books of Mearsheimer and Walt." *Security Studies* 18, no. 1 (January–March 2009).

Slater, Jerome. "Just War Moral Philosophy and the 2008–09 Israeli Campaign in Gaza." *International Security* 37, no. 2 (Fall 2012).

Smith, Hedrick. "U.S. Assumes the Israelis Have A-Bomb or Its Parts." *New York Times*, July 18, 1960.

Sobelman, Daniel. "Learning to Deter." *International Security* 41, no. 3 (Winter 2016/17).

Sokatch, Daniel. "Netanyahu Won the Election, Will He Now Dismantle Israel's Democracy?" *Haaretz*, April 10, 2019.

Spiegel, Steven L. *The Other Arab-Israeli Conflict: Making America's Middle East Policy from Truman to Reagan*. Chicago: University of Chicago Press, 1985.

Stavridis, James. "For a Narrow U.S.-Israel Defense Pact." Washington, DC: Jewish Institute for National Security of America, July 2019.

Stephens, Bret. "Six Days and Fifty Years of War." *New York Times*, June 2, 2017.

Stern, Yoav. "Following the Stretch from Concept to Dogma to Axiom." *Haaretz*, June 2004.

Sternhell, Zeev. "An Imposed Solution Is the Only Option." *Haaretz*, August 22, 2003.
Sternhell, Zeev. "Post-Zionist Settlement." *Haaretz*, June 20, 2003.
Sternhell, Zeev. "Subversive Action Against the Jewish People." *Haaretz*, July 4, 2013.
Sternhell, Zeev. "If I Were a Palestinian." *Haaretz*, January 2, 2015.
St. Fleur, Nicholas. "Fate of Ancient Canaanites Seen in DNA Analysis: They Survived." *New York Times*, July 27, 2017.
Stolberg, Sheryl Gay. "Concerns Raised over Power Wielded by a Pro-Israel Lobbying Giant." *New York Times*, March 5, 2019.
"Stop Shooting Gazan Protesters," editorial. *Haaretz*, April 23, 2018.
Strenger, Carlo. "Get Arab Leaders to Recognize Israel." *Haaretz*, June 7, 2003.
Strenger, Carlo. "Is the Law of Return Inherently Racist?" *Haaretz*, December 20, 2007.
Strenger, Carlo. "Why Israel Does Not Engage with the Saudi Initiative." *Haaretz*, June 8, 2007.
Strenger, Carlo. "Keepers at the Gates of Our Democracy." *Haaretz*, January 16, 2013.
Strenger, Carlo. "Meet the Worst Anti-Zionist of Them All." *Haaretz*, December 5, 2014.
Sullivan, Andrew. "The Daily Dish" (blog), March 13, 2009.
Swisher, Clayton, *The Truth about Camp David*. New York: Nation Books, 2004.
Talbott, Strobe, ed. *Khrushchev Remembers*. Boston: Little, Brown, 1974.
Taylor, Alan R. *The Superpowers and the Middle East*. Syracuse: Syracuse University Press, 1991.
Tessler, Mark. *A History of the Israeli-Palestinian Conflict*. 2nd ed. Bloomington: Indiana University Press, 2009.
Teveth, Shabtai. *Ben-Gurion and the Palestinian Arabs: From Peace to War*. New York: Oxford University Press, 1985.
Teveth, Shabtai. *Ben-Gurion: The Burning Ground, 1886–1948*. New York: Houghton Mifflin, 1987.
Thrall, Nathan. "What Future for Israel?" *New York Review*, August 15, 2013,
Thrall, Nathan. "Feeling Good about Feeling Bad." *London Review of Books*, October 9, 2014.
Thrall, Nathan. *The Only Language They Understand: Forcing Compromise in Israel and Palestine*. New York: Henry Holt, 2017.
Thrall, Nathan. "How the Battle over Israel and Anti-Semitism Is Fracturing American Politics." *New York Times Sunday Magazine*, March 28, 2019.
Tibon, Amir. "Obama's Detailed Plan for Mideast Peace Revealed." *Haaretz*, June 8, 2017.
Tibon, Amir. "Kerry Reveals Details of Assad's Secret Letter to Netanyahu in 2010." *Haaretz*, September 4, 2018.
Tibon, Amir. "House Democrats Chide State Department for Settlement Policy Reversal." November 24, 2019.
Tibon, Amir. "Most Americans Hold Negative View of Israeli Government, Pew Survey Shows." *Haaretz*, April 25, 2019.
Tibon, Amir. "Trump, Netanyahu Discuss Iran, Annexing Jordan Valley." *Haaretz*, December 2, 2019.
Tibon, Amir, and Amos Harel. "Netanyahu, Trump in Intensive Talks for Dramatic Diplomatic Gesture." *Haaretz*, September 3, 2019.
Tibon, Amir, and Noa Landau. "Netanyahu Suggested to U.S. Moving Israeli Arabs to Future Palestinian State, Sources Say." *Haaretz*, February 4, 2020.
Tillman, Seth. *The United States and the Middle East*. Bloomington: Indiana University Press, 1982.
Tivnan, Edward. *The Lobby: Jewish Political Power and American Foreign Policy*. New York: Simon and Schuster, 1987.
Trice, Robert. *Interest Groups and the Foreign Policy Process*. Beverly Hills, CA: Sage, 1976.
"Trump's Peace Plan." *Haaretz*, September 15, 2019.
"Two New Israeli Defense Brass Join in Support for Breaking the Silence." *Haaretz*, December 22, 2015.
Tyler, Patrick. *World of Trouble: The White House and the Middle East*. New York: Farrar, Straus and Giroux, 2009.
"United: The Palestinians Have Endorsed 1967 Borders for Peace." *Haaretz*, May 7, 2014.

Vance, Cyrus. *Hard Choices: Critical Years in America's Foreign Policy*. New York: Simon and Schuster, 1983.

Van Evera, Stephen. "Human Organizations of All Sorts." Manuscript, November 2003.

Verter, Yossi. "Not Peace-Shmeace. Not Syria-Shmyria." *Haaretz*, December 22, 2006.

Vital, David. *Zionism: The Formative Years*. Oxford: Clarendon Press, 1982.

Wakebridge, Charles. "The Syrian Side of the Hill." *Military Review* (February 1976).

Walsh, Declan. "Hamas Leaders Plays Final Hand: Trying to Lift Group's Pariah Status." *New York Times*, May 2, 2017.

Walt, Stephen M. *The Origins of Alliances*. Ithaca, NY: Cornell University Press, 1990.

Walt, Stephen. "Whiff of Desperation." *Foreign Policy*, April 25, 2011.

Waxman, Dov. *The Israeli-Palestinian Conflict: What Everyone Needs to Know*. New York: Oxford University Press, 2019.

Weinberger, Naomi. "The Palestinian National Security Debate." *Journal of Palestine Studies* 24, no. 3 (Spring 1995).

Whetten, Lawrence L. *The Canal War*. Cambridge, MA: MIT Press, 1974.

White House. *Peace to Prosperity: A Vision to Improve the Lives of the Palestinian and Israeli People*. https://www.whitehouse.gov/peacetoprosperity/.

"Why Not Hamas?" *New Republic*, March 26, 2010.

"Will the Relationship Change? Yes It Can." *The Economist*, February 12, 2009.

Wolfe, Alan. "Israel's Moral Peril." *Chronicle of Higher Education*, March 25, 2012.

Wolfe, Alan. *At Home in Exile: Why Diaspora Is Good for the Jews*. Boston: Beacon Press, 2014.

Worth, Robert F., and John Kifner. "The Destruction: Lebanese and Aid Groups Find Dangers in the Rubble." *New York Times*, August 25, 2006.

Wright, Lawrence. *Thirteen Days in September: Carter, Begin, and Sadat at Camp David*. New York: Knopf, 2014.

Yakobson, Alexander. "Not Israel's Policemen." *Haaretz*, July 14, 2008.

Yaniv, Avner. "Syria and Israel: The Politics of Escalation." In *Syria under Assad*, edited by Moshe Maoz and Avner Yaniv. London: Croom Helm, 1986.

Yaniv, Avner. *Deterrence without the Bomb*. Lexington, MA: D.C. Heath, 1987.

Yaniv, Avner. *Dilemmas of Security, Politics, Strategy, and the Israeli Experience in Lebanon*. New York: Oxford University Press, 1987.

Yizhar, S. *Khirbet Khizeh*. New York: Farrar, Straus and Giroux, 2008.

Zertal, Idith, and A. Eldar. *Lords of the Land. The War over Israel's Settlements in the Occupied Territories, 1967–2007*. New York: Nation Books, 2007.

"Zionism Is Not Racism, but Zionists Can Be Racists." *Foreign Policy*, May 1, 2012.

Ziri, Danielle. "2020 Candidates' Stand on Israel Is Lowest Priority for U.S. Jews, Poll Shows." *Haaretz*, May 24, 2019.

Zisser, Eyal. "June 1967—Israel's Capture of the Golan Heights." *Israel Studies* (Spring 2002).

Zoughbie, Daniel E. *Indecision Points: George W. Bush and the Israeli-Palestinian Conflict*. Cambridge, MA: Belfer Center, MIT Press, 2015.

Zreik, Raef. "Why the 'Jewish State' Now?" *Journal of Palestine Studies* 40, no. 3 (Spring 2011).

INDEX

Page numbers follwed by m, indicate the map on that page